Read this book online today:

With SAP PRESS BooksOnline we offer you online access to knowledge from the leading SAP experts. Whether you use it as a beneficial supplement or as an alternative to the printed book, with SAP PRESS BooksOnline you can:

• Access your book anywhere, at any time. All you need is an Internet connection.
• Perform full text searches on your book and on the entire SAP PRESS library.
• Build your own personalized SAP library.

The SAP PRESS customer advantage:

Register this book today at *www.sap-press.com* and obtain exclusive free trial access to its online version. If you like it (and we think you will), you can choose to purchase permanent, unrestricted access to the online edition at a very special price!

Here's how to get started:

1. Visit *www.sap-press.com.*
2. Click on the link for SAP PRESS BooksOnline and login (or create an account).
3. Enter your free trial license key, shown below in the corner of the page.
4. Try out your online book with full, unrestricted access for a limited time!

Your personal free trial **license key**
for this online book is:

SAP® Web Client

 PRESS

SAP PRESS is a joint initiative of SAP and Galileo Press. The know-how offered by SAP specialists combined with the expertise of the Galileo Press publishing house offers the reader expert books in the field. SAP PRESS features first-hand information and expert advice, and provides useful skills for professional decision-making.

SAP PRESS offers a variety of books on technical and business related topics for the SAP user. For further information, please visit our website: *www.sap-press.com*.

Horst Keller
The Official ABAP Reference (3rd edition)
2012, 1688 pp.
978-1-59229-376-6

Michael Füchsle, Matthias E. Zierke
SAP CRM Web Client—Customizing and Development
2010, 427 pp.
978-1-59229-297-4

James Wood
Object-Oriented Programming with ABAP Objects
2009, 357 pp.
978-1-59229-235-6

Thorsten Franz, Tobias Trapp
ABAP Objects: Application Development from Scratch
2008, 505 pp.
978-1-59229-211-0

Tzanko Stefanov, Armand Sezikeye, and Sanjeet Mall

SAP® Web Client

A Comprehensive Guide for Developers

Galileo Press

Bonn • Boston

Galileo Press is named after the Italian physicist, mathematician and philosopher Galileo Galilei (1564–1642). He is known as one of the founders of modern science and an advocate of our contemporary, heliocentric worldview. His words *Eppur si muove* (And yet it moves) have become legendary. The Galileo Press logo depicts Jupiter orbited by the four Galilean moons, which were discovered by Galileo in 1610.

Editor Kelly Grace Harris
Copyeditor John Parker
Cover Design Graham Geary
Photo Credit iStockphoto.com/pixalot
Layout Design Vera Brauner
Production Kelly O'Callaghan and Graham Geary
Typesetting Publishers' Design and Production Services, Inc.
Printed and bound in Canada

ISBN 978-1-59229-389-6

© 2011 by Galileo Press Inc., Boston (MA)

1st edition 2011

Library of Congress Cataloging-in-Publication Data
Stefanov, Tzanko.
SAP web client : a comprehensive guide for developers / Tzanko Stefanov, Armand Sezikeye,
Sanjeet Mall. — 1st ed.
    p. cm.
Includes index.
ISBN-13: 978-1-59229-389-6
ISBN-10: 1-59229-389-1
1. Web services—Computer programs. 2. Web site development—Computer programs.
3. Web-based user interfaces. 4. Management information systems. 5. Client/server computing.
6. SAP CRM. I. Sezikeye, Armand. II. Mall, Sanjeet. III. Title.
TK5105.88813.S75 2011
006.7'8—dc23
2011019542

FSC
www.fsc.org
MIX
Paper from
responsible sources
FSC® C011825

Contents at a Glance

Dear Reader,

Congratulations! You've just made the first step toward becoming an expert on the subject of SAP Web Client. With this book, you'll learn everything you need to know about developing and enhancing applications with the Web Client UI, from the basics to the functional and technical aspects of the framework. By the end of your journey, you will understand everything SAP Web Client has to offer to developers, and be able to build a full-fledged enterprise-ready application.

Writing a book is not an easy task, and—contrary to what you might think—having three people write a book is even less so. Tzanko Stefanov, Armand Sezikeye, and Sanjeet Mall, I'd venture to guess, discovered this the hard way. But thanks to their tireless efforts, super-human dedication, and I-don't-know-how-many sleepless nights, I'm confident that you will be truly impressed with the final results. Enjoy the wealth of knowledge contained in this book, and never doubt the energy and passion that went into it. (Or the many phone calls! Tzanko is still one of my only authors whose voice needs no introduction.)

We appreciate your business, and welcome your feedback. Your comments and suggestions are the most useful tools to help us improve our books for you, the reader. We encourage you to visit our website at *www.sap-press.com* and share your feedback about this work.

Thank you for purchasing a book from SAP PRESS!

Kelly Grace Harris
Editor, SAP PRESS

Galileo Press
Boston, MA

kelly.harris@galileo-press.com
www.sap-press.com

Contents

9   Enhancing Applications with Fields and Tables 417

10   Behavioral Extensibility 457

Introduction

This is a book about a framework. We, the authors, believe it is a great framework, and have been involved in developing and designing many of its features and pieces—which explains why we are so animated and enthusiastic about it. Our hope is that through this book we will pass on to you not only our knowledge of the product, but also our passion and excitement.

The name of the framework is SAP Web Client, though in the past it has been known as SAP CRM Web Client. Originally, it was created as part of SAP CRM; however, its openness and its focus on end users and application developers have since helped it become a full citizen of SAP's user interface technology stack.

This book will take you on a journey in which you learn how to develop and enhance applications with the Web Client UI. As you will see, the approach that we take is slightly different from what you would expect from a development guide book: instead of explaining the concepts and clarifying them with examples, we focus on the development tasks and clarify the technical concepts as part of the examples. As a result, each chapter provides you with just enough theory to accomplish the development task at hand. In order to get comprehensive knowledge of a given concept or feature, you will have to read through several chapters (sometimes not even sequentially). We start with the fundamentals, and, as we go through different programming layers, development activities, and phases, we cover more and more of the functional and technical aspects of the framework.

With each chapter, we deliver an example that has value on its own. There is plenty of ABAP code, screenshots, and explanations, so you can easily apply what you have learned in your projects, and recreate these comprehensive examples in your own development system. This not only fosters a sense of accomplishment, but will also allow you to experiment with something meaningful and easily drill deep into its technical intricacies.

In this book, you will learn that the Web Client UI has a lot to offer to developers. You can build a full-fledged enterprise ready application, or you can simply stick to small-scale development projects by enhancing existing objects, generating building blocks or even a complete business application. The framework allows you to leverage SAP and non-SAP technologies, and supports the exposure and consumption of enterprise services. After all, the Web Client UI is not just a framework, but an open platform with the potential to be extended in multiple directions.

Who This Book Is For

This book is aimed at developers and consultants who are new to SAP CRM and Web Client UI. The book assumes that you have some programming experience, as well as the passion necessary to learn how to build applications with the Web Client UI. There are even a few chapters that might be of interest to less technical users who are comfortable with SAP backend configuration activities. With respect to the general development background, we made the assumptions that you understand the principles of Web development and ABAP programming—and by Web development we mean HTML, some understanding of Cascading Style Sheets, Extensible Markup Language (XML), and client side dynamic languages such JavaScript. It will definitely help if you are familiar or willing to learn the basics of BSP application programming. In any case, in order to follow the technical discussions, you should have a general knowledge of the ABAP programming language, including ABAP objects.

What This Book Covers

This book mainly covers various programming and customizing topics related to the Web Client UI application development. The structure of the book is as follows:

▶ **Chapter 1**
This chapter provides an overview of the elements, concepts, and tools that constitute the SAP Web Client UI framework. If you are already familiar with the new Web UI paradigm of SAP CRM, you can skip this chapter. However, those new to SAP CRM should take the time to read it and learn about the UI concepts and interaction patterns. In addition to briefly discussing the topics that will be covered by the rest of the chapters, here we introduce the story around which all our examples and sample development tasks revolve.

▶ **Chapter 2**
This chapter introduces the GenIL layer. We discuss the foundation of GenIL programming and show you how to create a GenIL component, as well as how to model and code the functionality required to cover read-only scenarios.

► **Chapter 3**

In this chapter, we finalize the GenIL discussion. We discuss the foundation of GenIL programming and show you how to create a GenIL component, as well as how to model and code the functionality required to cover read-only scenarios.

► **Chapter 4**

In this chapter we introduce you to the BSP programming model, which is the technology that underlies the Web Client framework. We analyze the MVC paradigm in the context of BSP applications and we build an example that helps us to explore and understand the various components of a BSP application. And, before moving on to Chapter 5, we discuss the building blocks of a Web Client application.

► **Chapter 5**

In this chapter, we finally build a Web Client application. We start by doing BOL programming, from reading data all the way to sorting BOL collections, and then through the creation, modification, and deletion of data. We then proceed with the creation of a hotel booking application, which we use to discuss search and result pages as well as overview pages.

► **Chapter 6**

This chapter is a continuation of the exploration started in Chapter 5. We improve the application built in the previous chapter, add new, advanced features, and integrate it in the L-Shape after having analyzed such concepts as business roles and authorization profiles.

► **Chapter 7**

In this chapter, you will learn how to leverage existing SAP applications and add custom functionality to them. We show you how to develop upgrade-safe enhancements. We also take the opportunity to discuss some important aspects of UI configuration, such as configuration keys and text determination. Finally, as part of the example development tasks, we show you how to navigate across UI components.

► **Chapter 8**

In this chapter, we introduce the new productivity tools for application developers that are available as of CRM 7.0 EhP1. You will see how one can easily generate a fully functional Web UI on top of the GenIL component that we created in Chapters 2 and 3. We then fine-tune the new application and use the imaginary development tasks to conclude the topics of UI configuration and personalization, the design layer, and reusing components in a pop-up.

▶ **Chapter 9**

In this chapter, we will introduce you to the tools supporting the structural enhancements of standard SAP applications. This topic is also known as *extensibility*, and we will demonstrate via example how an end user can add new fields (including navigation links) and views to existing applications. We will also provide you with some practical usages of custom extensions in the context of SAP CRM reporting and the design layer.

▶ **Chapter 10**

CRM 7.0 EhP1 comes with updates that allow users to enhance not only the structure but also the behavior of existing applications. In the past, SAP technical consultants would often add their custom logic to application specific BAdIs. This chapter revises this approach, and introduces some of the specific Web Client UI mechanisms for behavior enhancements. The provided examples will show you how to add custom logic to table extensions, define calculated fields, expose application data via global attribute tags, and add new functionalities via custom BRF+ operations.

▶ **Chapter 11**

In this chapter, you will learn how one can easily consume custom data sources with the tools available in the Web Client UI (as of CRM 7.0 EhP1). The imaginary assignments provided in this chapter demonstrate how you can fully produce operational UI applications from existing database tables and Web services. You will also learn how to create application mash-ups from both newly generated and existing standard SAP applications.

▶ **Chapter 12**

In this chapter, you will see how SAP CRM can expose its rich functionality via Web services. We also talk about the Web service tool that lets you expose business objects in a convenient Web service interface without writing a single line of code. Finally, we briefly look at making your custom objects available to the Web service tool.

▶ **Chapter 13**

In this chapter, we dig down into one of the most-used features of any SAP CRM implementation: document templates. We cover both Adobe and Microsoft Word templates, and discuss the underlying concepts and technologies that make templates work. As part of this discussion, we create both Adobe and Microsoft templates from scratch, so that you can understand the concepts in detail.

▶ **Chapter 14**

In this chapter, you will get an overview of SAP CRM's groupware integration. The chapter focuses on what is possible and supported in the latest version of SAP CRM. In addition, the customizing requirements for both IBM Lotus and Microsoft Outlook are covered.

▶ **Chapter 15**

This chapter is dedicated to additional topics. We discuss heterogeneous features including task-based UI, field actions, Flash Islands and the Transaction Launcher. We finish the chapter by discussing the very important topic of performance and session management. We also give a quick overview of the tag libraries used in the Web Client framework.

All coding samples and screenshots were prepared using the commercially available SAP CRM 7.0 EhP1 IDES system.

Each of us (the authors) probably has a different story to share when it comes to what it took to write this book. However, we all agree that it was a lot more work that we originally thought. There were sleepless nights, stressful weekends, and extremely upset family members and friends. But through this whole endeavor, we kept on hearing the voice of our editor Kelly Grace Harris from Galileo Press (SAP PRESS), encouraging us to move forward, praising our work, and leading us to the successful completion of what seemed at times to be a mission impossible project.

Tzanko Stefanov
Armand Sezikeye
Sanjeet Mall

Acknowledgments

The framework that we write about in this book was conceived and developed by teams of people. Without them, there would have been no framework and therefore no book. All three of us have worked for years with these developers, architects, development managers, and product managers. It was hard work, but it was also great fun. We have not met a more enthusiastic and committed crowd. Thank you, guys, for the fantastic job!

We would not have been able to get to know these great developers, managers, and their product if it were not for Peter Conrad and Florian Weigman—the people in charge of development and product management. We would like to convey our sincere thanks for trusting and mentoring us.

The framework's architects, Uwe Raimitz, Tim Back, Alexandre Trottier, and Arman Voskanian, have been extremely helpful over the years. We owe them a lot for helping us gain a better understanding of the product, as well as for their guidance and the provided materials.

Last but not least, we would like to thank our editor, Kelly Grace Harris. She worked closely with us, and it was her valuable input that helped us convert our ideas into something readable. Kelly, all three of us are indebted to you for your efforts and constant encouragement.

From Tzanko Stefanov

This project would not have been possible without the support of my loved ones—my wife Dora and daughter Stephanie. I would like to thank them for their understanding, consideration, and for spending many evenings and weekends without me. Thank you for encouraging and bearing with me when things did not go smoothly. I am dedicating this book to you.

There are several SAP colleagues that made direct contributions to this book by reviewing some of our work and providing us with feedback. My thanks go to Daniel Rochon and Matthias Schmalz. You played a significant role in writing this book.

I would also like to express my appreciation and gratitude to my fellow authors, Armand and Sanjeet. Guys, without you this book would not exist. Thank you for your hard work, professionalism, and for making this journey not only smoother but also a lot more fun.

From Armand Sezikeye

First and foremost, I want to thank my daughter Annie-Laurine and my wife Lesya. They are certainly the people who showed the most support and understanding, especially during those moments, weekends, and evenings when they would simply accept that I had to be absent and that I had to carry out this project and lead it to completion at their expense. I also want to thank Marina for believing in me and encouraging me.

I dedicate this book to my mother. I will not even try to say what for, since this would be another book by itself. I just know she would be proud to see this book out there.

I also want to thank my friends and relatives for their understanding and encouragement.

Last but not least, I want to thank my good friend Tzanko, who started this project and who, thanks to his persistence, made it happen.

From Sanjeet Mall

This project would be bits and pieces scattered somewhere over my laptop without the loving support of my wife Veena. I would like to say I would not have been able to do this if she was not around as a constant source of inspiration. I would like to dedicate this book to her.

I would like to thank Ankan Banerjee for helping me write a key chapter in this book. Simone Schoenemann and Silke Arians also deserve my special thanks for answering my millions of questions over the years.

I would also like to take this opportunity to thank my fellow author and friend, Tzanko, for kick starting this project and, more importantly, making sure we delivered!

*The success of SAP Customer Relationship Management (SAP CRM)
would not be possible without an up-to-date, Web-based, flexible, and
highly configurable user interface. At the heart of it lies the Web Client UI
framework. It is available not only to SAP CRM developers but to everyone
who wants to easily build Web applications in the SAP NetWeaver ABAP
stack.*

1 Introducing the Web Client UI Framework

As of SAP CRM 2006s, SAP consolidated the *user interface* (UI) technologies available in SAP CRM. SAP chose one Web-based UI technology for all end user scenarios, namely the *Web Client UI*. *People Centric UI* would not be supported anymore, and *SAP GUI* would be used only for customizing and development.

The new UI concept was based on the proven *Interaction Center Web Client*. It incorporated many best practices pertinent to standard Web applications. To end users, it provided a look and feel and navigation that matched their experience with the Web. As a result, the learning curve was reduced and the rate of adoption was increased.

The Web Client UI served the purpose of UI unification. It came with a new underlying architecture that offered a great deal of flexibility when building UIs. The new framework covered all the application variants, such as Interaction Center and *On Demand*. In addition, the framework provided multi-browser support, *UI skin* modeling via style sheets, and—most important—one *configuration tool* for all CRM applications.

The new UI framework provided a *BSP tag library* to facilitate development of views. The tags not only defined a standard set of UI elements, but also helped address performance issues and supported out-of-the-box Web-development best practices such as *AJAX*-based interaction. Over the next year, SAP continued its investment in the Web Client UI. CRM 2007 was released with a more refined and complete version of the UI framework. Not only was the framework more mature, but it also showed SAP's commitment to Web 2.0 concepts such as personalization and configuration of content. With CRM 7.0, SAP decided to open the framework to further enhancement and extensibility. The tools and concepts that followed in enhancement pack 1 (EhP1) capitalized on the earlier investments and delivered tools supporting user and developer productivity. As a result, one can refer to the Web Client UI not just as a highly extensible framework but also as a platform for building custom applications (even outside of the CRM context).

This book will focus on the latest features of the Web Client UI. Although some of them exist only in EhP1, you can follow the discussion and understand many of the examples if you have been exposed to CRM 7.0 or even CRM 2007.

We thought for some time about how to structure this first chapter. We needed to introduce the terminology and outline the overall concepts. At the same time, we could not accomplish this merely by providing an entertaining example. So, if you are familiar with the Web Client UI already, feel free to skim quickly through this chapter and take note of the few EhP1 features that we discuss here. If this is the first time you have encountered the Web Client UI, take the opportunity to understand the main UI components, patterns, and concepts. Take encouragement from the fact that once you grasp these, the best is yet to come.

To begin, we should establish a common understanding of the basic concepts of the Web Client UI. We already mentioned that the new UI comes with a new framework—but Web Client UI also defined a brand-new layout and interaction paradigms. It is important to highlight the main elements of the new UI before diving deep into the technical details. In this chapter, we will outline the main building blocks of the Web Client UI. Later on, we will discuss the details in the context of examples.

1.1   Main Components of the Web Client UI

If you have a CRM system at your disposal (version 2007 or higher) please log onto it. You will land on something that we call a home page. Take a close look. It contains the main screen elements: the *header area*, the *navigation area*, and the *work area*. An example of a home page is provided in Figure 1.1.

The header and the navigation areas, together, are also known as the *L-shape* (due to the resemblance with the letter "L"). The L-shape always stays fixed, so the user always has access to common functionalities and never gets lost. The work area changes its content based on the navigation or functions a user executes.

Corporate branding can generally be applied to all areas via the CSS files, while the upper area is often used to place corporate images or color schemes. We will talk about styles later in this chapter.

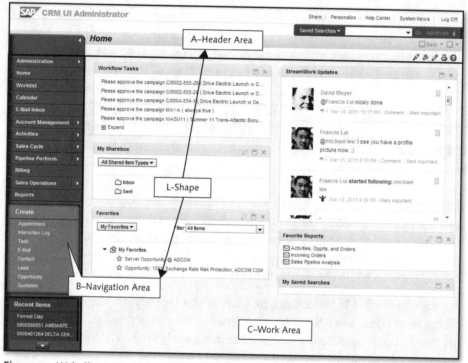

Figure 1.1 Web Client UI's Main Screen Elements

We will now look into the outlined screen elements and their variations.

1.1.1 Header Area

The header area provides generic functionality normally available to all users (defined by business roles). The functionalities are grouped as follows (Figure 1.2):

▸ System links
▸ Central search

► Work area title

► History navigation (back and forward)

The system links are PERSONALIZE, HELP CENTER, SYSTEM NEWS, and LOG OFF. The names of these links are self explanatory. The PERSONALIZE link offers generic personalization options for the user. This is a very important concept, and we will discuss it in detail later on. The HELP CENTER offers direct access to online help using the knowledge warehouse. SYSTEM NEWS is the area where the user can always access SAP system messages (for example, if an administrator sends a message to all users about the planned downtime of the system). The LOG OFF link allows the users to terminate their current session securely (log off from the system).

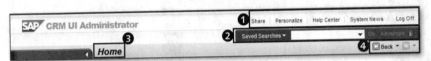

Figure 1.2   The Header Area

Business users can search through the system whenever they are in CRM via the *central search* component. The central search combines three main search capabilities that significantly facilitate searching and discovery of information by the user: *simple search* (via NetWeaver *Enterprise Search*), *advanced search,* and *saved searches.* The simple search (also known as *enterprise search*) will be discussed separately.

The saved search was introduced in CRM 2006s (see Figure 1.3). The user can choose from a dropdown list of search queries he had defined and saved in standard advanced search pages. Selecting a saved search and clicking on ADVANCED will take the user to the standard advanced search page, where the user can edit the query attributes. The DELETE button allows for the deletion of a saved search.

The (simplified) advanced search allows the user to quickly perform simple search on a given business object (for example account, opportunity, or sales order). Suppose that you want to look for an account with the name "Adcom." First, you have to select ACCOUNT from the dropdown list box (DDLB). In the second level of DDLB, pick the NAME attribute. Next, enter "Adcom" in the search input field. Once you click on the Go button, you will be taken to the search result page. Note that both advanced and saved searches show the result list in the standard advanced search page of the object.

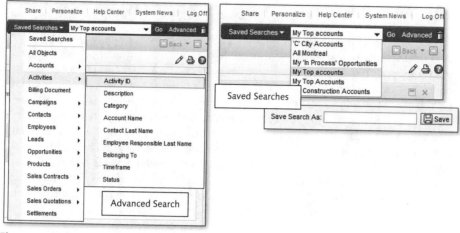

Figure 1.3 Advanced Search and Saved Search

The work area title provides an overview of the current context. It informs the user about the topic that is currently displayed. Here are some examples:

▶ SEARCH: ACCOUNTS will be displayed on the advanced search page for accounts

▶ CORPORATE ACCOUNT designates the corporate account overview page

▶ ACCOUNTS AND PRODUCTS could be displayed for a work-center page

The title also provides specific information about the object the user is looking at and helps identify it. The work area title also hosts the backward and forward histories: a DDLB that helps you select where to navigate (see Figure 1.4).

Figure 1.4 Work Area Title and History Navigation

We recommend that you try the search and the navigation yourself. You will find they work easily. They represent standard UI concepts, and you can find similar controls in most desktop and Web-based applications.

> **CRM Business Object**
>
> Throughout this book and also in your SAP documentation you will frequently encounter the term *business object* used in discussing different concepts. For example, we have just used it to refer to everyday business entities such as products, accounts, sales orders, opportunities, and campaigns. We will try to use the term *CRM business objects* when we refer to these entities (or applications). The term *"business object"* is used when we discuss the GenIL model. In general, "business object" is used in programming to refer to the backend model data. As you know, in programming an *object* is a construct that combines methods and attributes. It often contains business logic. The GenIL model adopts this definition because there are similarities between its nodes and the objects in programming. In SAP documentation, the GenIL nodes are officially referred to as "business objects." We will try to use the same terminology. Nevertheless, we ask you to pay attention to the context in which the term "business object" is used.

1.1.2 Navigation Area

The navigation area can consist of several elements. You can control via customizing what is presented to the end user. These elements are as follows (Figure 1.5):

❶ Navigation bar

❷ Quick create links

❸ Recent items

❹ Open/close navigation bar

The most important element is the navigation bar. It allows direct navigation to all *entry pages* and the most important searches. The navigation bar can include application searches, a URL link, SAP NetWeaver BI reports and analysis, and transactions from other systems.

The navigation bar provides a maximum of two levels for navigation. The first-level navigation entries lead to corresponding entry pages or role-specific *work centers*. Second-level navigation entries normally represent searches for the most important applications. It is up to the customer to define the number of entries available in the first level of the navigation bar. This is controlled by business-role customizing, so that different users will be presented with different sets of links. It is also possible to remove second-level navigation if a customer requires this. In the second-level entry, the SAP standard delivery only shows links to search pages, even though technically any kind of links can be embedded there. The navigation bar can also be collapsed to enlarge the work area.

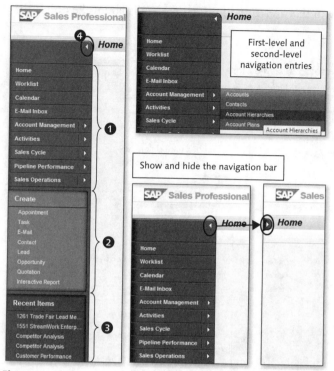

Figure 1.5 Navigation Area

The navigation area could contain (depending on the business-role customizing) QUICK CREATE and RECENT ITEMS. The first of these is technically called a *direct link group*. We will talk about these concepts when we discuss business-role customizing. The QUICK CREATE area allows users to start creating an object quickly, no matter where the user is located. Links allow users to navigate to the corresponding standard created pages. This area is not only configurable but can also be personalized by the user. Its entries of direct link groups can be equipped with an icon. You will notice that some UI components have icons, though this feature is not available for all skins. Figure 1.6 not only shows QUICK CREATE and RECENT ITEMS, but also gives you an idea of how they can look in different skins. As you will see later, when customizing the business role, you can also modify these visual identifiers in line with the customer's branding policy.

The RECENT ITEMS area allows users to easily navigate with one click to the topics they have worked on recently. The number of objects visible in the recent items can be personalized (PERSONALIZE • PERSONALIZE NAVIGATION BAR • RECENT ITEMS).

The tooltip of each entry in this area provides further details about the object that it points to.

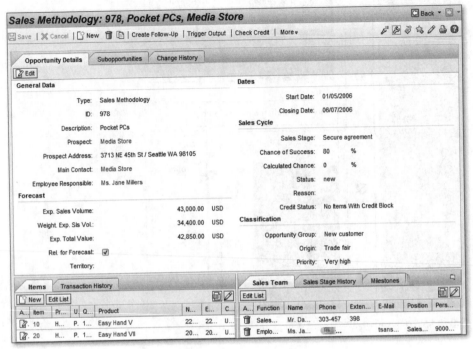

Figure 1.6 Quick Create and Recent Items

1.1.3 Entry Page

The term "entry page" was used already when describing the navigation bar. Before we elaborate on this, we will describe the navigation flow in Web Client UI. More details will be provided throughout the book. The navigation bar contains links to the business applications and reports your user is allowed to use. Figure 1.7 depicts the basic idea. Namely, that the first level navigation typically takes you to work centers, while the second level navigation provides further specialization and allows you to directly access a search page. Both work centers and search pages are what we call entry pages.

You will notice that in the example shown in Figure 1.7, the product search page is not only accessible through the second-level navigation menu, but also through the work center page. This is quite logical, given that the work center page is accessible through first-level navigation. From both the work center and first-level navigation, you can access more specialized functionality, such as the search page of a particular business object.

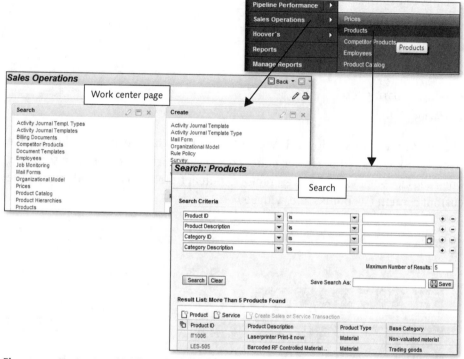

Figure 1.7 Navigation Flow from Navigation Bar

You do not even have to use the navigation bar to see an entry page. As soon as you log into SAP CRM you will land on the home page. This is the first entry page that you will have to deal with. Similar to work centers, it also contains links to other pages.

Home

The home page is the starting point for every user doing daily business on the Web. It contains the most important personal information and access to the most frequently used tools.

The main building blocks of the home page are called trays. Some examples of trays are:

- Hyperlinks to more detailed information

- Predefined content for appointments, tasks, reports

- Alerts and workflow tasks

- Links to external applications (Web links)

- Widgets

- Tag cloud

- Favorites

- Central sharing tool

- Dashboards

The commitment of SAP towards Web 2.0 is probably best seen on the home page (Figure 1.8). Users can personalize the tray design, rearrange content on the page, open and close blocks on the page, remove content from the screen, and incorporate custom content (Web links and widgets).

Figure 1.8 CRM Home Page

In SAP CRM 7.0 EhP1, users can enable one or more dashboards on their homepage without coding. The dashboard on the homepage is a powerful tool that users can select from a repository via the personalization of the home page. Users can choose from their favorite reports or all reports available for their business roles. The home page dashboard supports all valid report types.

Tag clouds and favorites were introduced in SAP CRM 7.0. Millennium users have been using these concepts on the Web for quite some time. As one can expect, tagging is a way to assign a semantic identifier to an SAP CRM business object. Tags are displayed on the home page via a tag cloud, which gives yet another dimension to data discovery and retrieval. Everyone who is using a Web browser is familiar with the idea of having favorite Web pages. SAP CRM users can apply this concept to business applications. In EhP1, tagging and favorites have been enhanced even further. The users are able to share them (and saved searches) via the *central sharing tool*. The latter is the first of its kind in CRM solutions. It allows users to collaborate with respect to business content.

Work Center

A work center is a flexible grouping of applications and information that logically belong together. We already saw an example of such a page when discussing the navigation in the beginning of this section. Figure 1.9 shows the SALES CYCLE WORK center and the various objects grouped on it.

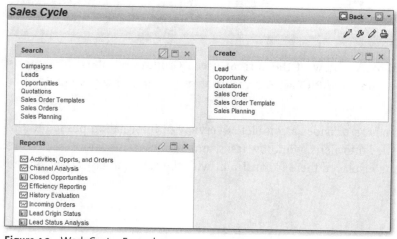

Figure 1.9 Work Center Example

A work center typically provides access to the different application searches, direct creation options, and links to related reports. The grouping of work centers and the content of a work center page are configurable per business role.

Calendar, Email, and Work List

CRM calendar is a Microsoft Outlook-like time organizer. Its page provides a graphical overview of appointments for today and of open tasks. Users can reschedule via drag and drop (Figure 1.10).

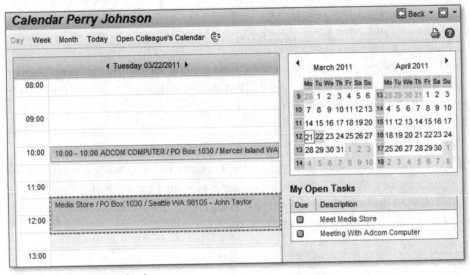

Figure 1.10 SAP CRM Calendar

The email inbox is a view of the current user's Groupware inbox. It supports transferring emails to SAP CRM. A screenshot of this entry page is provided in Figure 1.11.

The WORKLIST page provides a complete overview of information pushed to the user. It is divided into alerts, workflow tasks, and business transactions (see Figure 1.12). The data displayed there is consistent with the alert and tasks trays on the home page.

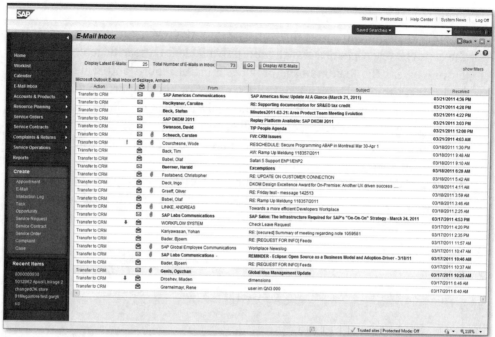

Figure 1.11 SAP CRM E-Mail Inbox

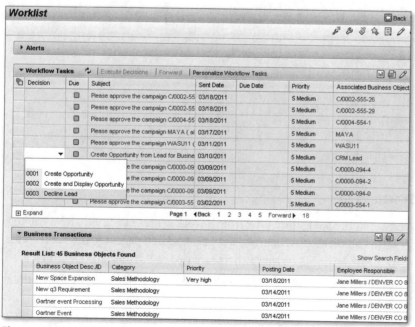

Figure 1.12 Worklist Page

Reports

Another standard entry page that comes with SAP CRM is the REPORTS page. It is the central entry page to access all reports available for a specific role, grouped by business area. The REPORTS page provides a list of reports and analysis grouped by business topic (see Figure 1.13). Examples of such reports include account analysis, campaign analysis, and pipeline analysis. Clicking a link will call the full page of analysis. It can have second-level navigation entries providing direct access to important analysis or dashboards. Content and grouping are configurable by business role. The report's content could be based on *SAP BI* and *CRM interaction reporting*. We will show you how to modify a CRM interactive report in one of our examples, but we recommend that you refer to your SAP documentation for more details on this.

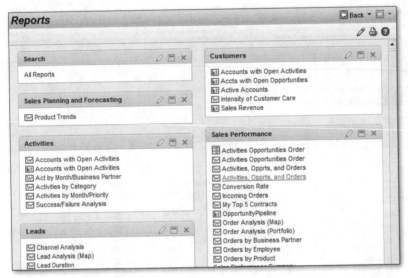

Figure 1.13 Reports Page

1.1.4 Search Page

Earlier, we saw that the navigation flow from a work center page could take you to a search page (also known as an *advanced search page*). Search pages are the main access points to SAP CRM business objects. The search page enables an operator-based search, which combines ease of understanding with great flexibility in specifying a search. There are very few search pages in SAP CRM that differ from this approach to visualizing the search field area and the search result list area. This is because SAP studied various business use cases and developed this search pattern based on the most common user needs.

The content in the search field and the search result list for each application can be flexibly configured by business role. Figure 1.14 shows an example of a search page.

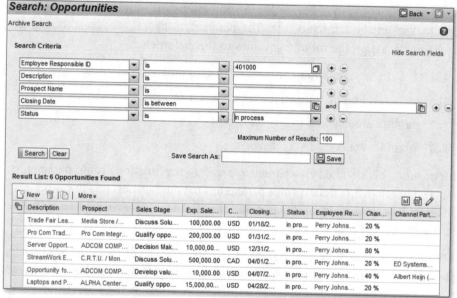

Figure 1.14 Advanced Search Page

Once the user executes a search, the results come back in the RESULT LIST block. It is optimized for quick overview and easy navigation to detailed information of the business object found. Business users can benefit from state-of-the-art sorting and filtering of the results. In addition, the result list block offers actions such as create, delete, mass update, and Microsoft Excel export. Users can fine-tune the page using various personalization options, such as defining the column sequence via drag and drop.

The TABLE GRAPHICS button in the search result block deserves special attention. You can find this button in any other assignment block that renders table data, but it is in search results that you can enjoy its benefits to the fullest. There, it helps you understand patterns and schemes behind the found search results in a graphical manner.

Via customizing, it is possible to enable or disable the use of charts. The settings are accessible by following the menu path CUSTOMER RELATIONSHIP MANAGEMENT • UI FRAMEWORK • TECHNICAL ROLE DEFINITION • DEFINE PARAMETERS. Once there, select the PROFILE DEFINITION TABLE GRAPHICS and afterwards double click PARAMETER ASSIGNMENT on the left-hand side. The parameter ENABLE_FTG_USAGE can be set here. You can assign the following values to this parameter:

▸ ASSIGNMENTBLOCK: graphics are enabled in assignment blocks only

▸ SEARCHRESULT: graphics are enabled in result lists only

▸ ALL: graphics are enabled in any table type

▸ NONE: graphics are completely disabled

This parameter is assigned via a *parameter profile* to the function profile parameters. You need to assign functional profile parameters to your business role in customizing for CUSTOMER RELATIONSHIP MANAGEMENT • UI FRAMEWORK • BUSINESS ROLES • DEFINE BUSINESS ROLE.

In EhP1, the functionality for export to Microsoft Excel can be modified by business role. To disable the export to spreadsheet in a particular business role, you need to define parameter EXPORT_DISABLE with parameter value TRUE in customizing, following the menu path CUSTOMER RELATIONSHIP MANAGEMENT • UI FRAMEWORK • TECHNICAL ROLE DEFINITION • DEFINE PARAMETERS.

Another improvement that comes with EhP1 is the presences of *multi-value fields* in the search criteria block. When a search page is called, the multi-value feature directs the user to a multi-value help dialog box. There the user can select multiple filter criteria for advanced search operation. In addition, this prevents users from entering values manually in the multi-value input field. Instead, the user gets more guidance on how to enter the data correctly.

1.1.5 Overview Page (OVP)

If you find the required data in the search page, chances are that you will want to take a detailed look at it and even modify it. That is why the search result block contains means to navigate to what is known as an *overview page* (OVP). Each SAP CRM business object has an overview page. An example of an OVP is shown in Figure 1.15.

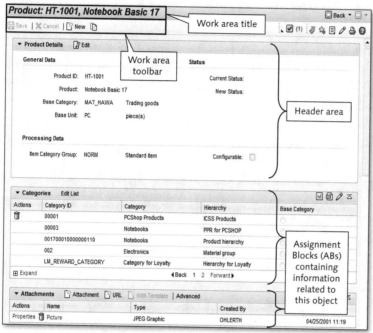

Figure 1.15 CRM Overview Page

An overview page displays all the information related to one SAP CRM business object instance; for example, one sales order, one service ticket, or one marketing campaign.

OVPs are scrollable as this is a format that internet users are quite familiar with. The most important information is shown in the first assignment block. The other blocks contain what is often called dependent data.

The main components of every overview page are:

▶ The *work area title* always identifies the object at which the user is looking.

▶ The *overview page toolbar* (also called *work area toolbar*) provides all the functionality available to the complete object (left-aligned buttons). The right-aligned buttons offer CRM generic functionality such as *personalization* and *printing*.

▶ The *assignment block (AB)* specific functionality is located in the title bar of every assignment block. This makes editing possible and also can contain additional actions pertinent to the data in that block.

As of SAP CRM 7.0, the layout of an OVP can be changed from single column to *tile layout* (Figure 1.16). This has already been used intensively in the Interaction Center Web Client environment to design pages that display all the information without any page scrolling.

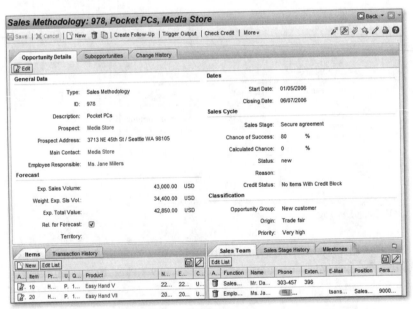

Figure 1.16 Tile Layout in CRM Overview Pages

System administrators and power users can open any OVP and configure it right from the Web Client UI. One configuration aspect that they can control is the layout. We will discuss the configuration paradigm later in this book.

1.1.6 Assignment Blocks

As you already saw in the search and overview pages, data is grouped by assignment block (AB). The behavior and capabilities of an AB are designed to make it easier to read and understand an overview page and thus the complete business object. Figure 1.17 shows the two main types of assignment blocks: *table* and *form views*. As the names suggest, the former is suited for tabular data, while the latter allows you to work with information that has a 1:1 cardinality with respect to the business object.

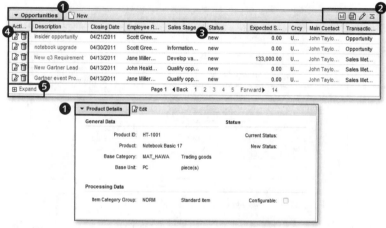

Figure 1.17 Assignment Blocks

The main elements of an assignment block are:

❶ The title identifying the content of the AB

❷ Column personalization (also via drag and drop)

❸ Comprehensive sorting and filtering in tables

❹ One-click actions for fast and easy deletion or editing

❺ Expand function, which appears if the default number of visible rows is exceeded

You could configure your page to show less important ABs as closed. The user can open them when he or she needs their content. In addition to helping visualize the overall data, this improves the performance of the page.

1.1.7   Interaction Concept

Now that we have covered the main components in the Web Client UI, let's conclude this section by looking into the role of interaction. The different navigation flows we described already give you some idea of this. Now we can build on what we have learned so far.

The basic interaction concept is captured in Figure 1.18. As discussed, the user always has access to the L-shape. This contains navigation links that typically take you to a search page or a page for creating objects.

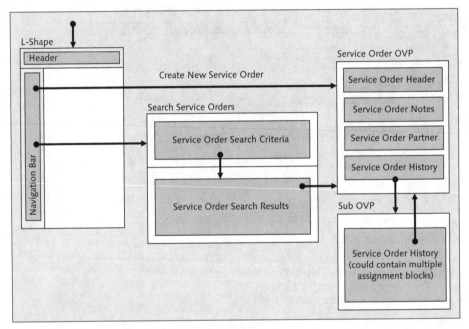

Figure 1.18   Interaction Patterns

If you choose to search for existing data, the results appear in a dedicated assignment block. From there you could navigate to an overview page that contains all the information about the selected SAP CRM business object. This information is grouped into assignment blocks. Some of these blocks can contain links themselves. Such links might take you to overview pages of dependent business objects (*sub-OVPs*).

In the past, when editing data in an assignment blocks, the user would be redirected to a separate *edit view*. Although most of the OVPs now can be edited, you might still find views that require dedicated editing pages. This pattern is appropriate when the AB contains a summary of the most important information, but more data is available when editing. Figure 1.19 displays this pattern.

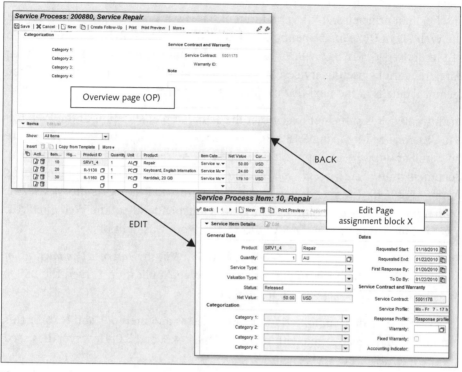

Figure 1.19 Editing a CRM Business Object Pattern

The trend is clearly towards editing without leaving the OVP. As we will see later in the book, editing requires locking business-object data. As we do not want to lock each object entity that we view, OVPs are typically shown in display mode. The user might be able to differentiate between editing all the data on the OVP or only the data in a particular assignment block (for example, when the data there belongs to a different business object). In either case, the framework might present to the user the same page where all the relevant assignment blocks are editable.

1.2   Architecture

SAP CRM is a Web-based application, and as such it runs on the *SAP Web Application Server*. The latter contains two runtime environments: *ABAP* and *Java EE (Java*

Enterprise Edition). The Web Client UI is based on the ABAP stack and does not make use of Java technology.

The framework follows the WebDynpro architecture. While it complies with overall architectural principles, it is a very different framework. The biggest differences in the Web Client UI lie in its openness and extensibility. In addition, it is built on top of the *Business Object Layer (BOL)*, which offers uniform access to the underlying data and various useful services. We will talk about the BOL and the rest of the technical details in the next few chapters of this book.

At this point, it is sufficient to say that the actual implementation of the Web Client UI is realized by using SAP's *Business Server Pages (BSP) framework*. If you are not familiar with the BSP application paradigm, we recommend that you use SAP documentation, visit *www.sdn.sap.com*, or get one of the BSP development books from SAP PRESS. The rest of you already know that BSP supports the *Model View Controller (MVC)* concept. Although this exists independently of the Web Client UI, it is the foundation on top the SAP CRM framework was built on.

The user interface is a *Business Server Page* (BSP). Via the *Internet Communication Manager* (ICM), which is also part of the SAP Web Application Server, the BSP is transferred as a Web page to the frontend client.

In general, BSPs are a combination of ABAP classes and methods and HTML. This technology was already used within SAP CRM 3.1, 4.0, and 5.0. However, it is used very differently in the Web Client UI.

Figure 1.20 shows the main architectural components that affect the delivery of the SAP CRM content to the end user. As you can see, the SAP CRM user interface can be rendered as a standalone Web application or as part of SAP's *Enterprise Portal*.

In this book we will not focus on the portal integration. Once you know how to develop and configure Web Client UI applications, you could learn this from your documentation and SDN.

Figure 1.21 shows the high-level architectural layers in the Web Client UI.

We now need to expand our earlier description of a Web Client UI application as a BSP application. Server applications typically include three main layers: presentation, logic, and data. Those of you familiar with Web application development can easily recognize them. The end user communicates with SAP CRM via the browser, so the first layer is the HTML code rendered by the browser. This HTML code is produced by the software component in the presentation layer. This is where the BSP programming model comes in.

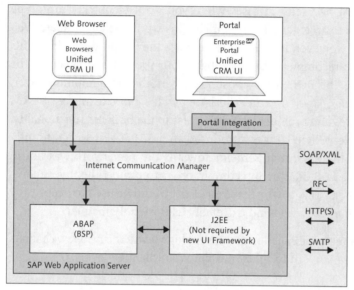

Figure 1.20 Main Software Components

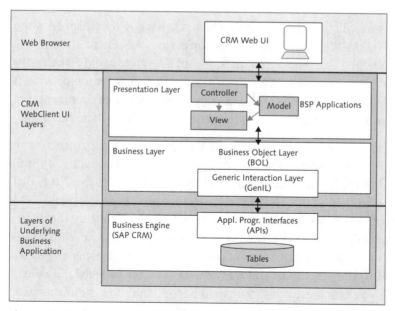

Figure 1.21 Web Client UI Architecture Layers

The Web Client UI sits on top of BSPs but has its own set of application programming interfaces (APIs), concepts, and development tools. You can create a Web Client UI application that retrieves data directly from the data source in the presentation layer itself. This might be useful in cases when you want to quickly prototype something or connect to an external data source. This would be a legitimate Web Client UI application. However, in order to experience the full power and benefits of the framework, we recommend that you base your presentation layer on the business object layer. The BOL is the consumer of another programming layer, called *Generic Interaction Layer (GenIL)*. The latter wraps the existing SAP CRM programming interfaces and provides uniform access to the backend functionality. Remember that the Web Client UI was introduced after SAP invested significantly in SAP CRM. One of the main requirements towards the framework was not to change the underlying SAP CRM architecture in order to protect the investments of the existing customers. That is why the Web Client UI can be used to expose any ABAP functionality in a real-world and extremely user friendly manner.

We will leave the architecture discussion at this very high level. The next few chapters will provide you with plenty of insights into the Web Client UI layers.

1.3   Tools in Web Client UI

In these sections we will look into the tools which you have at your disposal when developing SAP CRM Web Client UI applications. The Web Client UI is in the ABAP stack. Therefore, you will use all the standard ABAP tools and transactions available in SAP NetWeaver. The Web Client UI tools are built on top of what is already available in SAP NetWeaver. The existing development environments are complemented with tools that allow you to produce Web Client UI applications.

As of SAP Business Suite 7.0, the Web Client UI is made available to the entire business suite. You can now develop custom applications that run on top of ECC, CRM, SRM, and other solutions. The drawback of SAP Business Suite 7.0 is that although the Web Client is there, the relevant access points are not visible and organized for you. Therefore, you have to know and execute explicitly the different transactions, maintenance views, and view clusters required to develop a Web Client UI application. The situation improves significantly in EhP1, when the access to the various Web Client UI tools and registries is available in SPRO. There is a small catch: The access to these transactions can be found in the customizing path for FI-CA, but activation is required via FI-CA switch.

The Web Client UI recognizes four distinct categories of users, whose use of the technology is illustrated in Figure 1.22:

- ▶ End users (business users)
- ▶ Developers (technical consultants)
- ▶ Administrators
- ▶ Power users

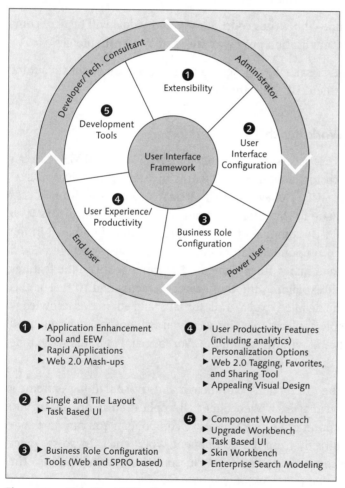

Figure 1.22 Web Client UI Tooling

Everything we discussed in the previous sections is intended for the end user (business user). Personalization and configuration of the UI are related, and we will cover configuration first.

Administrator and power user roles are often merged in organizations. Hence we will use these terms interchangeably. We sometimes distinguish them in order to indicate the level of authorization required. The administrator needs more permissions than the power user. The power user also requires less technical knowledge and might be a business user who is somewhat technology-savvy.

The developer is someone who writes code. Such an individual will be very comfortable with ABAP, BSP application programming, and Web technologies.

With the above in mind, we can take a closer look at the tools you might encounter when developing Web Client UI applications.

1.3.1   Component Work Bench

The *Component Workbench* is accessible via Transaction BSP_WD_CMPWB. You can also access it from the customizing in SPRO, via the menu path CUSTOMER RELATIONSHIP MANAGEMENT • UI FRAMEWORK • UI FRAMEWORK DEFINITION • ACCESS UI COMPONENT WORKBENCH. This tool facilitates the development of the Web Client UI components. A UI component is the uppermost building block in the Web Client UI. Within a component, you can develop controllers and views, and define navigation links and many other elements. We cannot explain the features of this tool without first explaining the framework elements and APIs. For this reason, we will leave the detailed explanation for later and share this knowledge as we develop our sample applications. This way, you will not feel overwhelmed by the various concepts and wizards within the Workbench, but at the same time be learning how to use them.

For now, let us open the Component Workbench and try something extremely simple. You just learned that each Web Client UI application is organized into components. The entry point of SAP CRM is also a component. You can start your SAP CRM application directly from the Component Workbench. To do so, enter the name of the frame component, CRM_UI_FRAME, and click the TEST button. The SAP CRM Web UI will open in a new browser window.

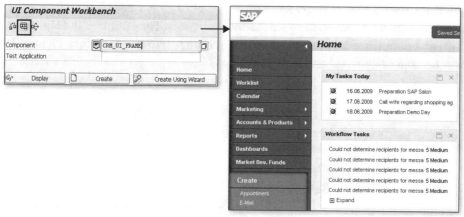

Figure 1.23 Running CRM_UI_FRAME Component from Component Workbench

You just learned how to test and run UI components. You will do this frequently while developing.

How to Start CRM UI

If you test component CRM_UI_FRAME and are using a newer version of SAP CRM, you will see a page telling you that there is a better way to start the Web Client UI. For instructions on how to start SAP CRM, see SAP Note 1173951. However, you can save some time in the future by using Transaction WUI (or bookmarking the URL).

1.3.2 Skins and Skin Work Bench

The *skins* allow you to adjust the visual layout of the user interface to match your customer's preferences (for example the corporate identity). SAP CRM comes with five standard skins:

▸ Signature Design (cross-SAP standard design)

▸ Default

▸ Serenity

▸ New Hope

▸ High Contrast (a skin suitable for visually impaired users)

The end user can personalize the layout via skins via the PERSONALIZE link in the header area of the L-shape. Once on the PERSONALIZATION page, you need to follow the PERSONALIZE LAYOUT link. As of CRM 7.0 EhP1, the user can also change the dominant color of each skin to suit individual tastes. For example, the Signature Design is dominated by blue. The user might change it to green, and the end result will be as per Figure 1.24.

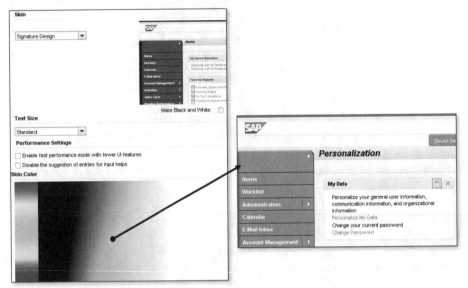

Figure 1.24 Selecting a Skin and Changing Its Color

Adjusting skins in SAP CRM 2007 involved direct manipulations of BSP applications. However, SAP CRM 7.0 provides a workbench in IMG that facilitates exploring and copying of SAP default skins. You can access this tool by following the menu path CUSTOMER RELATIONSHIP MANAGEMENT • UI FRAMEWORK • UI FRAMEWORK DEFINITION • SKINS • ACCESS SKIN WORKBENCH or via Transaction CRMC_SKIN_WB.

The standard skins are stored in the MIME repository of the BSP application THT-MLB_STYLES. Depending on the skin, the files are automatically uploaded by the thtmlb:content tag (we will discuss BSP tags later in this book).

Each skin consists of a number of *style sheets*. The styles and pictures used to create the *THTMLB* controls are separated into CSS style sheets. The latter is a standard technology (CSS) and is accepted by the industry and development community.

Skinning also means that you can create custom skins in a modification-free manner, meaning that the next upgrade should not affect them. The Skin Workbench helps you achieve that.

Here is a summary of what you need to do in order to create a custom skin:

1. Create a BSP application (in your namespace).

2. Start the skin workbench.

3. Select an SAP skin.

4. Click on the COPY SAP SKIN button and provide the details about the new skin's name and your BSP application.

5. If you want to start using your skin right away, select the ADD SKIN TO CUS-TOMIZING option. We recommend doing this. The skin will become available on the central personalization page of the CRM Web Client, under the layout settings.

The Skin Workbench displays the standard and custom skins (see Figure 1.25). Your skins are displayed in a separate area below SAP SKINS. You can make your adjustments to the copied skin. The actions you can perform on each element are available in the context menu (right-click). If you select an image folder, you can also display an overview of the available images (name and picture).

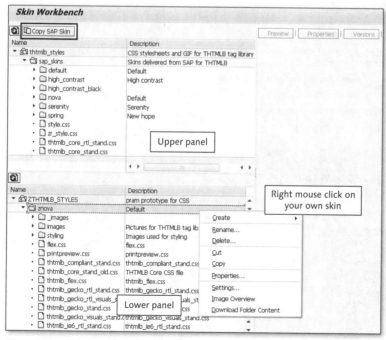

Figure 1.25 Skin Workbench

We will not go into the details of how the Skin Workbench works. The documentation in SPRO provides sufficient information for you to start exploring the features on your own.

If a skin is not needed any more, but you do not want to delete it, the skin can be deactivated. Run Transaction SM30 and maintain Table CRMC_THTMLB_SKNE. Each entry there specifies a skin that will be excluded from the skin dropdown box on the PERSONALIZATION page. You can use this functionality for a temporary deactivation of a skin; for example if you want seasonal layouts.

Often all you need to get started with your custom project is to change the logo and the text in the header area. At least in the beginning, the standard SAP skins will be adequate for this. Prior to EhP1, you had to go through the above procedure and create your custom skin. There, you would have to allocate the logo file and change it. In EhP1, you can exchange the logo (browser specific, skin specific, or across skins) without having to create custom skins. You don't have to worry about CSS files. All you need to do is upload your logos and register them using standard customizing (see Figure 1.26).

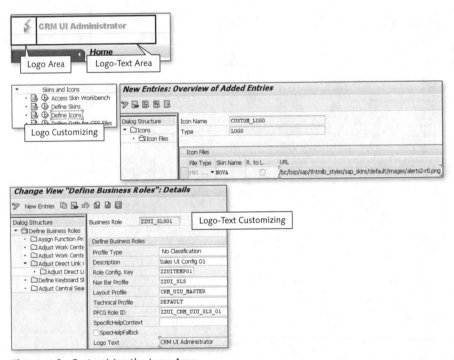

Figure 1.26 Customizing the Logo Area

In EhP1, the logo area has been enhanced with a freely definable text accompanying the image. You can define the logo text as part your business role customizing (in SPRO or in the Web UI).

1.3.3 Configuration and Personalization

The *UI configuration* concept facilitates the configuration of views and pages. You can control aspects such as positioning, adding, removing and/or relabeling of fields on views. The same applies to assignment blocks in overview pages. In addition you can define different configurations for different occasions (for example, one business role might see fields or views that another does not).

In this section, we will introduce the main concept behind the UI configuration tool. We will provide details along with practical examples later in the book.

Whenever you want to change the layout and texting of pages, blocks, and fields, we recommend that you use the UI configuration tool. Before you can access it, make sure that you have enabled the configuration mode in the PERSONALIZATION page and have the right permissions.

In the header area, next to the history buttons, you will find three new buttons (see Figure 1.27).

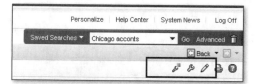

Figure 1.27 Configuration and Personalization Buttons

The first one, SHOW CONFIGURABLE AREAS, allows you to configure views. The second is CONFIGURE PAGE and is used to control the assignment blocks that are displayed on the current page. The third button, PERSONALIZE, allows end users to personalize the current page. A variant of this button also exists on most assignment blocks. Thus, end users can fine tune the content on each block.

We will start with view configuration. If you click this button, the display will suddenly change and you will be able to select each view that is configurable. Once you click on such a view, you will get the view configuration. As you know, there are two types of standard views in CRM: forms and tables. The configuration tool will reflect that. In the case of forms, you will be working with fields, while in the case of tables you will be working with columns. Figure 1.28 shows what you will see when configuring a form view.

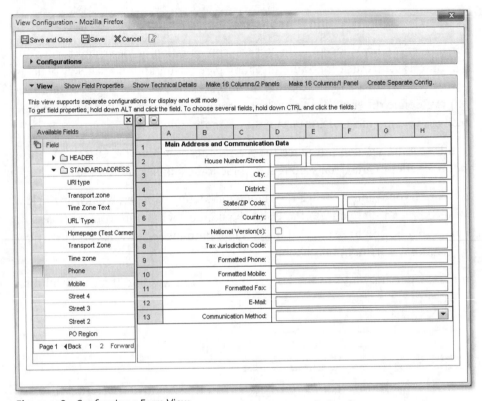

Figure 1.28 Configuring a Form View

You could select fields from the AVAILABLE FIELDS block on the left and move it to the grid on the right. Web Client UI allows you to work with three types of grids:

▶ 8 columns 1 panel guided mode

▶ 16 columns 2 panel guided mode

▶ 16 columns 1 panel freestyle mode

In the freestyle mode there are rules for moving up, down, left, and right (as long as there is enough space).

It is important to note that as of SAP CRM 7.0 one can move fields and columns via drag and drop. Figure 1.29 shows a table view configuration.

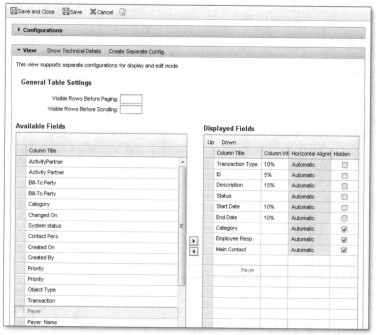

Figure 1.29 Table View Configuration

The configuration tool is very intuitive once you start using it. Moreover, you will have plenty of practice with the examples in this book.

The overview pages can have a single column or tile layouts. Configuring the first one should be fairly easy to visualize. You have a list of assignment blocks and you move them (drag and drop is available) into a single column. When configuring a tile layout, you need to select your layout first: 2 by 2, 2 by 4, and so on. In general, you can define any type of tile layout using the customizing activity CUSTOMER RELATIONSHIP MANAGEMENT • UI FRAMEWORK DEFINITION • FACT SHEET • MAINTAIN FACT SHEET. You might be wondering why the layout definition is next to the fact sheets. This is purely due to historical reasons (in the past, tile layout configuration made sense only for fact sheets). A screenshot of a tile layout configuration is presented in Figure 1.30.

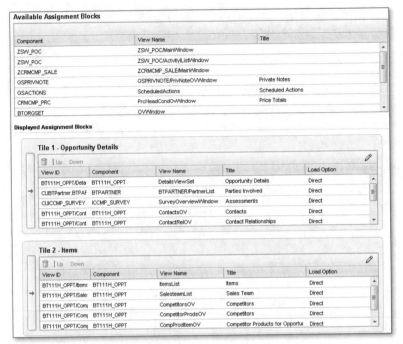

Figure 1.30   Tile Layout Configuration

In general when configuring, you are specifying what will be available to the end user. Each user belongs to a business role. You can define different configurations for different business roles, but it is not necessary to deal with that now.

Based on the configuration, the end user might fine-tune the layout of pages and views. These changes will affect only the end user who performs them. This concept is called *personalization*; you can consider it a limited version of the configuration tool. When defining the view or page configuration, we do not only specify the layout but also control the labels and the visibility of the fields and blocks. Thus, if we mark a given column in a table view as hidden, the user will not see it the first time he or she opens that view. However, the end user could click on the PERSONALIZE button of that view and enable the hidden column to appear. They will not see the columns that you left in the AVAILABLE FIELDS block (not part of the DISPLAYED FIELDS block). Similarly, you could configure a given assignment block to have a LAZY LOAD OPTION. The end user will see that block as collapsed each time he or she loads the page. Should the user always need the information in that block, it will be very frustrating to expand the block each time he or she visits the page. By personalizing the load settings for that assignment block, the end user can solve this problem.

Figure 1.31 displays the personalization options for the home page.

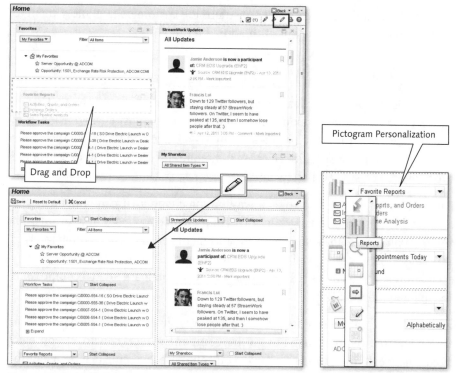

Figure 1.31 Personalization of the Home Page

Business users can position the content on each screen easily via drag and drop. Unwanted content can be easily removed via the X in the top right corner of the view. In EhP1, the users can personalize pictograms per views (though only on home, work center pages, and for the reports page). These pictograms serve as content identifiers and differ across skins (some skins, like Signature Design, do not have pictograms).

1.4   Extensibility

SAP is a leader in business automation software and provides comprehensive solutions targeting various industries. However, no matter how extensive the standard functionalities are, businesses will always end up enhancing and customizing standard offerings. This is entirely natural, because each business has specific needs and possesses unique features that make it stand out among its competitors. Therefore, SAP applications and solutions don't constraint the customers, but allow them to innovate and add value to the out-of the-box offerings.

1.4.1   Overview

Extensibility is the principle that allows for the addition of extensions that range from customizing to the development of add-ons or composites. Extensions can either be made by customers, partners, or by SAP. Extensibility allows customers and partners to support specific use cases and requirements that cannot, or should not, be covered by standard software.

Enhancement is often referred to as a way of enhancing a UI component. If you want to make functional changes in a UI component—to create new events, for example—you can use the component enhancement concept. This is often referred to as *enhancement set* and is available in the BSP Component Workbench. It is a very specific approach that allows customers to modify the standard SAP UI components in an upgrade-safe manner.

In addition to the enhancement sets, SAP offers ways to enhance applications from the Web UI itself (with no need to go the Component Workbench). If you have created a new extension (*field* or a *table*) you could use it to enhance the views of the corresponding applications. You could enhance a standard SAP CRM application with content from an external data source (for example a custom DB table).

As you can see, the difference is subtle. Depending on how you look at the process, extensibility and enhancement could be used interchangeably. One good way to differentiate them is this: When you are creating something new you are extending; when you are adding value to something, you are enhancing.

Figure 1.32 depicts all the paradigms that are part of or related to the realm of extensibility. It also shows that the level of flexibility often comes with increased complexity. Those experienced with SAP CRM 2007 and SAP CRM 7.0 know how easy it is to configure a page or a view. Personalization is also a very intuitive process. However, if you have tried to add a new field or table with the *Easy Enhancement Workbench* (prior to SAP CRM 7.0), you know that only a technical user can do that. Extending the standard behavior of applications often requires implementing a *business add-in* (*BAdI*), something that is a task for an ABAP developer.

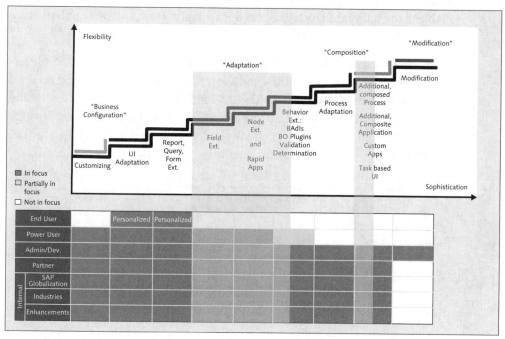

Figure 1.32 Orchestrated Extensibility

SAP CRM 7.0 and especially EhP1 have introduced tools and concepts that aim at reducing complexity. The areas of investment are highlighted in Figure 1.32. SAP has a comprehensive solution when it comes to new fields and tables (known as *structural extensibility*); the tool that supports these activities is known as the *Application Enhancement Tool* (AET). As of EhP1, AET contains an important feature known as *calculated fields* that targets some aspects of the *behavior extensibility*. Last but not least, SAP enables its customers to create and integrate new content with the *Rapid Applications* and Web 2.0 *mash-ups*. These tools support the composition of applications.

Application Enhancement Tool

AET supports the structural extensibility scenarios. It allows power users to create new fields and tables quickly without deep technical knowledge. A new field, for example, can be easily enabled as a search criterion in mobile interfaces, R3 adapters, BI Data Source, and even CRM Interactive Reporting. The user does not have to know about the complex technical steps. For example, each new field becomes available in the relevant BDocs. The tool does this automatically without bothering the user with the technical details.

As mentioned earlier, AET supports calculated fields as of EhP1. This support leverages the power of NetWeaver's BRF+ and allows definition of complex expressions based on operations and operands. The operands come from the corresponding business object, while the operations are defined in BRF+. The formula expressions are evaluated at runtime by BRF+, and the result is delivered to the UI. Figure 1.33 shows screenshots from AET (enhancements overview and a calculated field).

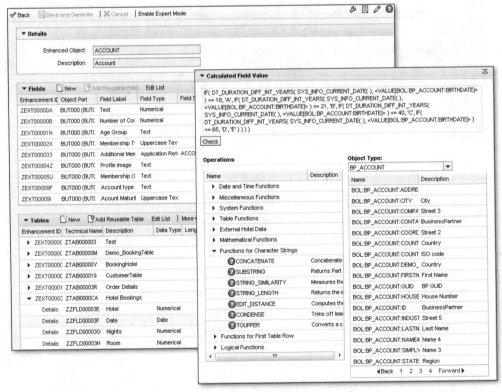

Figure 1.33 Enhancements Overview and Calculated Field Screenshots

Some of the most important features of AET are outlined in Table 1.1.

Feature	Description
Field Extension	Creates new fields that complement existing applications and best match your specific business needs.
Table Extension	Extends a business object with a form or table view (1:1 vs. 1:N cardinality). Each table extension consists of fields.
Calculated Fields	Defines calculation expressions as part of the field definition. The result is a read-only field that is part of the business object layer (BOL), but is not persisted in the database.
Search Relevance	Specifies whether a given field will become part of the search criteria or search result view.
Migration of Manual Fields	Migrates existing fields, created manually or via EEWB, to the new format (AET).
Extension Artifacts	Extends the supported external interfaces such as Mobile, R/3, BW, and OLTP reporting.
Field Reusability	Easily reuses custom fields and tables in applications that share common extension places.
How To Deploy	Produces a comprehensive report on what transports are affected by a given extension.

Table 1.1 Application Enhancement Tool Features

The fields and tables are created in a way that all the tiers of an application are aware of their existence. For example, the fields are created in dedicated enhancement includes and thus become part of the data structures used by the application APIs, BADIs, etc. These fields and tables become an integral part of the application. Therefore, this scenario is often referred to as tight coupling.

Rapid Applications

As of EhP1, SAP CRM users can take advantage of a new tool and concept called Rapid Application (RAP). RAP facilitates the generation of applications based on existing data sources. In the Web UI, users have access to a subset of RAP that allows even the business users to quickly generate standalone applications based on a Web service or a database table (existing in DDIC). The Component Workbench in SAP

GUI provides access to a wizard that helps developers to easily generate a fully functional UI application based on existing BOL models. Both tools allow users to influence the input (data model) and the result (UI model) via wizards that guide them throughout the process. The tools produce dedicated UI components that can be further modified as per the specific business requirements.

However, because the target user group is different, the RAP tools differ in terms of usability and features. In the Web UI tool, for example, the user can enable the new application for any business role and can start using it immediately. The Component Workbench wizard, on the other hand, does not affect the navigation profiles. Additional customizing is required before the applications can be presented to end users.

Once RAP applications are created, they can be used as standalone applications, or integrated within existing business applications. This process is facilitated by an *Embedding View* tool. During the embedding, the user can map the attributes of the target application to those of the RAP. When rendered, the embedding view will present content that is pertinent to the hosting applications. As a result, one can create application mash-ups. The procedure is shown in Figure 1.34.

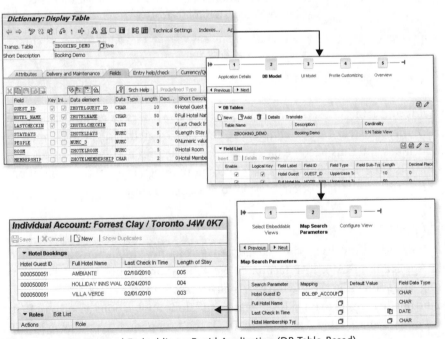

Figure 1.34 Creating and Embedding a Rapid Application (DB Table-Based)

Mash-ups

The concept of mash-ups and embedding of views has been enhanced with the support of widgets based on URLs or JS/HTML. This feature is known as *Web 2.0 mash-up*. It allows users to create new functionality that is based on content that exists on the Web and is mixed with data from the SAP CRM business applications. The result is a brand new functionality that was not planned by either SAP CRM or by the Web resource providers (see Figure 1.35).

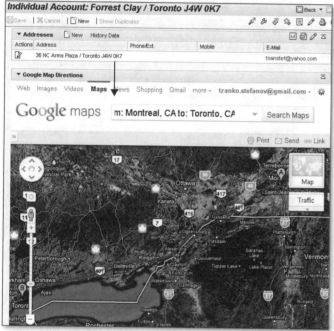

Figure 1.35 A Web 2.0 Mash-up Between Google Maps and CRM Accounts

The embedding of views (mash-ups) happens at a UI level. The layers of the RAP and business applications below the UI are completely unaware of each other. Therefore, this paradigm is often referred to as *loose coupling*.

Conclusion

Figure 1.36 provides an architectural overview of the extensibility paradigms discussed so far. For example, it shows that all RAPs that are generated from DB tables use a common GenIL component. In contrast, each Web-service- based RAP has a dedicated GenIL component. The Web 2.0 mash-ups exist solely in the UI layer (with no backend logic).

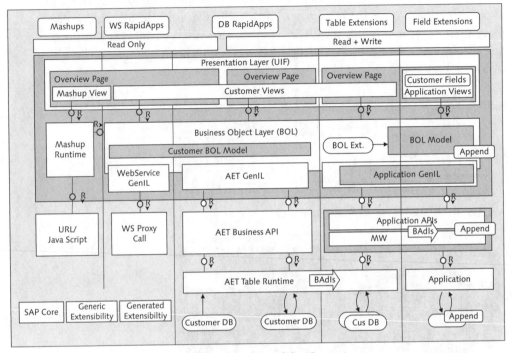

Figure 1.36 Architectural Overview of the Extensibility Concepts

All the tools discussed above offer an easy-to-use interface that can be easily understood by users who do not have deep technical knowledge. Many of the basic scenarios can be covered by using these concepts. SAP is aware that there will be cases that go beyond the existing extensibility tools. Therefore, there is always a way for the technical experts to fine-tune the results and enhance them to meet actual requirements. Even in cases when further development is required, we believe that the available tools offer productivity gains and a solid foundation upon which one can build additional features.

1.4.2 Design Layer

When we presented the architecture layers, we saw that the presentation layer can be based on what we call a business object layer (BOL). The *design layer* is positioned

64

between the UI layer and the BOL. It facilitates the semantic definition of the SAP CRM business object.

The design layer stores these semantic definitions into *design objects*. The latter specify which attributes from a given BOL are relevant to which SAP CRM application. The first question that we need to address is: How is an SAP CRM application modeled? From a UI perspective, it is represented by a page and a set of views. However, each page can actually be used to visualize data from different applications. A good example is the BP_HEAD component that is used for CRM accounts and contacts. It is clear that there must be something else that uniquely defines the semantic of entities. This is the so called *UI object type* (often, simply *object type*). Each CRM application (business object) has a unique UI object type. Therefore, the entry point into the modeling of design objects is the UI object type. Each object type contains a list of design objects. Some of them refer to the same object parts but expose different subsets of the available attributes. This is because the different scenarios in CRM require variations of the business applications. For example, the account object is represented via BP_ACCOUNT object type. It has many design objects. Each points to a different BOL object. However, if you look at them closely you will see that many design objects point to the same BOL object. For example, BP_NOTES and BP_NOTES_PH are associated with BOL object name BuilNotes. The reason is simple: The second design object was introduced to expose the attributes relevant to the pharmaceutical scenario (industry). Both design objects can expose attributes from BuilNotes, but they can expose a different subset of these attributes.

In order to access the standard SAP design objects you can use Transaction BSP_DLC_SDESIGN. This functionality is also available through customizing via the menu path CUSTOMER RELATIONSHIP MANAGEMENT • UI FRAMEWORK • UI FRAMEWORK DEFINITION • DESIGN LAYER • DEFINE DESIGN OBJECTS.

When creating your views you can associate one or more design objects to them. At runtime, the framework will check this assignment and determine what fields from which design object are relevant for the current SAP CRM application. The UI object type plays a key role in determining the relevant design objects. However, developers could do the assignments to the design objects in a very free manner (though this is rarely used). The important thing to remember at this point is that there is an association between the view models in the presentation layer and the design objects. This allows you to achieve the main functionality behind the design layer, which is to control:

- Field visibility (by hiding the irrelevant fields)
- Field label assignment
- Generic value helps from DDIC
- Field types from DDIC

All of the above activities are done centrally and affect all the related CRM applications. This increases efficiency by simplifying the task of maintaining the same settings for the semantically identical fields in different views and applications.

Here is a short example (Figure 1.37). If you open a CRM account, you might find a field called E-Mail. Suppose that your customer wants to see Email Address instead of E-Mail. You can open the related design object (this happens to be STANDARDADDRESS) and change the Field Label of the attribute E_MAILSMT to "Email Address." From now on, each view (not only the account application) that points to this design object and the email attribute will show Email Address in the UI.

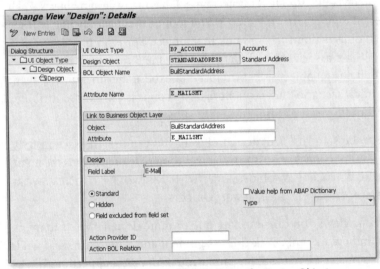

Figure 1.37 Changing the Settings of an Attribute of a Design Object

To view the design layer assignments in the Web UI, mark a given field with your cursor and press the [F2] button on your keyboard. The technical settings window will appear. At the bottom of it you will see the design layer settings for the selected field.

1.4.3 Web Service Tool

The benefits of Web services are widely documented. Their essential value is that they give you a standard way to access business data. You don't have to worry about the way the functionality was developed or implemented. To the Web-service consumer, the service is a black box that returns information when invoked. The invocation happens over HTTP(s), so you do not need to implement any proprietary communication protocols.

As part of SAP's service-oriented architecture initiative, SAP CRM provides many well-documented Web services to expose business functionality to the outside world. At the same time, new Web services need to fit the specific needs of an organization. SAP has always provided many ways to do this, and the process is well-documented and efficient. For example, one can expose an ABAP function module as a Web service. SAP CRM, however, has gone one step further to make this process more user friendly and less challenging technically. A tool, called *Web Service Tool* (WST) allows you to expose CRM business objects as Web services.

The key benefits of using the WST are:

- Ability to define services for your exact needs
- Simple four-step wizard for quick service definition and provision
- Model-driven workbench, so no need for additional coding
- Flexible service management
- Integrated with SAP NetWeaver
- Support for Web-service templates

Web-service creation involves the use of a wizard that lets you select the business object and its attributes (see Figure 1.38), the operation you want to support (query, create, read, and update), set default values (optional) for attributes, and give aliases to attributes (optional). The wizard ultimately generates a Web service that is consumable by an appropriate client. The tool also lets you test Web services before publishing it to the outside world. We will cover WST in Chapter 12.

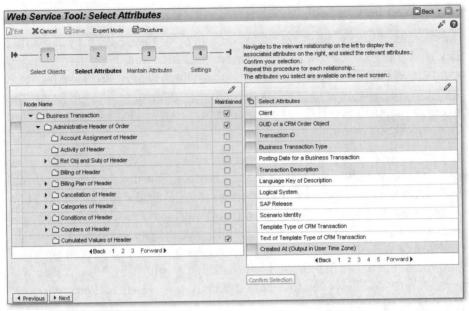

Figure 1.38 Web Service Tool

1.4.4 Groupware

One of the most popular features of any application, at least among information workers, is the ability to use features and applications that integrate tightly with their tool of choice: their email and calendaring application.

No SAP CRM implementation can do without this feature. The idea is very simple: to let users have one central calendar and task list, one place to see contacts and accounts, and an easy and intuitive way to link business emails to the central CRM system. There are many strategies for making this feature available, and each has its strengths and limitation. We have chosen to describe in detail the preferred way—client-side integration—later in this book (Chapter 14). SAP CRM supports server-side integration as well, but that method is outside scope of this book. We will only focus on Microsoft Outlook.

Technically, SAP has developed plug-ins for Microsoft Outlook to communicate with CRM server. Chapter 14 focuses solely on this topic. There, we will provide a detailed overview of the architecture and discuss ways of customizing and enhancing this integration.

1.4.5   Office and Adobe Integration

Microsoft Office and Adobe integration are crucial to the success of any implementation that needs output management in a traditional format such as paper. In order to keep the overall architecture consistent and to use standards such as Web services, XSLT, etc., the Microsoft Office integration in SAP CRM (starting from CRM 2007) uses custom XML feature of Word 2003+ and Adobe XML to define document templates. The goal of such integration is to give power users an environment in which to define templates in native editors (Microsoft Word for Word templates and Adobe Lifecycle designer for Adobe templates). The power user defines a template that the end user can use to create an actual document. The template consists of static text and dynamic variables. Dynamic variables point to SAP CRM business application data and are resolved when the document is created. The final document can be printed or saved in the SAP CRM system (they become attachments to a SAP CRM business object). We will cover this integration in detail in Chapter 13.

1.5   Enterprise Search

Previously, we introduced the central search component and discussed simplified advanced search and saved search functionalities. We deliberately left out the so-called simple search. The latter utilizes a dedicated search engine: *SAP TREX*. The result is a fast, almost real-time, Google-like search feature. End users can enter a free text in the central search component, and the simple search will deliver all the matching results across all available SAP CRM business objects. The best part is that the search criteria do not have to be exact; the simple search will try to find close matches.

1.5.1   Overview

From a search functionality perspective, the simple search delivers a free text search that implements a fuzzy search algorithm. The latter yields results even when there is no exact match. In addition, users can provide wild cards as part of the free text. The search will scan across CRM business objects and across multiple attributes. For example, if you search for "perry," the results could contain all the employees where the name is "perry," all the opportunities where someone called "perry" is involved, and so on (Figure 1.39).

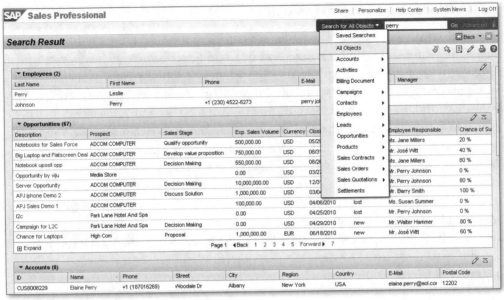

Figure 1.39 Simple Search Results

From a user-interface perspective, the simple search results are presented in a special page where all the hits are grouped per SAP CRM business object type. These groups are assignment blocks that can be personalized and configured. As a result, one can configure and/or personalize the search result page so that it contains results from specific business objects only. In addition, the blocks support column filtering, which helps the end user drill down quickly through the results.

As mentioned, the simple search requires a TREX engine. There are two ways to utilize the SAP TREX search engine. The first one is the so called *embedded search*. It requires that SAP TREX be installed along with SAP CRM and will produce results from that system only. The second option is the *enterprise search*. It requires a separate search appliance (a server). One can configure the enterprise search appliance to scan through structured data across multiple systems. Unfortunately, results from other systems will not be available in SAP CRM. This does not mean that you cannot get the results through the enterprise search server itself.

Before you can use the simple search and even the central search, you need to perform certain configurations. In customizing (IMG), the menu path CUSTOMER RELATION MANAGEMENT • UI FRAMEWORK • TECHNICAL ROLE DEFINITIONS will lead you to DEFINE CENTRAL SEARCH. There you can specify which business objects will be available in the central search component and the types of searches users can perform on them. Then you can create business-role specific customizations as part of the business role configuration.

1.5.2 Search Modeling Workbench

Not all the SAP CRM objects are enabled for simple search. One can open the *SAP CRM Enterprise Search (ES) Modeling Workbench* (Transaction CRM_ES_WB) and see what business objects are modeled there. The *search models* are based on the CRM GenIL/BOL models. If you are experienced in using BOL, you could easily find which attributes are marked as search criteria and search results (see Figure 1.40). If you have enough knowledge of the enterprise search technology, you could also create custom search models. The SAP CRM ES Modeling Workbench generates *search templates* which are used by NetWeaver Enterprise Search to index and retrieve information.

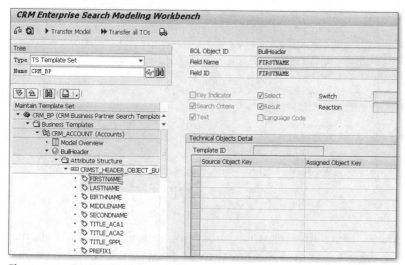

Figure 1.40 CRM ES Modeling Workbench

If you want to administer the search models in SAP TREX, you have to launch the *Enterprise Search Administration Cockpit* via the Web Dynpro application ESH_ADMIN_ UI_COMPONENT. There you can start and track initial loading of data from SAP CRM to the search engine. You could also define and track the schedule for updating search indexes with changed data from SAP CRM. Before you attempt any of these, you should consult your SAP documentation.

1.6   Collaboration

In SAP CRM 7.0, SAP enabled users to take advantage of various Web 2.0 features. Users can personalize blocks and pages and even add widgets to the home page. SAP invested further in Web 2.0, and as of EhP1 provided tools that promote collaboration and community sharing.

1.6.1   RSS Feeds

There is also the option to subscribe to an *RSS feed* from the PERSONALIZE page. An end user can subscribe to different types of notifications (see Figure 1.41). The notification can be delivered to any standard RSS feed reader.

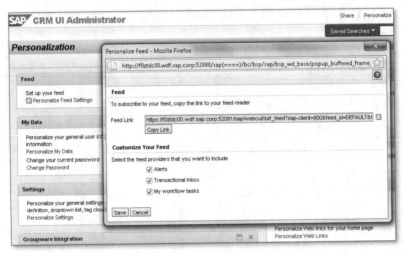

Figure 1.41   RSS Feeds Personalization

The administrator can control what is available in customizing (IMG) via the menu path CUSTOMER RELATION MANAGEMENT • UI FRAMEWORK • UI FRAMEWORK DEFINITION • FEEDS.

1.6.2   Favorites and Tags

As of EhP1, SAP CRM users can mark business objects as *favorites* (with one click of a button). In addition, they can *tag* an object. As you know from using the Web, tagging is a way to assign a semantically meaningful identifier to a Web resource. The results of tagging are often visualized in so-called *tag clouds*. If many users use the same identifier (tag name) for a given resource, it appears more prominently (bolder) in the cloud than the tags created by fewer users. As a result, the tag cloud helps users to quickly find relevant information that is considered important by the community. The ideas of tagging and tag clouds have been adopted in SAP CRM. Moreover, users have ways to organize both tags and favorites and may share them with the user community. The home page can contain two new trays: one for favorites and the other for tags (see Figure 1.42).

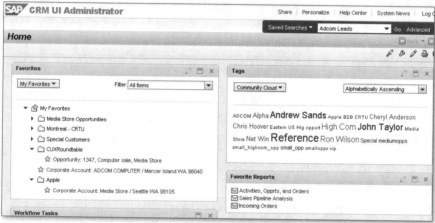

Figure 1.42   Favorites and Tags on SAP CRM Home Page

1.6.3   Central Sharing Tool

If you have EhP1, you will see that the header area contains a new link called SHARE. It is the entry point of the *Central Sharing Tool* (CST) that allows user to share information with their colleagues. CST provides ways of sharing tags, favorites, saved searches, and favorite reports. Users can share across business roles, users, organizations, and positions (see Figure 1.43). This is also the place where users receive items shared by others. It is the first collaboration tool in SAP CRM.

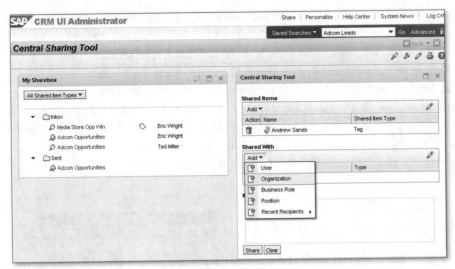

Figure 1.43 Central Sharing Tool

To activate the CST feature, you must assign the *function profile* CENTRAL_SHARING_TOOL to the desired business roles. The function profile can have the following values:

▶ RECIPIENT: The feature is enabled but users cannot initiate shares. They can only receive shares.

▶ SHARER: The feature is enabled and users can share data.

▶ SUPERSHARER: Same as SHARER except that users can also push the saved search directly to the recipients' central search without any necessary action from the recipients.

You can also add the CST tray to the homepage. To do so, simply add UI component WCF_UST_SH_BOX (interface view USTSH) in your runtime repository component usages.

The above explanations contain a few terms that probably are new to you. We will tackle them later in the book, and you can then revisit this section if you are interested in the topic.

1.7 Sample Business Scenario

In the previous sections we introduced different tools and concepts. As with any introduction, this probably provided more questions than answers. The subsequent chapters will flesh on the details, but we also will describe them in the context of a sample business scenario. As we will be constantly referring to this scenario, it makes sense to outline it now. You may find the examples oversimplified, but this is intentional as we want to focus on the technologies and also target a very diverse audience.

Imagine that you are supporting the systems of a company in the hospitality industry. Your company operates several hotels. This involves providing services to the hotel guests and running a loyalty program. The activities of your guests are tracked via a dedicated reservation system (it could be even custom-built).

Your company has just purchased SAP CRM 7.0 EhP1. Some of the challenges include customizing the SAP standard deliveries to meet your company's specific business needs. As the existing reservation system is doing a great job, no one wants to change it. However, it will be a great advantage if you can bring some of the data into the SAP CRM system.

It is safe to assume that there will be mapping between the business partners (accounts) in SAP CRM and the hotel guests from the existing systems. You can expect that the business partner (BP) ID in SAP CRM will be mapped to an identifier from the reservation system called "Guest ID." Many of the examples will be based on this assumption.

The reservation system keeps track of all guest bookings. It is easy to find out in what hotel, room, on what dates, and for how long your guests have stayed. One of the challenges is to bring this information into SAP CRM. One option would be to create dedicated database tables and replicate the data from your reservation systems on a regular basis (with *SAP CRM Middleware* for example). Another option would be to expose your reservation data with a Web service and call this service from your SAP CRM system. Both approaches have advantages and disadvantages. Regardless of which option you choose, you will have to overcome the challenge of building your UI, integrating the content into SAP CRM, and even enhancing existing CRM objects.

From now on, when we discuss the Web Client UI tools and concepts, we will always stick to these use cases as much as possible. We believe they are simple enough to understand and suitable for building sample applications. You will be able to see different solutions to the same problem and also find recommendations on the best approaches for given situations.

1.8   Summary

In this chapter, we gave you a crash course in Web Client UI basics. It is not expected that you understand everything outlined here. This should serve as an overview of the different concepts that made the Web Client UI so appealing to users of SAP CRM and other solutions. We tried to split this overview into UI components, architecture, tools, and extensibility. We also looked at the enterprise search and the collaboration support in SAP CRM.

The user interface consists of predefined building blocks that are based on different data presentation patterns. The smallest element block element is the so called view (of forms or tables). These are grouped into assignment blocks. The latter can be positions vertically one below each other or grouped in tiles.

The main interaction pattern for accessing CRM business objects typically starts with a search page. Once the user identifies the desired object, he or she navigates to an overview page. We defined the latter as an entry page. Other such pages are the home page, reports, email, and calendar.

The UI pages change based on user's interaction. The area where this happens is called the work area. It is encompassed by the so called L-shape, which is static and contains navigation links and a header area with system functionality.

The Web Client UI provides access to various productivity and usability tools. Some of them (personalization and collaboration tools) target the business end users, while others (configuration, WST, AET, etc.) are used by the so-called power users or administrators.

The development tools are available in SAP GUI. The framework comes with its own component development workbench with is integrated with the standard ABAP development tools.

We will describe the architectural details in the next few chapters. For now, it is sufficient to remember that the Web Client UI comes with its own framework and set of APIs that sit on top of the existing SAP architectures and APIs (GenIL, BOL, and the UI layers).

The Web Client UI provides various means of integration and customization. We have dedicated chapters on Groupware, Microsoft Office and Adobe integration, extensibility, and mash-ups.

Although we will explore further most of the topics introduced here, we will leave some of them out. For example, we will not explain the details of the simple search. This involves work with SAP TREX and SAP NetWeaver, and these deserve a book of their own. We advise you to check SAP Help and SDN.

We recommend that you get acquainted with the various collaboration tools (tagging, favorites, CST). They are intuitive, and with the help of your SAP documentation you will get up to speed in no time.

Although we could not describe all that the Web Client UI has to offer, we believe that you now have enough to get started.

Web applications call for extensive programming, and complex systems like these require heavy-duty code. Data buffering, caching, transactions and various kinds of runtime optimization can add a lot to your workload. You need some help in terms of services, APIs, and programming best practices.

2 Introducing the GenIL Component

In this chapter, we will examine what it takes to develop custom business logic. We will use the hotel guest-booking scenario to present the technical concepts and tools introduced by the Web Client UI framework in SAP CRM to help expose application logic in a uniform and elegant way. These concepts are known as Business Object Layer (BOL) and Generic Interaction Layer (GenIL). We already mentioned them in the first chapter. However, even if you are already familiar with SAP CRM, the chances are that BOL and GenIL are still unfamiliar. In this chapter, we hope to clear up some of the mystery. We will start with a simple example and work from the backend up to the UI. Along the way, we will show some of the latest features that simplify and speed up GenIL component development.

This and the next few chapters will probably be the most technically challenging ones. Therefore, our example might seem too primitive at times. However, our main goal is to explain the GenIL programming model as comprehensively as possible, rather than to deliver great business value. Our explanations are accompanied by plenty of code, so we urge you to try to reproduce the sample yourself (if you have a development SAP CRM system at hand). This way you can experiment on your own and eventually master the best application development practices of SAP CRM (Web Client UI) application.

In addition to explaining the architecture of the GenIL layer, in the next sections we will show you how to build a custom GenIL model. We will demonstrate what it takes to implement data query and read operations. Last, we will look at the tools available for testing GenIL components.

2.1   Introduction

While we do not want to repeat the architecture discussions from the previous chapter, we feel that you should constantly keep the big picture in mind and know exactly where you are in terms of application layering. In this section, we review the overall Web Client UI architecture, and then briefly introduce the concepts of BOL and GenIL.

2.1.1   Web Client UI Architecture

By now you should be fairly comfortable with the concept of multi-tier software architecture. You know that the Web Client UI facilitates the development of classical three-tier applications. These consist of the user interface (presentation layer), business-logic implementation layer, and data access layer (persistency layer).

Those of you familiar with enterprise application development know that data buffering and transaction control are not only very important, but also complex. Any mistakes in these will impose a heavy penalty when developing an enterprise-ready application. By enterprise-ready, we refer to systems plugged into a complex landscape, accessible simultaneously by many users at the same time and across different channels. By users, we mean other systems as well as human beings. In the context of our business scenarios, if SAP CRM was consuming data from the existing booking system via Web services, it would be considered a user.

One has to distinguish between developing user interfaces and manipulating transactional data. In big projects, you may often find separate development teams focus on the presentation layer (frontend) and the underlying business-logic implementation (backend). This is often because the heavy-duty backend logic is implemented in a dedicated layer and uses completely different concepts and infrastructures than the frontend. Some might argue that one can build a backend as part of your UI. We respond that in programming we take pride in reusability. It is important to develop common logic once and use it everywhere. For example, service and sales orders involve the same users. Do you really want to code the logic to retrieve the related business partners in each page that contains a list of parties involved? Ideally you will create instead a reusable piece of code and plug it in wherever needed. As a matter of fact, you can look at the whole one-order implementation and see that the objects there are used across most of the SAP CRM business applications. If you have to code the logic for retrieving the one-order data in the presentation layer, you could easily multiply the code in SAP CRM by a factor of hundreds. The worst consequence will be maintaining that code. It will be "mission impossible."

Hopefully, we now agree on the need to encapsulate your business rules and logic in a separate layer. In addition, we need to do it in an object-oriented manner and keep the semantics of the SAP CRM business objects. This is what we will focus in this chapter. Figure 2.1 gives a high level overview of the different layers/tiers available in SAP CRM, but puts the focus on the business layer. In Web Client UI, this layer is supported by two frameworks: the Generic Interaction Layer (GenIL) and the Business Object Layer (BOL).

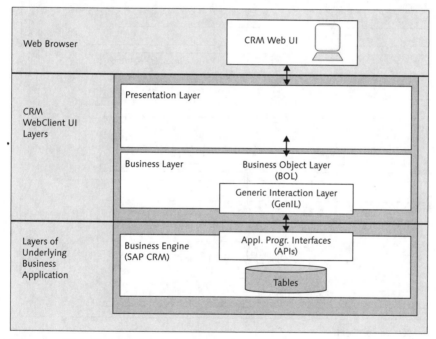

Figure 2.1 Web Client UI Multi-Tier Architecture

2.1.2   Introduction to BOL and GenIL

The BOL provides a uniform API that is used by the presentation layer (UI Components) to access the required SAP CRM business data. Behind the BOL sits the GenIL. The latter wraps the SAP CRM application logic. You can think of the two frameworks as different faces of the same coin. When you are building a UI and reading backend data, you will be working with the BOL APIs. When you are coding the backend logic (often wrapping existing application APIs) you will be implementing the GenIL APIs. In both cases, your business objects will be described via metadata as in the GenIL object model. Some might find it confusing that both BOL and GenIL use the same model, but in the end metadata is API-agnostic and both layers should be working with the same semantics. Figure 2.2 illustrates the concepts that we will examine in depth.

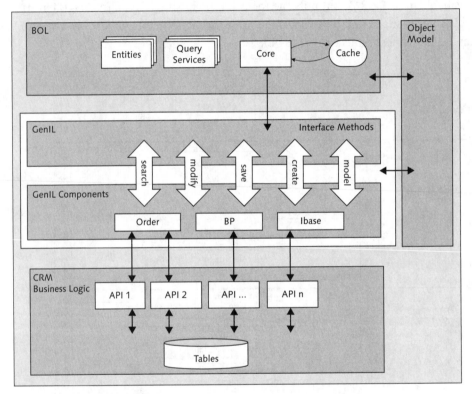

Figure 2.2   BOL versus GenIL

BOL allows you to work with entities. From an API point of view, you will be dealing with generic programming objects (for example `CL_CRM_BOL_ENTITY`, `CL_CRM_BOL_QUERY_SERVICE`, and so on). You should not expect specialized classes that represent concrete business objects (such as orders, items, business partners, etc). The concrete type of BOL entity will come from the GenIL model information associated with it (its metadata). You will be traversing a tree of entities connected via *relations* and requesting *attribute* values as per the defined model. All the entities will be represented by the same ABAP class (CL_CRM_BOL_ENTITY). But you will distinguish and access an entity by its object name (part of its metadata). The same applies to the entity attributes and the relationships between the entities. Those of you familiar with reflection should be comfortable with this concept. If you are not one of those, do not despair. We will provide plenty of examples. Apart from accessing entities and their properties, BOL allows you to execute *queries*. A query returns a result that is nothing but a collection of entities.

Let's provide a simple example of BOL programming. Suppose we have a reference to a business transaction (an order); namely, the object ID attribute value. Our goal is to retrieve the description of the order. We will execute a query called BTQUERY10 and retrieve the DESCRIPTION attribute from the order's header. The latter is represented via a GenIL business object called BTORDERHEADER. The sample code to achieve that task is provided in Listing 2.1.

```
Lv_query_service = cl_crm_bol_query_service=>get_instance( 'BTQuery10' ).
Lv_query_service ->set_property( iv_attr_name = 'OBJECT_ID'  iv_value =
'12345' ).
lv_search_result ?= qs->get_query_result( ).
lv_entity ?= lv_search_result ->get_first( ).
lv_entity = lv_entity ->get_related_entity( 'BTOrderHeader' ).
lv_entity ->get_property_as_value ( exporting iv_attr_name =
'DESCRIPTION' importing ev_resutl = descr_string).
```

Listing 2.1 Querying and Reading Transaction Data with BOL API

In addition to allowing you to work with entity and queries, BOL also has an in-memory cache service that reduces the unnecessary calls to the GenIL.

The GenIL layer dispatches the requests to the appropriate GenIL component(s) and bundles the results before it returns the request. You can think of the GenIL components as an implementation of your business objects. Each GenIL component is represented by a dedicated class that implements a set of interfaces. In classical object-oriented programming, you would probably write one class per entity. Then you probably would link the entities in your hierarchy via composition and aggregation. For example, you might have a field property in each class that points to a concrete instance of another class (creating a relationship between classes). This is not how the GenIL works. GenIL requires only one class: the GenIL component class. This class has dedicated methods for reading, modifying, saving and searching for entities (all entities). The entity hierarchy is captured in the GenIL (object) model, namely as metadata. Your implementation of create, read, modify, and search methods takes the model into consideration and retrieves whatever is requested by the consumer. The consumer is the BOL API.

The examples in this chapter will help you understand this. We will focus on the GenIL and ignore the BOL until later in the book. For now, it is important to remember that the BOL provides a uniform and yet simple way to access the SAP CRM business data. BOL is nothing but an add-on layer on top of GenIL. Among other things, BOL caches the retrieved data and provides transaction management. GenIL wraps the SAP CRM application APIs and delivers a uniform interface to retrieve and make persistent the application data. The later is semantically described via an object model used by both GenIL and BOL. We will refer to the entities in this model as business objects, or BOs.

> **GenIL Business Object**
>
> The GenIL model defines the semantics of a business application. Object- oriented programming implies that a business application is implemented via the objects. Each object is defined in a programming class. In GenIL, you have only one class: the GenIL component class. It is typically designed to work with a specific set of metadata: the GenIL model. The latter consists of nodes that are connected via relationships. Each node has attributes; this is where the data comes from. There is clearly a parallel between the nodes/entities in the GenIL model and an object in object-oriented programming. Therefore, in the SAP documentation, these entities are called Business Objects (BOs). Unfortunately, this is pretty close to another term, namely the SAP CRM business objects (applications such as account, opportunity, and campaign).

2.2   Creating your First GenIL Model

We often hear in computer science classes that the first thing we need to do when writing an object-oriented application is to define our objects. From there, we can easily create a class diagram that contains our object types, their attributes, and the relationships between the objects. The equivalent of this process in a database design exercise is the entity relationship diagram. Implementing GenIL components is no different. You need to start with the object model (also known as the GenIL model).

2.2.1   GenIL Model Overview

The GenIL model defines a hierarchy of objects. We agreed to refer to these objects as business objects (BOs). Each BO has a flat structure of attributes associated with it. There is always at least one *root object* node.

The object nodes are related to each other via GenIL relations. The relations could be *aggregation*, *composition,* and *association*. Aggregation and composition are possible between nodes of the same object model, while association is possible between nodes of different object model hierarchies. Relationships are unidirectional: They have a source and target object. They can also be one-to-one (1:1) or one-to-many (1:N).

Apart from root object and relationships, a GenIL model also contains *access* and *dependent* objects. Root, access, and dependent objects constitute the entities of an object model. A dependent object cannot be determined uniquely by its ID. Instead you will need also the ID of its parent. Sometimes only the ID of the parent will suffice, and sometimes you might need both the ID of the dependent and the ID of the parent. We recommend that you always add the keys of the parent to the key of the dependent object. An access object is a special kind of object. It is not a root object, but it can be accessed by its own ID. Therefore an access object can be used to retrieve its dependent children. One can conclude that a root object is also an access object.

There are also node types that facilitate the process of searching for entities. A *query object node* is an object whose attributes are used as parameters of entity search requests. The result of such a query would be access objects or *query result objects*. One severe limitation of query objects is that a search parameter can take only a single value or pattern and use it to produce a match.

This limitation of the query objects is overcome by *dynamic query objects*. A search parameter in this case can also be associated with a logical operator, such as greater than, less than, or in between. As a result the match does not have to be a direct one.

As mentioned already, a query can return a special node type called query result object. Why not return an access or root object? This is also a valid approach, but imagine what will happen when you want to return a set of attributes from more than one object (a subset of the whole) for faster access. Alternatively, you might wish to return fewer attributes than in the original root or access BO, for performance reasons. Being able to return a lean read-only object type will allow you to implement such scenarios.

One can also define *view objects*. These node types represent a named part of the object model. They are read-only. When they are requested, a hard-coded set of objects will be returned.

As of CRM 7.0 EhP1, one can define *abstract objects*. The idea is to promote reuse of the modeled data. An abstract object is defined in an object model just like any other node type. There needs to be at least one real access or dependent object inheriting from the abstract one. At runtime, only the concrete node is used.

If you want to explore an existing object model, take a look at the SAMPLE GenIL component. You need to run Transaction GENIL_MODEL_BROWSER and provide SAMPLE as a component name. You should see something very similar to Figure 2.3.

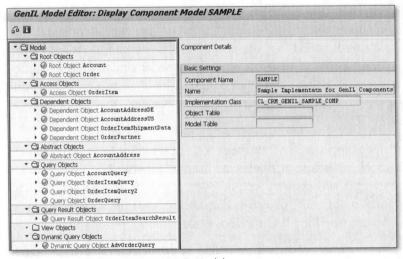

Figure 2.3 SAMPLE Component GenIL Model

2.2.2 Defining a GenIL Model

How can you define a GenIL model? You could implement the IF_GENIL_APPL_MODEL interface. Although this approach offers lots of flexibility it is not the easiest one. As of EhP1, you can use Transaction GENIL_MODEL_EDITOR and define your model interactively there. You edit an existing model by simply clicking the EDIT button in GENIL_MODEL_EDITOR. There is another transaction that is identical to the model editor: GENIL_MODEL_BROWSER. The "browser" precedes the "editor" (before EhP1). In the past, one had to define the model manually. In this book, we will use the model editor. The easiest way to use this approach is to ensure that your GenIL component class extends the default implementation of IF_GENIL_APPLM-ODEL_PERSISTENCY, namely CL_WCF_GENIL_ABSTR_COMPONENT. We will discuss the GenIL interfaces and classes in more detail later in this chapter

There are three model implementation strategies that we would like to quickly describe:

▶ You can have dynamic models based on a custom IF_GENIL_APPL_MODEL implementation

▶ Using the model editor, you can easily create static models. An alternative to the model editor is to implement IF_GENIL_APPLMODEL_PERSISTENCY and store your model metadata in custom tables.

▶ You can also have a static model with dynamic parts. To do this, use the model editor but extend IF_GENIL_APPL_MODEL methods to enhance the model dynamically.

2.2.3   Creating a GenIL Model

In case you are confused at this point, let's create a simple GenIL model. We will use our favorite example, namely the hotel guest-booking application. In our database model, we have two tables. One will store the hotel bookings of our guests and the other will have all the products and services used by our guests during each stay. The booking table will be the master and the products used will be the details. If you browse these tables in Transaction SE11 you will have something similar to Figure 2.4.

Our guest-booking data (table ZBOOKING_RESERV) consists of the ID of the guest, the name of the hotel (the assumption is that it is unique), the check-in date, the stay-in days, the number of people who stayed in the room, and the membership type at the time of booking. As part of each booking, we will keep track of the products used by the guest, the date of use and how the guest rated the product or service (ZBOOK_PRODUCTS). As you can see, the key of ZBOOKING_RESERV (our booking table) participates in the key of ZBOOK_PRODUCTS. In addition to this, we will limit the possible entries for membership and rating via a check table and domain fixed values respectively (see Figure 2.5).

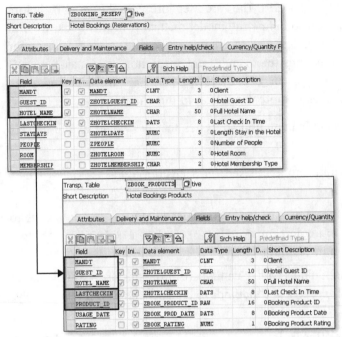

Figure 2.4 Data Tables Used for the Exemplary GenIL Implementation

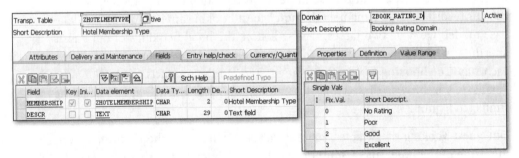

Figure 2.5 Check Table for Membership Values and Fixed Values of the Rating Domain

It is time to do some modeling. In this simple example, it is easy to deduce that there will be two GenIL business objects: Bookings and ProductsUsed. They will be connected via a composition relationship, in which ProductsUsed will be part of Bookings. Many products can exist for the same booking. In the GenIL world, the root object will be the Bookings and ProductsUsed will be a dependent object.

Creating and Registering the GenIL Component

At this point you might be tempted to start the model editor and define your model. But first we will create a GenIL component. You will recall, however, that a GenIL component implies that there is an implementation class. Below are the activities that you have to perform.

1. The first task is to start Transaction SE80 or SE24 and create a new ABAP class.
2. As we want this class to use a statically defined model in the model editor we will inherit from CL_WCF_GENIL_ABSTR_COMPONENT (as discussed previously).
3. Give this class a name; in our example it will be ZCL_ZGENIL_COMP_BOOKINGS.
4. Save and activate the class.
5. Once done, you can register the GenIL component. Go to Transaction SM34, enter the view-cluster name CRMVC_GIL_APPDEF and hit the MAINTAIN button (you can also use maintenance view CRMV_GIL_COMP). You will notice many other component definitions; for example the SAMPLE component should be there.
6. Define your component as per Figure 2.6.

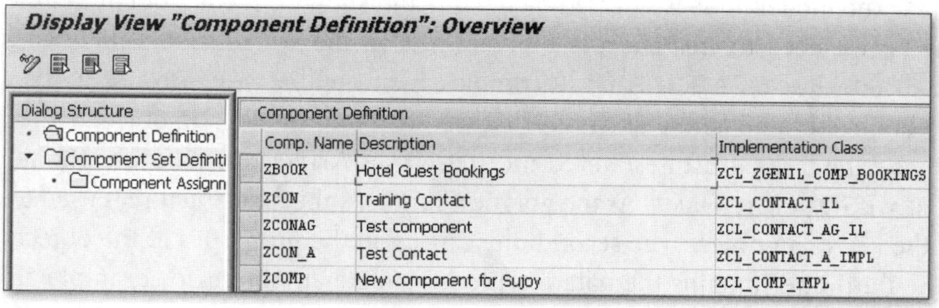
Display View "Component Definition": Overview
Dialog Structure
Component Definition
Component Set Definiti
Component Assignn
Component Definition
Comp. Name
Description
Implementation Class
ZBOOK
Hotel Guest Bookings
ZCL_ZGENIL_COMP_BOOKINGS
ZCON
Training Contact
ZCL_CONTACT_IL
ZCONAG
Test component
ZCL_CONTACT_AG_IL
ZCON_A
Test Contact
ZCL_CONTACT_A_IMPL
ZCOMP
New Component for Sujoy
ZCL_COMP_IMPL

Figure 2.6 ZBOOK Component Definition

In the view cluster there is a node called COMPONENT SET DEFINITION. A *GenIL component set* is a predefined set of components that will be used together. For example, when you want to use BOL/GenIL in your UI components, you need to provide a component set. Once a component set is loaded, all its components get loaded. Why not load all the available components in your system? Fortunately, you cannot do that (unless you include all the components in a dedicated component set). This would lead to an unnecessary high system load and is usually not required. The *GenIL core* (CL_CRM_GENERIC_IL_NEW) requests a component set as a parameter when it is instantiated. After instantiation, it is possible to load further

GenIL components and component sets dynamically (LOAD_COMPONENT, LOAD_COM-PONENT_SET). The model exposed by each component is integrated into the overall runtime model. In our example, see Figure 2.7, we will create a component set called ZBOOK and assign our *ZBOOK* component to it (we use the same name for the component and the component set).

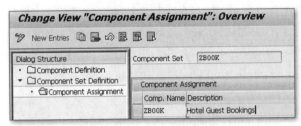

Figure 2.7 ZBOOK Component Set

Creating GenIL Business Objects

It is time to start the model editor and create our model. Launch Transaction GENIL_MODEL_EDITOR, enter "ZBOOK" as a component name and click on CHANGE. The model node is selected by default and shows our component definition. First we need to create a root object. Click on the ROOT OBJECTS node and select CREATE ROOT OBJECT. A fairly complex menu will appear. Do not worry; we do not need to fill all the entries. What we need to provide is an object name, Bookings, and three structures: KEY STRUCTURE NAME, ATTRIBUTE STRUCTURE NAME, and CREATE STRUCTURE NAME. As the notation suggests, the first structure is used to store the key of an object. The second one carries all the properties of the object, and the third one contains the data required to create an object (for example all the required fields). In our example, we use the same structure as key and creation data. The attribute structure exposes all the attributes from our table. Let's take a short detour and create these structures in the DDIC. While we are there, let us also define table types based on these structures (as line types). Figure 2.8 shows what we have used in our example.

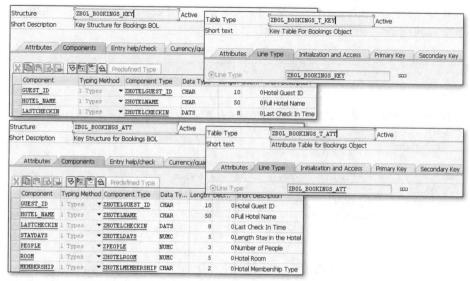

Figure 2.8 DDIC Elements Used by Bookings GenIL BO

With all the above in place, we can return to our model and finish the definition of our Bookings object. Once you are done, your definition should look very similar to Figure 2.9. Note that we have checked the WEBSERVICE ENABLED checkbox, as we want to be able to generate Web services out of this object node. We will talk about the Web Service Tool (WST) later.

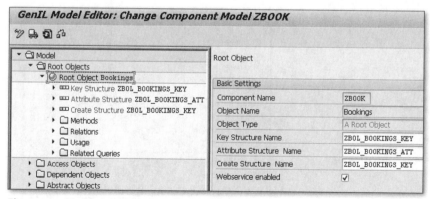

Figure 2.9 Bookings BOL Node Definition

We could define some methods on a BOL node, but we will leave this exercise for later. For now we will stick to the basics and create a dependent object for our used products. As this is a dependent BO, we will need key and attribute structures only. Make sure you have them in DDIC as per Figure 2.10.

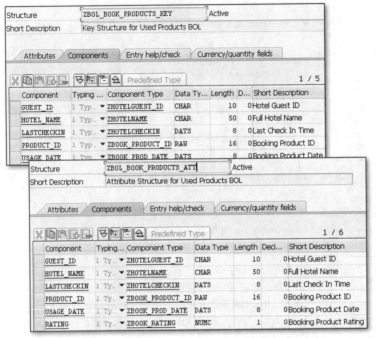

Figure 2.10 DDIC Structures for the Used Products BOL Node

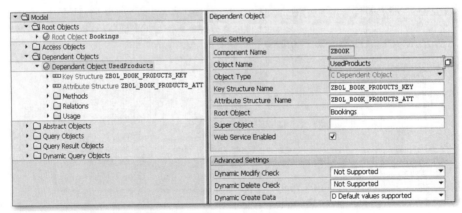

Figure 2.11 Used Products BOL Node Definition

As with the Bookings we will go ahead and create table types using the above structures as line types. The name of these tables will be ZBOL_BOOK_PRODUCTS_T_KEY (for the keys) and ZBOL_BOOK_PRODUCTS_T_ATT (for all used product attributes).

In the model editor, right click on the DEPENDENT OBJECTS node and select to create a dependent object. Fill in the required data as per Figure 2.11.

Note that we are specifying a root object, namely our Bookings BOL node. The WEB SERVICE ENABLED box is checked.

Creating GenIL Relations

Once we have the root and dependent objects, we have to connect them via a relation. We briefly described the concept of relations before, but let's dig a bit deeper. The relation between a root object and a dependent object is expected to be an aggregation or composition. What if we need to specify a relation between two root objects? In that case, we shall define a relation of type association between them. The association in general can be used to link any kind of object. It can be used across components with root or access objects as a target.

A relation (aggregation, composition, or association) is always unidirectional; that is, it starts from a source (parent) object and points to a target (child) object. In addition a relation has cardinality. Although there are more options, stick to 1:1 or 1:N relations.

In our example we will define a 1:N aggregation between Bookings and UsedProducts. We could have used composition, but this would imply that there is always a child object (i.e., a guest will always use a product, something we do not assume). Figure 2.12 shows our relation definition.

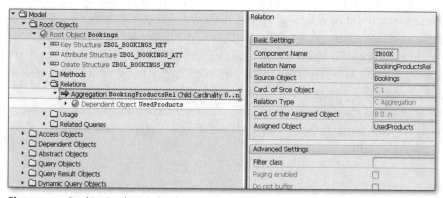

Figure 2.12 BookingProductsRel Relation

GenIL Business Object Attribute Properties

Let's go back to our booking object and expand the ATTRIBUTE STRUCTURE node. You will see all the attributes. If you double-click on an attribute, the attribute details will open on the right. There is one property that we want to specify there: ATTRIB. It could take several possible values such as Read-Only, Changeable, Hidden, Required Entry, and Technical Field. The names of the options are largely self-explanatory. We want our key fields to be read-only, while the others are changeable. Figure 2.13 shows how the STAYDAYS should look. You can modify the rest of the fields according to whether they are part of the key. Do the same for the UsedProducts object.

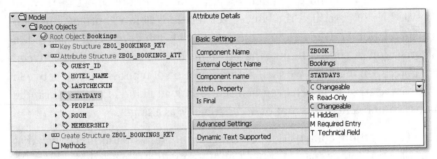

Figure 2.13 Setting Attribute Properties

Modeling GenIL Dynamic Queries

We also need queries to search for data. We will show you how to create a query that returns a collection of bookings matching certain criteria. As we want to use logical operators such as GREATER THAN, we will define a dynamic query. If you recall, the attributes of a query object are used as search parameters. In our example we want to search by guest ID, hotel name, check-in date, and products used. Therefore we will define a new attribute structure that contains these attributes. We chose to name it ZBOL_SEARCHBOOKINGS_ATT. The query will return a collection of Bookings. Hence, this will be our result object. A result object can be of THE typeS root, access, or query result. Queries require knowing which root object within the component they relate to. We have only one root object: Bookings. In the model, we will specify that we will use all the possible query logical operators, although we will not implement all of them. Figure 2.14 shows what the final result should look like.

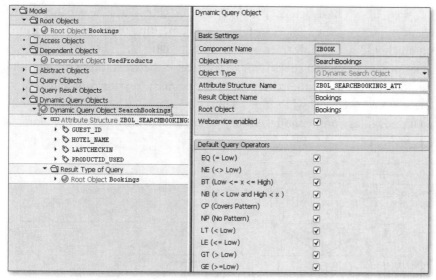

Figure 2.14 Exemplary Dynamic Query Result

Our simple GenIL model is complete. You can press the CONSISTENCY CHECK button, and if there are no errors save the model. We will look at some of the more advanced settings later.

2.3 Implementing a GenIL Query

The minimum that you need in order to read data via GenIL is an implementation of a query and a method that retrieves the attributes of an object identified by a query. Before we implement anything, it will help to make a quick overview of the GenIL interfaces and classes that we will use. These are shown in Figure 2.15.

IF_GENIL_APPL_MODEL is related to the GenIL object model. Because we are using the Genil Model Editor to define our model, we do not need to worry about this one. Recently, SAP added an optional interface for dynamic metadata: IF_GENIL_APPL_DYN_META_INFO. We will not be focusing on this either. However, we will be dealing extensively with IF_GENIL_APPL_INTLAY because it defines the way we access our data. So does IF_GENIL_APPL_ALTERNATIVE_DSIL. DSIL stands for Delete Save Init Lock. We will use both of them, although some of the methods in

IF_GENIL_APPL_INTLAY have been deprecated, and you should use the versions from IF_GENIL_APPL_ALTERNATIVE_DSIL. Instead of implementing these interfaces from scratch, you should use the abstract base classes CL_CRM_GENIL_ABSTR_COMPONENT and CL_CRM_GENIL_ABSTR_COMPONENT2. A key difference between these two classes is that the first one restricts the data type of the primary key for root and access objects to a RAW16 GUID, while the second one allows arbitrary keys. If you want to take advantage of the model editor you should ensure that you implement IF_GENIL_APPLMODEL_PERSISTENCY.

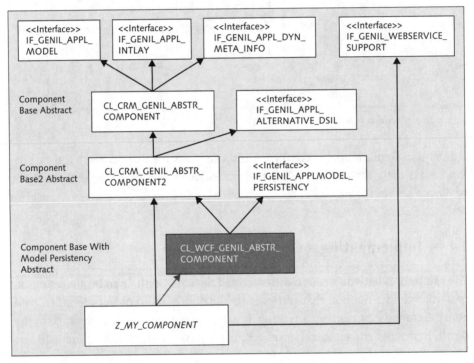

Figure 2.15 GenIL Class Diagram

By simply assessing our requirements about the GenIL Model Editor and understanding the above class diagram, it is clear that it will be best to use CL_WCF_GENIL_ABSTR_COMPONENT as a super class. SAP recommends that you either use this abstract class or CL_CRM_GENIL_ABSTR_COMPONENT2. We will discuss IF_GENIL_WEBSERVICE_SUPPORT later in Chapter 12.

> **CL_WCF* vs. CL_CRM* Classes**
>
> You might have noticed that the naming convention of the GenIL classes changes from CL_CRM* to CL_WCF*. In the past, Web Client UI was used only in the context of SAP CRM. Later, it was declared an SAP user interface technology in its own right.

Based on the above discussion, it should be clear why we chose CL_WCF_ GENIL_ABSTR_COMPONENT to be the superclass of our GenIL component class (ZCL_ZGENIL_COMP_BOOKINGS).

In order to produce a dynamic query we need to implement IF_GENIL_APPL_ INTLAY~GET_DYNAMIC_QUERY_RESULT. This method requires the following parameters:

▶ IV_QUERY_NAME

Contains the name of the query currently processed. As all of the queries will be handled by this method, you need the query name to trigger different implementations/APIs.

▶ IS_QUERY_PARAMETERS

Some additional query parameters, like maximum number of hits, are passed through this structure.

▶ IT_SELECTION_PARAMETERS

Contains the selection parameters (along with operations) passed to the query.

▶ IV_ROOT_LIST

A reference to an empty data container. You should fill it with the result objects from your query.

For SearchBookings we will have to query our database tables using the query selection and query parameters provided by the user. We need to then process the result, and for each found entry to create a Bookings object instance. This sounds fairly easy, but we need to get familiar with the GenIL APIs that will help us achieve that. But before we do so, we will walk you through the backend APIs that will wrap the database access logic of our application.

2.3.1 Defining the Backend APIs

The backend APIs should be GenIL-agnostic (not depend on any GenIL interfaces and classes). We will resort to static methods in a class called ZCL_BOOKINGS_BACK-END_API. Feel free to do this in another way. For the query, we will have a method

97

called `SEARCH_BOOKINGS`. It will accept a string that contains the `WHERE` clause of a `SELECT` statement and the maximum number of records. The method will return the matching records in internal `table ZBOL_BOOKINGS_T_KEY` (represented by keys of the found `Bookings`). The complete programming code can be found in Listing 2.2.

```
method SEARCH_BOOKINGS.
  REFRESH et_results.
  IF iv_string IS NOT INITIAL.

    SELECT GUEST_ID HOTEL_NAME LASTCHECKIN
      FROM ZBOOKING_RESERV
      UP TO iv_max_hits ROWS
      INTO CORRESPONDING FIELDS OF TABLE et_results
      WHERE (iv_string).
  ELSE.
    SELECT GUEST_ID HOTEL_NAME LASTCHECKIN
      FROM ZBOOKING_RESERV
      UP TO iv_max_hits ROWS
      INTO CORRESPONDING FIELDS OF TABLE et_results.
  ENDIF.
endmethod.
```

Listing 2.2 Retrieving Bookings from Database

The above code is simple and has nothing to do with GenIL programming. It does highlight what we believe is the recommended approach: Put your persistence and business logic in backend APIs and use the GenIL component only as a wrapper that contains Web Client UI specific code.

2.3.2 Implementing GET_DYNAMIC_QUERY_RESULT

In order to implement a dynamic query we have to redefine IF_GENIL_APPL_INTLAY~GET_DYNAMIC_QUERY_RESULT. You can see the result in Listing 2.3

```
DATA: lr_msg_cont TYPE REF TO cl_crm_genil_global_mess_cont,
      lv_num_hits     TYPE i,
      lt_results      TYPE ZBOL_BOOKINGS_T_KEY,
      lv_max_hits         TYPE char5,
      lv_max_hits_tmp     TYPE int4,
      lr_root_object      TYPE REF TO if_genil_cont_root_object,
      lt_request_obj      TYPE CRMT_REQUEST_OBJ_TAB.
   FIELD-SYMBOLS: <fs_results>   TYPE ZBOL_BOOKINGS_KEY.
```

```
*    Retrieve the message container to log eventual messages
     lr_msg_cont = iv_root_list->get_global_message_container( ).

*    When the max hits is set to 0.
     IF is_query_parameters-max_hits IS INITIAL.
       lv_max_hits_tmp = 100. "100 when no max_hits is set
     ELSE.
       lv_max_hits_tmp = is_query_parameters-max_hits.
     ENDIF.


*    select the rigth query
     case IV_QUERY_NAME.
       when 'SearchBookings'.
*        Call the API and get the result.
         CALL METHOD SEARCH_BOOKINGS
           EXPORTING
             it_search_criteria = it_selection_parameters
             iv_max_hits        = lv_max_hits_tmp
           IMPORTING
             et_results         = lt_results.

         IF lt_results IS NOT INITIAL.
*          Log a message if search result exceed the max hit limit
           DESCRIBE TABLE lt_results LINES lv_num_hits.

           IF  lv_num_hits > lv_max_hits_tmp.
             lv_max_hits = lv_max_hits_tmp.
             lr_msg_cont->add_message(  iv_msg_type   = 'I'
                                        iv_msg_id = 'ZBOOKING_MSG'
                                        iv_msg_number    = '000'
                                        iv_msg_v1    = lv_max_hits
                                   iv_show_only_once = abap_true ).
         ENDIF.
*        Loop through the results to build search result objects
         LOOP AT lt_results ASSIGNING <fs_results>.

           TRY.
*            Try to create a new result object
             lr_root_object = iv_root_list->add_object(
                               iv_object_name = 'Bookings'
                             is_object_key  = <fs_results> ).
*            Flag it as direct query result
             lr_root_object->set_query_root( abap_true ).
```

```
                    CATCH CX_CRM_GENIL_DUPLICATE_REL CX_CRM_GENIL_MODEL_ERROR.
*    Since the given object name is correct this could not happen!
                ENDTRY.
          ENDLOOP.
*    Note: The request object restricts the attributes to read.
*          If there is no request object entry or the attributes
*          table is empty all attributes are requested.

*       read the attributes and relation using the GET_OBJECTS
        ME->IF_GENIL_APPL_INTLAY~GET_OBJECTS( IT_REQUEST_OBJECTS = LT_
REQUEST_OBJ                        IV_ROOT_LIST       = IV_ROOT_LIST ).
        ELSE.

          lr_msg_cont->add_message(    iv_msg_type       = 'W'
                                       iv_msg_id     = 'ZBOOKING_MSG'
                                       iv_msg_number     = '001'
                                    iv_show_only_once = abap_true ).
        ENDIF.

    when others.
       return.
  endcase.
```

Listing 2.3 Redefining IF_GENIL_APPL_INTLAY~GET_DYNAMIC_QUERY_RESULT

In our code, we first get a reference to the global message container. We will discuss this later. At this point, it's sufficient to say that you use the message container to register all kinds of messages (the error message being among the most popular). The framework will later propagate these messages to the user.

```
lr_msg_cont = iv_root_list->get_global_message_container( ).
```

Next we will put in a safety net and ensure that we will not overload the system by processing too many records. In case the maximum number of hits is not set, we will limit the result to 100 entries.

```
IF is_query_parameters-max_hits IS INITIAL.
  lv_max_hits_tmp = 100. "100 when no max_hits is set
ELSE.
  lv_max_hits_tmp = is_query_parameters-max_hits.
ENDIF.
```

As you know, our GenIL component will be used by all GenIL objects in the related models. Although we have only one query object, it is good practice to always evaluate the IV_QUERY_NAME. If its value is SearchBookings, we execute our query logic.

```
case IV_QUERY_NAME.
  when 'SearchBookings'.
```

In our example, we process the booking searches in a separate method in the GenIL component, SEARCH_BOOKINGS. Please do not confuse it with the SEARCH_BOOKINGS of the ZCL_BOOKINGS_BACKEND_API. We will see how these two are related in just a moment.

```
CALL METHOD SEARCH_BOOKINGS
          EXPORTING
            it_search_criteria = it_selection_parameters
            iv_max_hits        = lv_max_hits_tmp
          IMPORTING
            et_results         = lt_results.
```

The instance method SEARCH_BOOKINGS returns a table of the matching Bookings keys (lt_results of type ZBOL_BOOKINGS_T_KEY). If we get IF lt_results IS NOT INITIAL, we know that the search produced results and we need to process them. We want to inform the user when the number of results exceeds the maximum hits value (that is, when there are more results than the ones presented to the user). We will use the message container and log an informational message.

```
IF  lv_num_hits > lv_max_hits_tmp.
  lv_max_hits = lv_max_hits_tmp.
  lr_msg_cont->add_message(  iv_msg_type   = 'I'
                             iv_msg_id = 'ZBOOKING_MSG'
                             iv_msg_number     = '000'
                             iv_msg_v1     = lv_max_hits
                             iv_show_only_once = abap_true ).
ENDIF.
```

Using the message container is really simple: You simply add messages to it. You need to indicate the message type/severity (for example, "I" is an information message), message class, message ID, and so on. At the end the framework looks at all the message containers and ensures that the messages are presented to the user.

Next, we loop through the found keys.

```
LOOP AT lt_results ASSIGNING <fs_results>.
```

For each record in the result table we create a new `Bookings` GenIL object and add it to the list of container objects (we will discuss the container object concept in Section 2.5.2).

```
lr_root_object = iv_root_list->add_object(
   iv_object_name = 'Bookings'
   is_object_key  = <fs_results> ).
```

The structure that we pass to the `add_object` method must correspond to the create DDIC structure that we used when we declared our Bookings object. What you observe here is the creation of a data container object (`if_genil_cont_root_object`). This is a very important concept in GenIL programming. The data container is the way GenIL transports objects (remember that unlike object-oriented programming, the GenIL business objects do not have dedicated classes to represent them). The data container also has an API for setting and accessing the data. You can call `SET_ATTRIBUTES` and `GET_ATTRIBUTES` to set and read data. In our example, we are calling the data container's `SET_QUERY_ROOT` method to flag this object as root (you need to do this for root objects):

```
lr_root_object->set_query_root( abap_true ).
```

Once we have compiled a list of matching root objects, we call `IF_GENIL_APPL_INTLAY~GET_OBJECTS` to read the `Bookings` attributes (and maybe even the related objects). Remember, so far we have simply identified its keys. We will look at the `GET_OBJECT` implementation very soon.

```
ME->IF_GENIL_APPL_INTLAY~GET_OBJECTS(
   IT_REQUEST_OBJECTS = LT_REQUEST_OBJ
   IV_ROOT_LIST       = IV_ROOT_LIST ).
```

In our `IF_GENIL_APPL_INTLAY~GET_DYNAMIC_QUERY_RESULT` there is no application specific code (except for the name of the query). Everything is strictly related to what you need to do from a GenIL perspective.

2.3.3 Implementing Helper Methods

It is time to examine the private `SEARCH_BOOKINGS` method of our GenIL class (Listing 2.4).

```
DATA: LV_MAX_HITS TYPE I,
      LV_STRING TYPE STRING,
      LT_SEARCH_CRITERIA TYPE GENILT_SELECTION_PARAMETER_TAB,
```

```
      LV_LAST_ATTR_NAME TYPE NAME_KOMP.

FIELD-SYMBOLS: <SEARCH_CRITERIA> TYPE GENILT_SELECTION_PARAMETER.

* NOTE:
* This is a good place to implement Authority checks!!!
*

LV_MAX_HITS = IV_MAX_HITS.
IF LV_MAX_HITS EQ 0.
  LV_MAX_HITS = 100.
ENDIF.

LT_SEARCH_CRITERIA = IT_SEARCH_CRITERIA.
SORT LT_SEARCH_CRITERIA BY ATTR_NAME.
LOOP AT LT_SEARCH_CRITERIA ASSIGNING <SEARCH_CRITERIA>.
* NOTE: * The current implementation takes care only of CP and EQ
search criteria options.
*
  IF ( <SEARCH_CRITERIA>-OPTION EQ 'CP' OR <SEARCH_CRITERIA>-OPTION EQ
'EQ' ).
    IF LV_STRING IS NOT INITIAL.
      IF <SEARCH_CRITERIA>-ATTR_NAME NE LV_LAST_ATTR_NAME.
        CONCATENATE  LV_STRING ') AND (' INTO LV_STRING SEPARATED BY
SPACE.
      ELSE.
        CONCATENATE  LV_STRING 'OR' INTO LV_STRING SEPARATED BY SPACE.
      ENDIF.
    ELSE.
      LV_STRING = '('.
    ENDIF.
    CONCATENATE  LV_STRING <SEARCH_CRITERIA>-ATTR_NAME <SEARCH_
CRITERIA>-OPTION '''' INTO LV_STRING SEPARATED BY SPACE.
    CONCATENATE  LV_STRING <SEARCH_CRITERIA>-LOW INTO LV_STRING.
    CONCATENATE  LV_STRING '''' INTO LV_STRING.
  ENDIF.
  LV_LAST_ATTR_NAME = <SEARCH_CRITERIA>-ATTR_NAME.
ENDLOOP.
REFRESH ET_RESULTS.
IF LV_STRING IS NOT INITIAL.
  CONCATENATE LV_STRING ')' INTO LV_STRING SEPARATED BY SPACE.
ENDIF.
* retrieve data from the backend
```

```
CALL METHOD ZCL_BOOKINGS_BACKEND_API=>SEARCH_BOOKINGS(
    EXPORTING IV_STRING = LV_STRING
              IV_MAX_HITS = LV_MAX_HITS
    IMPORTING ET_RESULTS = ET_RESULTS ).
```

Listing 2.4 GenIL Component's SEARCH_BOOKINGS

The first thing we do is throw in another safety net related to the maximum number of returned results. The idea is that the SEARCH_BOOKINGS can be used by other methods. Next we make a copy of the query criteria and sort it by name.

```
LT_SEARCH_CRITERIA = IT_SEARCH_CRITERIA.
SORT LT_SEARCH_CRITERIA BY ATTR_NAME.
```

The largest section of code is inside the LOOP AT LT_SEARCH_CRITERIA. If you think in terms of SQL SELECT statements, this is where we build our WHERE clause string based on each search criterion. As you can see, the structure of the query parameter (GENILT_SELECTION_PARAMETER) is pretty comprehensive, storing not just name-value pairs, but also operators, lower and upper values, and so on.

At the end we finally call the backend API that we introduced earlier in this section, namely the ZCL_BOOKINGS_BACKEND_API=>SEARCH_BOOKINGS. It is the one that performs the DB select using the WHERE clause that we constructed in the helper method SEARCH_BOOKINGS from our GenIL component.

2.3.4 Conclusion

This concludes our query logic. To summarize, we evaluated the query name parameter, and when it was equal to SearchBookings we called the backend APIs to execute the search. We took into account the query parameters and limited our result list to the maximum number of hits. Once we obtained the keys of the matching Bookings records we filled in the root list data container with Bookings entities (container objects).

One might ask what happened to the GET_OBJECTS call at the end of our GET_DYNAMIC_QUERY_RESULT. Before we answer that, let's just comment it out and test our code without that call. But how can we test it? Some of you probably are already thinking about using BOL APIs. That would work, but there is an easier way.

2.4 Introducing the BOL Browser

Transaction GENIL_BOL_BROWSER is a convenient tool with which to test GenIL components. When you start the transaction, you have to provide a COMPONENT NAME (or COMPONENT SET NAME). In our example, we will use component ZBOOK.

You will be presented with a screen divided into several panels. In the left-hand panel, you will find all the query objects present in the GenIL model. In our example there is only one query object. When you double-click on it, the top of the right-hand panel will show the query parameters. Upon execution, they will be passed to the query method via IS_QUERY_PARAMETERS. Set the MAX_HITS to "5." Below the search criteria, there is a section where you can define the dynamic search selection parameters (the IT_SELECTION_PARAMETERS importing the table of method GET_DYNAMIC_QUERY_RESULT). The possible values correspond to the DDIC structure that we assigned to our SearchBookings BOL node in the GenIL model (ZBOL_SEARCHBOOKINGS_ATT). To execute the query, press the FIND button above the query parameters. To see if there are entries in the DB tables that match the query parameters, check the results in the left panel, just below the list of search objects (Figure 2.16).

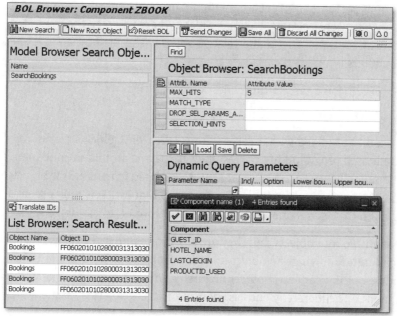

Figure 2.16 Executing SearchBookings in GENIL_BOL_BROWSER

If you double-click on one of the result entries, you should be able to see all your attributes. Recall, however, that we removed the call to the GET_OBJECTS method in our query method implementation. For this reason, do not double-click on the found entries. At this point you cannot see much, because the framework shows only the GUID (an internal ID assigned by GenIL to each entity instance). Once we implement the mechanics to retrieve all the Bookings data, we will come back to the BOL browser and execute the query again.

We will be using the BOL browser frequently in this and following chapters. So we do not want to waste precious time and explain something that will become obvious as our sample implementation progresses. In general, the tool is quite intuitive, and you can experiment with it even now. For example, you can open the SAMPLE GenIL component and try to traverse it. The left-hand panels will contain the GenIL nodes, and as you double-click on the entries there, the right-hand side will present the details of each selection. To move from a parent object down to its children, you can click the CHILDREN button above the object details.

2.5 Retrieving a BOL Entity

The IF_GENIL_APPL_INTLAY~GET_OBJECTS method is probably one of the most complex methods in your GenIL classes. This is the place where you read the requested attributes for your root and any of the related objects. The method accepts the following parameters:

▶ IT_REQUEST_OBJECTS is a table with request object entries.

▶ IV_ROOT_LIST is a reference to the data container.

IV_ROOT_LIST comes pre-filled with objects. Because the GenIL objects are not represented by dedicated programming classes, they are passed around in containers. Container objects can be packaged in *container lists*. You need to traverse the objects in the container and provide them with whatever they request. This might seem a bit confusing at first. The container always starts with root or access objects.

There can be multiple root objects, but they are all of the same type. These objects can contain children following the object-node hierarchy as defined in the GenIL model. The leaves of the container-object hierarchy do not necessarily match the leaves in the model. The hierarchy ends as soon as an access object is reached. The reason for such a realization is that the calling application demands data from the GenIL component in chunks.

2.5.1 BOL Splitting

The consumer splits the object model into containers of objects that always start with root or access objects. This procedure is called *BOL splitting*. You can actually control the level of splitting in the GenIL Model Editor in the advanced settings of the model node. You have three types of splitting:

► Split only at root objects

► Default (discussed above)

► No splitting

The container that is being split from the rest of the model contains access objects that are filled only with their key attributes. The keys are being retrieved and populated while processing the previous container (representing a higher level of the model hierarchy). Thus, each subsequent call to GET_OBJECTS passes in a container that starts with access objects that have their key attributes prefilled. The implementation has to fill in the rest of the attributes and continue traversing and populating the requested object hierarchy. Relations to other root or access objects appear as foreign relations (we will discuss these in Chapter 3). According to the above rules, a foreign relationship indicates a BOL split.

2.5.2 Container Objects

The query will return a collection of Bookings that match the search criteria. This will be realized as a container list filled with container objects. The key attributes of these objects will be populated, so that if we have such a container list we can pass it to GET_OBJECTS and read all the data.

If you are implementing a transactional buffer, you should keep the splitting in mind. You might want to buffer your data into chunks, starting with the root/access object, storing the data related to the dependent objects and finishing with an access object. Be aware that you should not buffer query data (or at least be careful when doing so). However, you should buffer your data when the objects are locked and a transaction is occurring. We will talk about this later.

When you get the container in your GET_OBJECTS implementation, there are two main scenarios that you will be dealing with:

▶ The container contains only one root object. The key of this object is initial. This is an indication that you need to read all the objects belonging to this GenIL object type (BO) and fill the container with it. This functions as a placeholder indicating that a full read is required. Consider the keys of the parent (if available) and pull only the relevant data. For example, if you receive a UsedProduct with an initial key, you will take a look at the parent Bookings instance and read all the products belonging to this booking.

▶ The objects found in the container have valid keys. You will need to retrieve the data based on these keys and set the object's attributes.

There is more to consider in the above two scenarios, as you will have to also consider the children relationships. Sometimes the related data is requested, and sometimes not. You need to check for this.

2.5.3 Implementing GET_OBJECTS

We will base the implementation of our GET_OBJECTS method on the data flow outlined in Figure 2.17. In this section we will implement the following data processing steps.

1. Retrieve an object from the received object list

2. Check if the object attributes are requested

3. If the attributes are requested, retrieve and set them on the current object

4. Check if the object relations are requested

5. If the relations are requested, retrieve the children from these relations. For each child repeat Steps 1 to 5.

Sometimes, depending on your model, you might find that you do not need to implement all these steps. We recommend, however, that you always consider the complete algorithm.

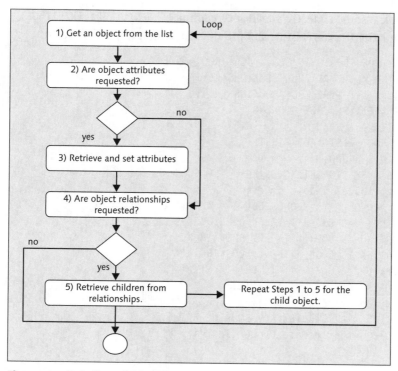

Figure 2.17 Data Flow of GET_OBJECTS

In order to implement the flow in Figure 2.17, you will have to work with interface IF_GENIL_CONTAINER_OBJECT. Every container object implements this interface.

Step 1 involves looping through the objects from the container list (IV_ROOT_LIST). In order to loop through a container object list, IF_GENIL_CONTAINER_OBJECTLIST interface exposes methods to get the first and the next container object in the list: GET_FIRST and GET_NEXT (among others). To check whether you should fill in object attributes (Step 2), call CHECK_ATTR_REQUESTED. For Step 3 (filling in attributes) you will use container object's SET_ATTRIBUTES (or GET_ATTRIBUTES to read what is set already). CHECK_RELS_REQUESTED will tell you if you need to pull the related child objects (Step 4). GET_RELS_REQUESTED and GET_RELATION will allow you to implement Step 5.

From an interface point of view, GET_OBJECT receives an IF_GENIL_CONTAINER_OBJECTLIST (IV_ROOT_LIST), which contains IF_GENIL_CONTAINER_OBJECT. GET_RELATION returns an IF_GENIL_CONTAINER_OBJECTLIST for the children linked via the specified relationship (passed as an argument to the method).

It is time to look at some code. Go ahead and redefine IF_GENIL_APPL_INTLAY~GET_OBJECTS in your GenIL class. Listing 2.5 provides an exemplary redefinition.

```
DATA LV_ROOT TYPE REF TO IF_GENIL_CONT_ROOT_OBJECT.
DATA LV_BOOKING_KEY TYPE ZBOL_BOOKINGS_KEY.
DATA LV_BOOKING_ATT TYPE ZBOL_BOOKINGS_ATT.
DATA LV_TEMP_ATT TYPE ZBOL_BOOKINGS_ATT.

LV_ROOT = IV_ROOT_LIST->GET_FIRST( ).
WHILE LV_ROOT IS BOUND.
  LV_ROOT->GET_KEY( IMPORTING ES_KEY = LV_BOOKING_KEY ).
* Check if attributes should be read
  IF LV_ROOT->CHECK_ATTR_REQUESTED( ) = ABAP_TRUE.
    ZCL_BOOKINGS_BACKEND_API=>READ_BOOKINGS(
        EXPORTING IS_BOOK_KEY = LV_BOOKING_KEY
        IMPORTING ES_BOOK_ATT = LV_BOOKING_ATT ).
*    Return the object only if it still exists
    IF LV_BOOKING_ATT IS NOT INITIAL.
*      Put attributes to the container
      LV_ROOT->SET_ATTRIBUTES( LV_BOOKING_ATT ).
*      You could set attribute properties like readonly.
    ENDIF.
  ENDIF.
* check if dependent objects should be read
  IF LV_ROOT->CHECK_RELS_REQUESTED( ) = ABAP_TRUE.
*    process the directly dependent objects
    PROCESS_CHILDREN( IT_REQUEST_OBJECTS = IT_REQUEST_OBJECTS
                      IV_ROOT           = LV_ROOT ).
  ENDIF.
  "process foreign relations
  PROCESS_FOREIGN( IV_ROOT = LV_ROOT ).
  "continue with the loop
  LV_ROOT = IV_ROOT_LIST->GET_NEXT( ).
ENDWHILE.
```

Listing 2.5 GET_OBJECTS Implementation

In accordance with the first step of the data flow from Figure 2.17, we have to loop through the root container list.

```
LV_ROOT = IV_ROOT_LIST->GET_FIRST( ).
WHILE LV_ROOT IS BOUND.
```

```
   ...
ENDWHILE.
```

Inside the loop, we will check whether we need to read the container object's attributes, and if the answer is yes we will do so (Steps 2 and 3 from the GET_OBJECTS data flow). However, we will not implement the logic that gets the data inside our GenIL component. We already agreed that we will try to assign such activities to a dedicated API that we refer to as the backend API. In this case, the robust backend logic takes place in ZCL_BOOKINGS_BACKEND_API=>READ_BOOKINGS. The code that implements Steps 2 and 3 inside GET_OBJECTS is as follows:

```
IF LV_ROOT->CHECK_ATTR_REQUESTED( ) = ABAP_TRUE.
ZCL_BOOKINGS_BACKEND_API=>READ_BOOKINGS(
            EXPORTING IS_BOOK_KEY = LV_BOOKING_KEY
            IMPORTING ES_BOOK_ATT = LV_BOOKING_ATT ).
*      Return the object only if it still exists
IF LV_BOOKING_ATT IS NOT INITIAL.
*         Put attributes to the container
          LV_ROOT->SET_ATTRIBUTES( LV_BOOKING_ATT ).
*         You could set attribute properties like readonly.
      ENDIF.
ENDIF.
```

In the above snippet, we pass the key to the backend API and get back the complete attribute structure of our Bookings BO. If the structure is not initial (that is if data already has been read), we will use it to set all the attributes of the Bookings object instance (represented by its container). We will discuss ZCL_BOOKINGS_BACK-END_API=>READ_BOOKINGS shortly.

IF_GENIL_CONT_ROOT_OBJECT~CHECK_ATTR_REQUESTED is part of the container's API. You can deduce its function from its name; it returns TRUE if the consumer has requested the object's attributes. Another helpful method of the container API is SET_ATTRIBUTES. It takes an importing structure IS_ATTRIBUTES and uses it to populate all the object's attributes. With this last call, we successfully complete Step 3 of the GET_OBJECTS data flow.

At this the point, you could set additional properties on the container object (for example mark some fields as read-only). For our sample implementation, we will keep the properties simple.

In Step 4, we need to check whether the related entities have been requested by the consumer (for example BOL). We will implement this step by checking whether

IF_GENIL_CONT_ROOT_OBJECT~CHECK_RELS_REQUESTED returns TRUE. If so, we need to retrieve the children of our container objects, as Step 5 from the data flow.

```
IF LV_ROOT->CHECK_RELS_REQUESTED( ) = ABAP_TRUE.
*   process the directly dependent objects
    PROCESS_CHILDREN( IT_REQUEST_OBJECTS = IT_REQUEST_OBJECTS
                      IV_ROOT            = LV_ROOT ).
ENDIF.
```

Step 5 is implemented in a separate helper method of our GenIL container class, namely PROCESS_CHILDREN (it is not part of the GenIL API). In our data-flow diagram we have indicated that inside Step 5 we will need to repeat all the previously discussed steps, but for the child object. This is exactly what our PROCESS_CHILDREN method does. According to the above snippet we are passing to it the IT_REQUEST_OBJECTS and the current root object LV_ROOT. But before we go into the details let's finalize our GET_OBJECTS. What is left is to continue looping through all the passed container objects and apply Steps 2 to 5 to each one.

```
LV_ROOT = IV_ROOT_LIST->GET_NEXT( ).
```

Finally we close the WHILE loop and complete the method implementation.

2.5.4 Bookings Backend API

It is time to go into the details of ZCL_BOOKINGS_BACKEND_API=>READ_BOOKINGS and the PROCESS_CHILDREN method of the component class.

Listing 2.6 shows the code of READ_BOOKINGS.

```
DATA LS_BOOK_ATT_N LIKE LINE OF GT_BUFFER_BOOKINGS.
FIELD-SYMBOLS <LINE> LIKE LINE OF GT_BUFFER_BOOKINGS.

IF IS_BOOK_KEY IS NOT INITIAL.
*   Try to read from the buffe
    READ TABLE GT_BUFFER_BOOKINGS
      WITH KEY GUEST_ID = IS_BOOK_KEY-GUEST_ID
               HOTEL_NAME = IS_BOOK_KEY-HOTEL_NAME
               LASTCHECKIN = IS_BOOK_KEY-LASTCHECKIN
      ASSIGNING <LINE>.
ELSE.
*   Late key assignment case
*   Get created booking => Only one object creation possible at a time
    READ TABLE GT_BUFFER_BOOKINGS WITH KEY NEW = 'C'
```

```
                  ASSIGNING <LINE>.
      if sy-subrc <> 0.
        RETURN.
      endif.
ENDIF.
* Check if the read from the buffer was successful
IF SY-SUBRC = 0.
* If the object is new or modified, return from the buffer
    IF <LINE>-NEW EQ 'C' OR <LINE>-NEW EQ 'M'.
      MOVE-CORRESPONDING <LINE> TO ES_BOOK_ATT.
      RETURN.
    ENDIF.
ENDIF.


* Read from the DB
SELECT SINGLE * FROM zbooking_reserv INTO CORRESPONDING FIELDS OF ES_
BOOK_ATT
      WHERE guest_id EQ IS_BOOK_KEY-guest_id
      AND hotel_name EQ IS_BOOK_KEY-hotel_name
      AND lastcheckin EQ IS_BOOK_KEY-lastcheckin.
CHECK SY-SUBRC IS INITIAL.
* return the data read
MOVE-CORRESPONDING ES_BOOK_ATT TO LS_BOOK_ATT_N.
```

Listing 2.6 READ_BOOKINGS Method

For now, do not spend too much time on the first 26 lines of READ_BOOKINGS code. Their purpose will become crystal clear when we discuss the transaction behavior (LOCK_OBJECTS, SAVE_OBJECTS, CREATE_OBJECTS, and MODIFY_OBJECTS). Remember GET_OBJECTS is not only called when the consumer (BOL) explicitly requests to read business object data. At this point, you need only know that at the beginning of the method we are checking the GenIL buffer (our custom implementation) to see if the requested Bookings entity is a new one or is being modified, but is still not persistent in the database. If we find matching data in the buffer (new or in the process of being modified), we return it from there (no database read). We buffer the data when we lock it before we start a new transaction. We will explain this topic further when we go through the data modification procedure.

In the read-business-data scenario, there will be no modifications and no new entities. Therefore, what is important for us is the database read. It is quite straightforward:

We use the object's key attributes to find a matching record via a select statement. Once we find one we return it via the export structure ES_BOOK_ATT:

```
SELECT SINGLE * FROM zbooking_reserv INTO CORRESPONDING FIELDS OF ES_
BOOK_ATT
        WHERE guest_id EQ IS_BOOK_KEY-guest_id
        AND hotel_name EQ IS_BOOK_KEY-hotel_name
        AND lastcheckin EQ IS_BOOK_KEY-lastcheckin.
CHECK SY-SUBRC IS INITIAL.
* return the data read
MOVE-CORRESPONDING ES_BOOK_ATT TO LS_BOOK_ATT_N.
```

For now, ignore the rest of READ_BOOKINGS and focus on the last snippet. The effect is that we return a fresh snapshot of the data in our database. We could have performed optimizations related to data caching but this is the safest bet when it comes to avoiding data inconsistencies.

2.5.5 Reading Dependent Object Data

Listing 2.7 shows the implementation of the PROCESS_CHILDREN method (our helper method). Note that we will stick to Steps 2 to 5 from the GET_OBJECTS data flow, but this time we will apply to it to the children of the Bookings object, UsedProducts.

```
data: LV_CHILDREN      type ref to IF_GENIL_CONTAINER_OBJECTLIST,
      LV_PRODUCT         type ref to IF_GENIL_CONTAINER_OBJECT,
      LV_BOOKING        type ref to IF_GENIL_CONTAINER_OBJECT,
      LV_NAME           type CRMT_EXT_OBJ_NAME,
      LT_FOREIGN_RELS type CRMT_RELATION_NAME_TAB,
      LT_REQ_RELS       type CRMT_RELATION_NAME_TAB,
      LV_PRODUCT_KEY   type ZBOL_BOOK_PRODUCTS_KEY,
      LV_PRODUCT_ATT   type ZBOL_BOOK_PRODUCTS_ATT,
      LT_PRODUCTS_KEYS type ZBOL_BOOK_PRODUCTS_T_KEY,
      LV_BOOKING_KEY   type ZBOL_BOOKINGS_KEY.

    field-symbols: <REL> type CRMT_RELATION_NAME.


* check which relations to dependent objects are requested
    LT_REQ_RELS = IV_ROOT->GET_RELS_REQUESTED( ).

    LOOP AT LT_REQ_RELS ASSIGNING <REL>.
```

```
      CASE <REL>.
        WHEN 'BookingProductsRel'.
*          get the list of all directly dependent objects (children)
           LV_CHILDREN = IV_ROOT->GET_RELATION(
                   IV_RELATION_NAME = <REL>
                                  IV_AS_COPY      = ABAP_FALSE ).
*          Note: WE set the IV_AS_COPY flag to FALSE so that our
*           list gets updated if new children were created.
*          Loop over the list
           LV_PRODUCT = LV_CHILDREN->GET_FIRST( ).
           WHILE LV_PRODUCT IS BOUND.
*            get the key of the child object
             CALL METHOD LV_PRODUCT->GET_KEY
               IMPORTING
                 ES_KEY = LV_PRODUCT_KEY.
*            check if child's key is given
             IF LV_PRODUCT_KEY IS INITIAL.
*          no key was given, object is just place holder -> read all
*              get the parent object and its key first
               LV_BOOKING = LV_PRODUCT->GET_PARENT( ).
               CALL METHOD LV_BOOKING->GET_KEY
                 IMPORTING ES_KEY = LV_BOOKING_KEY.

               CALL METHOD ZCL_BOOKINGS_BACKEND_API=>READ_PRODUCT_KEYS(
                 EXPORTING IS_BOOKING_KEY = LV_BOOKING_KEY
                 IMPORTING ET_PRODUCT_KEYS = LT_PRODUCTS_KEYS ).

*              create new objects for the other products  (except the
first) by copying the place holder
               LOOP AT LT_PRODUCTS_KEYS INTO LV_PRODUCT_KEY FROM 2.
                 TRY.
                   LV_PRODUCT->COPY_SELF_WITH_STRUCTURE( IS_OBJECT_KEY =
LV_PRODUCT_KEY ).
                 CATCH CX_CRM_GENIL_MODEL_ERROR.
*                 this can only happen if the optional parameter IV_
RELATION_NAME was given
*                 but did not fit to the model.
                 CATCH CX_CRM_CIC_DUPLICATE_ENTRY.
*                 this can only happen if the method was called on an
object which has a
*                 1:1 relation to its parent and no other relation name
was given.
                 ENDTRY.
```

```
          ENDLOOP.

*      set new key for place holder object from the first product
          READ TABLE LT_PRODUCTS_KEYS INTO LV_PRODUCT_KEY
                        INDEX 1.
          IF SY-SUBRC = 0.
            TRY.
              LV_PRODUCT->SET_KEY( LV_PRODUCT_KEY ).
            CATCH CX_CRM_GENIL_DUPLICATE_KEY.
*             This happens if an object with the same key already
exists in the container.
            ENDTRY.
          ENDIF.
*          now we have created an object for each found used product,
but only the keys were set.
*          normaly we would also set the attributes directly, but here
we want to demonstrate
*          how to work with the automaticly updated child list. So we
proceed only
*          with the current product, because all new objects were
appended to the list and will normaly
*          processed later on.
        ENDIF.

*        proceed only if at least one product was found
        IF LV_PRODUCT_KEY IS NOT INITIAL.

*          check if attributes should be read
          IF LV_PRODUCT->CHECK_ATTR_REQUESTED( ) = ABAP_TRUE.
            CALL METHOD ZCL_BOOKINGS_BACKEND_API=>READ_PRODUCT(
              EXPORTING IS_PRODUCT_KEY = LV_PRODUCT_KEY
              IMPORTING ES_PRODUCT_ATT = LV_PRODUCT_ATT ).
            IF SY-SUBRC = 0.
*             put attributes to the container
              LV_PRODUCT->SET_ATTRIBUTES( LV_PRODUCT_ATT ).
            ENDIF.
          ENDIF.
        ENDIF.

*        You could check if dependent objects should be read
*        but as we know that such do not exist we will stop here

        LV_PRODUCT = LV_CHILDREN->GET_NEXT( ).
```

```
      ENDWHILE.

    ENDCASE.
  ENDLOOP.
```

```
* If there were relationships to an access object we could have
explored the FOREIGN relations.
```

Listing 2.7 PROCESS_CHILDREN Method

One BO can have many relations. With this in mind, we have to loop through the requested relations and assess them individually. In our case, there is only one relation, `BookingProductsRel`.

```
  LT_REQ_RELS = IV_ROOT->GET_RELS_REQUESTED( ).
LOOP AT LT_REQ_RELS ASSIGNING <REL>.
  CASE <REL>.
    WHEN 'BookingProductsRel'.
  … (steps 1-5)
    ENDWHILE.
  ENDCASE.
ENDLOOP.
```

For each found relationship, you will need to implement specific logic. Therefore, it is best if you move that in a separate method/class. For our implementation, we will sacrifice best practices for the sake of simplicity and we will put all our code in one method. Once we find a `BookingProductsRel` we need to retrieve all the container objects associated with it and loop through them.

```
LV_CHILDREN = IV_ROOT->GET_RELATION( IV_RELATION_NAME = <REL>
                                     IV_AS_COPY  = ABAP_FALSE ).
* Note: WE set the IV_AS_COPY flag to FALSE so that our list
*        gets updated if new children were created.
*        loop over the list
LV_PRODUCT = LV_CHILDREN->GET_FIRST( ).
WHILE LV_PRODUCT IS BOUND.
… (steps 2-5)
ENDWHILE.
```

The above snippet corresponds to Step 1 of our data-flow algorithm. Next, we need to check whether the retrieved container objects (within `UsedProducts`) have key values. If the key is `initial`, then we need to read all the objects of this type. This is something missing from our data-flow diagram, but it is an important part of the

GenIL protocol. Passing an empty child container object (you can think of it as a dummy object)—as shown below—is the way to signal to the GenIL container that all the children associated with the requested relation will be read and returned.

```
CALL METHOD LV_PRODUCT->GET_KEY
          IMPORTING ES_KEY = LV_PRODUCT_KEY.
* check if child's key is given
IF LV_PRODUCT_KEY IS INITIAL.
… (read all children)
ENDIF.
```

Inside `IF LV_PRODUCT_KEY IS INITIAL`, we will refer to the parent and get its key. Once we have it, we will read the related `UsedProducts` keys and populate our container with objects containing those keys. In essence, we need to create a new `UsedProduct` instance (container object) for each key found.

```
LV_BOOKING = LV_PRODUCT->GET_PARENT( ).
CALL METHOD LV_BOOKING->GET_KEY
          IMPORTING ES_KEY = LV_BOOKING_KEY.

CALL METHOD ZCL_BOOKINGS_BACKEND_API=>READ_PRODUCT_KEYS(
          EXPORTING IS_BOOKING_KEY = LV_BOOKING_KEY
          IMPORTING ET_PRODUCT_KEYS = LT_PRODUCTS_KEYS ).

* create new objects for the other products (except the first) by
copying the place holder
LOOP AT LT_PRODUCTS_KEYS INTO LV_PRODUCT_KEY FROM 2.
  TRY.
    LV_PRODUCT->COPY_SELF_WITH_STRUCTURE( IS_OBJECT_KEY = LV_PRODUCT_
KEY ).
  CATCH CX_CRM_GENIL_MODEL_ERROR.
  CATCH CX_CRM_CIC_DUPLICATE_ENTRY.
  ENDTRY.
ENDLOOP.

* set new key for place holder object from the first partner
READ TABLE LT_PRODUCTS_KEYS INTO LV_PRODUCT_KEY INDEX 1.
IF SY-SUBRC = 0.
  TRY.
    LV_PRODUCT->SET_KEY( LV_PRODUCT_KEY ).
  CATCH CX_CRM_GENIL_DUPLICATE_KEY.
  ENDTRY.
ENDIF.
```

None of this is as complicated as it might seem at this point. First, for the provided `Bookings` key, we read the product keys via the backend API (`ZCL_BOOKINGS_BACK-END_API=>READ_PRODUCT_KEYS`). We will look at this method later. For now, keep in mind that it returns a table of product keys (there could be many products for one booking). Then we loop through that table and create product container objects starting from the second entry. In the previous snippet, we created a new object by calling `COPY_SELF_WITH_STRUCTURE` on the `LV_PRODUCT` container object. By doing so, we replicated the whole container structure (its model) associated with the empty/dummy container object. The keys of this object might be `INNITIAL`, but there could be relationships associated with the object and we want to replicate these in each object that we are about to create. This is why we started from the second product in the table, rather than from the first. Once done creating (via copying) new container objects, we will come back to the first (empty) object and set its key attributes. This is exactly what happens after the loop. We read the first key found and call `SET_KEY` on the first container object (variable `LV_PRODUCT`).

The previous code snippet contains several exception-processing statements. They are empty, but we want to show what you should expect from the container object interface. It is sufficient to say that our implementation will not lead to an exception. We encourage you to look at the code and the comments in Listing 2.7 for additional information.

If our model had been more complex, there might have been relations from `Used-Products` to lower-level dependent objects. We would have to repeat the same process for them as well. For example, we could have done this for each newly created `UsedProduct` container object. But a freshly created object does not contain any links to its dependencies (by default). The only object that had information about the model beneath was that first "dummy": `UsedProducts`. That is why we did not populate it immediately, but used it as a template to create all the other product container objects.

So far, we have created a container object for each key found in the products table. However no attributes were set. Normally, we would also retrieve and set all the attributes, rather than just the keys, but here we want to demonstrate how to work with the automatically updated child list and stick to our data flow from Figure 2.17.

We set the attributes of the current product in the same way that the other objects (if any) will be processed later on by the same loop.

```
IF LV_PRODUCT_KEY IS NOT INITIAL.
* check if attributes should be read
  IF LV_PRODUCT->CHECK_ATTR_REQUESTED( ) = ABAP_TRUE.
    CALL METHOD ZCL_BOOKINGS_BACKEND_API=>READ_PRODUCT(
             EXPORTING IS_PRODUCT_KEY = LV_PRODUCT_KEY
             IMPORTING ES_PRODUCT_ATT = LV_PRODUCT_ATT ).
    IF SY-SUBRC = 0.
*      put attributes to the container
      LV_PRODUCT->SET_ATTRIBUTES( LV_PRODUCT_ATT ).
    ENDIF.
  ENDIF.
ENDIF.
```

The previous snippet completes the realization of Steps 2 and 3 from the GET_OBJECTS data flow. We rely on ZCL_BOOKINGS_BACKEND_API=>READ_PRODUCT to fetch the UsedProduct's attributes based on the key values. We will discuss all the backend APIs very soon.

In our sample implementation, we will not check whether we need to read the children of UsedProducts (Step 4), as we know very well they do not exist. By following our code in GET_OBJECTS, however, it is easy to imagine what needs to be done. If the product had children objects and they were requested by the consumer, the corresponding relationships could be found in each product container object that we created earlier. This is guaranteed by the fact that we copied the empty (or also called placeholder) object with COPY_SELF_WITH_STRUCTURE.

Before we test our implementation, we will examine the backend API methods that we saw earlier. Let's start with READ_PRODUCTS (see Listing 2.8).

```
DATA: LT_PROD TYPE TABLE OF ZBOOK_PRODUCTS,
      LS_PROD_ATT_N TYPE ZBOL_BOOK_PRODUCTS_ATT_N,
      DB_READ_FLAG TYPE ABAP_BOOL.

FIELD-SYMBOLS: <LINE> TYPE ZBOL_BOOK_PRODUCTS_ATT_N,
               <FS_PROD> LIKE LINE OF LT_PROD,
               <PROD_ATT> TYPE ZBOL_BOOK_PRODUCTS_ATT.

REFRESH ET_PROD_ATT.
*check if there is something in the buffer
READ TABLE GT_BUFFER_PRODUCTS
  WITH KEY GUEST_ID = IS_BOOK_KEY-GUEST_ID
```

```
      HOTEL_NAME = IS_BOOK_KEY-HOTEL_NAME
      LASTCHECKIN = IS_BOOK_KEY-LASTCHECKIN
      TRANSPORTING NO FIELDS.
IF sy-subrc EQ 0.
* There is data in the buffer
    LOOP AT GT_BUFFER_PRODUCTS ASSIGNING <LINE>
      WHERE   GUEST_ID = IS_BOOK_KEY-GUEST_ID
      AND HOTEL_NAME = IS_BOOK_KEY-HOTEL_NAME
      AND LASTCHECKIN = IS_BOOK_KEY-LASTCHECKIN
      AND NEW <> 'D'.

      APPEND INITIAL LINE TO ET_PROD_ATT ASSIGNING <PROD_ATT>.
      MOVE-CORRESPONDING <LINE> TO <PROD_ATT>.
    ENDLOOP.

  ELSE.
* Read from the DB
SELECT * FROM ZBOOK_PRODUCTS INTO TABLE LT_PROD
  WHERE GUEST_ID EQ IS_BOOK_KEY-GUEST_ID
    AND HOTEL_NAME EQ IS_BOOK_KEY-HOTEL_NAME
    AND LASTCHECKIN EQ IS_BOOK_KEY-LASTCHECKIN.
  IF SY-SUBRC EQ 0.
   LOOP AT LT_PROD ASSIGNING <FS_PROD>.
*    We need to return the data read....
      APPEND INITIAL LINE TO ET_PROD_ATT ASSIGNING <PROD_ATT>.
      MOVE-CORRESPONDING <FS_PROD> TO <PROD_ATT>.
   ENDLOOP.
  ENDIF.
ENDIF.
```

Listing 2.8 READ_PRODUCTS Backend API Method

As we did when reading Bookings, we first check our GenIL component buffer and then read from the database. The difference here is that the database read might augment (rather than simply replace) the data stored already in the buffer. You can easily imagine a scenario in which we have inserted a new product but have not yet made the data persistent. Such a new product will remain in the buffer until we commit the transaction. In this case, reading only from the database will not be sufficient as we also need the new entry from the buffer. Again, we ask you to keep in mind that GET_OBJECTS is used not just to read the data during queries but also plays a role in transactions. We will talk about the buffering when we implement the transaction behavior.

For now, please focus on the SELECT * FROM ZBOOK_PRODUCTS statement, as it is the one relevant for simply displaying the data in a read-only mode. We are selecting all the products for the key of the parent booking and are appending each record to the exporting table.

```
SELECT * FROM ZBOOK_PRODUCTS INTO TABLE LT_PROD
  WHERE GUEST_ID EQ IS_BOOK_KEY-GUEST_ID
    AND HOTEL_NAME EQ IS_BOOK_KEY-HOTEL_NAME
    AND LASTCHECKIN EQ IS_BOOK_KEY-LASTCHECKIN.
  IF SY-SUBRC EQ 0.
    LOOP AT LT_PROD ASSIGNING <FS_PROD>.
*     We need to return the data read....
      APPEND INITIAL LINE TO ET_PROD_ATT ASSIGNING <PROD_ATT>.
      MOVE-CORRESPONDING <FS_PROD> TO <PROD_ATT>.
    ENDLOOP.
  ENDIF.
```

You might be wondering why we are discussing READ_PRODUCTS, given that it is nowhere to be found in the PROCESS_CHILDREN method. Both READ_PRODUCT_KEYS and READ_PRODUCT rely on GET_PRODUCTS to do all the heavy lifting. For example, retrieving the product keys requires the code in Listing 2.9:

```
call method ZCL_BOOKINGS_BACKEND_API=>READ_PRODUCTS(
    EXPORTING IS_BOOK_KEY = IS_BOOKING_KEY
    IMPORTING ET_PROD_ATT = LT_PRODS ).

LOOP AT LT_PRODS ASSIGNING <PROD_ATT>.
  MOVE-CORRESPONDING <PROD_ATT> TO LS_PROD_KEYS.
  INSERT LS_PROD_KEYS INTO TABLE ET_PRODUCT_KEYS.
ENDLOOP.
```

Listing 2.9 READ_PRODUCT_KEYS Backend API Method

As we explained, you will normally pull all the attributes at one time, but we wanted to implement the data flow because sometimes the model you are coding against can be quite complex. That is why we split the product retrieval: reading the keys first and then reading the rest of the attributes. For simplicity, we are relying on READ_PRODUCTS in both scenarios.

Based on the prior listing, we can see that all READ_PRODUCT does is to get a matching entry from the internal table imported from GET_PRODUCTS and return it as a result (see Listing 2.10).

```
DATA: LT_PRODS TYPE ZBOL_BOOK_PRODUCTS_T_ATT,
      LS_BOOK_KEY TYPE ZBOL_BOOKINGS_KEY.

MOVE-CORRESPONDING IS_PRODUCT_KEY TO LS_BOOK_KEY.

CALL METHOD ZCL_BOOKINGS_BACKEND_API=>READ_PRODUCTS(
    EXPORTING IS_BOOK_KEY = LS_BOOK_KEY
    IMPORTING ET_PROD_ATT = LT_PRODS ).

READ TABLE LT_PRODS
    WITH KEY GUEST_ID = IS_PRODUCT_KEY-GUEST_ID
      HOTEL_NAME = IS_PRODUCT_KEY-HOTEL_NAME
      LASTCHECKIN = IS_PRODUCT_KEY-LASTCHECKIN
      PRODUCT_ID = IS_PRODUCT_KEY-PRODUCT_ID
      USAGE_DATE = IS_PRODUCT_KEY-USAGE_DATE
    INTO ES_PRODUCT_ATT.
```

Listing 2.10 READ_PRODUCT Backend API Method

2.5.6   Testing the Implementation

It is time to test our implementation in the BOL browser. Remember to add the call to the GET_OBJECTS to your query implementation in case you have removed it. Start the GENIL_BOL_BROWSER transaction and enter your component set (ZBOOK in our example). Then execute the SearchBookings query as explained in the previous section.

If you have placed a breakpoint in GET_OBJECTS, you see that the method is invoked and also that all the attributes of the found objects are requested and set by our implementation (LV_ROOT->CHECK_ATTR_REQUESTED is true). The BOL has its own buffer, so it would store the data. As a result, the next BO read will hit the buffer rather than the database.

In the LIST BROWSER section (that shows the search result) double-click on an entry. You should get the attributes as shown in Figure 2.18. Note that GET_OBJECTS will not be called, as the data is already in the BOL buffer.

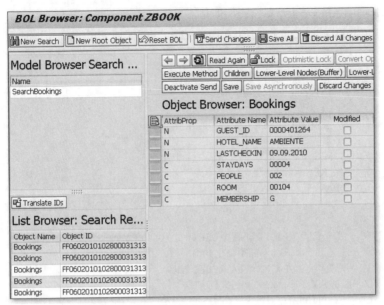

Figure 2.18 Reading a Booking in BOL Browser

In the button toolbar above the OBJECT BROWSER (right-hand side) you can click on the CHILDREN button. This will refresh the left-hand side, and instead of the list of queries you will see the list of relationships pertinent to the selected object. In our example, Bookings has only one relationship: BookingProductsRel. Go ahead and double-click on it. GET_OBJECTS is called again. Not surprisingly, LV_ROOT->CHECK_ATTR_REQUESTED is false (the Bookings attributes were populated during the first call). However, LV_ROOT->CHECK_RELS_REQUESTED is true and PROCESS_CHIL-DREN is executed. As expected, we see that the requested relationship is Booking-ProductsRel. Inside the container from that relationship, there is only one child object and its key is initial (a place holder for UsedProducts). Consequently, our implementation reads all the products for the current booking from the database and fills up the container list.

The BOL browser will show all the related UsedProducts in the LIST BROWSER below the relationships. If you double-click on one of them you will see a screen similar to Figure 2.19. GET_OBJECTS will not be called because the framework just read all the relevant products, set their attributes, and stored the result in the BOL buffer.

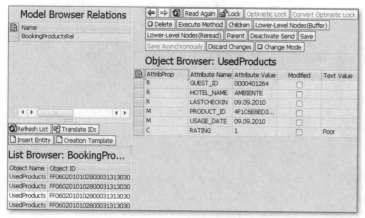

Figure 2.19 Reading a Product in BOL Browser

If you click on the PARENT button in the OBJECT BROWSER toolbar, the tool will show the attributes of the parent object. If you want to execute a new search, click on the NEW SEARCH button at the very top of the screen.

We will continue with the editing of our objects in Chapter 3. For now, we encourage you to experiment with the BOL browser, debug and even modify the GET_OBJECTS method.

2.6   Handling Container Lists and Objects

We have introduced and discussed the container object, and we now need to formalize and summarize all the information. The BOL/GenIL uses the container object to pass and request business objects. Semantically, the business objects are represented via their GenIL model and together with their relations form an object hierarchy. The container API facilitates the traversal of such a hierarchy. Figure 2.20 shows a class diagram of the container objects.

The root objects are always placed in a container list object of type IF_GENIL_ CONT_ROOT_OBJECTLIST. The other container list objects are of type IF_GENIL_CONT_ OBJECTLIST. You can think of IF_GENIL_CONT_ROOT_OBJECTLIST as a specialization of IF_GENIL_CONTAINER_OBJECTLIST for root objects.

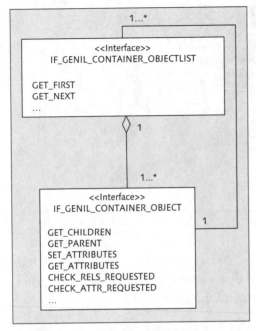

Figure 2.20 Container Objects Class Diagram

For example, both our query and GET_OBJECTS methods import IF_GENIL_CONT_ ROOT_OBJECTLIST. This is normal. Remember that because of the BOL splitting, the requested object hierarchy always starts with a root (or access) object.

The most important methods of your container list objects are:

▶ GET_FIRST

▶ GET_NEXT

▶ GET_GLOBAL_MESSAGE_CONTAINER

▶ GET_LAST

▶ REWIND

▶ ADD_OBJECT

▶ SIZE

▶ ADD_CHILDREN

The GET* methods allow you to traverse the container list; they all return IF_GENIL_CONT_ OBJECT. In our query implementation, we used the GET_GLOBAL_MESSAGE_CONTAINER to store the messages resulting from the business logic processing. We also used `ADD_OBJECT` to create a new object in the container list.

Always remember that a container list object only can be empty (`GET_FIRST` is not bound) inside a query method. In any other case it will always contain something.

If a container list holds only one container object with an initial key, you should consider this an indication to retrieve all the valid objects (all the root objects or all the objects referred to by the current relationship).

Every container object exposes, among others, the following methods:

- `GET_CHILDREN`
- `GET_PARENT`
- `GET_ROOT`
- `ADD_CHILD`

`GET_CHILDREN` will allow you to access any related container list object. The rest of the methods are self-explanatory.

Before we conclude this chapter, we want to discuss one more topic, namely filling the container list with objects. In the previous sections, we used `ADD_OBJECT` and `COPY_SELF_WITH_STRUCTURE`. You can also use the `ADD_CHILD` method from the container object.

The key difference between `COPY_SELF_WITH_STRUCTURE` and the other methods is that it preserves the object hierarchy associated with the container object on which it is invoked. You will need to traverse the full hierarchy in order to understand what has been requested by the framework (which dependent objects to return, for example). Remember that we retrieved `UsedProducts` by evaluating the relationships of `Bookings`. By doing so we found out that there is one `UsedProducts` object in the container list from `BookingProductsRel`. The key of this `UsedProducts` was `initial`, and this made us pull all the `UsedProducts` related to the current `Bookings` parent object.

Now, let's look at a more complex scenario. In the case of an order (sales or service), we typically have a header that contains items, which in turn could be linked to information about a ship-to party. Imagine a situation in which you receive a container list with one header object that has an item relation. The latter reveals a single item container object with `initial` key. Imagine also that from that dummy item, there is a relationship to a ship-to party. The party container object also has an `initial` key. Such a setup automatically means that you need to retrieve all the `items` along with their `ship-to party data`. Therefore, you would first read the keys of all the items and for each key you would create a new item container object. What happens if you add the new item to the item container list via `ADD_OBJECT`? Figure 2.21 depicts this scenario.

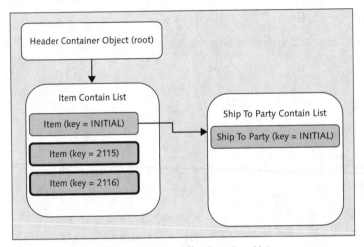

Figure 2.21 Using ADD_OBJECT to Fill a Container List

It is obvious that by using `ADD_OBJECT` (or `ADD_CHILD`) we will lose any related containers. As a result, we would never pull the ship-to party for the items we just added to the container (the ones with keys 2115 and 2116 in Figure 2.21). This is obviously not what we want. For this reason, use methods like `ADD_OBJECT` with care; for example, when populating a container list with leaves.

Let us look at the effects of using `COPY_SELF_WITH_STRUCTURE` (Figure 2.22 reflects the outcome of using the object with key `initial` as a template).

As one would expect, the container is populated with item objects that all point to a container list filled with placeholders of the ship-to-party type. As a result you can pull all the items and their related ship-to parties. Based on the above scenario, we recommend that your first choice for filling a container list is `COPY_SELF_WITH_STRUCTURE`.

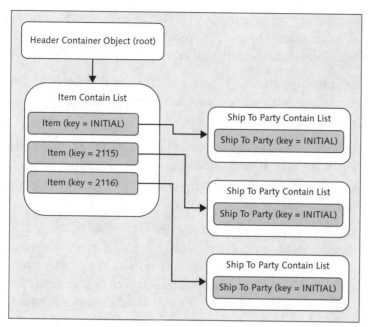

Figure 2.22 Using COPY_SELF_WITH_STRUCTURE to Fill Container List

2.7 Summary

In this chapter, we introduced two of the most challenging topics in this book, namely the BOL and GenIL layers. We saw that they can be used to implement and access the business logic of your application in a uniform way. The GenIL layer provides the implementation of the business logic, while the BOL layer is its consumer. The BOL/GenIL layers provide several services to the implementing applications, including message containers, transaction handling, and data buffering.

In this chapter we implemented querying and reading data: IF_GENIL_APPL_INTLAY~GET_DYNAMIC_QUERY_RESULT and IF_GENIL_APPL_INTLAY~GET_OBJECTS methods. Let's recap what we did.

The code inside GET_DYNAMIC_QUERY_RESULT accepts query parameters and search attributes. Based on these we tried to find matching bookings records in the database. For each match, we retrieved the keys and used them to create Bookings objects. We added these newly created objects (container) to a container list object.

We then passed the container list object to the GET_OBJECTS to do the complete reading and populating of the container objects. The container list was returned to the consumer. This concluded the implementation of GET_DYNAMIC_QUERY_RESULT.

GET_OBJECTS accepts a container list object. Each object inside that list is a root object (container). For each root container we checked whether the consumer wants us to get all the attributes.

Next, we checked whether the consumer is interested in the related entities (children). If so, we pulled all the related entities. We got another container list, but this one was holding the children of the current root object. We looped through that list of child objects.

If a child container contained initial key attributes (place holder) we treated it as a signal that the consumer wants us to read all the children of that type (connected to the root container object via the same relation). We queried the database and pulled all the keys for the matching dependent objects. For each key, we created a new child container object and added it to the container list of the related entities (child list).

We then continued with our loop and for each child object we checked whether we had to read the attributes, and if so we populated the container. We could also have checked for any related entities, but our GenIL model hierarchy has only two levels and the UsedProducts are leaf nodes. This concluded our GET_OBJECTS implementation.

While we tested our code in the BOL browser we saw that GET_OBJECTS is called once within GET_DYNAMIC_QUERY_RESULT and called again when we requested the details of the child entities (UsedProducts). The rest of the time, the data came from the BOL buffer.

If your custom application has to support only a read-only scenario, then you are finished at this point. However, if you want to edit our data you will have to do more coding. This is what we will discuss in Chapter 3.

We saw how to define the GenIL model via the GenIL Model Editor (for static models). If you would rather take care of the model persistency and definition yourself, you can study some of the existing CRM standard models (for example BT or even UIF_FL). SAP SDN also offers materials on this subject. One read that is easy to follow is the Create Your Own BOL Object blog by Harel Gilor (*http://www.sdn.sap.com/irj/scn/weblogs?blog=/pub/wlg/19914*).

Many failures in software design are preceded by prototypes that focus solely on retrieving and displaying data. Data modification embodies most of the complexities of your business logic and requires most of your attention.

3 Completing Your GenIL Component

In the previous chapter, we shared an overview of BOL and GenIL. We created a model with the Model Editor, and also implemented methods to query and read business data. As a result, we achieved a relatively comprehensive read-only scenario. Moreover, we learned how to test our GenIL implementation and model via the BOL browser.

Data modification is indeed the most complex logic that you will have to implement. There are a number of reasons for this. For one thing, you have many users accessing the same data at the same time, so you have concurrency problems to address. Unless your application is very simple, you will have to update many data sources (tables). Maybe some of the data is even in different systems. Failure in one of these processing steps means that everything updated so far in the current operation has to be invalidated. As professionals familiar with the basics of database transactions, you already have a good idea of the intricacies of enterprise data manipulation.

In this chapter, we will see what it takes to edit business data. We will dig deeper into the GenIL APIs, and successfully modify application data. We will start by discussing the transactional behavior of the GenIL component. A comprehensive overview will follow of the main GenIL methods that you need to implement in order to complete your business logic: locking, object creation, modification, saving, and deleting. As usual, we will be building on the previously introduced hotel guest booking example. Towards the end of the chapter we will introduce a fresh addition to SAP CRM 7.0 EhP1, the so-called GenIL handlers. These might significantly simplify GenIL component development.

3.1   Transaction Behavior

GenIL components implement transaction processing via the following interfaces:

- IF_GENIL_APPL_INTLAY~CREATE_OBJECTS
  Used to implement root object creation.

- IF_GENIL_APPL_INTLAY~MODIFY_OBJECTS
  Modifies data.

- IF_GENIL_APPL_INTLAY~ON_AFTER_COMMIT
  Event handler executed after transaction commit.

- IF_GENIL_APPL_INTLAY~ ON_AFTER_ROLLBACK
  Event handler executed after rollback.

- IF_GENIL_APPL_ALTERNATIVE_DSIL~INIT_OBJECTS
  Refreshes the GenIL component buffer.

- IF_GENIL_APPL_ALTERNATIVE_DSIL~LOCK_OBJECTS
  Requests a lock.

- IF_GENIL_APPL_ALTERNATIVE_DSIL~DELETE_OBJECTS
  Deletes data.

- IF_GENIL_APPL_ALTERNATIVE_DSIL~CHECK_OBJECTS_BEFORE_SAVE
  Performs one last check before calling the SAVE method.

- IF_GENIL_APPL_ALTERNATIVE_DSIL~SAVE_OBJECTS
  Performs the data save.

From the above, you can deduce that your GenIL component will implement both IF_GENIL_APPL_INTLAY and IF_GENIL_APPL_ALTERNATIVE_DSIL interfaces. Initially, IF_GENIL_APPL_ALTERNATIVE_DSIL did not exist, which is why you can find similar methods in IF_GENIL_APPL_INTLAY. However, soon you consider INIT_OBJECTS, LOCK_OBJECTS, DELETE_OBJECTS, CHECK_OBJECTS_BEFORE_SAVE, and SAVE_OBJECTS in IF_GENIL_APPL_INTLAY deprecated.

Your GenIL implementation will never initialize, commit, or rollback a transaction. The transaction context is owned by the framework, so you need not worry about it.

Another fact worth mentioning is that there is only a single instance of your GenIL component per user session. As a result, you could implement buffering mechanisms to improve the performance. Such buffering is not related to the BOL buffering service but rather should wrap the access to your database tables (or other data sources).

GenIL as a Transaction Buffer

The basic assumption is that a GenIL component encapsulates a business object API (also referred to as backend API), which handles the communication with the database. One of your components' major requirements is to act as a transactional buffer for the data of your objects. The GenIL component data containers therefore must reflect the latest data changes after each user interaction. We cannot call commit or rollback within the GenIL component, as the framework is handling the transaction contexts.

What can you expect when you want to edit your data? Your implementations of the methods from IF_GENIL_APPL_INTLAY and IF_GENIL_APPL_ALTERNATIVE_DSIL will be executed. The sequence of the API calls is as follows.

1. IF_GENIL_APPL_ALTERNATIVE_DSIL~LOCK_OBJECTS means that the framework will attempt to lock the affected root and dependent objects. This is a good place to refresh (reload) your buffer from the data source (if you have one). By default, the locking strategy is exclusive but the framework allows you also to implement optimistic locking. The locking mode will be passed via IV_LOCK_MODE parameter, and your implementation can respond to it accordingly. The parameter CT_OBJECT_LIST contains all the object names (root nodes) that will be locked. Remember that you can have more than one root object, and the GenIL is implemented via a single class. If you have successfully acquired a lock for a given object name, set the success flag on the corresponding object in CT_OBJECT_LIST to true ('X') before returning from the method.

2. IF_GENIL_APPL_INTLAY~GET_OBJECTS is called after locking the data in order to bring to the user a fresh snapshot of the data that is about to be modified. While you were viewing your data, someone might have modified it. By re-reading the data, the framework ensures that you have the opportunity to obtain the latest snapshot of your data.

3. IF_GENIL_APPL_INTLAY~MODIFY_OBJECTS is called by the framework to allow your GenIL component to evaluate and cache the data changes (your component is acting as a transactional buffer). The creation and deletion of dependent objects is handled via the same method. In order to improve the performance, the framework might bundle several modify calls. As a result, you might not be able

to predict when exactly MODIFY_OBJECTS will be called. During modification you should not only validate but also buffer the data changes. The reason is that in the subsequent calls you will not regain the changed and the original attribute values but only the keys of the objects that have been marked as new, modified or deleted. Therefore, it is very important that you buffer all the modifications. MODIFY_OBJECTS is a good place to reject the data changes based on your data validation rules. One of the parameters that will receive inside this method is a GenIL container list. Each container object inside that list contains only the attributes that have been changed (only the delta is sent back by the framework). You shall traverse all the container objects (root and the dependent ones), check for changes, validate, and buffer them. Upon successful processing of an object, you set the object name and its ID in exporting parameter ET_CHANGED_OBJECTS.

4. IF_GENIL_APPL_ALTERNATIVE_DSIL~CHECK_OBJECTS_BEFORE_SAVE is part of the save process. You can run some consistency checks and cancel the modification if needed. You will receive a table filled with data structures. Each structure contains the object name, internal ID, and a SUCCESS flag. The implementation of this method is optional.

5. IF_GENIL_APPL_ALTERNATIVE_DSIL~SAVE_OBJECTS is where you store the changes from your buffer into your data sources. As with CHECK_OBJECTS_BEFORE_SAVE, you will get the object's name and internal ID. Based on these, you should pull the corresponding data from your buffer (where you stored your changes during the execution of MODIFY_OBJECTS method) and persist it. Do not forget to set the SUCCESS flag for each successfully processed entry.

6. IF_GENIL_APPL_INTLAY~ON_AFTER_COMMIT and IF_GENIL_APPL_INTLAY~ON_AFTER_ROLLBACK are executed during the transaction commit or rollback process. If you have not cleaned your buffer and released your locks, this is the time to do so.

We mentioned several times that the framework passes or expects an internal ID. This ID is a unique combination of numbers and characters and is used by the framework to uniquely identify a GenIL object instance. For various reasons, the framework does not use the actual object key to look up entity instances. In SAP CRM we often work with a Globally Unique Identifier (GUID). For example, a GUID of a product helps you identify a specific product record. A GUID can be used as a primary key in a table.

Because of the conceptual similarities between the GenIL internal (object) ID and the GUID, some people might use these terms interchangeably. There are helper methods that allow you obtain the key from a GenIL object ID and vice versa. These are GET_KEY_FROM_OBJECT_ID and BUILD_OBJECT_ID from CL_CRM_GENIL_CONTAINER_TOOLS. You will see these in action as part of our examples.

3.2   Requesting a Lock

Let us implement the LOCK_OBJECT method of our GenIL class. We will rely on backend APIs to perform the work on the database level; namely to lock the relevant tables via the standard ABAP enqueueing.

3.2.1   Implementing LOCK_OBJECT

The implementation of IF_GENIL_APPL_ALTERNATIVE_DSIL~LOCK_OBJECT should check the locking mode (optimistic vs. exclusive) and take appropriate actions. We will only support exclusive locking, as do the majority of the SAP CRM business objects. We will then check the object name that needs to be locked and—based on its value—call the appropriate backend API. The latter will lock the relevant tables using standard ABAP enqueueing. Listing 3.1 shows how your code could look.

```
data LV_KEY type ZBOL_BOOKINGS_ATT.
field-symbols <OBJECT> like line of CT_OBJECT_LIST.
if IV_LOCK_MODE = IF_GENIL_APPL_INTLAY=>LOCK_MODE_EXCLUSIVE.
  loop at CT_OBJECT_LIST assigning <OBJECT>.
     if <OBJECT>-OBJECT_NAME = 'Bookings'.

        call method CL_CRM_GENIL_CONTAINER_TOOLS=>GET_KEY_FROM_OBJECT_ID
          exporting
            IV_OBJECT_NAME = <OBJECT>-OBJECT_NAME
            IV_OBJECT_ID   = <OBJECT>-OBJECT_ID
          importing
            ES_KEY         = LV_KEY.
        call method ZCL_BOOKINGS_BACKEND_API=>BUFFER_BOOKINGS
          changing
            CS_ATTR = LV_KEY.
        if LV_KEY is initial.
          <OBJECT>-SUCCESS = 'X'.
        endif.
     endif.
```

```
    endloop.
  endif.
```

Listing 3.1 GenIL Lock Method

The objects that we need to lock are in CT_OBJECT_LIST. Therefore, we start our method by looping through them:

```
loop at CT_OBJECT_LIST assigning <OBJECT>.
```

If you look at what is inside <OBJECT>, among other attributes, you will find OBJECT_NAME and OBJECT_ID. The latter is the internal ID that GenIL uses to uniquely identify object instances. All the methods that you have seen so far rely on the GenIL business object key structure. Therefore, we need to convert the ID into the object's key:

```
call method CL_CRM_GENIL_CONTAINER_TOOLS=>GET_KEY_FROM_OBJECT_ID
        exporting
            IV_OBJECT_NAME = <OBJECT>-OBJECT_NAME
            IV_OBJECT_ID   = <OBJECT>-OBJECT_ID
        importing
            ES_KEY         = LV_KEY.
```

The key of the currently processed root object (Bookings) will be returned in LV_KEY structure. Once we have the key, we call the backend API that performs the actual data locking.

```
call method ZCL_BOOKINGS_BACKEND_API=>BUFFER_BOOKINGS
        changing CS_ATTR = LV_KEY.
```

The backend API will lock the object via an enqueue function on the database tables. If this operation is successful, we will set the SUCCESS flag in CT_OBJECT_LIST.

```
if LV_KEY is initial.
  <OBJECT>-SUCCESS = 'X'.
endif.
```

3.2.2 Backend API

Listing 3.2 shows the exemplary code of ZCL_BOOKINGS_BACKEND_API=>BUFFER_BOOK-INGS. As discussed (and as its name implies), its main goal is to obtain and buffer the latest data snapshot. In addition, our implementation will perform the database locking.

```
DATA LS_BOOKINGS LIKE LINE OF GT_BUFFER_BOOKINGS.

CALL FUNCTION 'ENQUEUE_EZBOOKING_RESRV'
 EXPORTING
   MODE_ZBOOKING_RESERV      = 'E'
   GUEST_ID                  = CS_ATTR-GUEST_ID
   HOTEL_NAME                = CS_ATTR-HOTEL_NAME
   LASTCHECKIN               = CS_ATTR-LASTCHECKIN
 EXCEPTIONS
   FOREIGN_LOCK              = 1.
IF SY-SUBRC = 0.
  SELECT * FROM ZBOOKING_RESERV APPENDING CORRESPONDING FIELDS OF
  TABLE GT_BUFFER_BOOKINGS
  WHERE GUEST_ID = CS_ATTR-GUEST_ID AND
     HOTEL_NAME = CS_ATTR-HOTEL_NAME AND
     LASTCHECKIN = CS_ATTR-LASTCHECKIN.

  IF SY-SUBRC IS NOT INITIAL.
*    the key does not exist on the db
    LS_BOOKINGS-GUEST_ID = CS_ATTR-GUEST_ID.
    LS_BOOKINGS-HOTEL_NAME = CS_ATTR-HOTEL_NAME.
    LS_BOOKINGS-LASTCHECKIN = CS_ATTR-LASTCHECKIN.
    LS_BOOKINGS-NEW = 'C'.
    APPEND LS_BOOKINGS TO GT_BUFFER_BOOKINGS.
  ENDIF.

* buffer products
  SELECT * FROM ZBOOK_PRODUCTS APPENDING CORRESPONDING FIELDS OF
   TABLE GT_BUFFER_PRODUCTS
     WHERE GUEST_ID = CS_ATTR-GUEST_ID
        AND HOTEL_NAME = CS_ATTR-HOTEL_NAME
           AND LASTCHECKIN = CS_ATTR-LASTCHECKIN.
* clean the structure
  CLEAR CS_ATTR.
ELSE.
*   Implement suitable error handling here
ENDIF.
```

Listing 3.2 Backend API Lock Method

The name of the enqueue function that we created was ENQUEUE_EZBOOKING_RESRV. We will not discuss the enqueueing mechanism, as it is a well known standard mechanism for locking data in ABAP. You can read about it in the help or in any book on ABAP programming. For simplicity, we did not provide a full blown enqueue/dequeue implementation. We are locking only the ZBOOKING_RESERV table, assuming that the only way to modify data is through our GenIL component and there is no other way to modify the ZBOOK_PRODUCTS.

Upon successful enqueueing, we read the booking record that corresponds to the provided key and add it to the buffer. In our implementation we use the GT_BUF-FER_BOOKINGS GenIL component attribute as a buffer. We can do so because there is only one instance of the GenIL component class per user session.

```
SELECT * FROM ZBOOKING_RESERV APPENDING CORRESPONDING FIELDS OF
   TABLE GT_BUFFER_BOOKINGS
   WHERE GUEST_ID = CS_ATTR-GUEST_ID AND
       HOTEL_NAME = CS_ATTR-HOTEL_NAME AND
       LASTCHECKIN = CS_ATTR-LASTCHECKIN.
```

If there is no database record for the supplied key, we assume that the key belongs to a newly created booking object that has not yet been persisted (used during root object creation). If this is the case, we add it to the buffer but we set its NEW flag to 'C' (create), as shown in the following code snippet. Later in this chapter, you will see an implementation of a root object creation that follows this routine.

```
IF SY-SUBRC IS NOT INITIAL.
   LS_BOOKINGS-GUEST_ID = CS_ATTR-GUEST_ID.
   LS_BOOKINGS-HOTEL_NAME = CS_ATTR-HOTEL_NAME.
   LS_BOOKINGS-LASTCHECKIN = CS_ATTR-LASTCHECKIN.
   LS_BOOKINGS-NEW = 'C'.
   APPEND LS_BOOKINGS TO GT_BUFFER_BOOKINGS.
ENDIF.
```

Next we read all the products belonging to the current booking and add it to the GT_BUFFER_PRODUCTS (internal table), as shown in the following code snippet. The latter is also an attribute of our GenIL component class.

```
SELECT * FROM ZBOOK_PRODUCTS APPENDING CORRESPONDING FIELDS OF
   TABLE GT_BUFFER_PRODUCTS
      WHERE GUEST_ID = CS_ATTR-GUEST_ID
         AND HOTEL_NAME = CS_ATTR-HOTEL_NAME
            AND LASTCHECKIN = CS_ATTR-LASTCHECKIN.
```

When the above code executes without any errors, we can consider our database entries locked and buffered in the current user session. We signal this to the caller of the LOCK method by clearing the key structure: CLEAR CS_ATTR.

3.2.3 Testing LOCK_OBJECT

How do you lock an object? After opening a specific object in the BOL browser transaction, you can hit the LOCK button. An alternative is to click on the CHANGE MODE button. This is equivalent to opening a document/record in SAP CRM, for example an account, and clicking the EDIT button (see Figure 3.1).

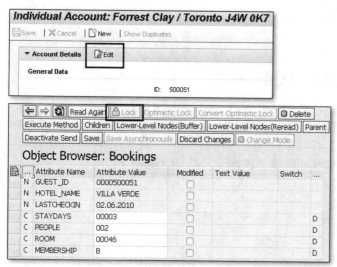

Figure 3.1 Locking a Business Object

If you put breakpoints in both the LOCK and GET_OBJECTS methods, you will see that the framework calls them one after the other. As we already mentioned GET_OBJECTS is called to ensure that the user is presented with the latest snapshot from the data source (after the data is locked).

3.3 Creating a Root Object

The most straightforward data-modification operation is probably CREATE_OBJECTS. This method is responsible for the creation of your root objects. The dependent ones are taken care of by MODIFY_OBJECTS. CREATE_OBJECTS has the following parameters:

▶ IV_OBJECT_NAME
The name of the root object to be created.

▶ IV_NUMBER

Defines how many root object instances shall be created.

▶ IT_PARAMETERS

Is of type `CRMT_NAME_VALUE_PAIR_TAB` and holds name-value pairs for each attribute that shall be used to create the root object.

▶ V_ROOT_LIST

Is an empty root list container that shall be filled with all the newly created object instances.

3.3.1 Implementing CREATE_OBJECTS

We know that our GenIL model has only one root business object (`Bookings`). Therefore we do not need to check the `IV_OBJECT_NAME`. If we had several root objects, we would have executed different creation procedures based on the object name. Our sample implementation is provided in Listing 3.3.

```
method IF_GENIL_APPL_INTLAY~CREATE_OBJECTS.
  data LV_BOOK_ATTR type ZBOL_BOOKINGS_ATT.
  data LV_BOOK_KEY type ZBOL_BOOKINGS_KEY.
  data LV_SUCCESS type CHAR1.
* We have only one Root Object - hence we know it is Bookings
* In more complex scenarios you need to check the OBJECT_NAME

* populate the BOL node create structure (in our case it is the same as
the key)
  FILL_STRUCT_FROM_NVP_TAB(
      exporting IT_PARAMETERS = IT_PARAMETERS
      changing  CS_PARAMETER  = LV_BOOK_KEY ).


  call method ZCL_BOOKINGS_BACKEND_API=>CREATE_BOOKING
    exporting
      IS_BOOKING_ATTR = LV_BOOK_KEY
    importing
      RV_SUCCESS  = LV_SUCCESS.
*   move-corresponding LV_SCARR_ATTR to LV_SCARR_KEY.
  if not LV_SUCCESS is initial.
    IV_ROOT_LIST->ADD_OBJECT( IV_OBJECT_NAME = IV_OBJECT_NAME
                              IS_OBJECT_KEY  = LV_BOOK_KEY ).
```

```
    endif.
endmethod.
```

Listing 3.3 CREATE_OBJECT method

Let us introduce an important helper method. `FILL_STRUCT_FROM_NVP_TAB` belongs to one of our base classes, `CL_CRM_GENIL_ABSTR_COMPONENT`. This method fills a structure based on the name-value pairs from table `CRMT_NAME_VALUE_PAIR_TAB`. We will use it to populate `LV_BOOK_KEY`, the create structures of `Bookings` (the one that we assigned in the GenIL model).

```
FILL_STRUCT_FROM_NVP_TAB( exporting IT_PARAMETERS = IT_PARAMETERS
      changing  CS_PARAMETER  = LV_BOOK_KEY ).
```

Next, we will call our backend API that will create the actual booking records. We will look at its implementation once we are done with `CREATE_OBJECTS`.

```
call method ZCL_BOOKINGS_BACKEND_API=>CREATE_BOOKING
    exporting
      IS_BOOKING_ATTR = LV_BOOK_KEY
    importing
      RV_SUCCESS  = LV_SUCCESS.
```

Upon successful database record insertion, we need to create a root object instance and add it to the root list container `IV_ROOT_LIST`. The framework expects to find the newly-created container objects there. If not `LV_SUCCESS` is initial.

```
  IV_ROOT_LIST->ADD_OBJECT( IV_OBJECT_NAME = IV_OBJECT_NAME
                            IS_OBJECT_KEY  = LV_BOOK_KEY ).
  endif.
```

3.3.2 Backend API

In the previous section, we completed the implementation inside our GenIL component class. As promised, let's look at our backend API (Listing 3.4).

```
DATA LINE LIKE LINE OF GT_BUFFER_BOOKINGS.
*first lock
CALL FUNCTION 'ENQUEUE_EZBOOKING_RESRV'
 EXPORTING
   MODE_ZBOOKING_RESERV      = 'E'
   GUEST_ID                  = IS_BOOKING_ATTR-GUEST_ID
   HOTEL_NAME                = IS_BOOKING_ATTR-HOTEL_NAME
   LASTCHECKIN               = IS_BOOKING_ATTR-LASTCHECKIN
```

```
    EXCEPTIONS
      FOREIGN_LOCK                    = 1.
  IF SY-SUBRC = 0.
  * ... then write into the buffer
      LINE-GUEST_ID = IS_BOOKING_ATTR-GUEST_ID.
      LINE-HOTEL_NAME = IS_BOOKING_ATTR-HOTEL_NAME.
      LINE-LASTCHECKIN = IS_BOOKING_ATTR-LASTCHECKIN.
      LINE-NEW = 'C'.
      APPEND LINE TO GT_BUFFER_BOOKINGS.
  * The operation was a success
      RV_SUCCESS = 'X'.
  ENDIF.
```

Listing 3.4 Create Booking Records in Backend API

First, take into account the fact that so far no one has requested a lock on the data. After all, we are not modifying existing records but creating new ones. Therefore, the framework leaves it up to the creation implementation to decide when and how to lock. In a way, the framework expects the create operation to implement locking, if required. We have done so in our backend API.

```
CALL FUNCTION 'ENQUEUE_EZBOOKING_RESRV'
  EXPORTING
    MODE_ZBOOKING_RESERV      = 'E'
    GUEST_ID                  = IS_BOOKING_ATTR-GUEST_ID
    HOTEL_NAME                = IS_BOOKING_ATTR-HOTEL_NAME
    LASTCHECKIN               = IS_BOOKING_ATTR-LASTCHECKIN
  EXCEPTIONS
    FOREIGN_LOCK              = 1.
```

If the enqueue is successful, we will add a new line to our buffer GT_BUFFER_BOOK-INGS. This line will have the values form the booking key (passed as a parameter) and a NEW flag set to C. Let's not forget to set the RV_SUCCESS parameter accordingly.

```
LINE-GUEST_ID = IS_BOOKING_ATTR-GUEST_ID.
...
LINE-NEW = 'C'.
APPEND LINE TO GT_BUFFER_BOOKINGS.
RV_SUCCESS = 'X'.
```

This concludes our CREATE_OBJECTS implementation. It is time to test it in the GENIL_BOL_BROWSER.

3.3.3 Testing CREATE_OBJECTS

Start the BOL browser and open your GenIL component. In order to test your cerate method, you will have to perform the following steps:

1. At the top of the page, click on the NEW ROOT OBJECT button.

2. The MODEL BROWSER ROOT OBJECTS in the left-hand side of the screen will list all the root objects present in your model. In our case we have only Bookings. Go ahead a double-click on it.

3. A new view will open below: the PARAMETER BROWSER. There you can specify the create parameters for the new booking. The framework uses the create structure form the GenIL model to determine what parameters you will need to provide. Enter some values.

4. Once done, you can click on the CREATE OBJECT button above and our CRE-ATE_OBJECT will be invoked.

If you have set a breakpoint in your method, you could see how the create parameters were being converted into ZBOL_BOOKINGS_KEY and how the backend API populated the buffer. If you still keep your breakpoint in the GET_OBJECTS method you will see that it is also invoked immediately after the CREATE_OBJECTS. Our implementation picks up the newly created booking record from the buffer table (it checks if the NEW flag is C). The following code from ZCL_BOOKINGS_BACKEND_API=>READ_BOOKINGS will be executed:

```
IF <LINE>-NEW EQ 'C' OR <LINE>-NEW EQ 'M'.
   MOVE-CORRESPONDING <LINE> TO ES_BOOK_ATT.
   RETURN.
ENDIF.
```

The retrieved attributes will be used to create a Bookings container object. The latter is passed back to the consumer, namely the GENIL_BOL_BROWSER (BOL API calls). The result is rendered inside the OBJECT BROWSER (on the right-hand side). Figure 3.2 illustrates your interaction in the BOL Browser.

Although we have executed the CREATE_OBJECTS method, we will not be able to find our new booking after we restart the BOL Browser. The reason is that we have not saved it. We will cover MODIFY_OBJECTS and SAVE_OBJECTS in the next sections.

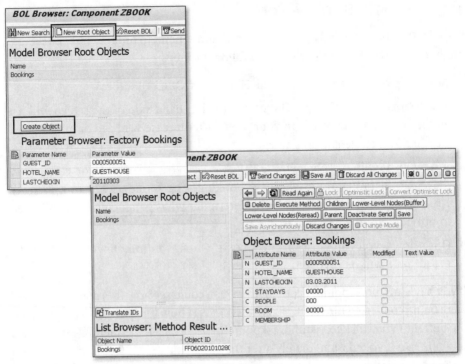

Figure 3.2 Creating New Root Object from BOL Browser

3.4   Implementing the Object Modification Logic

MODIFY_OBJECT is typically the most complex method in your GenIL implementation. Whenever you are creating, changing, or deleting dependent objects or changing the root object, the framework will rely on the MODIFY_OBJECT to perform the updates.

The method is defined in IF_GENIL_APPL_INTLAY. It has an importing reference parameter, IV_ROOT_LIST of type IF_GENIL_CONT_ROOT_OBJECTLIST. This is a GenIL container list that stores your component's root object instances. These root objects are just the tip of the iceberg, as the entire affected object hierarchy is being delivered through them. Unlike GET_OBJECTS there is no split on object level.

Each object instance in the container has a modification flag, and you have to call IF_GENIL_CONTAINER_OBJECT ~GET_DELTA_FLAG to get it. The value of this delta flag indicates whether the object has been created, modified, or deleted. If the delta flag is empty, this signals that the object has not been altered and is simply part of the object hierarchy structure affected by the modification (for example, it is a parent of a modified object). Therefore, even if the modification flag is initial you must process its dependent objects as they might have been changed.

Your implementation will traverse the container objects, check which objects have been modified, validate the correctness of the modifications, and buffer the changes. Please note that MODIFY_OBJECTS does not make the changes persistent. Instead, it extracts the changes, analyzes them, and stores them in a temporary (transactional) buffer. When the SAVE_OBJECT is executed later on (as part of a transaction), it will obtain the modifications from the transactional buffer and persist them. The successfully updated objects in the BOL buffer will be refreshed by a subsequent call of GET_OBJECTS.

Upon completion, MODIFY_OBJECTS returns ET_CHANGED_OBJECTS, which is an internal table of type CRMT_GENIL_OBJ_INSTANCE. The latter is a structure that contains an object name and object ID. By placing an object in that table, you are acknowledging that you have processed and accepted the modifications for that object. To make your life a bit simpler, the framework assumes that an entry in ET_CHANGED_OBJECTS implies that not only the corresponding object has changed but also its child objects. The framework uses the information from ET_CHANGED_OBJECTS to invalidate the BOL buffer. Therefore, it is very important that all the objects (at the top of the hierarchies) that you consider changed are in that table. As you know already, the BOL will read the data from the BOL buffer first. Therefore, if you change an object but do not inform the framework about it, the BOL consumers (UI layer) will get incorrect data.

You have to pay attention when handling object deletion. You should not put into ET_CHANGED_OBJECTS the objects that have been deleted implicitly because they were children of a deleted object instance. The framework will delete them from the buffer automatically.

Figure 3.3 outlines the data flow that your MODIFY_OBJECTS should implement.

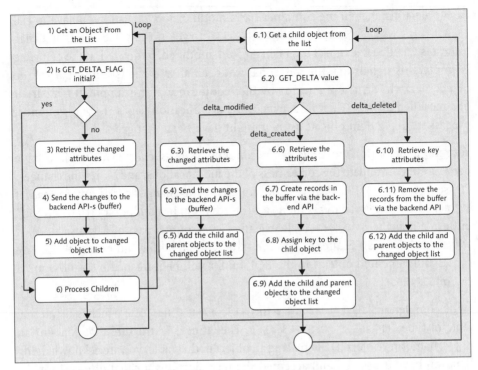

Figure 3.3 Object Modification Flow

The above diagram requires some explanation. As usual, we will do so with the help of code snippets.

3.4.1 Implementing MODIFY_OBJECTS

As previously mentioned, when updating your data the GenIL framework will call your component's implementation of IF_GENIL_APPL_INTLAY~MODIFY_OBJECTS. All the root container objects that have been modified will be passed to your IF_GENIL_APPL_INTLAY~MODIFY_OBJECTS implementation via the import parameter IV_ROOT_LIST. Note, that the root objects might be intact and it might be that some of the dependent/child objects have been changed. Therefore, you must process the children of the root containers. Listing 3.5 shows the complete implementation of our MODIFY_OBJECTS.

```
DATA: LV_BOOK_ATTR TYPE ZBOL_BOOKINGS_ATT,
      LV_ROOT TYPE REF TO IF_GENIL_CONTAINER_OBJECT,
      LV_PROD_CONTAINER TYPE REF TO IF_GENIL_CONTAINER_OBJECTLIST,
```

```
          LV_CHANGED_OBJECTS TYPE CRMT_GENIL_OBJ_INSTANCE,
          LV_PROPS_OBJ TYPE REF TO IF_GENIL_OBJ_ATTR_PROPERTIES,
          LT_CHANGED_ATTR TYPE CRMT_ATTR_NAME_TAB,
          LV_BOOK_KEY TYPE ZBOL_BOOKINGS_KEY,
          LV_SUCCESS TYPE ABAP_BOOL.

CHECK IV_ROOT_LIST IS BOUND.

LV_ROOT = IV_ROOT_LIST->GET_FIRST( ).
WHILE LV_ROOT IS BOUND.
  IF LV_ROOT->GET_DELTA_FLAG( ) IS NOT INITIAL.
    CASE LV_ROOT->GET_NAME( ).
      WHEN 'Bookings'.
        LV_PROPS_OBJ = LV_ROOT->GET_ATTR_PROPS_OBJ( ).
*        retrieve attributes which are modified (only the delta )
        LV_PROPS_OBJ->GET_NAME_TAB_4_PROPERTY(
                    EXPORTING IV_PROPERTY = IF_GENIL_OBJ_ATTR_
PROPERTIES=>MODIFIED
                    IMPORTING ET_NAMES = LT_CHANGED_ATTR ).
        LV_ROOT->GET_KEY( IMPORTING ES_KEY = LV_BOOK_KEY ).
        LV_ROOT->GET_ATTRIBUTES(
         IMPORTING ES_ATTRIBUTES = LV_BOOK_ATTR ).
        MOVE-CORRESPONDING LV_BOOK_KEY TO LV_BOOK_ATTR.
*        send changes to backend buffer
        ZCL_BOOKINGS_BACKEND_API=>CHANGE_BOOKING(
          EXPORTING IS_BOOK_ATTR = LV_BOOK_ATTR
                    IT_NAMES = LT_CHANGED_ATTR
         IMPORTING RV_SUCCESS = LV_SUCCESS ).
        IF LV_SUCCESS IS NOT INITIAL.
          LV_CHANGED_OBJECTS-OBJECT_NAME = 'Bookings'.
          LV_CHANGED_OBJECTS-OBJECT_ID = CL_CRM_GENIL_CONTAINER_
TOOLS=>BUILD_OBJECT_ID( LV_BOOK_KEY ).
          APPEND LV_CHANGED_OBJECTS TO ET_CHANGED_OBJECTS.
        ENDIF.
      WHEN OTHERS.
    ENDCASE.
  ENDIF.
* process the child objects
  LV_PROD_CONTAINER = LV_ROOT->GET_CHILDREN(
                IV_AS_COPY = ABAP_TRUE ).
  CALL METHOD MODIFY_CHILDREN
    EXPORTING IV_CHILDREN = LV_PROD_CONTAINER
    CHANGING CT_CHANGED_OBJECTS = ET_CHANGED_OBJECTS.
```

```
* procede to the next root object
  LV_ROOT = IV_ROOT_LIST->GET_NEXT( ).

ENDWHILE.
```
Listing 3.5 MODIFY_OBJECTS Implementation

Our implementation will start by looping through the root object list and looking for changes in each object. (Steps 1 and 2 from Figure 3.3).

```
LV_ROOT = IV_ROOT_LIST->GET_FIRST( ).
WHILE LV_ROOT IS BOUND.
  IF LV_ROOT->GET_DELTA_FLAG( ) IS NOT INITIAL.
    "... process root objects
  ENDIF.
    ".... proceed to the next root object
  LV_ROOT = IV_ROOT_LIST->GET_NEXT( ).
ENDWHILE.
```

The method GET_DELTA_FLAG indicates whether the container object has been modified. If the check is positive, we will process the root object changes. As our modification method will be called for any business object from our GenIL model, our code needs to implement specific handling based on the object's name. Therefore, our first task as part of root-objects processing is to call GET_NAME method and define a CASE statement based on its return value. We have only one root object—Bookings—but you can easily see how one can accommodate multiple root business objects in place of the WHEN OTHERS.

```
CASE LV_ROOT->GET_NAME( ).
  WHEN 'Bookings'.
    "... steps 3,4 and 5 for Bookings GenIL object
  WHEN OTHERS.
ENDCASE.
```

According to our modification flow diagram, Step 3 involves retrieving the changed attributes. If we try to retrieve all the attributes of the container object (by calling GET_ATTRIBUTES), we might get an initial or partially filled structure. The reason is that MODIFY_OBJECTS, unlike GET_OBJECTS, received only the data that has been changed. Therefore, we must find a way to find exactly which attributes have been altered. Luckily, this can be easily accomplished via IF_GENIL_OBJ_ATTR_PROPERTIES~GET_NAME_TAB_4_PROPERTY.

`IF_GENIL_OBJ_ATTR_PROPERTIES` defines ways of accessing attribute metadata. If you recall, when defining the GenIL model we had to provide attribute details for each element of the attribute structure. We were able to choose from a dropdown list box among values such as Read Only, Changeable, Hidden, and others. `IF_GENIL_OBJ_ATTR_ PROPERTIES` defines the corresponding constants of type `CRMT_GENIL_ATTR_PROPERTY` (see Figure 3.4). One can get an object reference of this interface directly from the container object by calling `IF_GENIL_CONT_SIMPLE_OBJECT~GET_ATTR_PROPS_OBJ`.

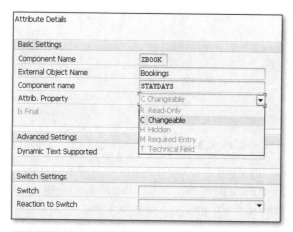

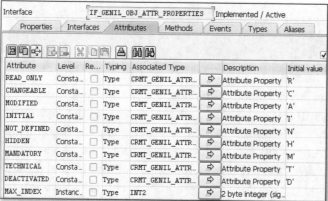

Figure 3.4 GenIL Model Attribute Properties

The number of constants in `IF_GENIL_OBJ_ATTR_PROPERTIES` exceeds the options available in the GenIL editor, given that the information available in runtime is greater than that during design time. In our implementation, we are interested in the MODIFIED constant. This is exactly what we are passing as an import parameter (IV_PROPERTY) to GET_NAME_TAB_4_PROPERTY.

We will rely on GET_ATTRIBUTES to get the attribute values. However, we first will obtain the object's key values. The object keys are not available during an update, so we need to take care of them explicitly. Next, we will combine the key with the modified attribute values. Here is how a typical implementation of Step 3 (retrieve the changed attributes) from the data flow might look:

```
LV_PROPS_OBJ = LV_ROOT->GET_ATTR_PROPS_OBJ( ).
* retrieve attributes which are modified.
LV_PROPS_OBJ->GET_NAME_TAB_4_PROPERTY(
               EXPORTING IV_PROPERTY = IF_GENIL_OBJ_ATTR_
PROPERTIES=>MODIFIED
               IMPORTING ET_NAMES = LT_CHANGED_ATTR ).
LV_ROOT->GET_KEY( IMPORTING ES_KEY = LV_BOOK_KEY ).
LV_ROOT->GET_ATTRIBUTES(IMPORTING ES_ATTRIBUTES = LV_BOOK_ATTR ).
MOVE-CORRESPONDING LV_BOOK_KEY TO LV_BOOK_ATTR.
```

LV_BOOK_ATTR has the key and the modified attributes of the current object instance. LT_CHANGED_ATTR has the names of the changed attributes. We will pass these to our backend API, which will perform Step 4 from the data flow (send the changes to the buffer).

```
ZCL_BOOKINGS_BACKEND_API=>CHANGE_BOOKING(
EXPORTING IS_BOOK_ATTR = LV_BOOK_ATTR
IT_NAMES = LT_CHANGED_ATTR
IMPORTING RV_SUCCESS = LV_SUCCESS ).
```

CHANGE_BOOKING performs the validation of the booking changes and stores them in the transactional buffer. If it is successful, we have to signal to the framework that we have accepted the modifications. We do so by returning the object name and object ID from IF_GENIL_APPL_INTLAY~MODIFY_OBJECTS via the export structure ET_CHANGED_OBJECTS. We calculate the internal GenIL object ID from the key attributes using CL_CRM_GENIL_CONTAINER_TOOLS=>BUILD_OBJECT_ID. This concludes the implementation of Step 5 (add object to changed object list) from our modification flow.

```
IF LV_SUCCESS IS NOT INITIAL.
  LV_CHANGED_OBJECTS-OBJECT_NAME = 'Bookings'.
  LV_CHANGED_OBJECTS-OBJECT_ID =
  CL_CRM_GENIL_CONTAINER_TOOLS=>BUILD_OBJECT_ID( LV_BOOK_KEY ).
```

```
   APPEND LV_CHANGED_OBJECTS TO ET_CHANGED_OBJECTS.
ENDIF.
```

3.4.2   Data Modification via Backend APIs

Let us examine how we are buffering the changed values in our example application. We are sure that you can come up with much better implementations, but ours might be a good starting point.

If you recall, our sample implementation in ZCL_BOOKINGS_BACKEND_API =>BUFFER_BOOKINGS stored the newly created or freshly read from database data into GT_BUFFER_BOOKINGS. We are using this static attribute as a buffer (see Listing 3.2). As BUFFER_BOOKINGS locks the data (via an enqueue function), it is safe to assume that our static table contains the same information as our database tables. Listing 3.6 shows the ZCL_BOOKINGS_BACKEND_API=>CHANGE_BOOKING implementation.

```
FIELD-SYMBOLS: <LINE> TYPE ZBOL_BOOKINGS_ATT_N,
               <OLD>  TYPE SIMPLE,
               <NEW>  TYPE SIMPLE,
               <NAME> TYPE NAME_KOMP.

READ TABLE GT_BUFFER_BOOKINGS
WITH KEY GUEST_ID = IS_BOOK_ATTR-GUEST_ID
HOTEL_NAME = IS_BOOK_ATTR-HOTEL_NAME
LASTCHECKIN = IS_BOOK_ATTR-LASTCHECKIN
ASSIGNING <LINE>.
CHECK SY-SUBRC IS INITIAL.
LOOP AT IT_NAMES ASSIGNING <NAME>.
ASSIGN COMPONENT <NAME> OF STRUCTURE <LINE> TO <OLD>.
CHECK SY-SUBRC = 0.
ASSIGN COMPONENT <NAME> OF STRUCTURE IS_BOOK_ATTR TO <NEW>.
CHECK SY-SUBRC = 0.
<OLD> = <NEW>.
ENDLOOP.
<LINE>-NEW = 'M'.
RV_SUCCESS = 'X'.
```

Listing 3.6 CHANGE_BOOKING Implementation

In Listing 3.6, we first retrieve the matching records in the buffer table, using the key attributes that we thoughtfully stored in the attribute structure. Then we update it with the values of the modified attributes (their names are in IT_NAMES). Last, we set the NEW flag of the changed record to 'M' indicating that it has been modified. Remember, MODIFY_OBJECTS can only update our root objects. You will use the NEW flag when in SAVE_OBJECTS.

3.4.3 Modifications to Child Objects

Now let's get back to the implementation of our modification method (in the GenIL component class). After processing the root objects, whether they have been altered or not, we will check their child objects. The modifications can actually be in the dependent objects, but we must always start drilling down from the root container. You recall the following snippet from the MODIFY_OBJECTS method:

```
LV_PROD_CONTAINER = LV_ROOT->GET_CHILDREN(IV_AS_COPY= ABAP_TRUE).
CALL METHOD MODIFY_CHILDREN
EXPORTING IV_CHILDREN = LV_PROD_CONTAINER
CHANGING CT_CHANGED_OBJECTS = ET_CHANGED_OBJECTS.
```

In line with the above code snippet, you can easily deduce that we have outsourced the dependent object processing logic to another method in our GenIL component: MODIFY_CHILDREN. This is where we can see the implementation of Steps 6 and further from our modification flow (Listing 3.7).

```
DATA:  lv_child        TYPE REF TO if_genil_container_object,
       lv_PARENT       TYPE REF TO if_genil_container_object,
       lt_changed_attr TYPE        crmt_attr_name_tab,
       lv_cl_object    TYPE REF TO object,
       lr_msg_cont     TYPE REF TO cl_crm_genil_global_mess_cont,
       lv_name         TYPE        crmt_ext_obj_name,
       ls_obj_inst     TYPE        crmt_genil_obj_instance,
       lr_props_obj    TYPE REF TO if_genil_obj_attr_properties,
       lv_success      TYPE        abap_bool VALUE abap_true,
       LS_PROD_ATT     TYPE        ZBOL_BOOK_PRODUCTS_ATT,
       LS_PROD_KEY     TYPE        ZBOL_BOOK_PRODUCTS_KEY,
       LS_BOOK_KEY     TYPE        ZBOL_BOOKINGS_KEY.
*Loop on the children list and process each
LV_CHILD = iV_CHILDREN->GET_FIRST( ).
WHILE LV_CHILD IS BOUND.
   LV_PARENT = LV_CHILD->GET_PARENT( ).
* First, get the global message container to add error messages
   CALL METHOD LV_CHILD->IF_GENIL_CONT_SIMPLE_OBJECT~GET_GLOBAL_MESSAGE_
CONTAINER
   RECEIVING
```

```
     RV_RESULT = LR_MSG_CONT.

     LV_NAME = LV_CHILD->GET_NAME( ).

    CASE LV_NAME.
    WHEN 'UsedProducts'.
*      process used product dependant object
*      Retrieve the delta flag. According to the delta flag. Dependent
objects may be created, modified or deleted.
       CASE LV_CHILD->GET_DELTA_FLAG( ).

      WHEN if_genil_cont_simple_object=>delta_changed.
*          Retrieve the attribute property object to get the modify
details
        lr_props_obj = LV_CHILD->get_attr_props_obj( ).
*          Which attributes were modified?
        CALL METHOD lr_props_obj->get_name_tab_4_property
        EXPORTING
          iv_property = if_genil_obj_attr_properties=>modified
        IMPORTING
          et_names    = lt_changed_attr.

        CALL METHOD LV_CHILD->GET_ATTRIBUTES
        IMPORTING ES_ATTRIBUTES = LS_PROD_ATT.
*      Modify product
        CALL METHOD ZCL_BOOKINGS_BACKEND_API=>CHANGE_PRODUCT
        EXPORTING IS_PROD_ATT = LS_PROD_ATT
          IT_NAMES = LT_CHANGED_ATTR
        IMPORTING EV_SUCCESS = LV_SUCCESS.
        IF LV_SUCCESS EQ ABAP_TRUE.
*          Add the PRODUCT to the changed objects list
          ls_obj_inst-OBJECT_NAME = LV_NAME.
          ls_obj_inst-object_id = LV_CHILD->get_object_id( ).
          APPEND ls_obj_inst TO ct_changed_objects.

*          Add the root object to the changed objects list

          ls_obj_inst-object_name = LV_PARENT->GET_NAME( ).
          ls_obj_inst-object_id = LV_PARENT->get_object_id( ).
          APPEND ls_obj_inst TO ct_changed_objects.
        ENDIF.
      WHEN IF_GENIL_CONT_SIMPLE_OBJECT=>DELTA_CREATED.
*      Get the attributes of the product as entered on UI
```

```
          CALL METHOD LV_CHILD->GET_ATTRIBUTES
            IMPORTING ES_ATTRIBUTES = LS_PROD_ATT.


        TRY.
*         Call the API to create the Product entry
          CALL METHOD ZCL_BOOKINGS_BACKEND_API=>CREATE_PRODUCT
            EXPORTING IS_PROD_ATT = LS_PROD_ATT
            IMPORTING EV_SUCCESS = LV_SUCCESS.
        ENDTRY.


        IF LV_SUCCESS EQ ABAP_TRUE.
*         Fill key structure before setting the key to the object
          MOVE-CORRESPONDING LS_PROD_ATT TO LS_PROD_KEY.
*         Set new key
          LV_CHILD->SET_KEY( LS_PROD_KEY ).
*         Add the product to the changed objects list
          LS_OBJ_INST-OBJECT_ID = CL_CRM_GENIL_CONTAINER_TOOLS=>BUILD_
OBJECT_ID( LS_PROD_KEY ).
          LS_OBJ_INST-OBJECT_NAME = LV_NAME.
          APPEND LS_OBJ_INST TO CT_CHANGED_OBJECTS.


*         Add the root object to the changed objects list
          LS_OBJ_INST-OBJECT_NAME = LV_PARENT->GET_NAME( ).
          LS_OBJ_INST-OBJECT_ID = LV_PARENT->GET_OBJECT_ID( ).
          APPEND LS_OBJ_INST TO CT_CHANGED_OBJECTS.
        ENDIF.

      WHEN IF_GENIL_CONT_SIMPLE_OBJECT=>DELTA_DELETED.
*       Get the Product key that was deleted from the UI
        CALL METHOD LV_CHILD->get_key
          IMPORTING
            es_key = LS_PROD_KEY.


        TRY.

          CALL METHOD ZCL_BOOKINGS_BACKEND_API=>DELETE_PRODUCT
            EXPORTING IS_PROD_KEY = LS_PROD_KEY
            IMPORTING EV_SUCCESS = LV_SUCCESS.

        ENDTRY.


        IF lv_success EQ abap_true.
*         Add the product to the changed objects list
```

```
      LS_OBJ_INST-OBJECT_ID = LV_CHILD->GET_OBJECT_ID( ).
      LS_OBJ_INST-OBJECT_NAME = LV_NAME.
      APPEND LS_OBJ_INST TO CT_CHANGED_OBJECTS.

*       Add the root object to the changed objects list
        LS_OBJ_INST-OBJECT_NAME = LV_PARENT->GET_NAME( ).
        LS_OBJ_INST-OBJECT_ID = LV_PARENT->GET_OBJECT_ID( ).
        APPEND LS_OBJ_INST TO CT_CHANGED_OBJECTS.
      ENDIF.
    ENDCASE.
  WHEN OTHERS.
*     If there are other children objects, implement the modification
logic here
    RETURN.
  ENDCASE.



  LV_CHILD = IV_CHILDREN->GET_NEXT( ).
ENDWHILE.



  LV_CHILD = IV_CHILDREN->GET_NEXT( ).
ENDWHILE.
```

Listing 3.7 MODIFY_CHILDREN Implementation

MODIFY_CHILDREN accepts a list of used products (the child objects of Bookings) and the table of changed objects: ET_CHANGED_OBJECTS. The latter will be populated with all the products that are processed and stored in the GenIL buffer. The code up to WHEN 'UsedProducts' should be familiar by now. Similarly to MODIFY_OBJECTS, MODIFY_CHILDREN will be used for any child of the any root object. Therefore we need to differentiate the behavior based on the child's name.

Once we have established the type of the business object— UsedProducts—we check the GET_DELTA_FLAG. However, unlike with the root object, this time we care about its value. Remember, we have to process the creating, updating, and deleting of dependent objects. Conveniently, the possible values can be found in the DELTA_* constants of IF_GENIL_CONT_SIMPLE_OBJECT.

Handling Child Objects Updates

The code for processing product updates can be found immediately under the `WHEN if_genil_cont_simple_object=>delta_changed` statement. This corresponds to the following steps in our data flow diagram:

- ▶ 6.3: Retrieve the changed attributes.
- ▶ 6.4: Send the changes to the backend API's buffer.
- ▶ 6.5: Add the child and parent objects to the changed object list.

In order to retrieve the changed attributes, we need to obtain an instance of `if_genil_obj_attr_properties` based on our product container object:

```
lr_props_obj = LV_CHILD->get_attr_props_obj( ).
```

The names of the updated attributes can be retrieved via `get_name_tab_4_property` method:

```
CALL METHOD lr_props_obj->get_name_tab_4_property
    EXPORTING iv_property = if_genil_obj_attr_properties=>modified
    IMPORTING et_names    = lt_changed_attr.
```

We need to fetch the attribute values (all of them):

```
CALL METHOD LV_CHILD->GET_ATTRIBUTES
    IMPORTING ES_ATTRIBUTES = LS_PROD_ATT.
```

Next, we pass the names of the changed attributes and all the attribute values to our backend API, which takes care of the buffering and data validation:

```
CALL METHOD ZCL_BOOKINGS_BACKEND_API=>CHANGE_PRODUCT
    EXPORTING IS_PROD_ATT = LS_PROD_ATT IT_NAMES = LT_CHANGED_ATTR
    IMPORTING EV_SUCCESS = LV_SUCCESS.
```

If the above operation is successful, we place the object name and its ID in the table of changed objects, as shown in the code snippet below. This will tell the framework that this object has been modified and will be removed from the BOL buffer.

```
ls_obj_inst-OBJECT_NAME = LV_NAME.
ls_obj_inst-object_id = LV_CHILD->get_object_id( ).
APPEND ls_obj_inst TO ct_changed_objects.
```

In Step 6.5, we also add the parent of the modified dependent object to the list of changed objects. The reason is simple: Any changes to a child object invalidate the current state of the whole object hierarchy.

```
LS_OBJ_INST-OBJECT_NAME = LV_PARENT->GET_NAME( ).
LS_OBJ_INST-OBJECT_ID = LV_PARENT->GET_OBJECT_ID( ).
APPEND LS_OBJ_INST TO CT_CHANGED_OBJECTS.
```

The backend API method — CHANGE_PRODUCT — is very straightforward (at least in our example). First, we fetch the matching records from the buffer (GT_BUFFER_PRODUCTS is a static table with attributes of ZCL_BOOKINGS_BACKEND_API). Next, we update the modified attributes with their new values. We set the NEW flag to 'M', thus indicating that the corresponding record has been modified. Do not forget to set the success flag at the end. Our code is shown in Listing 3.8.

```
DATA: ls_prod_n TYPE ZBOL_BOOK_PRODUCTS_ATT_N.
FIELD-SYMBOLS: <LINE> like line of GT_BUFFER_PRODUCTS,
                   <OLD>   TYPE SIMPLE,
                   <NEW>   TYPE SIMPLE,
                   <NAME> TYPE NAME_KOMP.

READ TABLE GT_BUFFER_PRODUCTS
    WITH KEY GUEST_ID = IS_PROD_ATT-GUEST_ID
             HOTEL_NAME = IS_PROD_ATT-HOTEL_NAME
             LASTCHECKIN = IS_PROD_ATT-LASTCHECKIN
             PRODUCT_ID = IS_PROD_ATT-PRODUCT_ID
             USAGE_DATE = IS_PROD_ATT-USAGE_DATE
    INTO <LINE>.
IF sy-subrc EQ 0.
  LOOP AT IT_NAMES ASSIGNING <NAME>.
     ASSIGN COMPONENT <NAME> OF STRUCTURE <LINE> TO <OLD>.
     CHECK SY-SUBRC = 0.
     ASSIGN COMPONENT <NAME> OF STRUCTURE IS_PROD_ATT TO <NEW>.
     CHECK SY-SUBRC = 0.
     <OLD> = <NEW>.
  ENDLOOP.
  <LINE>-NEW = 'M'.
  EV_SUCCESS = 'X'.
ENDIF.
```

Listing 3.8 CHANGE_PRODUCT Backend API Method

Handling Child-Object Creation

Let's go back to the MODIFY_CHILDREN method. What follows is the processing of the object creation case. The delta flag would be equal to 'N', but we recommend that you use the constant `IF_GENIL_CONT_SIMPLE_OBJECT=>DELTA_CREATED`. The steps that we need to implement (as defined in our data flow) are:

▶ 6.6: Retrieve the attributes.

▶ 6.7: Create records in the buffer via the backend API.

▶ 6.8: Assign key to the child object.

▶ 6.9: Add the child and parent objects to the changed object list.

Retrieving the attributes of a newly created object (Step 6.6) is rather trivial; we simply get the whole structure:

```
CALL METHOD LV_CHILD->GET_ATTRIBUTES

    IMPORTING ES_ATTRIBUTES = LS_PROD_ATT
```

Step 6.7 is implemented in a separate backend method. We will discuss it later.

```
CALL METHOD ZCL_BOOKINGS_BACKEND_API=>CREATE_PRODUCT
EXPORTING IS_PROD_ATT = LS_PROD_ATT
IMPORTING EV_SUCCESS = LV_SUCCESS.
```

Before we add the modified child and its parent object to the table with changed objects (Step 6.9), we need to set the key attributes of the created object (Step 6.8). This is done after ensuring that the buffering was successful.

```
MOVE-CORRESPONDING LS_PROD_ATT TO LS_PROD_KEY.
LV_CHILD->SET_KEY( LS_PROD_KEY ).
```

Remember that because this is a new object, the GenIL internal ID has to be built using the keys of the newly created object:

```
LS_OBJ_INST-OBJECT_ID =
    CL_CRM_GENIL_CONTAINER_TOOLS=>BUILD_OBJECT_ID( LS_PROD_KEY ).
```

Next we add the new dependent and the affected root object to the `CT_CHANGED_OBJECTS`.

As promised, let's review the code in `ZCL_BOOKINGS_BACKEND_API=>CREATE_PRODUCT`. This method handles the GenIL buffer update with newly created product data. First, we are ensuring that the newly created object has not been pushed in the buffer already. Next we simply append the attributes of the `UsedProduct` to the buffer table (`GT_PRODUCT_BUFFER`). Set the `NEW` flag to 'C', indicating that the record corresponds to a newly created product. The success flag shall be set at the end. Listing 3.9 shows all these steps.

```
DATA: LS_PROD_N LIKE LINE OF GT_BUFFER_PRODUCTS.

READ TABLE GT_BUFFER_PRODUCTS
    WITH KEY GUEST_ID = IS_PROD_ATT-GUEST_ID
             HOTEL_NAME = IS_PROD_ATT-HOTEL_NAME
             LASTCHECKIN = IS_PROD_ATT-LASTCHECKIN
             PRODUCT_ID = IS_PROD_ATT-PRODUCT_ID
             USAGE_DATE = IS_PROD_ATT-USAGE_DATE
    TRANSPORTING NO FIELDS.
IF SY-SUBRC NE 0.
  MOVE-CORRESPONDING IS_PROD_ATT TO LS_PROD_N.
  LS_PROD_N-NEW = 'C'.
  APPEND LS_PROD_N TO GT_BUFFER_PRODUCTS.
  EV_SUCCESS = 'X'.
ENDIF.
```

Listing 3.9 CREATE_PRODUCT Backend API Method

Handling Child Object Deletion

The last case left to cover is the deleting of a child object. The value of the delta flag is 'D' or IF_GENIL_CONT_SIMPLE_OBJECT=>DELTA_DELETED. The steps that we have to implement are:

▶ 6.10: Retrieve key attributes.

▶ 6.11: Remove the records from the buffer via the backend API.

▶ 6.12: Add the child and parent objects to the changed object list.

We get the key attributes of the deleted child object as follows:

```
CALL METHOD LV_CHILD->get_key IMPORTING  es_key = LS_PROD_KEY.
```

Next, we remove the corresponding records from the buffer:

```
CALL METHOD ZCL_BOOKINGS_BACKEND_API=>DELETE_PRODUCT
     EXPORTING IS_PROD_KEY = LS_PROD_KEY
     IMPORTING EV_SUCCESS = LV_SUCCESS.
```

Finally, we add the dependent object and its parent to the table of changed objects (we will not show the code as it is identical to the modify case).

Listing 3.10 shows the code in ZCL_BOOKINGS_BACKEND_API=>DELETE_PRODUCTS. In our implementation, we find the corresponding records in the product buffer table and set the NEW flag to 'D', thus marking the record for deletion.

```
FIELD-SYMBOLS: <LINE> LIKE LINE OF GT_BUFFER_PRODUCTS.

READ TABLE GT_BUFFER_PRODUCTS
    WITH KEY GUEST_ID = IS_PROD_KEY-GUEST_ID
             HOTEL_NAME = IS_PROD_KEY-HOTEL_NAME
             LASTCHECKIN = IS_PROD_KEY-LASTCHECKIN
             PRODUCT_ID = IS_PROD_KEY-PRODUCT_ID
             USAGE_DATE = IS_PROD_KEY-USAGE_DATE
    ASSIGNING <LINE>.
IF sy-subrc EQ 0.
  <LINE>-NEW = 'D'.
  EV_SUCCESS = 'X'.
ENDIF.
```
Listing 3.10 DELETE_PRODUCT Backend API Method

You might be tempted to call GENIL_BOL_BROWSER and run some test. However, please note that all we have done so far is to accept the modifications and insert these in the corresponding buffer tables (transaction buffer). Before we see the results of our efforts, we need to implement the SAVE_OBEJCTS method.

3.5   Persisting the Changes

When an object save is triggered, the framework will call IF_GENIL_APPL_ALTERNA-TIVE_DSIL~CHECK_OBJECTS_BEFORE_SVE first. This is your last chance to check for inconsistencies and to cancel a save operation. By now, all your data is in the transaction buffer. In our example, we will not implement this method. Our component is quite simple and the fact that MODIFY_OBJECTS went smoothly is sufficient.

If CHECK_OBJECTS_BEFORE_SAVE goes through without errors, then IF_GENIL_APPL_ALTERNATIVE_DSIL~SAVE_OBJECTS will be called. This is where your data persistency logic resides. Please note that, in the past, implementations used to redefine IF_GENIL_APPL_INTLAY~SAVE_OBJECTS. The latter is obsolete and you should use IF_GENIL_APPL_ DSIL~SAVE_OBJECTS instead. Its parameters are explained next.

▶ CT_OBJECT_LIST is a table of object instances (of type Changing). Each instance is represented by its name and ID. There is also a success flag that must be set to ABAP_TRUE when the operation was successful. The table can also be filled with additional objects, indicating to the framework that other objects have been changed by the process. If you do not do so, the framework might not be aware of such changes and the BOL buffer might end up containing outdated information. You do not need to pass all objects that have been changed but only the uppermost object of the object hierarchy. Remember that saving is always related to root-object instances and affects all the related data below them.

▶ ET_ID_MAPPING is used in special cases when you do not know the actual key of an object while creating it. In that case, you would create a temporary key and map this key to the actual one in SAVE_OBJECTS. In other words, the actual key would be determined during save.

▶ IV_MSG_SERVICE_ACCESS can be used to issue a message in case the save failed.

Transaction Commit and Rollback

You must save your object using the statement 'IN UPDATE TASK'. You shall never explicitly trigger a commit or rollback. In order to indicate success or failure, you have to set a dedicated flag in the changing parameter CT_OBJECT_LIST of your SAVE_OBJECTS method.

After successfully saving the data, the method IF_GENIL_APPL_INTLAY~ON_AFTER_ COMMIT is called. This is where you are expected to remove the lock and to clear the backend-API buffers. In case of failure, the framework will execute IF_GENIL_ APPL_INTLAY~ON_AFTER_ROLLBACK. For simplicity, we will clean our buffer as part of the save, so we will skip the implementation of these two methods. However, feel free to experiment with them as an exercise. In this section we will focus on implementing SAVE_OBJECTS (including the required backend APIs).

The SAVE_OBJECTS is much simpler than MODIFY_OBJECTS, which does all the heavy lifting. Figure 3.5 shows a typical data flow that you should implement as part of the save.

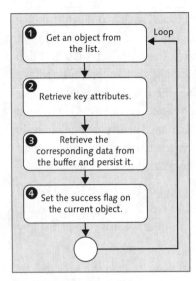

Figure 3.5 Save Data Flow

In the next sections, we will provide a reference implementation for the following save-data-flow steps:

❶ Get an object from the list.

❷ Retrieve key attributes.

❸ Retrieve the corresponding data from the buffer and make it persistent.

❹ Set the success flag on the current object.

3.5.1 Implementing SAVE_OBJECTS

As discussed earlier, the change table CT_OBJECT_LIST contains the list of the objects that must be saved. In keeping with our data flow, we will be looping through these objects and processing them one by one. The complete code is presented in Listing 3.11.

```
field-symbols <OBJECT> type CRMT_GENIL_OBJ_INST_LINE.
data LV_BOOK_KEY type ZBOL_BOOKINGS_KEY.

loop at CT_OBJECT_LIST assigning <OBJECT>.
   case <OBJECT>-OBJECT_NAME.
     when 'Bookings'.
       call method
```

```
   CL_CRM_GENIL_CONTAINER_TOOLS=>GET_KEY_FROM_OBJECT_ID(
      exporting IV_OBJECT_NAME = <OBJECT>-OBJECT_NAME
         IV_OBJECT_ID = <OBJECT>-OBJECT_ID
      importing ES_KEY = LV_BOOK_KEY ).
    call method ZCL_BOOKINGS_BACKEND_API=>SAVE_BOOKINGS(
            changing CS_KEY = LV_BOOK_KEY ).
    if LV_BOOK_KEY is initial.
      <OBJECT>-SUCCESS = ABAP_TRUE.
    endif.
  endcase.
endloop.
```

Listing 3.11 SAVE_OBJECTS Implementation

As you already know, the GenIL component methods are responsible for handling all the business objects defined in the component's model. Therefore, our first task within the loop is to retrieve the object name and process it accordingly. In our example, we have only one root object, namely Bookings. Recall that, while handling the modification of its children objects (UsedProducts), we also buffered the parent object (Bookings) of each modified child. Therefore, in our save we can focus only on the Bookings as they would appear if only their dependents had been modified.

The CT_OBJECT_LIST is based on line type CRMT_GENIL_OBJ_INST_LINE. The latter carries the object representation via its OBJECT_NAME and OBJECT_ID. In addition there is the SUCCESS flag that we will set at the end (Step 4). In order to retrieve the key attributes and implement Step 2, we can make the following method call:

```
CL_CRM_GENIL_CONTAINER_TOOLS=>GET_KEY_FROM_OBJECT_ID(
   exporting IV_OBJECT_NAME = <OBJECT>-OBJECT_NAME
         IV_OBJECT_ID = <OBJECT>-OBJECT_ID
   importing ES_KEY = LV_BOOK_KEY ).
```

The key attribute structure will appear in LV_BOOK_KEY. Next, we pass it to a dedicated method of our backend API that carries on the actual data persistence (Step 3).

```
call method ZCL_BOOKINGS_BACKEND_API=>SAVE_BOOKINGS(
   changing CS_KEY = LV_BOOK_KEY ).
```

Our backend API will clear LV_BOOK_KEY if the operation is successful. We will respond to that by setting the success flag of the current entry (current Bookings) of CT_OBJECT_LIST.

```
if LV_BOOK_KEY is initial.
   <OBJECT>-SUCCESS = ABAP_TRUE.
endif
```

3.5.2 Backend API for Data Persistence

In our example, we have implemented step 3 (persisting data) from our data flow in our backend API layer. You can see the code of ZCL_BOOKINGS_BACKEND_API=>SAVE_ BOOKINGS in Listing 3.12.

```
DATA:   WA_BOOKING TYPE ZBOOKING_RESERV,
        WA_PROD TYPE ZBOOK_PRODUCTS,
        LV_SUCCESS TYPE CHAR1.
FIELD-SYMBOLS: <BOOKING_ATTR_N> LIKE LINE OF GT_BUFFER_BOOKINGS,
               <PROD_ATT_N> LIKE LINE OF GT_BUFFER_PRODUCTS.

LV_SUCCESS = 'X'.
READ TABLE GT_BUFFER_BOOKINGS ASSIGNING <BOOKING_ATTR_N>
WITH KEY GUEST_ID = CS_KEY-GUEST_ID
         HOTEL_NAME = CS_KEY-HOTEL_NAME
         LASTCHECKIN = CS_KEY-LASTCHECKIN.
CHECK SY-SUBRC = 0.
CASE <BOOKING_ATTR_N>-NEW.
WHEN 'C' OR 'M'.
  MOVE-CORRESPONDING <BOOKING_ATTR_N> TO WA_BOOKING.
  MODIFY ZBOOKING_RESERV FROM WA_BOOKING.
WHEN 'D'.
  DELETE FROM ZBOOKING_RESERV
          WHERE GUEST_ID = CS_KEY-GUEST_ID
          AND HOTEL_NAME = CS_KEY-HOTEL_NAME
          AND LASTCHECKIN = CS_KEY-LASTCHECKIN.
  DELETE FROM ZBOOK_PRODUCTS
          WHERE GUEST_ID = CS_KEY-GUEST_ID
          AND HOTEL_NAME = CS_KEY-HOTEL_NAME
          AND LASTCHECKIN = CS_KEY-LASTCHECKIN.

WHEN OTHERS.
ENDCASE.

LOOP AT GT_BUFFER_PRODUCTS ASSIGNING <PROD_ATT_N>
WHERE  GUEST_ID = CS_KEY-GUEST_ID
AND HOTEL_NAME = CS_KEY-HOTEL_NAME
```

```
  AND LASTCHECKIN = CS_KEY-LASTCHECKIN.

IF SY-SUBRC = 0.
  CASE <PROD_ATT_N>-NEW.
  WHEN 'C' OR 'M'.
    MOVE-CORRESPONDING <PROD_ATT_N> TO WA_PROD.
    MODIFY ZBOOK_PRODUCTS FROM WA_PROD.
  WHEN 'D'.
    DELETE FROM ZBOOK_PRODUCTS
            WHERE GUEST_ID = <PROD_ATT_N>-GUEST_ID
            AND HOTEL_NAME = <PROD_ATT_N>-HOTEL_NAME
            AND LASTCHECKIN = <PROD_ATT_N>-LASTCHECKIN
            AND PRODUCT_ID = <PROD_ATT_N>-PRODUCT_ID
            AND USAGE_DATE = <PROD_ATT_N>-USAGE_DATE.
  WHEN OTHERS.
  ENDCASE.
ENDIF.


ENDLOOP.

DELETE GT_BUFFER_BOOKINGS
        WHERE GUEST_ID = CS_KEY-GUEST_ID
        AND HOTEL_NAME = CS_KEY-HOTEL_NAME
        AND LASTCHECKIN = CS_KEY-LASTCHECKIN.
DELETE GT_BUFFER_PRODUCTS
          WHERE GUEST_ID = CS_KEY-GUEST_ID
          AND HOTEL_NAME = CS_KEY-HOTEL_NAME
          AND LASTCHECKIN = CS_KEY-LASTCHECKIN.

CALL FUNCTION 'DEQUEUE_EZBOOKING_RESRV'
EXPORTING
  GUEST_ID                  = CS_KEY-GUEST_ID
  HOTEL_NAME                = CS_KEY-HOTEL_NAME
  LASTCHECKIN               = CS_KEY-LASTCHECKIN.

CLEAR CS_KEY.
```

Listing 3.12 Persisting Bookings Data in the Backend API

In our method, the first thing we do is to retrieve the matching booking record from the GenIL component buffer:

```
READ TABLE GT_BUFFER_BOOKINGS ASSIGNING <BOOKING_ATTR_N>
WITH KEY GUEST_ID = CS_KEY-GUEST_ID
          HOTEL_NAME = CS_KEY-HOTEL_NAME
          LASTCHECKIN = CS_KEY-LASTCHECKIN.
```

Next, we evaluate the NEW flag. If the changes are to create or modify ('C' or 'M') we simply modify the records in our database table.

```
WHEN 'C' OR 'M'.
  MOVE-CORRESPONDING <BOOKING_ATTR_N> TO WA_BOOKING.
  MODIFY ZBOOKING_RESERV FROM WA_BOOKING.
```

If the value of the NEW flag indicates deletion, we not only remove the booking records but also delete the products, as shown in this code snippet.

```
WHEN 'D'.
  DELETE FROM ZBOOKING_RESERV
          WHERE GUEST_ID = CS_KEY-GUEST_ID
          AND HOTEL_NAME = CS_KEY-HOTEL_NAME
          AND LASTCHECKIN = CS_KEY-LASTCHECKIN.
  DELETE FROM ZBOOK_PRODUCTS
          WHERE GUEST_ID = CS_KEY-GUEST_ID
          AND HOTEL_NAME = CS_KEY-HOTEL_NAME
          AND LASTCHECKIN = CS_KEY-LASTCHECKIN.
```

We repeat the above procedure for the UsedProducts. We LOOP AT GT_BUFFER_PRODUCTS (the transactional buffer) and for each matching product we evaluate the NEW flag. In case of create and modify we will simply update the ZBOOK_PRODUCTS database table. Unsurprisingly, when NEW = 'D' we delete the matching records from the database.

In our sample implementation, we always clear the transactional buffer tables, both for Bookings and UsedProducts (GT_BUFFER_BOOKINGS and GT_BUFFER_PRODUCTS). Finally, we remove the lock on our data:

```
CALL FUNCTION 'DEQUEUE_EZBOOKING_RESRV' EXPORTING
  GUEST_ID                = CS_KEY-GUEST_ID
  HOTEL_NAME              = CS_KEY-HOTEL_NAME
  LASTCHECKIN            = CS_KEY-LASTCHECKIN.
```

The above step is extremely important because we do not have ON_AFTER_COMMIT and ON_AFTER_ROLLBACK implementations. Let us not forget to signal to the caller that the data has been handled successfully by clearing the keys: CLEAR CS_KEY.

3.5.3   Testing SAVE_OBJECTS

In this section, we will test the implementation of the SAVE_OBJECTS method. Set breakpoints in your CREATE_OBJECTS, SAVE_OBJECTS, MODIFY_OBJECTS, and GET_OBJECTS in order to observe the framework's execution flow.

▶ Start GENIL_BOL_BROWSER, and open your GenIL component (ZBOOK in our example).

▶ You can repeat the steps from the create object section and click on the CREATE OBJECT button (Figure 3.2).

▶ The debugger will open the CREATE_OBJECTS method, and there you can see that FILL_STRUCT_FROM_NVP_TAB will populate LV_BOOK_KEY with the values you have entered in the UI. The backend API will lock the booking data and push the new entries into the buffer.

▶ Once CREATE_OBJECTS returns, your breakpoint in GET_OBJECTS will get called as well. The framework will fetch the data from the buffer and pass it to the UI.

You can now enter data for the non-key attributes (STAYSDAYS, PEOPLE, ROOM and MEMBERSHIP). Figure 3.6 shows sample data.

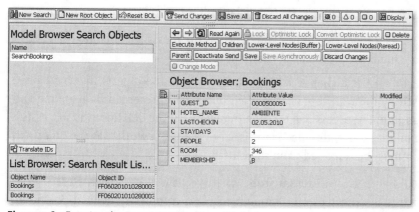

Figure 3.6   Entering the Remaining Bookings Attributes

If you click the SAVE ALL or SAVE buttons, the MODIFY_OBJECTS will be called. In the debugger, you can see that GET_NAME_TAB_4_PROPERTY returns only the names of the new attributes. ZCL_BOOKINGS_BACKEND_API=>CHANGE_BOOKING pushes these changes to our buffer table. The ID of the modified Bookings is placed in

ET_CHANGED_OBJECTS. Next, the SAVE_OBJECTS will be executed. It takes the data from the buffer and persist it in the database. The transactional buffers are flushed, and the lock is removed. As we set the SUCCESS flag on each processed booking from CT_OBJECT_LIST in SAVE_OBJECTS, the BOL's buffer is refreshed and GET_OBJECTS is called. The data is loaded from the database, and you get the fresh content from ZBOOKING_RESERV and ZBOOK_PRODUCTS.

3.6 Deleting a Root Object

So far, we have described how dependent or child objects are deleted as part of the object's modification. Remember that inside the modification procedure you always start with a root object, and you have to drill down in order to find any changes to its children. As a result, adding and deleting new children can be viewed as modifications to the root object. However, creating new and deleting existing root objects must be handled differently. We already saw how the CREATE_OBJECT method is responsible for creation of new root objects. In this section we will focus on root object deletion.

In order to delete a root object, you first need to implement method IF_GENIL_APPL_ ALTERNATIVE_DSIL~DELETE_OBJECTS. The latter has the following parameters.

- ▶ IV_MSG_SERVICE_ACCESS allows you to access the message container (you might want to issue error messages if your delete fails).

- ▶ CT_OBJECT_LIST is a change table that contains all the objects that have been processed by the DELETE_OBJECTS. Each object is represented by its name and ID. In addition, a success flag tells the framework if the deletion was successful. As you might expect, the idea is to signal to the framework that the objects in question must be removed from the buffer.

DELETE_OBJECTS is a bit different from what we have seen so far. Here, a root object instance is expected to be immediately and completely deleted (including its dependent or child objects). The deletion in the database must take place in an update task. Therefore, you will need to take care of the enqueueing and dequeueing of the data. However, note that the commit work is given externally and you should not perform commit or rollback (just set the success flag in CT_OBJECT_LIST accordingly).

> **DELETE_OBJETCS Shall Not Depend On LOCK and SAVE_OBJECTS**
>
> Make sure that you lock your data and make the deletion persistent in the database as part of DELETE_OBJECTS process. You should not expect that either LOCK has been called prior to the operation, or that SAVE_OBJECTS will be invoked to make the changes in the database.

The framework will not execute SAVE_OBJECTS before the commit. However, if you want persistence of the deletion to be effected as part of the SAVE_OBJECTS procedure, you have to set the root object property NO DIRECT ROOT DELETION to ABAP_TRUE. You can do so in the ADVANCED SETTINGS of the root object definition in the GenIL Model Editor.

The DELETE_OBJECTS data-flow diagram is shown in Figure 3.7 and involves the following steps.

❶ Get an object from the list.

❷ Retrieve key attributes.

❸ Lock the corresponding data.

❹ Delete the data and persist the changes.

❺ Remove the lock.

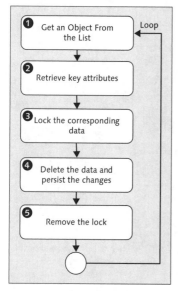

Figure 3.7 Root Object Deletion Data Flow

In the next sections, we will take you through our implementation of the above steps and as usual will complete the discussion by testing DELETE_OBJECTS in the BOL browser.

3.6.1 Implementing DELETE_OBJECTS

The complete ABAP code of the method is shown in Listing 3.13.

```
DATA: lr_msg_cont TYPE REF TO cl_crm_genil_global_mess_cont,
      ls_book_key TYPE         ZBOL_BOOKINGS_KEY,
      lv_success  TYPE         abap_bool VALUE abap_true.
FIELD-SYMBOLS: <fs_object_list> TYPE crmt_genil_obj_inst_line.

"get access to the message service
lr_msg_cont =
      iv_msg_service_access->get_global_message_container( ).

"loop through all objects subject to deletion
LOOP AT ct_object_list ASSIGNING <fs_object_list>.
  "we know that we have only one root object - Bookings and
  "we do not check if <fs_object_list>-object_name = 'Bookings'
  TRY.
    "Retrieve the key attributes
    CALL METHOD cl_crm_genil_container_tools=>get_key_from_object_id
      EXPORTING
        iv_object_name = <fs_object_list>-object_name
        iv_object_id   = <fs_object_list>-object_id
      IMPORTING
        es_key         = ls_book_key.
  CATCH cx_crm_genil_general_error.
    lv_success = ABAP_FALSE.
    lr_msg_cont->add_message(  iv_msg_type       = 'E'
                               iv_msg_id         = 'ZBOOK_MSG'
                               iv_msg_number     = '001'
                               iv_show_only_once = abap_true ).
  ENDTRY.

  IF lv_success EQ abap_true.
    "Call the delete API (remove from the buffer).
    call method ZCL_BOOKINGS_BACKEND_API=>DELETE_BOOKING
      exporting
        IS_BOOK_KEY = LS_BOOK_KEY
```

```
    importing
      RV_SUCCESS   = LV_SUCCESS.

   IF lv_success EQ abap_false.
     "process error
     lr_msg_cont->add_message(  iv_msg_type      = 'E'
                                iv_msg_id        = 'ZBOOK_MSG'
                                iv_msg_number    = '02'
                                iv_show_only_once = abap_true ).
   ELSE.
     "object successfully removed from the buffer
     <fs_object_list>-success = lv_success.
   ENDIF.
  ENDIF.
ENDLOOP.
```
Listing 3.13 DELETE_OBJECTS Implementation

In the above implementation, we are using the message service. In order to do so, we have to first retrieve the message container via the following call:

```
iv_msg_service_access->get_global_message_container( ).
```

The texts of our messages are stored in a message class called ZBOOK_MSG (see Figure 3.8). There are two examples in the code that issue messages by referencing the text IDs from that message class.

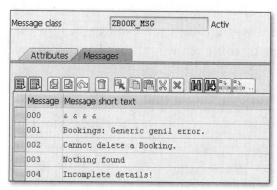

Figure 3.8 Example of a Message Class

In our code we loop through the list of objects in CT_OBJECT_LIST and assign each entry to a field symbol (Step 1 from our data flow):

LOOP AT ct_object_list ASSIGNING <fs_object_list>. Because the `CT_OBJECT_LIST` contains the object name and the internal ID of the object, we need to retrieve the key attributes based on this information (Step 2), as shown in this code snippet.

```
CALL METHOD cl_crm_genil_container_tools=>get_key_from_object_id
    EXPORTING
      iv_object_name = <fs_object_list>-object_name
      iv_object_id   = <fs_object_list>-object_id
    IMPORTING
      es_key         = ls_book_key.
```

To make things more interesting, we have encapsulated the above in a try-catch block. In case of failure, we log a generic GenIL error message via the message container:

```
lr_msg_cont->add_message(  iv_msg_type      = 'E'
                           iv_msg_id        = 'ZBOOK_MSG'
                           iv_msg_number    = '001'
                           iv_show_only_once = abap_true ).
```

We have delegated Steps 3 to 5 to a dedicated method in our backend APIs, namely `ZCL_BOOKINGS_BACKEND_API=>DELETE_BOOKING`.

3.6.2 Backend API

Our `DELETE_BOOKING` method will access the keys of the booking object that needs to be deleted and will issue a success flag upon completion.

In case of an error we log an error message (text `002` in `ZBOOK_MSG`). If the operation is successful, we set the success flag of the corresponding entry from `CT_OBJECT_LIST`:

```
<fs_object_list>-success = lv_success.
```

Our implementation of `ZCL_BOOKINGS_BACKEND_API=>DELETE_BOOKING` is shown in Listing 3.14.

```
FIELD-SYMBOLS: <LINE> TYPE ZBOL_BOOKINGS_ATT_N,
               <OLD>  TYPE SIMPLE,
               <NEW>  TYPE SIMPLE,
               <NAME> TYPE NAME_KOMP.

DATA:   LS_ATT TYPE ZBOL_BOOKINGS_ATT,
        LS_KEY TYPE ZBOL_BOOKINGS_KEY.
```

```
MOVE-CORRESPONDING IS_BOOK_KEY TO LS_ATT.

* lock entity
BUFFER_BOOKINGS( CHANGING CS_ATTR = LS_ATT ).
* ls_key should have been cleared
CHECK LS_ATT IS INITIAL.

move-corresponding IS_BOOK_KEY TO LS_KEY.
* mark the buffered line as Deleted
READ TABLE GT_BUFFER_BOOKINGS
  WITH KEY GUEST_ID = LS_KEY-GUEST_ID
    HOTEL_NAME = LS_KEY-HOTEL_NAME
    LASTCHECKIN = LS_KEY-LASTCHECKIN
  ASSIGNING <LINE>.
CHECK SY-SUBRC IS INITIAL.
<line>-new = 'D'.
* free buffer and persist
SAVE_BOOKINGS( CHANGING CS_KEY = LS_KEY ).

CHECK LS_KEY IS INITIAL.
RV_SUCCESS = 'X'.
```

Listing 3.14 Deleting Bookings in Backend API

You might notice right away that we are reusing two previously introduced methods: BUFFER_BOOKINGS and SAVE_BOOKINGS. The call to BUFFER_BOOKINGS contains the object-locking procedure; we have just implemented Step 3 of the data flow.

Next, we will find the matching records in the Bookings object buffer (GT_BUF-FER_BOOKINGS) and mark them for deletion:

```
READ TABLE GT_BUFFER_BOOKINGS WITH KEY GUEST_ID = LS_KEY-GUEST_ID
     HOTEL_NAME = LS_KEY-HOTEL_NAME
     LASTCHECKIN = LS_KEY-LASTCHECKIN ASSIGNING <LINE>.
  CHECK SY-SUBRC IS INITIAL.
  <line>-new = 'D'.
```

Finally, we will call SAVE_BOOKINGS. If you revise its implementation (shown in Listing 3.11), you will see that it removed both the Bookings and the relevant UsedProducts when records contained NEW='D'. After its execution, neither buffer (GT_BUFFER_BOOKINGS and GT_BUFFER_PRODUCTS) nor the database tables (ZBOOK-ING_RESRV and ZBOOK_PRODUCTS) will contain any entries that match the keys of the

`Bookings` object from `CT_OBJECT_LIST` (assuming the `COMMIT` goes through). Here is the snippet from `SAVE_BOOKINGS` that implements what we just described:

```
WHEN 'D'.
      DELETE FROM ZBOOKING_RESERV
              WHERE GUEST_ID = CS_KEY-GUEST_ID
              AND HOTEL_NAME = CS_KEY-HOTEL_NAME
              AND LASTCHECKIN = CS_KEY-LASTCHECKIN.
      DELETE FROM ZBOOK_PRODUCTS
         WHERE ...
      DELETE GT_BUFFER_PRODUCTS
         WHERE ...
...
DELETE GT_BUFFER_PRODUCTS
      WHERE ...
```

In addition, `SAVE_OBJECTS` contains a call to our dequeue function, which leads to releasing the database lock. As you can see, Steps 4 and 5 have been implemented as part of our `SAVE_OBJECTS`.

3.6.3 Testing SAVE_OBJECTS

We are now ready to go and test the changes. Do not forget to set a breakpoint in the `DELETE_OBJECTS` method. Open the BOL browser and find a record that you would like to delete. Click on the DELETE button in the right-hand side panel and observe your implementation being invoked. If you execute the booking search again, you will not find the deleted booking. You can exit, reopen the BOL browser and check the results from `SearchBookings` again. You will see that the result list contains one fewer entry. Your changes have persisted simply by pressing the DELETE button. If you check the content of the database tables (both for `Bookings` and `UsedProducts`) you will not find records with keys matching those of the deleted objects. All the children of that booking have been removed as well.

3.7 The Handler Concept

Our GenIL component implementation class derives from `CL_WCF_GENIL_ABSTR_COMPONENT`. In the previous chapter, we provided a justification for this choice. If you recall, we did not want to implement `IF_GENIL_APPL_ALTERNATIVE_DSIL`, `IF_GENIL_APPL_INTLAY`, and `IF_GENIL_APPL_DYN_META_INFO` from scratch. Moreover, we did not want to deal with the definition and persistency of the GenIL model. As a result, we were looking for a based class that implements `IF_GENIL_APPLM-ODEL_PERSISTENCY` and allows us to take advantage of the functionalities of the GenIL Model Editor. The abstract class `CL_WCF_GENIL_ABSTR_COMPONENT` allowed us to achieve all the above.

The approach presented so far involves implementing different methods for object discovery, retrieval, creation, modification, and deletion. All these methods have to be in the same class; namely, the GenIL component class. At the same time, they need to serve all the business objects within the GenIL component.

One can implement the GenIL class as a dispatcher. Based on the object name, the component could delegate to dedicated handlers that specialize in handling the operations of different business objects. For example, you can have one handler class that takes care of the `Bookings`, another that is responsible for the `UsedProducts`, and so on. Given the complexity of the `MODIFY_OBJECTS`, you might be tempted to put it into a handler class of its own. We can go on and on with the possible refactoring options. However, the important point is that you have to implement such an infrastructure yourselves. And this takes time and adds complexity to your code.

As of SAP CRM 7.0 EhP1 SP02, the Web Client UI framework has introduced a new feature called the *GenIL Handler Concept* that simplifies the GenIL component development. In this section, we will discuss the classes involved, how handlers are resolved, and give you an overview of the supported operations.

3.7.1 Overview of the GenIL Handler APIs

Figure 3.9 shows the main classes that constitute the GenIL handler APIs.

Three interfaces and two classes have been introduced in order to support the GenIL handlers. You can probably guess their use from their names.

▶ `IF_GENIL_NODE_HANDLER_BASE` defines the behavior for non-transactional nodes. You can match some of its methods to those in your GenIL component class (`ZCL_ZGENIL_COMP_BOOKINGS` in our example). For example `GET_OBJECTS` and `MODIFY_OBJECTS` exist in both places.

▶ CL_GENIL_NODE_HANDLER_BASE is the base handler class for the non-transactional scenario. It enriches the behavior defined by IF_GENIL_NODE_HANDLER_BASE and provides methods for root object creation and deletion (CREATE_OBJECT and DELETE_OBJECT). When implementing a handler you will be redefining these methods. You could also intercept the GenIL flow earlier by redefining the EXECUTE methods from the IF_GENIL_NODE_HANDLER_BASE, but you will not need this for the straightforward scenarios.

▶ IF_GENIL_NODE_HANDLER_TX defines the behavior required to support transactional nodes. As with IF_GENIL_NODE_HANDLER_BASE, its methods can be matched against the methods of the GenIL component class.

▶ CL_GENIL_NODE_HANDLER_TX is the base handler class for the transaction behavior. It is not to be used with root or lockable business objects.

▶ IF_GENIL_NODE_HANDLER_QUERY facilitates query handlers. When creating a handler responsible for the query operations, you have to implement this interface.

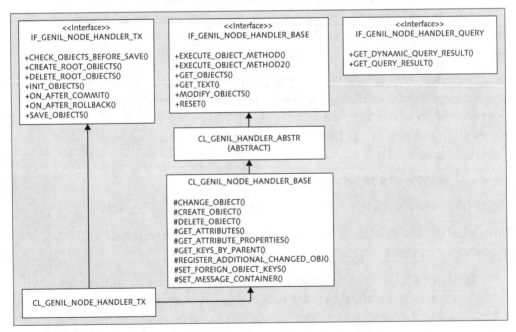

Figure 3.9 GenIL Handler Class Diagram

Based on the desired behavior, your handler will derive either from CL_GENIL_ NODE_HANDLER_TX for transaction scenarios or CL_GENIL_NODE_HANDLER_BASE when transaction support is not required. In case of a query, you will have to implement IF_GENIL_NODE_HANDLER_QUERY (Figure 3.10).

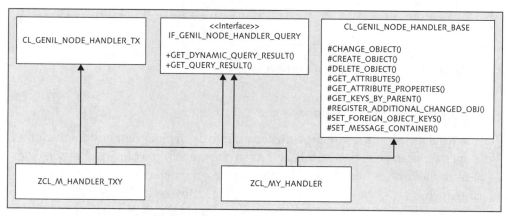

Figure 3.10 Custom GenIL Handler Class Diagram

3.7.2 Handler Factory and Registration

We mentioned already that the default implementation in CL_WCF_GENIL_ABSTR_COM- PONENT class delegates to the corresponding handler classes. This is the superclass that our GenIL component class derived from, and we will maintain the model in the GenIL Model Editor. This will also allow us to register handler classes for business objects directly in the model editor (you will see how very soon).

As per the handler concept, you do not have to implement core GenIL methods like GET_OBJECTS, MODIFY_OBJECTS, etc. in your GenIL component class. You need to implement the specialized handlers and assign them to the corresponding business objects. CL_WCF_GENIL_ABSTR_COMPONENT will use a factory class—called CL_GENIL_NODE_HANDLER_FACTORY—to obtain the handler object reference and execute the corresponding method on it (Figure 3.11). Each GenIL component has a dedicated handler factory instance. You can obtain the factory instance via the HANDLER_FACTORY attribute in the GenIL component. The HANDLER_FACTORY is also available in all handler classes.

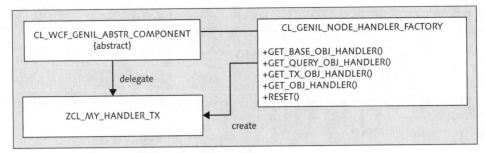

Figure 3.11 GenIL Component and Handler Factory

3.7.3 Handler Operations

What does the handler concept offer apart from decoupling your business logic into specialized and independent classes? As we mentioned, you can match the methods from the handler interfaces and classes to the core methods in the GenIL component class (GET_OBJECTS, MODIFY_OBJECTS, etc.). However, although the signature is pretty much the same, the use of these methods is different. The intent of the whole handler concept is simplification. As you know already, the implementation of methods like GET_OBJECTS and MODIFY_OBJECTS can be quite cumbersome. The handler concept reduces the complexity of implementing these operations. They are now split into simpler, easier-to comprehend-methods such as CREATE_OBJECT, DELETE_OBJECT, and CHANGE_OBJECT.

Reading and Modifying Data

The default implementation of GET_OBJECTS and MODIFY_OBJECTS in the handler base class will detect the type of operation and the business object for which it has been requested, and will delegate to the corresponding method in the right handler class. For example, the MODIFY_OBJECT of CL_GENIL_NODE_HANDLER_BASE will check the modification operation (create, delete, update) and based on its type will call the CREATE_OBJECT, DELETE_OBJECT, or CHANGE_OBJECT in your handler class (ZCL_MY_HANLDER according to the diagrams in this section). Something very similar will happen when GET_OBJECTS is called. Figure 3.12 shows the handler sequence diagram for GET_OBJECTS and MODIFY_OBJECTS.

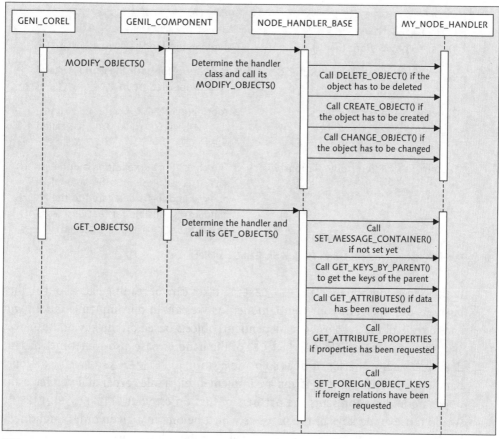

Figure 3.12 Sequence Diagram For GET_OBJECTS and MODIFY_OBJECTS

We just briefly covered how MODIFY_OBJECTS in handlers works. We believe that this, together with the sequence diagram, should be sufficient for now.

Reading Dependent Object Data

Let's take a look at GET_OBJECTS, as it is a bit more complex. In the previous chapter we introduced the data flow that your GET_OBJECTS shall implement. Table 3.1 tries to relate that flow to the way the handler concept works.

GET_OBJECTS in Components	GET_OBJECTS in Handlers
1) Get an object from the list.	Implemented in the NODE_HANDLER_BASE
2) Are object attributes requested?	The checks for both the attributes and their properties are in NODE_HANDLER_BASE
3) Retrieve and set attributes.	Your handler's GET_ATTRIBUTES( ) and GET_ATTRIBUTE_PROPERTIES( ) are called if needed
5) Retrieve children from relationships.	The check for the relations is done in the NODE_HANDLER_BASE, but the dependent object handling is delegated to the handler responsible for that business object (its GET_OBJECTS( ) is called)

Table 3.1 Standard GET_OBJECTS Flow vs. GenIL Handler

In the GenIL component class, GET_OBJECTS takes care of reading data about all the business objects from your GenIL model. As we saw in our implementation, we had to read all the UsedProduct (dependent) objects based on the key of the Bookings (parent) object. The GET_OBJECTS of the handler base also sometimes has to deal with such scenarios. It does so by delegating to GET_KEYS_BY_PARENT of your handler class. For example, if you are implementing a sales order and you have an object node that represents the partners of that order, your GET_KEYS_BY_PARENT would retrieve the keys of the partners which belong to a given order (identified by the order GUID). Your code might look like the following:

```
data: LV_PARENT    type ref to IF_GENIL_CONTAINER_OBJECT,
      LV_ORDER_GUID type CRMT_GENIL_OBJECT_GUID.
  IV_PARENT->GET_KEY( importing ES_KEY = LV_ORDER_GUID ).
*   call the API to get all partner keys
  call method CL_CRM_GENIL_SAMPLE_API=>ORDER_PARTNERS_GET
    exporting IV_ORDER_GUID   = LV_ORDER_GUID
    importing ET_PARTNER_KEYS = CT_CHILD_KEYS.
```

Processing Foreign Relations

The last method that we will mention is GET_FOREIGN_OBJECT_KEYS. It requests keys of objects linked to your GenIL model via a foreign relation. We mentioned foreign relations earlier, but we never examined them in a context of a specific example. We will do so shortly. If you recall, foreign relations are all relations having roots or access objects as target objects. The latter can be from another GenIL component.

Supporting Transactions

CL_GENIL_NODE_HANDLER_TX consist of methods which fully match the methods in the GenIL component class. We will not cover the following in detail, as you should be able to grasp the ideas based on the examples we covered so far.

▶ CREATE_ROOT_OBJECTS is responsible for creation of root objects. As you already know, the GenIL distinguishes between the creation of a dependent and root object instances.

▶ DELETE_ROOT_OBJECTS is responsible for deletion of root objects.

▶ LOCK_OBJECTS locks root or lockable access object. This method is called before you can change the object data.

▶ INIT_OBJECTS is called when the buffer in GenIL component has to be reset (initialized).

Handler Queries

When it comes to GenIL query objects, you need to implement IF_GENIL_NODE_HAN-DLER_QUERY. It contains two methods: GET_DYNAMIC_QUERY_RESULT and GET_QUERY_RESULT. They behave the same way as the corresponding GenIL component methods (dynamic and regular queries).

If you have SAP CRM 7.0 EhP1 SP02 or a higher version at hand, you can take a look at GenIL component SAMP_N. It contains an exemplary implementation of GenIL handlers. In the next section, we will implement a custom GenIL component via handlers.

3.8   Implementing GenIL Handlers and Foreign Relationships

In our sample application, we deal with hotel guest booking data. Imagine that there is also a basic loyalty program in place. The hotel loyalty program has three membership types: gold, silver, and bronze. Different membership status implies different services and rates for the hotel guests. The membership type could be assigned to the member based on the number of points he or she accumulates. As a result, a member might have different membership types at different times, and therefore the membership type of a guest might vary across hotel bookings. Therefore, it is not surprising that we have a dedicated field that captures the membership data in table ZBOOKING_RESERV. The name of the field is MEMBERSHIP, and until now the assumption was that the end user can enter any character data there.

Clearly, this is error prone, given that the possible membership types have been predefined and limited to three possible values: gold, silver, and bronze ('G',' S' and 'B'). Hence it would make sense to use a DDIC checktable and fix those values. The name of this checktable is ZHOTELMEMTYPE, and we have established the foreign key constraint over its MEMBERSHIP attribute. The checktable is displayed in Figure 3.13.

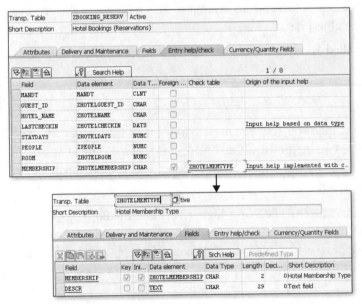

Figure 3.13 Membership DDIC Checktable

We will create another GenIL component to handle the membership data. It will be unrealistically simple, but our goal is to demonstrate the foreign relationships and GenIL handler concepts without too much complexity. In this section we will revise the GenIL component creation, demonstrate the GenIL handlers, and show you how to process foreign relations.

3.8.1 Creating a GenIL Component

This will be a good opportunity to recap some of the things that we learned so far. Go ahead and create a GenIL component class. We would like to define our model in the GenIL Model Editor and use the handler concept. Therefore, you must make sure that you derive from CL_WCF_GENIL_ABSTR_COMPONENT. In our example, we have given the class the name of ZCL_ZGENIL_COMP_MEMBERSHIP.

We will define two additional structures in DDIC to accommodate the key and the rest of the membership attributes. The key will be the MEMBERSHIP field. Figure 3.14 shows the DDIC entries.

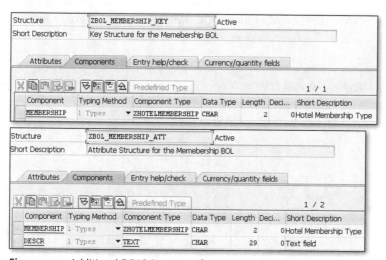

Figure 3.14 Additional DDIC Structures for GenIL Membership Model

Before we define the GenIL model, we need to register a GenIL component. Start transaction GENIL_MODEL_EDITOR, and click the CREATE button. You will be taken to Transaction WCF_GENIL_COMP. Create a new entry and provide a name, description, and implementation class for the new component. We have chosen ZMEMB as a name (Figure 3.15).

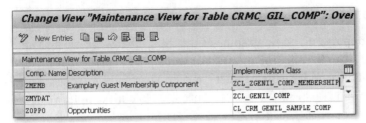

Figure 3.15 Registering GenIL Component ZMEMB

3.8.2 Define the GenIL Model and Handler

You can go back to the GenIL Model Editor's start page, enter the name of your component, and click on the CHANGE button. Our component will have one root object—Membership—and one query object, MembershipQuery.

Right-click on the ROOT OBJECTS node in the Model Editor and enter the required data. You can use Figure 3.16 as a reference.

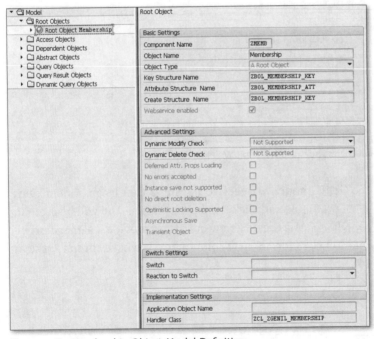

Figure 3.16 Membership Object Model Definition

Next, we will create a regular QUERY OBJECT instead of a DYNAMIC QUERY OBJECT, just to show you the difference between the two types. It will allow us to search for membership data. To keep things really simple, we will reuse the ZBOL_MEMBER- SHIP_KEY structure as a search attribute structure. Figure 3.17 will give you an idea how your end result should look.

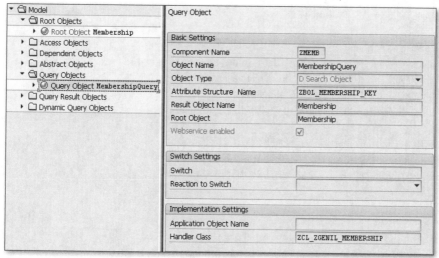

Figure 3.17 MembershipQuery Object Model Definition

We hope that you noticed that we registered our GenIL handler class with both model nodes. Make sure that you create a GenIL handler class (the implementation discussion is just around the corner) via Transaction SE24 or Transaction SE80. Because we would like to support the transaction behavior, we will use CL_GENIL_NODE_HAN- DLER_TX as a superclass. In addition, we will use the same handler class for the query logic. In order to do so, we need to implement IF_GENIL_NODE_HANDLER_QUERY. In our example we have given our handler the name of ZCL_GENIL_MEMBERSHIP.

3.8.3 Implementing Query Operations

In the previous section, we have successfully defined a GenIL component ZMEMB. Unlike the ZBOOK component, it uses a handler class to facilitate the business object data manipulation. It is time to move to the difficult part: implementation of the handler class. Listing 3.15 shows what the redefinition of IF_GENIL_NODE_HAN- DLER_QUERY~GET_QUERY_RESULT could look like.

```
data: LS_PARAMETERS  type ZBOL_MEMBERSHIP_KEY,
      LT_RESULT      type table of  ZBOL_MEMBERSHIP_KEY,
      LV_KEY         type ZBOL_MEMBERSHIP_KEY,
      LV_OBJECT      type ref to IF_GENIL_CONT_ROOT_OBJECT,
      LV_MSG_CONT    type ref to CL_CRM_GENIL_GLOBAL_MESS_CONT.

* move parameters for typed access
LS_PARAMETERS = IS_PARAMETERS.

* perform search
* Normally, you will have an API to delegate the call
IF LS_PARAMETERS-MEMBERSHIP is initial.
SELECT MEMBERSHIP FROM ZHOTELMEMTYPE
  INTO CORRESPONDING FIELDS OF TABLE lt_result.
ELSE.
SELECT MEMBERSHIP FROM ZHOTELMEMTYPE
  INTO CORRESPONDING FIELDS OF TABLE lt_result
  WHERE MEMBERSHIP = LS_PARAMETERS-MEMBERSHIP.
ENDIF.

if LT_RESULT is initial.
*    no orders where found -> send a message
LV_MSG_CONT = IV_ROOT_LIST->GET_GLOBAL_MESSAGE_CONTAINER( ).
LV_MSG_CONT->ADD_MESSAGE(
           IV_MSG_TYPE       = IF_GENIL_MESSAGE_CONTAINER=>MT_ERROR
              IV_MSG_ID        = 'ZBOOK_MSG'
              IV_MSG_NUMBER    = '003' "'Nothing found'
              IV_SHOW_ONLY_ONCE = ABAP_TRUE ).
else.
*    fill data container
loop at LT_RESULT into LV_KEY.
*     Add an new object for each found order
  LV_OBJECT = IV_ROOT_LIST->ADD_OBJECT(
           IV_OBJECT_NAME = 'Membership'
                IS_OBJECT_KEY  = LV_KEY ).
*     flag it as direct query result
  LV_OBJECT->SET_QUERY_ROOT( ABAP_TRUE ).
endloop.
endif.
```

Listing 3.15 Handler's GET_QUERY_RESULT Implementation

You can see that we are not living up to the best practices that we preached so far. In order to keep things simple, we do not have a backend API. Instead we have our select statements directly in the handler class. The query parameters can be found in the IS_PARAMETER import structure. We copy it into a ZBOL_MEMBERSHIP_KEY and use it to select the matching data from ZHOTELMEMTYPE. If there are no query attributes (LS_PARAMETERS-MEMBERSHIP is initial), we simply retrieve all the Memberships.

```
IF LS_PARAMETERS-MEMBERSHIP is initial.
   SELECT MEMBERSHIP FROM ZHOTELMEMTYPE
      INTO CORRESPONDING FIELDS OF TABLE lt_result.
ELSE.
   SELECT MEMBERSHIP FROM ZHOTELMEMTYPE
      INTO CORRESPONDING FIELDS OF TABLE lt_result
      WHERE MEMBERSHIP = LS_PARAMETERS-MEMBERSHIP.
ENDIF.
```

If no results are found (LT_RESULT is initial) a message will be issued via the global message container:

```
LV_MSG_CONT = IV_ROOT_LIST->GET_GLOBAL_MESSAGE_CONTAINER( ).
LV_MSG_CONT->ADD_MESSAGE(
   IV_MSG_TYPE      = IF_GENIL_MESSAGE_CONTAINER=>MT_ERROR
   IV_MSG_ID        = 'ZBOOK_MSG'
   IV_MSG_NUMBER    = '003' "'Nothing found'
   IV_SHOW_ONLY_ONCE = ABAP_TRUE ).
```

If there are results, we loop through them and create a container object for each entry. By calling ADD_OBJECT on the container object list IV_ROOT_LIST, we ensure that the new object is also added to the list and thus returned to the framework.

```
LV_OBJECT = IV_ROOT_LIST->ADD_OBJECT(
         IV_OBJECT_NAME = 'Membership'
IS_OBJECT_KEY  = LV_KEY ).
```

Last we set the query root flag: LV_OBJECT->SET_QUERY_ROOT(ABAP_TRUE).

3.8.4 Implementing Data Read

Once an object is discovered by our query, you should be able to read it and display its data via the BOL browser. Reading object data requires redefinition of at least the GET_ATTRIBUTES method. Do not forget to create a backend API and decouple your specific business logic there. At the very least, this promotes reusability, portability, and encapsulation.

```
data: LV_KEY        type ZBOL_MEMBERSHIP_KEY,
      LS_ATTRIBUTES type ZBOL_MEMBERSHIP_ATT.

LV_KEY = IS_KEY.
"call the backend API to retrieve the data
SELECT SINGLE MEMBERSHIP DESCR FROM ZHOTELMEMTYPE
    INTO CORRESPONDING FIELDS OF LS_ATTRIBUTES
    WHERE MEMBERSHIP = LV_KEY-MEMBERSHIP.

if SY-SUBRC <> 0.
  "issue an error
else.
  IV_CONT_OBJ->SET_ATTRIBUTES( LS_ATTRIBUTES ).
endif.
```

Listing 3.16 Handler's GET_ATTRIBUTES Implementation

In our over-simplified implementation we will perform a database SELECT on the ZHOTELMEMTYPE where key (MEMBERSHIP) matches the one passed to the GET_ATTRIBUTES method (IV_KEY parameter). If a record is found—and it should be—we set the retrieved attributes on the current container object (the IV_CONT_OBJ import parameter).

As we do not want the user to edit the master data membership, we will make all of its attributes read only. This can be easily achieved by redefining GET_ATTRIBUTE_PROPERTIES using the following code:

```
IV_PROPERTY_OBJECT->SET_ALL_PROPERTIES(
    IF_GENIL_OBJ_ATTR_PROPERTIES=>READ_ONLY ).
```

3.8.5   Testing the New GenIL Component

Now, you can open the BOL browser and test the newly created component (ZMEMB in our example). Double-click on the MembershipQuery in the MODEL BROWSER SEARCH OBJECTS panel and enter a valid attribute value in the right-hand side panel. After clicking the FIND button, you should get the expected result. If you have placed debug statements in GET_ATTRIBUTES and GET_ATTRIBUTE_PROPERTIES methods, you will see them being executed in this order. The ATTRIBUTE PROPERTY of each Membership attribute should be set to 'R' (read-only). Figure 3.18 contains screenshots from the BOL browser.

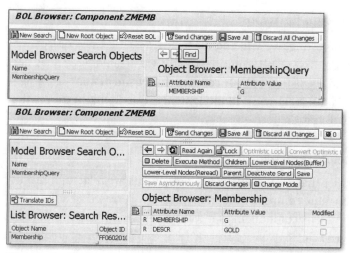

Figure 3.18 Executing Membership Query

If you enter a non-existing membership value as a search parameter of `Member-shipQuery`, you will not get any results. In our implementation, an error message is issued. The BOL browser will display it ("Nothing found") as shown in Figure 3.19.

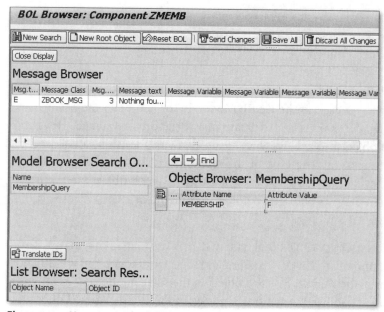

Figure 3.19 Messages in the BOL Browser

3.8.6 Processing Foreign Relations

To make things more interesting, we will add the Membership business object as a foreign relationship to the first GenIL component that we created — ZBOOK as per our example. We will add ZMEMB to the ZBOOK component set and define the foreign relation in the Model Editor. Next, we will implement the code that retrieves the related data. Last, we will test the foreign relation.

Updating the GenIL Component Set

Because the above implies that ZMEMB and ZBOOK components are related, it makes sense to put them in the same component set. Previously, we created a component set ZBOOK and added the ZBOOK component to it. We will add the ZMEMB component there as well. Start the view cluster CRMVC_GIL_APPDEF in Transaction SM34 and assign the new component to the existing ZBOOK component set (Figure 3.20).

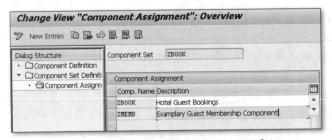

Figure 3.20 Adding ZMEMB to ZBOOK Component Set

Defining a Foreign Relation

Save your changes, go back to the GenIL Model Editor and open the ZBOOK component for editing. Our next task is to create an association between Bookings and Membership root objects. To achieve that, create a new relationship called MembershipType under Bookings. The type of the relationship shall be an association and the cardinality 1:1. Specify Membership as the assigned object (you will not find Membership in the [F4] help as it belongs to component ZMEMB). These actions are shown in Figure 3.21.

If you run the CONSISTENCY CHECK tool, you will get a warning saying that Membership belongs to component ZMEMB. Go ahead and save your model. You will still not be able to see the associated Membership object in the ZBOOK model as it belongs to another component. Go back to the starting page of the GenIL Model Editor and instead of opening a COMPONENT, open the COMPONENT SET ZBOOK (Figure 3.22).

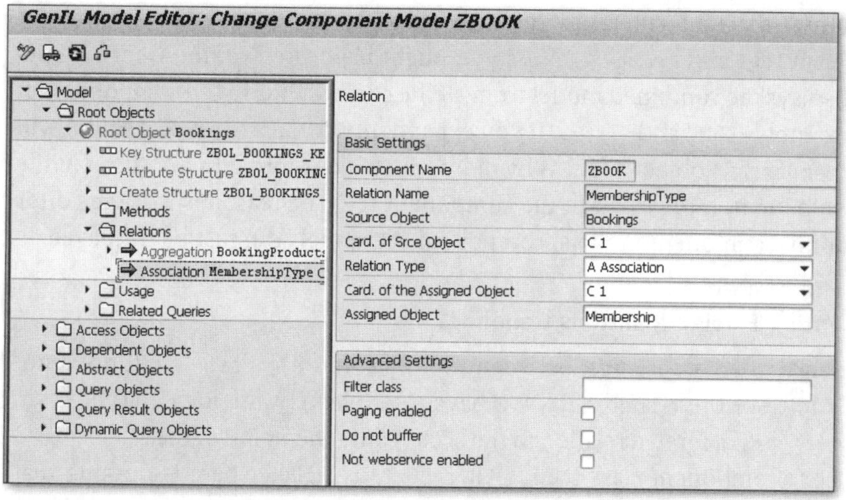

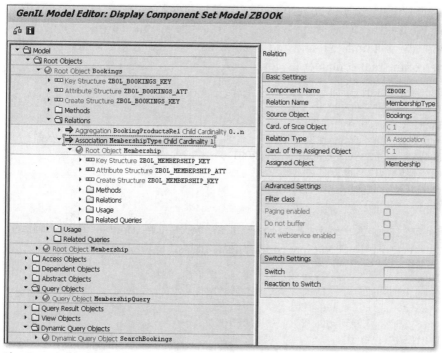

Figure 3.21 Association between Bookings and Membership

Figure 3.22 Display the GenIL Model of a Component Set

The first thing that you will notice, once the model opens, is that you have two root objects: Bookings and Membership. As you might have guessed, the GenIL Model Editor displays the combined model from all the components in the component set (in our example ZBOOK and ZMEMB). If you expand, the MembershipType relation will find the Membership object node. Why did we define our foreign association in the ZBOOK component, rather than in the component set? The reason is that the editor can edit only component models; component set models can just be displayed.

Implementing Foreign Relations Handling

The presence of an association between Bookings and Membership will not automatically retrieve the related data. We have to implement the logic that does so. MembershipType is a foreign relation in the ZBOOK component. But in the GET_OBJECTS of the ZBOOK component class (ZCL_ZGENIL_COMP_BOOKINGS) there is nothing that handles foreign relations. To facilitate this process, we will create a separate (custom) method in the component class called PROCESS_FOREIGN. It will accept a root container object that will be responsible for handling the foreign relations of that object. We have to ensure that PROCESS_FOREIGN is being called by the GET_OBJECTS method. We will update it and add a call to the PROCESS_FOREIGN method as the last step of the root container list loop:

```
LV_ROOT = IV_ROOT_LIST->GET_FIRST( ).
WHILE LV_ROOT IS BOUND.
    … same as before
    "process foreign relations
    PROCESS_FOREIGN( IV_ROOT = LV_ROOT ).
    "continue with the loop
    LV_ROOT = IV_ROOT_LIST->GET_NEXT( ).
ENDWHILE.
```

The PROCESS_FOREIGN method handles all the foreign relations of the container object it receives. The complete code appears in Listing 3.17.

```
data: LT_FOR_RELS    type CRMT_RELATION_NAME_TAB,
      LT_MEMB_KEY     type ZBOL_MEMBERSHIP_KEY_T,
      LS_BOOK_KEY   type ZBOL_BOOKINGS_KEY,
      LS_BOOK_ATT   type ZBOL_BOOKINGS_ATT.
FIELD-SYMBOLS: <rel>        TYPE crmt_relation_name.

"get the list of foreign relationships
LT_FOR_RELS = IV_ROOT->GET_FOREIGN_RELATIONS( ).
```

```
"loop over the list of foreign relationships
LOOP AT LT_FOR_RELS ASSIGNING <rel>.
  CASE <rel>.
    WHEN 'MembershipType'.
      "call the backend API and retrieve related Membership data
      iv_root->GET_KEY( importing ES_KEY = LS_BOOK_KEY ).
      zcl_bookings_backend_api=>READ_BOOKINGS(
exporting IS_BOOK_KEY = ls_book_key
      importing ES_BOOK_ATT = ls_book_att ).
lt_memb_key = zcl_bookings_backend_api=>get_membership(
IV_BOOK_ATT = LS_BOOK_ATT ).
    TRY.
      "Set the foreign key
      iv_root->set_foreign_relation( iv_relation_name = <rel>
                                     it_child_keys    = lt_memb_key ).
    CATCH cx_crm_genil_duplicate_rel cx_crm_genil_model_error.
   "Since the given object name is correct this could not happen!
    ENDTRY.
  ENDCASE.
ENDLOOP.
```

Listing 3.17 PROCESS_FOREIGN in GenIL Component Class

First, we need to get the list of the current object's foreign relations (all objects but `Bookings` will have an empty list):

```
LT_FOR_RELS = IV_ROOT->GET_FOREIGN_RELATIONS( ).
```

Then we loop over the list of relations and acts according to the relation name. In our example we have only one foreign relation (`MembershipType`):

```
LOOP AT LT_FOR_RELS ASSIGNING <rel>.
  CASE <rel>.
    WHEN 'MembershipType'.
  ... process the relation
```

The procedure that we need to follow is rather simple. We have to retrieve the key of the target object (`Membership`) and use it to set a foreign relation on the current container object (`Bookings`). How do we do this? The only data that we have at our disposal is the container object `Bookings`. Remember that the key of the `Membership` attribute of `Bookings` points to a record in the membership table (a foreign key DDIC relation). Therefore, if we have all the attributes of a booking we can retrieve the corresponding `Membership` object. Let's get all the `Bookings` attributes by calling our `READ_BOOKINGS` backend API.

```
iv_root->GET_KEY( importing ES_KEY = LS_BOOK_KEY ).
zcl_bookings_backend_api=>READ_BOOKINGS(
exporting IS_BOOK_KEY = ls_book_key
        importing ES_BOOK_ATT = ls_book_att ).
```

The attributes of `Bookings` are in the `LS_BOOK_ATT` local structure. We have created a backend API that fetches the key of a `Membership` from the complete attribute structure of `Bookings`. We will use it in our GenIL class.

```
lt_memb_key = zcl_bookings_backend_api=>get_membership(
IV_BOOK_ATT = LS_BOOK_ATT ).
```

We will use the key attribute structure of `Membership` to set the foreign relation and enable the framework to retrieve the `Membership` container object.

```
iv_root->set_foreign_relation( iv_relation_name = <rel>
                               it_child_keys    = lt_memb_key ).
```

Backend API

The code of the backend API method—`ZCL_BOOKINGS_BACKEND_API=>GET_MEMBER-SHIP`—is quite trivial (Listing 3.18). All we do is to select all the membership data for a given membership key and insert it into a table that we return to the caller. The result will always contain one record with one attribute, namely the membership value. In your code, instead of selecting from the database every time, you could store the selection in an internal table and query the database only when that table is empty.

```
SELECT * FROM ZHOTELMEMTYPE
    INTO CORRESPONDING FIELDS OF TABLE RT_MEMBERSHIP_KEY
    WHERE MEMBERSHIP = IV_BOOK_ATT-MEMBERSHIP.
```

Listing 3.18 GET_MEMBERSHIP Method from the Backend API

Testing Foreign Relations

Set a breakpoint in `PROCESS_FOREIGN` method of the GenIl component class. Once done, run the BOL browser, but instead of entering a GenIL COMPONENT, DISPLAY the GenIL COMPONENT SET ZBOOK.

The BOL browser will display all the business objects from both ZBOOK and ZMEMB components. First you will see that there are two queries (SearchBookings and MembershipQuery).

▶ Execute the SearchBookings, and select a booking that has membership data.

▶ If you click on the CHILDREN button in the OBJECT BROWSER, you will get both BookingProductsRel and MembershipType relations.

▶ Double-click on the MembershipType.

In the debugger, one can observe the PROCESS_FOREIGN method being executed. In PROCESS_FOREIGN we set the foreign relation MembershipType along with the Membership keys. This will help the framework retrieve the membership data. It will call the GET_OBJECTS of the ZMEMB component class. The latter will delegate the call to the handler class that we implemented earlier. If you still keep your breakpoints from the Membership handler class (ZCL_ZGENIL_MEMBERSHIP), you will see that GET_ATTRIBUTES and GET_ATTRIBUTE_PROPERTIES are being executed. The result of these steps is shown in Figure 3.23.

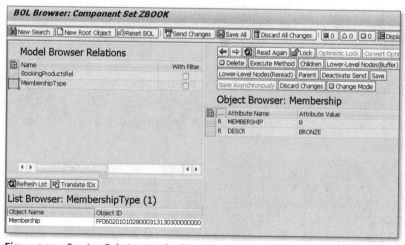

Figure 3.23   Foreign Relations in the BOL Browser

The BOL browser, the OBJECT BROWSER block will show the Membership and Description fields from the retrieved Membership object. They are read only as dictated by ZCL_ZGENIL_MEMBERSHIP~ GET_ATTRIBUTE_PROPERTIES.

3.9 Summary

Congratulations! You have just successfully implemented your first GenIL component. You are now equipped with all the knowledge you need to continue experimenting and tackling complex scenarios on your own.

In this chapter, we demonstrated how you can implement the transactional behavior of a GenIL component. We implemented the required methods from the two interaction interfaces: IF_GENIL_APPL_INTLAY and IF_GENIL_APPL_ALTERNATIVE_DSIL. We saw that in order to update a business object from your model, you have to implement MODIFY_OBJECTS. This method requires you to lock the relevant data sources. The framework delegates this procedure to a method called LOCK_OBJECT. The MODIFY_OBJECTS is also responsible for creating and deleting dependent objects. However, the creation and deletion of root objects is handled by separate methods: CREATE_OBEJCT and DELETE_OBJECT respectively.

As part of the data modification, the GenIL component should validate the data and store it in an internal (transactional) buffer. At some point, the GenIL consumer triggers data save. The framework will delegate this call to your component's SAVE_OBJECTS. Upon successful data persistence, the method also will release the data lock. You must never perform transaction commit or rollback explicitly. It is the responsibility of the framework to do so.

One peculiarity of the CREATE_OBJECT is that it handles data locking on its own (LOCK_OBJECT will not be called). The same is true for DELETE_OBJECT. In addition, the latter is also expected to finalize the data deletion, including that of the dependent records (SAVE_OBJECTS will not be called).

If you find implementing all these methods and their data flow overwhelming, you can use the new GenIL handler concept. It significantly simplifies GenIL component development. The catch is that it is available only in the latest Web Client UI releases.

We will continue to explore some additional details of GenIL and BOL. We will show you how to build user interfaces on top of the GenIL component that we created in this chapter. In our model, we checked the Web service enablement flag but haven't yet discussed it. You might also find the concept of BOL methods useful. We will talk about these and more throughout the rest of this book.

Underlying the Web Client Framework is the BSP technology. Understanding the basics of BSP is a major step toward mastering UI development in Web Client Framework.

4 Creating a Web Application with Business Server Pages

Business Server Page (BSP) is SAP's proprietary programming model for designing, developing, and implementing Web applications. As you know from your BSP programming training, BSP applications are standalone development objects that are developed on the SAP Web Application Server using the Web Application Builder. As an integrated part of the SAP Web Application Server, BSP applications can read and write data to and from the database, call function modules, or perform complex transactional operations. There are two techniques for creating interactive BSP-based HTML pages: page with flow logic and the *Model View Controller (MVC)* design pattern. The Web Client is built using the more commonly used MVC. A BSP application can comprise the following components:

▸ BSPs

▸ Application class

▸ MIME objects

▸ Navigation structure

▸ Controllers

Figure 4.1 represents a schematic view of a BSP application.

The use of controllers and views follows the MVC design pattern that will be discussed in the following sections. For more details on the BSP programming model, consult *http://help.sap.com*, using the following menu path: SAP NETWEAVER • SAP NETWEAVER 7.0 (2004s) • DEVELOPMENT • DEVELOPER'S GUIDE IN SAP LIBRARY • FUNDAMENTALS • USING ABAP • CORE DEVELOPMENT TASKS • UI TECHNOLOGY • BUSINESS SERVER PAGES.

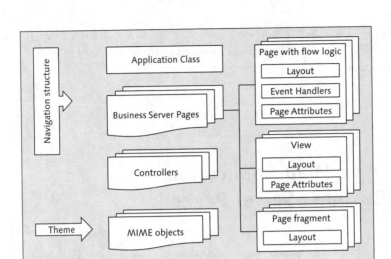

Figure 4.1 BSP Application Structure

In this chapter, we will provide an overview of the BSP programming model that underlies the Web Client framework. In Section 4.1, we will analyze the MVC paradigm in BSP. In Section 4.2, we will use our new theoretical understanding to build a small BSP application that will help us understand its various components as well as their interactions. Finally, in Section 4.3, we will dive deep into the presentation layer of Web Client applications so that we can understand their building blocks well enough to build a real Web Client application in the next chapter. That, after all, is the ultimate goal of this book.

4.1 Model View Controller in BSPs

The MVC design pattern clearly isolates the data model, the presentation logic in the views, and the process control. In BSPs, the formal separation of these three areas is implemented using three distinct objects: the model, the view, and the controller. This gives us an easy and straightforward way to divide complex BSP applications into logical units.

In a well-designed BSP application based on the MVC design pattern, the model manages application data. It is only used for internal data processing and can have different views that are implemented using different view pages. Because the model does not recognize either the view or the controller, internal data processing is detached from the user interface. As a result, changes to the user interface have no effect on internal data-processing and the data structure.

The view represents the graphical and textual output of the model data on the user interface, using appropriate user interface elements. The view takes care of the display by using buttons, menus, input fields, and other user-interface controls. To display the application data, the view queries the model, or the model informs the view about possible status changes. Because the view is decoupled from the model, it can display the data in different formats; you can display selection results as a table, a bar chart, or as a pie chart. During the processing, BSP views are compiled into HTML pages and displayed in the browser.

The controller interprets the mouse and keyboard inputs from the user, informing the model and/or the view about required changes. Input data is passed on, and changes to the model are initiated. The controller uses the methods of the model to change the internal status and then informs the view. The controller thus defines the reactions to user input and controls processing. Figure 4.2 depicts the MVC design pattern.

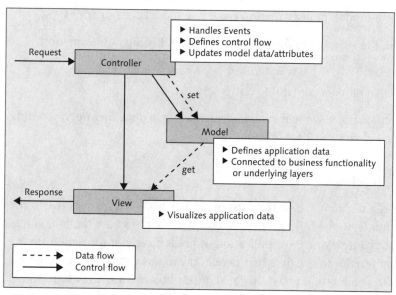

Figure 4.2 MVC Pattern in BSP Applications

When using the MVC pattern in the BSP environment, controllers are implemented using classes that are subclasses of the CL_BSP_CONTROLLER2 class. Every controller has a URL that points to it and that can be addressed externally; for instance, from a browser. This does not mean that calling a controller from its URL will necessarily lead to meaningful results, given that controllers can depend on each other to maintain a valid internal state. When it makes sense, a controller can be used as the entry point to a BSP application.

In the Web Application Builder, a view is created as a sub-object of a BSP application. A BSP view is usually built with a number of BSP elements from one or more BSP libraries. A view can contain native HTML, JavaScript, and ABAP statements. However, in a well-designed BSP view, the number of ABAP statements should be kept to a minimum because—in a true MVC implementation—the business logic should not be included in the view. At runtime, a BSP view is represented by an instance of a locally generated class. Although traditionally the layout has been built using the BSP extension HTMLB, the Web Client is based on a different BSP extension: the *THTMLB tag library* that will be discussed later in this book.

A model is created using the Object Navigator in the Class Builder. In order to simplify programming with the MVC design pattern, the framework provides a basis class, CL_BSP_MODEL, for the model of an application. Therefore, a model is represented by a model implementation class. The model class provides:

▶ Data used in the views with the relevant type and dictionary information

▶ Input conversion

▶ Information about data containing errors

In the following sections, we will explain data binding in detail before proceeding with the process flow in BSP applications.

4.1.1 Data Binding

Data binding is a technique used to transport values back and forth between the view and the model in the form of input and output data. Because the model represents the data context of a BSP application, it holds a copy of the data from the database or a reference to the data that is relevant to the view. Similar to the list of sub-controllers, a controller has a list of all model instances with unique model IDs. As we will see throughout this book, data binding is a fundamental feature element of the Web Client framework.

In the simplest case, the data that is required by the view is added to the model class as public attributes. This data can be:

- Simple variables
- Structures
- Tables

In this simple case, together with the controller, the model class provides the following functions:

- The controller creates a model instance and initializes its attributes because they are public attributes.
- The controller transmits a reference to the model instance to the view. The view defines in its page attribute a variable of the same type as the model, which will be used to hold this reference.
- The data binding to the model attributes is specified in the view using the notation `//model_variable_name/attribute_name`.

With the example in the following section, we will come back to the process flow that is related to data binding.

Simple model classes are sufficient if there are no special requirements or complex logic needed to send the data to the model or to retrieve the data from the application context. If you are working with generic data or if you need special logic for setting and getting attributes, you can use `SET` and `GET` methods to determine the data retrieval and data update logic that is specific to your application.

In applications with complex logic for data manipulation, the base class contains copy templates for the `SET` and `GET` methods: `_SET_<attribute>` and `_GET_<attribute>`. All of these templates begin with `_`. The naming conventions for the actual SET methods are as follows:

- `SET_<attribute>` for a field
- `SET_S_<attribute>` for a structure
- `SET_T_<attribute>` for a table

For the actual getter methods, the naming conventions are as follows:

- `GET_<attribute>` for a field
- `GET_S_<attribute>` for a structure
- `GET_T_<attribute>` for a table

Fields, for which GET and SET methods have been defined, can be addressed in the view using the following syntax:

▸ Simple field attribute
alue="//<field name>"

▸ Structure attribute
value="//<structure name>.<field name>"

▸ Table attribute
value="//<table name>[<line index>].<field name>"

Once you have defined the GET and SET methods and have addressed the corresponding model attributes in your view, the respective model methods will be invoked automatically based on the similarity in the name. In method DO_HANDLE_DATA of class CL_BSP_CONTROLLER2 all controllers automatically fill the form fields with data.

Data binding provides the static part of a BSP application. However, to make sure that data is handled effectively, you need to understand the process flow between the view and the application context—represented by the model—and the handling of events that are triggered in the view by the end user and that potentially trigger updates in the model. The following section presents the dynamics in a BSP application built on the MVC pattern.

4.1.2 Process Flow in a BSP Application

In BSP applications built using the MVC design pattern, the controller inherits directly or through its parent classes from class CL_BSP_CONTROLLER2. Methods of this class are used—among other things—to create controllers and components of the BSP application. The DO_REQUEST method of this class is central to the whole flow of execution in a BSP application. With every request, the following hierarchy of calls is processed.

1. The first method—DO_INIT—is called once at the start and is used for initialization, much as we would do with a constructor.

2. Method DO_INITATTRIBUTES is then called with every request to initialize the attributes. This method can also be used to perform initializations that are required with every request.

3. Then follows method `DO_REQUEST`. Within the main controller, this method takes care of both the input and output processing, but only handles the output processing within sub-controllers. The `DO_REQUEST` method performs the following actions:

   ▶ During input processing, the browser request is sent to the top-level controller, which dispatches the input to the sub-controllers in `DISPATCH_INPUT` method. This is done by reading form fields from the request and dispatching them after adding prefixes corresponding to the respective controller IDs. Data that does not belong to any of the sub-controllers must be processed in the main controller's `DISPATCH_INPUT` method. Furthermore, methods `DO_HANDLE_DATA`, `DO_HANDLE_EVENT`, and `DO_FINISH_INPUT` are called by the main controller for each of the sub-controllers. The main controller passes to sub-controllers only data that is relevant for them. In the method `DO_HANDLE_DATA`, the BSP runtime fills a two-column internal table, in which the name/value pairs from the query string are stored.

   ▶ During output processing, the content of the view that is to be displayed is determined, and that view is created and displayed. At this stage, depending on internal application status and conditions and specific business logic in the top-level controller, you can create a new controller or set one of the other sub-controllers to inactive. This is useful when, for instance, you have hidden views and don't want their corresponding controllers to be called. `DO_REQUEST` takes care of the following tasks:

      — Fetching data from the model and from the global attributes, if required. This can be data that is to be shared with or send to the views or to sub-controllers, if any.

      — Fetching the table with the object keys from the top-level controller for the benefit of the views.

      — Requesting the view that is to be displayed.

      — Setting the necessary attributes of the view.

      — Calling the view for display.

Figure 4.3 illustrates the hierarchy of calls during output processing.

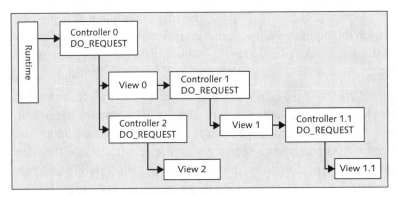

Figure 4.3 Process Flow during Page Output

When a component contains events, the method DISPATCH_INPUT will call the HTMLB manager, which will collect all the relevant information about the object that triggered the event. All active controllers will then call method DO_HANDLE_DATA, and the model class will be filled. Note that if the model class inherits from CL_BSP_MODEL and the relevant GET and SET methods have been defined properly, the form fields will be filled automatically.

After DO_HANDLE_DATA has filled all the data, the controller that is responsible for the event will be called via method DO_HANDLE_EVENT with the relevant event information passed in the object HTMLB_EVENT. This object is filled only if the event is an HTMLB event.

Once methods DO_HANDLE_DATA and DO_HANDLE_EVENT have been processed, method DO_FINISH_INPUT is called. This method is always called for all controllers of all active components. This can be useful if you want to react on an event in a given component that occurred in a different component. In order to broadcast to all components the current event, you can use the parameter GLOBAL_EVENT that is set in method DO_HANDLE_EVENT.

Figure 4.4 illustrates the process flow of methods DO_HANDLE_DATA, DO_HANDLE_EVENT, and DO_FINISH_INPUT.

When writing the code of your controller, you must overwrite method DO_REQUEST in order—among other things—to branch to the correct view or controller. We also recommend overwriting methods DO_HANDLE_DATA, DO_HANDLE_EVENT, and DO_FINISH_INPUT in order to determine how to handle input and user events. You also could overwrite methods DO_INIT and DO_INIT_ATTRIBUTES depending on the particular initialization logic in your application.

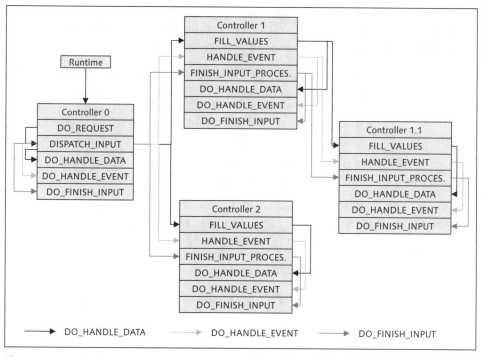

Figure 4.4 Method Call Sequence of Input and Event Processing

With this theoretical understanding of data binding and process flow, we will now apply the BSP programming model to an example that uses the THTMLB BSP extension and that illustrates the different aspects of an MVC BSP application that we have seen so far.

4.2 Building a Search Application Using the BSP Programming Model

In this section, we will build a simple search application using the THTMLB tag library. We will focus on different elements of an application that uses the MVC design pattern. The need to use the MVC pattern is dictated by the fact, as we will see later, that each individual part of a Web Client application consists of a complex

BSP application that contains precise application logic and well-defined presentation logic. Because these components are reused in different Web Client applications and components, it makes sense to build them as reusable BSP components. Building a search-result BSP application while strictly following the BSP programming model will help you understand the structure of applications and components that are built using the Web Client Framework Workbench wizard.

Following the MVC design pattern described earlier, our search application will consist of the following components:

▶ The main component serves as the entry point to our application. It comprises the main view and the main controller.

▶ The search view is used to select search criteria and to launch the search. It comprises the search view, the search controller, and the search model.

▶ The result view is used to present the results of the search to the user. It comprises the result view, the result controller, and the result model.

Besides explaining these components, we will analyze in the last section how events triggered in the search view are processed.

Figure 4.5 represents the search application with the interactions between different components.

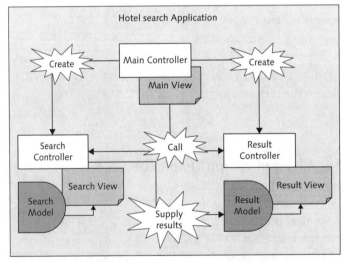

Figure 4.5 Structure of the Search and Result BSP Application

4.2.1 The Main Component

In the main component, the main view is used as a container that gives shape to the entire page. It serves as the entry point to the search application. Listing 4.1 shows the code of the main view:

```
<%@page language="abap" %>
<%@extension name="bsp" prefix="bsp" %>
<%@extension name="thtmlb" prefix="thtmlb" %>
<%@extension name="htmlb" prefix="htmlb" %>
<htmlb:content id           = "content"
        design       = "design2003"
        controlRendering = "sap"
        rtlAutoSwitch  = "true" >
<thtmlb:content renderBody = "true"
        renderHead = "true" >
 <htmlb:form>
 <chtmlb:pageType type="SEARCH">
 <thtmlb:searchFrame showSearchFields = "TRUE"
          personalizable  = "FALSE"
          resultListTitle = "Hotel Bookings" >
    <thtmlb:searchHeaderArea>
     <thtmlb:searchCriteriaFrame>
      <bsp:call comp_id = "search"
            url   = "search.do" />
     </thtmlb:searchCriteriaFrame>
     <thtmlb:searchResultFrame>
      <bsp:call comp_id = "result"
            url   = "result.do" />
     </thtmlb:searchResultFrame>
    </thtmlb:searchHeaderArea>
   </thtmlb:searchFrame>
   </chtmlb:pageType>
  </htmlb:form>
 </thtmlb:content>
</htmlb:content>
```

Listing 4.1 View main.htm

The main view is almost entirely built using tags from the THMTLB tag library. There are two main tags in the main view: the thtmlb:searchFrame tag and the thtmlb:searchResultFrame tag. The thtmlb:searchFrame tag introduces the area in which the search view will be included. The thtmlb:searchResultFrame tag introduces the frame, which will include the result view. We can view the main view as a shell that will contain the actual views—the search and the result views—that will contain the data retrieved from or to be sent to the model. In order to insert the search and the results components into the main view, we use <bsp:call>.

To create the main view, follow these steps:

1. Using the Web Application Builder in the ABAP Workbench (Transaction SE80) create a BSP application ZCMP_SRCH_MAN1. For details on how to create a BSP application, refer to the help page of Web Application Builder for BSPs at *http://help.sap.com*.

2. Create a page-type *View* as a sub-object of the BSP application ZCMP_SRCH_MAN1. In our example, this page is called main.htm.

3. On the PROPERTIES tab, specify CL_BSP_CONTROLLER as the controller class. We use the generic controller class because the main view will have no role other than calling the two sub-controllers that are included in it and will be under full control of the main application controller main.do.

4. Copy and paste the listing provided above onto the LAYOUT tab.

5. Save and activate.

The main view is now created. However, you will notice that the TEST/EXECUTE button is not active because you cannot run a view. We still need a controller.

In order to create the main controller, follow these steps:

1. Using the Web Application Builder in the ABAP Workbench, create a controller object, main.do, as a sub-object of the BSP application ZCMP_SRCH_MAN1. To do this, you will have to enter the controller name and the name of the controller class. In our example, the class name is ZCL_CMP_SRCH_MAN1_MAIN_CTRL. The URL that points to this controller will be derived from the BSP application and the controller names.

2. In Transaction SE24, create class ZCL_CMP_SRCH_MAN1_MAIN_CTRL. Alternatively, you can use forward navigation by double-clicking on the controller class in the property page of the controller that you created previously. The advantage of using forward navigation to create the controller class is that class CL_BSP_CONTROLLER2 automatically will become the default super class of your controller.

3. Redefine method DO_INIT. We will use this method to create the two controllers that are dependent on the main controller. The sub-controllers are created

using the service method CREATE_CONTROLLER as shown in the following code snippet.

```
create_controller( controller_name = 'search.do'
        controller_id  = 'search' ).
  create_controller( controller_name = 'result.do'
        controller_id  = 'result' ).
```

4. As we have seen earlier, method DO_REQUEST has to be overwritten and will control c branching to the right view. Therefore, redefine method DO_REQUEST and add the code shown in Listing 4.2.

```
DATA: main_view TYPE REF TO if_bsp_page.
dispatch_input( ).
CHECK is_navigation_requested( ) IS INITIAL.
main_view = create_view( view_name = 'main.htm' ).
call_view( main_view ).
```

Listing 4.2 Code of Main Controller DO_REQUEST Method

5. Save and activate.

At this point, we will leave the main view and controllers in order to focus on the components that will be included within the main components. We will start with the search view and then proceed with the result view.

4.2.2 The Search View

The search view has to give the user a way to specify search parameters and execute the search. The user might want to specify a maximum number of results to be returned. They might also want to clear the search criteria in order to start over. Without appropriate BSP tags, one would need to program this layout manually. However, using the THTMLB tag thtmlb:searchArea we get all this layout standard-delivered. In a similar way, we can use the thtmlb:cellerator tag to represent the results of the search triggered in the search view in a tabular form. Following the steps outlined in the creation of the main view above, create your search view with the name search.htm. Specify ZCL_CMP_SRCH_MAN1_SRCH_CTRL or a name of your choice as the name of the controller class and copy-and-paste the code in Listing 4.3 onto the layout tab.

```
<%@extension name="thtmlb" prefix="thtmlb" %>
<thtmlb:searchArea>
 <thtmlb:searchTagArea>
```

```
<thtmlb:advancedSearch
  id          = "AdvSearchBooking"
  fieldMetadata = "<%= controller
              ->GET_DQUERY_DEFINITIONS( ) %>"
  header      = "<%= model
              ->get_param_struct_name( ) %>"
  fieldNames  = "<%= controller
              ->GET_POSSIBLE_FIELDS( ) %>"
  values      = "//model/PARAMETERS"
  maxHits     = "//model/max_hits"
  onEnter     = "search" />
</thtmlb:searchTagArea>
<thtmlb:searchButtonsArea>
  <thtmlb:button id   = "Searchbtn"
        design = "EMPHASIZED"
        onClick = "search"
        text  = "Search" />
  <thtmlb:button id   = "Clearbtn"
        onClick = "clear"
        text  = "Clear" />
</thtmlb:searchButtonsArea>
</thtmlb:searchArea>
```

Listing 4.3 Code Snippet of view search.htm

Before continuing, we need to explain concepts that are used in the listing of view search.htm. First, we can see that the tag thtmlb:advancedSearch requires many attributes. The attribute id is used to identify the element in the result HTML page. The value that you give this attribute is arbitrary. However, we will see that when one needs to access dynamically different elements of the HTML page, duplicate IDs can cause problems. If you double-click on the thtmlb:advancedSearch tag, you will navigate to the BSP element screen like the one in Figure 4.6 where you can analyze the different attributes of that tag.

From the analysis of the attributes of the thtmlb:advancedSearch tag, we see that the attribute header that we encountered in the listing of the search.htm view has to be assigned a value of type CRMS_THTMLB_SEARCH_HEADER. In the listing of the view search.htm we have used the notation <%= model->GET_PARAM_STRUCT_NAME( ) %> to assign this value. The notation <%= > is used to identify BSP directives or other ABAP statements and variables that need to be interpreted by the server at runtime. In this case, we are instructing the server to execute method GET_PARAM_STRUCT_NAME( )

using the instance that is stored in the variable `model` and to assign the result to the attribute `header`. Doing a similar analysis, we see that the attribute `fieldMetadata` has to be assigned a value of type `CRMT_THTMLB_SEARCH_FIELD_INFO`. In the listing, we see that the value of this attribute is assigned by calling method `GET_DQUERY_DEFI-NITIONS( )` on the instance of a class stored in the variable `controller`. Naturally, we want to know where this variable is defined. The BSP environment automatically provides a BSP page with a handle to its controller under the variable name `controller`. We will see later on how this controller is instantiated. In Listing 4.3, we saw that beside the method `GET_DQUERY_DEFINITIONS( )`, there is another call to method `GET_POSSIBLE_FIELDS( )` that is made using the same controller instance. We realize that these methods have to exist in the search view controller.

Attribute	R...	D...	C...	Bi...	Typing me...	Associated Type	Dflt value	Description
ajaxDeltaHandling	☐	☑	☐	☐	TYPE	▾ STRING	false	Supports AJAX Delta Handling (input .
disabled	☐	☑	☐	☐	TYPE	▾ STRING	false	When true, all UI elements are disabl..
fieldMetadata	☑	☑	☐	☐	TYPE	▾ CRMT_THTMLB_SEA...		Field metadata (input only)
fieldNames	☑	☑	☐	☐	TYPE	▾ CRMT_THTMLB_SEA...		Field names (input only)
header	☑	☑	☐	☐	TYPE	▾ CRMS_THTMLB_SEA...		Header information (input only)
id	☑	☑	☐	☐	TYPE	▾ STRING		Element ID (input only)
maxHits	☐	☑	☐	☑	TYPE	▾ STRING		Maximum hits displayed in result list
onEnter	☐	☑	☐	☐	TYPE	▾ STRING		Server event triggered when Enter k.
showMaxHits	☐	☑	☐	☐	TYPE	▾ STRING	true	Show the Max Hits input field
switchId	☐	☑	☐	☐	TYPE	▾ STRING		switch id
values	☑	☑	☐	☑	TYPE	▾ CRMT_THTMLB_SEA...		Search criteria (input/output)
widthField	☐	☑	☐	☐	TYPE	▾ STRING	207px	Width of field selector
widthOperator	☐	☑	☐	☐	TYPE	▾ STRING	147px	Width of operator selector
widthValue	☐	☑	☐	☐	TYPE	▾ STRING	152px	Width of value input control

Figure 4.6 Attributes of BSP Element thtmlb:advancedSearch

Unlike the reference to the controller instance, which is automatically provided by the BSP environment, we have to explicitly assign in the page attributes a reference to the model (or to the models, if we have opted to use more than one class to represent the model). Therefore, as we have seen in Section 4.1.1 on data binding, we have to define the variable `model` that is used in providing values to attributes of the `thtmlb:advancedSearch` tag.

Follow the following steps to create a model class:

1. Using the class builder—Transaction SE24—create class ZCL_CMP_SRCH_MAN1_DATA with super class CL_BSP_MODEL.

2. On the INTERFACES tab, add the interface IF_BSP_WD_MODEL_BINDING. This interface is not required in the basic BSP applications but it is required when using THTMLB tags.

3. Add these public instance attributes to your class:
   - ▶ PARAMETERS of type CRMT_THTMLB_SEARCH_CRITERION
   - ▶ MAX_HITS of type I with initial value 100

4. Redefine method IF_BSP_MODEL~INIT and copy-and-paste the code snippet in Listing 4.4.

```
METHOD if_bsp_model~init.
 CALL METHOD super->if_bsp_model~init
  EXPORTING
   id  = id
   owner = owner.
 FIELD-SYMBOLS:
     <fs_params> TYPE crms_thtmlb_search_criterion.

 APPEND INITIAL LINE TO parameters
 ASSIGNING <fs_params>.
 <fs_params>-field = 'GUEST_ID'.
 <fs_params>-operator = 'EQ'.

 APPEND INITIAL LINE TO parameters
 ASSIGNING <fs_params>.
 <fs_params>-field = 'HOTEL_NAME'.
 <fs_params>-operator = 'EQ'.
ENDMETHOD.
```

Listing 4.4 Code of Method IF_BSP_MODEL~INIT of Class ZCL_CMP_SRCH_MAN1_DATA

5. Add method GET_PARAM_STRUCT_NAME with returning parameter RV_PARAM_STRUCT_NAME of type STRING and the following code:rv_param_struct_name = 'ZBOOKING_RESERV'.

6. Redefine method IS_ATTRIBUTE_ACTIVE of interface IF_BSP_WD_MODEL_BINDING and make it return true. This is for simplification. In a real business application, we implement logic to determine whether a given attribute that is passed in the input parameter is active.

7. Save and activate.

Now that we have a model class, we have to remember that we used a reference to it—model—in the search view in Listing 4.3 without declaring it (it would have been impossible to declare it before creating it). Therefore, go back to your view search.htm and, on the PAGE ATTRIBUTES tab, declare the attribute model of type reference to ZCL_CMP_SRCH_MAN1_DATA. Save and activate.

As we have seen earlier, the search component has its own controller. We have already created the view, we just created the model, and now we need a controller. Follow these steps to create the search view controller:

1. Either using forward navigation by double-clicking on the name of the controller class or using the class builder—Transaction SE24—create class ZCL_CMP_SRCH_MAN1_SRCH_CTRL that inherits from class CL_BSP_CONTROLLER2.

2. As we have seen, one of the tasks of the controller is to communicate to the model any changes that occurred in the view. This implies that the controller knows what model or models it has to handle. In more technical terms, this means that the controller needs a reference to the model. Therefore, add the private instance variable m_model of type ZCL_CMP_SRCH_MAN1_DATA to link our model to our controller.

3. We have seen that method DO_INIT is used for initialization. At the very beginning of the process flow, the controller creates a model and stores a reference to it as shown in the listing below. Overwrite method DO_INIT and copy-and-paste this code snippet:

```
m_model ?= create_model(
model_id = 'm'
class_name = 'ZCL_CMP_SRCH_MAN1_DATA' ).
```

4. As we have seen in the process flow of BSP applications, the DO_REQUEST method creates and calls the views under control of the controller. Overwrite method DO_REQUEST and copy-and-paste the code snippet in Listing 4.5. Remember that, before calling the view, the search controller sets the model attribute of the search view page to have it pointing to the model instance that it just created.

```
DATA: search_view TYPE REF TO if_bsp_page.

dispatch_input( ).

IF is_navigation_requested( ) IS NOT INITIAL.
 RETURN.
ENDIF.
```

```
search_view = create_view( view_name = 'search.htm' ).
search_view->set_attribute(
          name = 'model' value = m_model ).
call_view( search_view ).
```

Listing 4.5 Code Snippet of Method DO_REQUEST of class ZCL_CMP_SRCH_MAN1_DATA

5. Create instance public method GET_DQUERY_DEFINITIONS with returning parameter RT_FIELD_METADA and copy-and-paste the code from Listing 4.6:

```
DATA: lt_metadata TYPE crmt_thtmlb_search_field_info.

FIELD-SYMBOLS:
    <ls_metadata> TYPE crms_thtmlb_search_field_info,
    <ls_operator> TYPE CRM_THTMLB_SEARCH_OPERATOR,
    <ls_ddlb_nvp> TYPE crms_thtmlb_search_ddlb_nvp.

APPEND INITIAL LINE TO lt_metadata
ASSIGNING <ls_metadata>.

<ls_metadata>-field = 'GUEST_ID'.
<ls_metadata>-data_type = 'STRING'.
<ls_metadata>-max_length = 30.
APPEND INITIAL LINE TO
<ls_metadata>-operators ASSIGNING <ls_operator>.
<ls_operator> = 'EQ'.
APPEND INITIAL LINE TO
<ls_metadata>-operators ASSIGNING <ls_operator>.
<ls_operator> = 'NE'.

APPEND INITIAL LINE TO lt_metadata
ASSIGNING <ls_metadata>.
<ls_metadata>-field = 'HOTEL_NAME'.
<ls_metadata>-data_type = 'STRING'.
<ls_metadata>-max_length = 30.
APPEND INITIAL LINE TO
<ls_metadata>-operators ASSIGNING <ls_operator>.
<ls_operator> = 'EQ'.
APPEND INITIAL LINE TO
<ls_metadata>-operators ASSIGNING <ls_operator>.
<ls_operator> = 'NE'.
APPEND INITIAL LINE TO
```

```
<ls_metadata>-ddlb_options ASSIGNING <ls_ddlb_nvp>.
<ls_ddlb_nvp>-key  = '1'.
<ls_ddlb_nvp>-value = 'Holidays Inn'.
APPEND INITIAL LINE TO
<ls_metadata>-ddlb_options ASSIGNING <ls_ddlb_nvp>.
<ls_ddlb_nvp>-key  = '2'.
<ls_ddlb_nvp>-value = 'Marriott'.
APPEND INITIAL LINE TO
<ls_metadata>-ddlb_options ASSIGNING <ls_ddlb_nvp>.
<ls_ddlb_nvp>-key  = '3'.
<ls_ddlb_nvp>-value = 'Intercontinental'.

rt_field_metadata = lt_metadata.
```

Listing 4.6 Code Snippet of Method GET_DQUERY_DEFINITIONS of class ZCL_CMP_SRCH_MAN1_DATA

6. Create instance public method `GET_POSSIBLE_FIELDS` with returning parameter `RT_RESULT` and copy-and-paste the code from Listing 4.7.

```
DATA: lt_fields TYPE crmt_thtmlb_search_field_name.
FIELD-SYMBOLS: <ls_field> TYPE crms_thtmlb_search_field_name.

APPEND INITIAL LINE TO lt_fields ASSIGNING <ls_field>.
<ls_field>-field = 'GUEST_ID'.
<ls_field>-description = 'Guest ID'.

APPEND INITIAL LINE TO lt_fields ASSIGNING <ls_field>.
<ls_field>-field = 'HOTEL_NAME'.
<ls_field>-description = 'Hotel'.

rt_result = lt_fields.
```

Listing 4.7 Code Snippet of Method GET_POSSIBLE_FIELDS of Class ZCL_CMP_SRCH_MAN1_DATA

7. Save and activate.

At this point, the search view can be used to display static data but still cannot handle user input and react to events triggered by the user. Remember, though, that on the main view the search view was called through its controller `search.do`.Therefore, follow the same steps that we used to create the `main.do` controller and create the search controller with the name `search.do` and the controller class

ZCL_CMP_SRCH_MAN1_SRCH_CTRL that we created previously. After saving and activating the search controller, we focus on the result list. We will come back later to add some interactivity to the search controller.

4.2.3 The Result View

We have chosen to represent the results of a search triggered in the search view in a tabular form. Like the search view or any other view, the result view has its own controller and its own model. The result view will contain only one table. This table can be built using the cellerator tag. This tag handles the proper formatting of data passed to it and basic interaction events that are related to tabular data, such as paging and row selection.

Before creating the BSP page itself, let's create the various components that it requires, namely the model and the controller. To create the model, follow these steps:

1. Using the class builder—Transaction SE24—create class ZCL_CMP_SRCH_RES_MAN1_DATA with super class CL_BSP_MODEL. As we have seen, having a model class inheriting this base class simplifies coding and eliminates the need to manually carry out all the necessary operations to transfer the form fields to the model.

2. On the INTERFACES tab, add the interface IF_BSP_WD_MODEL_BINDING. This interface is not required in the basic BSP applications but it is required when using THTMLB tags.

3. Add the following public instance attributes to your class:
   - ▶ VISIBLE_FIRST_ROW_INDEX of type I with initial value 1
   - ▶ SELECTEDROWINDEX of type I with initial value 0
   - ▶ TABLE of type ZBOOKINGTABLE

4. Redefine method IF_BSP_MODEL~INIT to carry out any initialization that is required. In this example we simply clear the table attribute.

5. Redefine method IS_ATTRIBUTE_ACTIVE of interface IF_BSP_WD_MODEL_BINDING and make it return true.

6. Save and activate.

Now create the controller with the following steps:

1. Using the Web Application Builder in the ABAP Workbench, create a controller object, result.do, as a sub-object of the BSP application ZCMP_SRCH_MAN1. To do this, you will have to enter the controller name and the name of the controller class. In our example, the class name is ZCL_CMP_SRCH_MAN1_RESULT_CTRL.

2. Use forward navigation by double-clicking on the name of the controller class ZCL_CMP_SRCH_MAN1_RESULT_CTRL to create the class ZCL_CMP_SRCH_MAN1_RESULT_CTRL and make it inherit from class CL_BSP_CONTROLLER2.

3. Add the private instance variable m_model of type ZCL_CMP_SRCH_RES_MAN1_DATA.

4. Add the public instance variable gt_button of type CRMT_THTMLB_BUTTON_T. This is the variable that will contain action buttons and that we will pass to the table for display.

5. Overwrite method DO_INIT and copy-and-paste the following code snippet:

```
m_model ?= create_model(
model_id = 'm'
class_name = ' ZCL_CMP_SRCH_RES_MAN1_DATA' ).
```

6. Overwrite method DO_REQUEST and copy-and-paste the code snippet in Listing 4.8. Before calling the view, remember that the search controller sets the model attribute to have it pointing to the model instance that it just created.

```
DATA: result_view TYPE REF TO if_bsp_page.

dispatch_input( ).

IF is_navigation_requested( ) IS NOT INITIAL.
 RETURN.
ENDIF.

result_view = create_view( view_name = result.htm' ).
result_view->set_attribute(
        name = 'model' value = m_model ).
call_view( result_view ).
```

Listing 4.8 Code Snippet of Method DO_REQUEST of class ZCL_CMP_SRCH_RES_MAN1_DATA

7. Save and activate.

We have now created all the components required to run the view. Now create the result.htm BSP page with controller class ZCL_CMP_SRCH_MAN1_RESULT_CTRL and page attribute model of type reference to ZCL_CMP_SRCH_RES_MAN1_DATA. Listing 4.9 shows the listing of BSP page result.htm. Save it and activate the view.

```
<%@page language="abap" %>
<%@extension name="thtmlb" prefix="thtmlb" %>

<thtmlb:cellerator
  personalizable = "TRUE"
  id       ="Table"
  usage    = "SEARCHRESULT"
  onRowSelection ="select"
  table        ="//model/Table"
  fillUpEmptyRows= ' '
  headerText   = " "
  width        = "100%"
  actions      = "<%= controller->gt_button %>"
  actionsMaxInRow   = "20"
  visibleFirstRow   =
"<%= model->visible_first_row_index %>"
  selectedRowIndex  = "<%= model->selectedrowindex %>"
  selectionMode       = "SINGLE"
  enableTableGraphics  = "TRUE"
  hasExpander        = "true"
  hasPagerWhenCollapsed   = "false"
  horizontalScrolling     = "false"
  verticalScrolling       = "true"
  visibleRowCount     = "10"
  visibleRowCountExpanded    = "50"
  scrollRowCount       = "20"
  />
```

Listing 4.9 Code Snippet of View result.htm

Once you have activated all the components, you can start the search-result application by launching the main controller. For the time being we have a static application that does not react to the user input. In order to make our application dynamic, we have to add event-handling to our BSP application.

4.2.4 Handling the Search Event

There are two events—search and clear—that have been declared in the view search.htm as onClick attributes of the two buttons present on that view. As we have seen in Section 4.1.2 (Process Flow in a BSP Application), events are passed to the controller of the component that triggered those events and are processed in that controller. Therefore, in order to react to those two events, we have to implement the appropriate search and clear logic.

To simplify things, we leave method DO_HANDLE_DATA of our search controller untouched; that is, we do not redefine it because there is no special logic that we want to define here. However, as we have seen earlier, form parameters are collected from this method and set in the model if corresponding SET and GET methods have been properly defined. Therefore, we need to define the SET method for our bound attribute parameters. In order to define this method, we have to follow the naming convention mentioned in Section 4.1.1 (Data Binding) so that the SET method is called automatically. Therefore, the name of the setter method of table attribute parameters will be SET_T_PARAMETERS. To do this, copy method _SET_T_XYZ of class CL_BSP_MODEL to the search view model class and copy-and-paste the code in Listing 4.10. Note that the code in this listing is simple and does not perform data validation, white and black list checks, and other validations that shall normally be carried out in a real business application.

```
FIELD-SYMBOLS:
    <crit> TYPE CRMS_THTMLB_SEARCH_CRITERION,
    <compo> TYPE any.

READ TABLE parameters INDEX index ASSIGNING <crit>.
ASSIGN COMPONENT component OF STRUCTURE <crit> TO <compo>.
<compo> = VALUE.
```

Listing 4.10 Transferring Form Parameters to Model Attributes

The next step is to redefine method DO_HANDLE_EVENT, which will be called after the handling of the data. For the sake of modularization, it is a good idea to make this method a kind of dispatcher to individual event handling methods, which take care of exactly one event each. Listing 4.11 shows what a redefinition of method DO_HANDLE_EVENT can look like.

```
METHOD do_handle_event.
 IF htmlb_event_ex->event_server_name EQ 'search'.
  eh_onsearch( htmlb_event    = htmlb_event
        htmlb_event_ex = htmlb_event_ex ).
 ELSEIF htmlb_event_ex->event_server_name EQ 'clear'.
  eh_onclear( htmlb_event    = htmlb_event
       htmlb_event_ex = htmlb_event_ex ).
 ENDIF.
ENDMETHOD.
```

Listing 4.11 Redefinition of Method DO_HANDLE_EVENT to Process Search and Clear Events

In this redefinition, it is important to make sure that the server event name that is used to delegate to the appropriate event handler matches the name of the event that was assigned to the onClick attribute in the view.

The listing of method EH_ONSEARCH follows in Listing 4.12. This method is also simple and focuses only on showing what is done with the search event and how data can be retrieved from the database and set in the model. You will notice that the search view controller accesses the model of the result list. This can be seen as a shortcut. You can enhance the design of this application by making sure that any interaction between the search and the result components happens through the main controller. This can help ensure that there are no dependencies between two sister components.

```
METHOD eh_onsearch.

 FIELD-SYMBOLS <criterion> TYPE crms_thtmlb_search_criterion.
 DATA:
  ls_result TYPE TABLE OF zhotelbooking,
  lv_title TYPE string,
  lv_where TYPE string,
  lr_res_ctrl TYPE REF TO zcl_cmp_srch_man1_result_ctrl,
  lr_parent TYPE REF TO cl_bsp_controller2,
  lr_res_model TYPE REF TO zcl_cmp_srch_res_man1_data.

 LOOP AT m_model->parameters ASSIGNING <criterion>.
  IF <criterion>-value1 IS NOT INITIAL.
   IF lv_where IS INITIAL.
    lv_where = '('.
   ELSE.
```

```
    CONCATENATE lv_where ') AND (' INTO lv_where
          SEPARATED BY space.
    ENDIF.
    CONCATENATE lv_where <criterion>-field
          <criterion>-operator ''''
          INTO lv_where SEPARATED BY space.
    CONCATENATE lv_where <criterion>-value1
          INTO lv_where.
    CONCATENATE lv_where '''' INTO lv_where.
  ENDIF.
ENDLOOP.

CONCATENATE lv_where ')'
      INTO lv_where SEPARATED BY space.

SELECT * FROM zhotelbooking
      INTO TABLE ls_result
      WHERE (lv_where).

lr_parent ?= m_parent.
lr_res_ctrl ?=
   lr_parent->get_controller( controller_id = 'result' ).
lr_res_model ?= lr_res_ctrl->get_model( model_id = 'm' ).
lr_res_model->set_results( ls_result ).

ENDMETHOD.
```

Listing 4.12 Method for Handling Search Event

The last line in the method EH_ONSEARCH sets the result table. Define that method in the model and make sure to assign the import parameter to our model attribute table.

You can now define method EH_ONCLEAR. We will make sure to reinitialize the result table as well as the search criteria.

After saving and activating your changes, you can launch the application and run some tests to see how the application works. Once you have started the application and executed a search, you will see a screen that is very similar to the one in Figure 4.7.

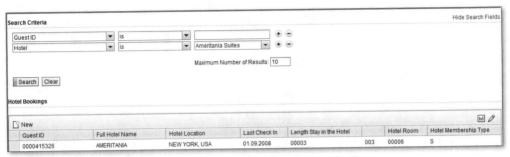

Figure 4.7 Search-Result View of the Hotel Booking BSP Application

We could enhance our application in many ways but—as we will see in subsequent chapters—enhancing applications has been made significantly easy by various tools available in Web Client Framework.

4.2.5 Conclusion

In this section, we have built a search-result application using the THTMLB extension and following a rather manual process in order to create all the individual components. This approach has two clear disadvantages. First, it is tedious and provides little reusability. One needs to carefully create all the components one by one, making sure that they do not omit anything necessary. Second, it does not give the developer the opportunity to focus on the actual business at hand: a search-result application. The developer has to constantly worry about various technical aspects of creating BSP components and has little time to focus on the actual business logic. It is for these and other reasons that the Web Client Framework Workbench was created. In order to prepare you for using the Workbench, the next sections will focus first on explaining the presentation layer of a Web Client application and on mapping the MVC concepts that we have just seen to Web Client components. Once we are prepared, we will be able, in the next chapter, to actually start creating an enhanced version of our application with a few of mouse clicks.

4.3   Presentation Layer of a Web Client Application

In terms of complexity, Web Client encompasses a wide range of applications. The range starts with very simple applications made with a small number of views and ends with very complex applications, in which many individual MVC applications interact and integrate with one another to provide a meaningful business application. Independently of their complexity, the presentation layer of most if not all Web Client applications leverages the MVC pattern. A Web Client application can be broken down to the smallest building blocks, which represent views. The elements of a Web Client view can be grouped as follows:

▶ *The layout*, which controls the rendering. It corresponds to the view of the MVC paradigm.

▶ *The context*, which deals with the application data. It corresponds to the model in the MVC paradigm.

▶ *The controller*, which connects the layout and the context and responds to users' actions.

Like the relatively simple BSP application we have built in Section 4.2, Web Client applications are based on the MVC pattern. However, the Web Client framework introduced a new concept, which is valid for all applications built on top of it and which makes it easier to encapsulate and reuse components. In the following sections, we will analyze in more details the presentation layer of a Web Client application. In Section 4.3.1, we will discuss the component concept in the Web Client framework. In Section 4.3.2, we will analyze how the MVC pattern applies to UI components. In Section 4.3.3, we will examine in more detail the structure of the UI component layout. In Section 4.3.4, we will discuss the context and context nodes, which form the model in UI components. Then, in Section 4.3.5, we will discuss the different types of controllers and their role in a UI component. Finally, in Section 4.3.6, we will discuss the Runtime Repository, which keeps the components of a Web Client application together.

4.3.1 Component Concept in Web Client Framework

A Web Client component is a bundle of view sets, views, and custom controllers that is self-contained, reusable, and has meaningful business content. It has its own runtime repository and exposes a clear, well-defined interface to the outside world. At runtime, a UI component can have multiple instances. From a logistical point of view, a UI component is mapped to a BSP, and thus it is assigned to a package.

Analysis shows that a UI component is represented by a component controller, which has a context that is partially visible to the outside as a public interface. A component consists of custom controllers and one or more windows that host the views and view sets.

An outside perspective reveals that a UI component can be reused by one or more other components. The embedding component defines component use in its runtime repository to formally declare the dependency. At runtime, the embedding component has access to the component usage in the runtime repository in order to access the interface of the embedded component. Each component use will get its own instance at runtime. This makes it possible to reuse the same component inside the same embedding component.

At the very minimum, each component contains the following objects:

▸ The component controller `BSPWDComponent.do`. This is a special controller that is available only in a UI component.

▸ The runtime repository `Runtime.xml`. This is an XML file that is present in each UI component and contains the details about all constituents of the component: views, view sets, windows, navigational links, etc.

▸ At least one window.

▸ A *document type definition* (DTD) for the runtime repository.

In the following sections, we will see in more details the structure of a UI component. We will analyze the individual objects of a UI component, their roles, and their interactions.

4.3.2 Model View Controller in Web Client Component

We have seen in Section 4.1 how the MVC pattern applies to BSP applications in general. We have also seen that the presentation layer of Web Client applications leverages the MVC pattern. Figure 4.8 illustrates how the MVC pattern illustrated on Figure 4.2 applies to UI components.

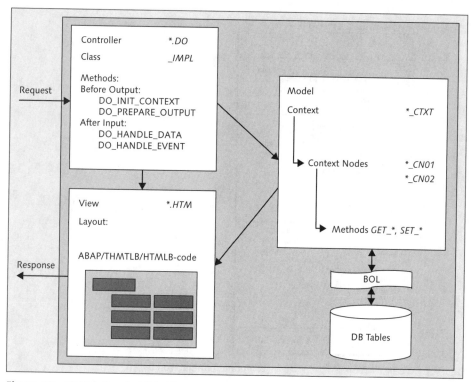

Figure 4.8 MVC Pattern in Web Client Components

Figure 4.8 introduces the naming conventions that are in effect in Web Client components.

- Views are represented in HTML files with the extension .HTM.

- Controller implementation classes have names with the suffix _IMPL. Their corresponding view controllers have the extension .DO.

- The context of the model is represented by a class with the suffix _CTXT. The hierarchies of context nodes that are bound to this context are classes with the suffix _CN01, _CN02, etc.

When you create a UI component, a wizard takes care of assigning the right names to each object. Typically, the name—or more accurately the prefix—is the same for all objects that relate to the same component. Figure 4.9 shows on a real business application in the Component Workbench the different components of the MVC design pattern as applied to a Web Client component.

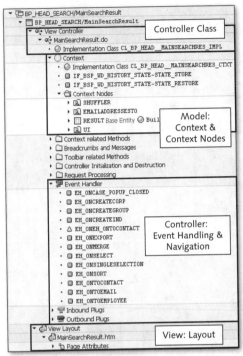

Figure 4.9 Identification of MVC Pattern Component in the Workbench

4.3.3 The Layout in a Web Client Component

The layout consists of a view or a view set. A view is represented by a standard BSP view, which in most cases defines the presentation of application data in an HTM file that can contain THTMLB, CHTMLB, HTMLB tags as well as pure HTML and JavaScript code. As with pure BSP applications, a view consists of a pair of BSP views—HTM files—and a corresponding view controller: a .DO controller. Through its attributes, a view has access to the associated controller, as well as to the model, represented by the context node. Each view is contained in a window, which is itself part of a component. A view contains UI elements that can be bound to a context node attribute. Thanks to the introduction of view configurations, a view can contain a minimal amount of coding and rather invoke its configuration XML, which contains all necessary information to render the view. The configuration is defined at design time in the component workbench. If you have to manually write your views, you always must use the THTMLB or CHTMLB tags when available and avoid using other tag libraries, such as HTMLB. We will discuss the use of THTMLB and CHTMLB libraries in more detail in Chapter 15.

A view set is used to group many views in one logical entity in order to design a more or less complex layout, while keeping logical and technical groupings of layout element. We can see the main view of our search-result example as a view set with two views: one that presents search criteria and search actions, and one that presents the results of the search. A view set contains view areas, in which views can be inserted.

The next section explains the model, which is the source of the data presented by the view.

4.3.4 The Model in a Web Client Component

The model is represented by the context and context nodes. Although the Web Client framework supports context nodes that are not based on BOL—the so called value nodes—it is preferable to use model nodes, which directly relate to Business Object Layer (BOL) entities. BOL was quickly covered in the first chapter and a detailed overview will follow later. At this point, you only need to know that the BOL layer facilitates access to the business logic in a uniform and object-oriented manner, as its name implies. With model nodes, each context node instance refers to a BOL collection through a collection wrapper. The collection wrapper encapsulates BOL objects, which hold the actual data. This setup gives an easy access to model data, which is accessed using the context node binding, similar to the data binding we have previously discussed. The setup also makes it possible to add value attributes to model nodes. Value attributes are attributes that are added to a node without any reference to an underlying BOL objects.

Model data, which is represented by the context and context nodes, is accessible through `GET` and `SET` methods. Attributes are not directly visible to the outside world. The type of the BOL object to which a context node relates is indicated by its attribute `BaseEntityName`, which makes it possible to use generic `GET` and `SET` methods. This means that, unless you have special processing requirements, you do not have to (re)define the individual `GET` and `SET` methods for your model attributes. Thanks to their well-defined interface, context nodes can be bound and their attributes accessed by other context nodes.

Like the model classes that inherit from the same class—`CL_BSP_MODEL`—to benefit from generic features, the context nodes inherit from a context node base class. The context node base class provides generic features that are common to all context nodes like data conversion error handling, conversion to and from string for all

ABAP data types, generic GET and SET methods that do not require any special processing, etc.

In order to provide generic access to context node attributes via GET and SET methods, the Web Client framework simulates the existence of a model attribute of type structure and with the name STRUCT. The model attribute STRUCT represents the BOL entity that was declared at design time in the attribute BaseEntityName. The access to individual BOL attributes is then realized in the format STRUCT.<attribute_name> that we have seen when discussing data binding. By BOL model lookup at runtime, the generic service of the context node takes care of resolving that format and retrieving the underlying BOL attribute using the BOL component set declared for each UI component.

Besides the generic context node, there exist other specialized context nodes:

▸ **Advanced search context node**
This context node is specially designed to be used with the thtmlb:advancedSearch tag. It provides all convenient methods to handle search criteria, search operators, etc. The advanced search context node works hand-in-hand with a special advanced search controller.

▸ **Table view context node**
This is a context node that was specialized to handle tabular data for table tags such as thtmlb:cellerator and chtmlb:configCellerator. In the same fashion the base context node introduces an artificial STRUCT attribute, the table view context node introduces the attribute TABLE along with such features such as sorting, filtering, and row selection.

▸ **Tree view context node**
Based on the table view context node, this node is a specialization that is designed to support tree tags thtmlb:tree and chtmlb:configTree.

▸ **Deep table view context node**
This is another specialization of the table view context node that handles nested tabular data.

The model is updated based on user input and it returns application data to the view for display. This interaction, as we have seen, is managed by the controller. The following section analyzes the controller.

4.3.5 Controllers in a Web Client Component

As we have seen earlier, a Web Client component contains at least one controller: the component controller. In real business applications, a component will contain more controllers. Different types of controllers can be found in different combinations in Web Client components, depending on their complexity. The base architecture includes the following types of controllers:

▶ **View controller**
This is a controller that has a visible part on the UI. The visual part is typically a view or a view set. The view controller reacts to events that occur in the corresponding view or view set. It also manages the view inbound and outbound plugs, which are the points of entry into and exit from the view, for handling navigational events.

▶ **Component controller**
The component controller has no visible elements. It contains all instances of the controllers—view, window, application, and custom—present in its component. Furthermore, it is responsible for managing the use of other components, if required.

▶ **Custom controller**
The custom controller acts as a central place for sharing data between views. The custom controller makes it convenient for one view to access another view's data without either of the views having to directly expose its internal model to the outside world. A custom controller has no visible element.

▶ **Window controller**
As we have seen, each view is contained in a window. The window provides a view with space for displaying its content. Like the view controller, the window controller manages the inbound and outbound plugs. Unlike the view controller, the window controller manages inter-component navigation instead of navigation between views inside the same window.

▶ **Application controller**
This is an optional controller that can be defined to enable an application to be called via a URL. If used, it manages the HTTP request-response cycle and manages access to all components that it hosts.

▶ **Global custom controller**
Used in conjunction with the application controller, the global custom controller is globally visible and not restricted to the component context.

Beside those standard controllers, it is worth mentioning three other specialized controllers:

▶ The advanced search controller is specially designed to work with the advanced search tag. This controller is responsible for the majority of the interactive features that you see in the advanced search view.

▶ The overview page controller is designed for dynamically configurable view sets.

▶ The guided maintenance controller is specially designed for sequencing views in a guided maintenance wizard.

4.3.6   The Runtime Repository

As we have seen, the UI component is a collection of views, controllers, context, and context nodes. The runtime repository, represented by the `Repository.xml`, is a file that is present in each UI component to bundle all its components and provide the UI component specifications. The runtime repository defines the following.

▶ **Models**
The models define the BOL component set that underlies the context and context nodes of the UI component. This is the BOL component set where the context nodes will "search" for the attributes either for read or for update.

▶ **Windows**
There can be more than one window in a component. The runtime repository describes the inbound, outbound plugs and the views that are embedded in each window.

▶ **View sets**
Their view areas and the views that are embedded or can potentially be embedded at runtime are included.

▶ **Navigation links**
The source view, the target view, and the outbound and inbound plugs for each navigational link are included. The name of a navigational link has to be unique.

▶ **Component interface**
These describe the public interface and its visibility to other components for potential reuse.

▶ **Component usage**
This describes the external components that are used and how they are used; for example, the inbound and outbound plugs, the window interface, etc.

Although the runtime repository is an xml file that is user readable, we strongly discourage manual editing. Instead the runtime repository editor, as seen in Figure 4.10, should be used to ensure consistency. A defective runtime repository makes a UI component unusable.

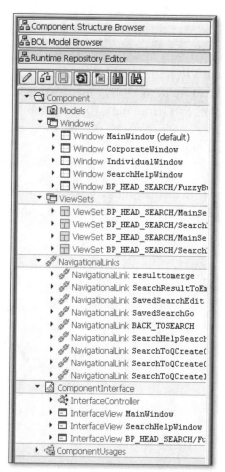

Figure 4.10 The Runtime Repository Editor

The runtime repository can be seen as the central coordination instance of a UI component.

4.4 Summary

Throughout this chapter, we have analyzed the foundation of the Web Client framework, BSP technology. We started by studying the important concept of the BSP programming model, which is the foundation of the presentation layer of Web Client. We then analyzed how the well-known MVC pattern is applied in BSPs. Before discussing the process flow in a BSP application, we discussed the fundamental concept of data binding, which will help us throughout this book in understanding how data is transferred back and forth between the view and the model.

Through an example, we familiarized ourselves with the MVC pattern as applied in BSP technology. Having mastered the MVC pattern in BSP, we discussed the presentation layer of a Web Client application. We started with the component concept that was introduced with the Web Client framework, and then analyzed the application of the MVC pattern in UI components, from the layout to the different types of controllers and to the unique way in which the UI framework uses the model. Finally we discussed the runtime repository: the glue that binds the building blocks of a UI component.

In the next chapter, we'll use our new knowledge to help us build a UI framework-based application, and we will see how easy it is to build such an application using the component workbench.

Software engineers focus on technology; application developers focus on business logic. In this chapter, you will learn how to build a Web Client application focusing on your business rather than your technology.

5 Creating a Web Client Application

As a true MVC BSP application, a Web Client application has three main components: the model, the views, and the controllers. In the process of creating a Web Client application, many features are available free if one is using the Component Workbench to build the UI. Thanks to the configuration tool, it is possible to build a UI and make it user-friendly look without spending too much time in manual coding. This task becomes even easier if we use the GenIL/BOL model for our model.

Figure 5.1 provides an overview of the architecture of a Web Client application with a focus on the presentation and the business-object layers. Although it adds more features that we will discuss later in the chapter, you already can see in Figure 5.1 that a Web Client application has all the components of a typical MVC application that we have discussed earlier in the book. The requests are interpreted by the controller, which communicates with both the model and the view. The view takes care of presenting the data from the model to the user. The model communicates with the business object layer to read data and write changes to data as instructed by the controller.

By the end of this chapter, we will have produced a full blown application for which we will build the UI in a semi-automated way, with very little code, using the Component Workbench. We will then be ready to take a step further in the next chapter and enhance our application. To achieve this, we will start in Section 5.1 by learning how to program access and modify the data exposed by our GenIL component via BOL programming APIs. In this section, we will learn how to read data, how to create and modify data, how to lock data for ensuring safe concurrent access, and how to sort data in the BOL. In Section 5.2 we will proceed with the actual creation of our UI component. We will first present the anatomy of our application, then create one by one the components of our application: the search page, the custom controller, the form and table view, and the overview page. We will finish by enabling navigation inside our component.

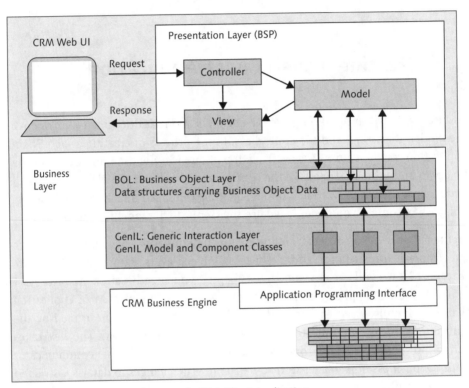

Figure 5.1 Top Architectural Layers of a Web Client Application

5.1 BOL Programming

By now you know that the Business Object Layer (BOL) can be viewed as a consumer of GenIL components. It serves as a uniform programming interface to access the application business logic. The key advantage of BOL is the uniformity that it delivers. As you will see in this chapter, accessing different GenIL business objects via the BOL API is extremely straightforward. In addition, BOL provides services such as message handling and its own buffer.

From a software engineering point of view, the BOL helps you achieve the so called *timeless* aspect of your code. As you know, different application layers evolve at a different pace. For example, the UI technologies change much faster than the SQL code in your stored procedures. The BOL serves as a firewall between the code in your presentation layer and the code in your GenIL components (backend). In this chapter, you will see that the BOL and the UI layer of the Web Client UI framework are designed to work hand in hand. This not only brings us closer to the timeless software paradigm but also allows you to develop UI applications faster. Later in this book we will talk about generating applications. This would also not be possible without the BOL (and GenIL to a certain degree). We will start with on overview of the BOL. Then in Section 5.1.2 we will learn how to read data using the BOL, before discussing the creation, the modification, the deletion and the locking of data. In Section 5.1.7 we will discuss sorting BOL collections. We will finish this chapter by making some recommendations in Section 5.1.8.

5.1.1 Overview

Although BOL is simple to use, its structure involves a number different interfaces and classes that are important to understand. Figure 5.2 summarizes the most important ones.

As the name suggests, CL_CRM_BOL_CORE is the most important class within the BOL layer. It communicates directly with the underlying business object implementations. Only one instance of this class exists per session. Using the BOL core instance, you can access all the BOL's functionality, but we recommend that you use the so-called dedicated *service providers*. The main BOL service providers are the *query* and the *entity*.

The query service is implemented via two classes: CL_CRM_BOL_QUERY_SERVICE (shown in Figure 5.2) and CL_CRM_BOL_DQUERY_SERVICE. The second class serves the dynamic queries from the GenIL component.

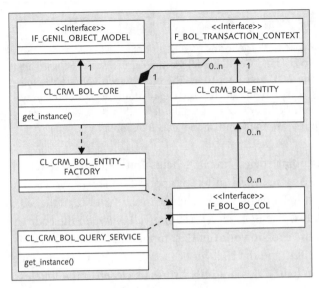

Figure 5.2   Overview of BOL API

CL_CRM_BOL_ENTITY serves as the entity service provider. Each business object is represented via this class. The BOL overview class diagram does not tell us how the entities are managed. Entities represent business object instances, and so they need to be unique. As explained earlier, the BOL has its own buffer, and that is where BOL entities are buffered. Figure 5.3 depicts the *entity manager*—CL_CRM_BOL_ENTITY_MANAGER—that holds the references of all the BOL entities in a table attribute (ENTITY_TAB).

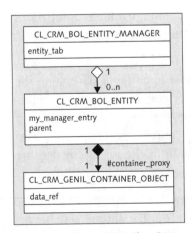

Figure 5.3   BOL Entities Class Diagram

An entity also has a reference to its entity manager. The business object represented by the BOL entity is defined in the GenIL layer. While implementing the GenIL component, we often refer to a data container (data vehicles). As you recall, the data container class is CL_CRM_GENIL_CONTAINER_OBJECT. In the context of BOL, the instance of the container class is referred to as CONTAINER_PROXY. A BOL entity contains a CONTAINER_PROXY reference. As a result, the entity serves as a wrapper around the underlying application data.

In the GenIL component, the entities (container objects) are typically passed around via collections (container object lists). The BOL entity collections shown in Figure 5.2 have to implement IF_BOL_BO_COL. Although this is the main interface, things are a bit more complicated. In Figure 5.4, you can see that there are two interfaces and two classes that make up the collection class diagram. IF_BOL_BO_COL is the generic one and IF_BOL_ENTITY_COL specializes in working with entities. Consequently, you have two collection classes (one generic and one specialized).

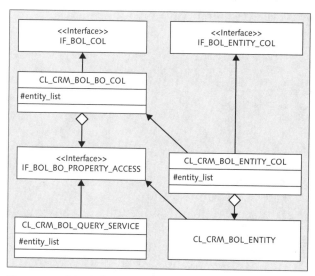

Figure 5.4 BOL Collection Class Diagram

The BOL entity class allows you to get important information about the business object data it represents and navigate to other entities. However, it does not provide a way to directly assess the application data properties. This has to be done through interface IF_BOL_BO_PROPERTY_ACCESS. The good news is that the CL_CRM_BOL_ENTITY class implements this interface and thus incorporates the attribute property access as part of the entity class.

The only class from Figure 5.2 that we have not discussed so far is the `IF_BOL_TRANS-ACTION_CONTEXT`. It represents the transaction context. This interface can serve different transaction scopes; for example, single root object, all modified object instances, or a custom scope. We will describe the transaction context in more detail later.

5.1.2 Reading Data

We now will describe the main BOL APIs. We will use the GenIL components that we created in the previous chapters in our examples. Remember that we had a component called `ZBOOK` where we handled the hotel guest booking data. This component was part of a component set also called `ZBOOK`.

Figure 5.5 displays an overview of our `ZBOOK` model. The root object was called `Bookings`, and we used BOL query `SearchBookings` to find and retrieve the desired information. From `Bookings`, we can drill through the `BookingProductRel` relationship and get the dependent `UsedProducts` objects.

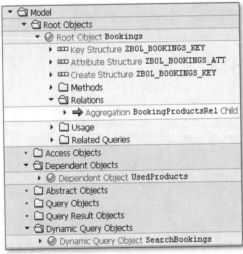

Figure 5.5 Overview of ZBOOK GenIL Model

In order to start retrieving data from a given GenIL component, you first need to load it. This is done via the `CL_CRM_BOL_CORE` (the heart of the BOL API). It is implemented as a singleton and you can always get a reference to it by calling its `GET_INSTANCE` method. Once you have a reference to the BOL core, you can load your component (see Listing 5.1).

```
data: lr_core type ref to cl_crm_bol_core.

TRY.
  lr_core = cl_crm_bol_core=>GET_INSTANCE( ).
  lr_core->START_UP( 'ZBOOK' ).

CATCH CX_CRM_GENIL_GENERAL_ERROR.
ENDTRY.
```

Listing 5.1 Loading GenIL Component Set

The START_UP method of the BOL core takes two parameters:

▶ IV_APPL_NAME is the name of the component set you would like to load.

▶ IV_DISPLAY_MODE_SUPPORT will tell the BOL what locking strategy to use. The default ABAP_FALSE value stands for optimistic locking. As a result, a business object will appear changeable even when the user is simply displaying it. The lock will be requested automatically when the user tries to modify the business object. The ABAP_TRUE value will open the component in a mode in which the user will have to explicitly request the lock before he or she can modify a business object.

Once the GenIL component set is loaded, you can start querying it (retrieving the relevant data). You will recall there are two types of queries: the regular and the dynamic query. SearchBookings is a dynamic query; Listing 5.2 shows how you can get results with it.

```
data: lr_core type ref to cl_crm_bol_core,
      lt_param type CRMT_NAME_VALUE_PAIR_TAB,
      ls_param type CRMT_NAME_VALUE_PAIR,
      lr_query type ref to CL_CRM_BOL_DQUERY_SERVICE,
      lr_result type ref to IF_BOL_ENTITY_COL.

TRY .
  lr_core = cl_crm_bol_core=>GET_INSTANCE( ).
  lr_core->START_UP( 'ZBOOK' ).

  lr_query = CL_CRM_BOL_DQUERY_SERVICE=>GET_INSTANCE( 'SearchBookings'
).
  ls_param-NAME = 'MAX_HITS'.
  ls_param-VALUE = '5'.
  append ls_param to lt_param.
```

```
lr_query->SET_QUERY_PARAMETERS( lt_param ).
lr_query->ADD_SELECTION_PARAM( IV_ATTR_NAME = 'HOTEL_NAME'
                               IV_SIGN = 'I'
                               IV_OPTION = 'EQ'
                               IV_LOW = 'AMBIENTE'
                               IV_HIGH = '' ).
lr_result = LR_QUERY->GET_QUERY_RESULT( ).
CATCH CX_CRM_GENIL_GENERAL_ERROR.
ENDTRY.
```

Listing 5.2 Executing Dynamic Query

In the above example, we instantiate the `SearchBookings` query from the BOL query service immediately after loading our GenIL component set, like this:

```
lr_query =
   CL_CRM_BOL_DQUERY_SERVICE=>GET_INSTANCE( 'SearchBookings' ).
```

A dynamic query accepts query parameters and selection parameters. Recall how we could specify `MAX_HITS`, `MATCH_TYPE` and two other attributes in the BOL browser. These were query parameters. To support our sample implementation, we prepare a structure of name-value pairs and use it to set these parameters:

```
ls_param-NAME = 'MAX_HITS'. ls_param-VALUE = '5'.
append ls_param to lt_param.
lr_query->SET_QUERY_PARAMETERS( lt_param ).
```

In the BOL browser, just below the query parameters, there was a block called DYNAMIC QUERY PARAMETERS. In order to set a dynamic (selection) parameter programmatically, you have to call `ADD_SELECTION_PARAM`:

```
lr_query->ADD_SELECTION_PARAM( IV_ATTR_NAME = 'HOTEL_NAME'
                               IV_SIGN = 'I'
                               IV_OPTION = 'EQ'
                               IV_LOW = 'AMBIENTE'
                               IV_HIGH = '' ).
```

The `IV_SIGN` could have values of INCLUSIVE and EXCLUSIVE. The `IV_OPTION` carries the query operation values (equal, not equal, less than, greater than, etc). The value that we want to match against is in `IV_LOW` (and `IV_HIGH` in case of operators like between).

Once you are done setting your parameters, you can execute your query and get the results in a BOL collection (`IF_BOL_ENTITY_COL`):

```
lr_result = LR_QUERY->GET_QUERY_RESULT( ).
```

If you run the above code in a report and set a breakpoint, you will see that the matching business objects are retrieved in the BOL collection. Naturally, you will not see this right away. You have to drill into the lr_result and see the value of the ENTITY_LIST attribute (Figure 5.6). This is consistent with our discussion of the elements in Figure 5.4.

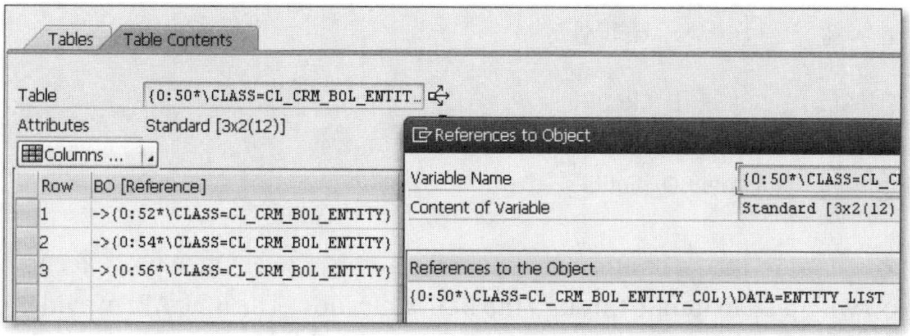

Figure 5.6 CL_CRM_BOL_ENTITY_COL-ENTITY_LIST in the Debugger

In line with our GenIL model, the result object of SearchBookings query was Bookings. Therefore, we can expect that the BOL collection that we receive from the query will allow us to obtain the booking data. So far we have been working with the specialized interface IF_BOL_ENTITY_COL. It specializes in handling entities. Therefore, what we will get as a result of this collection is a BOL entity, rather than a BOL property access. Remember that we explained that the way to access the underlying data is through the BOL property access. If you take another look at Figure 5.4, you will see that CL_CRM_BOL_ENTITY implements IF_BOL_BO_PROPERTY_ACCESS. Listing 5.3 demonstrates sample code for reading data from an entity.

```
data: "same as before
       lr_result  type ref to IF_BOL_ENTITY_COL,
       lr_iter    type ref to IF_BOL_ENTITY_COL_ITERATOR,
       lr_entity  type ref to CL_CRM_BOL_ENTITY,
       lv_guest   type string,
       lv_checkin type string.

TRY .
  "load the ZBOOK component set (same as before)
  ..
  "get and prepare the query service (same as before)
  ...
```

```
"execute the query and get the results
lr_result = LR_QUERY->GET_QUERY_RESULT( ).
"iterate through the resutls
lr_iter = lr_result->GET_ITERATOR( ).
lr_entity = lr_iter->GET_FIRST( ).
WHILE lr_entity is bound.
  lv_guest = LR_ENTITY->GET_PROPERTY_AS_STRING( 'GUEST_ID' ).
lv_checkin = LR_ENTITY->GET_PROPERTY_AS_STRING( 'LASTCHECKIN' ).
  write: / lv_guest, ', ', lv_checkin.
  lr_entity = lr_iter->GET_NEXT( ).
ENDWHILE.
CATCH CX_CRM_GENIL_GENERAL_ERROR.
ENDTRY.
```

Listing 5.3 Retrieving Data from BOL Entities

You now know how to load a component set and query service. Once you execute the query, you will need to iterate through the BOL collection. The BOL API provides IF_BOL_ENTITY_COL_ITERATOR, which implements the well-known *iterator* pattern. This allows you to access the BOL entity within the collection sequentially. To get the iterator, you need to call IF_BOL_ENTITY_COL~GET_ITERATOR. Once you have the iterator, you just need to loop through its elements:

```
lr_iter = lr_result->GET_ITERATOR( ).
lr_entity = lr_iter->GET_FIRST( ).
WHILE lr_entity is bound.

   …
   lr_entity = lr_iter->GET_NEXT( ).
ENDWHILE.
```

The BOL entity allows you to access its properties without worrying about the specific type of business object. All you need to know is the attribute name. In our implementation, we use GET_PROPERTY_AS_STRING to get this string representation of the object's attributes:

```
lv_guest = LR_ENTITY->GET_PROPERTY_AS_STRING( 'GUEST_ID' ).
```

If you run the above code, you will get the guest IDs and the check-in dates of the first five bookings for hotel AMBIENTE. Naturally, such data should exist in your database.

We just retrieved the data behind a root business object. A GenIL model, however, might consist of several objects. In our example, the relationship `BookingProductRel` leads to the `UsedProducts` object. The methods `GET_RELATED_ENTITY` and `GET_RELATED_ENTITIES` of `CL_CRM_BOL_ENTITY` allow you to access child objects. The former is suitable for cases when you know that there is only one instance behind a given relationship; that is, when the child is related to the parent via 1:1 cardinality. Listing 5.4 illustrates this discussion.

```
data: "same as before
      lr_booking type ref to CL_CRM_BOL_ENTITY,
      lr_product type ref to CL_CRM_BOL_ENTITY.

TRY .
  "same as before
  …
  lr_result = LR_QUERY->GET_QUERY_RESULT( ).
  "iterate through the resutls
  lr_iter = lr_result->GET_ITERATOR( ).
  lr_booking = lr_iter->GET_FIRST( ).
  WHILE lr_booking is bound.
    lv_guest = lr_booking->GET_PROPERTY_AS_STRING( 'GUEST_ID' ).
lv_checkin = lr_booking->GET_PROPERTY_AS_STRING( 'LASTCHECKIN' ).
    write: / lv_guest, ', ', lv_checkin.
    "used products
    lr_product = lr_booking->GET_RELATED_ENTITY(
        IV_RELATION_NAME = 'BookingProductsRel' ).
    lr_booking = lr_iter->GET_NEXT( ).
  ENDWHILE.
CATCH CX_CRM_GENIL_GENERAL_ERROR.
ENDTRY.
```

Listing 5.4 Getting a 1:1 Related Object

In order to retrieve a child object, you need to pass its relationship name to `GET_RELATED_ENTITY`. This will return the following single BOL entity:

```
lr_product = lr_booking->GET_RELATED_ENTITY(
        IV_RELATION_NAME = 'BookingProductsRel' ).
```

If you insert a breakpoint and drill into the `lr_product` instance, you will be able to see the actual data it is carrying. You probably need help finding your way through `CL_CRM_BOL_ENTITY`. Figure 5.7 shows how to do this.

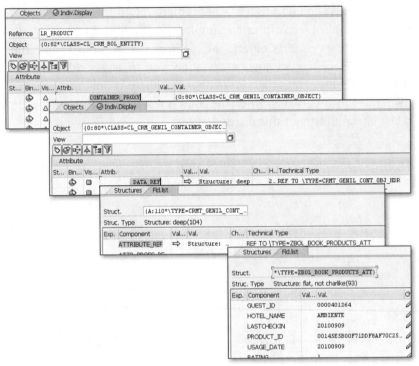

Figure 5.7 Debugging CL_CRM_BOL_ENTITY

As illustrated in Figure 5.7, the attribute CONTAINER_PROXY (of the BOL entity class) takes you to a CL_CRM_GENIL_CONTAINER_OBJECT. From there, you need to trace the content of the DATA_REF attribute. It will ultimately lead you to structure reference ATTRIBUTE_REF. In our example, this is the attribute structure of UserProducts GenIL business object, namely ZBOL_BOOK_PRODUCTS_ATT. As evident from Figure 5.7, the latter has been populated with some product data.

There is one problem with the last example: there are many products associated with one hotel booking. The cardinality of BookingProductsRel is not 1:1 but 0:N. We would need to use the GET_RELATED_ENTITIES method, which returns a collection of BOL entities. From there, you could use the iterator and loop through the dependent objects in a way similar to what you have seen already. Listing 5.5 provides you with a complete example.

```
data: "same as before
      lr_product type ref to CL_CRM_BOL_ENTITY,
      lr_products  type ref to IF_BOL_ENTITY_COL,
```

```
        lr_prod_iter type ref to IF_BOL_ENTITY_COL_ITERATOR,
        lv_prod_id  type string,
        lv_rating   type string.

TRY .
  "same as before

  ...
  lr_result = LR_QUERY->GET_QUERY_RESULT( ).
  "iterate through the resutls
  lr_iter = lr_result->GET_ITERATOR( ).
  lr_booking = lr_iter->GET_FIRST( ).
  WHILE lr_booking is bound.
     lv_guest = lr_booking->GET_PROPERTY_AS_STRING( 'GUEST_ID' ).
lv_checkin = lr_booking->GET_PROPERTY_AS_STRING( 'LASTCHECKIN' ).
     write: / lv_guest, ', ', lv_checkin, '{'.
     "used products
     lr_products = lr_booking->GET_RELATED_ENTITIES(
             IV_RELATION_NAME = 'BookingProductsRel' ).
     lr_prod_iter = lr_products->GET_ITERATOR( ).
     lr_product = lr_prod_iter->GET_FIRST( ).
     WHILE lr_product is bound.
 lv_prod_id = lr_product->GET_PROPERTY_AS_STRING( 'PRODUCT_ID' ).
 lv_rating =  lr_product->GET_PROPERTY_AS_STRING( 'RATING' ).
        write:  lv_prod_id, ', ', lv_rating , '; '.
        lr_product = lr_prod_iter->GET_NEXT( ).
     ENDWHILE.
     write: '}'.
     lr_booking = lr_iter->GET_NEXT( ).
  ENDWHILE.
CATCH CX_CRM_GENIL_GENERAL_ERROR.
ENDTRY.
```

Listing 5.5 Getting 0:N or 1:N Related Entities

We have covered the reading of application data. Now we will see how to create content. The BOL entity plays a key role in such operations. However, any modifications take place as part of a transaction and occur during global transactions unless explicitly specified. Such modification holds all the updated root object instances. The Web Client UI framework might perform optimizations and execute the updates in batches. As discussed previously, you should leave the job of triggering transaction commits to the framework.

5.1.3 Creating and Modifying Data

Let us create a new booking object. To do so you need a BOL object factory. Once you have a reference to the factory, you need to pass all the attributes described by the create structure from your GenIL model. As you did when testing `CREATE_OBJECTS` in the BOL browser, you have to initiate the save and transaction commit. Listing 5.6 shows an example of this procedure.

```
data: lr_core type ref to cl_crm_bol_core,
      lt_param type CRMT_NAME_VALUE_PAIR_TAB,
      ls_param type CRMT_NAME_VALUE_PAIR,
      lr_factory type ref to CL_CRM_BOL_ENTITY_FACTORY,
      lr_result  type ref to IF_BOL_ENTITY_COL,
      lr_booking type ref to CL_CRM_BOL_ENTITY,
      lr_tcontext type ref to IF_BOL_TRANSACTION_CONTEXT,
      lv_success type abap_bool.
TRY .
  "load the ZBOOK component set
  lr_core = cl_crm_bol_core=>GET_INSTANCE( ).
  lr_core->START_UP( 'ZBOOK' ).
CATCH CX_CRM_GENIL_GENERAL_ERROR.
  exit.
ENDTRY.
"prepare the creation parameters
ls_param-NAME = 'GUEST_ID'.
ls_param-VALUE = '0000401264'.
append ls_param to lt_param.
ls_param-NAME = 'HOTEL_NAME'.
ls_param-VALUE = 'VILLA VERDE'.
append ls_param to lt_param.
ls_param-NAME = 'LASTCHECKIN'.
ls_param-VALUE = '20101111'.
append ls_param to lt_param.
"obtain Bookings factory
lr_factory = lr_core->GET_ENTITY_FACTORY( 'Bookings' ).
"create Bookings instance
lr_booking = lr_factory->CREATE( lt_param ).
"save and commit
lr_tcontext = lr_core->GET_TRANSACTION( ).
lv_success = lr_tcontext->SAVE( ).
IF lv_success = abap_true.
  lr_tcontext->COMMIT( ).
ELSE.
```

246

```
  lr_tcontext->ROLLBACK( ).
ENDIF.
```
Listing 5.6 Creating Root Object

In order to prepare the data required by the create structure, we use name-value pairs of strings:

```
ls_param-NAME = 'GUEST_ID'.
ls_param-VALUE = '0000401264'.
append ls_param to lt_param.
```

CL_CRM_BOL_CORE helps us to retrieve an entity factory for the Bookings business object:

```
lr_factory = lr_core->GET_ENTITY_FACTORY( 'Bookings' ).
```

Next, we pass the table of name-value parameters to the CREATE method of the factory. The result is an entity instance that contains a reference to a Bookings container object:

```
lr_booking = lr_factory->CREATE( lt_param ).
```

Last, we obtain the global transaction context and trigger its save method. If it executes without errors, we perform a transaction commit:

```
lr_tcontext = lr_core->GET_TRANSACTION( ).
lv_success = lr_tcontext->SAVE( ).
IF lv_success = abap_true.
lr_tcontext->COMMIT( ).
```

If you have placed breakpoints in your GenIL component class, you will see that the framework calls CREATE_OBJECTS and SAVE_OBJECTS methods. This is quite consistent with what we observed when testing with the BOL browser.

You will typically create some dependent object data as well. To do so, you need to call the CREATE_RELATED_ENTITY method of a root object entity. It is extremely important to remember that this method requires a call to CL_CRM_BOL_CORE->MODIFY. Unlike the CREATE method of the BOL factory, the CREATE_RELATED_ENTITY does not call the underlying GenIL API (MODIFY_OBEJCTS does not get called automatically in this case). This allows you to create several dependent objects for a given root before delegating to the GenIL component; thereby grouping the backend API calls. Listing 5.7 extends Listing 5.6 and creates a product entry in addition to the booking.

```
data: lr_core type ref to cl_crm_bol_core,
      lt_param type CRMT_NAME_VALUE_PAIR_TAB,
      ls_param type CRMT_NAME_VALUE_PAIR,
      lr_factory type ref to CL_CRM_BOL_ENTITY_FACTORY,
      lr_result  type ref to IF_BOL_ENTITY_COL,
      lr_booking type ref to CL_CRM_BOL_ENTITY,
      lr_tcontext type ref to IF_BOL_TRANSACTION_CONTEXT,
      lv_success type abap_bool,
      lr_product type ref to CL_CRM_BOL_ENTITY,
      lv_guest  type string,
      lv_checkin  type string.

TRY .
  "load the ZBOOK component set
  lr_core = cl_crm_bol_core=>GET_INSTANCE( ).
  lr_core->START_UP( 'ZBOOK' ).
CATCH CX_CRM_GENIL_GENERAL_ERROR.
  exit.
ENDTRY.
"prepare the creation parameters
ls_param-NAME = 'GUEST_ID'.
ls_param-VALUE = '0000401264'.
append ls_param to lt_param.
ls_param-NAME = 'HOTEL_NAME'.
ls_param-VALUE = 'VILLA VERDE'.
append ls_param to lt_param.
ls_param-NAME = 'LASTCHECKIN'.
ls_param-VALUE = '20101111'.
append ls_param to lt_param.
"obtain Bookings factory
lr_factory = lr_core->GET_ENTITY_FACTORY( 'Bookings' ).
"create Bookings instance
lr_booking = lr_factory->CREATE( lt_param ).
"create product
TRY .
  lr_product = lr_booking->CREATE_RELATED_ENTITY(
      IV_RELATION_NAME = 'BookingProductsRel' ).
  LOOP AT lt_param into ls_param.
    lr_product->SET_PROPERTY(
      IV_ATTR_NAME = ls_param-name
      IV_VALUE     = ls_param-value ).
  ENDLOOP.
```

```
lr_product->SET_PROPERTY(
    IV_ATTR_NAME = 'PRODUCT_ID'
    IV_VALUE     = '4F1C6E8ED3CCD411858800902761A739').
lr_product->SET_PROPERTY(
    IV_ATTR_NAME = 'USAGE_DATE'
    IV_VALUE     = '20101111').
lr_core->MODIFY( ).
CATCH CX_CRM_GENIL_DUPLICATE_REL.
CATCH CX_CRM_GENIL_MODEL_ERROR.
ENDTRY.

"save and commit
lr_tcontext = lr_core->GET_TRANSACTION( ).
lv_success = lr_tcontext->SAVE( ).
IF lv_success = abap_true.
  lr_tcontext->COMMIT( ).
ELSE.
  lr_tcontext->ROLLBACK( ).
ENDIF.
```

Listing 5.7 Creating a Dependent Object

In order to create a dependent object, you need to know how it is related to the parent (its relation name). For example:

```
lr_product = lr_booking->CREATE_RELATED_ENTITY(
    IV_RELATION_NAME = 'BookingProductsRel' ).
```

Next we set all the required properties. We use the previously created name-value pair table which contains the Bookings key attributes. In addition we add the UsedProducts specific key attributes, for example:

```
lr_product->SET_PROPERTY( IV_ATTR_NAME = 'PRODUCT_ID'
          IV_VALUE     = '4F1C6E8ED3CCD411858800902761A739').
```

The above snippet demonstrates how to set properties on BOL entities. Each time you modify an entity, you can set individual attributes via the SET_PROPERTY method.

Do not forget to call MODIFY on the BOL core. It will trigger the MODIFY_OBJECTS in your GenIL class. The rest of the code is related to making the modifications persistent in the buffer and committing the transaction.

Based on the last example, it is easy to deduce that in order to modify application data via BOL you need to retrieve the relevant BOL entities, change their properties via SET_PROPERTY, call MODIFY, and save the changes. Instead of setting the properties one by one, you can also prepare a data structure with all the values (the attribute structure from your GenIL model node) and call SET_PROPERTIES. This method expects the attribute structure of your GenIL business object.

5.1.4 Deleting Data

Recall that when we were testing our GenIL component we differentiated between deleting a root object and removing dependent objects. The deletion of a dependent object is a modification of the corresponding root object. This is why, after calling DELETE of the dependent BOL entity, you have to call MODIFY and then perform the transaction commit.

In order to delete a GenIL root business object, we relied on the DELETE_OBEJCTS method of the component class. Unlike any other method in the GenIL, this one did not require a special call to SAVE_OBJECTS but was in effect able to complete the entire task. Listing 5.8 shows how you can delete a root object via the BOL API.

```
data: lr_core type ref to cl_crm_bol_core,
      lr_query type ref to CL_CRM_BOL_DQUERY_SERVICE,
      lr_result  type ref to IF_BOL_ENTITY_COL,
      lr_booking type ref to CL_CRM_BOL_ENTITY.

TRY .
  lr_core = cl_crm_bol_core=>GET_INSTANCE( ).
  lr_core->START_UP( 'ZBOOK' ).
  lr_query = CL_CRM_BOL_DQUERY_SERVICE=>GET_INSTANCE( 'SearchBookings'
).
  lr_query->ADD_SELECTION_PARAM( IV_ATTR_NAME = 'LASTCHECKIN'
                      IV_SIGN = 'I'
                      IV_OPTION = 'EQ'
                      IV_LOW = '20101111'
                      IV_HIGH = '').
  lr_result = LR_QUERY->GET_QUERY_RESULT( ).
  "get the first (and hopefuly the only one)
  lr_booking = lr_result->GET_FIRST( ).
  IF lr_booking is bound.
    lr_booking->DELETE( ).
  ENDIF.
CATCH CX_CRM_GENIL_GENERAL_ERROR.
ENDTRY.
```

Listing 5.8 Deleting a Root Entity

First we need to retrieve the entity we want to delete. We do this by executing this query:

```
lr_query->ADD_SELECTION_PARAM( IV_ATTR_NAME = 'LASTCHECKIN'
                               IV_SIGN = 'I'
                               IV_OPTION = 'EQ'
                               IV_LOW = '20101111'
                               IV_HIGH = '' ).
lr_result = LR_QUERY->GET_QUERY_RESULT( ).
```

We expect only one entry in the query result:

```
lr_booking = lr_result->GET_FIRST( ).
```

Now that we have found a matching entity, we call its DELETE method:

```
lr_booking->DELETE( ).
```

Note that you do not need to explicitly call a transaction commit. The changes are made persistent via an internal COMMIT WORK.

5.1.5   Locking

Although we created, modified, and deleted BOL entities, we never locked them. If you had inserted a breakpoint in the LOCK method of the GenIL component, you would have seen that it is actually being called. The truth is that you do not have to explicitly lock a BOL entity. For example, SET_PROPERTIES will try to lock the object if a lock has not been set.

Locks are always set on a root object. It takes just one line of code to do so:

```
lv_success = lr_root_entity->lock( ).
```

In order to see if the lock was successfully set you can check the value of the returned CRMT_BOOLEAN parameter (should be ABAP_TRUE).

5.1.6   Sorting BOL Collections

Suppose that you want to modify the results of the data manipulation prior to displaying them. A common operation is to sort the result; for example by date or price. Imagine that in our guest booking example, we want to sort the bookings by the membership type. Listing 5.9 should convince you that this is a very simple task.

```
data: lr_core type ref to cl_crm_bol_core,
      lr_query type ref to CL_CRM_BOL_DQUERY_SERVICE,
      lr_result  type ref to IF_BOL_ENTITY_COL,
      lr_iter   type ref to IF_BOL_ENTITY_COL_ITERATOR,
      lr_booking type ref to CL_CRM_BOL_ENTITY,
      lv_guest  type string,
      lv_checkin  type string,
      lv_membership  type string.
"load the ZBOOK component set
lr_core = cl_crm_bol_core=>GET_INSTANCE( ).
lr_core->START_UP( 'ZBOOK' ).
"get the query service
lr_query = CL_CRM_BOL_DQUERY_SERVICE=>GET_INSTANCE(
                    'SearchBookings' ).
"execute the query and get the results
lr_result = LR_QUERY->GET_QUERY_RESULT( ).
"sort
lr_result->SORT( IV_ATTR_NAME = 'MEMBERSHIP'
            IV_SORT_ORDER = IF_BOL_BO_COL->SORT_ASCENDING ).
"iterate through the resutls
lr_iter = lr_result->GET_ITERATOR( ).
lr_booking = lr_iter->GET_FIRST( ).
WHILE lr_booking is bound.
  lv_membership = lr_booking->GET_PROPERTY_AS_STRING(
                      'MEMBERSHIP' ).
  lv_guest = lr_booking->GET_PROPERTY_AS_STRING( 'GUEST_ID' ).
  lv_checkin =lr_booking->GET_PROPERTY_AS_STRING('LASTCHECKIN' ).
  write: / lv_membership, ', ', lv_guest, ', ', lv_checkin.
  lr_booking = lr_iter->GET_NEXT( ).
ENDWHILE.
```

Listing 5.9 Sorting of BOL Collection

The above example code should look quite familiar except for one section, namely:

```
lr_result->SORT( IV_ATTR_NAME = 'MEMBERSHIP'
            IV_SORT_ORDER = IF_BOL_BO_COL=>SORT_ASCENDING ).
```

With the above code, we tell the framework to sort the resulting BOL collection by MEMBERSHIP and in ascending order.

Please note that the sorting is alphabetical. Therefore, if you need to sort other data types, such as dates, you will have to provide your implementation of IF_BOL_COL_SORTING interface.

5.1.7 Final Recommendations

The above introduction to BOL programming should be sufficient to get you started. Take a look at the interfaces and classes outlined here, and practice on your own. When in doubt, write a simple report and see how the API behaves.

You can also check the SDN for *BOL Application Programming Guide*. It provides a comprehensive overview of the BOL API. The availability of that SDN resource is one reason we were able to stick to the basics without overburdening you with details.

Remember that you should try to work with the IF_BOL_BO_PROPERTY_ACCESS interface. This allows you to access collections in a generic way and work with both entities and queries. Any BOL entity object can be cast to IF_BOL_BO_PROPERTY_ACCESS.

5.2 UI Component Development

In the previous chapter, we have built a search-result application in a rather manual way using the basic means provided in the application builder (Transaction SE80). We have built one by one the individual parts of our application and connected them programmatically by adding the relevant commands in different parts of our code. As we have seen, this approach is error prone and does not enable the developer to focus on what really matters for them: business logic. The Component Workbench—Transaction BSP_WD_CMPWB—solves these issues. In the next sections, we will use it to build a new version of the search-result application, and we will enhance it with an overview page and editing capabilities.

In Section 5.2.1, we will briefly analyze the structure of the application that we are to build. In Section 5.2.2, we will create the main component of our application and assign it a model. Then, in Section 5.2.3, we will build a search page consisting of the actual search area and the result area. As we will see in the discussions that follow, a custom controller is necessary for data exchange inside the application. We will create a custom controller for our application in Section 5.2.4. In Section 5.2.5 and subsequent sections, we will create various views, forms, and tables, and we will configure the overview page that comprises a header area and an assignment block. Finally, in Section 5.2.9 we will enable navigation inside our application so that the user can navigate from the result page to the overview of a specific entry. By the end of this chapter, you will be able to use the Component Workbench to build a full blown application. For more advanced topics, you will need to wait until the next chapter.

5.2.1 The Anatomy of the Hotel Booking Application

The hotel booking application consists of a search page that contains a search area and a result area, and an overview page. Navigation from the result list to the overview page is done through a link. From a technical perspective, the search page consists of a view set that contains two views: the search view and the result view. The overview page is a special type of a view set and contains assignment blocks, which are essentially views that are added to the overview page through customizing. Both the search and the overview pages are contained in a window. Figure 5.8 gives an overall picture of the hotel bookings application.

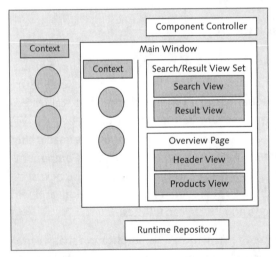

Figure 5.8 Hotel Bookings Application Technical Overview

As you can see in Figure 5.8, the individual components of the application are hosted in a Web UI component that represents the whole application. We start our journey by building this outer component.

5.2.2 Creating a Component and Defining the Model

As we have seen earlier, the Web UI component is the glue that keeps together the individual components of a Web UI application. To create the hotel bookings Web UI components:

1. Start Transaction BSP_WD_CMPWB.

2. Enter the name of the component, for example ZCMP_BOOK_HTL.

3. Click on CREATE.

4. Besides the name of the component, you will be asked for the description of the window and the name of the main window, as shown in Figure 5.9.

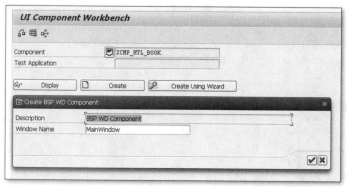

Figure 5.9 Creating a New Component

Once you have confirmed the data entered in the pop-up, you will get a pop-up window asking you repeatedly to specify the package and the transport request. You might wonder why this pop-up comes up more than once. The answer lies in the earlier definition of a UI component: a bundle of views, controllers, context nodes, and runtime repository. As you might have guessed, these are ABAP objects that are created one by one and each needs to be assigned an ABAP package and transport request. Because you might choose to assign different packages to different objects and require information about the objects that are created, you are asked to confirm for each and every one of them. The following two figures give you two different views of the objects that you have just created. Figure 5.10 gives the Component Workbench view, while Figure 5.11 gives the classical object navigation view (Transaction SE80).

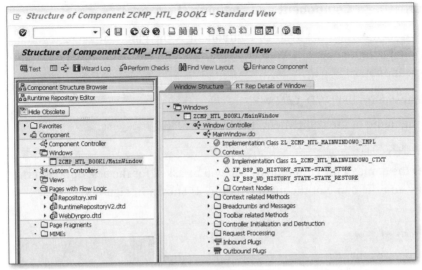

Figure 5.10 Structure of Component ZCMP_HTL_BOOK

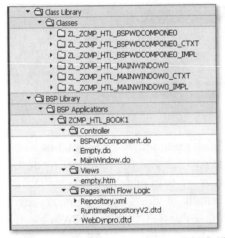

Figure 5.11 View of BSP Application ZCMP_HTL_BOOK in Repository Browser of Transaction SE80

In Figure 5.10 (and on your screen if you are recreating this example) you can see that once it is created, a new UI component contains the following elements:

▶ A window, which has its controller MainWindow.do and its implementation class ZL_ZCMP_HTL_MAINWINDOW_IMPL

- A window context implementation class `ZL_ZCMP_HTL_MAINWINDOW_CTXT`

- A component controller BSPWDComponent.do with its implementation class `ZL_ZCMP_HTL_BSPWDCOMPONEN_IMPL`

- A component controller's context implementation class `ZL_ZCMP_HTL_BSPWDCOMPONEN_CTXT`

- Three pages with flow logic: a runtime repository XML and two DTD files

The view in Figure 5.10 is the main view of your component that you will use while building and modifying your UI components.

Transaction SE80 offers an alternative view of the application. In Figure 5.11, we can see the different components of a MVC based BSP application: view, controllers, and models, as well as what makes this BSP application a true Web UI component: a runtime repository. Furthermore, this view helps us better understand why we were asked so many times to confirm the package and transport request. We will not come back to this view, because a much more convenient way of working with a UI component is through the Component Workbench. Furthermore, while this view uses simple ABAP nomenclature for different objects, the Component Workbench provides names that are more appropriate to the UI component.

Our hotel booking component has most of the elements that make it a real MVC BSP application. However, we did not yet define the data model our application will be based on. Remember that a UI component may be built on top of a GenIL component set. This will allow you to use the available GenIL business objects as models for your views (in the context of MVC). To define the model:

1. Click on the RUNTIME REPOSITORY EDITOR.

2. Switch to edit mode.

3. If not already expanded, expand the node COMPONENT.

4. Right-click on the node MODELS.

5. Choose ADD MODEL. You will be prompted to select a component set as shown in Figure 5.12. Enter the name of the component set ZBOOK that you have created in Chapter 4.

6. Save.

You could have achieved the same result as in the steps above by directly and manually editing the runtime repository XML. As a matter of fact, if you return to the COMPONENT STRUCTURE BROWSER and open the file `Repository.xml`, you will see that an entry was added to the node <Models>. Using the tools and wizards provided in the Component Workbench is more elegant and less error prone; manually editing the runtime repository XML is strongly discouraged.

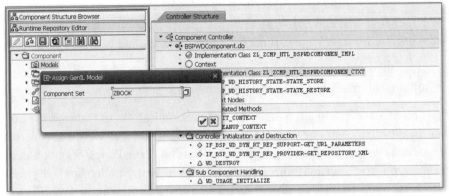

Figure 5.12 Assigning Component Set to UI Component

Now that we have created our UI component, defined the main window, and assigned a model, it is time to create the views that make our hotel booking application. The standard pattern of Web UI application is to search, display the results, choose among the retrieved objects with which you want to work, navigate to its overview page, and edit it, if necessary. This is exactly the sequence of activities we will follow.

5.2.3 Creating a Search Page

As you might have guessed, we have to create our search page in the node VIEWS of our component. As we know by now, a search page is a view set that hosts a search query view and a result view. To create the search page, follow these steps:

1. Right-click on the node VIEWS.

2. Select CREATE SEARCH PAGE. On the next pop-up (see Figure 5.13), you will be notified that only dynamic query objects can be used in this wizard.

3. Specify the view names and the window name. Most developers have adopted the practice of including some abbreviation of "advanced search" or "search query" in the name of the search area view, an abbreviation of "result view" in the result area view, and "VS" in the view set. This is a good practice, similar to code conventions, because it enhances the readability of the elements of the UI

component, making navigation through the code easy. Figure 5.14 shows how your views might look.

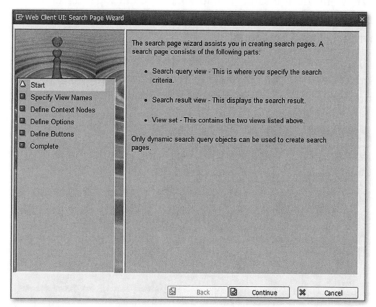

Figure 5.13 Search Page Wizard

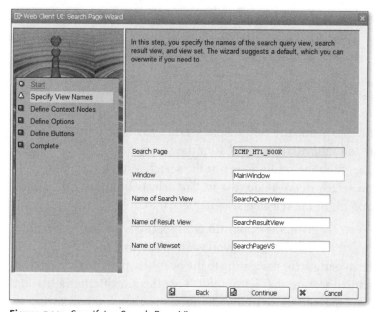

Figure 5.14 Specifying Search Page Views

4. At this point, although you can specify a new window name, we recommend that you specify the same window you did when creating the UI component. Creating all the views inside the same window keeps them together and—as we will see in handling navigational events—it makes navigation internal to the component rather than cross-component.

5. Specify the search query and result nodes. The search and query nodes are the model of the search page. Use the F4 help to retrieve the appropriate node, as shown in Figure 5.15.

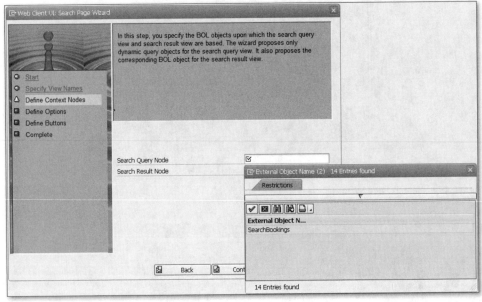

Figure 5.15 Selection of Search Query Node

6. The F4 help searches inside the component set that you have provided in the previous section and returns all nodes that fit the search query (for the search query node) or that fit to the result node (for the search result node). Once you have selected the search query node, the wizard selects by default the result node that corresponds to the selected search query node.

7. In the next step, you are given the opportunity to specify whether you want to use saved searches, the type of selection you want to use, and the field that you want to use as the hyperlink for navigating to the overview page. Saved searches are a very convenient feature that let the user save the search criteria that he uses frequently and execute those frequently used searches without having to

re-enter the search criteria. Furthermore, as we will see in discussing additional features, the saved searches can be shared among users. Using the ⟨F4⟩ helps, select the UI object type, under which the searches will be saved.

8. In order to prepare the ground for handling events, select the SINGLE SELECTION OPTION. We will use a button to navigate to the details of the selected object.

9. Use the APPEND ROW or INSERT ROW to add a new row to the list of fields that will be shown as navigation links. In the ⟨F4⟩ help, select HOTEL_NAME. Note that ⟨F4⟩ presents you with a limited list of fields. These are fields from the DDIC structure ZBOL_BOOKING_ATT. In line with our GenIL model, the SearchBookings query has a result node of type Bookings (we chose to return the root object instead of a query result object). ZBOL_BOOKING_ATT is the attribute structure of the Bookings business object. Note also that you can add as many navigational fields as you want. This is convenient when you want to navigate to different pages from the result page. For example, in the result list of some business opportunities you might want to navigate to the overview page of the opportunity, to the overview page of the business partner, or to the overview page of the employee responsible. The following figure shows our selection of options in the hotel booking application.

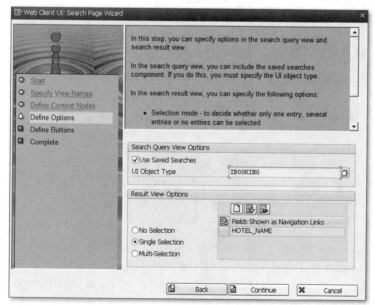

Figure 5.16 Defining Search and Result View Options

10. In order to define actions in the result list, add buttons. If you are following our sample implementation, add a button to navigate to the selected object and specify the name of the event. Your definition of buttons will look like the one in Figure 5.17.

11. Once you have defined the buttons, select CONTINUE and then COMPLETE. You will notice that once again you will be asked repeatedly to specify the package and the transport request. This happens for the same reasons as when we were creating the UI component.

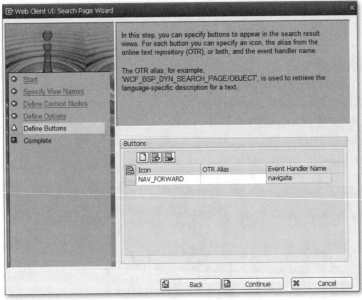

Figure 5.17 Defining Buttons in Search Result List

Once your objects have been created and activated, you are only a couple clicks away from finishing your search page. Note that the activation happens automatically and you don't need to manually activate anything. Before continuing, let's take a look at what actually happened.

First of all, under the node VIEWS in the Component Structure Browser, you will notice the three views that you have just created: the search query view, the search result view, and the search page view set. To see how they are bound together, go to the RUNTIME REPOSITORY EDITOR and expand the node VIEWSETS.You will see that the search page view set contains two view areas, one that contains the search query view and one that contains the search result view. Still in the RUNTIME REPOSITORY EDITOR, under WINDOWS, you will notice inbound plugs that are used to enter the search components and that are attached to their respective navigational links. The search page view set is currently set as the default view set for the main window. Figure 5.18 presents an expanded view of the runtime repository.

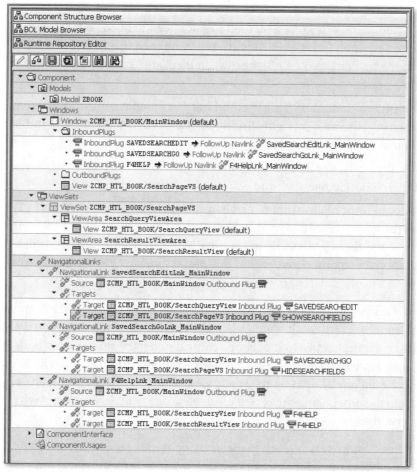

Figure 5.18 Runtime Repository View after Creating Search Page

You will also notice that each navigational link has a source and at least one target. This concept will become clearer once we are done with the example. At this point, it suffices to note that these links are basically connections between the two views (typically). The source is an outbound plug from one view and the target is the inbound plug to another view.

Go back to the COMPONENT STRUCTURE BROWSER and explore the various objects that have been created in each view. When you expand a node, you will notice different icons in front of methods, event handlers, and inbound and outbound plugs. Here is a brief description of the icons that you can influence:

▶ A gray diamond indicates that a method has not been defined; you can define it in the corresponding class, which is always mentioned in a higher node. For context node attributes, you can right-click on them and choose from the menu the one you want to generate.

▶ A yellow triangle indicates that a method has been implemented in a parent class; you can redefine it by right-clicking on it and choosing REDEFINE in the context menu.

▶ A green square indicates that the method is defined in the current implementation class; you can double-click and edit or modify it.

▶ A black dot in front of an attribute name means that none of the GET and SET methods (be it a V-, a P-, an I-, or any other getter) has been generated. You can generate any of them or all of them together by right-clicking on the attribute and choosing the appropriate entry in the context menu. We will discuss the GET and SET methods later on.

In the search query view, the wizard has inserted two context nodes: the search query node and the search result node. When you analyze the result view, you will notice that the wizard has inserted only one context node: the search result node. As with the example of the search page that we created manually, the search view needs to know the model used by the result view so that it can set the results of the search. On the other hand, the search result view does not need to know what the search criteria were.

This "awareness" of the search result model is brought to the search view through context node binding. In order to share data that would otherwise be internal and known only to the view, context nodes are bound to the main window context nodes. This ensures that when the search view has retrieved the search results and has set them into its own search result node, these will be visible right away in the result view because both views' result context nodes are bound to the same window context node. Besides the context nodes, you will notice in Figure 5.19

that the event handlers have been created. For the time being, we will skip the nodes CONTEXT RELATED METHODS, BREADCRUMBS AND MESSAGES, and TOOLBAR RELATED METHODS because we have no toolbars in the search view CONTROLLER INITIALIZATION AND DESTRUCTION and REQUEST PROCESSING.

The event handler EH_ONCLEAR is used to clear the search criteria and reset the result list. The event handler EH_ONSEARCH is used to trigger the actual search. The other event handlers are used to handle various events in the search query area. These include adding a new line to a group of search criteria, changing the search criteria by selecting a new one, pasting multiple search criteria from a spreadsheet, and deleting search criteria either as a group or individually.

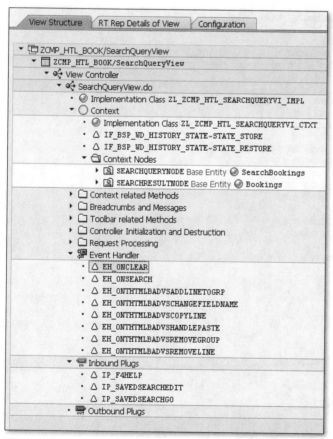

Figure 5.19 Expanded View of Search Query View

By double-clicking on the event handler EH_ONSEARCH, you can take a look at the code generated for the search event and compare to the code that we have written for our search event in the manual version of our search-result application.

Figure 5.20 gives a partial view of the generated search result view structure. First of all, we can see that method GET_TABLE_LINE_SAMPLE has been implemented. If you double-click on it, you will see the code in Listing 5.10.

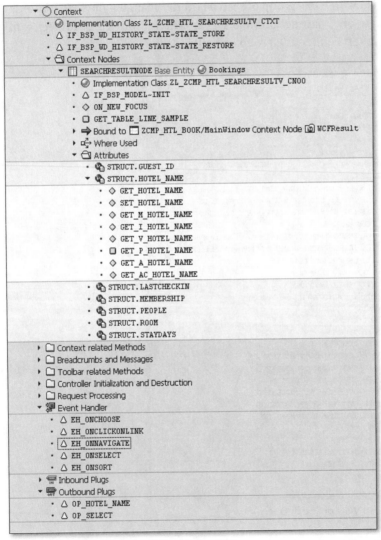

Figure 5.20 Expanded View of Search Result View

```
METHOD get_table_line_sample.
  TYPES: BEGIN OF line,
    include TYPE zbol_bookings_att.
  TYPES: END OF line.
  CREATE DATA rv_sample TYPE line.
ENDMETHOD.
```

Listing 5.10 Definition of Table Line

This method creates and returns a reference to a data type that it defined. The type line includes only the structure ZBOL_BOOKINGS_ATT. This is the same structure that populated the F4 help that we saw during the definition of fields to be used as navigational links in the result lists. As we mentioned, this is coming from our GenIL model. You can see also in the BOL MODEL BROWSER that this is the underlying structure of the dynamic query object SearchBookings. If you want to extend the result list with fields that are not included in the dynamic query object, you can add those new fields in the type line above. Those fields will appear in the configuration of your table.

You can see that method GET_P_HOTEL_NAME has been defined. This should look familiar: When creating the search page, we selected HOTEL_NAME as a navigational link. The definition of HOTEL_NAME as a navigational link has been translated in method GET_P_HOTEL_NAME into the code in Listing 5.11. Note that defining navigational links and events is not the only purpose of the GET_P_x methods. We will come back to this subject.

```
CASE iv_property.
  WHEN if_bsp_wd_model_setter_getter=>fp_fieldtype.
    rv_value = cl_bsp_dlc_view_descriptor=>field_type_event_link
  WHEN if_bsp_wd_model_setter_getter=>fp_onclick.
    rv_value = 'CLICKONLINK'.
ENDCASE.
```

Listing 5.11 Definition of Field as Navigational Link

In the listing above, you can see that the event attached to the navigation link is CLICKONLINK. Because this is an event, we can be sure that there is a corresponding event handler; otherwise nothing will happen when we click on the link. We find the event handler under the name EH_ONCLICKONLINK. We will come back to the implementation of this event handler as well as the outbound plug OP_HOTEL_NAME when we discuss navigation.

Now that we have created all the components that we need to have a full blown search page, we can proceed with configuring it. You might have noticed that the search query and the search result view structures have a tab called CONFIGURATION. This tab is present only in those views that are configurable. Because the search page view set is not configurable, it does not have such a tab.

Configuring a view amounts to defining what fields we want visible and how we want them to be displayed. We start with the search query view.

1. Click on the CONFIGURATION tab and wait until all the fields are loaded. You get a view where you are presented with a list of all available fields in one column and fields that have been selected as search criteria in another column.

2. Create a new configuration. Accept the proposed default values in the pop-up. We will come back later to the creation of multiple configurations.

3. Select the fields you want to be part of the search criteria and—using either drag and drop or the small yellow arrow—add them to the SELECTED SEARCH CRITERIA list.

4. Using the appropriate checkbox, specify those fields that you want to be visible. Those that you choose not to be displayed will still exist in the search query view, but on initial load they will remain in the search criteria dropdown list boxes without being directly visible.

5. Choose the default operator.

6. Save.

Once you have saved, your configured view will look like Figure 5.21.

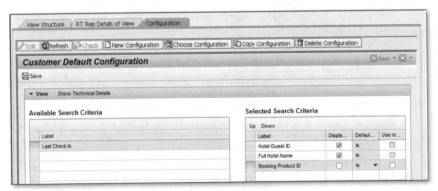

Figure 5.21   Configuration of Search Query View

In the example shown in Figure 5.21, the search view will start with three search criteria, and all of them will have the operator IS as the default operator. The LAST CHECK IN field will not be available in the search criteria, while the BOOKING PRODUCT ID field will remain the search criteria but will not be initially visible. We can now proceed with configuration of the result view.

1. Double-click on the search result view and choose the CONFIGURATION tab.

2. Switch to edit mode by clicking on the EDIT button.

3. Select the fields that you want to be displayed as part of the result list and specify whether they will be visible or hidden.

4. Save.

You can specify the VISIBLE ROWS BEFORE PAGING and the VISIBLE ROWS BEFORE SCROLLING. The first attribute will determine the number of rows that are displayed on each page of a table with a pager and the second attribute will determine the number of rows that are displayed before a scrollbar appears. Fields left on the AVAILABLE FIELDS tab will not be displayed and those that are marked as hidden will be available for personalization, even though they will not be visible upon initial load of the table. Furthermore, you can specify the column width as well as the field alignment. If you do not do this, the rendering tag will adjust the width of the columns depending on the length of the underlying data elements and the alignment will follow predefined rules. Once you have saved your configuration, your view will look like Figure 5.22.

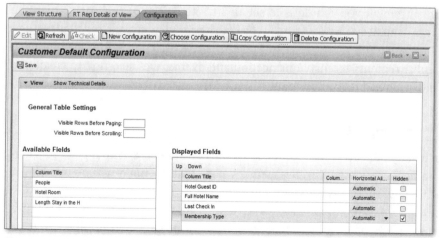

Figure 5.22 Configuration of Search Result View

You have just produced an operational Web Client UI advanced search page. Without writing a single line of code, we have created a full-blown search page. You can now click on the test button and watch the result unfold.

If you have followed our example, your application will look like the one in Figure 5.23.

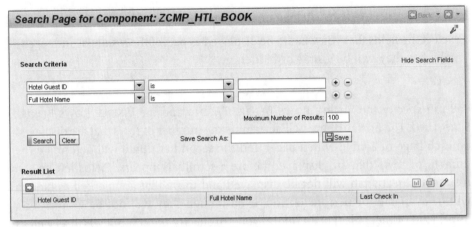

Figure 5.23 Hotel Booking Application Search Page

You can experiment with the application. Perform a search, clear the results, drag and drop the columns, or click on the personalization button to add or remove columns in the result lists.

One enhancement you can do is to set an attractive title for this page. Open the node BREADCRUMBS AND MESSAGES in the search page view set, and redefine method IF_BSP_WD_HISTORY_STATE_DESCR~GET_STATE_DESCRIPTION. Before making even more enhancements to enable navigation and events, we need first to create the overview page and its components.

5.2.4 Creating a Custom Controller

As discussed in the previous chapter, a custom controller is a central place for sharing data between views. On the overview page that we build will be two views, a header view, and an assignment block containing used hotel products. In order for these two views to share data, we have to create a custom controller. Later, we will bind nodes that are local to those two views to the custom controller. To create the custom controller, follow these steps:

1. In the Component Structure Browser, right-click on the node Custom Control-lers and choose Create.

2. Once you have provided a name—CucoBookings in our case—add the model name and the corresponding BOL entity using the [F4] help as illustrated in Figure 5.24.

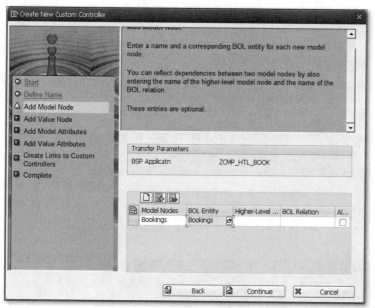

Figure 5.24 Definition of Model Node

3. You can base your custom controller on more than one node and use a combination of model and value nodes. The following step asks you to specify a value node. However, this is optional, and we do not use a value node in our sample implementation. Therefore, simply click on Continue.

4. You do not have to use all the attributes of a model node. Therefore, in the next step, you have to select the attributes of the model node that you want to use. To do this, click on the function Add Model Attributes. Because you have specified a model node, this function displays all the attributes of that model node. You only have to select those that you would like to see in the view. As illustrated in Figure 5.25, we select all the attributes. Note also that besides the attributes, the [F4] help displays any relationship between this BOL entity and other entities.

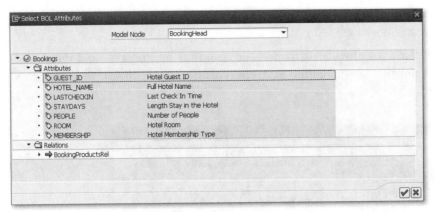

Figure 5.25 Selection of Model Node Attributes

5. Once you have selected the model node attributes you will see a screen similar to Figure 5.26. On that screen, you can change the name of the model nodes. You might want to do this to increase the readability of your components, especially if you find that the default names, which are those of the underlying BOL attributes, are not user friendly enough. Note, however, that you cannot change the BOL attribute name or the model node name.

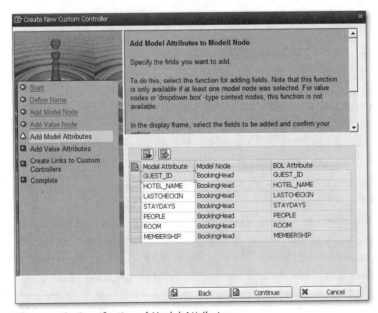

Figure 5.26 Specification of Model Attributes

6. In the next step you can add value attributes to any of the context nodes that you have specified previously. This is useful when you want to manipulate information that does not come from the BOL and that you can compute or retrieve manually. Note that if you add a value attribute to a model node, that node will be created as a mixed node. If you use multiple nodes in a view and you need to add value attributes, add them to the node that contains the any fields you need to use in order to deduct the value of your value attribute. This will ease the access to those fields. In this example, we will not use value attributes, therefore, click on CONTINUE to skip this step.

7. Click on CONTINUE to skip the next step that asks you to link your node to a custom controller.

8. Confirm the final steps.

Once you have created your custom controller, it will appear in the COMPONENT STRUCTURE BROWSER. You now have a node to which you can bind other nodes from different views to ease data exchange between them. The following step is to create those views.

5.2.5 Creating Form Views

The purpose of the search page that we have created in the previous section is to help the user retrieve objects and display a summary of the most important fields in a list view. For a deeper analysis of the object and eventually for editing it, the user needs a more detailed view. In this section we will create a view that contains details of a booking. Such a view is typically called a header view and contains the most important information that a user needs to have at one glance. In a way similar to the process of creating a search page, we have to specify the model on which the view will be based. This is the most important activity required from us from an MVC perspective, given that the controllers and the views will be automatically created by the wizard. Once the view is created, we will have the opportunity to configure it. To create the header view of the hotel booking application, follow these steps:

1. In the Component Structure Browser, right-click on the node VIEWS and choose CREATE.

2. You will notice that the wizard for creating a view looks like the wizard you used to create a custom controller. The reason is simple: Except for the visual part, which does not exist in the custom controller, the two wizards are similar.

Therefore, follow exactly the same steps as during the creation of the custom controller, up to the step in which you are asked to link your node to a custom controller.

3. As shown in Figure 5.27, link the context node that you have created to the custom controller. To do this, select the context node in the first column, enter the name of the BSP application ZCMP_HTL_BOOK, use the [F4] help in the third column to retrieve the custom controller and the [F4] help in the last column to retrieve the context node to which you want to bind your context node. This binding ensures that data will be shared between the view and the custom controller and with any other context node bound to the same context node.

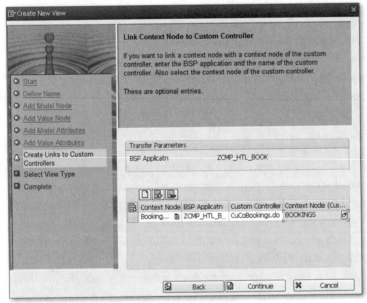

Figure 5.27 Linking Context Node to Custom Controller

4. The last step is to select the view type, as shown in Figure 5.28. Select the form view without buttons and ensure that the view is configurable by selecting the checkbox CONFIGURABLE. Because we want to use this view both for display and edit, also select the checkbox CHANGE/DISPLAY MODE.

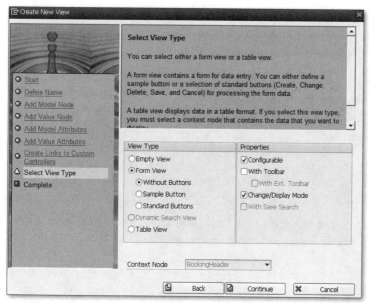

Figure 5.28 Selection of View Type

Once you have confirmed the last step, you have to assign packages and transport to the multiple objects—controller classes, context nodes, and views—that are created at the end of the wizard process. After activation, you will see a new view in the Component Structure Browser. Take time to explore the structure of your new view. You will note, among other things, that the binding of the context node BookingHeader is displayed in the component structure, that SET and GET methods have been implemented and that an htm view has been created. If you open the BookingHeader.htm file you will notice that it contains only one tag with two attributes. The first attribute specifies the display mode. This is related to the last checkbox that we set in the wizard. The second attribute indicates that the tag expects the controller to provide it with the view configuration data. For the time being, simply set the tag attribute displayMode to true. Unless you have very specific needs, you only have to configure your view in order to complete it. Let us set the layout of our header view.

5.2.6 Configuring Form Views

Now that we have added the fields that we want to display to the header view, it is time to design the view exactly as we would like it to be displayed. In order to

275

do this, we need to configure our view. The following actions will help complete the header of our hotel booking application. You can configure the header view on the CONFIGURATION tab in the Component Workbench.

1. Create a new configuration and accept all the defaulted values. Alternatively, you can simply click on the EDIT button.

2. Click on the SHOW AVAILABLE FIELDS button. You will see the context node BOOKINGHEADER. When you expand it, the fields that you can choose from are shown.

3. Select all fields or a subset of the fields that you want to display and click on the small plus sign to add the selected fields to the right panel.

4. Using drag and drop, rearrange the fields and redistribute them in two columns. Figure 5.29 shows how your configured view could look.

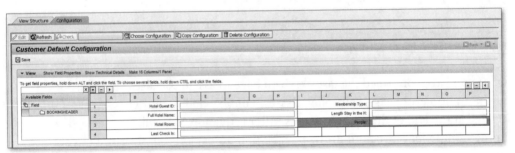

Figure 5.29   Configuration of Header View

5. Save your configuration.

You have configured your header view. We will see more details on configuration and how to create multiple configurations later in the book. For now, we will proceed with the creation of another view, this one to display additional bookings belonging to the same guest.

5.2.7   Creating Table Views

Creating table views is much like creating form views. However, there are two important concerns. First, we are not creating a totally independent view. The view we are creating will hold information that depends on the information displayed in the header view. In line with our example, we will show the products that the guest used during a stay in a hotel. This implies that there is a need for data exchange between the header view and the table of used products. Therefore, during the creation of the table view we have to ensure this master-slave relationship between the two views and the need for data exchange between them. To create the list of additional bookings, follow these steps below:

1. In the Component Structure Browser, right-click on the node VIEWS and choose CREATE and give a name to the view.

2. In the next step, add two model nodes. We do this in order to facilitate the data exchange, as you will see later. First, add a model node with BOL entity Book-ings. Then use the APPEND ROW button to add a new entry. Specify a name (we have chosen "MoreBookings") and choose the BOL entity UsedProducts. Using the [F4] help, select the higher-level node and the BOL relation. The higher-level node will be the one that you have added in the first row. This is automatically suggested because—if you look in the BOL Model Browser—you will see that there is a relationship between BOL entity Bookings and UsedProducts. Once you have added the two model nodes, your screen will look like the one in Figure 5.30.

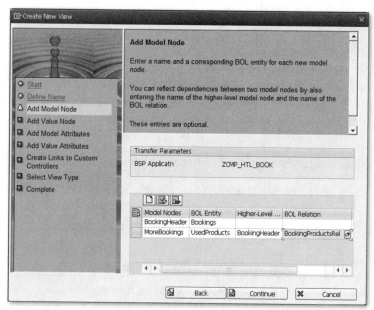

Figure 5.30 Adding Model Nodes to View, Showing BOL Relation

3. Continue with the next steps and add model attributes. In the ⌐F4⌐ help, select the model node `MoreBookings` from the dropdown list box and then select the fields you want to add to your view. Note that you can achieve the same result by selecting the `BookingHeader` model node and then selecting the same fields through its relation `UsedProducts`. Figure 5.31 shows the first approach.

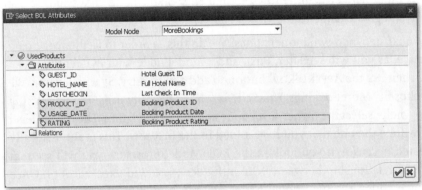

Figure 5.31 Selection of Fields to be Added to Additional Booking View

4. Continue with the next steps and create a link between the `BookingHeader` context node and the corresponding context node from the custom controller. This step is exactly the same as a similar step you performed when creating the header view.

5. Select the view type as being TABLE VIEW and configurable. Make sure also to choose the right context node: `MoreBookings`. As we do not plan to do editing in this view, we will not select the option to switch between display and change modes.

6. Complete the steps; confirm packages and transport requests, if applicable.

When you double-click on the newly created view, you might get a message stating that your view is not defined in the runtime repository that was loaded. This is understandable, because we did not yet add the newly created views to the runtime repository.

You now can proceed with configuration of the used-products view. To configure this view, you have to follow the same steps that we have followed to configure the search result list. Both this view and the result list view are based on the configurable table; therefore they are configured in the same way.

Now that we have the two views that are to be part of our overview page, we can create the overview page itself.

5.2.8 Creating an Overview Page

To create an overview page, right-click on the node VIEWS in the Component Structure Browser and chose CREATE OVERVIEW PAGE. The only information you have to provide is the name of the overview page. Once you have done this, switch to the RUNTIME REPOSITORY EDITOR. You will see that a new view set with the name of your overview page has been added with one view area called OverviewPage. As you know, an overview page is a collection of assignment blocks that are themselves based on views and view sets. Therefore, you need to add the two views that you created earlier to the overview page. To do this:

1. Switch to the RUNTIME REPOSITORY EDITOR if you have not already done so.
2. Switch to EDIT mode.
3. Expand the node that represents your overview page. If you are following our example this will be `ZCMP_HTL_BOOK/HotelBookingOVP`.
4. Right-click on the `OverviewPage` view and add the `BookingHeader` and `MoreBookings` views.
5. Right-click on the main window under the WINDOWS node and choose ADD VIEW to add your overview page.
6. Save.

Once you have added your views to the overview page and the overview page to the main window, your RUNTIME REPOSITORY EDITOR will look like the screen in Figure 5.32.

After having created the overview page, you need to configure it by following these simple steps:

1. Select the overview page in the COMPONENT STRUCTURE BROWSER.
2. Go to the CONFIGURATION tab.
3. Switch to EDIT mode.
4. Choose OVERVIEW PAGE as the configuration type and click on CONTINUE.

5. Select the two assignment blocks in the AVAILABLE ASSIGNMENT BLOCKS list and add them to the list of DISPLAYED ASSIGNMENT BLOCKS.

6. Give the two assignment blocks user-friendly titles.

7. Leave the two assignment blocks with the direct-load option enabled so that they are displayed upon load.

8. Save.

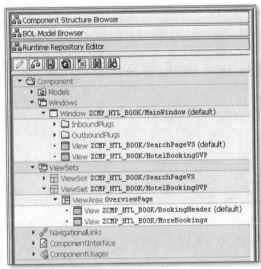

Figure 5.32 Runtime Repository Editor of Hotel Booking Application

Once you have configured your overview page, you will have a view similar to the one in Figure 5.33.

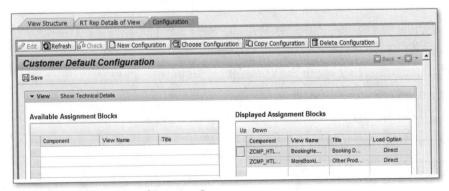

Figure 5.33 Configuration of Overview Page

Note that in Figure 5.32, the window default view—that is, the view that is loaded first when the window is launched—is the search page view set. This is because, unless one is performing navigation directly to an object's overview page, the standard pattern is to search, retrieve, and navigate to an object. In order to implement the navigation to the overview page of a booking, we need to go back to our result list and add the code that programs the click on the field that we have defined as a link. However, there is one more task that has to be done first. Because the navigation from the result list will have to transfer the BOL entity corresponding to the selected line to the overview page and this entity will have to be visible to the views of the overview page, it makes sense to use the technique of data binding so that this data is shared among all the relevant components. To create the context node on the overview page, follow these steps:

1. Open the overview page in the COMPONENT STRUCTURE BROWSER.

2. Expand the node CONTEXT.

3. Right-click on CONTEXT NODES and choose CREATE.

4. Follow the same steps as in Section 5.2.4. Make sure to bind the created context node to the context node BOOKINGS of the custom controller when performing the step CREATE LINKS TO CUSTOM CONTROLLER. By doing this binding, you ensure that data in the context nodes is shared among the overview page, the header, and the used products views.

Once you have created the context node, you are ready to enable navigation in your component.

5.2.9 Enabling Navigation inside a Component

Recall that we have decided to make the field HOTEL_NAME in the result list a hyperlink by adding it to the list of navigational fields, as shown in Figure 5.16. You remember also that as a result of that decision the wizard has added the appropriate coding to method GET_P_HOTEL_NAME and has attached the event name clickonlink as the onClick event of field HOTEL_NAME. You can see these actions in Listing 5.11. Furthermore, the event handler eh_onclickonlink has been predefined.

A close look at the event handler eh_onlickonlink (which you can see by double-clicking on it in the COMPONENT STRUCTURE BROWSER) shows that the search page creation wizard has taken care of retrieving the BOL entity corresponding to the link on which the user has clicked. This is done with the code snippet in Listing 5.12.

```
cl_thtmlb_util=>get_event_info(
    EXPORTING iv_event = htmlb_event_ex
        IMPORTING ev_index = lv_index ).
CHECK lv_index IS NOT INITIAL.

lr_entity = me->typed_context->
searchresultnode->collection_wrapper->find(
    iv_index = lv_index ).
```
Listing 5.12 Retrieving Current Entity from Navigational Event

The index of the line that was clicked is retrieved from the event info and then used to get the BOL entity from the collection. Besides the current entity, the event-handler method retrieves the name of the field, on which there was a click. This is done in the code snippet in Listing 5.13.

```
SPLIT htmlb_event_ex->event_id AT '].'
  INTO lv_temp lv_field.
TRANSLATE lv_field TO UPPER CASE.
me->navigate_to_link( ir_entity = lr_entity
                      iv_field  = lv_field ).
```
Listing 5.13 Retrieving Field that Triggered Click Event

Retrieving the field that triggered the click event is necessary in order to discriminate between fields because the event handler is generic and handles all navigational actions that were defined in the search page wizard. Once it has retrieved the field name, it calls the method `navigate_to_link`, passing the field name and the entity. We now have to implement the actual navigation by implementing the method `navigate_to_link`.

Listing 5.14 shows an example of the implementation of method `navigate_to_link`.

```
METHOD navigate_to_link.

  CHECK ir_entity IS BOUND.
  CASE iv_field.
    WHEN 'HOTEL_NAME'.
*       Add BOL data to data collection of the navigation
      DATA lr_data_col  TYPE REF TO  if_bol_bo_col.
      CREATE OBJECT lr_data_col TYPE cl_crm_bol_bo_col.
      lr_data_col->add( iv_entity = ir_entity ).
```

```
*          Call the outbound plug
        op_hotel_name( iv_data_collection = lr_data_col ).
      WHEN OTHERS.
    ENDCASE.
  ENDMETHOD.
```
Listing 5.14 Implementation of Method NAVIGAGE_TO_LINK

Because the method `navigate_to_link` is generic and can handle navigational events from different fields, we choose to use a `case…endcase` statement to take appropriate and specific actions for each field. For the hotel name, we add the BOL entity that was retrieved in the event handler to the collection and then pass that collection to the outbound plug `op_hotel_name` that was created by the wizard.

The next step is to implement the code of the outbound plug. The outbound plug is like a door, from which a navigational event goes outside a view. The code of our outbound plug is quite simple, as shown in Listing 5.15.

```
METHOD op_hotel_name.
  view_manager->navigate(
       source_rep_view = me->rep_view
       outbound_plug   = 'DisplayOverview'
       data_collection = iv_data_collection ).
ENDMETHOD.
```
Listing 5.15 Leaving Result view to Outbound Plug

Note that one of the parameters of the `navigate` method in the listing above is the name of the outbound plug `DisplayOverview`. We have to define this name in the runtime repository as a navigational link entry that establishes a connection from a source view and its outbound plug to a target view and its inbound plug within our UI component. Our target view is the overview page. However, you might remember that we did not create any inbound plug in the overview page. Therefore, to create the navigational link, follow these steps:

1. Select the `HotelBookingOVP` view in the COMPONENT STRUCTURE BROWSER.

2. Right-click on inbound plug and choose CREATE.

3. Specify the plug name, for instance `toOverviewPage`.

4. Go to the RUNTIME REPOSITORY EDITOR and switch to EDIT mode.

5. Right-click on NAVIGATIONAL LINKS and choose ADD NAVIGATIONAL LINK.

6. Enter `DisplayOverview` as the ID of the navigational link.

7. Using the ⎡F4⎤ helps, specify the source, target views, and their respective plugs as shown Figure 5.34.

8. Save.

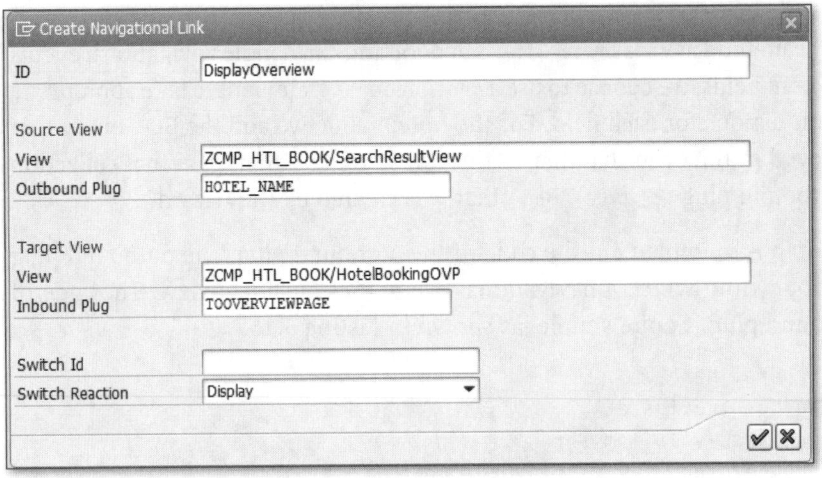

☞ Create Navigational Link		✕
ID	DisplayOverview	
Source View		
View	ZCMP_HTL_BOOK/SearchResultView	
Outbound Plug	HOTEL_NAME	
Target View		
View	ZCMP_HTL_BOOK/HotelBookingOVP	
Inbound Plug	TOOVERVIEWPAGE	
Switch Id		
Switch Reaction	Display	▼

Figure 5.34 Creation of Navigational Link

The necessary connection between the search result and the overview page has been established. The last step is to make sure that the object that is sent from the result page via the outbound plug is received in the overview page in the inbound plug and properly set in the context node of the custom controller. From there, it will be visible to all the views that bind their respective nodes against the custom controller. Listing 5.16 shows our implementation of the inbound plug ip_tooverviewpage of BookingsOVP. We retrieve the BOL entity that we receive and set it into custom controller.

```
METHOD ip_tooverviewpage.
  DATA: lr_entity TYPE REF TO cl_crm_bol_entity,
        lr_cuco   TYPE REF TO zl_zcmp_htl_cucobookings_impl.

  CHECK iv_collection IS BOUND.
  lr_entity ?= iv_collection->get_current( ).
  CHECK lr_entity IS BOUND.
  TRY.
      lr_cuco ?= me->get_custom_controller(
```

```
    'ZCMP_HTL_BOOK/CuCoBookings' ).
    CATCH cx_sy_move_cast_error.
  ENDTRY.
  lr_cuco->typed_context->bookings->collection_wrapper->
clear( ).
  lr_cuco->typed_context->bookings->collection_wrapper->add
( lr_entity ).
```

Listing 5.16 Receiving Entity and Setting It into Custom Controller

We've reached the climactic moment in our sample implementation. After you have activated the objects and methods that you created, you are ready to run your application. Test your application either by pressing [F8] or by clicking the TEST button from the Component Workbench. If you have followed carefully the steps described in this book, then once you have navigated from the result to the overview page you will see a page that looks like the one in Figure 5.35.

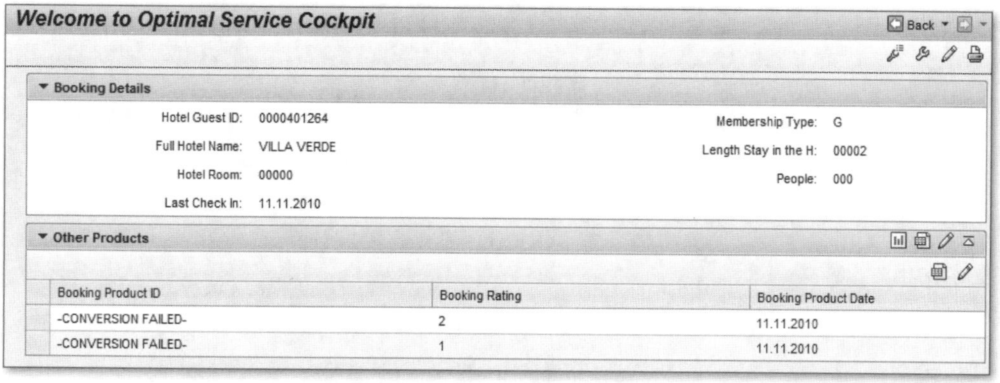

Figure 5.35 Overview Page of Hotel Booking Application

The application we have just created makes it possible to search for bookings and to navigate to the overview page of one of them. You will notice that there are many features that come for free on the overview page and in the assignment blocks: personalization, configuration, export to Microsoft Excel, and table graphics. On the other hand, our application can only display data. We do not yet have editing capabilities. Furthermore, you will notice that not every aspect is polished: The booking product ID is not properly displayed, there are unnecessary leading zeroes in some fields, and there are duplicate icons in the assignment block. We will address these issues and add new capabilities in the next chapter.

5.3   Summary

In this chapter, we learned how to create a BOL that represents the model of a Web UI framework-based application. We have covered aspects of BOL programming such as reading data, creating and modifying data, deleting, and locking. We have also explored creation of a UI component that follows the standard pattern of search, retrieve, and display. We produced a complete read-only hotel booking application. In order to leverage the various features of BOL that we have covered in this chapter, we will enhance our application in the next chapter to include editing and integration in the L-Shape.

The L-Shape is a powerful and convenient way of presenting to the user all the applications he or she needs when performing a given business role. Knowing how to integrate an application in the L-Shape is a must for anyone who wants to do end-to-end Web Client development.

6   Advanced Web Client Application Development and Integration

In the previous chapter, we created a hotel booking application, using as few manual tasks as possible and mainly focusing on using features that come standard in the component workbench. The resulting application was a display-only application that needed enhancements to give it a finished, user-friendly look. In the first section of this chapter, we will improve our application and build into it new capabilities. We will enable editing and Breadcrumb, implement a warning for potential data loss, learn how to use different GET methods to influence the look and the functionality of the fields, learn how to implement the very convenient F4 helps, and learn how to implement the one-click actions that you want to perform without leaving your current screen. Because Web Client applications seldom if ever run in standalone mode, in the second section we will integrate our application in the L-Shape. In order to do that, we will explain the concept of business roles and UI object types, create various profiles — navigational bar, layout, functional, technical — and explain how to create a home page and how to set direct link groups. But before proceeding with the integration, we first have to finish our application.

6.1   Improving the Web Client Application

The hotel booking application that we built in the previous chapter came pretty much out of the box as a read-only application with little functionality besides displaying data. We need to adjust the visualization of some fields that were not properly displayed and add convenient features that help the end user work with our application. We will start by enabling editing and then proceed to enhance our application with more advanced features.

6.1.1 Enable Central Editing

The standard pattern of Web UI-based applications is to specify search criteria, retrieve data, and then display details about the retrieved objects. However, in a business application it rarely happens that the end user simply displays details about an object for the sake of displaying it. Normally, the ultimate intent is to act on the displayed data, either by editing it or by triggering some actions from it. In this section, we enable editing of our booking object.

One can enable editing of each assignment block individually by implementing an EDIT button in the header of each editable assignment block. However, if you know that the end user will need to edit data in multiple assignment blocks, you might want to enable editing for the entire overview page. In most SAP-delivered applications, both options are offered: The user can switch the entire application to edit mode or they can edit content of assignment blocks individually. We will start by implementing a central EDIT button for the entire overview page. To achieve this, we need to:

► Add the edit button to the overview page

► Determine the number of buttons that we want displayed on the overview page

► Implement the appropriate logic to display the views in edit mode

► Handle the event triggered by the edit button

When it reaches a predefined number of displayed buttons, the Web Client UI Framework regroups all others under one pull-down menu button called MORE. Although it is not necessary to specify the number of buttons that are to be directly visible in the toolbar, it is always a good idea to find a tradeoff between displaying too many buttons that overcrowd the toolbar and too few buttons that force the user to click on the MORE button in order to access frequently used buttons. In order to define the number of visible buttons, redefine method `GET_NUMBER_OF_VISIBLE_BUTTONS` and simply return a numeric value, for example, `rv_result = 5`. This will ensure that at least five buttons are directly accessible and visible in the toolbar.

In order to add an edit button to the overview page of our hotel booking application, follow these steps:

1. Double-click on your overview page view in the Component Structure Browser to display its structure. If you are following our nomenclature, it is ZCMP_HTL_BOOK/ HotelBookingOVP.

2. Expand the node Toolbar related Methods.

3. Right-click on method GET_BUTTONS under node Toolbar related Methods and choose Redefine.

4. Double-click on the redefined method GET_BUTTONS to edit it.

5. Add the code in Listing 6.1 to your redefined method, save, and activate.

```
METHOD if_bsp_wd_toolbar_callback~get_buttons.
  DATA: ls_button TYPE crmt_thtmlb_button_ext,
        lr_booking TYPE REF TO cl_crm_bol_entity.

  lr_booking ?= me->typed_context->bookings->collection_wrapper->get_
current( ).
  ls_button-on_click = 'EDIT'.
  ls_button-type     = cl_thtmlb_util=>gc_icon_edit.
  ls_button-page_id  = me->component_id.
  IF lr_booking IS BOUND
     AND view_group_context->is_all_views_editable_set( ) = abap_
false
     AND lr_booking->is_change_allowed( ) = abap_true.
    ls_button-enabled  = abap_true.
  ELSE.
    ls_button-enabled  = abap_false.
  ENDIF.
  APPEND ls_button TO rt_buttons.
ENDMETHOD.
```

Listing 6.1 Adding a Button to Overview Page

In the listing above, we retrieve the current BOL entity from the Context node of the overview page. Remember that we decided to add this context node and to bind it to the custom controller in order to share the same data across all the views of the overview page. The current BOL entity of our overview page represents the object that the user might want to modify. Therefore, before enabling the Edit button, we want to make the following checks.

- ► First, we want to make sure that there is an object to edit.

- ► Second, we want to make sure that changes are allowed on the booking. This is done by calling method `is_change_allowed`.

- ► Finally, we want to make sure that the views on the overview pages are not yet in edit mode. This check is done by calling the appropriate method of the view group context.

The view group context is a feature of overview pages that is used to register each view that is in edit mode. As we will see when we switch the header view to edit mode, the view group context helps to determine the state of an assignment block: whether it is in edit or read-only mode. In the check, we are trying to establish whether all the views have already been put into edit mode. If the overview page — through its views — is already in edit mode, the EDIT button is disabled.

In order to use the button, we have to create a view-group context instance. The view-group context can be created in the highest view in the hierarchy, and as long as the subordinate views do not create their own view-group context instance, they will inherit their parent view-group context.

To create the overview page view-group context, redefine the method `set_view_group_context` (of `HotelBookingOVP`) under node PROCESSING REQUEST and simply add the code shown in Listing 6.2.

```
METHOD set_view_group_context.
  IF iv_first_time EQ abap_true AND
    me->view_group_context IS NOT BOUND.
   IF iv_parent_context IS INITIAL.
     CREATE OBJECT me->view_group_context
       TYPE cl_bsp_wd_view_group_context.
   ELSE.
     me->view_group_context = iv_parent_context.
   ENDIF.
  ENDIF.
ENDMETHOD.
```

Listing 6.2 Creation of View-Group Context

With the code in Listing 6.2, we make sure that we reuse the view group context of the parent view, if available. And once a view-group context has been assigned — which will happen the first time the view is loaded — we keep it intact and do not replace it on subsequent access. If you want to explore this topic in more detail, a quick look at class `cl_bsp_wd_view_group_context` will show you that a view-group context allows registration of editable views, switches all views at once or one view a time to edit mode, checks whether there is a view in edit mode at all, and uses some other convenient methods.

The button that we added to the toolbar of the overview page triggers the event that we called EDIT. We need to implement a handler of this event. To add the EDIT event handler do the following:

1. Right-click on the node EVENT HANDLER in the overview page view structure and choose CREATE.

2. Specify the event name — EDIT — and confirm.

3. Double-click on the newly created event handler EH_ONEDIT, add the code in Listing 6.3, save, and activate.

```
METHOD eh_onedit.
  DATA: lr_entity TYPE REF TO cl_crm_bol_entity.
  lr_entity ?= me->typed_context->bookings->collection_wrapper->get_
current( ).
  CHECK lr_entity IS BOUND.
  CHECK lr_entity->is_change_allowed( ) = abap_true.
  lr_entity->lock( ).
  IF lr_entity->is_locked( ) = abap_false.
    me->view_group_context->reset( ).
  ELSE.
    me->view_group_context->set_all_editable( ).
  ENDIF.
ENDMETHOD.
```

Listing 6.3 Handing the Edit Event

In Listing 6.3, in order to edit an object, we first have to lock it. However, a request to lock the object does not guarantee a successful outcome. Locking might fail, for instance, if the object is already being edited by another user. Therefore, before flagging all assignment blocks as being in edit mode, we have to make sure that the entity really has been locked.

Following the flagging, in the `eh_onedit` event handler of the assignment blocks to edit mode, we have to make sure that the relevant views take this flag into consideration and actually switch the visual design. Namely, in file `BookingHeader.htm`, replace `displayMode = "TRUE"`, which forced the view into display mode, with the following dynamic instruction that takes into account the state stored in the view group context:

```
displayMode = "<%= controller->view_group_context->is_view_in_display_
mode( controller ). %>"
```

We can now activate all the changes. If we run the application now, we will be able to navigate to the overview page and switch it to edit mode. This is the good news. The bad news is that, as we have seen in Listing 6.3, we must lock the object that we want to edit before switching the view to edit mode. Therefore, we will end up with locked objects and no way back, except for the hard way of using Transaction SM12 to manually delete the lock. Furthermore, we need a way to make persistent the changes that we might do in the header view. Therefore, we have to implement a CANCEL and a SAVE button. The implementation of the CANCEL button is relatively straightforward.

Add the CANCEL button to the overview page view by inserting the code in Listing 6.4 at the end of method GET_BUTTONS.

```
ls_button-on_click = 'CANCEL'.
ls_button-type     = cl_thtmlb_util=>gc_icon_edit.
ls_button-page_id  = me->component_id.
IF view_group_context->is_any_view_editable( ) EQ abap_true.
  ls_button-enabled = abap_true.
ELSE.
  ls_button-enabled = abap_false.
ENDIF.
APPEND ls_button TO rt_buttons.
```

Listing 6.4 Adding Cancel Button to Overview Page

Note that, although they are linked together, the status of the CANCEL button does not depend on that of the EDIT button but rather on the existence of at least one view in edit mode. The reason is clear: While the EDIT button switches the entire overview page to edit mode, different assignment blocks might be switched to edit mode individually. In this case, the user needs only to click on the central CANCEL button in order to cancel all edit activities taking place in the overview page.

We have to handle the event that we linked to the CANCEL button. Add the event handler of the CANCEL event to the EVENT HANDLER node and implement it. The code in Listing 6.5 shows how the event handler EH_ONCANCEL might look like.

```
METHOD eh_oncancel.
  DATA: lr_entity TYPE REF TO cl_crm_bol_entity,
        lr_tx     TYPE REF TO if_bol_transaction_context.

  lr_entity ?= me->typed_context->bookings->collection_wrapper->get_
current( ).
  lr_tx = lr_entity->get_transaction( ).
  lr_tx->revert( iv_suppress_buffer_sync = abap_true ).
  me->view_group_context->reset( ).
ENDMETHOD.
```

Listing 6.5 Canceling Edit Activities in Overview Page

In the listing above, we use the view-group context to reset the edit status of all assignment blocks and the transactional context to revert (discard) any changes that could have been made. As you might have guessed already, the transactional context is also used in order to make persistent the database changes made to an object.

Add a SAVE button with a SAVE event and the corresponding event handler to your overview page, making sure that the button is enabled only when the object is in edit mode—that is, as soon as method is_locked returns true—and disabled otherwise. To add the SAVE button, refer to the same steps you used previously for adding the CANCEL and EDIT buttons (in the GET_BUTTONS method). You can use the code in Listing 6.6 in the event handler to save the changes.

```
METHOD eh_onsave.
  DATA: lr_tx      TYPE REF TO if_bol_transaction_context,
        lr_booking TYPE REF TO cl_crm_bol_entity,
        lr_core    TYPE REF TO cl_crm_bol_core.
  lr_booking ?= me->typed_context->bookings->collection_wrapper->get_
current( ).
  lr_tx = lr_booking->get_transaction( ).
  IF lr_tx IS NOT BOUND.
    lr_core = cl_crm_bol_core=>get_instance( ).
    lr_tx = lr_core->begin_transaction( ).
  ENDIF.
  IF lr_tx IS BOUND.
    IF lr_tx->check_save_possible( ) EQ abap_true.
      CHECK lr_tx->save( ) EQ abap_true.
      lr_tx->commit( ).
    ENDIF.
  ENDIF.
```

```
  me->view_group_context->reset( ).
ENDMETHOD.
```

Listing 6.6 Event Handler for Saving Changes

In Listing 6.6, we use the transactional context to check if saving is possible; if it is, we save and commit the changes and reset the view-group context. This means that all the views and assignment blocks on the overview page are back in display mode. Furthermore, once save and commit are successful, the lock on the object that the user was editing is released. Now you can activate all your changes and run the application. Once you have retrieved a booking, navigate to its overview page and edit the booking, and cancel or save the changes to understand how the buttons behave. If you are following our example, you will see a screen like the one in Figure 6.1.

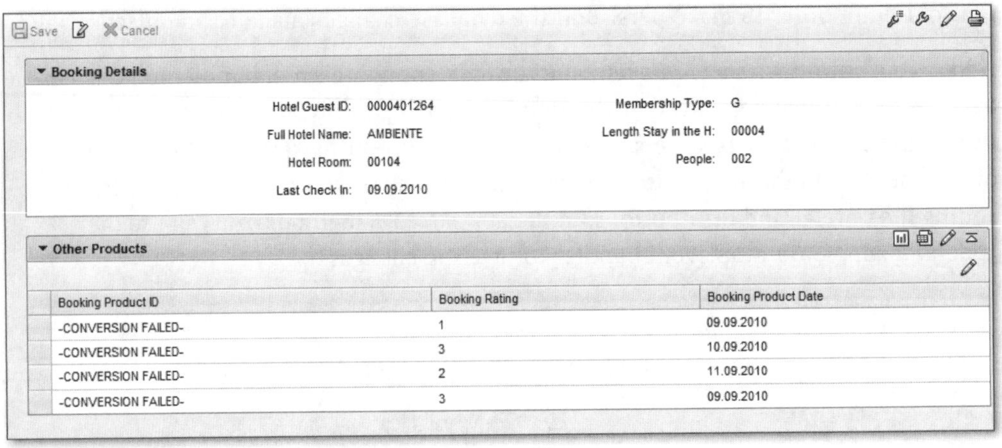

Figure 6.1 Editable Overview Page of Booking in Display Mode

You will notice that the buttons change their state depending on whether or not the object is being edited. Once you switch to edit mode, you get a screen that looks like the one of Figure 6.2.

In the header view, some fields are still not editable. You might wonder why. The answer will come in Section 6.1.4, when we analyze different mechanisms that are used to influence the behavior of fields. But before getting to that, let us integrate the page with the navigation history and implement a mechanism that prevents users from accidently losing their data.

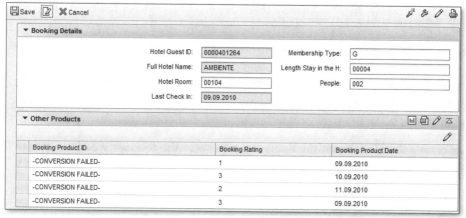

Figure 6.2 Editable Overview Page of Booking in Edit Mode

6.1.2   Enabling Breadcrumb

Navigation between different applications and objects can be achieved either by using links between components or inside the same component; or by using Breadcrumb for forward or backward navigation. We already saw how to implement links to navigate inside the component. Later on, we will see how to set up cross-component navigation. In this section, we see how you can implement Breadcrumb.

Breadcrumb creation during runtime is ensured by raising the event `history_trigger`. When you raise this event from a component, the framework writes an entry into the navigational history either under the backward or forward buttons depending on the direction of your navigation. The text of the entry is taken from method `get_state_description` that we discussed in the previous chapter and that determines the title of your current page.

In the overview page of your application, you might have already noticed an entry in the navigational history pointing to the search page, as seen in Figure 6.3.

Figure 6.3 Breadcrumb of Search Page on Overview Page

The display in Figure 6.3 assumes that you already adjusted the title of your overview page in a way similar to the way we have done it for the search page. The search page Breadcrumb entry is already there because the search-page creation wizard takes care of inserting code that raises the event `history_trigger` into method `wd_destroy` of the view set of the search page. You can take a look at method `wd_destroy` of class `cl_wcf_bsp_base_sp_2`, which is the super class of your search page view-set controller. The existence of this event in the search page explains why, once you have navigated to the overview page, you can navigate back to the search page using the back button in the upper right corner.

To enable Breadcrumb in the overview page, add the following code to method `wd_destroy` of your overview page:

```
RAISE EVENT history_trigger.
CALL METHOD super->wd_destroy.
```

Once you have activated this method, run the application, search and navigate to the overview page of a booking, and then go back to the search page. You will see that, as in Figure 6.4, the forward navigation button is active and clicking on it takes you to back to the already visited overview page.

Figure 6.4   Breadcrumb of Overview Page on Search Page

Note that the code we propose is rather simple and does not perform any validation to check if the object that we are leaving has been made persistent and still exists. If the object does not yet exist—for instance if the user was in the process of creating a new object—there is no point in storing it in the navigational history.

There is another important consideration. Although this is not the case for our hotel booking application, there are situations when you can navigate to an object of the same type as the already displayed object. In that case, one of the objects might be lost in the history entry. To ensure that in such cases you can navigate back and forth to all visited objects, you have to raise the `history_trigger` event in the `do_before_content_change` method of your controller implementation class. Note that you need first to redefine this method.

Navigation from objects that are being edited might cause the loss of the changes that have not yet been saved. In the next section, we see how to prevent such loss of data using the data loss pop-up.

6.1.3   Implement Data Loss Pop-Up

When a user is editing an object, he might navigate away from that edit screen without necessarily realizing that he did not yet save the changes that he made. If no mechanism is implemented to avoid this, the user ends up losing data, which is quite frustrating. In order to prevent this, you have to implement the data loss pop-up, which asks the user to choose between discarding the changes made and saving them before navigating away. However, you have to keep in mind that the framework handles only two scenarios where the data loss pop-up is triggered:

▶ Backward and forward navigation using Breadcrumb

▶ Cross-component navigation

In case navigation takes place inside a component and the user needs to save or discard changes, the application developer can still implement functionality similar to the central data loss pop-up. We will see later how this can be achieved.

In order for the two aforementioned scenarios to trigger a data loss pop-up, the component where editing takes place needs to notify the framework that there is a possibility for data loss and it must be ready to save, discard the changes, or cancel the navigation. In case the work area content has changed, the framework raises the event BEFORE_WORKAREA_CONTENT_CHANGE defined in class CL_BSP_WD_VIEW_MANAGER to ask work area components if there is any potential for data loss. It is then up to the components to notify the framework if there is indeed such a possibility and with what handler classes to handle it. To create the event handler that responds to this framework event, follow these steps.

1. Open the implementation class (controller) of your overview page in the repository browser (Transaction SE80). This can be done in different ways. If the Component Structure Browser is your starting point, simply double-click on the class and then press ⎡Ctrl⎤ + ⎡Shift⎤ + ⎡F5⎤.

2. Create a new method: right-click on Methods and choose Create.

3. Provide the method name. It is a good idea to give a name like ON_BEFORE_WORK-AREA_CONTENT_CHANGE that will let you easily recognize for what event this handler was created.

4. Specify for what event and class this method is created: the event is BEFORE_WORK-AREA_CONTENT_CHANGE, and the class is CL_BSP_WD_VIEW_MANAGER.

5. Confirm in order to create the event handler. Figure 6.5 shows the pop-up for creating the event handler.

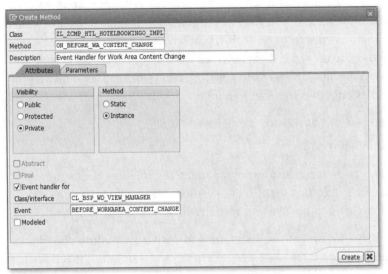

Figure 6.5 Creation of Event Handler Work Area Content Change

Once the event handler is created, it receives as an import parameter a reference to the interface IF_BSP_WD_DATA_LOSS_HANDLER. This interface provides methods for notifying the framework of the callbacks that will be used for the SAVE, REVERT, and CANCEL actions. In our example, we will handle all three actions in the view controller. To achieve this, the view (overview) controller has to implement the interface IF_BSP_WD_EVENT_HANDLER. Once you have added this interface to the list of interfaces that are implemented by your view controller class, your class will look like the screen in Figure 6.6.

A closer look at the interface IF_BSP_WD_EVENT_HANDLER that we added to the controller implementation class will show you that it has a method HANDLE_EVENT that accepts the event name as a parameter. We will have to implement this method, but we first must subscribe this handler to the event to which it will be listening. This can be done in method DO_VIEW_INIT_ON_ACTIVATION of your work area component (your overview page). You find this method under the node CONTROLLER INITIALIZATION AND DESTRUCTION in the COMPONENT STRUCTURE BROWSER. The method is DO_VIEW_INIT_ON_ACTIVATION, called to prepare the controller once a view has been activated and becomes visible (remember that the main controller can decide

298

to hide some views depending on the business logic). Here is a sample code that performs the activation of the event handler ON_BEFORE_WA_CONTENT_CHANGE.

```
METHOD do_view_init_on_activation.
 CALL METHOD super->do_view_init_on_activation.
 SET HANDLER on_before_wa_content_change ACTIVATION abap_true.
ENDMETHOD.
```

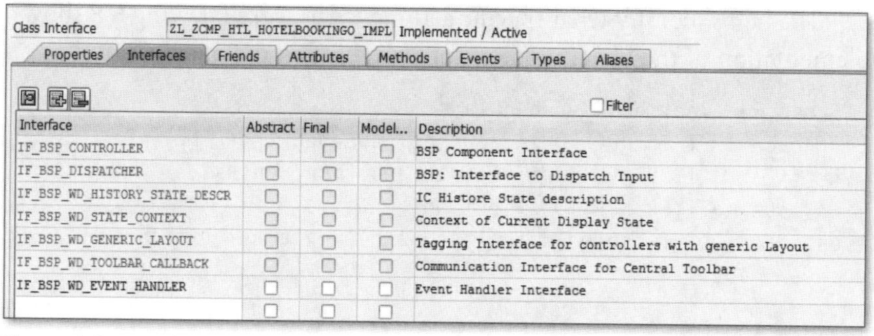

Figure 6.6 Interfaces Implemented by Overview Page Controller

Do not forget to unsubscribe, as shown below, from this event in method DO_CLEANUP_CONTEXT found under node CONTEXT RELATED METHODS. As its name suggests, you can use this method to do context-related clean-up when leaving a view. If you do not unsubscribe, inactive or invisible components might end up processing the data-loss event, causing errors in the application.

```
METHOD do_cleanup_context.
 SET HANDLER on_before_wa_content_change ACTIVATION abap_false.
ENDMETHOD.
```

Now that our view controller class qualifies for handling data-loss related actions, we can register it in the event handler we show in Figure 6.5.

Add the code in Listing 6.7 to the method ON_BEFORE_WORKAREA_CONTENT_CHANGE and activate it.

```
METHOD on_before_wa_content_change.
  data_loss_handler->set_save_handler( me ).
  data_loss_handler->set_revert_handler( me ).
  data_loss_handler->set_cancel_handler( me ).
  data_loss_handler->trigger_data_loss_handling( ).
ENDMETHOD.
```

Listing 6.7 Registration of Event Handlers and Handling Data Loss

In Listing 6.7, the controller implementation class is registered as the handler of the three events. If you have one central class that handles all the events, you could substitute me with the instance of your class as long as you have made sure that it implements the interface `IF_BSP_WD_EVENT_HANDLER`. The method `HANDLE_EVENT` of the interface `IF_BSP_WD_EVENT_HANDLER` is called from the data loss pop-up when the user selects YES or NO to save or discard and then navigate, or when the user selects CANCEL to stay on the same page. As we have seen earlier, the parameter `IV_EVENT_NAME` helps identify what specific action was triggered. Listing 6.8 shows our implementation of the handling of events triggered in the data loss pop-up.

```abap
METHOD if_bsp_wd_event_handler~handle_event.
  DATA: lr_cuco    TYPE REF TO zl_zcmp_htl_cucobookings_impl,
        lr_tx      TYPE REF TO if_bol_transaction_context,
        lr_booking TYPE REF TO cl_crm_bol_entity.
IF iv_event_name EQ if_bsp_wd_data_loss_handler=>cancel_event.
  rv_success = abap_false.
  RETURN.
ENDIF.
  TRY.
      lr_cuco ?= me->get_custom_controller( 'ZCMP_HTL_BOOK/
CuCoBookings' ).
    CATCH cx_sy_move_cast_error.
  ENDTRY.
  CHECK lr_cuco IS BOUND.
  lr_booking ?= lr_cuco->typed_context->bookings->collection_wrapper-
>get_current( ).
  CHECK lr_booking IS BOUND.
  IF lr_booking->alive( ) EQ abap_true.
    lr_tx = lr_booking->get_transaction( ).
  ENDIF.
  CASE iv_event_name.
    WHEN if_bsp_wd_data_loss_handler=>save_event.
      IF lr_tx IS BOUND AND lr_tx->check_save_needed( ) EQ abap_true.
        IF lr_tx->check_save_possible( ) EQ abap_true.
          IF lr_tx->save( ) EQ abap_true.
            lr_tx->commit( ).
            rv_success = abap_true.
          ELSE.
            lr_tx->rollback( ).
            rv_success = abap_false.
          ENDIF.
        ELSE.
```

```
              rv_success = abap_false.
         ENDIF.
       ENDIF.
     WHEN if_bsp_wd_data_loss_handler=>revert_event.
       IF lr_tx IS BOUND.
         lr_tx->revert( iv_suppress_buffer_sync = abap_true ).
       ENDIF.
       rv_success = abap_true.
   ENDCASE.
ENDMETHOD.
```

Listing 6.8 Handling Events Triggered in Data Loss Pop-Up

Without any surprise, you will notice that to the save event we react by saving the data, to the revert event we react by simply discarding all the changes made and with regard to the cancel event we take no action. In every case, if the operation—save or revert—was successful, we return a success flag indicating that processing can continue. If the choice is to cancel or if we were unable to make the object persist, we return a failure flag. The return flag lets the framework decide on further action: in case of a successful outcome, navigation continues; in all other cases, navigation is stopped and the user stays on the same page.

You will not be able to test the enhancements you added in this section until later when you integrate this application in the L-Shape. This is because the responsibility for opening the data loss belongs to the framework class CL_CRM_UI_CORE_APPL_CON-TROLLER, which can only run in an integrated, L-Shape environment. Meanwhile, let us see how to improve the look, feel, and functionalities of different fields using the getter methods.

6.1.4 Using the GET_X_ and SET_ Methods

The hotel booking application presented some obvious imperfections: the hotel guest ID and the length of stay in hours were not properly formatted, and so were the room number and the people fields, which were displayed with leading zeroes. In this section, we will see how to use different get methods to improve the look and feel of our application.

GET Method

The value of a field (or a context node attribute, depending on your perspective) is retrieved using the GET_<name_of_attribute>. The GET methods are automatically generated by the wizard during view creation. Therefore, they are generated with very generic code. Being generic, this code cannot always fit the needs of every single application. Even if the value retrieved is what is needed, the formatting might not necessarily be exact. If this is the case, as with our hotel guest ID, you can adjust the corresponding GET method to your needs. In the case of some of the fields displayed in the header overview, we see a need to trim the unnecessary leading zeroes.

If you open the GET methods, for example `get_guest_id`, you will see that the following generic code is used to retrieve the value of the attribute:

```
value = if_bsp_model_util~convert_to_string(
data_ref = dref
attribute_path = attribute_path ).
As we have seen, the value returned by this method for numeric values
has leading zeroes. In method get_guest_id, replace the code snippet
above with the code in Listing 6.9.
DATA lr_id TYPE REF TO zhotelguest_id.
lr_id ?= dref.
CALL FUNCTION 'CONVERSION_EXIT_ALPHA_OUTPUT'
    EXPORTING
      input  = lr_id->*
    IMPORTING
      output = value.
```

Listing 6.9 Formatting Hotel Guest ID

The code in Listing 6.9 is just an example of how you could change the GET method to influence the output value of an attribute. Use the same technique or other methods of your choice to adjust all values in the header that are not displayed properly.

If you look for better ways to format the field PRODUCT_ID of the assignment block, you will find your search is in vain. A look at the type of this attribute shows us that it is of type SYSUUID. In real applications, you do not display this type of fields. You would rather use it to get a more meaningful ID. For this exercise, in the GET method of the attribute PRODUCT_ID, we retrieve the hotel name and concatenate it with the usage date. You will see this result later in the chapter, in Figure 6.10.

GET_I Method

When you switched the header to edit mode, you noticed that some fields, for instance the field `GUEST_ID`, are not editable. To understand why, you have to open the corresponding `GET_I_<name_of_attribute>`. A closer look at the method `get_i_guest_id` shows that the wizard has created generic code that uses the method `is_property_readonly` of the interface `if_bol_bo_property_access` to decide whether or not the field `guest_id` will be editable. Because it is based on the underlying BOL object, this generated code ensures that the wizard does not give more edit permissions than allowed by the BOL. It is easy to imagine what would happen if it were allowed to edit a field that then cannot be persistent because the BOL does not allow any changes. On the other hand, even if the BOL allows a given field to be changed, you might want to add more checks before enabling the editing of a field. You will use the `GET_I` method to make your fields read-only or editable.

GET_P Method

Besides making fields read-only or editable, you might need to specify more advanced types. For instance, the hotel name in our application is a simple field containing a text string. However, hotels normally have Web sites. You might therefore want to redefine the field hotel name as a link. This can be achieved in method `get_p_hotel_name`. The method `GET_P_<name_of_attribute>` of a particular attribute is called repeatedly to determine the following.

▸ **The field type**

To request the field type the framework will call the `GET_P` method of the attribute with the import parameter `iv_propery` set to `IF_BSP_WD_MODEL_SET-TER_GETTER=>FP_FIELDTYPE`. The `GET_P` method returns one of the field types specified as constant in class `CL_BSP_DLC_VIEW_DESCRIPTOR` (input field, check box, radio button, etc.). Although under normal circumstances it is not necessary to define a `GET_P` method, this becomes necessary if you are implementing a table and want different cells of the same column to have different types. For performance reasons, if the framework does not find a `GET_P` method defined or if the `GET_P` method does not return a valid field type, the framework will calculate the field type, buffer it, and not ask the application anymore. This might lead to undesirable results if your table column contains mixed types.

▶ **Column sortability**

When the `GET_P method` is called with the import parameter set to `IF_BSP_WD_MODEL_SETTER_GETTER=>FP_SORTABLE`, the `GET_P method` of the column has to return `TRUE` or `FALSE` to indicate whether or not a column is sortable. In case you decide to make a column sortable, you will have to implement some additional steps as described in Section 6.1.5. On the other hand, if you do not want a column to be sortable, you have to explicitly implement the `GET_P method` and explicitly return FALSE, since failing to do so leaves it up to the framework to decide whether sorting is to be enabled based on the BOL implementation.

▶ **Server event**

There are situations when you want to trigger a server roundtrip with an event from fields that otherwise would not raise any event. This is the case, for instance, for a dropdown list box, in which you want the selected value to influence other parts of the screen. Under normal circumstances, selecting a value in a dropdown list box does not trigger a server event. If you want to influence this behavior, you have to use the `Get_P` model. With the import parameter `iv_propery` set to `IF_BSP_WD_MODEL_SETTER_GETTER=>FP_SERVER_EVENT` the framework asks the application to provide the name of the event that will be fired after a value is selected in a dropdown. You then have to implement the appropriate logic to handle that event. We will come back to this in Section 6.1.6.

▶ **Click event**

When the user clicks on a link, you can provide the name of the event that will be raised. Your `Get_P` method has to return the event name when it is called with import parameter `iv_property` set to `IF_BSP_WD_MODEL_SETTER_GETTER=>FP_ONCLICK`.

▶ **Tooltip**

You can provide a tooltip for a particular field by returning the value of your choice when the `Get_P` method is called with `iv_property` set to `IF_BSP_WD_MODEL_SETTER_GETTER=>FP_TOOLTIP`.

▶ **Disabled features**

You can disable features such as column filtering, smart value help, and table graphics by returning `FALSE` when the P-getter is called with the corresponding import value.

A list of the values that can be passed to the `Get_P` method in import parameter `iv_property` is provided as constants in interface `IF_BSP_WD_MODEL_SETTER_GETTER`.

Get_V Method

The Get_V method—also known as the value help getter—is used to provide a value help descriptor that will be used as an input help either in the form of a dropdown list box or in the form of a search help. We will see more details in Section 6.1.6.

Get_A Method

This method is used to retrieve the switch ID (as per the SAP enhancement package concept) for the current field. You will very likely never need to implement it.

Get_AC Method

This is used to provide an action menu for a specific field. An action menu is a contextual menu attached to a field. The Get_AC method has to return an action menu descriptor, which is a subclass of class CL_BSP_WD_ACTION_PROVIDER and at the very minimum implements method IF_BSP_WD_ACTION_DESCR_EXT~BUILD_ACTIONS. We will see how to implement action menus later with additional topics.

Besides the various GET methods, you have noticed that there is also a SET method. There is not much to say about this method except that it is used to set the value that comes from user input.

6.1.5 Enabling Sorting in Tables

As we have seen earlier, you can enable sorting for a specific column by implementing the Get_P method and by returning TRUE when the framework invokes that column's Get_P method with the import parameter set to constant IF_BSP_WD_MODEL_SET-TER_GETTER=>FP_SORTABLE. On the other hand, if you omit to implement the Get_P method or if you do not return a valid value—TRUE or FALSE—to indicate that the column is or is not sortable, the framework might still automatically enable sorting for that column if the underlying context node attribute is bound to a normal BOL entity. This explains why all the columns found the tables of our application are sortable. On the other hand, context node attributes that are bound to BOL via related entities and value node attributes are not automatically sortable and need to be sort-enabled via the Get_P method.

If a column is not automatically sortable and you enable sorting via the Get_P method, you will have to implement the following steps to handle the sorting:

- Create an event handler for the event sort (in lower case) on your view controller. If you are following our example, the event handler creation wizard has already added the event handler EH_ONSORT.

- Add the following instruction to the generated event handler: me->typed_context->\<context_node_name>->eh_on_sort(iv_htmlb_event_ex = htmlb_event_ex).

- Redefine the method EH_ON_SORT of the aforementioned context node \<context_node_name> and use the code snippet in Listing 6.10 as a guide for implementation of your custom sorting.

```
DATA: lr_table      TYPE REF TO cl_thtmlb_table_view,
      lv_attr       TYPE name_komp,
      lv_sort_order TYPE char1,
      lv_stable     TYPE abap_bool VALUE abap_false.
TRY.
    lr_table ?= iv_htmlb_event_ex.
  CATCH cx_sy_move_cast_error.
    RETURN.
ENDTRY.
IF lr_table IS BOUND.
  CHECK lr_table->event_type =
cl_thtmlb_table_view=>co_header_click.
  lv_attr  = lr_table->column_key.
  CHECK lv_attr IS NOT INITIAL.
  CASE lr_table->column_sort_direction.
    WHEN 'U'.
      lv_sort_order =
cl_bsp_wd_collection_wrapper=>sort_ascending.
    WHEN 'D'.
      lv_sort_order =
  cl_bsp_wd_collection_wrapper=>sort_descending.
    WHEN OTHERS.
      RETURN.
  ENDCASE.
  CASE lv_attr.
    WHEN <myattribute>.
      "implement your own sorting logic
    WHEN OTHERS.
      super->eh_on_sort( iv_htmlb_event    = iv_htlmb_event
              iv_htmlb_event_ex = iv_htmlb_event_ex ).
  ENDCASE.
ENDIF.
```

Listing 6.10 Implementation of Custom Sorting of Columns

As Listing 6.10 shows, you have to react only on the header click event `cl_thtmlb_table_view=>co_header_click`. You also have to retrieve the column to sort – `column_key` and the sorting direction from the table attribute `column_sort_direction`. Finally, you have to implement the sorting logic that is appropriate for each column and make sure that you delegate the sort event to the super class for any column that you do not handle explicitly.

6.1.6 Implement Dropdown List Boxes

We all know that there is nothing more frustrating for the user than having to manually enter values that are known to the system and that have fixed values. There are different ways to present fixed values to the users so that they can choose from a predefined set of values. In this section, we will see how to implement a dropdown list box. We will enhance our header view to make the field MEMBER-SHIP TYPE a dropdown list box.

As we have seen in Section 6.1.4, you use the `Get_V` method to provide a value help descriptor. Follow these instructions to implement a dropdown list box for the MEMBERSHIP TYPE field:

1. Open the booking header view and drill down to the context node attribute STRUCT.MEMBERSHIP.

2. Double-click on method placeholder GET_P_MEMBERSHIP and choose YES to create it.

3. Add the following code to indicate that you want this field to be a pick list. Notice that we isolate the response of the `Get_P` method to the sole case when the method is asked the field type.

```
CASE iv_property.
  WHEN if_bsp_wd_model_setter_getter=>fp_fieldtype.
    rv_value =
  cl_bsp_dlc_view_descriptor=>field_type_picklist.
ENDCASE.
```

4. Now you have to create the value help descriptor. If there is no need to use the same value help descriptor in many places, it is always a good idea to create it as a local class. Therefore, once you have navigated back to the COMPONENT STRUCTURE BROWSER, double-click on the implementation class of the context node used in the booking header view.

5. Click on LOCAL DEFINITIONS/IMPLEMENTATIONS or use `Ctrl` + `Shift` + `F6` to access the `include`, where we want to create our value help descriptor.

6. Insert the code in Listing 6.11 that defines and implements the value help descriptor as a local class. We assume that you are familiar with the structure of local class definition and implementation.

```
CLASS lcl_vhelp_for_membership DEFINITION FRIENDS
zl_zcmp_htl_bookingheader_cn00.
  PUBLIC SECTION.
    INTERFACES: if_bsp_wd_valuehelp_pldescr.
    METHODS: constructor
                IMPORTING
                  iv_source_type TYPE char1.
  PRIVATE SECTION.
    DATA: gt_selection_table
            TYPE bsp_wd_dropdown_table.
    METHODS: load_selection_table.
ENDCLASS.
CLASS lcl_vhelp_for_membership IMPLEMENTATION.
  METHOD constructor.
    me->if_bsp_wd_valuehelp_pldescr~source_type =
                iv_source_type.
  ENDMETHOD.
  METHOD if_bsp_wd_valuehelp_pldescr~get_selection_table.
    rt_result = gt_selection_table.
  ENDMETHOD.

  METHOD if_bsp_wd_valuehelp_pldescr~get_binding_string.
    RAISE EXCEPTION TYPE cx_bsp_wd_incorrect_implement.
  ENDMETHOD.

  METHOD load_selection_table.
    DATA: ls_ddlb TYPE bsp_wd_dropdown_line,
          lt_memb type TABLE OF ZHOTELMEMTYPE .
    field-symbols: <line> like line of lt_memb.
    CLEAR gt_selection_table.
    SELECT * FROM ZHOTELMEMTYPE
    INTO CORRESPONDING FIELDS OF TABLE lt_memb.
    LOOP AT lt_memb assigning <line>.
    ls_ddlb-key = <line>-membership.
    ls_ddlb-value = <line>-DESCR.
```

```
    APPEND ls_ddlb TO gt_selection_table.
    ENDLOOP.

  ENDMETHOD.
ENDCLASS.
```

Listing 6.11 Implementation of Value Help Descriptor in Local Class

In Listing 6.11, you notice that the constructor accepts as a parameter and sets the source type. This is because the value help descriptor interface if_bsp_wd_value-help_pldescr offers two methods that can be used to return dropdown list values. In our implementation, the method get_selection_table is used to return the values. This is communicated to the framework at the creation time of the value help descriptor. In other implementations, you can use method get_binding_string that will point to a context node of type CL_BSP_WD_CONTEXT_NODE_DDLB, which will hold the content of the dropdown list box.

1. Go back to the COMPONENT STRUCTURE BROWSER, double-click the placeholder get_v_membership and choose YES to create the Get_V method.

2. Insert the code in Listing 6.12 to return the value help descriptor.

```
METHOD get_v_membership.
  DATA: lr_descr TYPE REF TO lcl_vhelp_for_membership.
  CREATE OBJECT lr_descr
    TYPE
    lcl_vhelp_for_membership
    EXPORTING
      iv_source_type = 'T'.
  IF iv_mode EQ runtime_mode.
    lr_descr->load_selection_table( ).
  ENDIF.
  rv_valuehelp_descriptor = lr_descr.
ENDMETHOD.
```

Listing 6.12 Returning Value Help Descriptor

You will notice that the selection table is loaded only when the application is in runtime mode as opposed to when the application is in design mode. However, in all cases, the Get_V method returns the value help descriptor. This is done to enable the configuration view in the Workbench to display the membership field as a dropdown list box without needlessly loading the content of the dropdown list.

3. Activate your changes and test your application.

If you have followed our example, you will see, in edit mode, a screen like the one in Figure 6.7.

Figure 6.7 Dropdown List Box for Membership Type Field

If you select a value in the dropdown list box that we just implemented, you will notice that—except for the change of the value—there is no roundtrip triggered. As we saw in Section 6.1.4, you can force a roundtrip by adding a server event name in the Get_P method of the membership attribute in response to import parameter value FP_SERVER_EVENT. You would then need to add the following code to your GET method.

```
...
WHEN if_bsp_wd_model_setter_getter=>fp_server_event.
  rv_value = 'ddlb_value_changed'.
...
```

Dropdown list boxes are convenient when the number of entries is small. When there are many possible values, users might find it difficult to find specific values. In those cases, you can use either simple or complex search helps. We will come to complex search helps later. In the next section we implement a simple search help.

6.1.7 Implementing Simple F4 Help

[F4] helps (also known as search helps) are useful for filling fields that have pre-defined values. They are the recommended alternative to dropdown list boxes when the big number of entries would make dropdown lists less user friendly. In order to analyze how [F4] helps are implemented, we will enhance our application and add a search help on the room number. This makes sense, given that there are only a limited and predefined number of rooms.

Before implementing a search help in our application, we will have to create an ABAP search help. For the sake of brevity, we will not describe the detailed steps of ABAP search help creation; we assume that you are familiar with this activity from your ABAP classes. We simply present the prerequisites so that you can implement them yourself. In our example, we first created two database tables and a database view.

▶ The first table—room types—has two columns, the type and the description.

▶ The second table—hotel rooms—contains the hotel rooms with the room number, room type, capacity, date of check-in, and date of check-out. The type of the room is linked to the first table with a foreign relationship.

▶ The database view presents the room number, the capacity, and the room type description.

Based on the view, we created the search help that you see on Figure 6.8.

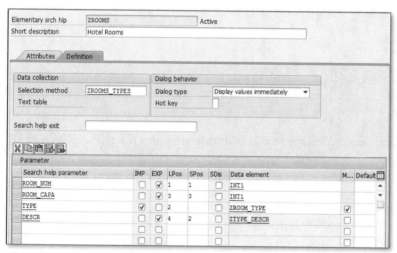

Figure 6.8 Search Help for Hotel Rooms

The search help is an elementary search help and accepts the room type as a search criterion to return the rooms of this specific type together with their capacity. Now that we have prepared the ground, follow these steps to enable a search help for hotel rooms:

1. Double-click on the method placeholder GET_V_ROOM in the context node BOOKINGHEADER in the header view and click YES to create the method.

2. Insert the code in Listing 6.13 into your `Get_V` method.

```
DATA:
  ls_map TYPE
if_bsp_wd_valuehelp_f4descr=>gtype_param_mapping,
  lt_inmap  TYPE
if_bsp_wd_valuehelp_f4descr=>gtype_param_mapping_tab,
  lt_outmap TYPE
if_bsp_wd_valuehelp_f4descr=>gtype_param_mapping_tab.

  CREATE OBJECT rv_valuehelp_descriptor TYPE
cl_bsp_wd_valuehelp_f4descr
    EXPORTING
      iv_help_id        = 'ZROOMS'
      iv_help_id_kind   =
if_bsp_wd_valuehelp_f4descr=>help_id_kind_name
      iv_input_mapping  = lt_inmap
      iv_output_mapping = lt_outmap.
```

Listing 6.13 Providing Simple F4 Help for Field

3. Save and activate.

When you run the application and switch to edit mode, you will notice that the hotel room now has an icon, on which you can click to get the list of rooms (Figure 6.9).

Upon selection, the room number will be transferred into the HOTEL ROOM field, from which the search help was triggered. We will explain the code we used to achieve this result and the different techniques used to implement search helps.

A generic value help descriptor utility class—`cl_bsp_wd_valuehelp_f4descr`—has been provided by SAP to ease the definition of F4 helps. To provide a search help for a specific field, you have to create an instance of that class—although you can create a class of your own—and provide the following information.

▶ The name of the search help, data element or custom search help to use as a basis for the current search help. In Listing 6.13, the search help ID is ZROOMS.

▶ A list of context node attributes used as sources to set search criteria in the search help and their corresponding target fields in the search help search fields. This list is called the input mapping. In our example, it is empty but is provided in the variable `lt_inmap` because it is a mandatory parameter.

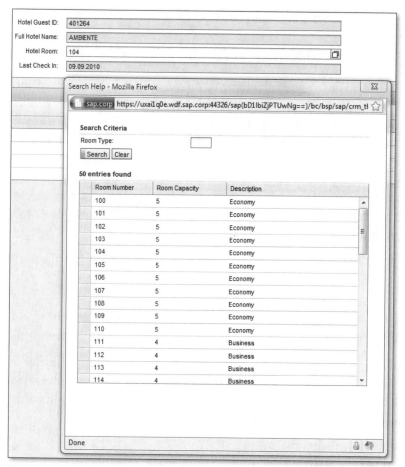

Figure 6.9 Search Help for Hotel Room

- A list of target context node attributes, into which values from the search help will be written along with their corresponding search help result fields. This list is called the output mapping. In our example, it is empty but is provided in the variable `lt_outmap` because it is a mandatory parameter.

- The type of search help. There are three types of search help, all identified by constants in the interface `if_bsp_wd_valuehelp_f4descr`. The search help `ZROOMS` used in our example is a DDIC search help and is identified as type `help_id_kind_comp`.

- The title of the search help.

▶ A flag indicating whether a roundtrip is required upon selection of a value in the search help.

▶ A reference object that will be used as a call back.

In our example, we do not provide any input or output mappings. In this case, the search help infrastructure assumes that the field that triggered the search help is the target while the key of the table underlying our DDIC search help contains the value to return. This explains why the room number is taken when we select an entry in the search help result list. In many cases, you might want to specify your own mapping. To do so, you reference the input and output context attributes using the STRUCT prefix and provide the name of the search help field. To come back to our example, we could also add the following code just before the creation of the value help descriptor (although it would change nothing).

```
ls_map-context_attr = 'struct.room'.
ls_map-f4_attr       = 'ROOM_NUM'.
APPEND ls_map TO lt_outmap.
```

This mapping instructs the search help infrastructure to put the value taken from the search help field ROOM_NUM into the context node attribute struct.room.

The Get_V method has an optional import parameter iv_index. This parameter is useful when dealing with table fields. In that case, the prefix of the context node attribute shall be TABLE[<index>]. Therefore, had we been in a table view the code would have been similar to the following code snippet.

```
lv_str_index = iv_index.
  CONCATENATE 'table[' lv_str_index '].room'
INTO ls_map-context_attr.
  ls_map-f4_attr       = 'ROOM_NUM'.
```

Within a tree, you have to prefix the name of the context node attribute with the name of the tree, then _TABLE [<index>]. If you want to send to the search help a constant to be used as a search criterion to limit the number of hits, you can use the following notation.

```
ls_map-context_attr = '\''E\'''.
ls_map-f4_attr       = 'ROOM_TYPE'.
APPEND ls_map TO lt_inmap.
```

Note that here we are presetting the room type in the input mappings because the room type is a search criterion, as we have seen earlier both in the ABAP search help and in the search help in our application. You can preset as many search criteria as there are import parameters in your search help. Note also that, although the search help is triggered from one specific field, there can be as many output mappings as you want. In other words, the values taken from the search help can be assigned to practically any attribute in the same context node.

We have seen that there are three types of search help types. The first one, the *reference structure field*, can be used to provide search help based on structure components or structure fields that have an underlying check table or a DDIC search help. A Get_V method based on this type of search help could look like Listing 6.14.

```
CREATE OBJECT rv_valuehelp_descriptor TYPE
cl_bsp_wd_valuehelp_f4descr
  EXPORTING
iv_help_id      = 'CRMST_ADDRESS_BUIL-COUNTRY '
iv_help_id_kind =
if_bsp_wd_valuehelp_f4descr=>help_id_kind_comp
iv_input_mapping = lt_inmap
iv_output_mapping = lt_outmap.
```
Listing 6.14 Creation of Search Help Based on Structure Component

The second type of search help, the *reference data element* is used when you want to base your search help on a data element, which is has a DDIC search help assigned to it. In that case, the Get_V method could look like the code in Listing 6.15.

```
CREATE OBJECT rv_valuehelp_descriptor TYPE
cl_bsp_wd_valuehelp_f4descr
  EXPORTING
iv_help_id      = 'ZCOUNTRY'
iv_help_id_kind =
if_bsp_wd_valuehelp_f4descr=>help_id_kind_dtel
iv_input_mapping = lt_inmap
iv_output_mapping = lt_outmap.
```
Listing 6.15 Creation of Search Help Based on Data Element

The third type, the DDIC name is used to provide a check table, a custom search help, or a DDIC search help, as we did in our example. You have to keep in mind that if you use a check table, its content is entirely displayed without to the option to first restrict the selection.

If you decide to use your own custom search help, you have to create a class that implements the interface `if_bsp_wd_custom_f4_callback`. If you use a custom search help, you have to signify that your search help ID represents a custom search help by putting it in parentheses so that your code will look like Listing 6.16:

```
CREATE OBJECT rv_valuehelp_descriptor TYPE
cl_bsp_wd_valuehelp_f4descr
  EXPORTING
iv_help_id      = '(CL_CUSTOM_F4)'
iv_help_id_kind =
if_bsp_wd_valuehelp_f4descr=>help_id_kind_comp
iv_input_mapping = lt_inmap
iv_output_mapping = lt_outmap.
```

Listing 6.16 Creating Custom Search Help Descriptor

To get familiar with the usage of a custom search help, you can go ahead and replace your DDIC-based implementation of the hotel room number search help with a custom search help.

6.1.8 Implementing One-Click Actions

One-click actions are a short cut typically used in tables to execute an action on an object without having first to navigate to its detail screen or selecting it. Typical actions are edit, delete, and release. In our example, we will implement a delete action on our table entries. To implement one-click actions, you need to add the action field to your collection, to define what actions are to be displayed and to handle the events raised by the click.

1. Go to the Component Workbench and open your component `ZCMP_HTL_BOOK`.

2. Open the view that contains the table of more bookings. In our example it is `ZCMP_HTL_BOOK/MoreBookings`.

3. Drill down to the context node `MOREBOOKINGS` and expand it.

4. Right-click on the note ATTRIBUTES and choose CREATE.

5. Add a value attribute with ATTRIBUTE NAME `thtmlb_oca` and DDICTYPE `crm_thtmlb_one_click_action`.

6. Click on COMPLETE to finish.

7. Double-click on method placeholder `GET_P_THTMLB_OCA` to create it.

8. Add the code in Listing 6.17 to specify the field type and the one-click event.

```
CASE iv_property.
  WHEN if_bsp_wd_model_setter_getter=>fp_fieldtype.
    rv_value = cl_bsp_dlc_view_descriptor=>field_type_oca.
  WHEN if_bsp_wd_model_setter_getter=>fp_onclick.
    rv_value = '_oca'.
ENDCASE.
```
Listing 6.17 Get_V Method of One-Click Action Field

9. Double-click on the implementation class of your context node. In our example it is ZL_ZCMP_HTL_MOREBOOKINGS_CN01 and redefine method GET_OCA_T_TABLE.

10. Add the delete button using the code in Listing 6.18.

```
DATA: ls_oca TYPE crmt_thtmlb_one_click_action.
ls_oca-icon    = 'delete.gif'.
ls_oca-text    = ''.
ls_oca-tooltip = 'Delete Booking'.
ls_oca-active  = 'X'.
APPEND ls_oca TO rt_actions.
```
Listing 6.18 Adding Delete Action to Possible One-Click Actions

11. Activate.

12. Now add the event handler for the one-click action_oca that we have defined in the Get_P method. After you have confirmed the event name in the pop-up, you will see a new event handler EH_ON_OCA under your EVENT HANDLER node. We will see how to handle this event shortly.

13. Open the configuration page and add the ACTIONS column to the list of displayed fields.

Run the application to see the visual result. If you click on the DELETE button, nothing happens. This is because we did not implement the handling of the event raised by the click on the DELETE button. To handle this event, we will use the pop-up to confirm.

14. Double-click on your view controller class and add a private instance attribute – delete_popup – of type reference to IF_BSP_WD_POPUP

15. Open the event handler EH_ON_OCA and add the following code in Listing 6.19 to open the confirmation pop-up.

```
    IF delete_popup IS NOT BOUND.
       DATA: lv_delete TYPE string
VALUE 'Alert! Deleting a booking',
            lv_text TYPE string
VALUE 'Do you really want to delete?'.
       CALL METHOD comp_controller->window_manager
->create_popup_2_confirm
        EXPORTING
          iv_title          = lv_delete
          iv_text           = lv_text
          iv_btncombination = if_bsp_wd_window_manager=>co_btncomb_yesno
        RECEIVING
          rv_result         = delete_popup.
      delete_popup->set_on_close_event(
iv_event_name = 'DELETE_POPUP_CLOSED' iv_view = me ).
    ENDIF.
    delete_popup->open( ).
```

Listing 6.19 Opening Pop-Up to Confirm

The code in Listing 6.19 creates a pop-up and sets the event that will be triggered when the pop-up is closed. It then will open the pop-up. As a result, we have a new event that needs to be handled: DELETE_POPUP_CLOSED. Create a new event handler for the event DELETE_POPUP_CLOSED and add the code in Listing 6.20.

```
    DATA: lv_answer       TYPE string.
    IF delete_popup IS BOUND .
      lv_answer = delete_popup->get_fired_outbound_plug( ).
      IF lv_answer EQ cl_gs_ptc_bspwdcomponent_cn01=>co_event_yes.
        " Well, let's not do it
      ENDIF.
    ENDIF.
```

Listing 6.20 Handling of Event DELETE_POPUP_CLOSED

When a pop-up to confirm is closed, it fires an outbound plug that depends on the button that the user clicked. In the event handler below, we check what outbound plug was fired—implicitly what button the user clicked: yes or no—and we react accordingly.

Once you activate and run the application, when you try to delete an entry in the table of other products, you will see a pop-up asking you to confirm, as shown in Figure 6.10.

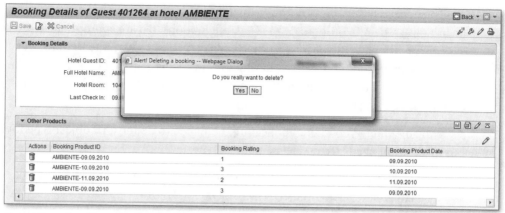

Figure 6.10   Pop-Up to Confirm One-Click Action Delete

Because we did not implement any logic to delete, clicking on any button will yield the same result. If you want to go a step further and implement the logic for deleting an object, you can use the `htmlb_event_ex` parameter to retrieve the index of the row that triggered the event. We used the same technique in the previous chapter to retrieve the current entity from the navigational event.

6.2   Integrating a Web Client Application

As we have seen earlier, the Web Client applications run inside the L-Shape. The L-Shape serves as a central point for accessing all the applications that the user uses on a regular basis to perform tasks related to a specific business role. The business role is a central concept to the usage of Web Client applications. It helps control the navigation bar, logical links, and user authorizations. In this section we will analyze the different aspects that serve to build a business role. But before getting to that, we need to understand one critical element of dynamic navigation and UI configuration: the UI object type.

6.2.1   UI Object Type

A UI object type is an object type that classifies the user interface with regard to the used business content. A UI object type is the best match for the end user's concept of an object. The concept of a BOL object is too generic, while that of a BOR object is too technical. A classic example is the complaint business object. From an end user's perspective, a complaint can be handled as a return, a simple complaint, or an in-house repair. In order to define UI configurations that are appropriate to each case, three different UI object types have been defined. In a way, the UI object type acts as a semantic identifier for your application. Using these UI object types, the developer can determine different configurations, different design layer settings, and dynamic navigation.

As with any other Web Client application, you need to define a UI object type for our application needs. To create a UI object type:

1. Go to IMG activity CUSTOMER RELATIONSHIP MANAGEMENT • UI FRAMEWORK • UI FRAMEWORK DEFINITION • DEFINE UI OBJECT TYPES.

2. Create a new entry and provide the object type, for example ZHTL_BOOK, a description, the GenIL Component Name—ZBOOK—and the BOL Object Name Bookings.

3. Save.

Once you have created it, your object type will look like the one shown in Figure 6.11.

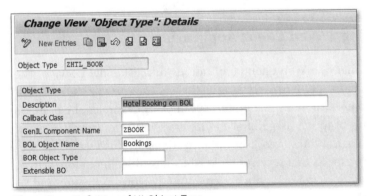

Figure 6.11 Definition of UI Object Type

As we will see soon, this object type will be used to help us integrate our application in the L-Shape. However, in order to specify for which components that we want to integrate the L-Shape, we need the work area component definition.

6.2.2   Create Entry Points to Application

When you want to access a building, you can force a window or you can use a more civilized and conventional way: entering through the door. With Web Client applications, it is no different. In order to facilitate access points, you have to declare access points. You can access an application with the primary intent to create, to search, to display, to edit, to print, or to delete an object. The access points to your object have to be specific to the action that the user wants to perform.

In our example, we want to access the application for searching and for displaying bookings. Note that once you are in the application you can always perform more actions depending on your permissions. However, we first want to control the way one enters the application. To create the display and the search access point, follow these steps:

1. Start the Component Workbench.

2. Go to the Component Structure Browser and add to your main window two inbound plugs called TOOVERVIEWPAGE and TOSEARCH, and an outbound plug called TOSEARCH.

3. Add an inbound called TOSEARCH to your search page view set.

4. Go to the RUNTIME REPOSITORY EDITOR of your application.

5. Add a navigational link with the following properties: ID TOOVERVIEWPAGE, source view ZCMP_HTL_BOOK/MainWindow, target view ZCMP_HTL_BOOK/HotelBookingOVP, and inbound plug TOOVERVIEWPAGE.

6. Add another navigational link with the following properties: ID TOSEARCH, source view ZCMP_HTL_BOOK/MainWindow, outbound plug TOSEARCH, target view ZCMP_HTL_BOOK/SearchPageVS and inbound plug TOSEARCH.

7. Add an inbound plug to the main window. Right-click on the node INBOUND-PLUGS and choose ADD PLUG WITH FOLLOW UP NAVIGATION and provide the following information: inbound plug TOOVERVIEWPAGE, navigational link ID TOOVERVIEWPAGE.

8. Add another inbound plug to the main window with inbound plug name =TOSEARCH and navigational link ID TOSEARCH.

9. Add a new component interface view ZCMP_HTL_BOOK/MainWindow with the two inbound plugs you have added to the main window: TOSEARCH and TOOVERVIEWPAGE (under the COMPONENTINTERFACE node).

10. Accept and save the changes.

If you have followed the same steps as described above, your runtime repository will look like the screen in Figure 6.12.

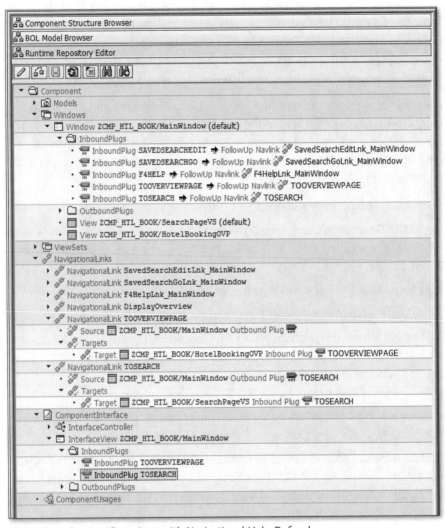

Figure 6.12 Runtime Repository with Navigational Links Defined

The follow-up navigational links defined in the inbound plugs on the figure above are a convenient way to define redirections directly in the runtime repository without having to do it programmatically. The inbound plugs in the component interface node are your access points from the outside world. You can now use those access points to customize how your component will be accessed.

6.2.3 Work Area Component Repository

The WORK AREA COMPONENT REPOSITORY serves as the one place where all components that can be included in the work area are defined with their inbound and outbound plugs. A component cannot be included in the work area unless it is specified in the WORK AREA COMPONENT REPOSITORY. To specify our application in the repository:

1. Go to IMG activity CUSTOMER RELATIONSHIP MANAGEMENT • UI FRAMEWORK • TECHNICAL ROLE DEFINITION • DEFINE WORKAREA COMPONENT REPOSITORY.

2. Create a new entry and provide the component for which you want to create a new entry (ZCMP_HTL_BOOK), a description, and the window name. Remember that we have created one window in our component. You have to provide the window name in the format *<component name>/<window name>*. If you have followed our example, the window name is ZCMP_HTL_BOOK/MainWindow. You can also provide a description.

3. Specify the INBOUND PLUG DEFINITION by providing the target ID (ZBOOK_BOL1), the inbound plug (TOOVERVIEWPAGE), the object type (ZHTL_BOOK), and the object action (Display). You can also provide a description.

4. Create a second inbound plug definition with the following attributes: target ID (ZHTLSRCH), inbound plug (TOSEARCH), object type (ZHTL_BOOK), and object action (Search).

5. Save.

In this section, we have enabled components of our application to be included in the work area. We have also prepared the ground for cross-component navigation by determining the inbound plugs through which external components can access our components. We now need to build what will later be the home page.

6.2.4 Work Center Page

The application that we have built can be integrated into the L-Shape and accessed directly from the navigation bar. However, in real business applications you often have a bundle of applications that a given user within a specific business role uses frequently. In order to present such a bundle in a user friendly way, you can build a work center page and put all the relevant views together on that page. On a work center page, links with similar functionality are grouped together: create, search, reports, favorites. For your convenience, there exists a reusable component—`CRMCMP_GS_WC`—that has views corresponding to those specific functionalities. We use that reusable component to build our work center page. To build a work center page that will contain our application, follow these steps:

1. Start the UI Component Workbench.

2. Create a component called `ZWCC_HTL_CMP`.

3. Create a new view of type Overview Page called `AgentHomePage`.

4. Adjust the overview page title and provide a new title by redefining the method `IF_BSP_WD_HISTORY_STATE_DESCR~GET_STATE_DESCRIPTION`.

5. Add the inbound plug `DEFAULT` to the main window.

6. Go to the Runtime Repository Editor and switch to edit mode.

7. Expand the Windows node and assign the view `AgentHomePage` to the main window `ZWCC_HTL_CMP/MainWindow`.

8. Expand the node ComponentUsage and add a new component usage with the following attributes: ID (`Search`), used component (`CRMCMP_GS_WC`), interface view (`IFVGroupLinks`). The result is a reusable component used to build work center pages, and the view we have selected is used for regrouping links of included applications.

9. Expand the node ViewSets and then the view set `ZWCC_HTL_CMP/AgentHomePage`, and add the view `Search.IFVGroupLinks` to the view area `OverviewPage`.

10. Declare entry points as we did in Section 6.2.2 by adding the main window `ZWCC_HTL_CMP/MainWindow` and the `DEFAULT` inbound plug to the component interface view. This is done in order to enable our work center page to be visible from outside.

11. Save. Your runtime repository will now look like the screen in Figure 6.13.

12. Go back to the Component Structure Browser and display the view `AgentHomePage`.

13. Go to the Configuration tab and switch to edit mode.

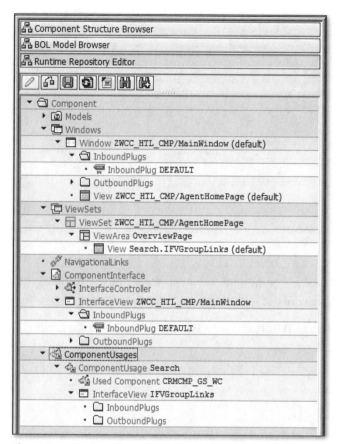

Figure 6.13 Runtime Repository of Work Center Page

14. Choose WORK CENTER PAGE and click on CONTINUE.

15. You will see now that there is one assignment block available, the assignment block `CRMCMP_GS_WC/IFVGroupLinks`.

16. Either using drag-and-drop or with the down arrow, add the assignment block to the LEFT VISIBLE COLUMN table and assign it a title; for instance, `Search` and the pictogram `SEARCH2`.

17. Save.

18. Your configured work center page will look like the screen in Figure 6.14.

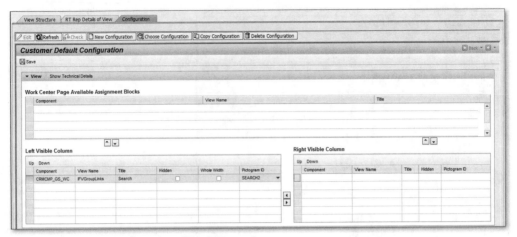

Figure 6.14 Configuration of Work Center Page

Because we are using a reusable component, we need to initialize it properly to give it the specific context in which it is running. In order to do this:

1. Go back to the COMPONENT STRUCTURE BROWSER and double-click on the node COMPONENT CONTROLLER.

2. Redefine method `WD_USAGE_INITIALIZE` that you find under the node SUB COMPONENT HANDLING.

3. Add the code in Listing 6.21.

```
METHOD wd_usage_initialize.
  DATA: wccontext TYPE REF TO cl_bsp_wd_context_node.
  CASE iv_usage->usage_name.
    WHEN 'Search'.
      TRY.
        wccontext = iv_usage->get_context_node(
'WORKCENTERINF' ).
        wccontext->set_s_struct(
attribute_path = ''
component = 'COMPONENT'
value = 'ZWCC_HTL_CMP' ) .
        wccontext->set_s_struct(
attribute_path = ''
component = 'INTERFACE_VIEW'
value = 'ZWCC_HTL_CMP/MainWindow' ).
        wccontext->set_s_struct(
attribute_path = ''
```

```
component = 'GROUP_TYPE'
value = 'BB' ) .
        CATCH cx_root.
     ENDTRY.
  ENDCASE.
ENDMETHOD.
```

Listing 6.21 Initialization of Reusable Component CRMCMP_GS_WC

4. Save and activate.

The code in Listing 6.21 serves to indicate to the reusable component what component is using it (ZWCC_HTL_CMP), with what interface view (ZWCC_HTL_CMP/Main-Window), and what type of group has to be considered to fill it (BB). The group type is important because the view can be reused to contain different types of links. In our case, we are looking for links of type search, code-named BB.

The component usage concept will be further clarified later in the book. For now, note that it a standard way of consuming views defined in other components. To expose views (windows, to be more precise) for external consumption you have to add them to the interfaces of their components (as we did previously for ZWCC_HTL_CMP/MainWindow).

If you test the component ZWCC_HTL_CMP that we just created, you will see that it is still empty. We need to populate it now with the link to the search page of our hotel booking application. However, before populating it, we need to make sure that it is included in the WORK AREA COMPONENT REPOSITORY. Therefore, we now have to repeat the steps from Section 6.2.3 for the component ZWCC_HTL_CMP, window ZWCC_HTL_CMP/MainWindow, and inbound plug definition with target ID WCCHTLHOME with action Display so that at the end of this operation our work center page is declared like in Figure 6.15.

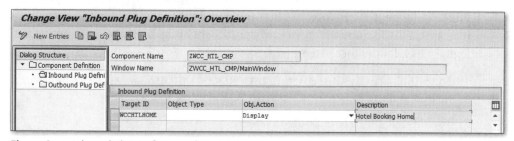

Figure 6.15 Inbound Plug Definition of Work Center Page

6.2.5 Navigation Bar Profile

When we tested our work center page in the previous section, we saw that it was empty. In this section, we will fill it with relevant entries as part of our steps to build the navigation bar profile. For a better understanding of what we want to achieve, Figure 6.16 presents the various components of a navigation bar. These were discussed in detail in our first chapter, but you can use the opportunity to refresh your memory.

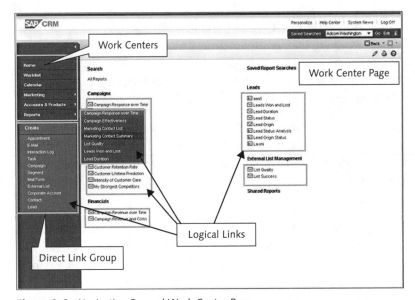

Figure 6.16 Navigation Bar and Work Center Page

From Figure 6.16, you can see that the work center page contains different groups that contain logical links. The work centers in the navigation area also contain links and groups, which when expanded reveal more logical links. The same goes for direct link groups. Therefore, the first thing to do is to define the logical links, as they are the basic components of each constituent of the home page. To define the logical links, follow these steps:

1. Go to IMG activity CUSTOMER RELATIONSHIP MANAGEMENT • UI FRAMEWORK • TECHNICAL ROLE DEFINITION • DEFINE NAVIGATION BAR PROFILE.

2. Double-click on DEFINE LOGICAL LINKS.

3. Click on NEW ENTRIES and provide the following information: logical link ID (ZHTL-WCP), type (Work Center), target ID (WCCHTLHOME or whatever name you have given to the target ID in the definition of the work center page for the work center component in the previous section).

4. Save.

Your definition of the logical link will look like the screen in Figure 6.17.

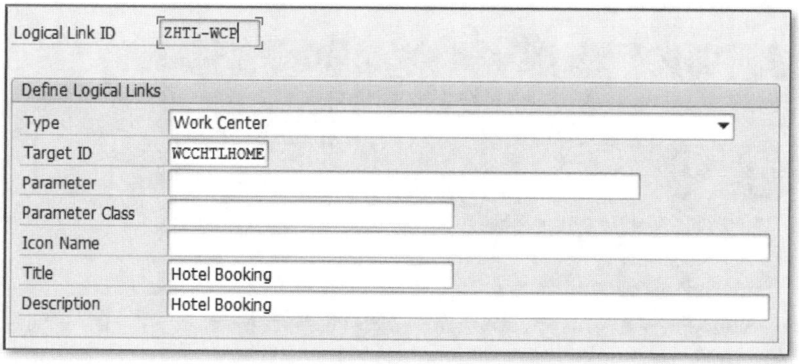

Logical Link ID	ZHTL-WCP	
Define Logical Links		
Type	Work Center	▼
Target ID	WCCHTLHOME	
Parameter		
Parameter Class		
Icon Name		
Title	Hotel Booking	
Description	Hotel Booking	

Figure 6.17 Definition of Logical Link for Work Center Page

Create another logical link for the search page with the following information: logical link ID (ZHTL-SRCH), type (Link), target ID (ZHTLSRCH or whatever ID you have given to the target ID in the definition of the WORK AREA COMPONENT REPOSITORY entry for the search page in Section 6.2.3). You can use the search help as shown in Figure 6.18.

Now that we have the logical links—a work center and a simple link—we can proceed with the creation of our work center groups, which we can later assign to the work center.

1. If not already there, go to IMG activity CUSTOMER RELATIONSHIP MANAGEMENT • UI FRAMEWORK • TECHNICAL ROLE DEFINITION • DEFINE NAVIGATION BAR PROFILE.

2. Double-click on DEFINE WORK CENTER LINK GROUPS.

3. Click on NEW ENTRIES and provide the following information: group ID (ZHTL-SR), group type (SEARCH), and a title and a description (for instance, "Booking Search").

4. Save.

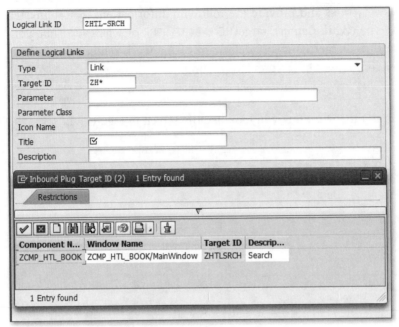

Figure 6.18 Retrieval of Target ID During Logical Link Definition

5. Double-click on Assign Links To Work Center Link Group.

6. Click on New Entries and provide the logical link ID (ZHTL-SRCH) with the title "Bookings."

7. Save.

In this activity, we have just declared that the search link that we created earlier can be part of the work center group of type Search. This for the time being is only a possibility because, as we will see later on, we still could exclude it for a particular business role. Now that we have grouped our links in a work center group, we can use it to define the work center (see Figure 6.16) that will be part of our navigation bar.

1. Double-click on Define Work Centers.

2. Click on New Entries and provide the work center ID (ZHTL-WCC), and logical link ID (ZHTL-WCP; this is the logical link to the work center page that we created in Section 6.2.4).

3. Double-click on Assign Work Center Link Groups to Work Center and click on the New Entries button.

4. Add the group ID ZHTL-SR that we created previously and specify the position 10.

5. Save.

We have just declared that we will have a work center (ZHTL-WCC) that will contain one group (ZHTL-SR) and that clicking on our work center will lead to the work center page, pointed to by the logical link ZHTL-WCP. It is time now to create the actual navigation bar profile.

1. Double-click on DEFINE NAVIGATION BAR PROFILES and click on the button NEW ENTRIES.

2. Provide the NAV BAR PROFILE (ZHTL-MGR), a description, and the link ID (ZHTL-WCP).

3. Save.

4. Double-click on ASSIGN WORK CENTERS TO NAVIGATION BAR PROFILE and click on the button NEW ENTRIES.

5. Add the work center ZHTL-WCC that we have created earlier to position 10.

6. Double-click on DEFINE GENERIC OUTBOUND PLUG MAPPINGS and click on the button NEW ENTRIES.

7. Specify the object type (ZHTL_BOOK; see Section 6.2.1), the object action (Search), and use the search help to retrieve the target ID ZHTLSRCH that we created earlier.

8. Save and exit.

We have now created a ready-to-use navigation bar profile. Before we create our business role, we need to understand some of the attributes of a business role, even though we will not need to modify them.

6.2.6 Layout, Technical, and Functional Profiles

When a user logs into SAP CRM, he or she is doing so within a specific business role. This will determine what is available to that user. In this section we will discuss what it takes to define a business role. Most important, you need to assign to the business role a navigation bar profile and specify the layout and the technical profiles. The layout profile contains the definition of the navigation frame: the header and footer area, the navigation bar and the work area. These are areas where you can define components such as the logo area, the message area, the menu area, and so on. To use a layout profile, you have to first create it and to assign components to it. In our example, we will use the layout profile `CRM_UIU_MASTER`, which is shipped standard. For more details on layout profiles, go to IMG activity CUSTOMER RELATIONSHIP MANAGEMENT • UI FRAMEWORK • TECHNICAL ROLE DEFINITION • DEFINE LAYOUT PROFILE.

Another profile that you may choose to assign to your business role is the function profile. The function profile helps define special functions that you want to grant to a given business role. For example, you can create a function profile that limits the level of personalization that users have within a specific business role. Or you can assign a functional profile to a role to specify how users use the central sharing tool: as simple recipients, as information sharer, or as super-sharers, for instance. Note that you can assign more than one functional profile to a business role. In the standard version, many functional profiles are available for all business roles. For more details on layout profiles, go to IMG activity CUSTOMER RELATIONSHIP MANAGEMENT • UI FRAMEWORK • TECHNICAL ROLE DEFINITION • DEFINE FUNCTION PROFILE.

Finally, you can assign a technical profile to a role. The technical profile deals with pure technical settings of a business role such as the ability to use or not use the browser back button, the time it takes before the wait notice appears, or whether closing the browser immediately ends the server session. In the standard profiles there are predefined technical profiles. For more details on layout profiles, go to IMG activity CUSTOMER RELATIONSHIP MANAGEMENT • UI FRAMEWORK • TECHNICAL ROLE DEFINITION • DEFINE TECHNICAL PROFILE.

For the sake of our exercise, we use the standard profiles. However, in real business applications, depending on your needs, you might have to create your own profiles and assign them to your business roles in order to fine-tune the look and feel of the applications used by your users. On the other hand, in order to grant users authorizations for business processes, you need to create or modify the authorization or Transaction PFCG roles assigned to them.

6.2.7 Define Authorization Role

As we have seen earlier, authorization roles determine what business authorizations users have. Every authorization role is linked to an authorization profile that contains detailed authorizations. It is very unlikely that you will ever have to create a new authorization role or build an authorization profile from scratch. This is because you always have a standard role that is shipped with a set of authorizations, and you either want to expand or restrict authorizations based on your business needs. Therefore, in our example, we also start with an existing authorization role and adjust it to our needs. To create our own authorization role, follow these steps:

1. Start Transaction PFCG.

2. Select an authorization role, for instance `SAP_CRM_UIU_CASE_WORKER`.

3. Copy the authorization role to the new role `ZHTL_MANAGER` and adjust the description.

4. Choose Copy Selectively and uncheck all the options.

5. Click on the change icon and go to the Menu tab.

6. Delete the folder under the node Role Menu.

7. Save the empty role that you just created.

With the empty role that you just created, you can proceed to the business role definition. However, in order for this authorization role to make sense, we will have to come back to it to adjust the different authorizations that it controls.

6.2.8 Business Role Definition

Now that we have prepared all the building blocks, it is time to put them together to build a business role. The business role is a fundamental concept in the Web Client UI framework that defines what the user can see in the browser, based on the navigation bar and what they can do in the system, and based on the authorizations associated with the business role. During the definition of the business role, you can make adjustments to the navigation bar and work center pages that you have previously defined. To create a business role, follow these steps:

1. Go to IMG activity Customer Relationship management • UI Framework • Business Roles • Define Business Role.

2. Click on New Entries and provide the following information: business role (`ZHTL-MGR`), description ("Hotel Manager"), role configuration key (`<*>`), navigational bar profile (`ZHTL-MGR`), layout profile (`CRM_UIU_MASTER`), technical profile (`DEFAULT`), and PFCG role ID (`ZHTL_MANAGER`).

3. Save.

Once you have saved, your business role will look like the one shown in Figure 6.19.

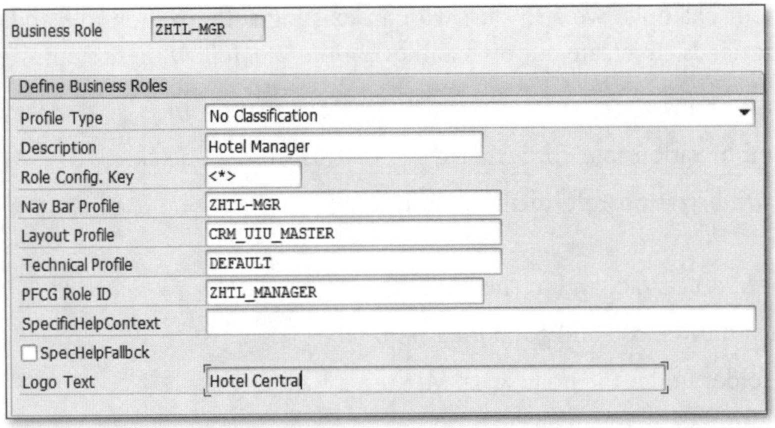

Business Role	ZHTL-MGR

Define Business Roles

Profile Type	No Classification
Description	Hotel Manager
Role Config. Key	<*>
Nav Bar Profile	ZHTL-MGR
Layout Profile	CRM_UIU_MASTER
Technical Profile	DEFAULT
PFCG Role ID	ZHTL_MANAGER
SpecificHelpContext	
☐ SpecHelpFallbck	
Logo Text	Hotel Central

Figure 6.19 Definition of the Hotel Manager Business Role

Note that we have assigned the default role configuration key <*>. If you have multiple configurations in your applications, they will be selected on runtime for a specific business role based on the role configuration key that you have specified. You can easily do so by following the IMG menu path CUSTOMER RELATIONSHIP MANAGEMENT • UI FRAMEWORK • TECHNICAL ROLE DEFINITION • DEFINE ROLE CONFIGURATION KEY and pasting its value in your business role. We will come back to the configuration determination later in the book.

We now have to adjust the work centers and the work center group links because the definitions we created earlier are generic and you might want to adjust them on a role-by-role basis.

Double-click on the node ADJUST WORK CENTERS and if you like, provide a work center title that is specific to this role. Double-click on the node ADJUST WORK CENTER GROUP LINKS and make sure that the checkboxes IN MENU and VISIBLE are checked. The first checkbox is responsible for ensuring that the link is available in the navigation bar, and the second checkbox makes the link visible in the tray in the work center page. Here you can also adjust the title and the position of the link in case you have many links.

We have now configured the business role, and it is ready to use. However, a user cannot use a business role unless it is assigned to him or her. Furthermore, as we have seen in the previous section, the authorization role that we created was empty. We need to adjust it and to assign ourselves the business role.

6.2.9 Adjust Authorization Role and Define Organizational Assignment

The authorization role contains an authorization profile that has all the authorizations required to access the business functionalities provided by applications launched in a specific business role. We have created an empty authorization role ZHTL_MAN-AGER, and we now have to declare the list of applications that are accessible in the business role linked to this authorization role. Follow these steps:

1. Start Transaction SE38.

2. Launch report CRMD_UI_ROLE_PREPARE.

3. Choose the option SELECT A BUSINESS ROLE and enter the business role ZHTL-MGR that we created earlier.

4. Specify the language.

5. Run the application either by clicking on the RUN icon or with F8.

Upon execution of the report, a file with the same name as your authorization role (ZHTL_MANAGER) is created on your local disk in the SAP directory. This file contains the details of the components that are accessed in this business role, including the component name, the window, and the inbound plug.

1. Start Transaction PFCG.

2. Select the role ZHTL_MANAGER and switch to edit mode.

3. Go to the MENU tab.

4. Click on the button COPY MENU and choose IMPORT FROM FILE.

5. Select the file that was created in the previous steps. The ROLE MENU folder is now populated with the entries corresponding to those found in the navigational bar profile definition.

6. Save.

7. Go to the AUTHORIZATIONS tab.

8. Click on the icon CHANGE AUTHORIZATION DATA.

9. Deactivate the authorization object S_SERVICE.

10. Choose GENERATE and save your role.

Executing these steps ensures that the authorization role that you have created contains authorization objects necessary for the execution of functionality provided by the corresponding role. As a prerequisite to the successful creation of your authorization role, you have to activate the trace function to determine all authorization objects. For more information see IMG activity CUSTOMER RELATIONSHIP MANAGEMENT • UI FRAMEWORK • BUSINESS ROLES • DEFINE AUTHORIZATION ROLE.

Although we have defined and fine tuned the authorizations and the business role that are necessary to access our application, we do not have those authorizations because we are not yet assigned to the business role that we just created. To make that assignment, follow these steps:

1. Go to IMG activity CUSTOMER RELATIONSHIP MANAGEMENT • UI FRAMEWORK • BUSINESS ROLES • DEFINE ORGANIZATIONAL ASSIGNMENT.

2. Search for your own user and double-click on your user name.

3. Click on the CREATE button in order to create a new position.

4. Choose GOTO • DETAIL OBJECT • ENHANCED OBJECT DESCRIPTION.

5. Select BUSINESS ROLE on the ACTIVE tab. You might need to scroll down to retrieve the BUSINESS ROLE entry.

6. Click on the button CREATE INFOTYPE.

7. Enter the business role `ZHTL-MGR`.

8. Save and exit.

Once you have performed the organizational assignment and have created your PFCG role, you can either manually assign the PFCG roles to the user on the ROLES tab or you can run the report CRMD_UI_ROLE_ASSIGN, which will perform the same operation based on user assignments in Organization Management.

You might want to run the application now, but if you can wait another five minutes we will add a direct-link group first.

6.2.10 Direct Link Groups

To increase productivity, the Web Client framework offers the possibility to group together what one can call the most used links in the navigation bar so that the user can assess them without having to go through the work centers and work center pages that host those links. These groups are called the direct link groups. In our example we want to add the possibility to directly access the search page from the navigation bar.

1. Go to IMG activity CUSTOMER RELATIONSHIP MANAGEMENT • UI FRAMEWORK • TECHNICAL ROLE DEFINITION • DEFINE NAVIGATION BAR PROFILE.

2. Double-click on DEFINE DIRECT LINK GROUPS.

3. Click on NEW ENTRIES and provide the following information: group ID (–ZHTL-DLG), group type ("Search"), and title ("Bookings").

4. Save.

5. Double-click on ASSIGN LINKS TO DIRECT LINK GROUP.

6. Click on NEW ENTRIES and provide the following information: logical link ID - ZHTL-SRCH.

7. Save.

8. Double-click on DEFINE NAVIGATION BAR PROFILE.

9. Select the navigation bar profile ZHT-MGR.

10. Double-click on ASSIGN DIRECT LINK GROUPS TO NAV. BAR PROFILE.

11. Click on NEW ENTRIES and add the group ID ZHTL-DLG.

12. Save and exit.

13. Go to IMG activity CUSTOMER RELATIONSHIP MANAGEMENT • UI FRAMEWORK • BUSINESS ROLES • DEFINE BUSINESS ROLE.

14. Select the business role ZHTL-MGR.

15. Double-click on ADJUST DIRECT LINK GROUPS and make sure that the direct link group ZHTL-DLG is flagged as visible.

16. Select the group ZHTL-DLG.

17. Double-click on ADJUST DIRECT LINKS.

18. Make sure that the link ZHTL-SRCH is flagged as visible.

19. Save and exit.

Now we have made the last adjustment that we need in our business role.

6.3   Summary

In this chapter we have seen how we can enhance our application by adding edit capabilities, enabling Breadcrumb, and also enabling accidental data-loss prevention. We added sorting capabilities to our tables and added a dropdown list and a simple [F4] help as means to ease data input.

In the second step, we recognized that an application does not run standalone but rather as part of a set of applications intended to provide users with a full set of tools to help them accomplish the tasks related to their roles. With this as our goal, we integrated our hotel booking application in the L-Shape. When you run your application using Transaction WUI, you will see screens similar to those in Figure 6.20 and Figure 6.21.

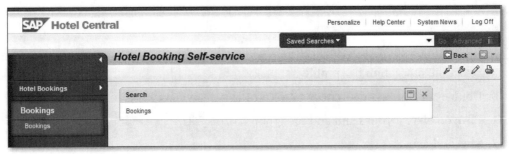

Figure 6.20   Home Page of Business Role Hotel Manager

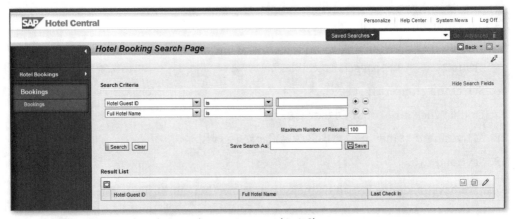

Figure 6.21   Hotel Booking Application Integrated in L-Shape

To achieve this integration, we have created entry points to our components and exposed the interface that we wanted to use for external communication. We have also defined our business role, which is the fundamental concept defining what is visible to the user. The attached authorization role determines what is allowed or prohibited from a business perspective.

This is just a starting point. An application runs as part of a set of applications intended to provide a certain kind of functionality. Therefore, you can use this business role as the basis and build much more functionality using the techniques and tools we have covered in this and previous chapters. However, before integrating more applications, you might want to look into an even more automated way to develop applications. This will be the focus of the next chapter, which will discuss the generation of fully functioning UI components.

In the past, consultants dreamed of reusing standard SAP components in order to create custom applications without modifying SAP code and worrying about upgrades. With the Web Client UI a technical consultant can make this dream a reality by creating an enhancement set.

7 Enhancing Existing UI Components

In the following sections, we will demonstrate and explain how to enhance SAP components without changing the SAP code. Web Client UI comes with *UI component enhancement*. It enables customers to modify standard UI components and their elements in a *modification-free* manner. As you know, modifying SAP code will get you in trouble as soon as you install a note or apply a service pack. Chances are good that you will lose the custom code investments.

Web Client UI's component enhancement concept takes advantage of object oriented programming (OOP) inheritance. The Web Client UI Framework follows the OOP paradigm, and as a result one can create views and controllers by inheriting from existing ones. After all, the views and controllers that we created so far always extended an existing base class. The UI component enhancements are nothing but derivatives of existing UI elements.

Most of the tools that facilitate the component enhancements are built into the Component Workbench. We will examine what is available and how to use it. Remember that a UI component contains more than just ABAP classes. For example, some metadata resides in the runtime repository XML. Therefore, modification-free component enhancement is not just an object programming extension of the standard SAP classes but also addresses tasks such as metadata handling and component element substitution at runtime.

We will continue with our imaginary custom implementation project. Our next task is to change the standard SAP CRM individual account page. Because we deal with hotel guests, we would like the application to be called GUEST rather than INDIVIDUAL ACCOUNT. Remember, in our scenario the system treats a hotel guest as a SAP CRM account. The business users complained that they often cannot quickly find the ID of a guest. Therefore, we were asked to make the ID field more prominent. Furthermore, we will bring into the account page a view from another application that shows the bookings of the current account. We also want to navigate to the bookings detail page (the one we developed earlier) from that new assignment block.

We will start the chapter by introducing the concept of an enhancement set, which we will use to enhance an existing UI component. We will show you how to use the UI configuration tool to further fine-tune the enhancement to meet specific requirements. This will allow us to explain the configuration determination procedure in the Web Client UI. Finally, we will bring content from our custom application into a standard SAP CRM business object and finalize the navigation discussion. We will look into something called *cross-component navigation*.

7.1 Enhancement Set Overview

In this section, we will briefly introduce the concepts in this chapter by first examining what is involved in enhancing an existing UI component. As you know, UI components are implemented as BSP applications. They contain standard BSP elements such as controllers and views. In addition, the Web Client UI framework uses some metadata; for example, the runtime repository XML file.

Component enhancement uses OOP inheritance extensively. However, one cannot inherit a BSP application and XML files. Therefore, each component enhancement has its own BSP application and a copy of the repository XML. The classes that you will create as part of the enhancement will be stored in that dedicated BSP application. Figure 7.1 summarizes the creation of a UI component enhancement.

Once you have a defined custom component enhancement, you can continue enhancing the original views and controllers. You even can create new views and controllers that were not part of the original component (see Figure 7.2).

This approach allows you to use any standard SAP CRM application as a foundation and build truly comprehensive custom logic and UI on top of it. In the next sections we will discuss what you need to do in order to enhance the standard SAP content.

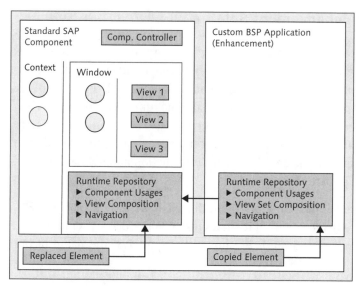

Figure 7.1 Creating Component Enhancement

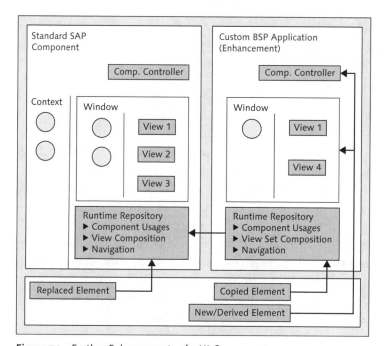

Figure 7.2 Further Enhancements of a UI Component

7.2   Create an Enhancement Set

Before we can enhance a UI component, we need to create an *enhancement set*. This is a placeholder that groups what are called *enhancement definitions*. Such a definition contains information about which component was enhanced, the name of the BSP application that hosts the enhanced objects, and the runtime repository. When enhancing a component, the Component Workbench first creates an enhancement definition and associates it with a given enhancement set. Later, the Workbench will automatically augment this definition with information about what has been enhanced (redefined) as part of the process.

If you are using a system with the Web Client (for example SAP CRM 7.0 EhP1), you can define a new enhancement set in view cluster BSPWDVC_CMP_EXT (you need to access it from Transaction SM34). As shown in Figure 7.3, the name of our enhancement set is ZBOOK_ES.

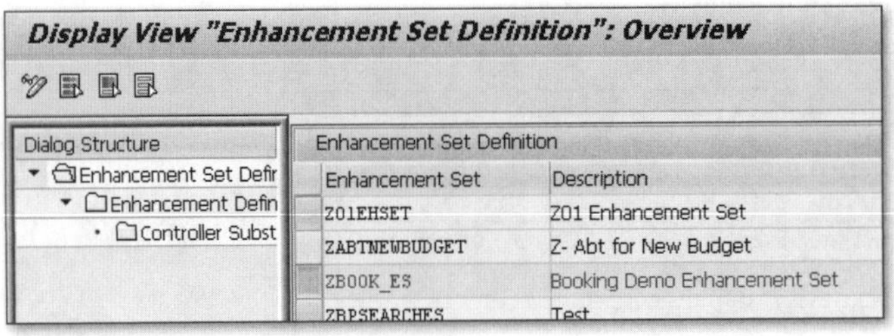

Display View "Enhancement Set Definition": Overview

Dialog Structure	Enhancement Set Definition	
▾ ⬜Enhancement Set Defin	Enhancement Set	Description
▾ ⬜Enhancement Defin	Z01EHSET	Z01 Enhancement Set
• ⬜Controller Subst	ZABTNEWBUDGET	Z- Abt for New Budget
	ZBOOK_ES	Booking Demo Enhancement Set
	ZBPSEARCHES	Test

Figure 7.3 Creating a New Enhancement Set

You can define many enhancement sets. However, only one will be used by the framework at runtime. By default, the Web Client UI will force you to associate an enhancement set with a system client. That way, the active enhancement set will be determined on the basis of the client number at runtime. However, you can implement BAdI COMPONENT_LOADING (enhancement spot COMPONENT_HANDLING) and determine an active enhancement set based on custom business rules. One frequently used criterion is the business role of the current user. The mapping between enhancement sets and roles can be defined in a customizing table. Your BAdI implementation will simply pick the one that that matches the user's role. Listing 7.1 shows a sample implementation for doing that.

```
DATA: lv_role    TYPE string,
      profile    TYPE REF TO if_crm_ui_profile.
* get the role of the current user
```

```
profile = cl_crm_ui_profile=>get_instance( ).
Lv_role = profile->get_profile( ).
* read enhancement from the customizing table (zmy_table)
SELECT SINGLE enhancement FROM zmy_table INTO rv_result
                         WHERE profile EQ lv_role.
```

Listing 7.1 COMPONENT_LOADING Sample Implementation

In our example, we will follow the default implementation for enhancement set determination. This means that we will register our enhancement set in view BSP-WDV_EHSET_ASG (through SM30). Figure 7.4 shows the registration of our enhancement ZBOOK_ES.

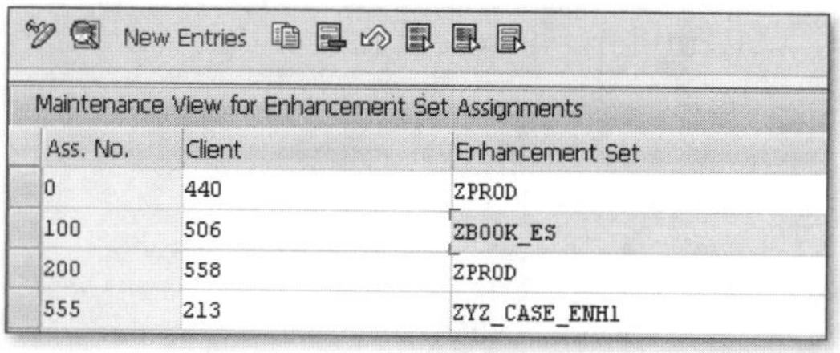

Ass. No.	Client	Enhancement Set
0	440	ZPROD
100	506	ZBOOK_ES
200	558	ZPROD
555	213	ZYZ_CASE_ENH1

Figure 7.4 Assigning an Enhancement Set to System Client

We just created a new enhancement set and declared it as the active one for our system client (Client 506). Now, each time you start the Web UI, the framework will try to substitute your requests according to any definitions in enhancement set ZBOOK_ES.

7.3 Enhancing a UI Component

Our assignment is to enhance the account application. The name of the UI component for this application is BP_HEAD. We will enhance it via the component workbench. On the starting page of the Workbench, we will provide not only the component name, but also the name of the enhancement set (Figure 7.5). If the ENHANCEMENT SET field is missing, you can enable it via the button just in front of the COMPONENT input field. In the latest releases of the Web Client UI, one can create or delete an enhancement set in the component workbench itself. In Figure 7.5 you will notice the NEW and DELETE buttons next to the COMPONENT SET input field.

Figure 7.5 Opening a UI Component with Active Enhancement Set

Let's click the DISPLAY button and open the component. A message will appear in the bottom of your screen telling you that this component does not have a definition in the selected enhancement set. You can create one by clicking on the ENHANCE COMPONENT button in the top of the page. You will have to provide the name of the BSP application that will be associated with your component enhancements. In addition, you can copy the repository XML under a different name. You can enter values for our example as shown in Figure 7.6.

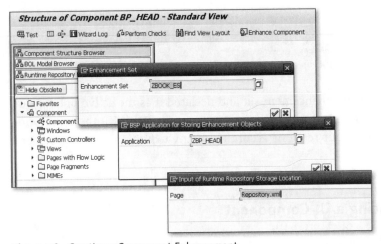

Figure 7.6 Creating a Component Enhancement

As of SAP CRM 7.0, most of the component enhancement tools are integrated in the component workbench. For example, if you click on ENVIRONMENT you will see that one of the options is ENHANCEMENT DEFINITIONS. Figure 7.7 shows the entry that our new component enhancement created in the ZBOOK_ES enhancement set.

Via Transaction SE80, you will be able to see that ZBP_HEAD BSP application (if you have used the same name) does exist and that it contains a file called Repository. xml. The latter is a copy of the repository XML from BP_HEAD component. We are now ready to enhance the elements of the SAP CRM account application.

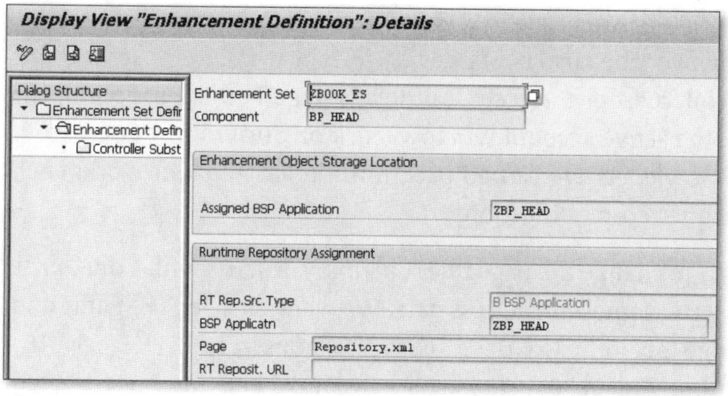

Figure 7.7 Enhancement Set Definition

7.3.1 Enhancing a UI Element

Although we have an enhancement, it behaves just like from the original component. Open an individual account and you will see that it looks the same as it did before we enhanced it. Watch what happens when you select the ID field and press the [F2] button. Figure 7.8 shows the technical details page.

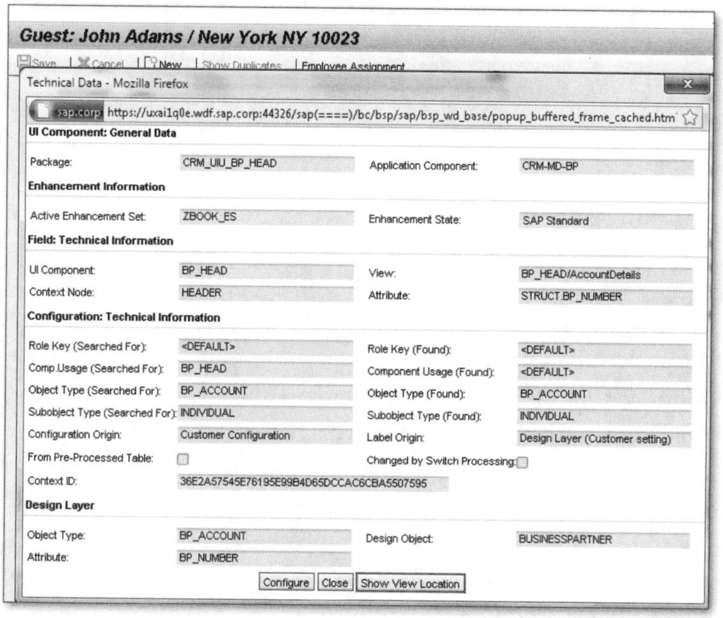

Figure 7.8 Technical Details of the Account's ID Field

In the ENHANCEMENT INFORMATION section, you will see that ZBOOK_ES is the active enhancement set. However the current state is SAP Standard. Other useful information that we can collect from the technical details page is the location of our ID field, its view, and the active account window (click on SHOW VIEW LOCATION). Equipped with this knowledge, we can go back into the component workbench and implement the requested modifications.

The first requirement is to change the page title. Currently, it starts with CORPORATE ACCOUNT: followed by the name and address data. We want the keep the name and address data, but change the prefix to GUEST:. The title comes from IF_BSP_WD_HIS-TORY_STATE_DESCR~GET_STATE_DESCRIPTION. As you know, this interface is used also by the Breadcrumb (navigation history). It has a method that allows you to retrieve the main entity of an application and use it to restore its BOL state. For now, let's stick to the title. We are interested in the IF_BSP_WD_HISTORY_STATE_DESCR implemented in the window element. We need to first enhance it and redefine GET_STATE_DESCRIPTION. Right-click on the BP_HEAD/MainWindow and select ENHANCE (Figure 7.9).

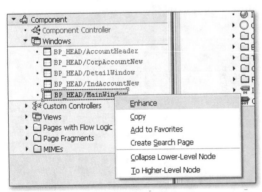

Figure 7.9 Enhancing Window Element

Once done, you will notice that the MainWindow element changes its color in the COMPONENT STRUCTURE BROWER. The Component Workbench detects and displays all the enhancements. Double-click on the MainWindow and expand its elements. Its controller and context classes now start with Z (see Figure 7.10). These new implementations inherit from the original controller and context node classes. As a result, they behave the same way as the ones in BP_HEAD, but they are part of your BSP application and you can modify them as you please.

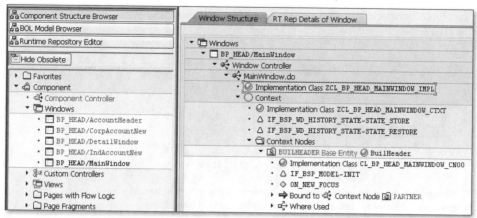

Figure 7.10 Enhanced Window Element

The redefinition of GET_STATE_DESCRIPTION could be as simple as the one in Listing 7.2.

```
data: lv_search_str type string,
      lv_search_count type i.
CALL METHOD SUPER->IF_BSP_WD_HISTORY_STATE_DESCR~GET_STATE_DESCRIPTION
  EXPORTING IV_CURRENT_DESCRIPTION = IV_CURRENT_DESCRIPTION
  RECEIVING DESCRIPTION           = DESCRIPTION.

lv_search_str = cl_wd_utilities=>get_otr_text_by_alias(
        'CRM_UIU_BP/INDIVIDUALACCOUNT' ).
lv_search_count = find( val = description sub = lv_search_str ).
IF lv_search_count >= 0.
  description = replace( val = description off = lv_search_count
                len = strlen( lv_search_str ) with = 'Guest' ).
ENDIF.
```

Listing 7.2 Redefining GET_STATE_DESCRIPTION

We are counting on the super method to figure out the title and we then rely on simple string replacement to change Individual Account (the OTR text 'CRM_UIU_BP/INDIVIDUALACCOUNT') with a hardcoded string Guest. In real life, you will replace with an OTR text rather than with a string literal.

Before we test the results, we will open the ENHANCEMENT DEFINITIONS view one more time (in the top ENVIRONMENT menu). Figure 7.11 shows that the framework has been instructed to replace the `MainView` from `BP_HEAD` with the `MainView` from `ZBP_HEAD`.

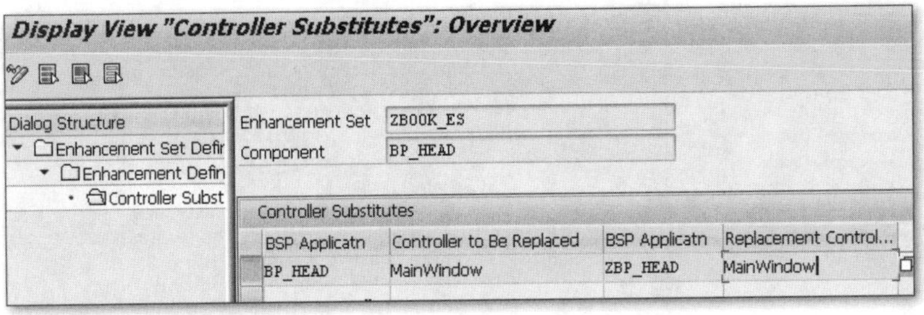

Figure 7.11 Controller Substitutions within Enhancement Definition

If you now start the Web UI you will see that our naïve implementation has done its job. The account page now says GUEST.

Next, we will change the appearance of the ID field. This is a bit tricky. We could probably come up with some Java Script code that changes the style of the corresponding HTML element. The problem is that there would be no way of knowing in advance the HTML names (IDs) of the different elements; you would have to scan all the elements and look for the ones that match some naming pattern. You would also have to enhance the `AccountDetails` view and add this elaborate and hard-to-maintain script to the HTM file. However, there is a more efficient way. As of SAP CRM 7.0 EhP1, you could use the form iterator interface. Prior to EhP1, the Web Client UI framework had only an iterator interface (`IF_HTMLB_TABLEVIEW_ITERATOR`) that allowed a developer to modify the rendering of table elements (for example, rows and cells). The framework now offers `IF_CHTMLB_FORM_ITERATOR`. Its method (`RENDER_CELL_START`) allows you to influence almost anything related to a UI element in a configurable form. In our example, we will make the label and text of the ID field bolder and larger. Listing 7.3 shows our implementation of `IF_CHTMLB_FORM_ITERATOR~ RENDER_CELL_START`.

```
DATA: LV_CURRENT TYPE REF TO IF_BOL_BO_PROPERTY_ACCESS.
DATA: LV_BEE     TYPE REF TO CL_BSP_BEE_TABLE.
DATA: LV_LABEL   TYPE REF TO CL_THTMLB_LABEL.
DATA: LV_DATA    TYPE STRING.
DATA: str1 TYPE STRING,
      str2 TYPE STRING,
      lv_attr_name TYPE NAME_KOMP.
IF IV_BINDING_STRING = '//HEADER/STRUCT.BP_NUMBER'.
```

```
"get the attribute name from the binding string
split iv_binding_string at '//' into str1 str2.
split str2 at '/' into str1 str2.
split str2 at '.' into str1 lv_attr_name.
LV_CURRENT = GV_CTX_NODE->COLLECTION_WRAPPER->GET_CURRENT( ).
LV_DATA = LV_CURRENT->GET_PROPERTY_AS_STRING( IV_ATTR_NAME = lv_attr_
name ).
  "reate the replacement element
  CREATE OBJECT LV_BEE.
  IF IV_ELEMENT_NAME   = 'label' .
    "wrap some CSS around the label
    LV_BEE->ADD_HTML( HTML = |<span style="float:right;">| LEVEL = 1 ).
    "emphasize the label with standard THTMLB label attribute DESIGN
    LV_LABEL ?= IV_ELEMENT_BEE.
    LV_LABEL->DESIGN = 'EMPHASIZED'.
  ELSEIF IV_ELEMENT_NAME   = 'inputfield'.
    LV_BEE->ADD_HTML( HTML = |<div style="font-weight:bold;"
title="Partner">| LEVEL = 1 ).
  ENDIF.
  "add original bee
  LV_BEE->ADD_BEE( BEE = IV_ELEMENT_BEE  LEVEL = 2 ).
  "close the added element
  IF IV_ELEMENT_NAME   = 'label' .
    LV_BEE->ADD_HTML( HTML = '</span>' LEVEL = 1 ).
  ELSEIF IV_ELEMENT_NAME   = 'inputfield'.
    LV_BEE->ADD_HTML( HTML = '</div>' LEVEL = 1 ).
  ENDIF.

  EV_REPLACEMENT_BEE = LV_BEE.
ENDIF.
```

Listing 7.3 IF_CHTMLB_FORM_ITERATOR Implementation

In Listing 7.3, we are checking the binding string of each form element. We are interested in the BP_NUMBER from context node HEADER (you can see this information in Figure 7.8):

```
IF IV_BINDING_STRING = '//HEADER/STRUCT.BP_NUMBER'.
```

Next, we extract the property name from the binding string and retrieve its value from the current BOL entity:

```
LV_CURRENT = GV_CTX_NODE->COLLECTION_WRAPPER->GET_CURRENT( ).
```

```
LV_DATA = LV_CURRENT->GET_PROPERTY_AS_STRING( IV_ATTR_NAME = lv_attr_
name ).
```

The GV_CTX_NODE attribute is being set in the constructor of our iterator class; you will see how shortly. What follows are some manipulations of the *BSP Element Expressions* (BEEs) that wrap the original HTML element with a span or div tags. The latter adds CSS styling to the form ID label and text field. As you will see later, there are no style conflicts, and we will achieve the desired result. Keep in mind that you could always completely substitute the BEE with your custom version. For more information on BEEs, you can study your SAP documentation.

It is time to register our form iterator class. We will do so in the corresponding HTM file. First, we need to enhance the view AccountDetails. By doing this, we ensure that it will be substituted at runtime with a controller, context classes, and HTM file from our BSP application. Once enhanced, we open the HTM file and add the initialization and activation of the custom form iterator class (before the chtmlb:config tag):

```
<% data: lv_iterator type ref to ZCL_BP_FORM_ITERATOR.
    create object lv_iterator exporting iv_ctx_node = HEADER.
    cl_chtmlb_config=>set_iterator( lv_iterator ). %>
```

As you can see, we pass the HEADER context node to the constructor of the form iterator class and use cl_chtmlb_config=>set_iterator to register it for the page.

Now if you open an individual account in the Web UI (Figure 7.12), you will see that not only is its title GUEST, but the ID field appears more prominent than the other fields.

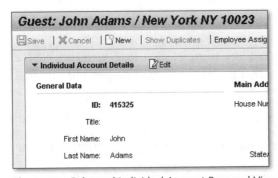

Figure 7.12 Enhanced Individual Account Page and View

If you want to be thorough about your project, you can open the page configuration tool and change the title of the INDIVIDUAL ACCOUNT DETAILS block to something like GUEST DETAILS. We will discuss the intricacies of the configuration paradigm later on.

7.3.2 Adding a New View

Component enhancements allow you not only to change the existing UI elements but also to add custom ones. Imagine that you have a custom component that shows all the bookings for a given SAP CRM business partner. Figure 7.13 shows a screenshot of such a component (called ZBOOK_VIEW) in the Component Workbench.

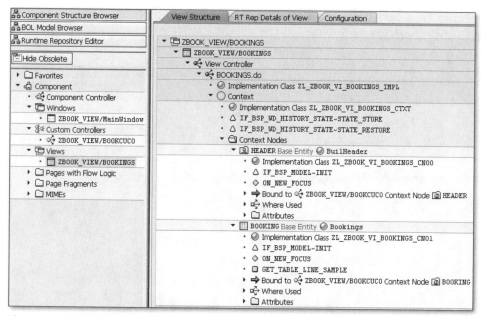

Figure 7.13 ZBOOK_VIEW UI Component

As you can see, the ZBOOK_VIEW contains one view element. The latter has two context nodes: HEADER and BOOKING. The first one uses the BuilHeader business object as a model, while the second works with our Bookings object. Figure 7.13 shows also that both the HEADER and BOOKING context nodes are bound to context nodes with the same name in a custom controller called BOOKCUCO. If you trace these nodes in BOOKCUCO, you will see that they in turn are bound to nodes also called HEADER and BOOKING but residing in the component controller. The effect of this data-binding chain is to ensure that if you set some data in the nodes in the component controller, this data will also appear in the context nodes of the custom controller and also in the BOOKINGS view. Remember that the context nodes of a component controller can be exposed as part of the component interface. As a result other components can see and work with these context nodes. This is particularly useful when you want to embed components via component usage and pass data from the embedding to the embedded component. We will use this technique when incorporating the view from ZBOOK_VIEW into the enhanced BP_HEAD.

For completeness, Listing 7.4 shows the DO_PREPARE_OUTPUT of ZBOOK_VIEW/BOOK-INGS. The code is extremely straightforward and uses the query SearchBookings to retrieve the bookings of a BP (guest) ID coming from the HEADER node.

```
data: lr_header type ref to IF_BOL_BO_PROPERTY_ACCESS,
      lr_query type ref to CL_CRM_BOL_DQUERY_SERVICE,
      lr_guest_id type ref to char10,
      lv_guest_id type string,
      lr_result  type ref to IF_BOL_ENTITY_COL,
      lr_iter    type ref to IF_BOL_ENTITY_COL_ITERATOR,
      lr_booking type ref to CL_CRM_BOL_ENTITY.

check me->TYPED_CONTEXT->HEADER is bound.

lr_header = me->TYPED_CONTEXT->HEADER->COLLECTION_WRAPPER->GET_FIRST(
).
check lr_header is bound.

lr_guest_id ?= LR_HEADER->GET_PROPERTY( 'BP_NUMBER' ).
lv_guest_id = lr_guest_id->*.
IF lv_guest_id = mv_guest_id.
  return.
ENDIF.
lr_query = CL_CRM_BOL_DQUERY_SERVICE=>GET_INSTANCE( 'SearchBookings' ).
lr_query->ADD_SELECTION_PARAM( IV_ATTR_NAME = 'GUEST_ID'
                    IV_SIGN = 'I'
                    IV_OPTION = 'EQ'
                    IV_LOW = lv_guest_id
                    IV_HIGH = '').

"execute the query and get the results
lr_result = LR_QUERY->GET_QUERY_RESULT( ).
```

```
me->TYPED_CONTEXT->BOOKING->COLLECTION_WRAPPER->SET_COLLECTION( IV_
COLLECTION = lr_result ).
MV_GUEST_ID = lv_guest_id.
```

Listing 7.4 ZBOOK_VIEW/BOOKINGS DO_PREPARE_OUTPUT

In the runtime repository of the enhanced BP_HEAD we will create a component usage for ZBOOK_VIEW. Let's call it GUEST_BOOKINGS. Remember that once defined, a component usage behaves like a normal view. Before we can display it in the UI, we need to assign it to a view set (or window). Our goal is to show the bookings in the guest (originally SAP CRM account) OVP. Therefore, we will add it to the BPHEADOverview (Figure 7.14).

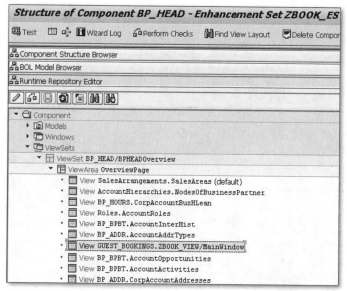

Figure 7.14 Adding GUEST_BOOKINGS to the Overview Page

You can configure the BPHEADOverview page from the Web UI or from the component workbench. From the Web UI, you should click on the CONFIGURE PAGE button in the top of the page (see Figure 7.15). If you prefer to stay in the Component Workbench, click on the CONFIGURATION tab in the view details screen (as we have done in the previous chapters).

Figure 7.15 Starting the UI Configuration Tool in the Web UI

After opening the UI configuration tool, you will find the newly added view in the AVAILABLE ASSIGNMENT BLOCKS. You could simply move it to the displayed assignment blocks and give it a meaningful title (see Figure 7.16).

Component Nam	Page	Role Config. Ke	Component Usage	Object Type	Object Subtyp	Standard Cont	Customer Con
BP_HEAD	BPHEADOVERV	<DEFAULT>	<DEFAULT>	<DEFAULT>	<DEFAULT>	✓	✓
BP_HEAD	BPHEADOVERV	<DEFAULT>	<DEFAULT>	BP_ACCOUNT	CORPORATE	✓	☐
BP_HEAD	BPHEADOVERV	<DEFAULT>	<DEFAULT>	BP_ACCOUNT	CREATE	✓	☐
BP_HEAD	BPHEADOVERV	<DEFAULT>	<DEFAULT>	BP_ACCOUNT	INDIVIDUAL	✓	✓
BP_HEAD	BPHEADOVERV	<DEFAULT>	WFDOverview	BP_ACCOUNT	CORPORATE	✓	☐

◀Back   1   2   3   Forward▶

▼ View   Show Technical Details

Available Assignment Blocks

Component	View Name	Title
BP_DATA_IDM	BP_DATA_IDM/MainWindow	User
BP_DATA	TaxNumbers	Tax Numbers
BP_DATA	TaxClassification	Tax Classifications
BP_DATA	Shareholders	Shareholders
BP_DATA	QualificationReqEOVP	Qualification Requirements
BP_DATA	Industries	
BP_DATA	IDNumbers	Identification Numbers
BP_DATA	ExclFunctions	
BP_DATA	CompetitorProducts	Competitor Products
BP_DATA	CompetitorOpportunities	Competitor Opportunities

Displayed Assignment Blocks

Up   Down

Component	View Name	Title	Load Option
BP_HEAD	AccountViewSet	Individual Account	Direct
ZBOOK_VIEW	ZBOOK_VIEW/Mai	Guest Bookings	Direct
BP_DATA	BP_DATA/Current	Current Work Add	Hidden
BP_DATA	BP_DATA/InvalidC	Invalid Work Addre	Hidden
BP_ROLES	MainWindow	Roles	Direct
BP_BPBT	AccountActivities	Planned Activities	Direct
BP_BPBT	AccountOpportuni	Opportunities	Direct
BP_ADDR	CorpAccountAddr	Addresses	Direct
BP_ADDR	BP_ADDR/Addres	Address Types	Lazy
BP_ADDR	AccountInactAddr	Inactive Addresse	Hidden

Figure 7.16 BP OVP Configuration

Once done, save and close the page configuration. The configuration changes are stored in customizing transport requests, and you will be prompted to provide one. As expected, the OVP contains a new block called GUEST Bookings but it is empty. The reason is that the HEADER context node of ZBOOK_VIEW/BOOKINGS is empty. Consequently, DO_PREPARE_OUT never calls the query. To remedy this, we should pass some BP data from the account page to our custom component.

Recall that the business object bound to the context node HEADER of ZBOOK_VIEW is BuilHeader. If you check the BP_HEAD component, you will find a node called PARTNER that is also bound to BuilHeader. The way to resolve this is to create a binding

356

between the `ZBOOK-HEADER` and `BP_HEAD-PARTNER`. Fortunately, the Web Client UI allows us to do this fairly easily. We need to redefine `WD_USAGE_INITIALIZE` in the `BP_HEAD`'s component controller. This method is responsible for initialization of component usages. Make sure you first enhance the component controller. You can find the `WD_USAGE_INITIALIZE` in the SUB COMPONENT HANDLING node of the CONTROLLER STRUCTURE page (double-click on the component controller to see it in the right-hand side of the Workbench screen). Listing 7.5 shows our sample implementation. Note that we call the super method first. After all, our goal is to enhance, not to remove any existing functionality.

```
CALL METHOD SUPER->WD_USAGE_INITIALIZE
  EXPORTING
    IV_USAGE = IV_USAGE.

IF IV_USAGE->USAGE_NAME eq 'GUEST_BOOKINGS'.
  iv_usage->BIND_CONTEXT_NODE(
      exporting IV_CONTROLLER_TYPE  = CL_BSP_WD_CONTROLLER=>CO_TYPE_
COMPONENT
        IV_TARGET_NODE_NAME = 'PARTNER'
        IV_NODE_2_BIND = 'HEADER' ).
ENDIF.
```

Listing 7.5 Implementation WD_USAGE_INITIALIZE

In the above listing, we perform data binding at the component controller level (`CL_BSP_WD_CONTROLLER=>CO_TYPE_COMPONENT`) when the component usage name is `GUEST_BOOKINGS`. The binding is between the `PARTNER` and `HEADER` context nodes of the embedding and embeddable components respectively.

If you now test the account application, the GUEST BOOKINGS block will show all the records related to the current business partner (see Figure 7.17).

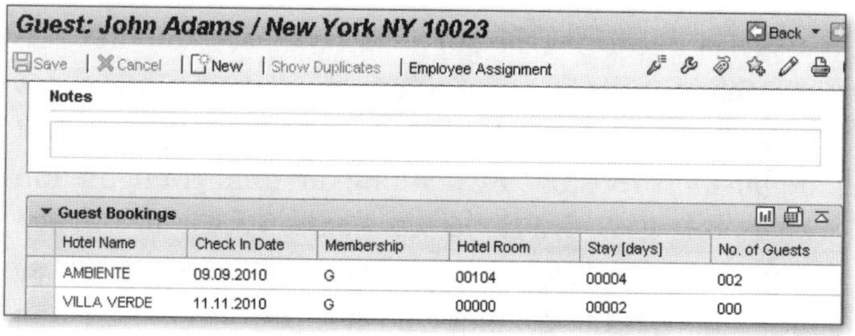

Figure 7.17 BP Account OVP with Custom Assignment Block

The `ZBOOK_VIEW\BOOKINGS` view has been configured already. We will continue our discussion of configuration in the next section.

7.4 View Configurations

To demonstrate the power of the UI configuration concept we will perform another configuration right from the account page. Click on the SHOW CONFIGURABLE AREAS button (Figure 7.15). The display mode of the page will change, and you can pick the view that you wish to configure (see Figure 7.18).

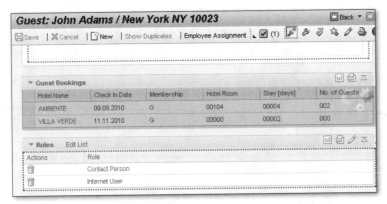

Figure 7.18 Select a View to Configure

Inside the UI configuration tool, you might have already spotted an assignment block called CONFIGURATIONS. The entries there are known as *configuration keys*. Let us look deeper into how they are handled by the framework.

7.4.1 Configuration Keys

Each configuration key is associated to a view layout definition. Based on the user- and application-specific information, the framework will pick one of those keys at runtime. When we discussed the business roles topic, we explained that one of the key values could be the business role key. By defining different configuration keys for the different business role keys, we can create dedicated layouts for the different user groups. Other key values are the object type and subtype. These are controlled by the application, as is the component usage key value. Based on the values of these parameters at runtime, the framework will find a matching configuration key and render its layout.

For our custom view, you will probably have only one default configuration key. This means that our view will look the same no matter who the user is and where the view is displayed. The <default> value is always a match. The framework gives precedence to the most specific configuration key.

We will create a specific layout that will be displayed only in the account OVP. Remember that we incorporated the ZBOOK_VIEW via a component usage GUEST_BOOK-INGS. Therefore, if we use the name of that component usage as a configuration key attribute we will ensure that the configuration in question will be matched only when the view is displayed in the BP_HEAD component.

You can create a new configuration by clicking on the NEW or COPY buttons. Always work with your own copy of a standard configuration. Remember that custom configuration keys have precedence over SAP keys.

In our example, we will remove the NO OF GUEST column from the configuration key with GUEST_BOOKINGS component usage (see Figure 7.19).

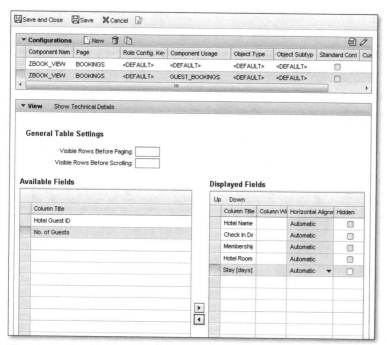

Figure 7.19 Creating View Configuration

Once you are done with the changes, you will notice right away the difference in the account OVP: The Guest Bookings has one fewer column (Figure 7.20). However, if you test the standalone `ZBOOK_VIEW` component, the configuration with `DEFAULT` key attributes will be used and there you will see the No. of Guests column.

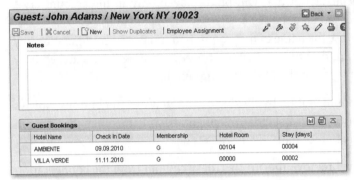

Figure 7.20 Guest Booking Based on Different Configuration Keys

If you have been trying to reproduce the examples in this book, you have noticed that the initial values of the field labels come from the DDIC. However, we can also change these labels in the configuration tool. The next section explains what can influence the labels presented to the end user.

7.4.2 Text Determination

At runtime, the Web Client UI framework tries to determine the actual field text based on different sources. First comes the DDIC, then the design layer, then configuration, and finally personalization. At the same time precedence is given to custom settings over SAP ones. To summarize, the text is determined based on multiples sources in the following order:

- Personalization (highest precedence)
- Customer configuration
- Customer design layer
- SAP configuration
- SAP design layer
- DDIC (lowest precedence)

We have talked about all the above, but have not gone in depth into personalization and design layer. We will provide you with some examples in the next chapter. For now, we would like to further enhance our custom view and wrap up the topic of navigation.

7.5   Cross-Component Navigation

You know that the guest booking data also contains information about the products and services used by the guest. This is tabular data and it could be awkward to display it in the account page (the guest page after our enhancements). Moreover, in real life you will probably have a more elaborate booking object with many fields and dependent objects. Therefore, it makes sense to show only a summary in the account page and to support navigation to the bookings page. This way, a business user can drill down in order to check the complete booking details. Because the booking is an independent object, it makes sense to handle it via a separate component. We already have such a component, and so our use case will be to implement navigation from the GUEST BOOKINGS view to the bookings overview page. One obstacle is that these are hosted by two separate components. The technique of cross-component navigation will help us implement this requirement. To make things more interesting, we do this through the enhanced BP_HEAD component.

Doss-component navigation is based on the settings in the WORK AREA COMPONENT REPOSITORY. The latter can be found via the IMG menu path CUSTOMER RELATIONSHIP MANAGEMENT • UI FRAMEWORK • TECHNICAL ROLE DEFINITION • DEFINE WORK AREA COMPONENT REPOSITORY. Cross-cross-component navigation is often called dynamic because it is determined at runtime.

We had to register our ZCMP_HTL_BOOK component in the Work Area Component Repository. We did this in order to enable the access to it through the navigation bar profile and the L-shape. Figure 7.21 shows the inbound plug definitions. These entries define target IDs.

The entries in the outbound plug definitions node of the Work Area Component Repository specify source IDs. They are a combination of component, view, and outbound plug. You also can provide a UI object type and action, but this involves a special case that we will not discuss in this book.

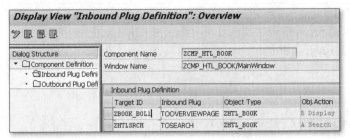

Figure 7.21 Inbound Plug Definition of ZCMP_HTL_BOOK

In order to navigate between components we will require all the above customizing (and more). We will discuss the different types of cross-component navigation, how to initiate it, and how to propagate it through the outbound plugs of the different UI elements (starting from the view and progressing to the window). Finally, we will test our work and explain what one can expect to see in the debugger.

7.5.1 Means of Cross-Component Navigation

There are three ways to perform cross-component navigation:

► A direct mapping between a source ID and a target ID.

► A generic mapping of a UI object type and an object action to a navigation target ID.

► Dynamic generic mapping of a UI object type and an object action to a target ID (via a descriptor object).

The first kind of navigation is very specific and involves extensive customizing. We do not recommend using it. The second kind allows you to define a link between a source and target view from different components through a layer of abstraction. Based on the settings in the Work Area Component Repository, the framework allows you to map combinations of UI object types to target IDs. As a result you do not have a specific mapping between outbound and inbound plugs.

The third kind of navigation is the one that we will discuss here. The idea is that you do not define dedicated outbound plugs but instead create a navigation descriptor object which helps the framework find the target component or view. You still rely on the level of abstraction that the Work Area Component Repository provides, but you do not have to worry about registering outbound plugs and you can perform the resolution of the target component at runtime.

7.5.2 Invoking Navigation

We will add a navigation link of the HOTEL NAME column in ZBOOK_VIEW/BOOKINGS view. Following the link will enable the user to navigate to and load the bookings overview page in the work area. The selected booking data will be displayed. Any actions on that link will trigger an event that will result in a navigation request through an outbound plug. The coding samples in this section should help you grasp the idea of cross-component navigation.

Creating a Link

In order to render a field as a link, we need to implement its P-getter method. We did this exercise previously but it does not hurt to revise. Go to the BOOKING context node of ZBOOK_VIEW/BOOKINGS view and right click on it. You should see the option GENERATE P-GETTER. Go ahead and select it. The framework will generate the getter's skeleton. Listing 7.6 shows our implementation of GET_P_HOTEL_NAME.

```
CASE iv_property.
  WHEN if_bsp_wd_model_setter_getter=>fp_fieldtype.
    rv_value = if_bsp_dlc_view_descriptor=>field_type_event_link.
    RETURN.
  WHEN if_bsp_wd_model_setter_getter=>fp_onclick.
    rv_value = 'GOBOOKING'.
    RETURN.
ENDCASE.
```

Listing 7.6 Hotel Name P-Getter

When the framework requests the field type property for the hotel name attribute, our P-getter returns a constant that tells the framework that this field shall be rendered by a link that is associated with an event. Next, the framework will ask what will happen when the user clicks on the link. The framework requests this information by calling our Get_P method with the attribute type FP_ONCLICK and our Get_P method indicates that an event called GOBOOKING will be called.

Implementing an Event Handler

Based on the above, it is clear that our view must have an event handler for GOBOOK-ING. To add the event handler, right-click on the node EVENT HANDLER, chose CREATE and specify the event GOBOOKING. Then open the event handler method and add the code as per Listing 7.7.

```
DATA: lv_index TYPE int4,
        lr_entity TYPE REF TO IF_BOL_BO_PROPERTY_ACCESS,
        lr_msg_srv TYPE REF TO cl_bsp_wd_message_service,
        lv_bo_coll   TYPE REF TO if_bol_bo_col.
CALL METHOD cl_thtmlb_util=>get_event_info
    EXPORTING iv_event = htmlb_event_ex
    IMPORTING ev_index = lv_index.
lr_entity = me->typed_context->BOOKING->GET_BO_BY_INDEX(
                                    iv_index = lv_index ).

IF lr_entity IS NOT BOUND OR lr_entity is initial.
    lr_msg_srv = me->view_manager->get_message_service( ).
    lr_msg_srv->add_message( iv_msg_type = 'E'
                             iv_msg_id = 'CRM_UIU_BT'
                             iv_msg_number = '010'
                             iv_important_info = abap_true ).
    RETURN.
ENDIF.

CREATE OBJECT lv_bo_coll TYPE cl_crm_bol_bo_col.
lv_bo_coll->add( lr_entity ).

OP_TOBOOKING( IV_DATA_COLLECTION = LV_BO_COLL ).
```
Listing 7.7 GOBOOKING Event Handler Implementation

First we get the index of the selected booking record via the static utility method `cl_thtmlb_util=>get_event_info`. Next we fetch the BOL entity that corresponds to this index from the `BOOKING` context node:

```
lr_entity = me->typed_context->BOOKING->GET_BO_BY_INDEX(
                                    iv_index = lv_index ).
```

We want to pass this BOL entity to the target component. We know that in order to display a complete booking record in `ZCMP_HTL_BOOK`, we must pass a `Bookings` object through the `TO_OVERVIEWPAGE` inbound plug. We retrieve the booking entity from the current component and put it in a collection. The collection is passed to an outbound plug (this is a clean way to send data out from the current component):

```
lv_bo_coll->add( lr_entity ).
OP_TOBOOKING( IV_DATA_COLLECTION = LV_BO_COLL ).
```

Triggering the Navigation in Outbound Plug

We do not have an outbound plug called TOBOOKING, so we have to create one. Make sure that you create two outbound plugs with the same name: one on the view and another on the component window. In order to create an outbound plug, right-click on the OUTBOUND PLUGS in the VIEW STRUCTURE and choose CREATE. Remember that the workbench will generate a method that starts with OP_ followed by the plug name. Listing 7.8 shows the outbound plug in the ZBOOK_VIEW/BOOKING view.

```
DATA: lr_window TYPE REF TO cl_bsp_wd_window,
      lr_descriptor TYPE REF TO  if_bol_bo_property_access,
      lr_nav_srv TYPE REF TO  if_crm_ui_navigation_service.

" create a descriptor object from a UI Object Type
CALL METHOD cl_crm_ui_descriptor_obj_srv=>CREATE_UI_OBJECT_BASED
   EXPORTING  iv_ui_object_type   = 'ZHTL_BOOK'
         iv_ui_object_action = 'B' " see CRMT_UI_ACTION
         iv_component        = 'ZCMP_HTL_BOOK'
   RECEIVING  rr_result           = lr_descriptor.

" if the navigation is supported according to the customizing
"then add the descriptor object to the data collection
lr_nav_srv = cl_crm_ui_navigation_service=>get_instance( me ).
IF lr_nav_srv->is_dynamic_nav_supported(
        ir_descriptor_object = lr_descriptor ) EQ abap_true.
   "CREATE OBJECT lr_data_collection TYPE cl_crm_bol_bo_col.
   "lr_data_collection->add( iv_entity = lr_descriptor_object ).
   iv_data_collection->INSERT( IV_BO = lr_descriptor
                               IV_INDEX = 1 ).
ELSE.
   " error handling
   RETURN.
ENDIF.

lr_nav_srv ->navigate_dynamically( iv_data_collection ).
lr_window = me->view_manager->get_window_controller( ).
lr_window->call_outbound_plug( iv_outbound_plug   = 'TOBOOKING'
                         iv_data_collection = iv_data_collection ).
```

Listing 7.8 Outbound Plug OP_TOBOOKING Implementation

We will use dynamic cross-component navigation, based on a descriptor object. In order to create one, we will use the UI descriptor object service class:

```
CALL METHOD cl_crm_ui_descriptor_obj_srv=>CREATE_UI_OBJECT_BASED
  EXPORTING  iv_ui_object_type   = 'ZHTL_BOOK'
         iv_ui_object_action = 'B' " see CRMT_UI_ACTION
         iv_component        = 'ZCMP_HTL_BOOK'
  RECEIVING  rr_result           = lr_descriptor.
```

In line with the work areas customizing (Figure 7.21), our target has an object type ZCMP_HTL_BOOK and action B. This is sufficient to identify it and generate navigational information from it. This navigational data is returned in the form of a descriptor object which implements the BOL property access interface.

Next we check if the customizing allows navigation to the desired target. In order for the framework to allow your users to navigate to a target, it must exist in their navigation profile. The profile that we use in our example is called SLS-PRO (you can get it from the business role customization). Figure 7.22 shows the required entry in the navigation profile. Please create this customizing if you have not done so already.

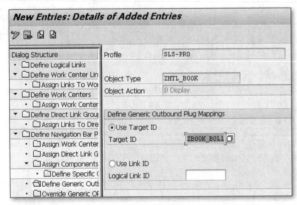

Figure 7.22 Adding the Target ID to Navigation Profile

The following code checks if the required customizations exist in the navigation bar profile:

```
lr_nav_srv->is_dynamic_nav_supported(
        ir_descriptor_object = lr_descriptor ) EQ abap_true.
```

The framework will pick the descriptor object from the BOL collection that we fire out of the outbound plug and process it. The framework expects to find this object in the beginning of the collection. Once the object is processed, the descriptor will be removed from the collection and the rest of the data will be handed over to the target inbound plug. Therefore, it is important that we insert our descriptor in the beginning of the collection:

```
iv_data_collection->INSERT( IV_BO = lr_descriptor
                            IV_INDEX = 1 ).
```

We will resort to the navigation service again and fire a dynamic navigation event:

```
lr_nav_srv ->navigate_dynamically( iv_data_collection ).
```

The last step will ignore the concept of the outbound plugs. As a result, we do not have to worry about this customization step.

Last, we will call the outbound plug of the window (make sure you create the plug):

```
lr_window->call_outbound_plug( iv_outbound_plug   = 'TOBOOKING'
                               iv_data_collection = iv_data_collection ).
```

The code of `OP_TOBOOKING` in the `MainWindow` controller is shown in Listing 7.9.

```
FIRE_OUTBOUND_PLUG( IV_OUTBOUND_PLUG = 'TOBOOKING'
                    IV_DATA_COLLECTION = IV_DATA_COLLECTION ).
```

Listing 7.9 MainWindow OP_TOBOOKING Implementation

Please note that so far we have been enabling a component (`ZBOOK_VIEW`) that will be nested inside another one. In such scenarios, the window of the embedded component is not the outermost. After all, it is wrapped by the views and/or window of the embedding component. The views or windows will be aware that the embedded component has outbound plugs through which it might navigate. Therefore, we shall expose the plug of the `ZBOOK_VIEW` component. Open the repository editor, and add `TOBOOKING` to the component interface.

Propagating the Navigation

Let us go back to the `BP_HEAD` component enhancement. The navigation request that has been fired by the `ZBOOK_VIEW` window (plug `TOBOOKING`) will be propagated to the embedding window `BP_HEAD\MainWindow`. This is one of the most frequent reasons for errors when embedding reusable views with links. The navigation request always has to leave through the outmost window. In this case, it is the `MainWindow` of the embedding component `BP_HEAD`. It is the parent window of `ZBOOK_VIEW`. In order to ensure that this takes place, we will add the `TOBOOKING` plug to the component usage `GUEST_BOOKINGS`. We can do this because we added the plug to the `ZBOOK_VIEW` component interface. We will then map it to an outbound plug of a parent window so that the navigation can proceed from inner to outer elements.

Let us first add an outbound plug `TOBOOKING` to the `MainWindow` of `BP_HEAD`. We will have to enhance the window and add such a plug. The code of this plug will be exactly the same as that in the `ZBOOK_VIEW`'s window (see Listing 7.9). We will also add the newly created plug to the component interface of `BP_HEAD` (see Figure 7.23).

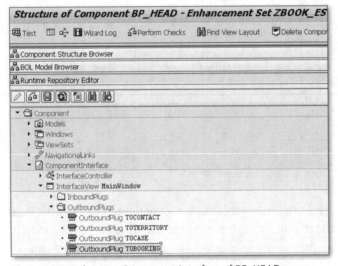

Figure 7.23 Enhancing Component Interface of BP_HEAD

`MainWindow` of `BP_HEAD` acts as a parent window to our component usage. We will right-click on the plug in the component usage and choose to delegate from `ZBOOK_VIEW` to an outbound plug `TOBOOKING` of the parent window (see Figure 7.24).

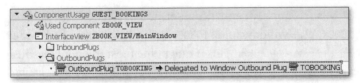

Figure 7.24 Delegating Embedded Outbound Plug to Embedding Plug

7.5.3   Testing the Navigation

It is time to test. We have placed debug breakpoints in the outbound plug methods. Open the account page. Make sure that the GUEST BOOKINGS block contains entries. The HOTEL NAME column will be rendered as links (see Figure 7.25).

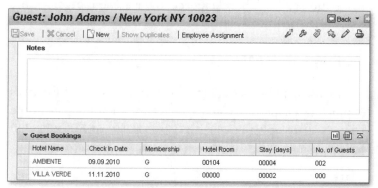

Figure 7.25   Guest Bookings with Hyperlinks

Clicking on it will start the debugger. We can detect that the frameworks goes through the event handler rather than through the outbound plug in ZBOOK_VIEW and gets into the TOBOOKING plug in BP_HEAD. If you take a look at the collection object, you will find two objects there. As you can see in Figure 7.26, the first entry is our descriptor object, and the second one is the Bookings entity that corresponds to the selected row from GUEST BOOKINGS.

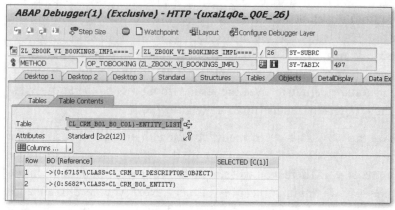

Figure 7.26   Content of Collection in Outbound Plugs

The framework will complete the navigation and eventually you will enter the TO_OVERVIEW inbound plug of ZBOOK_A. The BOL collection will contain only one entry: the booking. The descriptor will be gone. In the Web UI, the end user will be presented with the bookings overview page. The cross-component navigation has been performed successfully. Once the user is done reviewing the data, he or she can click the BACK button and will be taken back to the account page.

7.6 Outbound Plugs Delegation

In order to simplify the discussion of navigation we deferred some of the tasks needed a bit in the previous chapter. If you are recreating the examples in the book, please open the TOBOOKING plug in ZBOOK_VIEW\BOOKING view (Listing 7.8) and comment the following line:

```
lr_nav_srv ->navigate_dynamically( iv_data_collection ).
```

If you activate your changes and test again, you will get an error message related to missing navigation settings for TOBOOKING.

The reason is that IF_CRM_UI_NAVIGATION_SERVICE=>NAVIGATE_DYNAMICALLY does not strictly follow the concept of outbound plugs. As a matter of fact, only UI elements outside of the work area should rely on this method call. At the window level, you have to fire the outbound plug, which tells the UI runtime to leave the current UI component.

You might ask why we are getting the error after we have correctly mapped the outbound plug from the embedded view to that of the embedding window. The reason is that BP_HEAD is not the topmost component. BP_HEAD_MAIN is the one taking up the work area. BP_HEAD is included in it via a component usage. This may sound confusing but it is a common practice in UI component development. Therefore, you should carefully analyze the results from pressing the SHOW VIEW LOCATION in the F2 technical details pop-up (Figure 7.8).

In order to leave the BP_HEAD_MAIN correctly, you have to enhance it and create a new outbound plug in its MainWindow. You can use the same name as for the other plugs, namely TOBOOKING. There, you will simply fire your way out of that component in the same way we did in BP_HEAD\MainWindow. Next, you need to enhance the runtime repository and delegate the embedded outbound plug to the new embedding plug (from BP_HEAD's TOBOOKING to BP_HEAD_MAIN's \TOBOOKING).

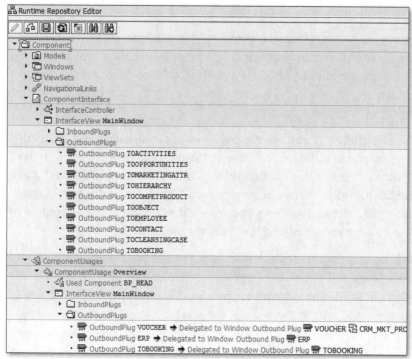

Figure 7.27 Outbound Plug Delegation in BP_HEAD_MAIN

Only after you complete the above steps will you be able to complete the cross-component navigation. At runtime, the outbound plug of ZBOOK_VIEW will delegate to the outbound plug of BP_HEAD, which will delegate to the outbound plug of BP_HEAD_MAIN and only then enter the ZCMP_HTL_BOOK component.

7.7 Summary

In this chapter we covered two very important topics: modification-free enhancement of UI components and cross-component navigation. The first allows you to change the default behavior of SAP-delivered business applications. You can change views, windows, code your custom logic, and even augment the original component with custom views. The best part is that you do all that in your own namespace and do not risk losing your changes during the next upgrade. Of course you have to be careful and always modify the derived elements. When redefining a method, you will often need to call the super method in order not to lose the original functionality.

We saw that the component enhancements are grouped in enhancement sets. You need to plan these definitions, as there could be only one active enhancement set during runtime. We showed you how you can create your custom rules for establishing the active enhancement set.

Towards the end of the chapter, we created a custom component and embedded it into the enhancement standard component. We used the opportunity to refresh your knowledge of plugs and component interfaces. The example evolved into a discussion about navigating between components. We used the components developed previously and showed you how you can use the concept of cross-component navigation to link the enhanced and the custom application.

All the frontend development presented so far in the book requires plenty of technical knowledge and skills. In the upcoming chapters, we will show you some tools the Web Client UI offers to ease the pain of development.

A developer's job would be much easier if he could quickly create a UI from a GenIL component. Even better would be a way to continuously enhance this UI based on feedback from customers.

8   Generating UI Components

In the previous sections, we demonstrated and explained how to build Web Client UI applications. By now, you know that the best way to expose your backend functionality in the Web UI is to wrap it with a GenIL component and then use the BOL APIs and the BSP Component Workbench to produce a UI component on top. We have discussed different tools and wizards that can speed up things and simplify your work. For example, the GenIL Model Editor allows you to easily define your model and business objects. The Component Workbench provides dedicated wizards that allow you generate a search page or a view from the GenIL component's model. Moreover, the context nodes in your views can be easily mapped against the business objects from your model, allowing you to seamlessly propagate your application data into the presentation layer.

Despite all these improvements, you still have to jump between different tools and perform various manual steps just to bring the data to the Web UI. Often, all you want to do when prototyping is to quickly show something to your customers, get their feedback, and continue working towards the final version of the application. If you are a SAP CRM consultant, the need for a tool that brings all these wizards into one homogenous environment must have been obvious.

If you look closely at how the search page and view wizards work, you will realize that they rely on metadata. In case of model context nodes, the source of this metadata is the GenIL model. In order to put all the pieces together and generate UIs out of the GenIL model, we need something that produces BSP applications and more ABAP code from the GenIL metadata.

Prior to SAP CRM 7.0, EEW was the closest thing to code-and-structure generation from metadata. In SAP CRM 7.0, SAP introduced the next generation extensibility tool: Application Enhancement Tool (AET). We saw it in action already. In addition to being user friendly and consistent across SAP CRM applications, AET is also quite extensible. It heavily relies on metadata and templates to generate code and structures. With this introduction, the idea of generating a complete application out of metadata became feasible.

In SAP CRM EhP1, SAP capitalized on its investments in BOL/GenIL and in extensibility and produced a set of tools allowing users to generate applications based on metadata. In this chapter, we will focus on resources available in the BSP Component Workbench to generate fully functional UI components from existing GenIL models. We also will look at how one can further enhance the output of the wizard and go beyond basic data visualization and prototyping. We will continue the exploration of the Web Client UI and present you with some new and useful features. We also will wrap up our discussion of UI configuration and the personalization topic. You are already familiar with the design layer concept, and this chapter will add the missing information on this subject. Last but not least, we will show you how to render UI components in a pop-up.

8.1 Generating a UI Component from BOL

To start with, we will assume that you already have a GenIL component. We will use the ZBOOK GenIL component set discussed in the earlier chapters. Previously, we showed what it takes to build a UI component around this manually via the Component Workbench. Therefore, you should know what is needed to bring application data to the end user. Our objective is to reproduce or come as close as possible to the frontend developed earlier, using the new code-generation tools. Figure 8.1 depicts schematically the UI that we have in mind.

As hinted in the introduction of this chapter, we will rely on the metadata already available in our GenIL model. We will show you how a technical user can define an UI application based on the GenIL model and produce a fully functional UI component without writing a single line of ABAP code. We will demonstrate a wizard that generates a complete component based on a GenIL model. Once the component is produced, we will take a look what is inside it, and finally we will test it. Last but not least, we will show how one can modify (fine-tune) the component's elements.

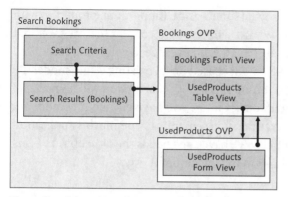

Figure 8.1 Schematics of User Interface

8.1.1 Using the Generation Wizard

As of SAP CRM 7.0 EhP1, the Component Workbench is equipped with a new wizard that facilitates UI component generation. If you start the Component Workbench (Transaction BSP_WD_CMPWB), you will see a new button called CREATE USING WIZARD. Clicking it will start a multi-step wizard with a title GENERATE UI FROM A BOL MODEL.

Step 1: Define Application Properties

Figure 8.2 shows Step 1 of the wizard.

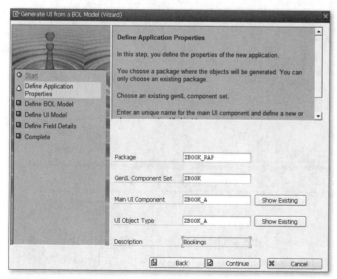

Figure 8.2 Define Application Properties in Wizard

375

As the name suggests, you have to provide some basic UI application properties with this screen. Upon completion, the wizard will generate code in the PACKAGE that you have to provide. So make sure you have a valid package in your namespace. The wizard will allow you to produce a UI model based on an existing GenIL model. By providing a GENIL COMPONENT SET, you are specifying what models will be available to the future application. In line with our example, we have given our component the name ZBOOK_A. The UI OBJECT TYPE that will semantically define this application is also called ZBOOK_A. The last property we have specified is the DESCRIPTION. This will be used to identify your application in a meaningful way.

Step 2: Define BOL Model

Clicking the CONTINUE button will take you to Step 2 of the wizard. Here you need to select the business objects and the queries that your application will be based upon. If you click on the ADD button, a pop-up will appear (Figure 8.3). In there you can find all the business objects from the GenIL models. You can navigate from parent to child objects via their relations.

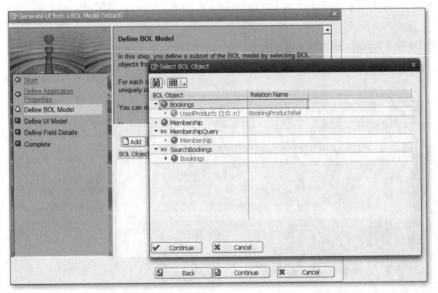

Figure 8.3 Define BOL Model

The SELECT BOL OBJECT pop-up is quite smart. In the beginning it will not allow you to pick anything other than a root object. Later, you will not be able to select an object whose parent is not already selected. For example, if you try to select `UsedProducts` before selecting `Bookings` you will get an error.

If you are following our example, please select the `Bookings` object and press CONTINUE. Another window will open, prompting us to provide an alias and thus confirm our selection (Figure 8.4). An alias serves as a semantically meaningful identifier for a given business object. It will also be used as a base name, suffix, or prefix when generating various artifacts. However, the strongest argument for having such an alias is the fact that the same business object can participate and have a different meaning at different levels in the model hierarchy. Take the business partner (BP) header, for example. This is one of the first objects that you will see when exploring the account GenIL model. As you drill deeper into the model hierarchy, you will again find the BP header as part of the contact data for a given account. Although the business object is the same, the data that it carries is quite different. In one account, you will have more than one instance of this BP head object. The only way for the wizard to differentiate between them is to name the first one as `Account Header` and the second occurrence as `Contact Header`, for example.

Figure 8.4 Entering BOL Object Alias Name

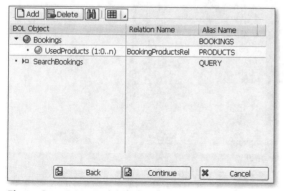

Figure 8.5 BOL Model Definition

Once you are done with the alias name, the `Bookings` entry will appear in the model definition. If you click on the arrow in front of it (as if trying to expand it), the SELECT BOL OBJECT will appear again, allowing you to easily find and choose the dependent `UsedProducts` object. Add the `SearchBookings` query as well. The result should be very similar to Figure 8.5.

Step 3: Define UI Model

In Step 3 of the wizard you get to model the UI elements of the future application. The BOL model defined in the previous step will serve as a foundation for the UI model. At this point, you might be wondering why you needed to select the business objects from the existing model and not use the complete model to define your UI. The answer may not be obvious in our sample implementation, but if you work with a complex component set the number of business objects can be overwhelming. Also, the wizard can automatically create a UI model based on the BOL model subset; imagine the outcome if you attempt to do so with a full-blown GenIL model such as a business transaction (BT); a sales order, for example. In order to take advantage of the automatic UI generation, you need to press the AUTO CREATE button. The result based on our example is shown in Figure 8.6.

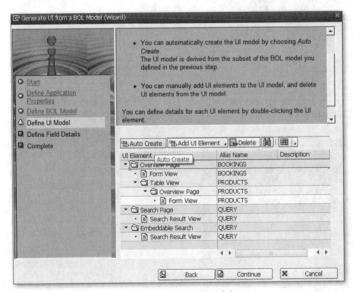

Figure 8.6 Automatically Generated UI Model

You could have defined the UI manually. The ADD UI ELEMENT button allows you to specify pages and views based on the BOL model objects from the previous step. As a matter of fact, if you want to combine more than one business object into a single view, you have to do so manually. The only condition is that the objects are connected via a 1:1 relation. In general, entities that are related to their parent via 0 or 1:M (one-to-many) cardinality will be rendered as table views. Those that have 1:1 cardinality will be displayed as a form.

Before you define views, you have to add pages. The tool distinguishes between an overview page, search page, and *embeddable search*. While the first two should be familiar, the last page type is new. The embeddable search page has a special use and could be integrated into other applications. We will see it in action later. For now, just take note of it and keep in mind that you can use it to enhance other applications.

As you know, an overview page (OVP) consists of assignment blocks. These could be form or table views. If you try to manually create such an OVP, the wizard will ask you to pick a root object. You can think of this as the header of the overview page. The wizard's auto create feature automatically picked the first object from our model, namely `Bookings`.

In an OVP, the first assignment block typically is a header form view, where the main details of the business object are presented. In our example, the header form view will be based on the `Bookings` object (the root object). If you select the first form view node (see Figure 8.6), and click ADD UI ELEMENT, you will see a menu where you can ADD A NODE. Such a node could be a dependent (1:1) object. This is how you can create views based on more than one business object (with multiple context nodes). In our simple example model, we do not have objects that have a 1:1 cardinality with `Bookings` and so we will not demonstrate this feature.

Now let's continue pretending that you are creating the UI manually. If you click on the overview page node and choose ADD UI ELEMENT, you would be able to add more views. Imagine that you choose to add a table view. The wizard would present a pop-up where you have to select an object for this view. Clearly, you have to choose an object that is connected to the header object via a 0 or 1:M cardinality. This would be the `UsedProducts` business object. The auto-create feature applies a similar logic when it generates the UI. For each object with multiple cardinality to the header, it generates a table view.

In order to define a search page or an embeddable search page, you need to have a query object in your model subset. The search pages are at the same level as the overview page. Make sure you have no UI node selected when clicking the ADD UI ELEMENT button. Our only query is `SearchBookings`, but if we had more you could define multiple embeddable search views, for example.

Once you have picked the main elements for your UI, you can specify certain additional characteristics. Let's double click on the SEARCH RESULT VIEW. A pop-up shown in Figure 8.7 will appear.

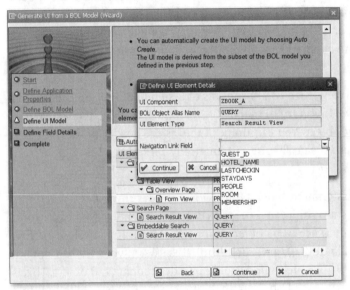

Figure 8.7   Search Result View Details

You can select a particular record from the search result page and open its overview page. This is typically done by clicking on a link in one of the columns and subsequent navigation to the OVP. In order to support this paradigm, the UI generation tool needs to know which column (field) should act as a navigation link. If you do not select one, the tool will pick the first key attribute. We will use the HOTEL_NAME as a navigation column. We will do the same for the embeddable search view (it also has a SEARCH RESULT VIEW node).

Figure 8.8 shows the details of a form view. We would like to be able to edit our bookings, so make sure that the EDITABLE checkbox is checked.

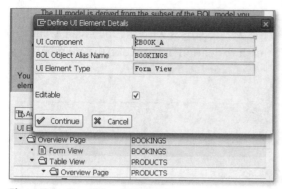

Figure 8.8 Form View Details

If you double-click on the OVERVIEW page, you will see that you can control if your end user can modify and or delete application data (see Figure 8.9). We want to give our end users full control, so ensure that all the options are selected.

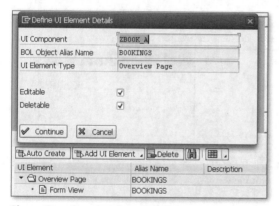

Figure 8.9 Overview Page Details

Step 4: Define Field Details

It is time to move to the next step. Once you have selected the elements of the user interface, you can go into each view and pick which fields will be presented to the user, which will be there but hidden, and which fields will not be available at all. Figure 8.10 shows the fields for the form view that displays our booking data. You can use the SHOW ALL and EXCLUDE ALL buttons to quickly mark all the fields as available or unavailable. We want users to modify all the booking data, so we will exclude none. Before launching the wizard, we have modified the attribute structure of the `Bookings` GenIL business object. It now has a DDIC check table assigned to the `Membership` field. As the wizard works with the metadata available in the GenIL model, it could pick this information and render the membership field with an ⎡F4⎤ help.

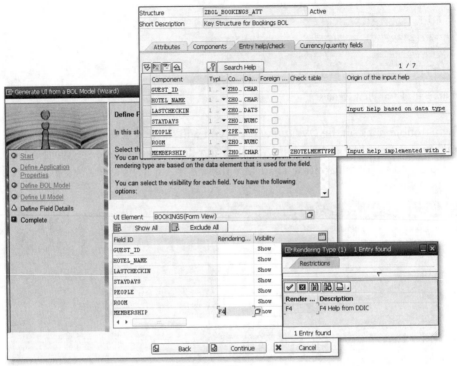

Figure 8.10 Field Details for BOOKINGS Form View

When it comes to the products table view (see Figure 8.11), it makes sense to exclude the key attributes of the parent object (`Bookings`). After all, we have these in the header (`BOOKINGS`) form.

You might wonder what fields are available as query criteria for our search and embeddable search pages. Figure 8.12 provides the answer. The tool will automatically read the search attribute structure from the GenIL model and use its fields in the search criteria view.

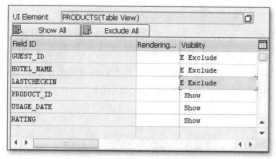

Figure 8.11 Field Details for PRODUCTS Table View

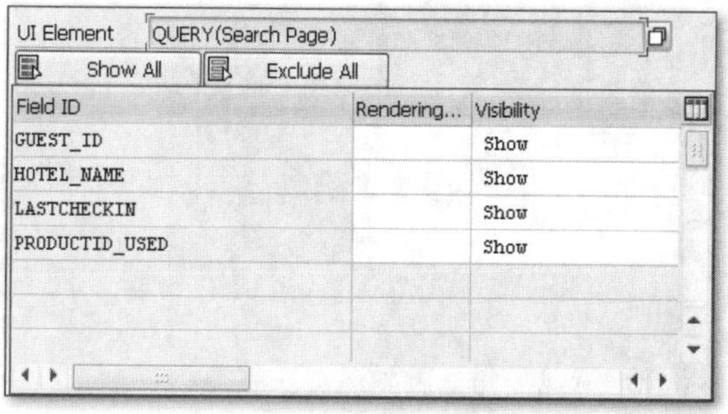

Field ID	Rendering...	Visibility	
GUEST_ID		E Exclude	
HOTEL_NAME		E Exclude	
LASTCHECKIN		E Exclude	
PRODUCT_ID		Show	
USAGE_DATE		Show	
RATING		Show	

UI Element: PRODUCTS(Table View) — Show All | Exclude All

Figure 8.12 Fields Used as Search Criteria

Field ID	Rendering...	Visibility	
GUEST_ID		Show	
HOTEL_NAME		Show	
LASTCHECKIN		Show	
PRODUCTID_USED		Show	

UI Element: QUERY(Search Page) — Show All | Exclude All

By default, the search result page will include all the attributes from the root object and any other object that has 1:1 cardinality with respect to the root (Figure 8.13). Let's exclude people and hide stay days and membership from the search result view. As a result, an end user will never be able to see the number of people who stayed in the room, but it will be possible to personalize the search page to show the number of days stayed and the membership type at the time of the booking.

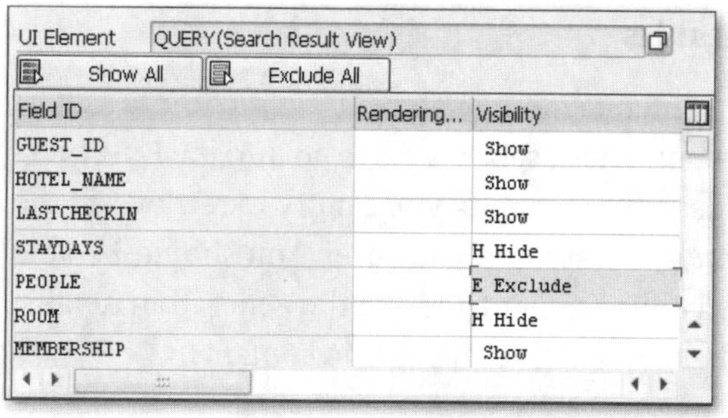

Field ID	Rendering...	Visibility	
GUEST_ID		Show	
HOTEL_NAME		Show	
LASTCHECKIN		Show	
STAYDAYS		H Hide	
PEOPLE		E Exclude	
ROOM		H Hide	
MEMBERSHIP		Show	

UI Element: QUERY(Search Result View) — Show All | Exclude All

Figure 8.13 Search Result View Fields

Step 5: Generate the Application

We are now ready for the last step. The confirmation page will give a preview all the artifacts that will be generated by the wizard (Figure 8.14). All the UI elements will be part of the ZBOOK_A UI component. As everything looks the way we expected, we will click the COMPLETE button and trigger the generation. The process might take several minutes.

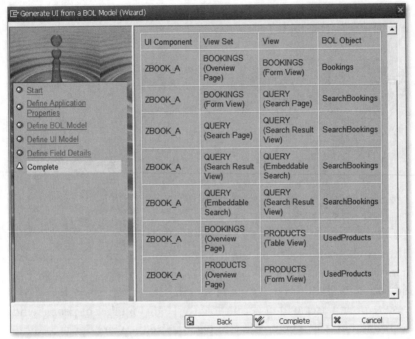

Figure 8.14 Preview of UI Elements to be Generated

8.1.2 Analyzing Generation Results

Upon completion, you can open the enhancement analyzer (Transaction AXTSHOW) and analyze the generated enhancement. The easiest way is to go into the ENHANCE-MENT ID field and press F4 . In the search value help, you can try to retrieve all the enhancement types BOL_UI that were generated by your user. You should be able to quickly select the newly produced enhancement and see the generation details. Figure 8.15 shows you what an enhancement overview page contains.

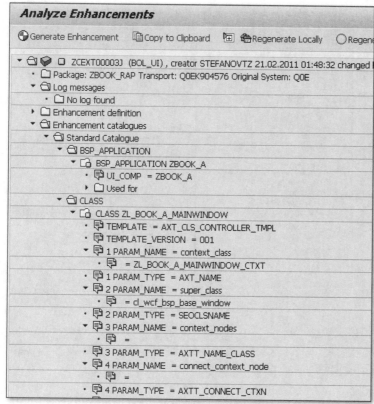

Figure 8.15 Analyze BOL_UI Enhancement

With the enhancement analyzer, you could get a complete overview of what has been generated. The most obvious way to use this transaction is to analyze the results when there is a generation error. You will be able to find the reason for the error and work to fix it. Once the issue is corrected, you can attempt to regenerate the enhancements via the GENERATE ENHANCEMENT button. Transaction AXTSHOW is delivered along with the Application Enhancement Tool. You can consult your SAP documentation on what other features are available.

Go back to the Component Workbench and try to open the newly generated UI component. Recall that we called ours ZBOOK_A. Figure 8.16 shows what you might find under COMPONENT STRUCTURE BROWSER, BOL MODEL BROWSER, and RUNTIME REPOSITORY EDITOR.

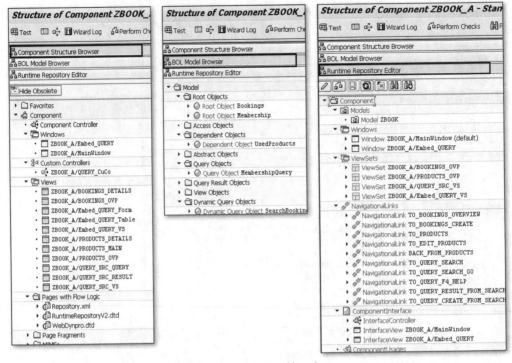

Figure 8.16 Newly Generated Component in Workbench

The BOL model included in the component is based on the business objects found in component set ZBOOK. The business data is displayed via two overview pages (one for Bookings and one for UsedProducts) and a search page (QUERY_SRC_VS). There are dedicated window and search pages for the embeddable scenario (we will discuss the embedding of views in Chapter 9). In general, you can find a match for each UI element that we defined in the wizard. The various artifacts in the component have names that contain the alias name they are related to, and this will help you to find your way within the UI component.

8.1.3 Testing the Generated UI Component

Press the TEST button in the UI component and test the generated application. Figure 8.17 gives you an idea of what you can expect. The entry page into a SAP CRM application is normally a search page.

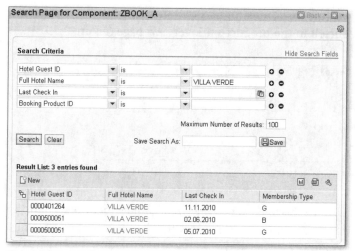

Figure 8.17 Search Page of Generated UI Component

You will probably see a message that there is no configuration for the views, but we will deal with this later. Take note that the labels of fields come from the DDIC. Enter valid search criteria and click SEARCH. As defined in the wizard, the hotel name column will contain a link to the OVP. Figure 8.18 shows the OVP of the booking application. The names of the views are definitely not user friendly, but we will fix this as part of the configuration.

Figure 8.18 OVP of a Generated UI Component

The generated pages are quite complete in terms of functionality. You have EDIT, SAVE, CANCEL, NEW, and DELETE (under MORE) buttons. In addition, the new application is Breadcrumb-enabled, and you can navigate to it through the navigation history buttons. Try out the application by editing the booking details and experimenting with the *one-click actions* (the Action column in the product table view). At some point, you will find yourself in the product sub-overview page (Figure 8.19).

Figure 8.19 Sub-OVP of Generated UI Component

Not only can you go back to the main OVP, but you also have dedicated buttons that allow you to go forward and backward across the dependent object entities (UsedProducts in our example).

You will also see that all the views and pages can be configured and personalized. Therefore, you can adjust the user interface directly from the Web UI without opening the component workbench. Try out this functionality. We will perform this exercise a bit later after we deal with a more critical issue. You should have noticed by now that one of the fields, namely Booking Product ID is rendered awkwardly. Its DDIC type is RAW16 and such fields are typically not visualized by the framework. This is why you see the Conversion Failed value.

8.1.4 Modifying the Generated UI Component

In order to address the Conversion Failed issue, you need to remember that the UI component produced by the wizard is in your namespace and you can do whatever you like with it (almost). So we can go inside and perform some fine-tuning.

One way to do this is to create a value node in the product context nodes, retrieve a meaningful description based on our RAW16 product ID, and display it instead. Another option is to actually overwrite the get and set methods of the product ID fields and convert the RAW16 into a product description. In this section, we will discuss the latter approach. First, we will add product information to our customer GenIL component set, and then we will implement the required getter and setter methods. We will also look into a remaining element from the GenIL programming topic, called default GenIL attribute values (upon creation). Finally, we will test the results of our work in the Web UI.

Updating GenIL Component Set

No matter how we choose to solve the conversion issue, we will need the product business object available within our UI component. The latter resides in a GenIL component called PROD. Therefore we need to load this GenIL component into our UI component. You can do so manually (CL_CRM_BOL_CORE->LOAD) or you can simply add the PROD component to the ZBOOK component set. If you do the latter and start the ZBOOK_A UI component, the BOL Model Browser will look like the screen in Figure 8.20. Now you can use any business object from PROD in the ZBOOK_A application.

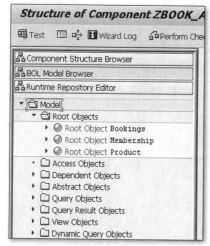

Figure 8.20   BOL Model Browser after Updating ZBOOK Component Set

Generating Attribute Getters and Setters

The product ID attribute (field) can be found in two views: PRODUCT_DETAILS (part of the OVP) and PRODUCT_MAIN (part of the sub-OVP). If you expand the product related content nodes of these views, you will be able to locate the PRODUCT_ID attribute. Right-clicking on it will open a menu where you can select to generate the attribute's get and set methods. The result of executing this action is shown in Figure 8.21.

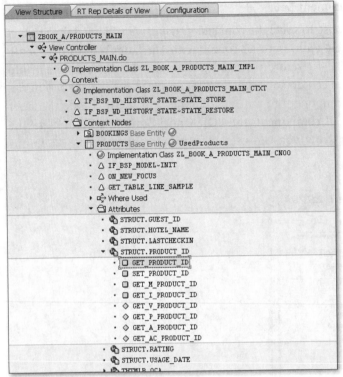

Figure 8.21 Generating PRODUCT_ID Get and Set Methods

Change the Product ID Getter Method

Double-click on the GET_PRODUCT_ID. You now can modify the get method code. Locate the following ABAP statement:

```
value = if_bsp_model_util~convert_to_string( data_ref = dref
            attribute_path = attribute_path ).
```

dref contains our product id value (RAW16). In line with the Product business object attribute structure, this is actually data element COMT_PRODUCT_GUID. Replace the above code with the following:

```
value = ZCL_BOL_BOOKINGS_UTIL=>GET_PRODUCT_ID( IV_DREF = DREF ).
```

We have encapsulated the logic for retrieving a product ID from a GUID in a separate class. Listing 8.1 shows the code of the GET_PRODUCT_ID method.

```
data: lr_product_id type ref to COMT_PRODUCT_GUID,
```

```
            lv_product_id type COMT_PRODUCT_GUID,
            lr_core type ref to CL_CRM_BOL_CORE,
            lr_product type ref to CL_CRM_BOL_ENTITY.
"convert ID to COMT_PRODUCT_GUID
lr_product_id ?= iv_dref.
lv_product_id = lr_product_id->*.
"get an instance of the core
lr_core = cl_crm_bol_core=>GET_INSTANCE( ).
"get the Product entity
lr_product = lr_core->GET_ROOT_ENTITY( IV_OBJECT_NAME = 'Product'
                               IV_OBJECT_GUID   = lv_product_id  ).
IF lr_product is not bound.
  RV_ID = ''.
ELSE.
  "return the PRODUCT_ID value
  RV_ID = lr_product->GET_PROPERTY_AS_STRING( 'PRODUCT_ID').
ENDIF.
```

Listing 8.1 Retrieving Product ID Based on COMT_PRODUCT_GUID

As evident in the last code listing, we rely on the BOL API to retrieve a Product entity. The key of this object is our RAW16 product ID (which we just learned was GUID). This is consistent with the key structure of the Product business object in the PROD GenIL component:

```
lr_core->GET_ROOT_ENTITY( IV_OBJECT_NAME = 'Product'
                          IV_OBJECT_GUID   = lv_product_id  ).
```

The rest of the code should be familiar from the BOL programming introduction. We do not need to load the PROD GenIL component, as this is already taken care of by including it into the ZBOOK component set. That component set is the basis for the whole ZBOOK_A application model.

> **Note**
>
> The GenIL component set assigned to the runtime repository of a UI component is loaded automatically by the framework. As a result you can call all its services and entities with the BOL API without having to explicitly initialize it. You can use the LOAD methods of the BOL core to load additional component when needed. You can check what is loaded by calling CL_CRM_GENIL_OBJ_MODEL->GET_COMPONENTS_LOADED. To get an instance of CL_CRM_GENIL_OBJ_MODEL, call CL_CRM_GENIL_MODEL_SERVICE->GET_RUNTIME_MODEL.

The last thing we do in the GET_PRODUCT_ID method is to return the value of the PRODUCT_ID property as a string, rather than as RAW16:

```
value = lr_product->GET_PROPERTY_AS_STRING( 'PRODUCT_ID').
```

You might be wondering why you wouldn't choose PROUCT_ID over the GUID as our product ID. The reason is that the Product-PRODUCT_ID is not unique. The PROD component has also been modeled around this assumption (the key structure of the Product object consists of the GUID only).

Make sure you repeat the above modifications for both PRODUCT_DETAILS and PRODUCT_MAIN view.

If you now test your application, you will find that instead of CONVERSION FAILED you get a user-friendlier product ID (Figure 8.22).

Figure 8.22 Booking OVP with Improved Product ID Rendering

Change the Product ID Setter Method

We still have more work to do on the product ID. What will happen if you try to edit a used product entity, but do not change the product ID value? During a round trip, the product ID attribute set method will compare what is coming from the UI with the RAW16 value. They will differ, and the framework will consider the product ID as changed. There are different strategies to handle such situations. First, you would probably just call the GET_PRODUCT_ID method and compare its return value with the one coming from the UI. If they are the same, there is no change. However, if they are different you have to update the attribute value with the GUID that corresponds to the new product ID. You could execute a BOL query search using the incoming value as search criteria. If you find a matching product, read its GUID and use it in the setter. Use the code in Listing 8.2 instead of the one in the default SET_PRODUCT_ID implementation.

```
DATA:
  current TYPE REF TO if_bol_bo_property_access,
  oval    TYPE string,
  dref    type ref to data,
  copy    TYPE REF TO data.


FIELD-SYMBOLS:
  <nval> TYPE ANY,
  <oval> TYPE ANY.
*get Old string value (real product id)
oval = GET_PRODUCT_ID( ATTRIBUTE_PATH = ATTRIBUTE_PATH
                            ITERATOR      =  ITERATOR ).
*get current entity
if iterator is bound.
  current = iterator->get_current( ).
else.
  current = collection_wrapper->get_current( ).
endif.


*only set new value if value has changed
IF value is not initial AND oval <> value.
  data: lr_product_guid type ref to COMT_PRODUCT_GUID,
        lv_product_guid type COMT_PRODUCT_GUID.
  "retrieve the GUID
  lr_product_guid ?= ZCL_BOL_BOOKINGS_UTIL=>GET_PRODUCT_GUID( IV_ID =
VALUE ).
  lv_product_guid = lr_product_guid->*.
  "set the guid
  current->set_property(
                  iv_attr_name = 'PRODUCT_ID'
                  iv_value     = lv_product_guid  ).
ENDIF.
```

Listing 8.2 Custom Implementation of SET_PRODUCT_ID

As mentioned we first call the get method to retrieve the actual product ID:

```
GET_PRODUCT_ID( ATTRIBUTE_PATH = ATTRIBUTE_PATH
                ITERATOR       =  ITERATOR ).
```

Next, we obtain the current object from the context node (part of the default setter code). Then, we compare the value coming from the UI with the old value retrieved from the get method. If they are different, we call use the value from the UI to retrieve an actual product GUID via a custom utility class:

```
lr_product_guid ?=
    ZCL_BOL_BOOKINGS_UTIL=>GET_PRODUCT_GUID( IV_ID = VALUE ).
```

The code of the above custom utility method is presented in Listing 8.3.

```
data: lr_product_guid type ref to COMT_PRODUCT_GUID,
      lv_product_guid type COMT_PRODUCT_GUID,
      lr_core type ref to CL_CRM_BOL_CORE,
      lr_product type ref to CL_CRM_BOL_ENTITY,
      lr_products type ref to IF_BOL_ENTITY_COL,
      lr_query  type ref to CL_CRM_BOL_QUERY_SERVICE.


"get an instance of the core
lr_core = cl_crm_bol_core=>GET_INSTANCE( ).
"get the Product query
lr_query = CL_CRM_BOL_QUERY_SERVICE=>GET_INSTANCE(
                               'ProdAdvancedSearchProducts' ).
lr_query->SET_PROPERTY( IV_ATTR_NAME = 'PRODUCT_ID'
                        IV_VALUE = IV_ID ).
"get the first matching product
lr_products = lr_query->GET_QUERY_RESULT( ).
lr_product = lr_products->GET_FIRST( ).
IF lr_product is bound.
  "retrieve the GUID
  RV_DREF = LR_PRODUCT->GET_PROPERTY( 'PRODUCT_GUID' ).
ENDIF.
```

Listing 8.3 Retrieving Product GUID from a Product ID

The code in our utility method relies on the `ProdAdvancedSearchProducts` BOL query from the `PROD` component to find a product based on its ID:

```
lr_query = CL_CRM_BOL_QUERY_SERVICE=>GET_INSTANCE(
                            'ProdAdvancedSearchProducts' ).
lr_query->SET_PROPERTY( IV_ATTR_NAME = 'PRODUCT_ID'
                        IV_VALUE = IV_ID ).
```

For simplicity's sake, we are interested in the first entity found. You might be tempted to check whether there are multiple matches and act accordingly, as follows.

```
lr_product = lr_products->GET_FIRST( ).
```

If there is a matching product, return its GUID:

```
RV_DREF = LR_PRODUCT->GET_PROPERTY( 'PRODUCT_GUID' ).
```

The last thing we do in our product setter method is to update the attribute value with the product GUID. This will trigger the business object modification process (MODIFY_OBJECTS in the GenIL component).

GenIL Default Attribute Values

Before you test the edit capabilities of the UI component, we will take a short detour. When defining the UsedProducts business object in the GenIL Editor, we set the DYNAMIC CREATE DATA attribute to D (Default Values Supported). We did not implement the elements required to support GenIL default values because we did not want to overwhelm you (also you do not need it when testing with the BOL browser). The effect of choosing to support default values is that the framework will try to create a new UsedProduct object based on a template. To support this, you have to implement the method IF_GENIL_APPL_DYN_META_INFO~GET_DYN_ATTR_DEFAULTS in your GenIL component. If you don't do so, you will get an exception when the framework tries to get the default attribute values. In our application, this will happen when a new empty row is added to the used products assignment block

Listing 8.4 provides our implementation of GET_DYN_ATTR_DEFAULTS.

```
IF cv_child_name = 'UsedProducts'.

  IF cv_parent_and_result-object_name = 'Bookings'
     AND iv_relation_name = 'BookingProductsRel'.

    DATA: ls_product TYPE ZBOL_BOOK_PRODUCTS_ATT,
          ls_book_key TYPE ZBOL_BOOKINGS_KEY.
    iv_container_object->get_attributes( IMPORTING es_attributes = ls_
product ).
      TRY.
        "Retrieve the key attributes of the parent
        CALL METHOD cl_crm_genil_container_tools=>get_key_from_object_
id
          EXPORTING
            iv_object_name = cv_parent_and_result-OBJECT_NAME
            iv_object_id   = cv_parent_and_result-OBJECT_ID
          IMPORTING
```

```
        es_key          = ls_book_key.
      "set the default attributes
      ls_product-USAGE_DATE = ls_book_key-LASTCHECKIN.
      ls_product-PRODUCT_ID = ''.
      "set the modified attribute structure
      iv_container_object->set_attributes( ls_product ).
      "set success flag
      cv_parent_and_result-success = abap_true.
    CATCH cx_crm_genil_general_error.
      "set success flag to FALSE
      cv_parent_and_result-success = abap_false.
    ENDTRY.
  ENDIF.
ENDIF.
```

Listing 8.4 GET_DYN_ATTR_DEFAULTS Implementation

We will return default attribute values only for the `UsedProducts` object. That is why we check the names of the parent and the relationship. Remember, the way to get from `Bookings` to `UsedProducts` was through the BOL relation `BookingProductsRel`.

First, we retrieve the attribute structure of the container object (namely `UsedProducts`):

```
iv_container_object->get_attributes(
    IMPORTING es_attributes = ls_product ).
```

Next we retrieve the booking key structure:

```
cl_crm_genil_container_tools=>get_key_from_object_id
        EXPORTING
          iv_object_name = cv_parent_and_result-OBJECT_NAME
          iv_object_id   = cv_parent_and_result-OBJECT_ID
        IMPORTING
          es_key         = ls_book_key.
```

The products and services used by the guest should fall within the duration of the stay. Therefore, it will be helpful if we preset the product usage date to something relevant, namely the check-in date from the booking record:

```
ls_product-USAGE_DATE = ls_book_key-LASTCHECKIN.
```

We also set the PRODUCT_ID to blank so that we do not confuse the Web Client UI with a RAW16 value.

Testing the Modified Application

Now we can test our UI component. Open a booking instance and click the EDIT LIST on the UsedProducts block. If you have a breakpoint in GET_DYN_ATTR_DEFAULTS, you will see it being executed as a new empty row gets appended to the assignment block. The values of USAGEDATE and PRODUCT_ID are set according to our implementation.

You can enter additional data in the empty line and click the SAVE button. The SAVE_OBJECTS of the GenIL component will be executed and the new used product entry will become persistent (see Figure 8.23).

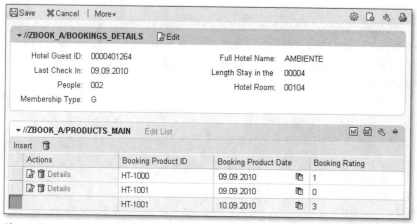

Figure 8.23 Adding a New Product Usage

8.2 Configuration and Personalization

Our application might do the job from a functional point of view, but we should improve its usability by giving titles to the views, setting proper labels, and even rearranging the view layouts. You already know how to perform page and view UI configuration, so we will cover these steps briefly. Discussing the personalization features should help us complete our understanding of the configuration concept of the Web Client UI.

First we will configure the overview page and enter meaningful texts in the TITLE column of the DISPLAYED ASSIGNMENT BLOCKS view (see Figure 8.24). Click on SAVE AND GENERATE and provide a customizing transport request when prompted.

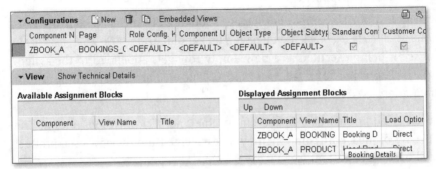

Figure 8.24 Page Configuration

Next we will configure the individual assignment blocks. Click on the SHOW CONFIGURABLE AREAS in the top of the page and select a view to configure. We already performed this exercise when enhancing the standard BP_HEAD component. Select the BOOKING DETAILS view as shown in Figure 8.25.

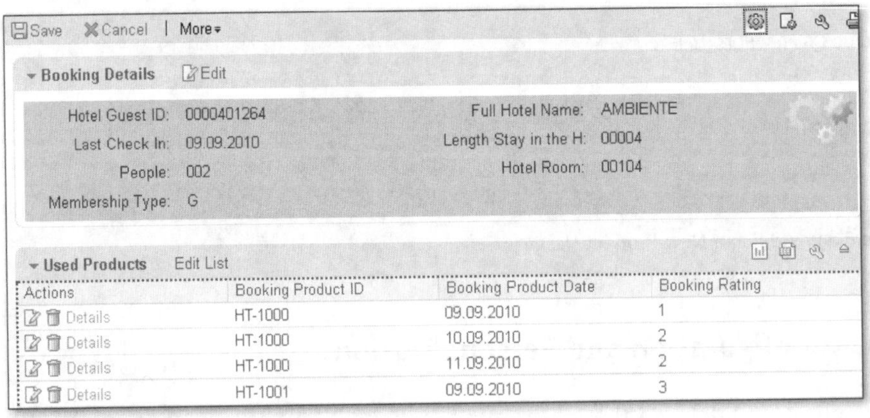

Figure 8.25 Pick View to Configure

In the form view configuration, you can change the labels, mark fields as mandatory, and rearrange fields. Using the mandatory checkbox will tell the framework to issue an error message if the user leaves the field blank (see Figure 8.26).

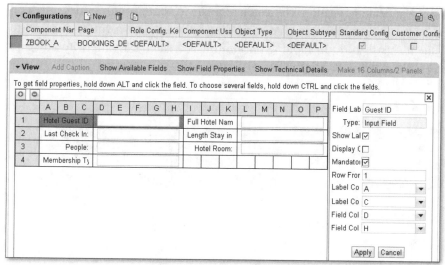

Figure 8.26 Changing Label of Field

If you click on SHOW AVAILABLE FIELDS, you will see the context nodes that constitute the selected view. As Figure 8.27 shows, the data in the bookings form is bound to one context node called BOOKINGS (the alias name that we provided in the wizard).

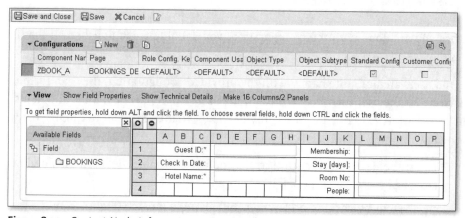

Figure 8.27 Context Node Information in View Configuration

The table view configuration should look like the screen in Figure 8.28. This screenshot shows what you can expect if you click the SHOW TECHNICAL DETAILS button. This will help you identify the actual structure attribute in the context node that is bound to the field in question. Notice that the first column comes from something called `THTMLB_OCA`, which stands for one-click action. By now, you know how to implement this feature. In rapid application it is a standard pattern to edit and display table data.

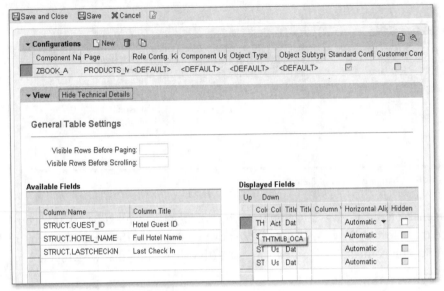

Figure 8.28   Table View Configuration

Once you are done with the configuration, you should have a polished UI that is easy to use.

If end users are not quite happy with the provided configuration, they can further personalize the user interface. For example, users can remove columns and fields. As of SAP CRM 7.0 EhP1 they can provide view variants. In order to do this, users should:

▶ Click on the personalize button in the toolbar of a table view. The table view personalization page will open in a pop-up.

▶ Copy a layout by clicking on SAVE AS and giving it a name (Figure 8.29).

▶ Modify the layout copy and save it.

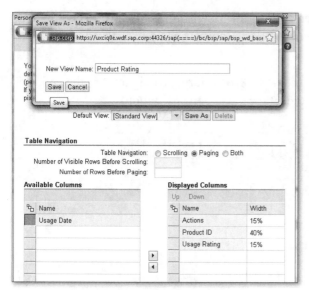

Figure 8.29 Creating a Personalization Variant

Figure 8.30 shows the personalized view. As you can see, the personalization variants appear in the dropdown list box in the table view. You can toggle between them, thus changing the layout of the view.

Save X Cancel	More ▾			⚙ 🗔 🔍 🖨

▾ Booking Details   🗋 Edit

Guest ID:	0000401264	Membership: G
Check In Date:	09.09.2010	Stay [days]: 00004
Hotel Name:	AMBIENTE	Room No: 00104
		People: 002

▾ Used Products   View: Product Rating ▾   Edit List

Actions	Product Rating	Usage Rating
🗋 🗑 Details	[Standard View]	1
🗋 🗑 Details	HT-1000	2
🗋 🗑 Details	HT-1000	2
🗋 🗑 Details	HT-1001	3

Figure 8.30 Table View with Multiple Personalizations

Before we leave this subject, let's configure the search result view of the search page (Figure 8.31). If you remember, in our wizard we marked some fields in the Search Result Page as hidden and we excluded the People attribute. The ones that are hidden will appear as such in the view configuration. Initially, the end users will not be able to see these fields. However, via personalization, they can enable the hidden fields.

If you leave a field in AVAILABLE FIELDS BLOCK during configuration, the end user will be never able to see it in the UI (even via personalization).

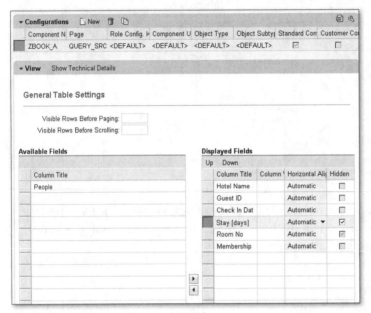

Figure 8.31 Configuring the Search Result View

As with our sample implementation, the business users will not be aware that one can show the number of people in the result view. Users will still be able to personalize the search result to show days stayed and room number. This demonstrates another aspect of the view configuration paradigm that we discussed in the previous chapter: User personalization ultimately takes precedence over the configuration.

8.3   Attaching a Design Layer Object

Hopefully you remember the design layer (DL) overview from Chapter 1. With the following example, we hope to shed some light on what it takes to integrate an SAP CRM application with the DL. We will use the opportunity to elaborate on the DL concept.

As discussed, the DL defines a layer that is logically positioned between the BSP view layer and the BOL. The main function of the DL is to provide modeling capabilities. These are based on business processes and not on the technical data model (such as BOL or UI context nodes).

You can always refer to SAP documentation for more details regarding the DL. However, it is worth explaining here how the DL assignments are resolved by the framework. How does the Web Client UI determine which DL attribute should be used and from which object to use it for a given UI element?

In this section, we will provide with an overview of the design layer assignment mechanism. To demonstrate it, we will create a custom design object and assign it to our newly generated UI component. We then will discuss what one can observe in the Web UI.

8.3.1 Design Object Assignments

It is important is to keep in mind that the DL assignments are made based on the following parameters:

▶ UI component

▶ View element

▶ Context node

▶ Context node attribute

▶ UI object type

▶ Component usage

Typically, a design object is assigned to a context node in a view in a component. In exceptional cases, one can assign DL attributes to context node attributes. But we recommend that you do not use this approach as it makes the DL assignments less obvious. Therefore, refrain from such assignments and ensure that the context node attribute is <DEFAULT>—meaning "any attribute."

The UI object type and component usage are resolved in a manner similar to the way the UI configuration determination matches these values. The <DEFAULT>

value indicates that the settings will be applied to all object types and component usages.

At runtime, the framework will pick the design object and its attributes based on the closest match to the above listed criteria. Therefore, you must keep all the above in mind when deciding which design object you will use.

8.3.2 Creating a Design Object

For our implementation, we will create a custom design object. It has to be assigned to a UI object type. The latter carries the application semantics and in addition contains a reference to a GenIL business object (the main BOL object). Luckily, the generation wizard created a UI object type for us. We specified it in Step 1 of the wizard (Figure 8.2) and you can now find an entry in table BSPDLCV_OBJ_TYPE (Figure 8.32).

Object Type	Description	Callback...	GenIL Co...	BOL Object Name	BOR Ob
WRAPPED_KNB1	ERP Customer		S02	ICBORWrapper	KNB1
WRAPPED_LFA1	ERP Vendor		S02	ICBORWrapper	LFA1
WRAPPED_LFB1	ERP Vendor		S02	ICBORWrapper	LFB1
WRAPPED_LIKP	ERP Outbound Delivery		S02	ICBORWrapper	LIKP
WRAPPED_MKPF	ERP Goods Receipt		S02	ICBORWrapper	MKPF
WRAPPED_MSEG	ERP Material Document		S02	ICBORWrapper	MSEG
WRAPPED_PROC	HCM P&F Processes		S02	ICBORWrapper	PROC
WRAPPED_REPORT	FSCM BOR object: REPORT		S02	ICBORWrapper	REPORT
WRAPPED_SCASE	FSCM SCASE		S02	ICBORWrapper	SCASE
WRAPPED_SSCSS	Self Service		S02	ICBORWrapper	
WRAPPED_VBRK	ERP Invoice		S02	ICBORWrapper	VBRK
WRAPPED_ZPROC	HCM Process		S02	ICBORWrapper	ZPROC
WSINCIDENT	SOLMAN INCIDENT		BT	BTOrder	BUS200
WS_SELECT_ATTRIBUTE	Attribute Selection Table	CL_WS_S...			
WS_TREE	Tree Structure	CL_WS_T...			
ZBOOK_A	Bookings		ZBOOK	Bookings	

Figure 8.32 UI Object Type Entries

Let us create a DL object for the ZBOOK_A object type. In customizing, you will need to follow menu path CUSTOMER RELATIONSHIP MANAGEMENT • UI FRAMEWORK • UI FRAMEWORK DEFINITION • DESIGN LAYER • DEFINE DESIGN OBJECTS. To illustrate some interesting concepts we will create the DL object for the UsedProducts business object. Create a new design object and give it a name, for example PRODUCTS. Make sure that the BOL object associated with this DL object is UsedProducts. Let us add an attribute for our RANKING business object field (see Figure 8.33). Make sure that the VALUE HELP FROM ABAP DICTIONARY is selected. As our domain ZBOOK_RATING_D has a value range associated with it, the DL will select this metadata and allow you to render the RANKING field as a dropdown list box.

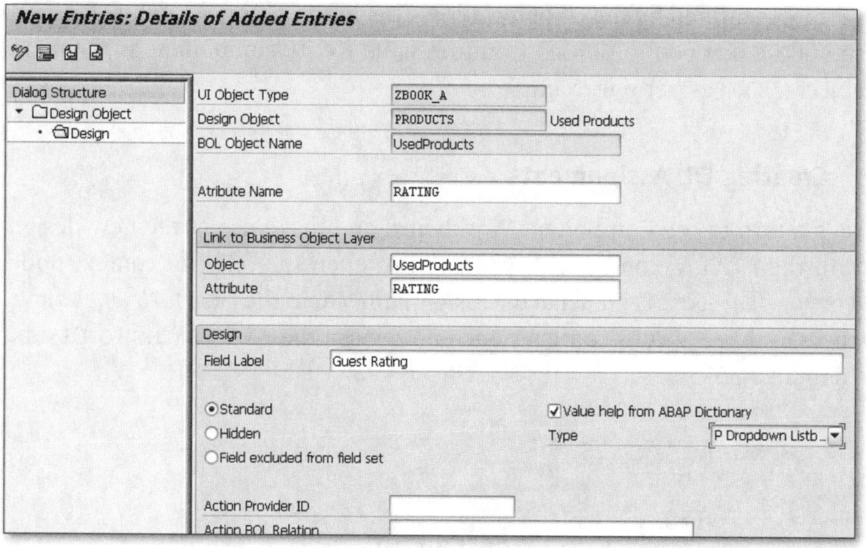

Figure 8.33 Creating a Rating Design Object Attribute

Add one more attribute to the PRODUCTS DL object called <default>. This is a special attribute that is present in each design object and specifies how the DL treats all the business object fields that are not explicitly exposed as DL attributes. Make sure that the visibility of <default> is Standard, otherwise the framework might hide all the attributes except of RATING. Figure 8.34 shows our design object definition.

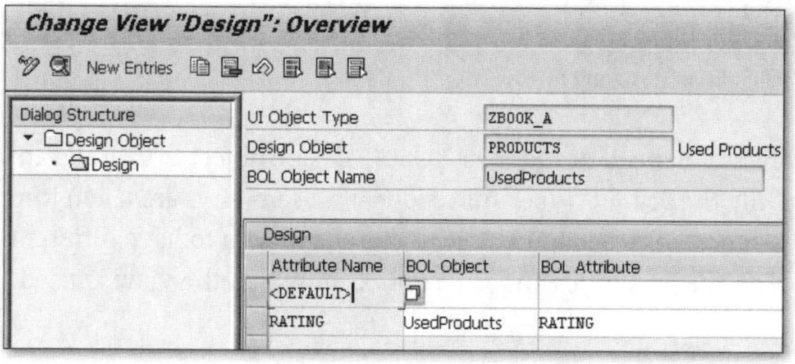

Figure 8.34 Complete Design Object Definition

You might be wondering why the ZBOOK_A UI object type points to the Bookings business object and how it relates to the newly created design object (based on UsedProducts). As we previously saw, the definition of a UI object type contains a BOL object name. This is the so-called main BOL object of the application that is semantically identified by the UI object type. The design objects under a UI object type should be mapped to objects from the same GenIL component as the main BOL object (ZBOOK as per our example).

8.3.3 Creating DL Assignment

Now let's return to the Component Workbench and make use of the new design object. In the ZBOOK_A component, you need to open the relevant context node (based on UsedProducts) and make the assignment. Go to the PRODUCTS_MAIN view, right-click on the PRODUCTS context node and choose the ASSIGNMENT TO DESIGN LAYER (Figure 8.35).

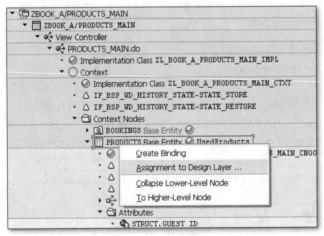

Figure 8.35 Call the Design Layer Assignment Tool

In the window that opens you need to add the PRODUCTS design object to the relevant configuration keys. Only the Object Type and Component Usage keys are taken into account for the DL assignments (see Figure 8.36). This allows you to have different design objects based on the semantics and the context in which the view is used.

Figure 8.36 Assigning Design Object to Context Node

This is all you need to assign a design object to a context node of a view. Now it is time to validate the results.

8.3.4 Testing the DL Assignment

Open the application in the Web UI and observe how the rating field is rendered with a dropdown list box (see Figure 8.37).

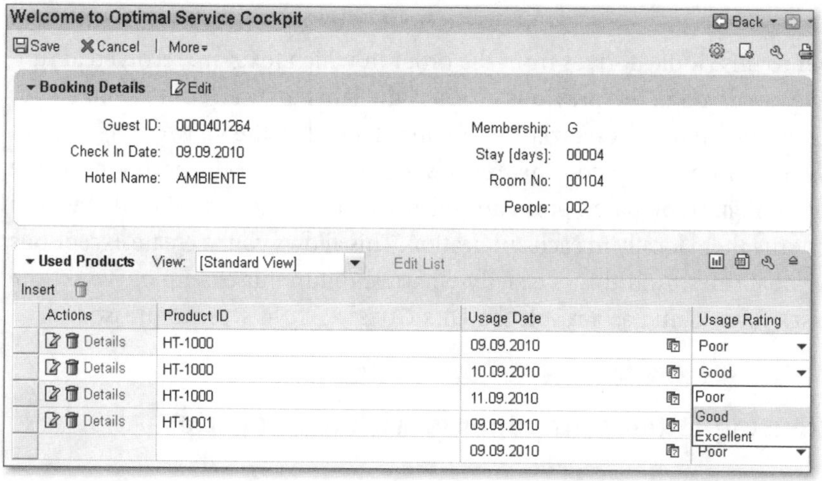

Actions	Product ID	Usage Date		Usage Rating
☑ 🗑 Details	HT-1000	09.09.2010	📋	Poor ▼
☑ 🗑 Details	HT-1000	10.09.2010	📋	Good ▼
☑ 🗑 Details	HT-1000	11.09.2010	📋	Poor
☑ 🗑 Details	HT-1001	09.09.2010	📋	Good
		09.09.2010	📋	Excellent
				Poor ▼

Figure 8.37 Rendering Product Rating According to DL settings

What you will notice immediately, is that the label text is not taken from the design object attribute. If you press F2 you will see that the technical details of the rating field indicate that there is a DL assignment and that the label text should come from there (Figure 8.38).

407

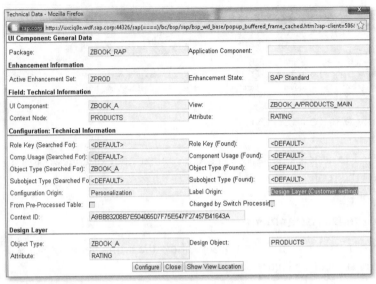

Figure 8.38 Technical Details of the Rating Field

The answer to this riddle derives from the order in which texts are resolved at run-time. As we discussed in the previous chapter, the label text can come from DDIC, DL, configuration, and personalization. If you set a text in the view configuration, the DL value will be discarded. This reveals a powerful concept pertinent to the DL and the configuration paradigm: The global settings come from the DL, but you could overwrite them locally in each application. This allows you to create exceptions from the global rules. And this is exactly what we did in our example. We set the label to USER RATING and as a result the DL's GUEST RATING was suppressed.

8.4   Reusing Other Components within a Pop-Up

In the previous sections, we have managed to solve obvious issues related to rendering a product GUID (RAW16). Despite the improvement, the situation is not ideal. End users have to know the product ID by heart. Moreover, the product ID is not unique. It would be better to allow users to search for and select products using a familiar UI. This would eliminate errors and improve the overall user experience. In this section, we will add a value help pop-up that will allow business users to perform searches against the product master data and select the desired records. We could go ahead and create a brand new search page that is based on one of the queries in the PROD component. Luckily, we can use an existing component.

In this section we will look inside a UI component that is meant for reuse. We will integrate it with our application and create a value help pop-up that works with the reusable component.

8.4.1 Analyzing the Reusable Component

As you know there are three types of pop-ups: confirmation, decision lists, and reused component. We will implement the last of these based on UI component PRD01QR. Let us open it and take a look at its component interface. We will be using the SearchHelpWindow shown in Figure 8.39. As you know, the inbound plugs are a way to pass data to the component interface. If you wish to influence the values of the search criteria of the SearchHelpWindow you should consider using inbound plug SEARCHPRODUCTS.

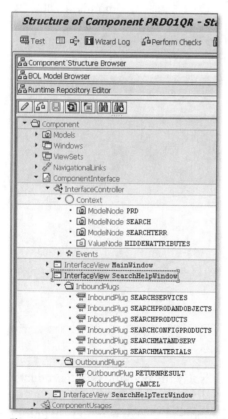

Figure 8.39 Component Interface of PRD01QR

You probably have some experience with SAP CRM and have created a sales or service order item at least once. For each item's product, you can call a F4 help pop-up that allows you to look up and select a product. The product's data must be passed back to the order page. This happens through outbound plugs. PRD01QR can pass information back though RETURNRESULT and CANCEL.

If you analyze further PRD01QR you will inevitably find that the view SearchHelpResult has an event handler that fires the RETURNRESULT outbound plug and passes a BOL collection with the selected Product entities. We will be relying on this plug to perform product selection. In the next section, we will enable PRD01QR for usage within our newly generated component and call it in a value help pop-up.

8.4.2 Value Help Pop-up

First we should create a component usage for PRD01QR in component ZBOOK_A (Figure 8.40). We gave it a name: ProductF4.

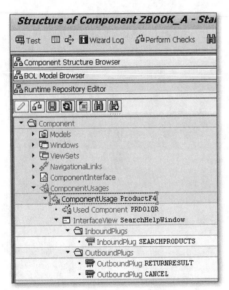

Figure 8.40 Component Usage for PRD01QR

Next, we will "improve" the table views that display the booking's used products. In our example, these are ZBOOK_A/PRODUCTS_MAIN (on the OVP) and ZBOOK_A/PRODUCTS_DETAILS on the sub-OVP. In our component the context node bound to the GenIL/BOL object UsedProducts is called PRODUCTS. We will make the framework render the PRODUCT_ID field of that component with an ⌞F4⌝ help (value help). In order to do that, we must redefine the Get_V method, which is GET_V_PRODUCT_ID. We will demonstrate how to change the PRODUCT_MAIN view but you could continue and enhance PRODUCTS_DETAILS. The implementation of the Get_V method will be a very short one, as evident in Listing 8.5.

```
create object RV_VALUEHELP_DESCRIPTOR type CL_BSP_WD_VALUEHELP_NAVDESCR
exporting IV_OUTBOUND_PLUG = 'OP_SEARCHPRODUCT'.
```

Listing 8.5 GET_V_PRODUCT_ID Implementation

The above listing implies that we need to define an outbound plug called SEARCHPRRODUCT. Make sure your outbound plug is implemented as a public method. After all, it has to be referenced from our value help descriptor, CL_BSP_WD_VALUEHELP_NAVDESCR.

Listing 8.6 shows our implementation of the outbound plug.

```
IF mr_popup is not bound.
  mr_popup = COMP_CONTROLLER->WINDOW_MANAGER->CREATE_POPUP(
       IV_INTERFACE_VIEW_NAME = 'SearchHelpWindow'
       IV_USAGE_NAME          = 'ProductF4'
       IV_TITLE               = 'Select a Product' ).
ENDIF.
CL_CHTMLB_CONFIG_UTILITY=>OUTBOUND_PLUG_EVENT_INFO(
          importing EV_INDEX = mr_index ).

mr_popup->SET_ON_CLOSE_EVENT( IV_VIEW = me
                              IV_EVENT_NAME = 'SELECT_PRODUCT' ).
mr_popup->OPEN( IV_INBOUND_PLUG = 'SEARCHPRODUCTS' ).
```

Listing 8.6 Outbound Plug SEARCHPRODUCT

MR_POPUP is an instance attribute of our controller of type IF_BSP_WD_POPUP and holds a reference to the pop-up window instance. Upon execution, the outbound plug creates it (in case this has not been done already) and stores it for future use:

```
mr_popup = COMP_CONTROLLER->WINDOW_MANAGER->CREATE_POPUP(
        IV_INTERFACE_VIEW_NAME = 'SearchHelpWindow'
        IV_USAGE_NAME          = 'ProductF4'
        IV_TITLE               = 'Select a Product' ).
```

The title of the new pop-up will be hardcoded to `Select a Product`, but you could use OTR. We also have to pass the component usage `ProductF4` and the name of the window interface that will be displayed `SearchHelpWindow`.

As you will see later on, we need to know on which table line the user clicked the `F4` help. The outbound plug is our last chance to collect this information and store it in a dedicated class attribute in the controller:

```
CL_CHTMLB_CONFIG_UTILITY=>OUTBOUND_PLUG_EVENT_INFO(
            importing EV_INDEX = mr_index ).
```

We want to be notified when the user closes the pop-up. After all, we want to collect a user's selection (if any) and use it to set the product ID field. We register an event handler that is activated when the pop-up closes:

```
mr_popup->SET_ON_CLOSE_EVENT( IV_VIEW = me
                              IV_EVENT_NAME = 'SELECT_PRODUCT' ).
```

The last line indicates that we need a new event handler called `SELECT_PRODUCT`. We will create it later. The last thing we do in the outbound plug is to open the pop-up through one of its plugs:

```
mr_popup->OPEN( IV_INBOUND_PLUG = 'SEARCHPRODUCTS' ).
```

The signature of the pop-up's `OPEN` method allows you also to pass a BOL collection to plug (`SEARCHPRODUCTS` in PRD1OQR). We will not do so, but it is an option that you may consider when you need to pre-populate the search help with query values.

If the user selects a product, its data will be passed back to our view through the `SELECT_PRODUCT` event handler of PRD01QR. However, if the user closes the pop-up, the event handler will be called again. So we need to differentiate between such cases in the `SELECT_PRODUCT` event handler. In addition to that, our event handler should be able to retrieve the user selection in the pop-up and set it in our view's context code. Listing 8.7 shows how you can achieve these requirements.

```
data: lr_node type ref to CL_BSP_WD_CONTEXT_NODE,
      lr_product type ref to IF_BOL_BO_PROPERTY_ACCESS,
      lr_used_product type ref to IF_BOL_BO_PROPERTY_ACCESS,
      lr_product_guid type COMT_PRODUCT_GUID,
      lv_plug type SEOCMPNAME.
  "check the plug that has been fired
  lv_plug = mr_popup->GET_FIRED_OUTBOUND_PLUG( ).
  check lv_plug = 'RETURNRESULT'.
```

```
"get the product node
lr_node = mr_popup->GET_CONTEXT_NODE( IV_CNODE_NAME = 'PRD').
lr_product = lr_node->COLLECTION_WRAPPER->GET_CURRENT( ).
check lr_product is bound.
lr_product->GET_PROPERTY_AS_VALUE(
       exporting IV_ATTR_NAME = 'PRODUCT_GUID'
            importing EV_RESULT = lr_product_guid ).
lr_used_product = TYPED_CONTEXT->PRODUCTS->GET_BO_BY_INDEX(
                  IV_INDEX = MR_INDEX ).
check lr_used_product is bound.
lr_used_product->SET_PROPERTY( IV_ATTR_NAME = 'PRODUCT_ID'
                                IV_VALUE = lr_product_guid ).
```

Listing 8.7 Event Handler SELECT_PRODUCT

If the user has selected a product line, data would be coming through the RETURN-RESULT plug of PRD01QR. This is the only case we are interested in:

```
lv_plug = mr_popup->GET_FIRED_OUTBOUND_PLUG( ).
check lv_plug = 'RETURNRESULT'.
```

The product data in PRD01QR can be found in the component's controller PRD context node. We have to retrieve the PRODUCT_GUID from there. Once we have it we can set the corresponding property of the current used product. Remember that we stored the index of the current line from where the [F4] was invoked in the MR_INDEX attribute. We will use it to get the current entity from the PRODUCTS context node and set its PRODUCT_ID property:

```
lr_used_product = TYPED_CONTEXT->PRODUCTS->GET_BO_BY_INDEX( IV_INDEX =
MR_INDEX ).
lr_used_product->SET_PROPERTY( IV_ATTR_NAME = 'PRODUCT_ID'
                                IV_VALUE = lr_product_guid ).
```

8.4.3 Analyzing the Results

Open our application in the Web UI and go into the booking OVP. The product column in the USED PRODUCTS block is rendered with a value help. We owe this to the Get_V method that we implemented. Clicking on the [F4] help icon will trigger the SEARCHPRRODUCT plug. There the pop-up window will be created and consequently displayed (see Figure 8.41).

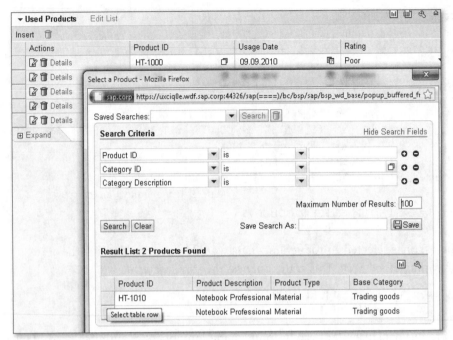

Figure 8.41 Reusing Product Search Pop-up in a Generated Component

When you select a line from the product result list in the pop-up, the SELECT_PROD-UCT event handler is called. The product GUID is set into the right entity from the PRODUCTS context node, and this triggers a call to MODIFY_OBJECTS of our GenIL component. If the SAVE button is pressed, a new used product will be permanently added to the Bookings.

8.5 Summary

In this chapter, we showed you how to generate a full-blown UI application from existing GenIL components. Once you have defined your GenIL/BOL model, you can use the GENERATE UI FROM BOL MODEL wizard and have a functional and comprehensive user interface in a matter of minutes. The only catch is that you need SAP CRM 7.0 EhP1.

You can show the freshly generated UI to the business users and discuss how it can meet the various use cases. Then you can go back to the drawing board, adjust your model, and generate the application once again. You can use the produced UI elements as a foundation or skeleton for your final application. As we saw, you can modify and adjust the UI component as you please. After all, the wizard generated a dedicated application in your namespace.

While elaborating on how you can add value to the new component, we discussed some interesting concepts. We showed you how to create custom design layer objects and assign them to your applications. To complete our discussion of the configuration and personalization paradigms, we explained the design layer assignments.

Finally, we showed you how to enhance your newly generated application with UI elements from another component. This allowed us to look in the custom view pop-ups. SAP CRM has plenty of standard components, and you can either use them to augment your custom application or use your applications to enhance the standard components. We will explore these components further in the next chapter.

There is no way to create a software product that covers every possible user scenario. The goal is to create a product that delivers enough standard features and at the same time is highly extensible.

9   Enhancing Applications with Fields and Tables

In Chapter 1 we introduced the overall topic of extensibility. As we explained, the ability to extend standard SAP content is of paramount importance to any SAP implementation. The Web Client UI takes these requirements and not only adopts best practices and concepts but also augments them with a set of comprehensive and user-friendly tools.

On several occasions, we demonstrated the power and ease of use of the UI configuration tools. We saw that not only can the administrator influence the UI layout but the end user can personalize the appearance of forms and views. Although the support of UI configuration and personalization is invaluable when it comes to the enhancement of the standard SAP content, it does not address one critical requirement: the frequent need to augment the standard content. Sometimes it is as simple as adding a single field that captures some very specific information. On other occasions, we need to add a complete view.

In this chapter, we will discuss the tools offered by the Web Client UI that allow power users to enhance standard SAP CRM content with fields and tables. We will start by giving you an overview of the tools available prior to SAP CRM 7.0. We look deeper into the new (as of SAP CRM 7.0) Application Enhancement Tool. We will work step by step through examples of how to create custom fields and views (tables). You will learn what kind of field types you can use. An important concept called *navigation fields* was introduced with EhP1, and we will discuss it as well. Finally, we will show you how to utilize the newly created fields in the design layer and the SAP CRM interactive reports.

9.1   Easy Enhancement Workbench

Creating a new field or view (table) in an existing application is referred to as structural extensibility. Prior to SAP CRM 7.0, consultants would use the *Easy Enhancement Workbench* (Transaction EEWB) to enhance the structures of standard SAP CRM applications. This development tool supports both field and table (view) extensions. Note that view extensions are often referred to as table extensions. This is because in most cases these new views render tabular data that has a one-to-many relation with the hosting business object. On a database level, the information is stored in custom DDIC tables (for example, Z-tables).

In EEW, the technical user selects a business object (application) and a wizard guides her or him through the process. Because of the technical differences between applications, the wizards can vary from one object to the other. Figure 9.1 shows screenshots from a project in EEW.

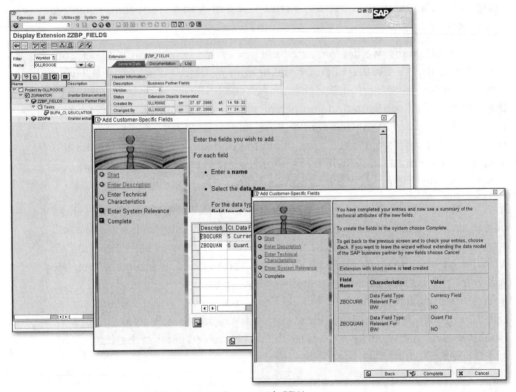

Figure 9.1   Adding Field to Business Partner with EEW

Adding new fields and tables in EEW leads to generating new data dictionary objects. The field extensions are typically added to dedicated customer includes that are part of the business object database model. Business object APIs might also be enhanced. The fields become part of the application's Business Object Layer (BOL) model and thus joins the available field list in the UI Configuration Tool. The consultant can enhance the related views with the newly created fields.

When a table extension is created, a new database table is created in the DDIC. This new structure results in generating new objects and relationships in the BOL model. The consultant then has to create new views in the BSP Component Workbench (Transaction BSP_WD_CMPWB) manually. The table fields become available in the view configuration.

Figure 9.2 outlines the steps that constitute the structural extensibility processes with EEW.

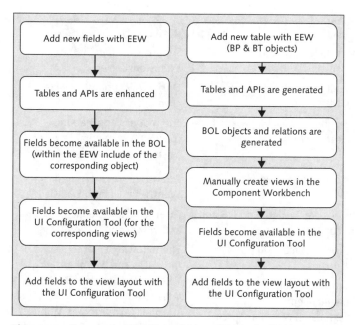

Figure 9.2 Steps in Creating New Fields and Tables in EEW

9.2   Application Enhancement Tool

You can see that EEW requires deep technical and application knowledge. Because of this and other shortcomings of the tool, SAP decided to launch a next generation extensibility tool called Application Enhancement Tool (AET). This new tool is part of the Web UI, accessible directly from the SAP CRM applications and providing seamless integration with the other power-user tools. AET is intuitive enough even for non-technical users.

As EEW has been on the market for quite some time, we will not describe it in detail here. If you are interested in learning more about it, you can consult your SAP documentation. Also, note that SAP is still supporting EEW and does not plan to discontinue it. Nevertheless, we believe that the features of AET make it the logical tool to use when it comes to structural extensibility. Table 9.1 compares EEW and AET.

	AET	EEW
Overall Scope	Supports field and table extensions.	Supports field and table extensions.
	Almost all applications are covered.	Only a few applications are covered.
	Universal but flexible approach for field extensibility.	The scope is application-specific. A configurable wizard exists for field extensions.
Features	Extensions can be used in SAP CRM WebUI.	Extensions can be used in WebUI, PC UI, and SAP GUI.
	Extensions are available on DB and within application logic.	Extensions are available on DB and within application logic.
	SAP CRM Interactive Reports can be enhanced.	The following external interfaces can be enhanced:
	The following external interfaces can be enhanced:	- R/3: extension of R/3 adapter + Generation in ERP
	- R/3: extension of R/3 adapter,	- Mobile: extension of Mobile Sync BDoc and CDB tables
	- Mobile: extension of Mobile Sync BDoc and CDB tables	- BW: extension of BW DataSource
	- BW: extension of BW DataSource	- XIF adapter (extended by default)
	- XIF adapter (extended by default)	

Table 9.1   AET vs. EEW

	AET	EEW
Tools	Integrated with SAP CRM WebUI Configuration Tool. Field creation and the corresponding UI configuration are done in the same place.	SAP GUI based. There is no integration with UI Configuration Tool (has to be started separately).
Target Audience	Easy to use and intuitive for power users (administrators). Could also be used by business users (no deep technical knowledge is required).	EEW is for users with deep technical knowledge.
Homogeneity	Consistent behavior across all applications (for example, the same data types are supported in all applications).	Inconsistent behavior and capabilities across different applications (for example, different data types are supported in different applications).
Value Helps	Custom dropdown list boxes can be defined for each field (as part of the field definition). Easy assignment of existing check tables and search helps for each field.	It is only possible to assign new and existing check tables and search helps to fields in some applications. Manual design layer adjustments are necessary.
Translation	Easy translation of labels and DDLB values in the tool (part of the field definition).	Translation has to be done separately in Transaction SE63.
Search	Use custom fields as search criteria and search result by simply selecting an option in the field definition.	Some applications allow search automatically but do not provide control over it.
Software Logistic	Use of standard transport system for generated objects.	Use of standard transport system for generated objects.

Table 9.1 AET vs. EEW (Cont.)

	AET	EEW
	Allows creation of extensions for a given application in different namespaces and packages (except BP). Extension include approach allows multi-layer extensibility. Extensions are defined cross-client. Transport of metadata fully supported.	Most applications are based on customer includes that do not support use of different namespaces. In the case of table extensions, there is a limit on the namespaces / multi-layer extensions. Supports the notion of projects. Extension definition is client specific (generation is not). No transport of metadata.
System Setup	Transaction AXTSYS allows definition of standard package for all applications.	Transaction EEWC is used to define roles and RFC connections to other systems. The package and namespace are assigned as part of the implementation projects.
Application Runtime	Provides extension metadata to applications. Complete runtime (buffer, API, GenIL) for table extensions (as of EhP1). Has WEBCUIF plug-ins for rendering tasks.	No runtime components. All generated objects are part of application runtime.
Tool Compatibility	EEW or manually created fields are accessible in read only mode. Migration of EEW and manual fields to the AET format is possible.	Works with EEW extensions only.

Table 9.1 AET vs. EEW (Cont.)

9.3 Creating New Fields and Tables with the Application Enhancement Tool

It is time to look at a specific example. We will be referring to the previously defined scenario from the hospitality industry. As you remember, we have two systems in our landscape: SAP CRM 7.0 EhP1 and a custom guest reservation system. The business partners in SAP CRM should correspond to the guests from the reservation system.

There is a basic loyalty program in place. Based on the services used, guests could have different membership statuses. When one signs up to the loyalty program, one receives a "bronze" membership status. For each service used, guests receive points. If a guest accumulates a certain level of points his or her status could become "silver" or "gold."

The information about the membership shall be brought into SAP CRM. Based on the above, your task could be summarized this way:

Create a new field in the ACCOUNT DETAILS assignment block in SAP CRM's account application. The name of the field will be MEMBERSHIP TYPE. The possible values for this field shall be "bronze,""silver," and "gold."

We will assume that your business role is configured correctly and you have all the required authorizations.

Note

SAP Note 1251796 contains details on how you can create an authorization role that will enable you to use the extensibility tools.

In the following sections, we will demonstrate how to start AET and how it integrates with the rest of the UI enhancement tools. We will show you how to create a custom field and a table.

9.3.1 Starting the Application Enhancement Tool (AET)

There are three ways to start the Application Enhancement Tool: starting the AET as a standalone application, starting the AET from the UI Configuration Tool, and using the SHOW CONFIGURABLE AREAS button.

Standalone Application

To start the AET as a standalone application, ensure that you have enabled logical link AXT_SEARCH in the administration work center (CT-ADM) as part of your business role customizing. When you start AET this way, you will be first presented with the SEARCH ENHANCEMENT page. Here you can view the objects that have already been enhanced and create new enhancements (custom fields). You can use this page to get an overview of all the objects that support structural extensibility. Click the NEW button in the result view and you will see a pop-up with all the objects that could be extended but that so far do not have structural extensions. The objects that already contain extensions will appear in the result view itself (you can trigger a search without any specific criteria). Figure 9.3 shows the enhancement search page.

UI Configuration Tool

Alternatively, you can start the AET from the UI Configuration Tool. The logical link VIEW CONFIGURATION (BSP-DLC-VC) must be enabled. The UI Configuration Tool has three guided steps when started in standalone mode. The last one is CREATE NEW FIELDS. To activate it, you need to select a UI component (you can skip the View Configuration step). Figure 9.4 shows what to expect in this case.

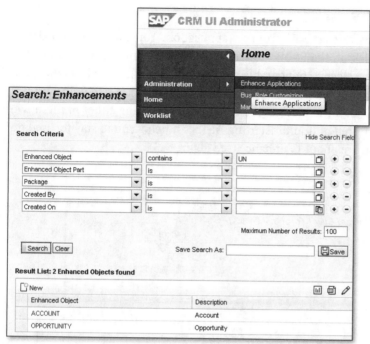

Figure 9.3 AET in Standalone Mode

Figure 9.4 Starting AET from UI Configuration Tool (View Configuration)

Show Configurable Areas

The third option is to start AET from an application. You can open an existing application and click on the SHOW CONFIGURABLE AREAS button. All you need to do afterwards is to select a configurable area and click on it. The view configuration pop-up will appear, and there you will see two buttons: one to quickly create a new field and the other to view all the enhancements. Using either of these two buttons is our preferred option for starting AET, as it helps you to stay focused on the object that you are about to enhance (see Figure 9.5).

Figure 9.5 Starting AET from Business Object Page

9.3.2 Creating a New Field

Let us go back to our example. We want to extend the ACCOUNT DETAILS of a SAP CRM account object. To do that, simply open any existing account. The SHOW CONFIGURABLE AREAS and CONFIGURE PAGE buttons should appear in the title bar. If this does not happen, open the global personalization page (by clicking on the PERSONALIZE link in the header area) and open the PERSONALIZE SETTINGS (part of the SETTINGS work center). Ensure that ENABLE CONFIGURATION MODE is checked.

Now back to the account overview page. Click on the SHOW CONFIGURABLE AREAS and select the ACCOUNT DETAILS view area (Figure 9.6).

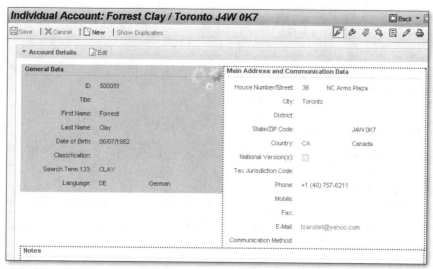

Figure 9.6 Selected Configurable Area in Account

Once you click on the ACCOUNT DETAILS, the UI Configuration for that view will appear in a pop-up. Figure 9.7 shows the view configuration pop-up.

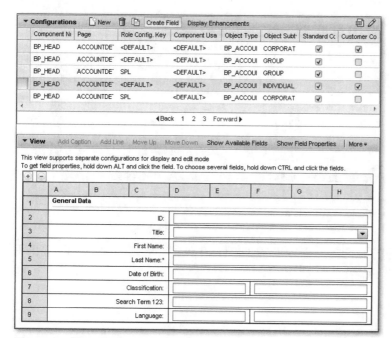

Figure 9.7 View Configuration for Account Details

We do not need to view all the existing structural enhancements. All we want to do is create a new field. Therefore, it makes sense to take a short cut and directly invoke the respective functionality by clicking on the CREATE FIELD button. This will start the AET and guide you to the view where you can define all the details for your new extension.

Select an Enhanced Object and Object Part

The configurable view area that we selected previously and that was displayed in Figure 9.6 serves more than one business object. For example, the ACCOUNT DETAILS view is shared by objects such as account, contact, and employee. Therefore, the first input that AET needs from the user is the concrete SAP CRM business object that will be enhanced. Such an object is sometimes referred to as *enhanced object*. The pop-up shown in Figure 9.8 illustrates this step.

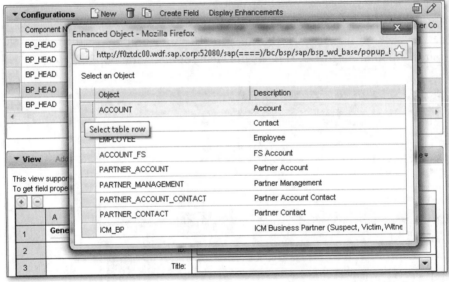

Figure 9.8 Selecting Business Objects to Enhance

Next you will have to select the so called *object part* (see Figure 9.9). In this particular case there is only one object part: Central Details.

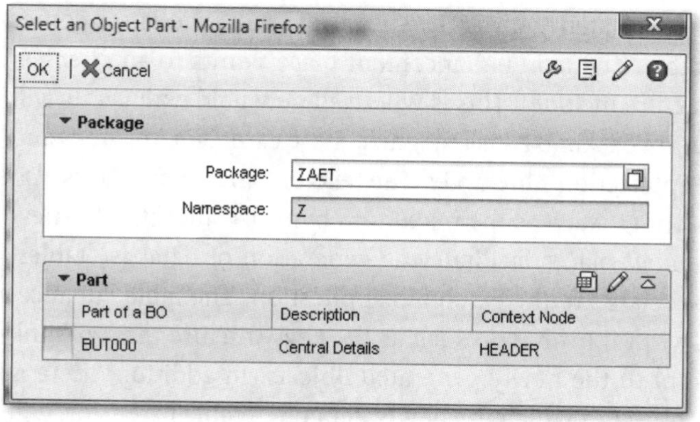

Figure 9.9 Selecting an Object Part

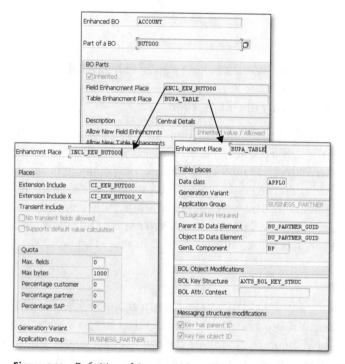

Figure 9.10 Definition of Account's Central Details (BUT000) Object Part

If you try to extend other SAP CRM applications, you might find that a given enhanced object contains multiple object parts. For example, if you try to extend the header of a sales order you will have to pick among object parts like Header, Item, Customer Header Data, Customer Item Data, Billing Data, and Organizational

Data. Each object part is associated with an *enhancement place*. The latter comes in two forms: field and table. The field enhancement place points to an *extension include* in the DDIC (a structure include). This is where all new field extensions will be generated. The application backend APIs recognize these extension includes and treats them as part of the application's life cycle. The field enhancement places also contain some technical settings, such as the maximum byte size allocated for new fields. The table enhancement places facilitate the generation of database tables. These new tables must be related to the extended application. The table enhancement places provide AET with information such as the key structure that will link the records from the parent to the newly generated objects. In addition, there is also a pointer to the BOL object to which the newly generated table extension will be attached via a BOL relationship. Figure 9.10 shows examples of the enhancement place definitions.

Extensibility Registry

If you want to see additional technical details behind a given enhanced object, you can use Transaction AXTREG (Extensibility Registry). Please note that it is maintained by SAP, and you should never modify the information there.

Let us consider another example of useful information one can find in AXTREG. If you follow the tree below the BUPA enhanced business object you will find a node called FURTHER GENERATION OBJECTS. Double-click on it to view all the registered generation objects. The first line has an enhancement indicator BW_REPORTING. This flag indicates that the corresponding data warehouse extractors could be enhanced with a new field. If you select and drill down to the GENERATION DETAILS NODE, you will find the name of the data source affected by this flag (see Figure 9.11).

The Runtime Information

Now we will resume creating a new field. If you look again at Figure 9.9, you will see that there is a column called CONTEXT NODE. Some entries have a value, and some do not. These values (when present) indicate the context node under which you can find your new field later when you configure your view. You shall always choose an object part that has a context node value. Otherwise, your newly created extension will not be available during the view configuration. The extensibility process has two steps. First, you create a new field or table, and then you enable it in the UI via the UI Configuration Tool (view or page configuration). If you start the

AET in a standalone mode (not from an application) you will not see the context node column because this information is only available as part of the application's runtime. That is why we strongly recommend that you create your fields or tables directly from the business application.

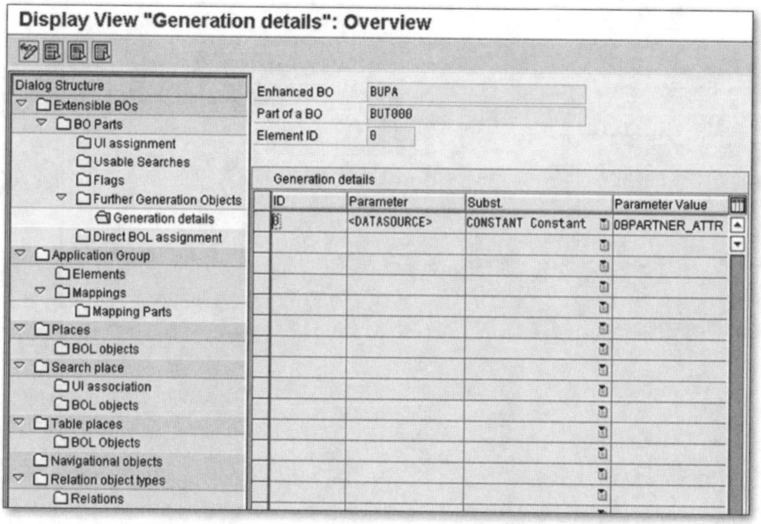

Figure 9.11 Finding Data Source Affected by BW Reporting Flag

The Field Details

After you select an object part, you will be presented with the FIELD DETAILS view. It allows you to define every single detail about your extension. Let us define the specifics of our MEMBERSHIP TYPE field as in Figure 9.12. Please note that we have specified valid membership values in the DROPDOWN LIST block. Remember that we want the end user to pick from a predefined list, rather than to enter arbitrary values. In the TRANSLATION block you can translate the field label and the dropdown list entries in any of the available system languages. In addition, you can enable the new field in other enhanced objects. Such objects must share the same enhancement place. For example, all the objects that you see when selecting an enhanced object (Figure 9.8) are available in the REUSED IN OBJECT assignment block. For example, we can enable our membership field in all SAP CRM business partner (BP) applications (account, contact, etc).

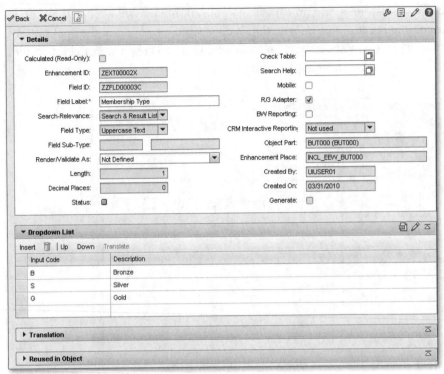

Figure 9.12 Membership Type Field Details

Enhancement Overview Page

Once you are done with the field details, you can click the BACK button and navigate to the ENHANCEMENT OVERVIEW. A screenshot is provided in Figure 9.13. This is the page that you would have seen if you had pressed the DISPLAY ENHANCEMENTS button in the view CONFIGURATION (from Figure 9.7).

Generating a Field Extension

If you press the SAVE AND GENERATE button, the new field will be generated. A pop-up regarding the transport request will be presented. You can select an existing or create a new workbench transport request (Figure 9.14).

Once a field has been generated, you will see a status message that the system has been restarted (or prompting you to do so). We strongly recommend that you close the current window and restart the session prior to using the system.

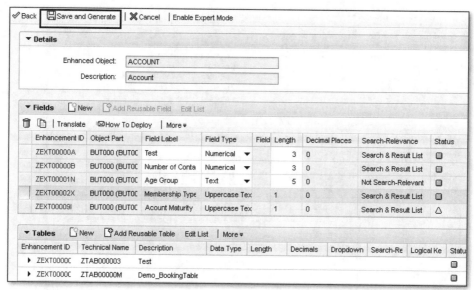

Figure 9.13 AET Enhancements Overview

Choose Request

	Extension	AXTE	
Request:	FDZK901606	Workbench request	
Short Description:	Extensibility Demo		

Choose   Create

Figure 9.14 Selecting a Workbench Transport Request

Configuring the New Extension

Once the session restarts, go back into your account object and open the view configuration for ACCOUNT DETAILS. The newly created field is available under the AVAILABLE FIELDS block. That view has many contexts, and you need to know where the new field is located. Remember the value in the CONTEXT NODE column of the pop-up where you selected the object part (Figure 9.9): It said HEADER. If we expand the HEADER context node, we will find the newly created field (see Figure 9.15).

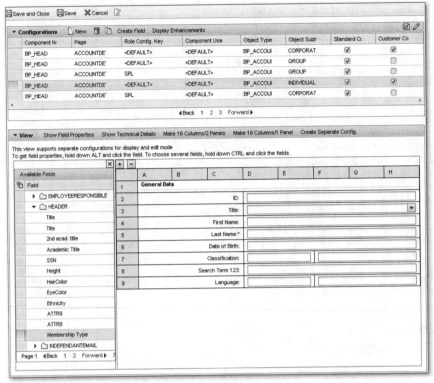

Figure 9.15 Configuring Enhanced View with New Field

You can move the field into the ACCOUNT DETAILS layout and save your configuration changes.

Using the New Extension

Once you exit the UI Configuration Tool and return to your account's overview page you will find the MEMBERSHIP TYPE field. It is fully operational, and your end users can start using it right away. They can select among the values that you defined in the DROPDOWN LIST block of the FIELD DETAILS pop-up. If they log into the system using a different language they will see the texts that you defined in the TRANSLATION block. Moreover, the new field is available as search criteria and search result. You just have to configure the corresponding views to get MEMBERSHIP TYPE in the account's search page. We achieved all that without writing a single line of code and without leaving the Web UI, working directly from the business object's overview page. Figure 9.16 provides screenshots that illustrate the final results.

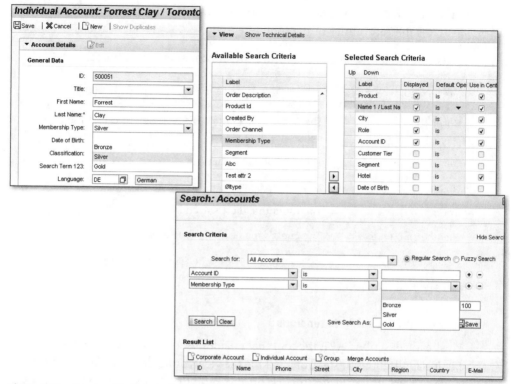

Figure 9.16 Membership Type in Account Overview and Search Pages

---

Handling the Transport Requests for the New Enhancements

When you are done testing, you might want to release the corresponding transports to your quality and productive systems. The *How to Deploy* functionality in SAP CRM 7.0 EhP1 delivers a comprehensive report of all the transports affected by your extension. All you need to do is go to the enhancement overview page, select the new field or table, and click on the How To Deploy button. You can export the content of the report to an MS Excel document and send it to the system administrator for further processing.

9.3.3 Creating New Tables with the AET

We showed how you can easily create a new field extension without leaving the Web UI. Imagine that a few days go by and you receive another request from the business process owners. The goal is to enhance the SAP CRM account application so that it stores the hotel bookings of the guests. Our solution is very simple but illustrates the capabilities of the tool.

Let us assume that we need to capture the information shown in Table 9.2.

Table Field	Details
Hotel	The name of the hotel. The assumption is that the hotel names are unique.
Date	The date of guest check-in.
Nights	How many nights (days) the guest stayed at the hotel.
Room	The room the guest stayed in.
Membership type	The guest's membership type at that date.
Points earned	How many points the guests earned during the stay.

Table 9.2 Hotel Bookings Table Requirements

Starting AET for Table Extensions

We already described AET, the tool that enables users to add new views (tables) to existing applications. Instead of invoking the view configuration (select configurable areas) to start it, you have to click on the PAGE CONFIGURATION button. The UI Configuration Tool will appear in a pop-up as shown in Figure 9.17. You can go to the enhancements overview by clicking the SHOW ENHANCEMENTS button. If you want to quickly create a table, press the CREATE NEW TABLE button. AET will start and you will have to select an enhanced object and an object part. The process is very similar to the one we used previously, but it is tailored for tables (views).

Providing Table Details

You create a table in a dedicated TABLE DETAILS pop-up. Here you specify information about the new view, such as the title. You also can specify the name of the UI component that will be generated. One important attribute is the RELATIONSHIP to the hosting business object. If you choose 1:1, a form view will be created. As we have multiple bookings for the same account, we need a table view: 1:N cardinality.

The bulk of the work will be done in the FIELDS block. A table consists of fields, and you define each one in the same way as a standalone field. The difference is the LOGICAL KEY flag. In the world of relational databases, a key identifies uniquely table entries. If after creating a table you try to enter data that has key values identical to those of an existing entry, the system will issue an error message.

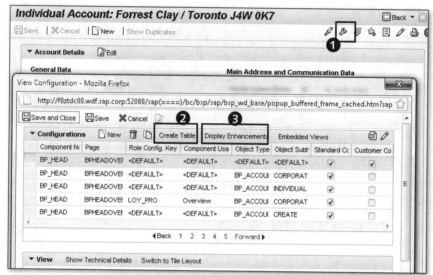

Figure 9.17 Account Page Configuration

Because the process of creating new tables follows the concepts and principles outlined in the previous sections, we will not go in so many details. First you should enter the table header data as shown in Figure 9.18.

Adding Fields

When you click on the ADD button, the familiar FIELD DETAILS page will appear. We do not want the users to enter arbitrary hotel names, so we will limit the possible choice via a dropdown list box. Enter the details for our first field as shown in Figure 9.19. You can also provide translations or mark a table field as searchrelevant. The latter will allow you to enable a field (HOTEL NAME in our example) as a search criterion.

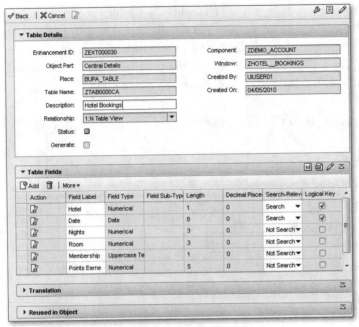

Figure 9.18 Creating a Table to Store Hotel Bookings

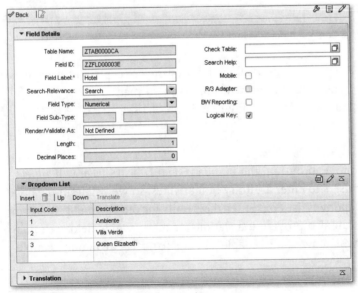

Figure 9.19 Create Table Field for Hotel Names

The fields HOTEL NAME and DATE are marked as logical keys. This reflects the requirement that a guest not check in to different hotels on the same date. (One could argue that this is not a very realistic requirement, but we are trying to keep things simple.)

Note that it is possible to define the fields directly in the FIELDS assignment block (Figure 9.18). This is useful for simple scenarios, when you need to quickly specify basic field properties.

Enabling a Table Extension

Once you are done with the table details, you have to go back to the ENHANCEMENT OVERVIEW page and press the SAVE AND GENERATE button. As mentioned earlier, we strongly recommend you close AET and let the system restart. Once the session restarts, you can re-open the account's overview page configuration (UI Configuration Tool). Under AVAILABLE BLOCKS, you will find the newly created view (Figure 9.20). You need to move it to the DISPLAYED BLOCKS and save your page configuration.

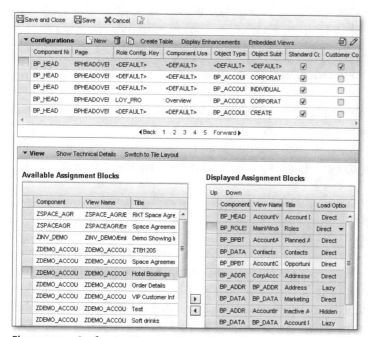

Figure 9.20 Configuring New Booking Table in SAP CRM Accounts

Using the New Table Extension

Once you complete the last step, you will get a new assignment block in the SAP CRM account business object. You can start using it immediately. As you remember, we have marked both hotel and date fields as logical keys. If you try to enter two bookings for the same hotel under the same date, you will get an error message (see Figure 9.21).

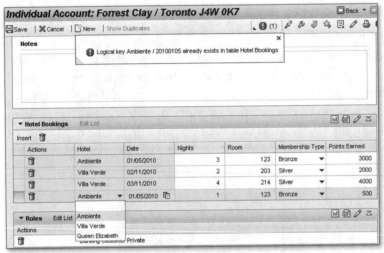

Figure 9.21   Using the Newly Created View in SAP CRM Account

The newly created table enhancement is fully integrated with the hosting business application. Whenever you save an account, the content of the BOOKINGS view will be persistent. Errors in BOOKINGS will put the account instance into an erroneous state as well. Deleting an account will delete the booking entries that belong to it.

9.4   Field Types

Whenever we define a standalone or a table field, we have to provide a data type. A field data type could be rendered differently during runtime. For example, you can choose to display a text field as an email or a hyperlink. As one can expect, the runtime will also validate that the text can be rendered as specified. Table 9.3 summarizes the existing data types as per SAP CRM 7.0 EhP1.

Field Type	Field Sub-Type	Render/Validate As	Comments
Uppercase Text	N/A	Input field, email, hyperlink, checktable as DDLB	Only uppercase text is allowed.
Text	N/A	Input field, email, hyperlink, checktable as DDLB	Accepts any text.
Indicator	N/A	N/A	A checkbox flag (for example representing true or false).
Currency	N/A	N/A	Amount and currency reference fields will be generated.
Date	N/A	N/A	Date field (rendered with a date picker value help).
Time	N/A	N/A	Time field (rendered with a time picker value help).
Decimal Number	N/A	N/A	Supports decimal numbers (decimal places become active).
Numerical	N/A	Input field, checktable as DDLB	Supports numerical data.
Quantity	Dimension	N/A	Value and unit-of-measure (UoM) reference fields are generated. The sub-type specifies the UoM dimensions and is rendered at runtime as a value help.
Application Reference	Navigation Object	N/A	Creates a navigation link to existing SAP CRM business applications. A value help that allows searching for the corresponding application object instances is rendered at runtime.

Table 9.3   Field Types in Application Enhancement Tool

The field type property is mandatory. In SAP CRM 7.0, the name of that attribute was *data type*.

Based on a field type, you might get different options for rendering and validating the information at runtime. For example, texts could be rendered as email links in display mode. When editing, the field will behave as an input field, but an additional validation will ensure that the text entered is a valid email address.

The field sub-type depends on the field type. Currently there are only two field types that have sub-types: Quantity and Application Reference. You are not required to provide unit-of-measure (UoM) dimensions for quantity fields. However, you must specify an object when you choose an application reference.

The advanced power users (administrators) could choose to use a custom data type. If you want to do so, you have to enable the expert mode in the enhancement overview page (press the ENABLE EXPERT MODE button).

9.5   Navigation Fields

Most of the types discussed in Table 9.3 do not require further elaboration. However, there is one special field type that deserves special attention. *Application references* (also known as *navigation fields*) allow you to define links between two SAP CRM business objects. For example, you could host a reference of a specific campaign, order, or product within an account. When editing an account, the reference field will be rendered along with a value help. The latter is the standard search value help for the referenced SAP CRM business object, and allows you to find easily the desired instance. For example, if you are creating a link to a product, you will get the same search value help as you would get when adding product items to an order. You can search for a specific product ID, browse the product categories, and so on. When you switch to display mode, the referenced object instance will appear as a hyperlink. By clicking on it you can navigate to the overview page of the referenced instance. That is why the concept is often referred to as navigation fields.

Let us look at a specific example. Suppose that a hotel loyalty program member could add someone as an additional cardholder. Both the primary and additional member will be accumulating points against the same account. The business process owner would like to capture the additional member information as part of the account header data. Therefore, your task is now to create a new field called ADDITIONAL MEMBER that allows the user to assign existing business partners to an account.

What you need to do is to create a new field called ADDITIONAL MEMBER and to choose its type as APPLICATION REFERENCE. AET will prompt you to specify a sub-type. The business user will assign an existing business partner to the ADDITIONAL MEMBER field. Therefore, we will define the sub-type as Account. Figure 9.22 shows the field details required to fulfil this requirement.

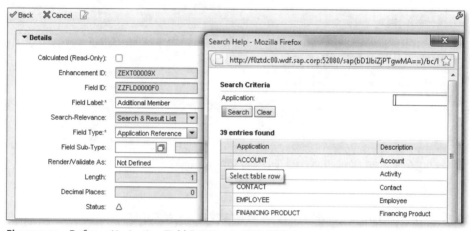

Figure 9.22 Define a Navigation Field Pointing to SAP CRM Accounts

Upon successful generation and session restart, you can open the ACCOUNT DETAILS view configuration and enable the newly created field. Once you save the view configuration, you can go back to account overview pages and start using the new navigation field (see Figure 9.23). Instead of working with account IDs, the end user can click on the F4 help, search for an account, and select one. The account field will show a user friendly description of the selected account. The end user can click on it and navigate to the account overview page.

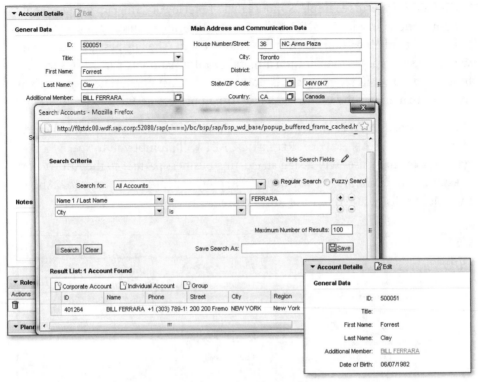

Figure 9.23 Account Navigation Field (Edit and Display Mode)

9.6 Extending SAP CRM Interactive Reports

While providing some guidance on Transaction AXTREG (AET Registry), we talked briefly about the BW data source flag. If you browse through the registry, you will find other flags (as per the options in the FIELD DETAILS page).

Extending Middleware Interfaces

More experienced technical users might be wondering what happened to extending middleware messages (BDocs). As a matter of fact, each successfully generated extension automatically registers in the corresponding BDoc. The users of the tool do not even have to flag this operation.

In this section, we will explain the flag OLT_REPORTING in AXTREG. This flag denotes the support for *SAP CRM Interactive Reports*. For some SAP CRM business objects, you can propagate the custom fields to the SAP CRM reports and use them as a key figure or characteristic (Figure 9.24). Note that these are not the BI reports, but the local SAP CRM reports.

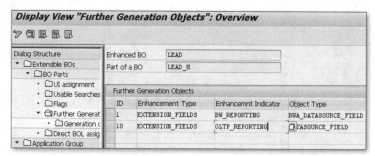

Figure 9.24 Further Generation Details of LEAD/LEAD_H

Please note that in order to use SAP CRM interactive reporting, you need authorization role *SAP CRM Operative Reporting User Role* (SAP_CRM_OR_USER) in SAP BI and SAP CRM clients. Enhancing SAP CRM interactive reports with the newly created extensions requires authorization role *Activation of SAP CRM OLTP Reporting InfoTypes* (SAP_CRM_OR_ACTIVATE) in the SAP BI client.

Let us illustrate the concept via a concrete example. Imagine that the business users want to track how many times a given lead has been contacted. Obviously, if there are many interactions for a given lead with little or no result, the lead should be reevaluated. In order to meet this requirement, you have to create a new field and make it available in a report in SAP CRM.

Create a New Field

If you use AET, all you need to do is create your field in SAP CRM leads (in the Lead Data object part) and select the option SAP CRM INTERACTIVE REPORTING. Because our field measures the number (quantity) of interactions, we will enable it as a key figure (see Figure 9.25).

Bringing that field to the view layout is something that we covered in the previous chapter when we discussed configuration and personalization. Complete the view configuration on your own. Once done, enter test data in several leads. If you are not familiar with SAP CRM Interactive Reporting you should be aware that the leads that will appear in your reports must be assigned to your user. For this, you must have a business partner (BP) associated with your user and that BP must be the employee responsible for your leads (Figure 9.26).

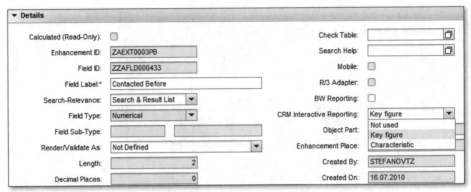

Figure 9.25 New Field Exposed as Key Figure in SAP CRM Interactive Reporting

Figure 9.26 Contacted Before Field in SAP CRM Leads Application

Creating a Report

Next, you need to modify an existing report or create a new one. To access this functionality, you have to have logical link ANA-REP-AP (the report search page) in your role and the right authorization and functional profile settings (for these, consult your SAP documentation). We will create a new report. Go to the search reports page and click on the NEW button (see Figure 9.27).

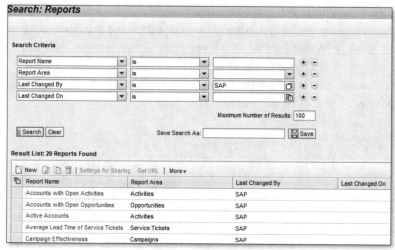

Figure 9.27 Search: Reports

The Interactive Report wizard will open. On the first page, you need to give the report a meaningful name and description, specify the report area (we are interested in the leads business object) and the default display format. Follow the entries on Figure 9.28.

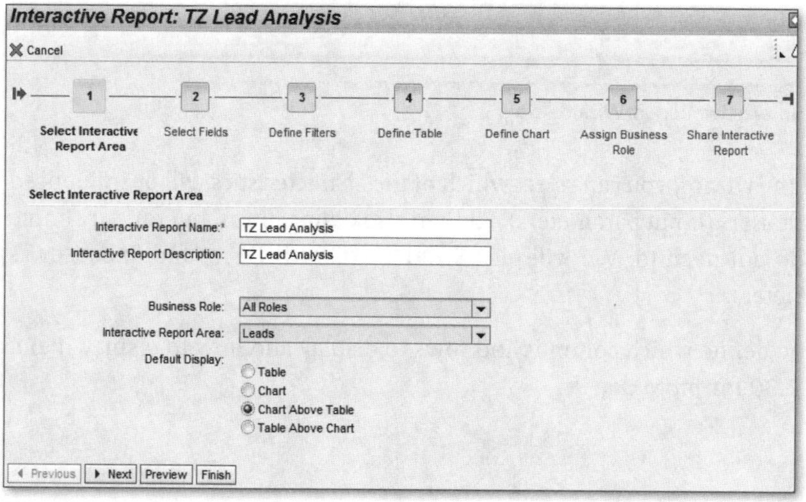

Figure 9.28 Interactive Report Wizard—Step 1

Step 2 of the wizard is where all the action takes place. Here you will need to pick the report's characteristics and key figures. You can follow the selections as per Figure 9.29. We have picked the lead ID, employee responsible, start and end dates, prospect, and status as the characteristics for which our data will be provided. In AVAILABLE KEY FIGURES you will find the newly created field CONTACTED BEFORE. Make sure you select it and click the NEXT button.

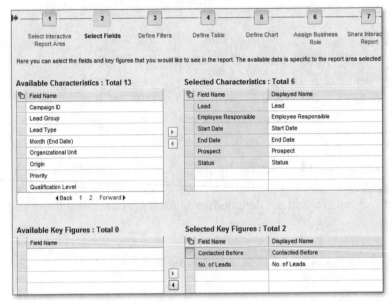

Figure 9.29 Interactive Report Wizard—Step 2

In Step 3 of the wizard, you can select which of the characteristics will be influenced by the report users (input parameters). You can also define filters, but for our simple report we do not need to. We will pick START DATE, END DATE, and PROSPECT as input parameters.

In Step 4 you define which columns and rows to display and how to display them. See Figure 9.30 for more details.

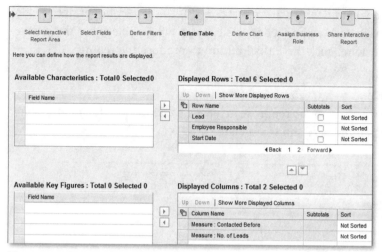

Figure 9.30   Interactive Report Wizard—Step 4

In Step 5 we will specify that the report will be displayed as Column Chart. In
Step 6 we will assign the report to the required business roles (Figure 9.31).

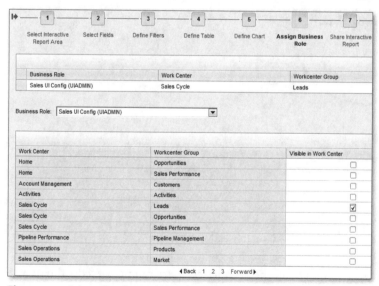

Figure 9.31   Interactive Report Wizard—Step 6

Last but not least, you must share the report (Step 7). This is very important because only those that have been authorized in this last step will be able to use the interactive report. Once done, click the FINISH button to produce the report.

Running a Report

You can run the report from the report search page by clicking on the report name. You shall get something very similar to Figure 9.32.

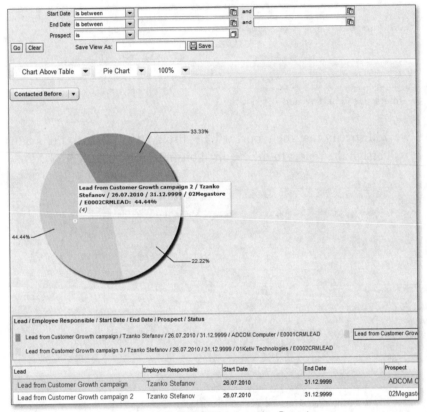

Figure 9.32 Sample Leads Analysis SAP CRM Interactive Report

Based on the settings in Step 6, all the authorized users can now access the newly created report through the LEADS work center.

9.7 Extending the Design Layer

Whether we are dealing with standalone fields or tables, the BOL model is extended accordingly. As a consequence, you can enhance the design layer objects based on the corresponding BOL objects with the newly created extensions.

As we already saw, the UI relevant settings can be made with the UI Configuration Tool. Technical consultants (developers) can create configurations in the Component Workbench. Whatever the method, if you want to introduce a new field, you need to add it to all relevant view layouts. If a given field needs to appear in many views, enabling it in multiple view configurations might be a tedious task. The design layer (DL) solves this problem by making it possible to make settings once and have them reflected in all views containing the new field.

As we saw previously, the DL allows customers to centrally manage fields that are seen in multiple views on the Web Client UI without maintaining them individually for every view. This allows for an increase in the efficiency and usability (by requiring fewer repetitive operations in the UI Configuration Tool). Customers can now maintain all relevant settings for field labels in a single place. For example, you can rename labels, hide or exclude fields from field set, and set value help from DDIC.

You also know that you can reuse a field extension across multiple business objects. Imagine that after a few months you are asked to change the label on one of the newly added fields. The last thing you would want is to change the label in each existing view configuration. The best way to tackle this imaginary scenario is through the DL. Let us see how you can add the MEMBERSHIP TYPE field to an existing DL object.

If you select the MEMBERSHIP TYPE field and press F2, you will get the TECHNICAL DATA pop-up. There you could see the name of the field, the view and context node it belongs to, and also the DESIGN LAYER assignments (among other details). As evident in Figure 9.33, MEMBERSHIP TYPE belongs to the HEADER context node and is represented by the context node attribute EXT.ZZFLD000003C.

If you now open the technical details of another field, for example DATE OF BIRTH, you will see something similar to Figure 9.34. The DL assignment is not empty. Instead, the field is associated with BUSINESSPARTNER design object under object type BP_ACCOUNT.

451

Figure 9.33 Technical Data for Membership Type Field

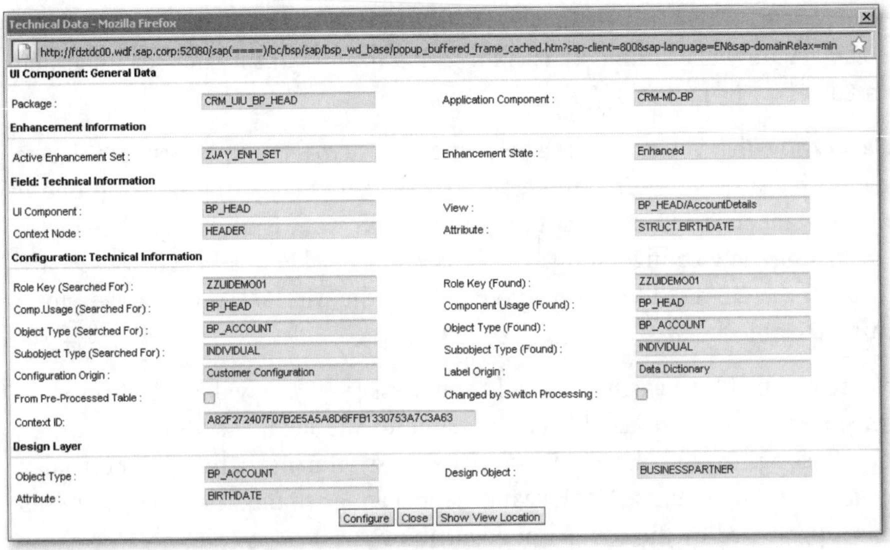

Figure 9.34 Technical Data for Date-of-Birth Field

The DL assignment in our current example (context node HEADER, view BP_HEAD/
AccountDetails) is at a context node level. Take a look at this assignment in the
component workbench. Open the BP_HEAD component, AccountDetails view and

drill down to the HEADER content node. After you right-click on it, you can go to the DL assignment (Figure 9.35).

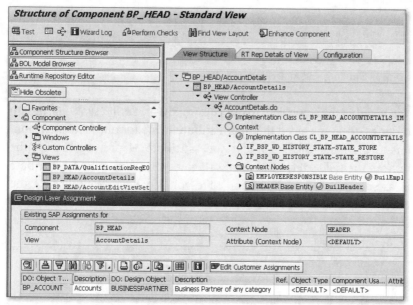

Figure 9.35 DL Assignment for Context Node Header in BP_HEAD/AccountDetails

DATE OF BIRTH belongs to the same component, view and context node as MEMBERSHIP TYPE. If you compare the data in CONFIGURATION: TECHNICAL INFORMATION (Figure 9.33 and Figure 9.34) you will see that object type and component usage for both fields are the same. The object type and component usage in the configuration of the fields match those of the DL assignment in the workbench (see Figure 9.35). Therefore, you can expect that adding MEMBERSHIP TYPE to the BUSINESSPARTNER design object will result in a proper design layer assignment for the newly added field.

The BUSINESSPARTNER design object is delivered via the standard SAP CRM content. Therefore, you cannot change it directly. Instead, you need to go to the customizing menu path CUSTOMER RELATIONSHIP MANAGEMENT • UI FRAMEWORK • UI FRAMEWORK DEFINITION • DESIGN LAYER • COPY SAP DESIGN OBJECTS and copy the SAP DL object in your namespace (Figure 9.36). Once done, you can click on the GOTO COPIES button and add your field(s) to the copied DL object.

Figure 9.36 Display and Copy an SAP Delivered DL Object

Let us add the membership type field to our copy of SAP's BUSINESSPARTNER design object. In order to do so, we need the BOL attribute name for our field extension. It is the same as the name of the context node attribute. Hence, we can use the information from the field's technical details (Figure 9.33). Enter the DL attribute information as shown in Figure 9.37 and save your changes. We will take the opportunity to change the label of our field to Membership.

Figure 9.37 Adding New Field to DL object

If you start a new session in the Web UI and navigate to the account page, you will see that the label of your field has been changed to MEMBERSHIP. If you open the technical details for that field [F2], you will see that it is assigned to the design layer and its label is retrieved from the DL (see Figure 9.38).

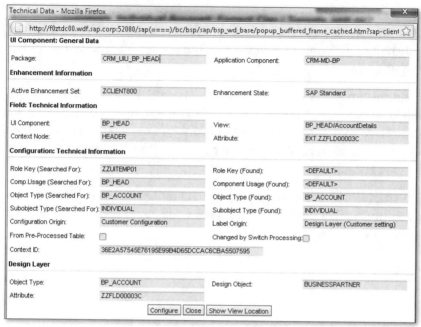

Figure 9.38 Technical Data for Membership Type after DL Assignment

What we have shown is of little value unless you plan to use your new field in different objects and want to maintain its consistency through the DL. In real life, we often want to assign the same structural extensions to many business objects. The design layer can make a real difference in maintaining such scenarios.

9.8 Summary

By now you can see why AET is the logical tool of choice when it comes to extensibility. It is quite easy to use and hides many of the complexities of the generation process. AET is also integrated with the UI Configuration Tool. Once you successfully create an extension, the tool guides you straight to the view or page configuration step. Moreover, you can initiate the whole process directly from the business application and test the newly added field or view right away.

We also touched briefly on how to provide additional value on top of custom extensions. The concepts presented here will allow you to quickly build custom scenarios not covered in the standard SAP delivery. We saw how one can propagate the structural extensions into the SAP CRM interactive reports, enabling the end user to perform analysis factoring in the new enhancements. The design layer can significantly reduce the effort needed to configure and maintain cross-application enhancements centrally.

For more information on AET you should consult the SAP Help documentation. In addition there are blogs on SDN that deal with different aspects of the tool. Our goal was not to go into every single detail of AET (or any other tool), but rather to demonstrate its main capabilities. We hope that we have convinced you of its usefulness, power, and ease of use.

In the next chapter we will continue our discussion of extensibility. Rather than focus only on structural extensibility, we will show you how one can enhance some aspects of the business logic processing.

Structural extensibility supports data enhancements, but when it comes to adding new logic one has to consider other options for enhancing the standard behavior.

10 Behavioral Extensibility

In the previous chapters, we showed you how to create new fields and tables within existing business applications. We also discussed practical examples related to building custom functionality on top of field extensions. It is time to look into enhancing applications with custom logic. We will refer to this as *behavior extensibility*.

The most powerful mechanism for adding custom logic remains creation and implementation of enhancement spots and BAdIs. Writing ABAP code in BAdIs is often the only way to achieve what we call behavior extensibility. In this chapter, you will find out how to add behavior to field and table extensions using dedicated standard enhancement spots.

As of SAP CRM 7.0 EhP1, you can add some custom logic without having deep technical knowledge of SAP CRM applications and frameworks. This could be done via the so called calculated fields, which we briefly introduced in the beginning of the book. Using concrete examples, we will demonstrate how easy it is to define a calculated expression and to deliver some custom intelligence to a SAP CRM business object without understanding the technical intricacies of the application and even without writing a single line of ABAP code.

In addition, in this chapter we will show you how to add intelligence to your custom table extensions. A dedicated section will clarify the concept of the global attribute tags. We will conclude by demonstrating how one can extend the standard SAP functionality through BRF+.

10.1 Behavior Extensibility via BAdIs

If you remember, the field and table extensions affect not only the UI but all the application layers. Therefore, the application APIs and BAdIs are aware of such structures. As a result, you can implement your custom logic in one of the available BAdIs. Clearly, you have to know the specifics of an application and also be prepared to write ABAP code. Information about the implementation of BAdIs in the context of the enhancement concept is available in the SAP Library for SAP NetWeaver under BADIs • EMBEDDING IN THE ENHANCEMENT FRAMEWORK.

Let us demonstrate this in a very simple example. Imagine that one of the requirements related to our membership type field is to ensure that an agent should not be able set the field when the account owner's age is less than 18. One might argue that the system should not allow creation of such accounts in the first place, but again our goal is to demonstrate the concepts rather than to provide comprehensive solutions.

The SAP CRM account object is a type of a business partner (BP). Therefore, what you need to do first is to review the available BP related documentation and find the correct extension places (BAdIs). In order to find a BAdI (or an enhancement place), go to Transaction SE18 and search in the REPOSITORY INFORMATION SYSTEM ($\boxed{\text{F4}}$ help). One can do the same in Transaction SE80. For our example, we need a BAdI that will be triggered each time a business partner gets updated. One candidate is a BAdI called BUPA_FURTHER_CHECKS (see Figure 10.1).

Once you open the BAdI definition, you can go to the IMPLEMENTATION menu and trigger the CREATE action. An empty class based on IF_EX_BUPA_FURTHER_CHECKS will be generated. Listing 10.1 shows an example of a BAdI implementation.

```
method IF_EX_BUPA_FURTHER_CHECKS~CHECK_CENTRAL.
  data: lv_dat type i,
        ls_ret_line type BAPIRET2.

  CALL FUNCTION 'FIMA_DAYS_AND_MONTHS_AND_YEARS'
    EXPORTING
      i_date_from   = IS_BUT000-BIRTHDT
      i_date_to     = SY-DATUM
      i_flg_separate = 'X'
    IMPORTING
      e_years       = lv_dat.

  IF lv_dat < 18 AND IS_BUT000-ZZFLD00003C IS NOT INITIAL.
    ls_ret_line-TYPE = 'E'.
*   add your error message here
    INSERT LS_RET_LINE INTO TABLE ET_RETURN.
```

```
    ENDIF.
endmethod.
```

Listing 10.1 Implementation of BUPA_FURTHER_CHECKS BAdI

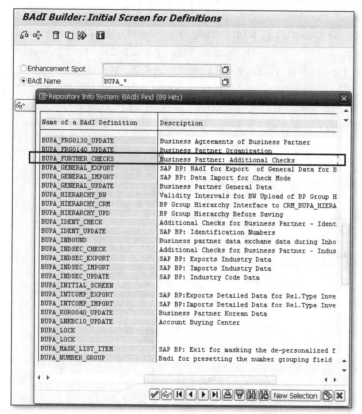

Figure 10.1 Looking Up the Right BAdI (Transaction SE18)

The BP header data is passed to the BAdI as a structure of type BUT000. We use it to retrieve the account's birth date and compare it with the current system date by calling function FIMA_DAYS_AND_MONTHS_AND_YEARS. The latter can return the difference between two dates in years. If this difference is greater than 18, and if the membership custom field (IS_BUT000-ZZFLD00003C) is not blank, we trigger an error.

Once done, we have to activate our BAdI. Now if we try to set the membership for a business partner who was born less than 18 years ago, we will get an error.

10.2 Adding Logic to Table Enhancements

Let us start Transaction SE18 again and look for an enhancement spot called AXT_RT_TABLES. Feel free to review the documentation of the different BAdI definitions there. Most of them are related to the so-called Rapid Applications, a concept that we will examine later. For the time being, let us concentrate on the classical structural extensibility. The BAdI AXT_RT_TABLE_API allows you to add some intelligence to your table extensions (see Figure 10.2). You can intercept the creation or update of table records and enhance them. If you are not happy with the way records of table enhancements are retrieved (for example for performance reasons) you can substitute the default query behavior. You can also add custom validation logic.

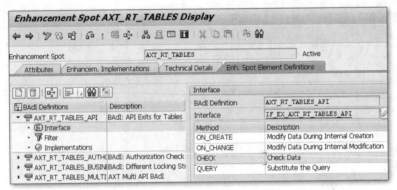

Figure 10.2 Enhancement Spot AXT_RT_TABLES and Table API Interface

As usual, we will demonstrate the potential of this feature with a simple example. It makes sense to prevent the end user from entering 0 (or fewer) nights in the HOTEL BOOKINGS assignment block (table enhancement). The default behavior of your table is such that every entry that does not violate the specifics of the underlying data types is persistent. By simply observing the table API interface, you might have guessed already that you will have to implement the CHECK method of the IF_EX_AXT_RT_TABLES_API (the interface behind the AXT_RT_TABLE_API BAdI).

Right-click on the AXT_RT_TABLES_API entry in the BAdI definitions tree and choose CREATE BAdI IMPLEMENTATION. The first step is to select or create an enhancement implementation. In our example, we have created a new one called ZDEMO_BOOKING_TABLE_API. Feel free to do the same if you are following along with our example. You need to choose it and create a BAdI implementation with an implementation class (for example ZCL_DEMO_BOOKING_TABLE_API).

The AXT_RT_TABLES_API BAdI allows you to specify filters so that implementations are associated with table names. If you open the definition of our newly created table in Transaction SE11, you can find out the name of the underlying DDIC table created by AET. In our example, AET gave it the name of ZTAB0000CA. We will use that name as filter value. Figure 10.3 summarizes this step.

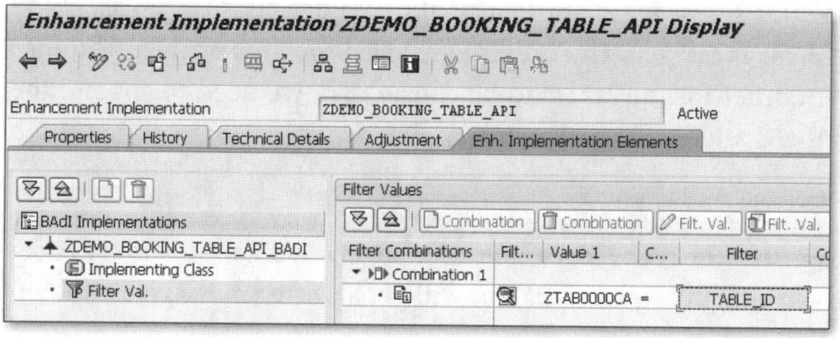

Figure 10.3 Sample AXT_RT_TABLES_API BAdI Implementation

Now you can double-click on the implementation class name and open the class builder. Go ahead and implement method IF_EX_AXT_RT_TABLES_API~CHECK. You can refer the implementation provided in Listing 10.2.

```
DATA lv_message type line of BAPIRETTAB.
FIELD-SYMBOLS <fs_nights> type ZDTEL0000CD.

ASSIGN COMPONENT 'ZZFLD00003G' of structure IS_WORK_STRUCTURE TO <fs_
nights>.

if SY-SUBRC = 0 AND <fs_nights> < 1.
    lv_message-ID     = 'ZHOTEL_BOOKING'.
    lv_message-NUMBER = 000.
    lv_message-TYPE   = 'E'.
    "lv_message-message = 'The stay (nights) shall be greater than 0.'.
    APPEND lv_message to CT_MESSAGES.
ENDIF.
```

Listing 10.2 IF_EX_AXT_RT_TABLES_API~CHECK Implementation

If you analyze the generated table in Transaction SE11, you should be able to figure out which field name corresponds to which attribute (check the short description). In our example, the nights-stayed attribute has the name ZZFLD00003G, and its type is `ZDTEL0000CD`. The table data accesses the `CHECK` method via the parameter `IS_WORK_STRUCTURE`. We will store the value of the night field in a field symbol:

```
ASSIGN COMPONENT 'ZZFLD00003G' of structure IS_WORK_STRUCTURE TO <fs_
nights>.
```

Next, we check if the value of the nights attribute is less than 1, and if the answer is yes we issue an error message. We make use of a message class `ZHOTEL_BOOKING` that contains the error message: "The stay (nights) shall be greater than 0" under the number `000`. In order for the errors to be considered, we need to append the error message to the change table parameter `CT_MESSAGES`:

```
APPEND lv_message to CT_MESSAGES.
```

Once done, you can start the SAP CRM application, open an account, and try to set a booking record with nights equal to 0. You will get an error message, as shown in Figure 10.4.

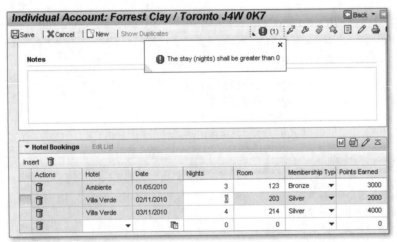

Figure 10.4 Hotel Bookings Validates the Number of Nights Entered

If you study the BAdI and interface documentation, you will understand clearly how to use this API. For example, in `ON_CREATE`, `ON_CHANGE`, and `CHECK`, you get a parameter structure containing one table record. If you put a breakpoint in the code in Listing 10.2, you will see that it is called once for each existing record. Here are some parameters that you might find useful:

- OBJECT_ID: The GUID identifier of the hosting application (for example business partner, order).

- PARENT_ID: The ID of the parent object to which the table extension is attached (for example, this could be the BP or order header).

- RECORD_ID: The GUID identifier of the current table record.

- WORK_STRUCTURE: Contains one complete table record (including the RECORD_ID, PARENT_ID and OBJECT_ID).

For example, the PARENT_ID and OBJECT_ID in the case of our CHECK method implementation will contain the BP_GUID of the current account object.

10.3   Creating a Calculated Field

Imagine that your company uses an image server to store all its multimedia content. Today, that idea is far from revolutionary. Image servers are often used along Web servers in order to speed up image retrieval and reduce the load on the application servers.

Let us assume that all the members of your hotel loyalty program have their pictures taken when they sign up. These pictures are stored on an image server.

You have been asked to incorporate the guest profile pictures into SAP CRM. The requirement is that every time an agent pulls up the SAP CRM account page, the picture of the guest appears there as well. Before SAP CRM 7.0 EhP1, you would have to roll up your sleeves and write code. For example, you would have to create an enhancement set of the BP_HEAD component. In the component, you probably would create a new value context node. In its get methods you would have to identify the URL that links to the image and instruct the Web Client UI framework to render the result as an image (read-only).

However, if you have SAP CRM 7.0 EhP1, you can skip all those tasks. You can define a calculated field that determines the URL at runtime and renders it as an image. In the following section, we will show you how to do that.

To keep things simple, we are simulating the image server locally. We have created a BSP application and stored all the images there as MIME content. The name of each image will contain the SAP CRM account ID. We can describe the URL to an image consisting of a static part followed by the account ID and ending with the image file extension (say JPG):

`'/sap/bc/bsp/sap/zwui_demo' + <ACCOUNT_ID> +'.JPG'`

To better visualize this scenario, take a look at Figure 10.5.

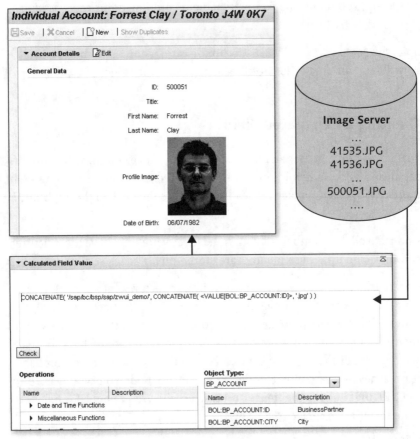

Figure 10.5 Calculated Image Field Scenario

Let us implement the above requirement. First, we need to open a SAP CRM account (for which you have a guest photograph) and start the configuration tool for a view where you want to add the new field. In our example we want to place the new field in the GENERAL DATA view. In the configuration tool, start AET by clicking on the CREATE FIELD button. Select the ACCOUNT enhanced object and the Central Details object part.

A pop-up with the details of the future field will open. The first field property that you will see is the CALCULATED (READ ONLY) checkbox. You have to select it in order to create a calculated field. The tool will bring a new assignment block called CALCULATED FIELD VALUE. There we will define the calculation expression (formula). Before you do so, you need to fill all the required fields in the DETAILS block. Select the field type as Text. If you expand the RENDER/VALIDATE AS attribute, you see an entry called Calculated Image. This option is only available for calculated fields. If you select it, the field length will be set to 255.

You might be wondering how you can define fields longer than 60 characters for calculated fields but not for the standard fields. If you tried to set a length greater than 60 before, AET would have issued an error. However, calculated fields are not like regular field enhancements. They exist only in the BOL layer and do not interact with the application DDIC structures (they are not part of the GenIL implementation, underlying API, and persistence layer). As the name suggests, calculated fields are read-only. Their value is always calculated at runtime. Therefore, they are not persistent and AET does not have to worry about the size and performance of the underlying data structures.

As we now know, the BOL layer provides a uniform way to access the application logic. The only way to enable the calculated fields feature globally is by integrating it into a layer that acts as a sole gateway into applications. The BOL layer is the most appropriate place to deliver this feature. The drawback of such an approach is that the application-specific APIs are not aware of these enhancements. However, because calculated fields will be used mostly by SAP CRM end users from the Web UI, this limitation is acceptable.

But let's go back to our example. Once you fill in all the required fields, you can define the calculation formula (expression). The latter consists of operations, operands, and constants. As you probably do not know all the operations at your disposal, you can browse the OPERATIONS block. Under FUNCTIONS FOR CHARACTER STRINGS, you will find the CONCATENATE operation. You can click on the question mark icon (❓) to read more about each calculation operation. The tooltip will provide a summary of the operation's parameters. By clicking on an operation, you copy the name of the operation into the current cursor position in the formula text area (the same applies to the operands/attributes in the block on the right). This way, you can mix manual entry with selecting operations and attributes via mouse clicks. Simple arithmetic operations such as +, -,* (multiply), / (divide), etc. are not present in the

OPERATIONS block. But they are easy to deduce and enter directly in the formula text area. Once you are done, your field will look similar to Figure 10.6.

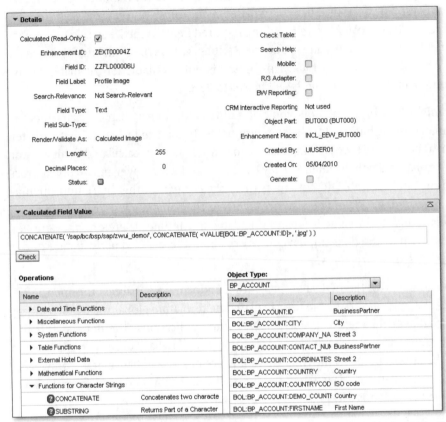

Figure 10.6 Calculated Image Field Details Page

The calculated field concept is powered by BRF+. All the operations that you see in the FIELD DETAILS page come from there. Those of you familiar with BRF+ might be tempted to use & instead of CONCATENATE. Please feel free to do so.

The more interesting question is where the application attributes (operands) come from. Moreover, you will notice that there are several types of attributes: BOL, USER, and CONST (constants). In order to facilitate business object attribute exposure, SAP CRM 7.0 EhP1 introduced the concept of *global attribute tags*. We will look into the topic later on in this chapter. If you do not see the account ID attribute, you can jump to the next section and read how to add new or activate existing attributes. Let us wrap up our example. We need to save and generate the newly created field.

The SAP CRM session will be restarted. Once the session is reopened, we will be able to open the account page and start the UI configuration tool for the ACCOUNT DATA view. As we saw before, the new field enhancements appear under the corresponding context node in the AVAILABLE FIELDS block. In our example, this would be the HEADER node. You need to move the Profile Image field into the view layout and save the UI configuration. Note that the placeholder for calculated image fields in the view layout appears in a distinct way and says IMAGE (see Figure 10.7).

▼ View	Show Field Properties	Show Technical Details	Make 16 Columns/2 Panels	Make 16 Columns/1 Panel	Create Separate Config.

This view supports separate configurations for display and edit mode
To get field properties, hold down ALT and click the field. To choose several fields, hold down CTRL and click the fields.

Available Fields		A	B	C	D	E	F	G	H
▫ Field	1	**General Data**							
▸ ☐ EMPLOYEERESPONSIBLE	2			ID:					
▾ ☐ HEADER	3			Title:				▾	
Title	4			First Name:					
Title	5			Last Name:*					
2nd acad. title	6			Profile Image:		**Image**			
Academic Title	7			Date of Birth:					
SSN	8			Classification:					
Height	9			Language:					
HairColor									

Figure 10.7 Configuring Newly Created Calculated Field

The final result of this simple exercise is a new image that appears in the account details, as shown in Figure 10.8.

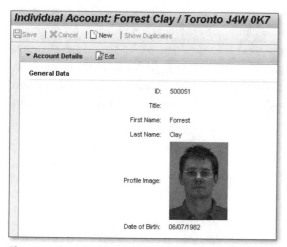

Figure 10.8 Calculated Image Field in SAP CRM Account Application

It should be clear that calculated fields offer new possibilities when it comes to adding value on top of the standard SAP solutions. Now, non-technical users can implement simple business logic without requiring in-depth application knowledge. Even ABAP developers can benefit from this quick, easy, and non-intrusive way of enhancing the behavior of SAP CRM business objects.

We would like to show two additional examples that illustrate more advance capabilities of the calculated fields. First, imagine that you want to display the age-group information based on the business partner's birth date. The age group values are shown in Table 10.1.

Age	Age Group Text
Less than 18	Adolescent
From 18 to 21	Young Adult
From 21 to 40	Adult
From 40 to 65	Middle Aged
After 65	Senior

Table 10.1 Age Group Values

It is obvious that we would need condition logic that selects the age group text based on the age of the account. The SAP CRM BP does not have an age field, but it has a date of birth. In order to calculate the age, we could subtract the current system date from the BP's birth date. Naturally this cannot be the normal mathematical subtraction but a specialized one that can return the year value. A bigger problem is how to get an age group text value that is local sensitive. The good news is that you could reference the dropdown list values from the field details in the calculation formula. As you know, you can translate these values as part of the field definition (in the translation assignment block). The realization of this business requirement is shown in Figure 10.9.

In the formula text area we have provided the following expression:

```
IF( DT_DURATION_DIFF_INT_YEARS( SYS_INFO_CURRENT_DATE( ),
<VALUE[BOL:BP_ACCOUNT:BIRTHDATE]> ) <= 18, 'A', IF( DT_DURATION_DIFF_
INT_YEARS( SYS_INFO_CURRENT_DATE( ), <VALUE[BOL:BP_ACCOUNT:BIRTHDATE]>
) <= 21, 'B', IF( DT_DURATION_DIFF_INT_YEARS( SYS_INFO_CURRENT_DATE( ),
<VALUE[BOL:BP_ACCOUNT:BIRTHDATE]> ) <= 40, 'C', IF( DT_DURATION_DIFF_
```

```
INT_YEARS( SYS_INFO_CURRENT_DATE( ), <VALUE[BOL:BP_ACCOUNT:BIRTHDATE]>
) <= 65, 'D', 'E' ) ) ) )
```

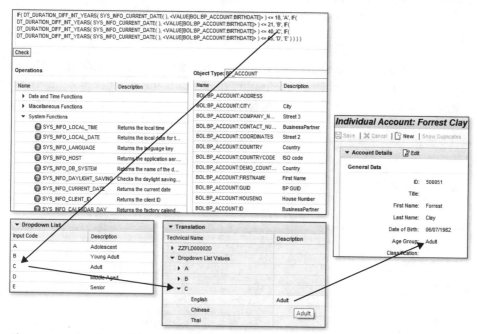

Figure 10.9 Age Group Calculated Field

Let's look at another example. The SAP CRM corporate accounts have contact information (contact persons). We will count the number of contacts of a given corporate account. As you know, an account can have many contacts. They are rendered as a table view (assignment block). In the GenIL model, one can access them via the 1:M relation `BuilContactPersonRel`. If you try to access an attribute of the contacts object from a calculated field at the BP header level and display its value, you will get an error because the contacts dependant object points to many entries (a collection of contact data).

In terms of data structures, a collection is represented as a table. This is exactly how the calculated field feature and BRF+ see it. Luckily, there are BRF+ operations that specialize in tables (table operations).

Imagine that you want to access the IDs of contacts in a calculated field expression. The result will be a table that contains only one column filled with the contact IDs of all contact entities. Therefore, in order to calculate the number of contacts of a given account, we could simply count the records returned by contact ID attribute. BRF+ provides an operation that counts table rows: `TABLE_ROW_COUNT`. Our requirement could be implemented via the following formula expression:

```
TABLE_ROW_COUNT( <VALUE[BOL:BP_ACCOUNT:CONTACT_NUMBER]> )
```

Make sure that the operand you pass to `TABLE_ROW_COUNT` yields a table at runtime. Figure 10.10 illustrates our field definition that counts the number of contacts of a given SAP CRM account business object.

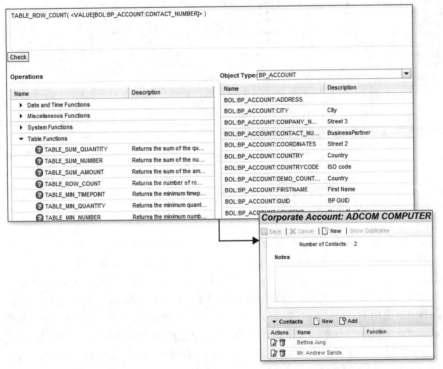

Figure 10.10 Number of Contacts Calculation in SAP CRM Account Object

Although the presented examples give you a good idea of how powerful the calculated field feature is, you should review the available documentation before trying something complex. It is very important to be comfortable with the content of collective SAP Note 1457617 before exploring the intricacies of the AET calculated-field concept.

10.4   Introducing Global Attribute Tags

In the previous section, we used and briefly discussed the operands (attributes) available at your disposal when defining a calculated field formula. It is time to take a look at where these attributes come from.

As of SAP CRM 7.0 EhP1, the framework introduces a new concept called *global attribute tags*. The idea is to allow administrators to tag attributes from the BOL/GenIL model. This allows them to expose the application data for consumption in different tools (AET, Rapid Applications, mash-ups, and tag clouds).

According to Wikipedia: "A tag is a non-hierarchical keyword or term assigned to a piece of information (such as an Internet bookmark, digital image, or computer file). This kind of metadata helps describe an item and allows it to be found again by browsing or searching." The Web Client UI uses the concept of tagging in a similar way. The global attribute tags paradigm supports tagging of application (BOL) attributes, system user profile attributes (Transaction SU3), and even definition of constants.

The attribute tags are defined in customizing via the menu path CUSTOMER RELATIONSHIP MANAGEMENT • UI FRAMEWORK • UI FRAMEWORK DEFINITION • GLOBAL ATTRIBUTE TAGS. There you will find two transactions: DEFINE ATTRIBUTE TAGS and COPY SAP ATTRIBUTE TAGS. As the names suggest, the first transaction is used to tag data within the customer's namespace. We will illustrate the creation of tags via concrete examples.

SAP CRM comes with some basic tags for many business applications. You can copy these into your namespace by calling Transaction COPY SAP ATTRIBUTE TAGS. The process is reasonably intuitive, and we recommend that you refer to the available documentation for more details.

There are three types of tags: BOL, user profile, and constants. The BOL tag is a non-translatable identifier that caries semantic meaning and points to an attribute of a BOL entity (GenIL business object). These tags are always defined in the context of an UI object type. The type of tag represents the application semantics and groups all the tags relevant for the given application. When defining such a tag, the power user needs to specify a path that points to a BOL attribute. The path is derived from the GenIL model of the business application.

In the context of the previous examples, let us look at the account's ID tagged attribute. In the CALCULATED FIELD VALUE block it appears as BOL:BP_ACCOUNT:ID. This notation signifies that this is a BOL attribute from the BP_ACCOUNT object type and its tag name is ID. Now let us start the DEFINE ATTRIBUTE TAGS transaction. It will first ask you for an OBJECT TYPE. Type in BP_ACCOUNT and press ⌷Enter⌷. A maintenance view will appear. On the left you can see all tag types you can define. The BOL ATTRIBUTES will be selected by default, and on the right you will see all the BOL attributes you have tagged within BP_ACCOUNT. In your case it might be empty. For our example we have defined a tag called ID that points to the BP_NUMBER attribute of the BuilHeader BOL entity (BuilHeader@BP_NUMBER).

In order to define a BOL tag you need to fill in the ATTRIBUTE NAME property (with ID), specify a BOL path, and check the ACTIVE flag. You can pick a BOL path from the BOL model via the ⌷F4⌷ help available along the BOL PATH input field. Figure 10.11 illustrates the ID tag example. If the ACTIVE flag is unchecked, the tag definition could be saved but it will not appear in any of the tools that utilize the tag concept (for example the CALCULATED FIELD VALUE block).

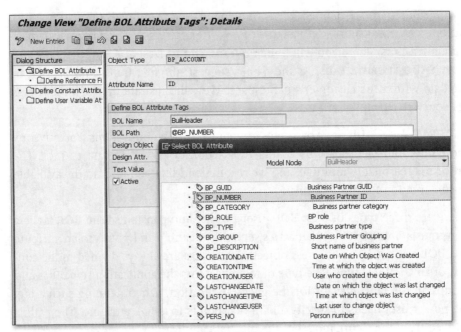

Figure 10.11 Tagging the BOL attribute BP_NUMBER

Another example will be the contact number of the account (`BOL:BP_ACCOUNT:CONTACT_NUMBER`). This is a bit more complicated because the contact information is represented by the `BuilContactPerson` GenIL business object. This entity is accessible through the `BuilContactPersonRel` relation. In our example, the BOL path that is tagged via the `CONTACT_NUMBER` tag name is `BuilHeader/BuilContactPersonRel/@CONP_NUMBER` (see Figure 10.12).

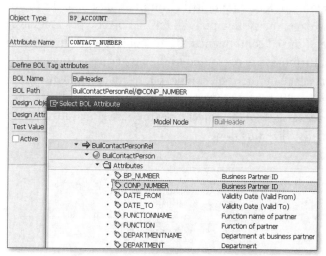

Figure 10.12 Tagging BOL Attribute CONP_NUMBER

As you might have already noticed, we use a special syntax to describe the tagged BOL paths, for example, `BuilHeader/BuilContactPersonRel/@CONP_NUMBER`. A relation always leads to exactly one object for which we do not have to provide the object name as part of the BOL path. For example, we use `BuilContactPersonRel/@CONP_NUMBER` instead of `BuilContactPersonRel/BuilContactPerson@CONP_NUMBER`.

The BOL Path property of a tag does not contain the first (main or root) BOL entity: `BuilHeader` in our example. Before we examine this further, let us explain where this main (root) entity comes from. The definition of each UI object type that we consider valid contains a BOL entity name. You can check the value of field `OBJECT_NAME` in table `BSP_DLC_OBJ_TYPE`. This BOL entity name should match the so called main BOL entity of the corresponding application overview page. You can think of the main BOL entity as the entry point to the application's BOL. It is the entity that will get loaded before anything else (hence the root entity of the loaded model). Typically it is returned by `IF_BSP_WD_HISTORY_STATE_DESCR~GET_MAIN_ENTITY` in the window controller. Hopefully, you recall this from some of our previous discussions. If you look into the implementation of the GET_MAIN_ENITY in the controller class of BPHEADOverview (overview page) in component BP_HEAD (class CL_BP_HEAD_BPHEADOVERVIEW_IMPL), you will see that it returns an instance of the GenIL/BOL business object BuilHeader (stored in the PARTNER context node). BuldHeader is also the BOL entity defined for the BP_ACCOUNT UI object type.

Based on the above, you might have already grasped how the application attributes in the calculated fields assignment block are pulled at runtime. Based on the main BOL entity of the overview page, the system pulls all the UI object types that have the same BOL object name. If the UI component sets an UI object type, this is used as a default and its tagged attributes are presented to the power user. However, if necessary, the user still can select another object type (with a matching BOL entity name) and work with its tagged attributes. The tagged user profile attributes and tagged constants are pulled regardless of the object type (they are global attributes). Figure 10.13 will help you visualize this flow.

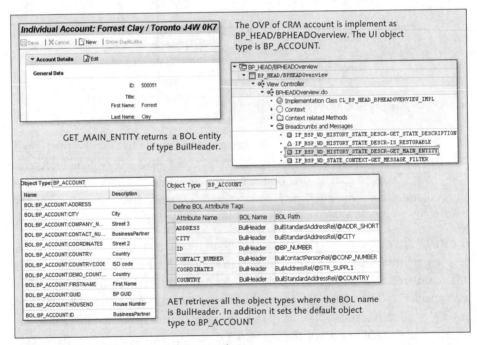

Figure 10.13 Retrieving the Tagged BOL Attributes

There are three properties in the tag attribute definition that we have not discussed yet: the DESIGN OBJECT, DESIGN ATTRIBUTE, and the TEST VALUE (see Figure 10.14).

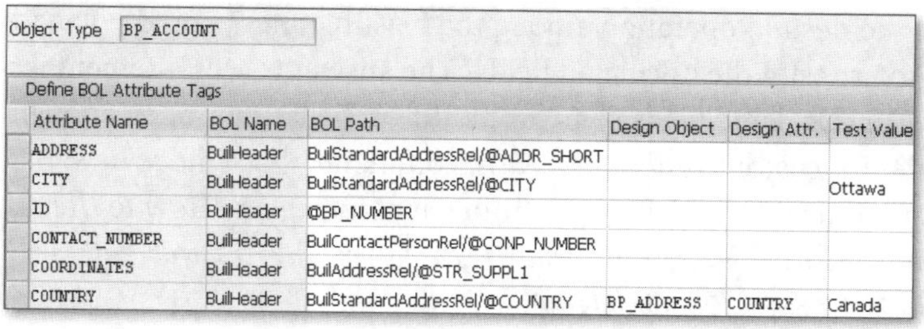

Object Type BP_ACCOUNT

Define BOL Attribute Tags

Attribute Name	BOL Name	BOL Path	Design Object	Design Attr.	Test Value
ADDRESS	BuilHeader	BuilStandardAddressRel/@ADDR_SHORT			
CITY	BuilHeader	BuilStandardAddressRel/@CITY			Ottawa
ID	BuilHeader	@BP_NUMBER			
CONTACT_NUMBER	BuilHeader	BuilContactPersonRel/@CONP_NUMBER			
COORDINATES	BuilHeader	BuilAddressRel/@STR_SUPPL1			
COUNTRY	BuilHeader	BuilStandardAddressRel/@COUNTRY	BP_ADDRESS	COUNTRY	Canada

Figure 10.14 BOL-based Global Attribute Tags with DL Assignment

As the name suggests, the DESIGN OBJECT designates a design layer object name. The design objects that you can assign must have the same BOL object name as the UI object type. Once you select a design object, you can associate a design layer object attribute to a tag. The effect of this assignment will be that the label of the design layer attribute will be used as a description for the tagged attribute. For example, in the DESCRIPTION column of the CALCULATED FIELD VALUE assignment block, the framework will pull the DL label. As a result, the users will get a consistent labeling (description) across the SAP CRM applications. If there is no design layer assignment, the DDIC text of the underlying data element will be used.

The test value is currently used only by the Web 2.0 mash-ups, a topic that we will discuss in the next chapter. However, at this point it is sufficient to say that the values there are string literals that could be used when testing the potential output of a component (like a mash-up) that uses tagged attributes.

The constant and the user profile attributes are not restricted to UI object types. They do not have an application context and are available in each application regardless of the selected object type. SAP CRM comes with a fixed list of user profile attributes that you can activate. In effect, the process of tagging them is equivalent to activating these attributes. The tagged constants can be viewed as aliases for data values. When specifying them you need to indicate the DDIC type of your constant and its value.

10.5 Adding Custom BRF+ Operations

So far we learned how to use calculated fields and how to expose application data (attribute tagging). Apart from attributes (operands), a calculated field formula also contains operations (mathematical, logical, table, date, and other functions). What if you cannot find the desired operation among the existing ones? Could you add custom functions to use with the calculated fields? The answer is "yes." Remember that the operations in calculated fields come from BRF+. The latter is open enough to allow you to define custom functions. We recommend that you review the available documentation and the SDN paper from Carsten Ziegler: "How to Create Formula Functions" (*http://www.sdn.sap.com/irj/scn/go/portal/prtroot/docs/library/ uuid/10e9c96f-0c8b-2b10-6885-f00adbeb314b*).

We will also walk you through an example in which we will add a new function in BRF+ and integrate it with the AET calculated field operations. Let us consider a scenario in which the membership type of a BP must not be entered by an end user. Instead it will be pulled from an external system and displayed in the account overview page. You could create an enhancement set for the BP_HEAD component, add a model node attribute, and pull the membership data from the external system via custom ABAP code. Another less intrusive alternative might be to create a custom operation that reads the membership data and uses it in a calculation field. We will now explain how to implement this.

A BRF+ formula can be implemented in a custom class with a static method. The formula (its logic) is in the static method. It must be also registered in what is called an *application exit class*. Application exit classes are used to implement application specific features in BRF+. The application exit class needs to implement the interface IF_FDT_APPLICATION_SETTINGS. When you create an application in BRF+ that needs to use certain custom features (your functions, for example), you have to make it use your application exit class.

For each calculated field, AET creates a BRF+ application using the default application exit class CL_AXT_BRFPLUS_APPL_EXIT. This is done behind the scenes and you cannot add your application exit class to it by following the standard BRF+ procedure. The good news is that there is a BAdI called AXT_BRFPLUS_APPL_EXIT (part of enhancement spot AXT_BRFPLUS_EXIT). You can use this BAdI to return your application exit class. However, you do not want to interfere with the standard behavior of AET (calculated fields). Instead of implementing an application exit that simply conforms to BRF+'s IF_FDT_APPLICATION_SETTINGS, you derive from the default AET exit class, namely CL_AXT_BRFPLUS_APPL_EXIT.

Let us follow the above steps in detail. First, we will create a class with a static method. The name of our class is ZCL_HOTEL_BRF and the method is FUNCTIONAL_ EXT_PROPERTY. Here you could pull the membership information from your external system and return its value. However, we will keep things as simple as possible and return a hardcoded value. The method accepts a property name parameter. You could make this function a bit more generic so that it returns other properties (not just membership) from our reservation system. The implementation works only with a property called MEMBERSHIP (see Listing 10.3).

```
CASE IV_PROP_NAME.
   WHEN 'MEMBERSHIP'.
*     make a call to the exterbnal system and get the value of the
property
*     for our demo hardcode to Silver
         RV_PROP_VALUE = 'S'.

   WHEN OTHERS.
         RAISE EXCEPTION TYPE cx_foev_error_in_function.
ENDCASE.
```

Listing 10.3 Custom BRF+ Formula Implementation

The importing parameter IV_PROP_NAME is of type STRING and so is the return value RV_PROP_VALUE.

We strongly encourage you to write class and method documentation (SAPScript). Remember, chances are that others might also use your operation when defining calculated fields. This documentation will be used by AET to populate the pop-up triggered via the question mark icon (?) in the OPERATIONS block of a calculated field.

Next, you need to create an application exit class. We have named this class ZCL_HOTEL_BRF_APP_EXIT. As our exit will register functions (one function to be precise) we have to indicate so in the constructor (Listing 10.4).

```
method CLASS_CONSTRUCTOR.
   if_fdt_application_settings~gv_get_formula_functionals = abap_true.
endmethod.
```

Listing 10.4 Constructor Method of ZCL_HOTEL_BRF_APP_EXIT

Registering our formula implementation is done in method IF_FDT_APPLICA-TION_SETTINGS~GET_FORMULA_FUNCTIONALS (see Listing 10.5).

```
DATA: ls_func_def TYPE if_fdt_formula=>s_functional_def,
      ls_func_categ TYPE if_fdt_formula=>s_functional_categ.
" make sure you do not loose any of the default AET
```

```
CALL METHOD CL_AXT_BRFPLUS_APPL_EXIT=>IF_FDT_APPLICATION_SETTINGS~GET_
FORMULA_FUNCTIONALS
    EXPORTING
      IV_ID                     =  IV_ID
    CHANGING
      CT_FUNCTIONAL_DEFINITION = CT_FUNCTIONAL_DEFINITION
      CT_FUNCTIONAL_CATEGORY   = CT_FUNCTIONAL_CATEGORY .

ls_func_categ-category = 'HOTEL_DATA'.
"you should probably get the texts from OTR
ls_func_categ-description = 'External Hotel Data'.
APPEND ls_func_categ TO ct_functional_category.


ls_func_def-category = 'HOTEL_DATA'.
ls_func_def-token = 'GET_EXTERNAL_PARAMETER'.
ls_func_def-class = 'ZCL_HOTEL_BRF'.
ls_func_def-method = 'FUNCTIONAL_EXT_PROPERTY'.
APPEND ls_func_def TO ct_functional_definition.
```
Listing 10.5 GET_FORMULA_FUNCTIONALS Implementation

In our implementation we first retrieve the tables containing the existing (from AET) function definitions and categories. We do so by calling the default implementation of GET_FORMULA_FUNCTIONALS from CL_AXT_BRFPLUS_APPL_EXIT. This ensures that we will not lose any of the standard functions defined in AET.

```
CL_AXT_BRFPLUS_APPL_EXIT=>IF_FDT_APPLICATION_SETTINGS~GET_FORMULA_
FUNCTIONALS
```

Next, we create a new category with an internal name HOTEL_DATA and add it to the global function category table:

```
ls_func_categ-category = 'HOTEL_DATA'.
ls_func_categ-description = 'External Hotel Data'.
APPEND ls_func_categ TO ct_functional_category.
```

Last, we register a new BRF+ operation and give it a name GET_EXTERNAL_PARAMETER. This new operation will be associated with our BRF+ function implementation (ZCL_HOTEL_BRF->GET_EXTERNAL_PARAMETER) and be part of the function category HOTEL_DATA. We append this newly created definition to the existing function definitions table:

```
ls_func_def-category = 'HOTEL_DATA'.
ls_func_def-token = 'GET_EXTERNAL_PARAMETER'.
```

```
...
APPEND ls_func_def TO ct_functional_definition.
```

We now have the application exit class. The only thing left is to make AET use it instead of CL_AXT_BRFPLUS_APPL_EXIT. As mentioned, we need to implement BAdI AXT_BRFPLUS_APPL_EXIT. The implementation will return the name of the new application exit class. The BAdI interface IF_AXT_BRFPLUS_APPL_EXIT has only one method, GET_APP_EXIT_CLASS. Our sample implementation is provided in Listing 10.6.

```
method IF_AXT_BRFPLUS_APPL_EXIT~GET_APP_EXIT_CLASS.
  "register your brfplus application exit
  CV_CLASS = 'ZCL_HOTEL_BRF_APP_EXIT'.
endmethod.
```

Listing 10.6 Implementation of BAdI AXT_BRFPLUS_APPL_EXIT

After you save and activate your classes and the BAdI implementation, you can log into the SAP CRM system and try to create a calculated field that uses the new operation. If you have provided a method documentation, please check the tooltip of the operation name and the content of the information pop-up (click the question mark icon (?)). Figure 10.15 shows the result of the procedure we just followed.

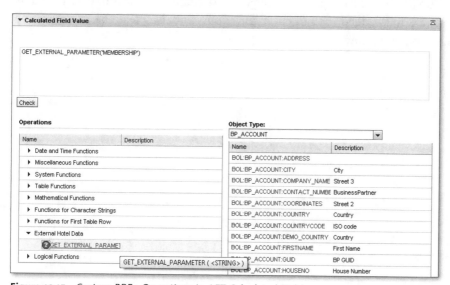

Figure 10.15 Custom BRF+ Operations in AET Calculated Fields

479

10.6 Summary

In this chapter, we described several techniques for behavior extensibility in SAP CRM. All of them except for BAdI BUPA_FURTHER_CHECKS come with SAP CRM 7.0 EhP1. Compared to the previously delivered BAdIs, the new ones show a clear trend towards unification and simplification.

The interfaces in enhancement spot AXT_RT_TABLES deliver an API that is easy to understand and works with any table extension, no matter which application it belongs to. If you need to add logic that is specific to your enhancement, you do not have to look for the right application-specific BAdI.

If you are not ABAP savvy and you have a simple scenario in mind, you can try the calculated fields feature. The integration with BRF+ offers a great degree of flexibility. Moreover, if you have very specific needs that are not covered by the standard SAP solutions, you could consider implementing a custom BRF+ operation. In conjunction with the calculated fields this might be a less labor-intensive but still powerful way to add custom behavior to standard applications.

In the next chapter we will show you how to generate applications from data sources in SAP CRM EhP1. The tools that we will use are based on AET, but they explore a new area of the structural enhancements paradigm. You will not only be able to generate full-fledged Web Client applications, but also create basic application composites, also known as mash-ups.

The key differentiator in SAP CRM 7.0 EhP1 is the provisioning of tools that allow users to enhance existing applications and build new one quickly, intuitively, and—most important—without a single line of code, so that no deep technical knowledge is required.

11   Rapid Applications and Mash-ups

In the following sections, we will demonstrate how to build full fledged applications quickly based on existing data sources. SAP has already promised customers that they can consume and add custom content. However, this often requires using different systems (for example, NetWeaver CE or PI) and writing programming code, which requires that businesses retain technical consultants with different backgrounds. As a result, even the simplest integration scenarios are perceived as costly. Therefore, even though SAP is capable of supporting a multitude of different types of customers and industries, once a system is implemented, SAP is sometimes considered inflexible and cumbersome to adjust or enhance.

SAP has recognized this problem and in the past few years has invested a lot in simplification, openness, and extensibility. Various tools are appearing across stacks and applications that support users in their efforts to customize the standard delivery. SAP CRM EhP1 is no exception. It has introduced tools that allow customers to consume content from database tables, Web services, and even resources available on the Web. Tasks that normally take hours can be accomplished in minutes. And the best part is that you do not have to write a single line of programming code.

In this chapter, we will show you how you can take the database model used by our hotel booking implementation and generate a complete application on top of it. We will explain *Rapid Applications* (RAPs) and show how it can be used to generate an application from a database table and from a Web service. Some sections will discuss the configuration and modification of a newly-generated rapid application. We will embed the booking data into the SAP CRM account application in the application mash-ups section. Finally, we will demonstrate how one can integrate resources freely available on the Web into the Web Client UI. This is known as *Web 2.0 mash-ups*, and can be done without having to start SAP GUI and use the Component Workbench. The whole process can be performed in the Web UI. Writing ABAP code is also not mandatory, but might be required for some complex scenarios. Therefore, we will cover the available BAdIs.

11.1 Rapid Applications

A RAP can be created from a data source such as a database table or a Web service. As a matter of fact, the UI generation from a BOL model that we saw earlier in the book is also a rapid application. Any database table defined in the DDIC can be used as a source. When it comes to Web services, these must comply with the WS-I (*http://www.ws-i.org*) standard. In general we recommend using simple Web-service definitions, where the response is represented via a flat structure. Moreover, with Web services, the produced application is read-only.

We will explore in detail the database-table-based RAPs because using them makes more features available. For this example, we have made a copy of the booking table and called it ZBOOKING_RESERV1 (see Figure 11.1).

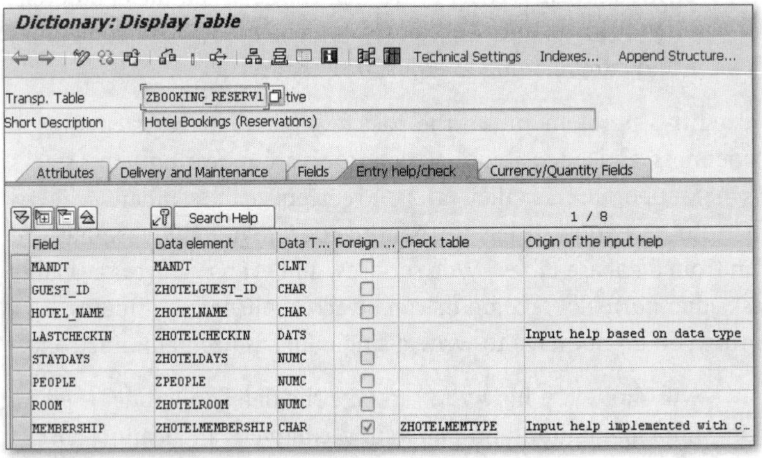

Figure 11.1 ZBOOKING_RESERV1 DDIC Table

To make things more interesting, we will assume that the table for used products does not exist, and we will create it on the fly. To summarize, our imaginary assignment is to bring the content from ZBOOKING_RESERV1 into the Web UI and augment it with product data.

In the following sections, you will first learn how to manage your RAPs. We will show you how to create a new RAP from a database table and how to customize it via configurations. Sometimes such customization will not address all your requirements, so we will describe ways to extend the newly generated application. Last, we will discuss the scenario of generating a RAP on top of a Web service.

11.1.1 Managing Rapid Applications

You can create a RAP directly from the Web UI. The logical link AXT_RAPP_S allows you to start the MANAGE RAPID APPLICATIONS application. Figure 11.2 illustrates the result of adding it to the ADMINISTRATION work center in our navigation profile.

Figure 11.2 Starting Manage Rapid Applications

Once inside the MANAGE RAPID APPLICATIONS, you can search for an existing application and delete or modify it. You can also create a new application from a Web service or a DDIC table as we will see in the next section (see Figure 11.3).

Manage Rapid Applications

Restart

Search Criteria

Rapid Application Type	is	
Rapid Application Name	starts with	
Rapid Application Description	contains	

Maximum Number of Results: 100

Search   Clear   Save Search As: _____ Save

Result List

Rapid Applications   Delete   How To Deploy   Regenerate

Create from DB Table		
Create from Web Service	Rapid Application Description	Rapid Application Type
New		

Figure 11.3 Create RAP from Manage Rapid Applications

An alternative way to create a RAP is to open an existing Web Client UI application and to go into the page configuration. There you will see an action menu button called EMBEDDED VIEWS. Its second option, SHOW ALL, will take you to the Embedded Views page where you can quickly embed the existing or create new rapid applications (see Figure 11.4).

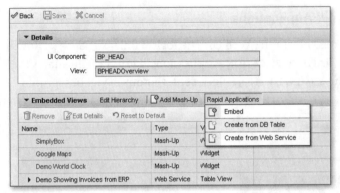

Figure 11.4 Create RAP from Application Overview

We will use the Manage Rapid Application option to create a RAP. It will start the RAP wizard that guides the user through several steps.

11.1.2 Creating a Rapid Application

When you create a RAP, you are supported by a user-friendly wizard that guides you through the whole process. The default mode of the wizard hides many of the technical details and therefore could be used even by business users, although some technical knowledge would probably be required. This section will take you through the different process steps and show you how to implement the previously discussed requirements.

Step 1

The first step of the RAP creation wizard prompts the user to provide application details such as name, description, and development package. The default package name comes from customizing (Transaction AXTSYS is shared with AET) but can be overwritten by the more technical users. These users can also press the SHOW TECHNICAL DETAILS button and control parameters such as the navigation target IDs for new and search pages, and the authorization group that can control which users have access to the application. Figure 11.5 displays the values that we used in our example. If you plan to write code that navigates to the new RAP, you should take note of the target IDs. The default authorization implementation is based on the authorization object S_TABU_DIS. You can use BAdI AXT_RT_TABLES_AUTHORITY_CHECK to use a different authorization object. Because the table name is a BAdI filter, you can provide different implementations for each database table.

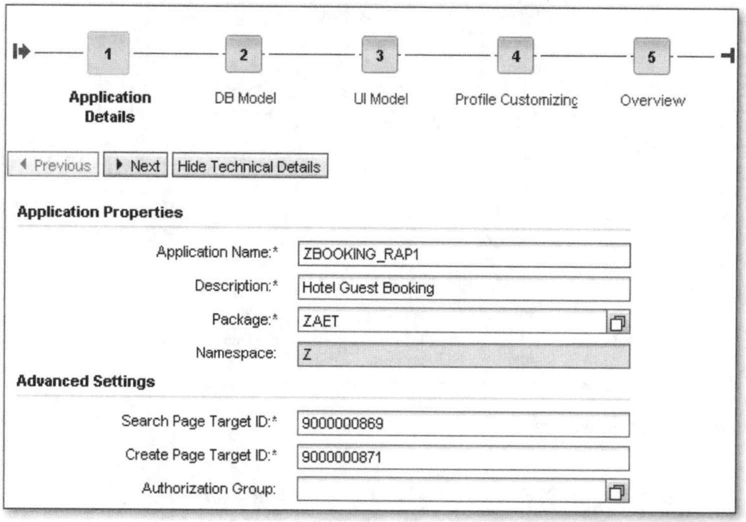

Figure 11.5 Step 1 of Create RAP Wizard

Step 2

In the next wizard step, the user defines the database model. You can pick either existing DDIC tables or define new tables on the fly. In our example, we will use the previously created ZBOOKING_RESERV1 and specify a new table with a user-friendly description Products. To add an existing table, use the ADD button. The wizard will read the DDIC metadata and display it. It not only will try to identify existing fields, but also will pick up the keys, DDIC check tables, and search helps. You cannot change the names of the fields, but you can control their appearance and even select which fields to exclude from the new the application (see Figure 11.6).

If you select a row from the FIELD LIST (you should select the table first), you will be able to click on the DETAILS button. It brings the FIELD DETAILS pop-up from AET (a slightly modified version). Let's do so for the membership field. As you can see in Figure 11.7, a checktable gets picked up by the RAP tool. The default visualization of check tables is a value help. Let's change the rendering as to Show checktable as DDLB.

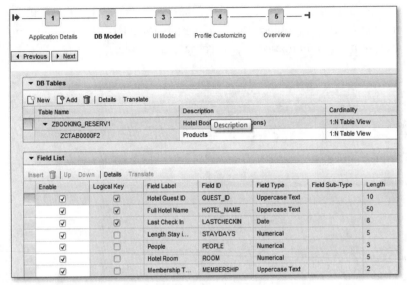

Figure 11.6 Retrieved DDIC Table Model

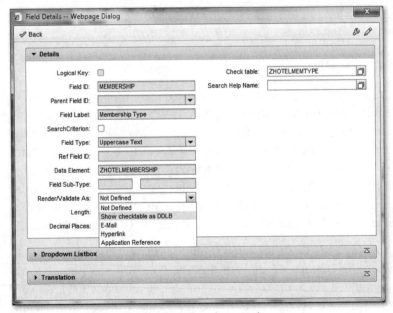

Figure 11.7 Displaying Checktable as Dropdown Listbox

The NEW button in the DB TABLES block will prompt you to define a new table. The table must have a name and description; we chose the description `Products` and let the wizard generate a table name. It also must have at least one key field. Our products table will have two key fields: the product and the date used. In addition, there will be a ranking field. We will define a fixed value list for it. Select the row with the ranking field and click the DETAILS button. Figure 11.8 displays the dropdown list box settings that we used in our example.

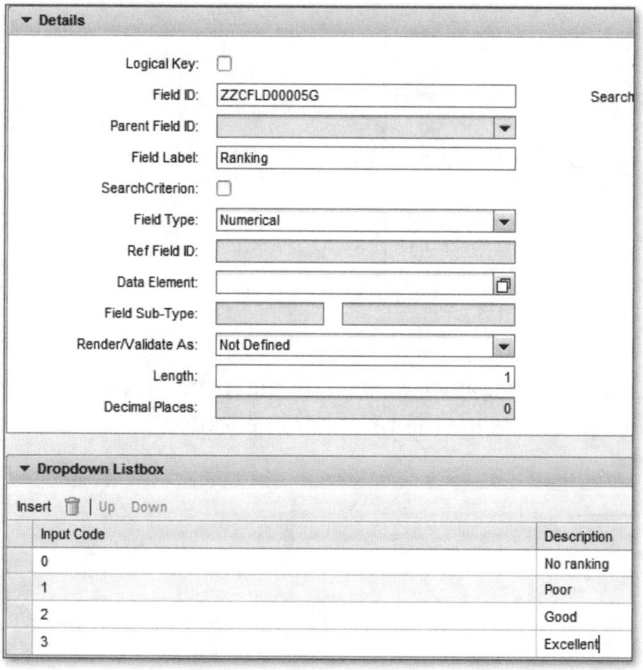

Figure 11.8 Field With Fixed Values

As you remember, we used product GUID as a unique identifier for the used products table. It proved difficult to handle from a usability and UI point of view. That is why we redefined the get and set methods to work with a product ID and provided an advanced search value help to facilitate product selection. How can we do something similar without writing a line of code? We will use the concept of navigation link fields and define a reference to the product application. In the wizard, we will select the table row with the product ID field and click the DETAILS button. In the FIELD DETAILS view we will change the type of the product field to `Application Reference` and will select PRODUCT as a sub-type. As a result, we will create a navigation field to SAP CRM product application (see Figure 11.9). End users will not have to type the product GUID manually but can conveniently select it from a standard advanced search value help.

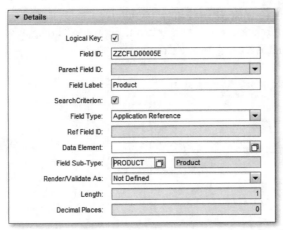

Figure 11.9 Application Reference to SAP CRM Product

Figure 11.10 illustrates the DB model that we defined for our example. In the next step of the wizard, we will use it to define the UI of our application.

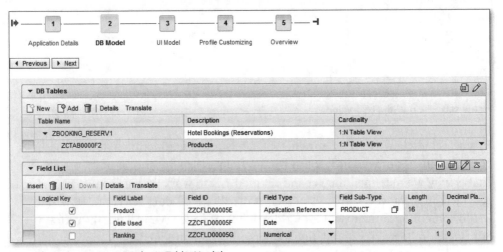

Figure 11.10 New Products Table Model

Step 3

In Step 3, you can define the application's UI model manually (using the ADD button) or simply by clicking the AUTO GENERATE button. The tool will look at your database model and suggest a UI element structure. For example, there will always be a search page and embedded view. The latter is analogous to what we saw when generating a UI out of a BOL.

In addition, the wizard will produce a view for each database table. When cardinality is 1:1, the result will be a form view. For multiple cardinalities there will be a table view. In addition, for each subordinate table (products in our example), the tool will generate a sub-overview page. Our example produced a UI model shown in Figure 11.11.

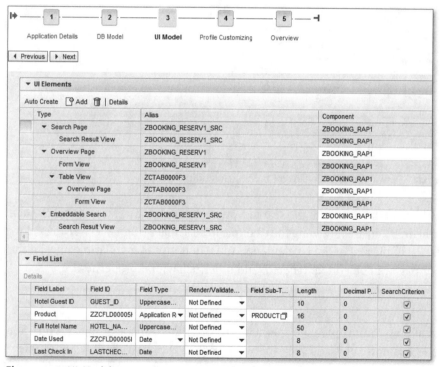

Figure 11.11 UI Model

If you select the SEARCH PAGE row in UI ELEMENTS block, you will see the search criteria fields. By default, the wizard marks all the key fields as search criteria. You can select more search attributes if needed.

Selecting the SEARCH RESULT VIEW element will allow you verify the fields that will constitute the search result. As you know, the search page shows search criteria and results and allows users to navigate to the overview page of a particular business object. The question is which column from the result view will be used as a navigation link. The tool will select one of the keys, but you can pick a navigation link column if you work within the view details. Click on the DETAILS button and define additional properties for the selected UI element. Figure 11.12 shows our selections for the search result view: We want to use the hotel name as a navigation field.

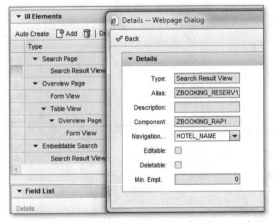

Figure 11.12 Defining Navigation Link for the Search Result View

We will repeat the above for the search result view under the EMBEDDABLE SEARCH UI element. If you are following the example in an actual system, feel free to explore the details of the rest of the UI elements. You will notice that you can control if the view or page can be edited, deleted, and other behavioral properties.

Step 4

Step 4 allows you to integrate the new RAP into the L-shape. You can do so for multiple business roles and pick the work centers that host the links to the new application. You can specify the appearance of two links: the direct creation and search page. We saw their target IDs in the technical details of Step 1 (see Figure 11.5). In our example, we will expose only the search link in the account management work center (Figure 11.13). When enabling a link, the tool enables the end users to add it to the navigation profile or to both the navigation profile and the business role. We saw earlier that in order to integrate a target ID in the L-shape, we have to first create a logical link and assign it to a navigation profile. Once done, we could make it visible in the business role customizing. Because many business roles share the same navigation profile, enabling a link for one of them will automatically make it available to all roles. The wizard will reflect this by selecting the `Navbar Profile` option for all the other business roles that share the same navigation profile. You might also want to add the link in the navigation profile and do business role customizing as a separate step.

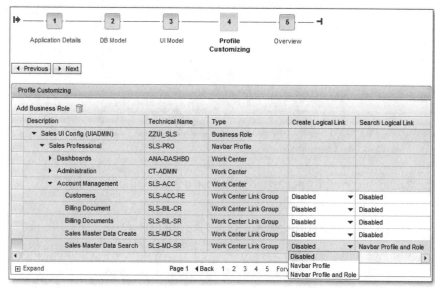

Figure 11.13 Step 4 of RAP Creation Wizard

Step 5

The last step allows you to review the definitions, the UI elements, and settings that are about to be created (see Figure 11.14). Clicking the SAVE AND GENERATE button will generate the application, DDIC structures, and the necessary customizing.

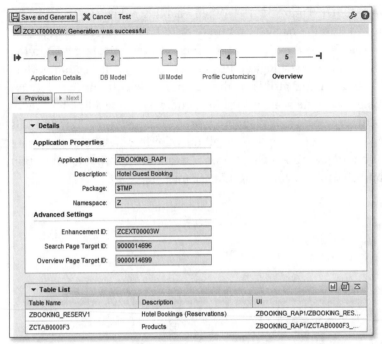

Figure 11.14 Step 5 of RAP Creation Wizard

Once the RAP is successfully generated, the Test button will be enabled.

11.1.3 Using and Configuring Your Rapid Application

In this section, we will show you how to test and use your newly generated application. We also will describe ways to configure and fine-tune your application so that it becomes more user-friendly.

Testing and Using a Rapid Application

As we saw in the previous section, the RAP wizard features a Test button. This will launch the application in the test UI component (in a separate window and session). You will be presented with the advanced search page (see Figure 11.15). Its search criteria and result views will exactly match the UI model we defined in the wizard. You will notice that there is a message telling us that there are no view configurations. We will create this later. Note that the field labels of the booking attributes come directly from the DDIC.

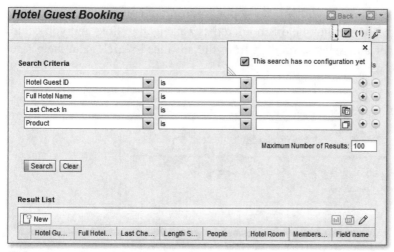

Figure 11.15 Advanced Search Page of New RAP

Clicking on the NEW button will take us to the overview page in a creation mode (see Figure 11.16). Apart from the need for view configuration, you will notice that the key attributes are marked as mandatory fields, the field types are rendered accordingly (for example date has a date picker), and the checktable of the membership field is displayed as a dropdown list box. There is one unusual read-only field called FIELD NAME that displays the description of the selected membership type. We will address this feature of the RAP concept during configuration.

Figure 11.16 Create New Guest Booking

The products view comes with an empty-line insertion in edit mode and one-click action column. The product field is rendered as a navigation link, and you could easily search for and select a product from the advanced search value help (see Figure 11.17).

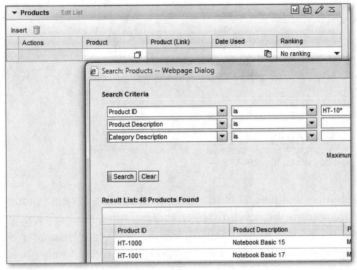

Figure 11.17   Product Application Reference Field

Not surprisingly, the end user can select from among the predefined ranking values, using a dropdown list box (see Figure 11.18).

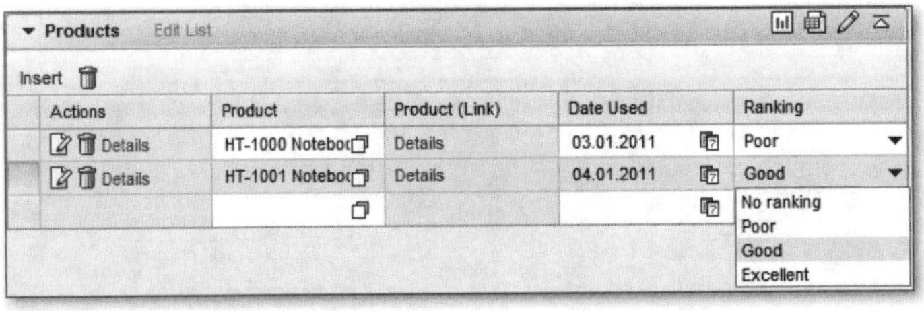

Figure 11.18   Ranking Dropdown List Box Values.

Once you are done, you can click the SAVE button and a new booking will be created.

Figure 11.19 shows the integration of the RAP's search target ID within a work center. We chose to enable only the search link, but if we want to add the create link we can return MANAGE RAPID APPLICATIONS, edit the profile customizing, and regenerate the RAP.

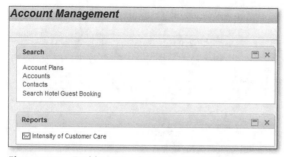

Figure 11.19 Enabling Search Link in Work Center

Configuration

It is probably a good idea to configure the views and improve the usability of the application. Note that the generated RAP is a full-fledged application and supports configuration and personalization. We will remove the read-only description for the membership, change some field labels, and rearrange the fields (see Figure 11.20).

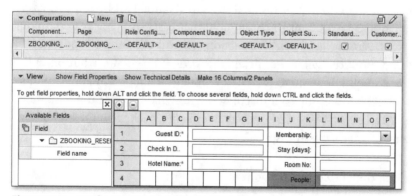

Figure 11.20 Configuring Booking Header Form View

Next we will change the table view configuration and also rename the titles of the assignment blocks in the page configuration. Figure 11.21 displays the results.

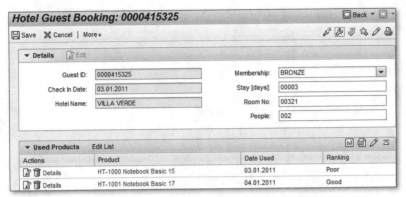

Figure 11.21 Configured Booking Overview Page

We now have a fully functional application that looks almost perfect. We would probably need to play a bit with the GET and SET methods in the UI component in order to get rid of the trailing zeros. It would help to add custom validation logic for tasks such as checking whether that the date of the used product falls within the booking timeframe. But we will discuss these in the next section.

11.1.4   Extending the Default Implementation

Let's look back at the last step of the RAP wizard (Figure 11.14). You can easily spot the name of the Web Client UI component that is about to be created. In our example this is ZBOOKING_RAP1. In this section we will take an in-depth look at what the wizard produced when we clicked the SAVE AND GENERATE button in the previous step. As you know, there is a UI component behind each application in the Web Client UI. We will start our discussion with what is inside it. In addition, we will give you an overview of the L-shape customizing, backend implementation, and enhancement areas at your disposal.

Overview of the Generated UI Component

Let us start the ZBOOKING_RAP1 application in the Component Workbench (BSP_WD_CMPWB). In Figure 11.22, you can see that the wizard produced a fairly sophisticated application structure. There are two windows. The MainWindow is used by the standalone RAP that we saw earlier. The Embed_ZBOOKING_RESERV1_SRC window is used for application mash-ups (we will discuss this later). The wizard also created an overview page, ZBOOKING_RESERV1_OVP, which hosts the form view from the

496

booking database table, ZBOOKING_RESERV1_DETAILS, and the table view from the new table that we created on the fly, namely ZCTAB0000F3_MAIN. The name of the existing database table, ZBOOKING_RESERV1, is used to form the name of the relevant UI elements. However, the name of the newly created database table, ZCTAB0000F3, is not very user-friendly. Neither are the names of the related UI elements. You can actually control the table name in Step 2 of the wizard. In our example we simply accepted the default value, but you can choose a different name. The MainWindow also hosts the advanced search page, ZBOOKING_RESERV1_SRC_SRC_VS and the products sub overview page, ZCTAB0000F3_OVP. The context nodes of the views are bound through the context of the custom controller, ZBOOKING_RESERV1_SRC_CuCo.

The bottom line is that if you want to influence the presentation logic of your application, you can do so through the Component Workbench. The generated RAP follows Web Client UI development best practices. You can implement GET and SET methods on context node attributes, add event handlers, and redefine the DO_PRE-PARE_OUTPUT of views (in this case, do not forget to call the super method).

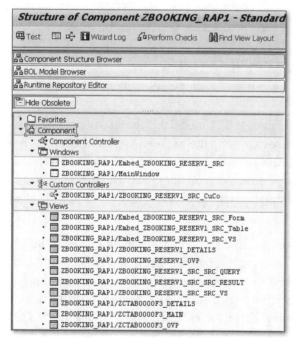

Figure 11.22 Structure of Newly Generated UI Component

Work Area Customizing

In the Work Area Component Repository (in customizing via menu path CUSTOMER RELATIONSHIP MANAGEMENT • UI FRAMEWORK • TECHNICAL ROLE DEFINITIONS), one can find the various target IDs produced by the RAP wizard (see Figure 11.23). For our `ZBOOKING_RAP1` application, the wizard generated a dedicated UI object type (same name as the application name) and four target IDs. We already discussed the target IDs for the search and create entities. The other two are used internally by the RAP. The `TO_OVERVIEW` navigates to the main OVP, and the other target is used to execute the search functionality.

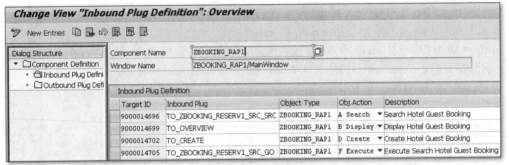

Figure 11.23 Inbound Plug Definitions for New Rapid Application

The Generated BOL Model

Some of you might be wondering if there is BOL model that the UI component uses. After all, this might give you a way to modify the backend application logic. The reality is that for each RAP, the wizard generates dedicated GenIL business objects, but they become part of a generic, GenIL component `AXT_CA`. The latter has also a generic GenIL component class implementation: `CL_AXT_CA_GENIL_BOL_COMP` (see Figure 11.24).

The fact that RAP is based on a generic backend implementation makes it almost impossible to add custom business logic through the GenIL layer. Keep in mind that the RAP tools were introduced to help non-technical users generate custom applications easily. Forcing even those with some ABAP skills into the GenIL paradigm would move the learning curve for enhancing RAPs quite high. The assumption is that the RAP will cover basic scenarios, will be simple to use, and will not require in-depth knowledge of the Web Client APIs. All the same, there is a need to enhance the behavior of the generated applications. The next section deals with this task.

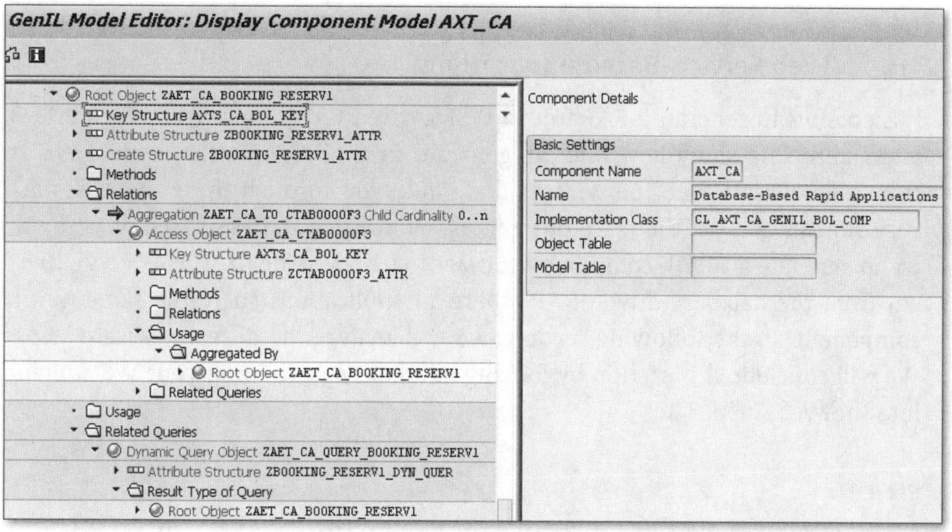

Figure 11.24 Generated GenIL Business Object

Available BAdI

Remember that RAP and AET share a lot in common. It makes sense that the enhancement area AXT_RT_TABLES can be used to add custom logic to your RAPs. We discussed this already when we showed you how to add custom logic to the table extensions.

You can influence the behavior of your RAP by implementing BAdI AXT_RT_TABLES_ API. It provides methods that allow you to validate data, optimize and modify the data retrieval queries, or introduce logic executed upon create or save. In order to identify the implementation specific to a given application, the BAdI accepts the table name as a filter value. Based on that, the correct BAdI implementation is executed in runtime.

You can change the locking behavior of your applications via BAdI AXT_RT_TABLES_ BUSINESS_LOCK. The default implementation locks based on whole database key. In order to change the default implementation (for example, to use an existing lock object), you can provide a custom BAdI implementation for each table name.

The discussions around GenIL implementation and the BAdIs apply only when you generate a RAP from database tables. The Web service scenario is quite different, as you will see in the next section.

11.1.5 Web Service-Based Applications

It is possible to generate a RAP from a WSDL based Web service (WS). Figure 11.3 and Figure 11.4 show how one can generate an application either from a WS or from a database table. The wizards that guide you through these two cases are very similar, and yet there are differences. Notice that the WS-based wizard will try to generate a GenIL component (COMPONENT NAME field). This is very different from the database-driven RAP where all applications share the same GenIL component. In the following sections we will analyze the different wizard steps. We will conclude this section by looking at other ways to bring your WS content into the Web Client UI.

Step 1

Figure 11.25 shows the first step of the WS based RAP wizard. As with the database case, the end user shall provide the application details.

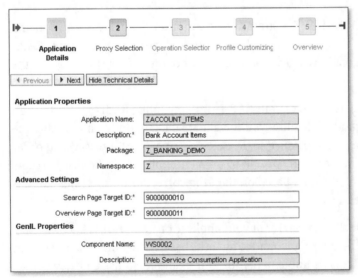

Figure 11.25 Application Details of a WS Based RAP

The fact that the backend logic is implemented in a dedicated GenIL component means that you do not need BAdIs to add custom logic. It is true that this is more complex and requires GenIL knowledge, but dealing with WSDL based Web services is not a trivial matter either. Again, for the basic integration scenarios, you do not have to worry about changing the GenIL component class, but you have the option to do so.

Step 2

Step 2 of the wizard allows you to select an existing WS proxy. SAP NetWeaver allows you to generate ABAP proxy classes based on existing Web services (more precisely based on their WSDLs). This standard functionality is part of Transaction SE80 (see Figure 11.26) and we will not discuss it further in this book. We will just mention that once the consumer proxy class is created in Transaction SE80, you would have to start Transaction SOAMANAGER and configure the logical port for the proxy. Only when you have completed this last step can you make a call to that Web service.

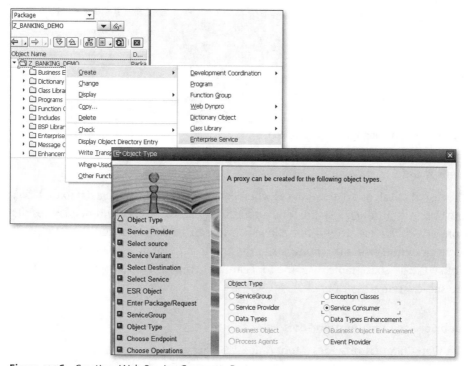

Figure 11.26 Creating Web Service Consumer Proxy

Step 2 of the wizard also allows you to generate a proxy directly from the UI. Although this approach is certainly more user-friendly, it does not have the advanced option of the wizard in Transaction SE80. Therefore, if you get an error, you should try to generate the proxy from the ABAP Workbench.

Step 3

The third step of the wizard allows you to pick the WS operation and select the field that will serve as navigation links between the search results view and the overview page (see Figure 11.27).

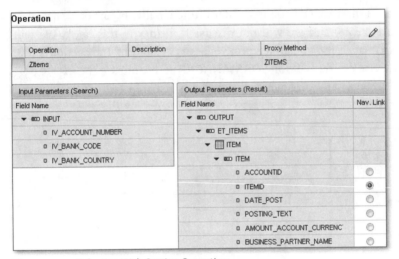

Figure 11.27 Selecting Web Service Operation

Steps 4 and 5

The rest of the steps are the same as when generating an RAP from a database table. The tool will produce a standalone application that can query and display results from a Web service. It will not allow you to edit the data. In addition, the Web service's output structure should be fairly simple and not include nested elements. Unlike the database table case, the tool cannot handle dependent business objects (no sub-overview pages).

Web Service Consumption Tool

The Web Client UI provides a tool called Web Service Consumption Tool (WSCT). You can access it through customizing at CUSTOMER RELATIONSHIP MANAGEMENT •

UI FRAMEWORK • UI FRAMEWORK DEFINITION • WEB SERVICES • WEB SERVICE CONSUMPTION TOOL: CREATE BOL OBJECTS or via Transaction CRM_GENIL_WSC.

This tool is based on the ABAP proxy generation functionality (from Transaction SE80) and produces a full-fledged GenIL component from an existing WS definition. The RAP tool actually uses it behind the scenes.

Although the WSCT is not as user friendly as the RAP, it offers much more flexibility to the technical user. You can use it to produce dedicated GenIL components that are based on complex WSDLs. You can then take advantage of the UI generation from BOL wizard and produce a RAP from the new GenIL model, as explained earlier.

The steps involved when consuming a Web Service using the WSCT are as follows:

1. Request Web service definition (WSDL).

2. Generate WS client proxy.

3. Create logical port.

4. Register client proxy to a GenIL component.

5. Generate a RAP or consume using BOL programming.

The first three steps can be achieved by the standard SAP NetWeaver functionality for consuming Web services. This includes functions for generating a proxy from a WSDL file (in Transaction SE80) and logical port maintenance (in SOAMANAGER). An ABAP client proxy is used in SAP NetWeaver to communicate with the Web service. It represents a typed ABAP interface and hides the technical Web service details.

The SAP NetWeaver service runtime handles the SOAP-based communication with the Web service provider. The communication details, such as host name and port, are configured separately in logical ports.

The last two steps are Web Client UI specific. The GenIL components are based on one generic implementation GenIL component class, CL_CRM_WSC_GENIL_BOL. However, the Web service consumer proxies that these components use could be generated in your own namespace. Therefore, you can modify them as you please and thus influence the behavior of your application. For more details on the WSCT topic, consult your SAP documentation. By now you know all the concepts involved and should be able to use this tool with little trouble.

11.2   Application Mash-ups

Whenever we generate a RAP (whether based on a BOL model or on a database table) we always end up with something called an embeddable search. These allow you to create what we call application mash-ups. We will start by explaining the mash-up concept, and then give an example in which we will create a new mash-up (embeddable view). We will conclude this section by enabling the new mash-up view in the Web UI.

11.2.1   Mash-ups Overview

Mash-ups allow you to combine content from different applications and create something new. We will continue with our hotel booking example and integrate the RAP that we generated in the previous sections into the SAP CRM account application. The embeddable search UI elements play a key role in this feature. You can think of the attributes of embeddable search criteria as input parameters that influence the content rendered by the embeddable view (a search result view). The application mash-up feature allows even a non-technical user to map application-specific attributes against the embeddable search criteria. At runtime, the corresponding attribute value will be passed to the embeddable search influencing the search result. The content from the result view will be rendered as part of the overview page of the hosting application. This feature is only available as of SAP CRM EhP1.

11.2.2   Creating a Mash-up

Figure 11.4 shows the overview page with all the embedded views (all the mash-ups). In order to create a new application mash-up, select the EMBED button from the RAPID APPLICATIONS action menu. A wizard will start prompting you to pick an existing RAP.

The Embed View Wizard

Note that an RAP can contain multiple embeddable searches. For example, when you generate a UI component from a BOL model you might choose to work with several BOL queries. Each query can produce a different embeddable search. In our example, we have only one embeddable search view (see Figure 11.28).

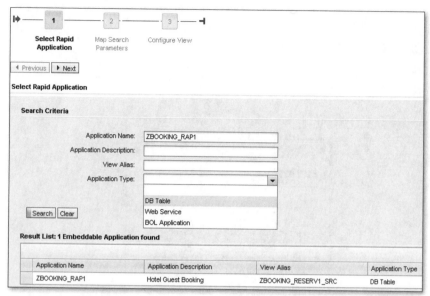

Figure 11.28 Select Rapid Application for Embedding

As you can see, the tool supports all types of rapid applications: DB-based, Web-service based, and BOL models. The VIEW ALIAS column indicates the embeddable search view that you are about to mash up against.

After you select an embeddable view, you can start mapping the attributes of the hosting application against the input parameters of the RAP. Here again, you will be working with global attribute tags (as in the case of calculated fields). You can also set default string values (see Figure 11.29).

The last step of the wizard will allow you to select how to display the new assignment block. You can enter the view's title and also select whether the result should be rendered as a form view or as a table view. Suppose you know that the mapping selection from Step 2 will always yield one result object. In such a case, it does not make sense to display that content as a table. In our example, we can have many bookings per account (guest), and so the results should be rendered as a table (Figure 11.30).

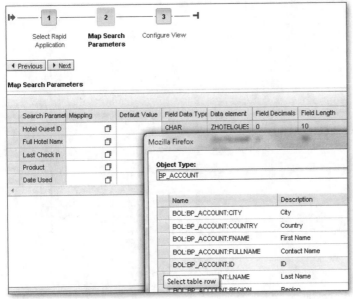

Figure 11.29 Mapping Application Attributes to Embeddable Search Criteria

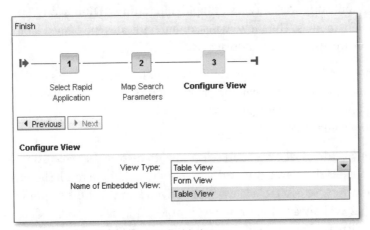

Figure 11.30 Configuring the Embedded View

Embedded Views Page

Once you click the FINISH button, the tool will take you back to a page showing you all the existing mash-ups (EMBEDDED VIEWS). Here you can once again review and edit the details. As evident in Figure 11.31, the APPLICATION NAME column is rendered as a link. You can click on it and start the RAP creation wizard, but this time in edit mode. This allows the users to edit certain properties of the generated applications directly from the SAP CRM business objects overview pages.

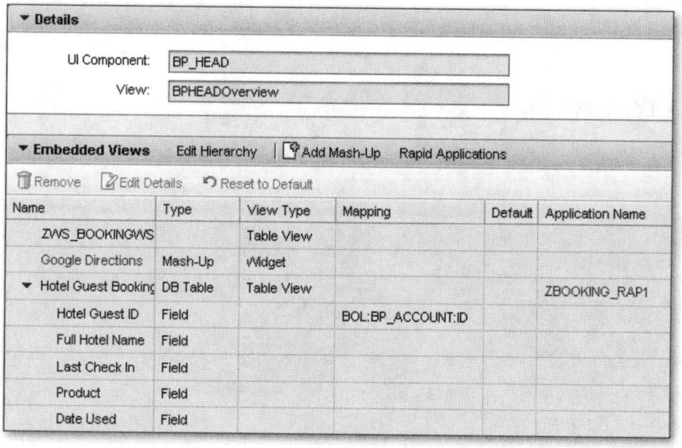

Figure 11.31 Overview of All Embedded Views

11.2.3 Enabling and Using a Mash-up

Pressing the SAVE button on the EMBEDDED VIEWS page will make your modifications persistent and bring you back to the page configuration tool. The newly added block will appear among the AVAILABLE ASSIGNMENT BLOCKS. Its title will match the NAME OF EMBEDDED VIEW property from Figure 11.30.

Once you move the view into the DISPLAYED ASSIGNMENT BLOCKS (Figure 11.32), you could save and generate the page configuration and go back to the account overview page.

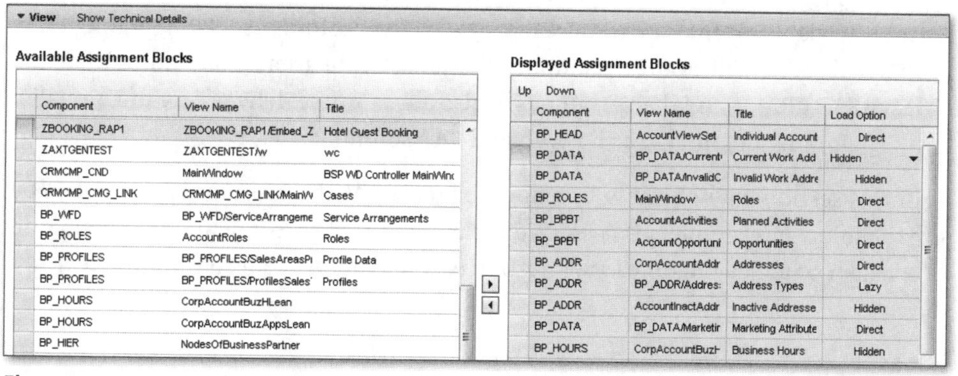

Figure 11.32 Page Configuration

The results from our example are presented in Figure 11.33. The new assignment block can be configured and personalized. If you click on the FULL HOTEL NAME column you will open the overview page of the previously generated HOTEL GUEST BOOKINGS RAP.

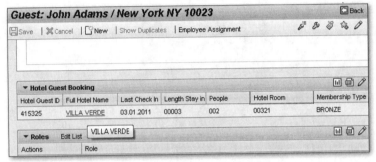

Figure 11.33 Application Mash-up Based on RAP

11.3   Web Mash-ups

The Web started as a network of static addressable documents (for example HTML pages). Over time, people developed dynamic Web resources that are not only addressable, but also behave differently based on parameters that get passed to them (for example, via HTTP GET parameters). Nowadays, we have REST-enabled Web services that use the standard HTTP protocol methods to expose a resource. It is not unheard of that a REST service can return even a ready-to-display HTML response. We will limit our discussion to Web resources that are ready to consume and could be influenced by URL parameters. Some examples would be the Google search engine, or various financial, news, and weather widgets. Such resources are often available for free and are already used by the business users. Integrating them into SAP CRM will not only simplify the job of your users (they do not have to leave SAP CRM to use them), but might also allow you to deliver new functionality by combining the forces of the Web and SAP solutions.

In this section we will show you how to create a Web mash-up. We will start by explaining an example scenario. We believe this will give you an idea of what to consider when evaluating a Web resource candidate for your mash-ups. Next, we will create a new Web mash-up. We will conclude the discussion by testing and enabling the new mash-up in the Web UI.

11.3.1 A Mash-up Example

Suppose that many sales agents in your organization use Google Maps to get directions to the address of their accounts. You observe them for some time and discover that they key in your company address as a start address and the account's address as a destination address. This gives you an idea: Add a new assignment block in the SAP CRM account page that will take the address associated with the currently logged-in user (the one visible in Transaction SU3), and the address from the account entity being displayed, pass them to Google Maps, and display the results. You also noticed that Google Maps allows you to pass the starting and destination address as URL parameters, like this:

http://maps.google.com/maps?saddr=<SU3_ADDRESS>&daddr=<BP_ADDRESS>

The task is fairly simple, but you would still have to enhance the account application, create a new view, figure out how to retrieve Transaction SU3 and BP account attributes, among other things. Because this is your own initiative, you would have to convince your boss to allocate some time for this. However, if you have SAP CRM 7.0 EhP1 you do not have to worry about all that. This release comes with a new functionality called Web 2.0 Mash-ups. We will implement our example using it.

11.3.2 Adding a Web Mash-up

Web mash-ups are a special kind of embeddable view. Therefore, you can start the mash-up tool from the embedded view overview page by clicking on the ADD MASH-UP button (see Figure 11.4). You will be prompted to provide a title and description for your mash-up. The former will be used as a title for the new assignment block. The mash-up tool will try to determine the optimal height of the block by scanning the mash-up script. If it finds a string that resembles height (h or height) it will use the numeric value that follows it as the height for the view. If the tool does not find a height definition it will assume the value of 300 pixels. You can manually specify the desired height.

In the Source Code text area, you can specify the mash-up script and inject it with global attribute tags from the right panel. We have pasted our Google Map URL string and woven in the desired user and application attributes (see Figure 11.34). Note that in our screenshot we have filtered the Name column with a `custom filter = 'USER'`. As a result we see only the user attribute tags.

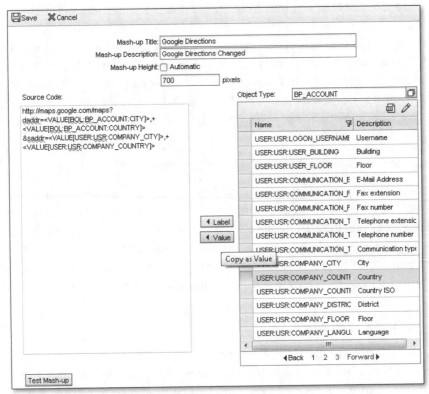

Figure 11.34 Web Mash-up Tool

While you can manually type in the attributes in the source code, you can also position the cursor in the desired location, select an attribute, and click the Value button. This will add the selected attribute in the desired location. The Label button will inject the value of the attribute label. At runtime it will be picked either from the DDIC or the design layer.

There are two types of mash-ups scripts you can define. In our example, we have used a plain URL (starts with HTTP or HTTPS). But you can create a widget script that produces an output by combining HTML with Java Script.

11.3.3 Testing and Enabling a Web Mash-up

The mash-up result can be tested by clicking the TEST MASH-UP button. A test pop-up (see Figure 11.35) will open. There you can experiment with different values and observe the results.

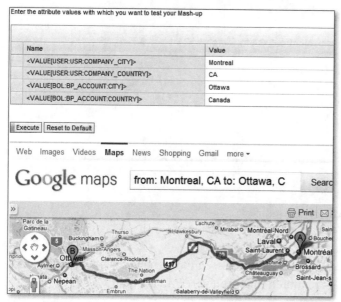

Figure 11.35 Testing Web Mash-up

The test values come from the global attribute tag customizing. If you remember, there was an option to specify a test value when tagging BOL and user attributes.

Once you are done with your mash-up, you need to click SAVE in the embedded view page and go back to page configuration. A new block with the mash-up's title will be available. Adding it to the DISPLAYED ASSIGNMENT BLOCKS will enable the new view in the account page (Figure 11.36).

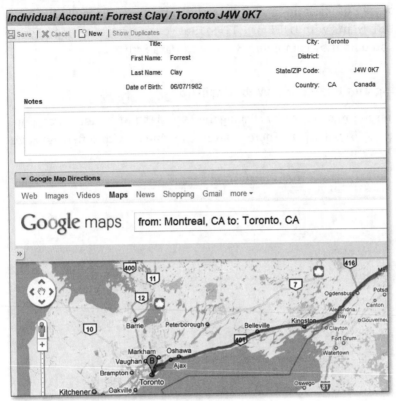

Figure 11.36 Google Map Mash-up in SAP CRM Account Page

The user and account BOL attributes are passed to the new view, their values are resolved, and the result is rendered in an iView HTML element.

11.4 Summary

In this chapter, we demonstrated how the rapid application tool allows you to quickly build a full-fledged application from existing data sources (database tables and Web services). The result is a custom UI component that contains all the necessary UI elements. For the database table case, the user can define the UI model based on the selected database tables. For the Web-service case, the UI elements are fixed and strictly follow the definitions in the WSDL.

All the rapid applications come with an advanced search page. From there, one can browse, display, and create new entries. For each rapid application, there is an overview page that displays one or more assignment blocks, depending on the complexity of the data source.

In addition to the advanced search page, one can define multiple embedded searches. The latter facilitate integration and mash-up with existing SAP CRM applications.

Custom code can be added to each rapid application. This allows you to realize more complex scenarios and deeper integration with the underlying infrastructure. The technical consultants can also modify the generated UI elements in the Component Workbench and augment them according to the business requirements.

Power users can also create a widget based on an URL or HTML/JS script. Application and system data (label or value) can be incorporated into the widget's script. The result is a mash-up that can be added to the application's overview page as a regular assignment block.

All these features are seamlessly integrated with the Web UI and the rest of the extensibility tools. Business users rather than technical consultants are enabled to adapt the software. Enhancing and creating new applications becomes quick and intuitive. One does not have to wait for the IT department to allocate resources and execute such initiatives. This contributes to successful and speedy implementation custom projects.

Web services can be considered one of today's most important technologies because it revolutionized the way we consume and create data. Today, it is the interoperability standard between systems.

12 Web Service Tool

In alignment with SAP's roadmap for enterprise service-oriented architecture, SAP CRM 2006s provided enterprise services that you can use out of the box for key business objects. In addition, you and your partners can now model your own Web services without additional programming. The Web service tool (WST) allows you to quickly create new services tailored to the specific needs of your organization, which you can use to extend your SAP Customer Relationship Management (SAP CRM) system. SAP CRM 7.0 brought plenty of improvements to the Web service tool.

Suppose, for example, that you need to consume or modify your business data from outside SAP CRM. The easiest way (without extensive coding or complex integration) is through a Web service, assuming one exists. The good news is that even if you do not have a Web service suitable for your needs, the chances are that the Web service tool will allow you to create one in minutes. The tool also allows you to expose your newly created structural enhancements to the outside world. As a result, you can read the data from the enhanced SAP CRM applications and also update them. Suppose that you have to add new fields to your SAP CRM account application after you have used the system for some time. Chances are that you have hundreds if not thousands of accounts already. You have to find a way to mass-populate your new field. You can write an ABAP report that uses some of the business add-ins (BAdIs) to load the required data. Alternatively, if your source data already is available in another system, you can quickly create a Web service that exposes the new field and write a simple application to update SAP CRM's accounts.

In this chapter, we will create a Web service that can handle our membership-type field. Before we do, let's take a quick look at the Web service tool itself.

12.1 Using the Web Service Tool

The Web services tool is provided in the form of a wizard, which guides you through the process of creating a Web service. The tool allows you to create standard service operations—such as read, create, or query services—for the main SAP CRM business objects. The Web service tool allows you to model your Web services in accordance with business objects within the business object layer (BOL). Each object has a set of defined attributes and relations, which provides the basis for defining and generating Web services. The services created are stateless and synchronous.

When modeling a Web service, you are creating the *service design object*. You do so by selecting the business objects and the attributes you require (from BOL). During generation, the tool transforms the service design object into a Web service interface by plugging into the standard SAP NetWeaver Web service application programming interface (API).

The customer can influence the service with the BAdI CRM_WST_RT_BADI. The BAdI is called for all read, change, create, and query operations, and is filtered via the name of the service. You can use it to influence the inbound data (before internal conversion) or to change the outbound data (after internal conversion).

Let's see how we can expose our membership type field and generate a new Web service that allows third-party applications to integrate with the SAP CRM account object. Before you start the Web service tool, you will configure it in your business role by including logical link CT-WS-SR. We have done so for the administration work center. As with any SAP CRM application, the entry point into the Web service tool is a search page. Here you can access and modify existing services or create new ones (Figure 12.1).

SAP delivers predefined service objects that you can use as templates to create your own objects. You can think of these as best-practice Web services, which you can adapt to your specific needs by copying and enhancing them. To find such predefined services, you need to filter via the usage type LEVEL 1 SERVICES. Once you select a Web service, the COPY button becomes active.

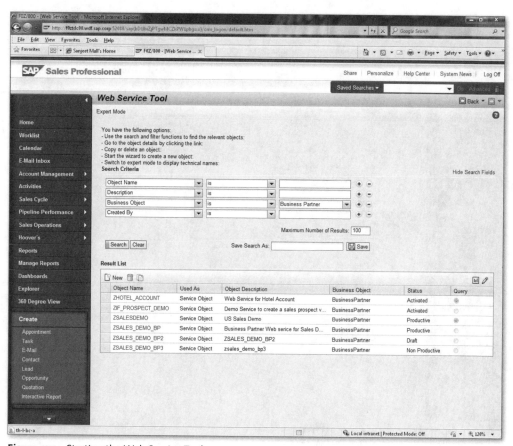

Figure 12.1 Starting the Web Service Tool

In our example, we will create a new service (even though copying is easier). Let's click on the NEW button and start the creation wizard. You will see Step 1 of the wizard (Figure 12.2). You need to provide a name and a description for the new service object. Then choose the necessary operations, desired business object (or BOL component), and relevant root object for the service. You also can select search operations from a list of predefined queries for your service. In this example, we created a Web service with two operations: to read and change a business-partner account. We also selected a query object to help us search for accounts. Click on the

Next button to navigate to the next wizard screen. Alternatively, you can navigate directly with the wizard 1-2-3-4 icons on top of the screen.

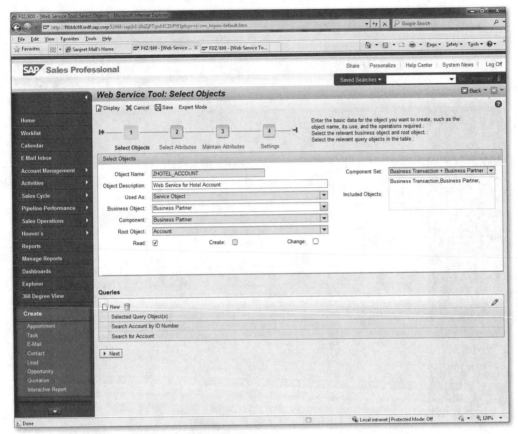

Figure 12.2 Web Service Tool Wizard—Step 1

In the next step, choose all the attributes needed for your service. Open the BOL model tree in the left part of the screen and select the ACCOUNT line item (the first one). The attributes belonging to the selected node appear in the right part of the screen. You have to choose the necessary attributes and confirm them by clicking on the CONFIRM SELECTION button at the bottom of the screen. If you want to choose from other BOL nodes, you have to go to the corresponding line item in the left part of the screen and repeat the selection process. After you have chosen all necessary attributes, you navigate to the next screen. In our example, we will select the following attributes: business partner category, business partner number, first name of business partner (person), last name of business partner (person), date of birth of business partner, full name, search term 1 for business partner, search term 2 for business partner, business partner GUID, and finally our newly created membership type. See Figure 12.3 for more details.

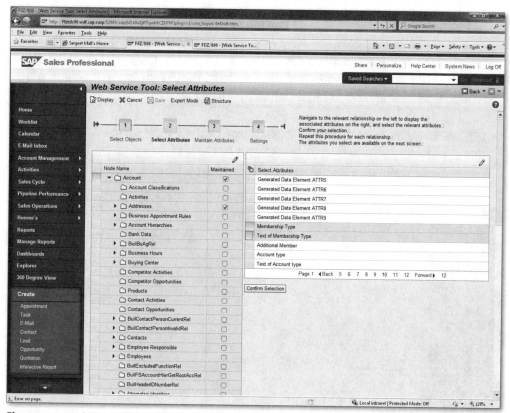

Figure 12.3 Web Service Tool Wizard—Step 2

In the third step (Figure 12.4), you can exclude attributes from the WSDL file, rename them, and set attribute default values. If necessary, you can prevent changes to the default values or allow the service consumer to overwrite them. This flexibility allows you to hide the internal service structure and customizing from consumers of your data. You can also set attributes for query objects. SAP delivers a predefined set of attributes for each query object for query operations. If you have chosen to create one or more query-service operations in Step 1, you can now exclude unnecessary attributes from the query object or change them to suit your needs. In our example, we will set a default value for the category attribute so that the service searches only for individual accounts. Here is a tip: If you are wondering about a specific key value, you can go to the global PERSONALIZE page and open the PERSONALIZE settings. You will find a block called DROPDOWN LISTS. Select the SHOW KEYS IN DROPDOWN LISTS checkbox. Next time you open a dropdown list box (such as the one next to SEARCH FOR on the accounts search page) you will see the key values next to the text description ("1" is the key of individual accounts).

In addition to the above, we have excluded all but the following query- operation attributes: BIRTHDATE, CATEGORY, CITY1, COUNTRY, CREATION_DATE, CREATION_USER, MAX_HIT, PARTNER_GUID, PARTNER, ZZFLD00003C. The last attribute is for our membership type. As you recall, we have defined our new field as search-relevant.

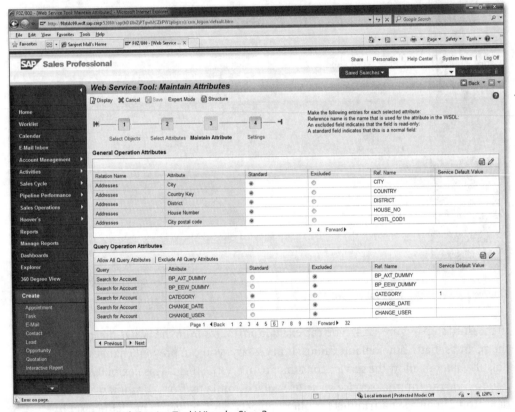

Figure 12.4 Web Service Tool Wizard—Step 3

In the last step (Figure 12.5) you can check, save, and activate your Web service. Once the service is saved and activated, the WSDL file becomes available. The test tool allows you to test the new Web service immediately. Let us save and activate the service.

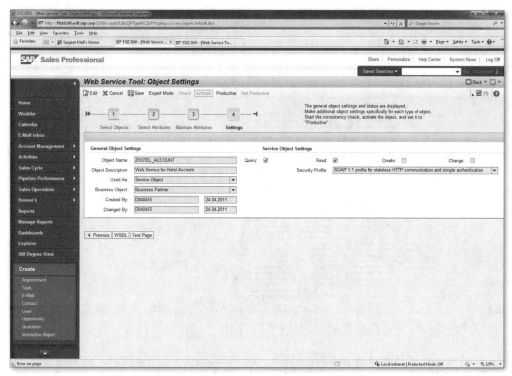

Figure 12.5 Web Service Tool Wizard—Step 4

Upon successful activation, you will see two new buttons: WSDL and TEST. The first one allows you to view the WSDL. Click on it and you see something similar to Figure 12.6. Take your time and review the generated WSDL.

It is time now to test the service. By doing so, you can get an idea what one could expect in a third-party application that uses the newly generated Web service to get (or update) SAP CRM account data. After you press the TEST button, the NW Web Service Navigator will open. You might have to log in using your ID. In the header area of the page you can find a TEST button. Click on it and the test page will come up. There, you can select an operation from our ZHOTEL_ACCOUNT Web service. Let's select operation _-crmost -zho001builheader001dq (in accordance with our WSDL, this corresponds to SEARCHFORACCOUNT—THE GENIL QUERY). The only value that we will set is 100 FOR MAXHITS, because we want to get the first 100 entries. Let's trigger the search now. The Web service will return a result and the NW Web Service Navigator will bring up a page that contains the request and response to/from our service, as shown in Figure 12.7.

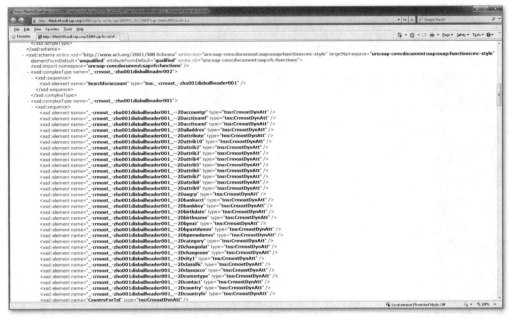

Figure 12.6 Snippet of WSDL of Generated Web Service

Figure 12.7 Sample Web Service Test Request/Response

Note the value of the first log-item element. It says "Field CATEGORY was assigned the default value 1." Recall that we set a default value in our query operation attributes in order to limit the results to individual account objects (CATEGORY=1). If you check all the BP numbers returned by this request, you will find out that they all are individual accounts. You can use the BP number value to read the details of a particular account. To do so, go back in the NW Web Service Navigator and select the `_-crmost_-zhotelAccountRead` operation. There, you can specify a BP number and read the data of the corresponding SAP CRM account. Modifying data works in a similar way.

If you again check the result shown in Figure 12.7, you can see that it contains the HTTP POST request and response. Take time to examine both. They can help you when building an application that works against the generated Web service.

We are not going to build a custom application as part of this book, but doing so would be fairly simple. Most of the current development environments offer tools to generate proxy clients from a WSDL. From there, it is a matter of simply passing and reading the right data.

If you go back to the Web Service tool, you can see that in Step 4 there is an active button called PRODUCTIVE. This is part of the status and life cycle management of a service object. Depending on the status of the objects, you can edit, delete, or change objects. Service objects can have four different statuses. The initial status is DRAFT. In this status you can change your service, delete it, or copy it. After you have finished the definition process, you activate a Web service. Then the status switches to ACTIVATED. Now the service is available, and the WSDL can be generated and tested. Whenever you want to change the service definition, for instance by adding further attributes, you can set it back to DRAFT. After you have successfully tested your service, you can set the status to PRODUCTIVE to prevent anybody from making further changes. A service with the productive status cannot be changed or deleted, but you can copy it and change the copy. The last status is NOT PRODUCTIVE. If a service has this status, it can be deleted but not changed.

12.2   Enabling the Web Service Tool

So far we have been using existing SAP CRM objects as data sources for our Web services. However, it is also possible to use custom applications in the WST. The prerequisite is that the application is based on a GenIL implementation.

When we created the GenIL model of our ZBOOK component, we set the WEBSERVICE ENABLED flag on all GenIL business objects (Figure 12.8). This is just one of the required steps to enable our custom objects in WST, however.

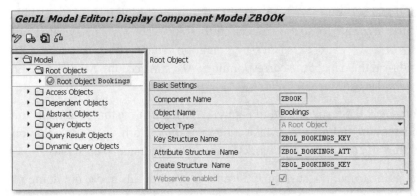

Figure 12.8 The BOOKINGS GenIL Model Object Settings

You also have to ensure that your GenIL component class implements the interface IF_GENIL_WEBSERVICE_SUPPORT. Last, you must register the component in the WST customizing: maintenance view CRMV_WS_METHODS (Transaction SM30).

12.2.1 Implementing the GenIL Adaptations

In our simple example, we will use the ZBOL_BOOKING_KEY structure as the Web service logical key. As explained earlier, we first need to implement IF_GENIL_WEBSERVICE_SUPPORT in our component class (in our example this is ZCL_ZGENIL_COMP_BOOKINGS).

```
DATA: ls_booking_key TYPE zbol_bookings_key.
IF iv_object_name = 'Bookings'.
ls_booking_key = is_logical_key.
"Use the GenIL FWK method to get the BOL object ID
RV_RESULT = cl_crm_genil_container_tools=>build_object_id( ls_booking_
key ).
ENDIF.
```

Listing 12.1 GET_OBJECT_ID_FROM_LOGICAL_KEY Implementation

```
DATA: ls_logical_key TYPE zbol_bookings_key.
IF iv_object_name = 'Bookings'.
   "Converts the BOL object ID into bookings key
   CALL METHOD cl_crm_genil_container_tools=>get_key_from_object_id
   EXPORTING
      iv_object_name = 'Bookings'
      iv_object_id   = iv_object_id
   IMPORTING
      es_key         = ls_logical_key.
   "export the key structure
   es_logical_key = ls_logical_key.
ENDIF.
```

Listing 12.2 GET_LOGICAL_KEY_FROM_OBJECT_ID Implementation

The last step is registering our bookings object in CRMV_WS_METHODS (Figure 12.9).

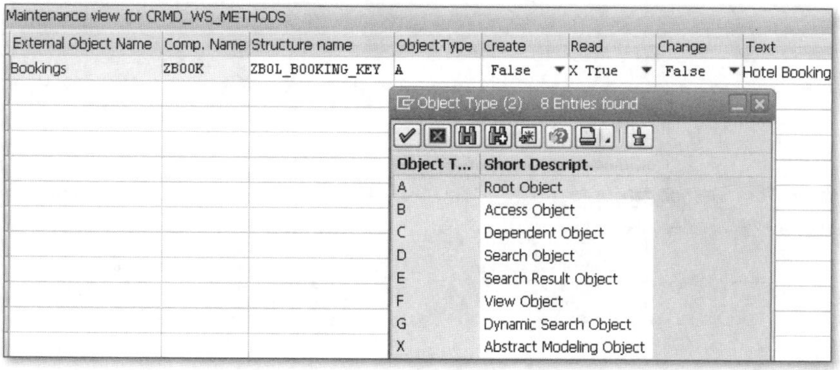

Figure 12.9 WST Customizing

Normally you would also expose your query (object type D or G), but this step requires only another entry in CRMV_WS_METHODS.

12.2.2 Creating a Web Service in WST

Let's discuss the process of creating a Web service in WST. Just as we did before, click on the NEW button in the WST page and follow the wizard (Figure 12.10 and Figure 12.11).

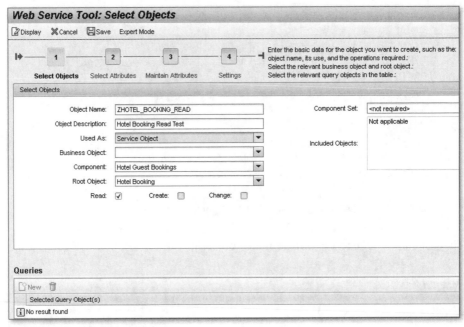

Figure 12.10 Select Objects Step

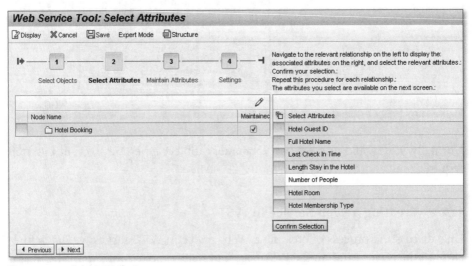

Figure 12.11 Select Attributes

In Step 3 (MAINTAIN ATTRIBUTES), click NEXT and go to the last step. Here you will have to save and activate YOUR Web service (Figure 12.12).

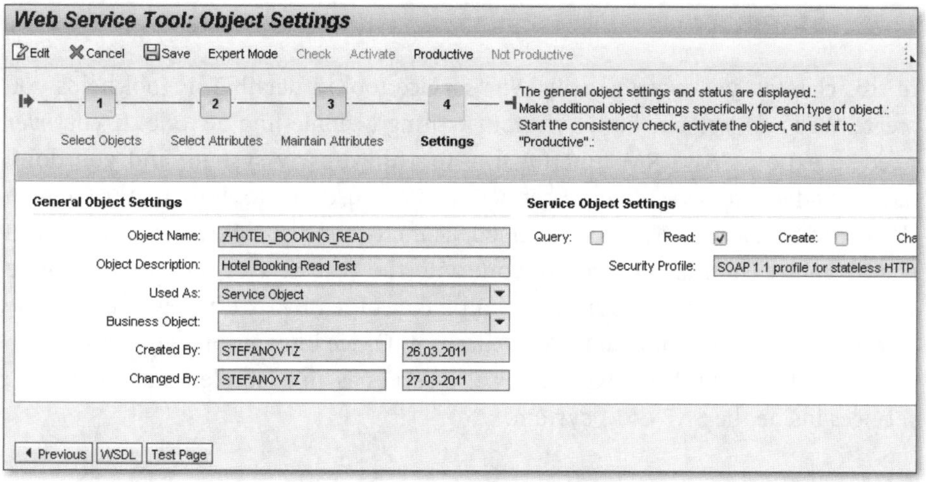

Web Service Tool: Object Settings

Edit | Cancel | Save | Expert Mode | Check | Activate | Productive | Not Productive

| ⇥ | — 1 — | — 2 — | — 3 — | — 4 — |⊣ |

Select Objects   Select Attributes   Maintain Attributes   **Settings**

The general object settings and status are displayed.:
Make additional object settings specifically for each type of object.:
Start the consistency check, activate the object, and set it to:
"Productive".:

General Object Settings

Object Name:	ZHOTEL_BOOKING_READ
Object Description:	Hotel Booking Read Test
Used As:	Service Object ▼
Business Object:	▼
Created By:	STEFANOVTZ 26.03.2011
Changed By:	STEFANOVTZ 27.03.2011

Service Object Settings

Query: ☐	Read: ☑	Create: ☐	Che
Security Profile:	SOAP 1.1 profile for stateless HTTP		

◀ Previous | WSDL | Test Page

Figure 12.12   Select Settings

In this last step, you can test the newly created Web service. As explained earlier, you need to click the TEST PAGE button and follow the steps in the WS Navigator. You select an operation, enter input parameters, and execute the Web service. The results should be similar to those shown in Figure 12.13. Now you have a fully functional Web service on a custom object.

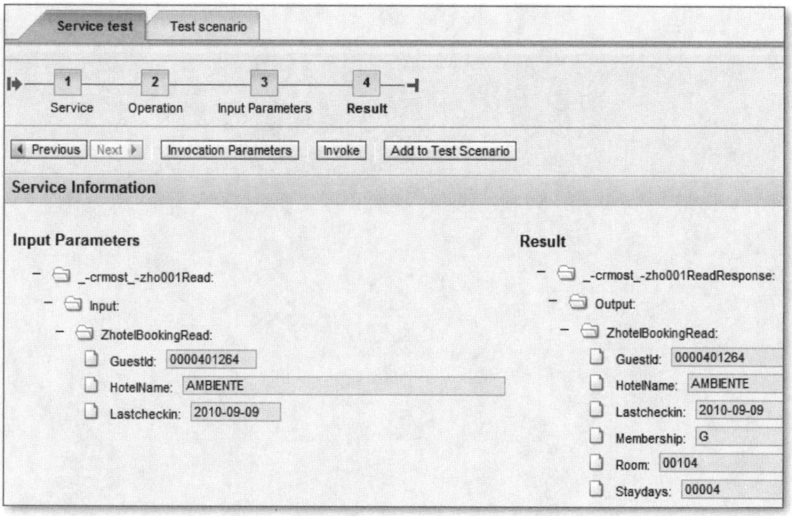

| **Service test** | Test scenario |

| ⇥ | — 1 — | — 2 — | — 3 — | — 4 — |⊣ |

Service   Operation   Input Parameters   **Result**

◀ Previous | Next ▶ | Invocation Parameters | Invoke | Add to Test Scenario

Service Information

Input Parameters

- _-crmost_-zho001Read:
  - Input:
    - ZhotelBookingRead:
      - Guestid: 0000401264
      - HotelName: AMBIENTE
      - Lastcheckin: 2010-09-09

Result

- _-crmost_-zho001ReadResponse:
  - Output:
    - ZhotelBookingRead:
      - Guestid: 0000401264
      - HotelName: AMBIENTE
      - Lastcheckin: 2010-09-09
      - Membership: G
      - Room: 00104
      - Staydays: 00004

Figure 12.13   Executing Custom Web Service

12.3   Summary

In this chapter, we described the Web service tool in detail. This tool helps you create Web services on the fly without writing a single line of code. If you ever need to expose SAP CRM functionality to a third-party system, and you don't have an adequate pre-delivered service, you can use this tool to create a custom Web service that exactly fits your need. The chapter also covered ways you can enable your customized object to work with the Web service tool, which can be very helpful if you want your object to be consumed by external systems. In the next chapter, we are going to look at Microsoft Office integration, which uses Web services extensively. The next chapter also serves as an example on usage of Web services inside the SAP CRM system.

There is one thing common to almost all CRM RFPs—Microsoft Office integration. This seemingly simple functionality becomes a key criterion in many implementations of SAP Customer Relationship Management (SAP CRM). To get it exactly right is surprisingly difficult; however, it doesn't have to be that way.

13 SAP CRM Integration with Microsoft Word and Adobe

Office integration is generally understood to consist of following three key elements:

▶ Word integration

▶ Excel integration

▶ Outlook integration

Some will also include PowerPoint in that list. InfoPath is another recent addition to the traditional line-up. For this chapter, we cover Word integration in depth; it is implied by the very term Office integration, and we point out any exceptions to that rule. Outlook is covered in Chapter 14. SAP CRM does not support templates for Excel, but it provides a generic feature that can export all tabular data to Excel. OneNote might make into some future edition; at present it is not natively supported by SAP CRM.

For the purpose of this chapter, Adobe integration is restricted to print forms (where the end user simply gets the document in a PDF form and cannot change anything). Interactive forms, though very similar to print forms, are outside the scope of this chapter. Most of the discussion in this chapter is applicable both to Microsoft Word and Adobe. We explain any differences between the two.

This integration is not strictly a feature of Web Client UI; however, it uses that framework to make it work. We cover it here to show what you can do with the framework and also because it is a very important feature of SAP CRM, the primary and the most important consumer of Web Client UI framework. The framework was specifically developed for SAP CRM.

13.1 Integration Scenarios

If you have done a few SAP CRM projects, you already know some common use cases that are requested by most if not all customers. Microsoft Office integration is one such requirement. It would not be an overstatement to say that if you don't have Office integration, you really don't have a viable SAP CRM product. Most CRM vendors support Microsoft Office integration. This integration broadly attempts to expose and consume data to and from Microsoft products. Most users use Microsoft Word, Outlook, and Excel on a daily basis, so it makes perfect sense to let them have access to CRM information through their familiar environment. Outside the obvious benefit of less effort training end users, one very positive side effect is that integration encourages collaboration and vastly superior data quality in SAP CRM. Let's explain that by taking examples that illustrate a common use case.

Email is probably the most common interaction channel in business today. Suppose as a SAP CRM user you get an email from your customer asking for a quote for a particulate product or service you offer. Assuming you don't have Office integration, you would need something like the following rough process in order to respond to the request.

1. Read the mail to understand the request.

2. Turn on the browser and log into SAP CRM.

3. Search for the customer.

4. Create a quote for the customer.

5. Save the quote.

6. Summarize, in a reply to the original email, the final quote (your customer doesn't have access to your SAP CRM system). This step would be manual, time-consuming, and very error-prone.

7. Create an activity to record that you responded to the request.

8. Attach the incoming mail and outgoing mail to the activity above.

Assuming you are an experienced SAP CRM user, the whole process might take between five and ten minutes. That would not include Step 4, the quote-creation process. The time needed for that step would depend on the complexity of your product or service. Worse, during this intensively manual process you would make mistakes and data quality would suffer. If you were exhausted or pressed for time, you might not do Step 7 and Step 8, and the whole interaction would be lost forever.

Now look at the same scenario with Office integration in place. Here would be the approximate steps:

1. Read the mail to understand the requirement.

2. Associate the mail (in Outlook itself) to SAP CRM.

3. Create quote and press SEND TO CUSTOMER.

With that, you are done.

So let's analyze what happened. Associating the email to SAP CRM triggered a lookup in SAP CRM for the customer (via email address of the incoming mail). Already, you have saved some time typing and clicking. Now you create the quote. The difference this time is that SAP CRM already knows the context (the original mail) so it can create an interaction history automatically. Once you are done creating the quote, you press another button and a nicely formatted Microsoft Word document (with your company logo and the correct text and quote details) is created and an email response triggered. Steps 7 and 8 here are automatic, so SAP CRM would be doing the work for you in the background.

Compared to the manual process, this would take at most one minute, and data quality would be impeccable. Even better, your customer would receive a polished, professional document that describes the quote in every detail, rather than your rough notes. As a bonus, this interaction of yours would be recorded in SAP CRM for future reference and would be available to all channels (your call center for example, if the customer happens to call to further discuss the quote, thus improving customer satisfaction).

Customers demand Word Integration to meet a simple need: They want to print and mail (both snail and email) information residing in SAP CRM. Among their reasons for doing this:

1. Sending quotes to customers via mail.
2. Printing sales orders for your files.
3. Printing service confirmations in order to get old-fashioned handwritten signatures from your customers.

13.2 Technologies Involved in Integration

It helps to understand some of the technologies involved in making this integration work. The list below is not exhaustive, but rather a quick overview of the main solutions.

▶ **WordML**
The Microsoft Office XML formatting consists of XML-based document formats (or XML schemas) introduced in versions of Microsoft Office. In short, you can use WordML to fully describe a DOC file in an XML format. This means that if you know the WordML specification, you can create a valid Microsoft Word Document without having Microsoft Word. WordML is a lossless format, meaning there is nothing lost in translation from WordML to DOC format and vice versa. In Office integration, we use this feature to create documents on the SAP CRM server, without even having Microsoft Word installed; the SAP CRM server could actually be running on a UNIX machine. WordML only applies to Microsoft Word integration.

▶ **XSD**
XML schema is an XML-based alternative to DTD. An XML schema describes the structure of an XML document. The XML Schema language is also referred to as XML Schema Definition (XSD). The purpose of XSD is to validate your XML with a given schema. In Office integration, we use XSD to create the final document that conforms to the template. It also is used at design time to add SAP CRM data elements to the template.

▶ **WebDAV**

Web-based Distributed Authoring and Versioning (WebDAV) is a set of methods based on the Hypertext Transfer Protocol (HTTP) that facilitates collaboration between users in editing and managing documents and files stored on a Web server. It is governed by the IETF (*www.ietf.org*). In Office integration, we use this to save and retrieve Word documents and templates in SAP CRM Content Management. Adobe does not use WebDAV.

▶ **XSLT**

Extensible Stylesheet Language Transformations is a declarative, XML-based language used for the transformation of XML documents. The original document is not changed; rather, a new document is created based on the content of an existing one. The new document may be serialized (output) by the processor in standard XML syntax or in another format, such as HTML or plain text. XSLT is most often used to convert data between different XML schemas or to convert XML data into web pages or PDF documents. In Office integration, we use it to transform SAP CRM data to WordML. In Adobe, this transformation happens in ADS (Adobe Document Services).

13.3   Design Time and Run time

There are two stages in doing Word integration: design time and run time. *Design time* is the definition phase; namely, the creation of a Word/Adobe template. Normally this is done by the power user (SAP consultant, in-house experts, or administrator). The output of this exercise is one or more Word/Adobe templates that define the layout of the final document. A template really is a collection of static text (such as the address of the company), pictures (such as a logo), and dynamic elements that are place holders for the data loaded at run time (such as the name of the customer, or line items in the case of a sales order). Templates don't change often. To design them, you need to know where the run time data comes from. Typically, you also have access to how the data is generally presented, based on the stationery or other documents that your company already uses. Templates need to be localized to be effective.

Run time is when the design-time definitions are used by the business- process implementations. In other words, the template becomes an actual document with real

SAP CRM information. This activity is generally performed by end users of the SAP CRM system (sales staff, service staff, and often by the customers themselves).

All the processing, both at design time and run time, happens on the server side. The client only displays the document. For example, you can actually create the whole run time document without having Word installed on your machine, though naturally you won't be able to see the generated document.

Let us look a little deeper into what is going on during each of these stages of integration.

13.3.1 Design Time

The data flow of the design time phase, for Microsoft Word, is summarized in Figure 13.1. As a power user, you will not have to deal with all that complexity, as SAP CRM does the heavy lifting behind the scenes. However, it makes sense to get acquainted (even at a high level) with the process.

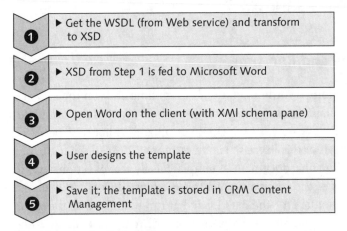

Figure 13.1 Design-Time Flow

As indicated previously, the application data is delivered via a Web service. The latter is described via a WSDL file. Therefore the first thing that the design-time tool does is to retrieve the WSDL of the associated Web service. The WSDL is parsed and transformed into an XSD file (Step ❶). Microsoft Word is selective about the kind of XSD it uses. Therefore the design-time environment needs to transform the output from Step ❶ into a format that Word can use (Step ❷). The newly created XSD has to be stored somewhere. IETF invented WebDAV Directory with that purpose in mind. The tool will store the XSD there (the SAP implementation of it) as part of Step ❸. Finally, the design-time process will rely on the power user to design the template (Step ❹). (We will explain how one can do that later in the book.) What is important at this point is to note that the result of this end-user interaction has to be saved. The template is stored as an XML file in the SAP CRM content management and this concludes the design time procedure (Step 5).

For Adobe, Step ❷ and Step ❸ take place in Adobe Live Cycle Designer.

13.3.2 Run Time

Run time is triggered when the end user is on an object in SAP CRM UI (for which one or many templates exists) and clicks on the WITH TEMPLATE button. Again, quite a bit happens in the background (Figure 13.2). The following steps are performed by the system, without the end user having to be aware of them.

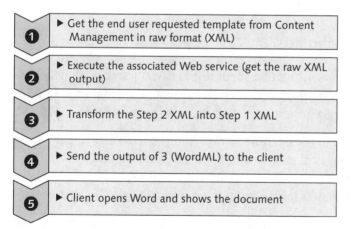

Figure 13.2 Run-Time Flow

1. SAP CRM recognizes the loaded object's unique ID. The nature of this ID depends on the loaded object (the SAP CRM business object on the page). For one order object, this is the GUID of the record.

2. SAP CRM shows a template selection pop-up screen to the user, with template name and language as the output.

3. With the ID as the key, a Web service is activated (in the case of a Web service tool, this means that the associated function module is executed), and the Web service returns the run-time XML data.

4. On the resulting XML, a custom transformation is performed with the template's XMLs generating a WordML (also called WML) file.

5. A business add-in (CRM_OFFICE_TEMPLATE_BADI) is fired for key value pair-type transformation.

6. The final document is then placed in a WebDAV location. (This is not the case with EHP1 because of enhanced security. In that case, Word is opened as Read Only.)

7. The document is shown to the end user.

The process is slightly different for Adobe. In Step ❸, the XML data from Step ❷ and Step ❶ is sent to ADS, which returns the final document in a PDF form. Step ❹ sends this document to the client. Step ❺ opens the PDF in Adobe Reader.

13.4   Creating a Template

Armed with all this information, it's time for us to get busy. Our task as administrator or power user is to create a template that end users would use to print SAP CRM quotes for their customers. To start, we will create a Microsoft Word template.

Before we start, we need to consider the so-called official template. This is a static document. Organizations generally have official templates that typically include logo, address, name of the company, and so on. The template also has some official text that the organization uses to streamline communication with its customers.

We also need a Web service that would provide us with the data at run time and structure at design time. In our example, we use a Web service created by WST and called ZBT_CTR_QUOTE_READ. It accepts a quote ID as an input and returns header and item (among other data). Figure 13.3 shows some of the Web service's information.

We need to know in advance which elements can have multiple occurrences and which can have single occurrences. We will refer to these, respectively, as having 1:1 or 1:N cardinality. In our example, some 1:1 elements are:

▶ PROCESSTYPE

▶ DATE OF ORDER

▶ EMPLOYEE RESPONSIBLE

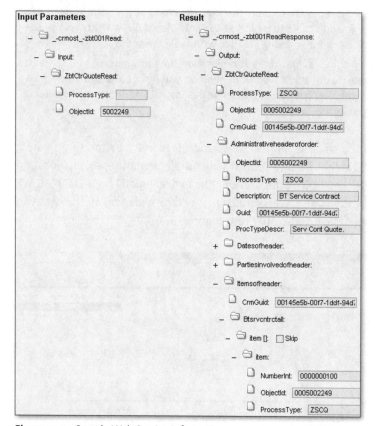

Figure 13.3 Sample Web Service Information

Examples of 1:N elements are:

▶ ITEM NUMBER

▶ DESCRIPTION

▶ PRICE

The price element is worth considering, because every SAP CRM veteran knows that this is actually not a 1:N type but 1:N:M type. That means that each line item can have many prices.

> **Note**
>
> In SAP CRM, whenever you have 1:N type, it needs to go in a table. This is a hint to the run-time engine to expect n (unknown at design time) entries. The format of the table is very simple: The first row is the header (static text), and the second row is the run time elements. If your official template dictates that the 1:N type goes in a list (instead of a table), you still need to add a table to indicate to SAP CRM that it is a 1:N type. You can get the table to look like a list by being creative with table formatting.
>
> You can nest a table inside a table. There is no limit on the nesting level; you can nest as many as you like. Actually, this does not depend on you but on the structure of the SAP CRM object. In practice, you can expect to be dealing with multiple nesting almost in every meaningful template.

To begin, we need to start the Template Designer. Figure 13.4 shows you where you can find it. This might be different in your implementation, as this location depends on your business-role configuration. The logical link ID is CT-DTD-SR. We assume that you already have a Web service that will provide you all the data you need (in our example, we use the one from Figure 13.3).

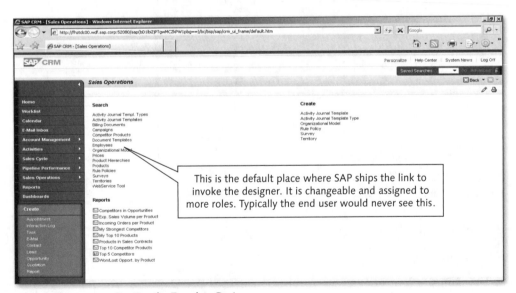

Figure 13.4   Starting the Template Designer

You should start by creating a NEW template. In the page that opens, you will have to provide the template details (see Figure 13.5). The FILE TYPE can be Microsoft Word or Adobe depending on your desired format. The NAME OF THE TEMPLATE needs to be unique across the system. This is used by SAP CRM to save and locate the template. The DESCRIPTION is a human-readable name for end users. This typically should indicate the intended use (for example "Quote for New Customers"). The OBJECT TYPE is the BOR object name. At run time, this helps to reduce the number of templates shown to users for selection, as only valid templates (based on what is loaded on the screen) are presented for selection. In our example we will select BUS20001 (business transaction). The LANGUAGE helps the end user (at run time) to select the right template, in case he or she is dealing with multiple languages. Each language variant needs to be designed separately. There is no automatic conversion.

Document Template Designer - Detail: New

Back | Web Service Tool | WSDL | Call BADI

Template Details

File Type:*	Microsoft Word
Name:*	Quatation Template
Description:	Quatation Printout Template
Object Type:*	BUS20001
Language:	EN
	○ No Webservice ● Webservice Name ○ Own WSDL URL
WS Name:	ZBT_CTR_QUOTE_READ
Download Schema:	Download
Download Template:	Download
Upload template to CRM:	Browse... Upload
Start tool for designing template:	Start Designer

Figure 13.5 Template Details

The WEB SERVICE NAME is key piece of information that serves as the data source for the template. At design time, the associated WSDL determines the structure of the template. In other words, the WSDL elements are placed at a desired location in the document. These elements might be key-value pairs, and at run time the key would be replaced by its value. It also can be of the 1:N:M type, where the element would become multiple entries at run time. To understand this last point, think of a table: At design time, you don't know how many rows will be needed at run time; you only know you want column 1 to be this element and column N to be that element. You can choose not to use a Web service if your template is static (or the values you need are very simple and not coming from a Web service). The Web service here must have a read operation.

Via a set of checkboxes the user can select the type of the Web service.

This way, one can tell the system whether the Web service is designed by the Web Service Tool (WST) or is a custom Web service (in the latter case, a URL is required to locate the Web service). This is a new feature in EHP1. Previously, the template could only be designed from a Web service exposed by WST. In EHP1, this restriction is taken away. You can design your templates from any Web service. While use of a custom Web service is very powerful, it is slightly more involved than using a Web service generated by the WST (we will provide you with some tips later on). Most of the additional work is related to properly exposing a Web service so that it can be consumed by an external process (MS Word). In our example, we select a service created by the WST.

Once you are done defining details, you click on the START DESIGNER button. As of EhP1 and depending on the ActiveX support of your browser, you might be required to download the XSD (the schema) and the template files.

Figure 13.6 shows the details of what is available in Word for creating the template. Everything in the illustration is standard Word; there are no changes to your standard Word installation.

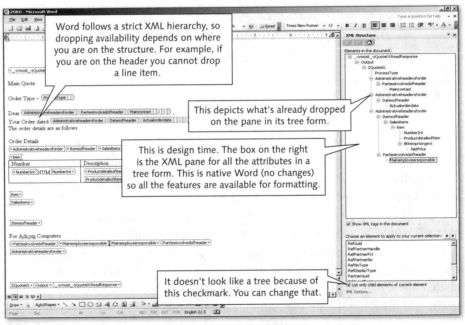

Figure 13.6 Design Time – XML Pane in Word

To drop elements, place the cursor where you need the element to appear in Word and click on the desired element from the bottom right box. As you navigate around the document you can see that this box's values changes. That is because Word follows a strict hierarchy. Only the elements that are available in the present context are visible. The tree on the right (ELEMENTS IN THE DOCUMENT) actually shows you what elements are dropped in its correct hierarchy.

Adding Content Not Available in the Selected Web Service

CRM_OFFICE_TEMPLATE_BADI enables you to put extra text (outside from the Web service) in the final document. The additional text variables are denoted via a name in the form of [[[VAR1]]]. These can only be 1:1 replacement and not of another cardinality

---

The goal of our exercise is to create a template that shows information from the quote header and item details. Let us start the template by adding all the Web service elements that will lead us to the quote header data. At first, the only element you can choose is the XML topmost element of the Web service response as specified by the WSDL (see Figure 13.3). In reality, Word uses the XSD obtained from parsing that WSDL. Figure 13.7 shows the blank template. You add elements to the document by clicking on the available elements in the box on the right. The selection is context-aware. We have to start with the root element (as per the response definition in the WSDL) and make our way down to the desired quote data.

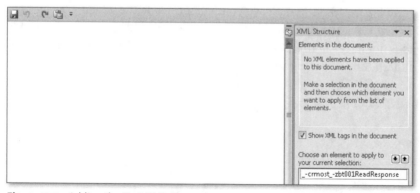

Figure 13.7 Adding the First XML Element

If you click on the _-crmost_-zbt001ReadResponse element in the bottom right box, you will see the selected element appear in your cursor location. Now that your cursor is inside the inserted element, the content of the selection box (bottom right) will change and display the element's children. You need to keep on drilling (selecting elements) in order to reach the quote header data. As you do so, the available element selection would also change. For example, the `_-crmost_-zbt001ReadResponse` has only one child, namely `Output`. Select it and continue until you find the `ProcessType` and its siblings (quote header). We will add the process type but we will enter some text so that the consumer of the template knows what the displayed data refers to (see Figure 13.8).

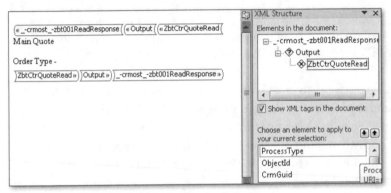

Figure 13.8 Preparing to Add Quote Header Data

If you are following our example, please place your cursor after the `Order Type` string literal and select the `ProcessType` element. The result should be similar to that shown in Figure 13.9. If you leave your cursor inside the added `ProcessType` element, you will see that the available selection is empty. The reason is that this element does not have children. However, if you step out of that element you will see the children of the element within which the cursor is placed.

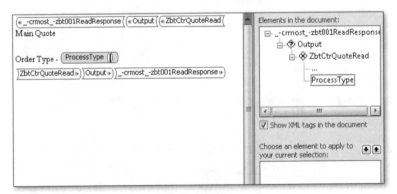

Figure 13.9 Adding the Process Type Element

As we have seen, you can keep on typing static text in the way you normally do in Word. Feel free to use formatting and even insert images (for example your company's logo). The key here is to keep in mind the hierarchy of your XSD document (WSDL).

Adding 1:1 elements, such as our `ProcessType`, is very easy. You just drop it in and you are done. The manipulation of elements with 1:N cardinality requires some consideration. To begin with, such elements have to be placed in a table. To demonstrate, let us add some quote item data in which the item is an 1:N element. Therefore, we will drill down to it and place its content in a table. You will insert the table in the way you normally do in Word. But in the cells that need to display the application data at run time, you will place the required XML elements. As shown in Figure 13.10, we will display the item number, description, and price. Note that the price can have multiple cardinality with respect to an item (overall cardinality of 1:N:M). One can handle such cases with nested tables. However, in our example we will not create a nested table because we are sure that there is only one price per item (1:N:1).

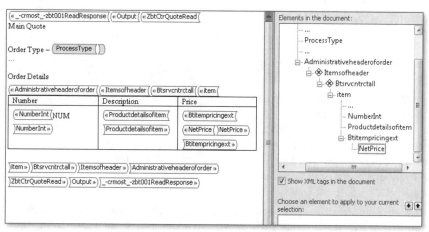

Figure 13.10　Inserting a 1:N Element Via a Table

You might have noticed that in our example we have typed "NUM" within the `NumberInt` element. By default, all data types in Word are treated as strings. To format the output in a different type, we need to provide hints to the template at design time. There are a few keywords that let you do it. They go into the template as place holder between the violet markups. NUM is one such example and it is used mostly to drop the leading zeros. Another value that you might use is DATE.

This keyword would force the output to format as a date. The actual date format used is based on logged-in user's date settings.

> **Tip**
>
> If you want to format the text, you need to actually get inside the markup (the two violet boxes) and type something, for example "formattext," then apply the formatting to it. At run time, this text "formattext" would be dropped and your format would be applied to the real text.

As we saw, not all Web service response elements are going to be converted to text in the final document. Most of them are inserted (dropped) to follow the WSDL hierarchy and thus to locate the text you want to appear in the final document. All such markup would be deleted at run time.

Once done with your template design, you have to save the document. If you are using SAP CRM 7.0 or lower, just press SAVE in Word and the template would be saved in SAP CRM. Remember to keep saving it every now and then so that your session doesn't expire. SAP CRM is using the WebDAV feature of Word to save it to content management. With EHP1 (due to enhanced security), you need to manually upload the template to SAP CRM once you are done.

> **Using Custom Web Services**
>
> Staring with EHP1, you can use any Web service to create your templates. The process of designing the template is exactly the same. The difference is that instead of using a WST generated service, you are using a custom one. Make sure your custom Web service has a read operation. You need to select it in the Template Designer before you can start the creation of templates. Creating a custom Web service that Template Designer can use is beyond the scope of this chapter and is covered by available SAP documentation. Locate the WSDL you want to use.
>
> Create a consumer proxy (this can be done in Transaction SE80). You will have to implement CRM_OI_WEBSERVICE_BADI from enhancement spot CRM_OFFICE_INT_ENHANCEMENT. The BADI uses the interface IF_EX_CRM_OI_WEBSERVICE_BADI. This interface exposes a method called CALL_WEB_SERVICE. Inside this method implementation, you will have to call your custom Web service and return its payload (as defined in the Web service's WSDL). The easiest way to do so is to generate a consumer proxy from your Web service (you can do so in Transaction SE80) and use it in your implementation.

We have completed our example. The end users can access our template whenever they select an object that the template is connected to. They just press the WITH

TEMPLATE button on the ATTACHMENTS block and choose the correct template (see Figure 13.11).

Figure 13.11 Creating a New Document from a Template

All the data from the presently loaded business object would be used to fill the template, and the final document would be opened in Word.

13.5 Adobe Integration

Adobe integration is very much like Microsoft Word integration in terms of the business use case. What to use depends more or less on your preference. Functionally there are some minor differences. Both forms of integration can be made to work exactly the same way, but the effort required is different, depending on what you are trying to achieve. At the end of the chapter, we will give you some hints on when to use Microsoft Word and when to use Adobe.

Technically there are some differences between Adobe and Microsoft Word for the purpose of this integration. For starters, If you wanted to use Adobe, you need to have an extra server—ADS (Adobe document services)—that actually converts your SAP CRM run-time data in to a PDF format with reference to your template. The design time template is an XML file known as Adobe XML form; it has file extension .xdp. It is important to remember this extension as this is the format in which you need to save your template (not PDF, which is another option that the LiveCycle Designer gives). LiveCycle Designer is an Adobe product that helps design Adobe forms. To get more information, you can visit Adobe LiveCycle at *http://www.adobe. com/products/livecycle/designer/*. SAP also provides a variant of this designer as part of SAP Interactive Forms by Adobe (more information can be found at *http://www. sdn.sap.com/irj/sdn/adobe*). We will use this tool to design the template. Please make sure this is installed on the machine where you want to design the template.

Internally, the flow at design time is almost similar to that in Microsoft Word (see Figure 13.1 at the beginning of this chapter). The real change is instead of using Mictosoft Word we are using the LiveCycle Designer.

13.5.1 Creating the Template in Adobe

The best way to learn the differences in the design processes is to create the exact same template we just created for Microsoft Word in Adobe.

The first step, just as with Word, is to start the Template Designer (see Figure 13.4) and create a new template. This time, however, we will choose TYPE as ADOBE. The rest of the information remains exactly the same as before (naturally, you need to choose a different name for the template). We will use the same Web service so the data source also remains the same. Once you have provided all the information, it's time to download the XSD document by pressing the button next to DOWNLOAD TEMPLATE (refer back to Figure 13.5). Save this XDS file somewhere on your local drive and remember the path. We will need to refer to this location later. The next step is to press START DESIGNER (refer back to Figure 13.5).

If everything is set up correctly, Adobe LiveCycle designer will open (Figure 13.12).

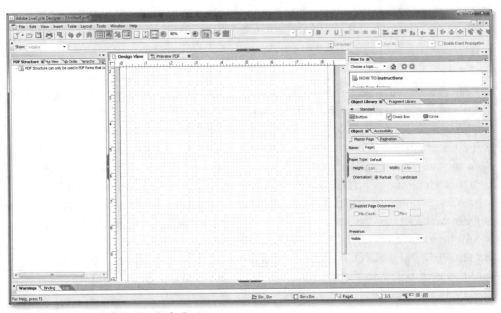

Figure 13.12 Adobe LiveCycle Designer

The next step in the process is to click on File • New in Adobe LiveCycle Designer. This would bring up a wizard. We want to select Use blank form in the first step of the wizard, click Next and then accept the defaults for page layout (in the second step of the wizard). The next step is to connect the XSD file we just downloaded to this form; for that, click File • New Data Connection.... This also brings up a wizard. In the first step of the wizard, type a name for your connection and select the option XML Schema and click Next. In Step 2 of the wizard, browse the location of the file (Hint: SAP gives the XSD file an XML extension, so don't filter on XSD but on XML in the file dialog), and press Finish.

This should give open a screen like the one shown in Figure 13.13.

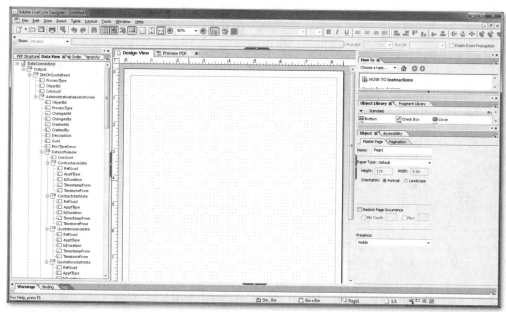

Figure 13.13 LiveCycle Designer with Our Schema

Just as before, the goal of our exercise is to create a template that shows information from the quote header and item details. Let us start the template by adding all the Web service elements that will lead us to the quote header data. Unlike in Microsoft Word, you can drop elements in arbitrary order (in Adobe LiveCycle Designer, context is implied). Start by dropping the first element. As you can see from Figure 13.14 the Process Type element is dropped. To get to this stage, we have:

1. Dropped a TextBox from the Object Library (see the second box on the right in Figure 13.14 named Object Library) and gave it the text "Main Quote." Object library gives you many features to customize your layout; for example, you can drop an image if you need logo or any other pictures in your layout.

2. Dragged and dropped the element ProcessType from the SCHEMA pane. Adobe LiveCycle Designer by default also includes the description of the element on the form. We can rename this description to match our template in Microsoft Word. Click on the label containing the text PROCESS TYPE and type "Order Type."

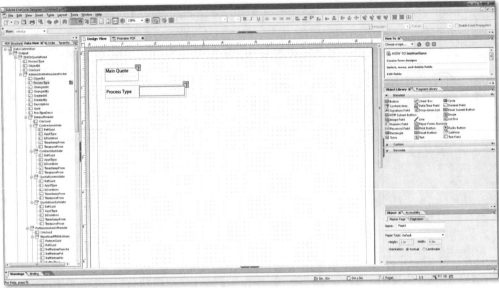

Figure 13.14 Adding the Process Type Element

You can always preview the way your document will look by clicking TAB PREVIEW PDF (Figure 13.14). You can toggle between design view and preview PDF view to make sure you exactly get the layout right (see Figure 13.15). In that screenshot, we have already changed the label to ORDER TYPE.

Now it is time to add quote item data. There are many ways to do it, but we will use the one that's closest to Microsoft Word. To drop a 1:N cardinality object we would use a table. To do that, follow menu path menu TABLE • INSERT TABLE. In the resulting pop-up screen, choose CREATE TABLE USING ASSISTANT. This brings up a wizard. In the first step in the wizard choose the option BODY ROWS VARY DEPENDING ON DATA (see Figure 13.16). Run through all the steps of the wizard by taking all the defaults.

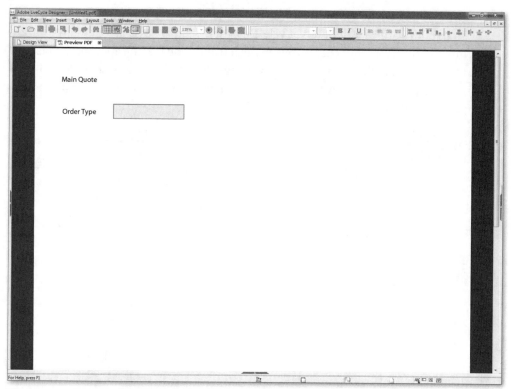

Figure 13.15 Preview of Template in PDF Form

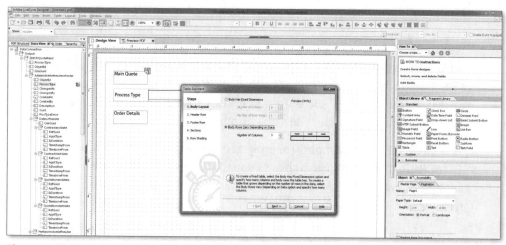

Figure 13.16 Dropping a Table in Adobe LiveCycle Designer.

Once you have the basic table, it is time to add 1:N (or 1:N:M) elements. This is straightforward in Adobe LiveCycle Designer. Simply take the element you are interested in from the schema tree on the left and drop it at the appropriate place in the table. Naturally, we would like to change the headers to give them meaningful name. Figure 13.17 shows our final template with correct header descriptions and all elements in the right place in the table.

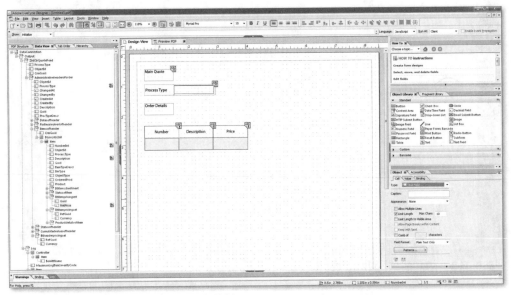

Figure 13.17 Inserting Elements via Table

Notice that Adobe LiveCycle Designer does not mark up the run-time text. To see what elements are bound on the form, choose the form element and look at the bottom right box on the Adobe LiveCycle Designer to view its details (see Figure 13.18). In the details of the object, you can perform exact formatting as well as patterns, change data type, and view its binding.

This completes our example. The only task left is to upload the template to SAP CRM. To do that, save the template to your hard drive as an Adobe XML form (XDP extension). Go back to SAP CRM UI and browse this file and press upload (refer back to Figure 13.5). This uploads the template to SAP CRM content management.

Now end users can access this template exactly was they would the Microsoft Word template (refer back to Figure 13.11).

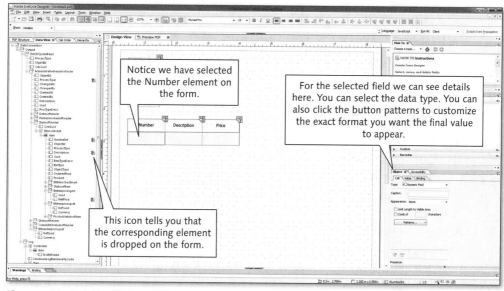

Figure 13.18 Details of Selected Element

13.5.2 When to Use Adobe

This chapter is really about print forms and not interactive forms. However, you can use Adobe LiveCycle Designer to create interactive forms. It actually is quite simple: You just need to change the source Web service that supports updates. Please make sure you have the right licenses to do so, as Adobe has definite policy on how the exact usage is charged. Even when you are only interested in print forms, it can be tough to decide on what to select. The following guidelines should help you decide which one to use, assuming you have the choice.

Adobe or Microsoft Word?

▸ If you want your end users to edit the final document freely, choose Microsoft Word.

▸ If your document is very complex (with client-side processing with macros in Microsoft Word or Adobe-script in Adobe), work what you are comfortable programming.

▸ If you are creating an interactive document, choose Adobe. Microsoft Word is not really an option for this. Microsoft InfoPath is a better alternative. Check with Adobe the pricing structure for your organization.

▸ If you are planning lot batch-document creation, use Adobe.

▸ If the final document needs to be only read-only, use Adobe.

▸ If formatting needs are outside the ordinary, Adobe has more options.

13.6 Summary

This chapter covered the details of Microsoft Word and Adobe Integration. Specifically, it introduced all the technologies you need to know to design your next template. It also walked you through an example template, by which you should have understood all the details of Template Designer, both in Microsoft Word and Adobe. The best way to refine the skills you learned in this chapter is to design a few templates and experiment. In the next chapter we are going to look at Groupware integration, which completes our discussion of the integration of SAP CRM with third-party software.

Today, real competitive advantage can only be achieved through personal collaboration. SAP Customer Relationship Management (SAP CRM) offers comprehensive tools such as Client-based Groupware Integration to address this growing demand for enterprise collaboration.

14   Introduction to Client-based Groupware Integration

In this chapter, we will explain the basics of Client-based Groupware Integration (cGWI). We will describe the functionality and architecture of the component and show you how to quickly get started using it.

In the context of our discussion, the term Groupware is used to refer to a non-CRM system that can store information in SAP CRM objects. In the case of cGWI, the Groupware system refers to mail clients such as Microsoft Outlook and/or IBM Lotus Notes.

We will be discussing the new version of Client-based Groupware Integration 10.x, which was launched recently and is available in SAP CRM 2007 and above.

14.1   Business Processes Covered by cGWI

You can use cGWI for two main processes—account management and appointments and tasks—in ways that allow a deeper integration of SAP CRM and Groupware systems. These processes allow collaboration between customer-facing professionals.

14.1.1   Account Management

For account management, you can maintain account and contact information in Groupware and SAP CRM, including automatic synchronization. This ensures complete data consistency and transparency in Groupware and SAP CRM. For account management, Groupware supports the following processes:

▶ Creating an account and contact in SAP CRM and replicating them in a contact in Groupware

▶ Creating a contact in Groupware and replicating it in SAP CRM as an account and contact

▶ Changing an account or contact in SAP CRM that originates in Groupware and synchronizing changes with Groupware

▶ Changing a contact in Groupware that was created in an account and contact in SAP CRM and synchronizing the changes with SAP CRM

▶ Deleting contacts in Groupware and removing corresponding contacts in SAP CRM, and vice versa

14.1.2 Appointments and Tasks

Second, for appointments and tasks, you can plan and record CRM-relevant activities in both Groupware and SAP CRM and update them as required. Tasks can be planned and tracked in both Groupware and SAP CRM. All such activities are exchanged between the Groupware platform and SAP CRM. For appointments, Groupware supports the following processes:

▶ Creating an appointment in the Groupware system with a specific category and synchronizing it with SAP CRM

▶ Creating an appointment in SAP CRM and synchronizing it with Groupware

▶ Changing an appointment in Groupware that was originally created in SAP CRM and replicating changes in SAP CRM

▶ Changing an appointment in SAP CRM that was created in the Groupware system and replicating changes in Groupware

▶ Deleting an appointment in Groupware that was created in SAP CRM and removing it from SAP CRM

▶ Deleting an appointment in SAP CRM that was created in the Groupware system and removing it from Groupware

▶ Attaching documents to the appointment and replicating them in SAP CRM and Groupware

▸ Viewing appointments in both the Groupware calendar and SAP CRM calendar

For tasks, Groupware supports the supported processes:

▸ Creating a task in the Groupware system with a specific category and synchronizing it with SAP CRM

▸ Creating a task in SAP CRM and synchronizing it to Groupware to the person responsible

▸ Changing a task in Groupware (e.g., setting a new status) that was created in SAP CRM and replicating changes in SAP CRM

▸ Changing a task in SAP CRM (e.g., setting a new status) that was was created in the Groupware system and replicating changes in Groupware

▸ Deleting a task in Groupware that was created in SAP CRM and removing it from SAP CRM

▸ Deleting a task in SAP CRM that was created in the Groupware system and removing it from Groupware

▸ Attaching documents to tasks, including replication

▸ Viewing tasks in both Groupware calendar and SAP CRM calendar

With cGWI, all the synchronized information for accounts, contacts, appointments, and tasks is available offline. You can view this data without any connection to the related SAP CRM system. However, you do need a connection to the SAP CRM system in order to make any changes in the data.

A key point to remember is that on the Groupware client, you must manually decide which object is relevant for SAP CRM by using the RELATE TO CRM button. Once an object is related, it is marked for synchronization with SAP CRM. All further updates, both on SAP CRM and Microsoft Outlook, will flow to the other system automatically.

14.2 cGWI Architecture

The synchronization functionality is encapsulated within an ActiveX control, so it is accessible directly from the browser. This ActiveX control provides interfaces for starting the synchronization as well as opening the Customizing forms. The Groupware client calls these interfaces using JavaScript, communicates with the server using HTTP(S) requests, and communicates with Microsoft Outlook/Notes using the corresponding objects models. On the SAP CRM side, the SICF framework is used for communication with the Groupware client. On the Groupware client, the .NET Framework is used to handle all communication and data exchange. This mechanism provides a secure and scalable infrastructure for the solution.

In Figure 14.1, we show a high-level diagram of all the major components in the cGWI architecture. Most of the components are reused in Microsoft Outlook or IBM Lotus Notes based Groupware systems. The Javascript and ActiveX components are invoked and used only when you invoke cGWI from the SAP CRM WebClient UI.

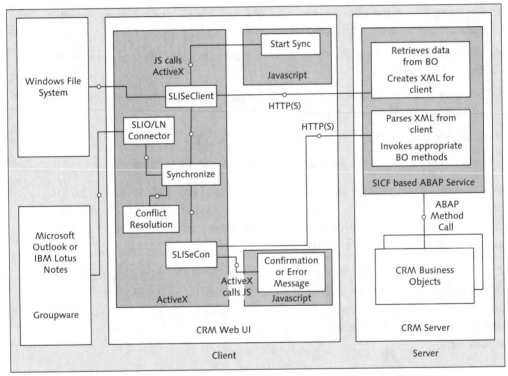

Figure 14.1 Client-Based Groupware Integration Architecture

When you look at the flow of data in the cGWI architecture, it is important to understand the underlying sequence. When you make any change in the cGWI client, the client sends a message to both the Groupware server (this can be Microsoft Exchange Server or IBM Domino) where the change is committed. Simultaneously, the data will then be sent to the SAP CRM server during the next synchronization run. When the data is committed in the SAP CRM server, it sends back the status and any changes to the cGWI client. The client would then repeat this update to the Groupware server if required.

The entire flow is shown in Figure 14.2. For each Groupware client, the sequence we described occurs when a change is made on the client.

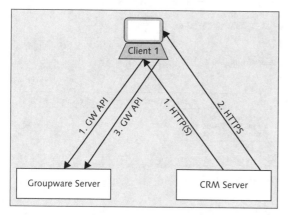

Figure 14.2   Client-Based Groupware Integration Architecture Data Flow

14.3   Configuring Client-based Groupware Integration

The cGWI solution consists of one part on the server and one part on the client side. We will explain how you can put client-server integration to work, starting with backend configuration, followed by installation on the client, and ending with configuration to your specific needs. We will first show how you can prepare the SAP CRM server and check whether it is configured to allow Groupware synchronization. We will then describe how the synchronization behavior can be governed and controlled by customizing settings on the SAP CRM. The behavior of Groupware can be controlled extensively, apart from the customizing settings, and we will describe another powerful way of doing this: using profiles.

14.3.1   Preparing the SAP CRM Server

Before installation, you need to make settings in the SAP CRM backend. In Transaction SMICM, you can configure the settings required. Because most of the infrastructure used by Groupware is used by other components as well, your SAP CRM server probably will already be configured largely for Groupware. First, you should check whether the HTTPS port for secure communication between the clients and the SAP CRM server is enabled. The server name and port number can be identified here and used to set which server the clients will communicate to, as shown in Figure 14.3 and Figure 14.4.

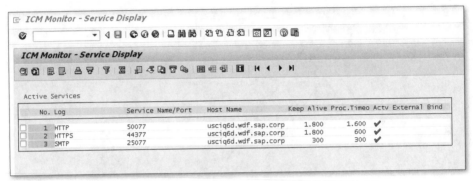

Figure 14.3 Port Settings for Use in cGWI Setup

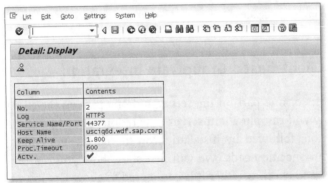

Figure 14.4 Server Host Name for Use in cGWI Setup

Next, you need to ensure that the service for synchronization is running on the SAP CRM server. The service that takes care of synchronization is *CRM_ACT_GWSYNC*. The status of the service can be checked in Transaction SICF, and you can activate it if required. The status of the service is shown in Figure 14.5.

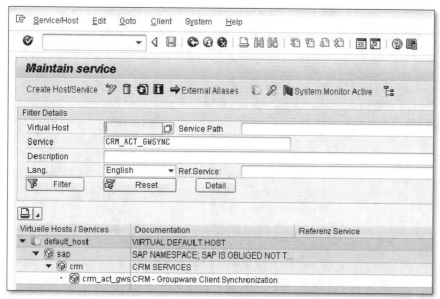

Figure 14.5 Checking Synchronization Service Status for cGWI

In this case, the server URL for communication would be *usai2q6d.wdf.sap. corp:44377.*

14.3.2 Synchronization Behavior

We can control the behavior and the results of a synchronization by a few customizations that cGWI supports. With these options (described in Table 14.1), you can define behavior on the SAP CRM server for events including contact creation, account creation, address creation, appointment types, and text types. This customization is accessible through Transaction SPRO.

Property	Description
BLOCK_CONT_NEW_(SPECIFIED BUSINESS ROLE)	This blocks creation of new contacts. This also blocks the associated actions of creating a new account and adding a new address to an existing account.
BLOCK_ACNT_NEW_(SPECIFIED BUSINESS ROLE)	This blocks creation of all new accounts.

Table 14.1 Possible Customization to Change Behavior of Groupware

Property	Description
BLOCK_ACNT_ADDR_NEW_ (SPECIFIED BUSINESS ROLE)	This blocks creation of a new address for an existing account.
BLOCK_CONT_WO_ACNT_RELN_ (SPECIFIED BUSINESS ROLE) used with BLOCK_ACNT_NEW_ (SPECIFIED BUSINESS ROLE)	This blocks creation of contacts with personal information (private address and communication details) when account creation is disabled.
DEFAULT_APPT_PROC_TYPE	Defines the process type for an appointment that is created in Microsoft Outlook. In the SAP CRM server, SAP CRM categorized appointments (from Outlook) will be created with this process type.
DEFAULT_TASK_PROC_TYPE	Defines the process type for a task that is created in Microsoft Outlook. In the SAP CRM server, SAP CRM categorized tasks (from Outlook) will be created with this process type.
DEFAULT_APPT_TEXTTYPE	Defines the text type of an appointment text (body) created in Microsoft Outlook. In the SAP CRM server, SAP CRM categorized appointment text (from Outlook) will be put as the defined text type in the Note section.
DEFAULT_CONT_TEXTTYPE	Defines the text type of contact text (body) created in Microsoft Outlook. In the SAP CRM server, SAP CRM categorized contact text (from Outlook) will be put as the defined text type in the Note section.
DEFAULT_TASK_TEXTTYPE	Defines the text type of task text (body) created in Microsoft Outlook. In the SAP CRM server, SAP CRM categorized task text will be put as the defined text type in the Note section.
DEFAULT_TASK_CANCELLED	Defines the status of the task maintained in Microsoft Outlook. This task status refers to the deferred state in Microsoft Outlook. In the SAP CRM server, SAP CRM categorized tasks that are deferred'(in Outlook) will be set to the value that is defined in the task mapping.
DEFAULT_TASK_COMPLETED	Defines the status of the task maintained in Microsoft Outlook. This task status refers to the completed state in Microsoft Outlook. In the SAP CRM server, completed tasks (in Microsoft Outlook) that are categorized for SAP CRM will be set to the value that is defined in the task mapping.

Table 14.1 Possible Customization to Change Behavior of Groupware (Cont.)

Property	Description
DEFAULT_TASK_INPROCESS	Defines the status of the task maintained in Microsoft Outlook. This task status refers to the in-progress state in Microsoft Outlook. In the SAP CRM server, SAP CRM categorized tasks that are in progress (in Outlook) will be set to the value that is defined in the mapping.
DEFAULT_TASK_OPEN	Defines the status of the task maintained in Microsoft Outlook. This task status refers to the not-started state in Microsoft Outlook. In the SAP CRM server, SAP CRM categorized tasks that are not started (in Outlook) will be set to the value that is defined in the mapping.
MAX_SEARCH_HITS_ACCOUNT	Defines the number of search items for an account to be displayed in RELATE TO CRM search results.
MAX_SEARCH_HITS_CONTACT	Defines the number of search items for a contact to be displayed in RELATE TO CRM search results.
MAX_SEARCH_HITS_EMPLOYEE	Defines the number of search items for an employee to be displayed in RELATE TO CRM search results.
MAX_SEARCH_HITS_REFDOC	Defines the number of search items for a reference document to be displayed in RELATE TO CRM search results.
REL_NAME_MY_ACCOUNTS	Defines the relationship category of employee responsible for accounts.
REL_NAME_MY_CONTACTS	Defines the relationship category of employee responsible for contact.

Table 14.1 Possible Customization to Change Behavior of Groupware (Cont.)

14.4   Synchronization Profiles

Starting with SAP CRM 7.0EhP1, you can create synchronization profiles for use with cGWI. A profile is a collection of settings used by the client-side component of cGWI that control its behavior. Because the client-side component has to be deployed to users and certain groups of users would use the synchronization to meet similar needs, it makes sense to have their settings bundled and sent to them. With profiles, this can be achieved easily. In SAP CRM, you can create multiple profiles, each one suited to a particular combination of roles, country, and language. When a user tries to synchronize for the first time from the SAP CRM WebClient UI, the profile is downloaded automatically, based on which role, country, and language match the logged-on user's details on the SAP CRM server. Deployments to groups of users can easily be controlled. Table 14.2 shows the parameters present in the profile and how they affect the behavior.

Property	Description
AccountSearchResults	Default value should be empty. The value pair I can get the default value from User Field XML.
AdditionalCheckfor ModifiedMicrosoft OutlookItem	To be removed.
AlwaysShowConflict	If the value is 1, any conflict or confirmation will be shown in a pop-up message in the conflict-resolution screen. This value corresponds to the UI field ALWAYS SHOW CONFIRMATION/CONFLICT RESOLUTION WINDOW in THE CONFLICTS AND CONFIRMATION tab in the synchronization settings screen.
ApptAttachment	▶ Appointment with attachment: Enable attachments sync for appointments. ▶ Without attachment: Disable attachment sync for appointments. To enable attachment sync for appointments, attachment sync should be enabled.
ApptSyncEnable	▶ True: Appointment synchronization enabled. ▶ False: Appointment synchronization disabled.
AutoSyncConflictOption	▶ 0: False ▶ 1: True Auto sync will use the manual sync conflict options.
CertificateOrIssuerName	Certificate name or issuer name, which will be used to filter certificate from certificate store when single sign-on is enabled.

Table 14.2 Profile Parameters Governing Synchronization Behavior in Groupware

Property	Description
Change	Any change/edit/modification related to appointments/tasks/contacts. ▸ True: Any change/update will appear in the confirmation screen. ▸ False: Any change/update will not appear in the confirmation screen. The default action will be taken.
CollectCertificateBy	States the process which should be used to collect certificate from certificate store: ▸ Subject name ▸ Issuer name ▸ Windows authentication ▸ Serial number ▸ Browse from path
Conflict	▸ SAP CRM has priority ▸ Open conflict resolution ▸ GWI has priority
ConflictAutoSync	If AUTOSYNCCONFLICTOPTION is false, the CONFLICTAUTOSYNC will take priority.
ContactAttachment	▸ Contact with attachment: Enable attachment sync for contacts. ▸ Without attachment: Disable attachment sync for contacts. ▸ To enable attachment sync for Contacts, contacts sync should be enabled.
ContactSearchResults	Default value should be empty. The value pair I can get the default value from user field XML.
ContactSyncEnable	▸ True: Contact synchronization enabled. ▸ False: Contact synchronization disabled.

Table 14.2 Profile Parameters Governing Synchronization Behavior in Groupware (Cont.)

Property	Description
CreateNew	Any new creation of appointments/tasks/contacts. ▶ True: Any new creation will appear in the confirmation screen. ▶ False: Any new creation will not appear in the confirmation screen. The default action will be taken.
CRMClient	SAP CRM server client number.
CRMServer	SAP CRM server for an active profile that is a concatenated string of <server_name>:<port number>.
Delete	Any deletion related to appointments/tasks/contacts. ▶ True: Any deletion will appear in the confirmation screen. ▶ False: Any deletion will not appear in the confirmation screen. The default action will be taken.
DeleteRemainingAccounts	Delete account on deletion of contacts when no other contacts exist.
DownloadContactsFromCRM	▶ Owned contacts: Bring down contacts for which the logged-in SAP CRM user is a responsible employee. ▶ Contacts of account: Bring down contacts assigned to the account team to which the logged-in SAP CRM user belongs. ▶ Both: Enables both owned contacts and contacts of account synchronization.
EmployeeSearchResults	Default value should be empty. The value pair I can get it from user field XML.
EnableAutoSync	▶ True: Enable auto synchronization feature. ▶ False: Disable auto synchronization feature.
EnableLog	▶ 1: Enables log files creation for Client GWI. ▶ 0: No log files are created for Client GWI. Log files are created in a default location: i.e., *%userprofile%\Local Settings\Application Data\SAP AG\ Client Groupware*

Table 14.2 Profile Parameters Governing Synchronization Behavior in Groupware (Cont.)

Property	Description
EnableSSOAuthentication	▶ True: Enable single sign-on feature. ▶ False: Disable single sign-on feature.
FormFolder	To be removed.
From	▶ csyncDays = 1 ▶ csyncWeeks = 2 ▶ csyncMonths = 3
IdleInterval	Idle time.
LastDays	A numeric value. This value depends on the FROM parameter, so we define the LastDays value as "2" and FROM as "Weeks"; then the sync will cover the previous two weeks.
LogonSyncEnable	If enabled, auto synchronization should be done when logging on to the system.
MaxNoOfContactToBeSynced	Maximum number of contacts to be synchronized in a single request. This is used during mass synchronization of contacts to avoid time-out errors.
NextDays	A numeric value. This value depends on the To parameter, so we define the NEXTDAYS value as "2" and To as "Weeks"; then the sync will cover the next two weeks.
OnConflict	Conflict resolution options: If SAP CRM or Microsoft Outlook has priority, or the conflict resolution screen is open, the value will be 1 for OTHER CALENDAR (Microsoft Outlook or Lotus Notes), 2 for OPEN CONFLICT, or 3 for SAP CRM.
PrivateHandlingCRM	▶ Ignore: Ignore all the private appointments/tasks from SAP CRM. ▶ Synchronize: Consider private appointments/tasks from SAP CRM. ▶ Synchronize as normal: Private appointments/tasks will be synchronized as normal appointments/tasks to Groupware. ▶ Synchronize frame only: Only the basic information is synchronized.

Table 14.2 Profile Parameters Governing Synchronization Behavior in Groupware (Cont.)

Property	Description
PrivateHandlingGroupware	▶ Ignore: Ignore all the private appointments/tasks from Groupware. ▶ Synchronize: Consider private appointments/tasks from Groupware. ▶ Synchronize as normal: Private appointments/tasks will be synchronized as normal appointments/tasks to SAP CRM. ▶ Synchronize frame only: Only the basic information is synchronized.
ReferenceDocSearchResults	Default value should be empty. The value pair I can get it from user field XML
Reminder	When appointments are synchronized from SAP CRM to Groupware, the reminder value is set by default to the value defined for this parameter.
Savepword	To be removed.
ShowErrorMessage	▶ True: Error message window will be populated with error details. ▶ False: No error message window.
ShowSyncResult	▶ True: Shows synchronization result when it's completed. ▶ False: No synchronization result window.
SyncAtComputerIdle	Auto synchronize if this is enabled when the computer is idle. Works along with IdleInterval value.
SyncAtInterval	If enabled, auto synchronize will be enabled after every interval as defined in SYNCINTERVAL value.
SyncDirecAppointment	▶ SAP CRM to GW: Synchronize appointments only from SAP CRM to GW. ▶ GW to SAP CRM: Synchronize appointments only from GW to SAP CRM. ▶ Both: Synchronize appointments from both SAP CRM to GW.

Table 14.2 Profile Parameters Governing Synchronization Behavior in Groupware (Cont.)

Property	Description
SyncDirecContact	► SAP CRM to GW: Synchronize contacts only from SAP CRM to GW. ► GW to SAP CRM: Synchronize contacts only from GW to SAP CRM. ► Both: Synchronize contacts from both SAP CRM to GW.
SyncDirecTask	► SAP CRM to GW: Synchronize tasks only from SAP CRM to GW. ► GW to SAP CRM: Synchronize tasks only from GW to SAP CRM. ► Both: Synchronize tasks from both SAP CRM to GW.
SyncInterval	This is the numeric value and should always be more than 5.
SyncIntervalUnit	Minutes or hours.
SyncOnDays	Which day of the week (Monday/Tuesday/Wednesday).
TaskAttachment	► Task with attachment: Enable attachments sync for tasks. ► Without attachment: Disable attachment sync for tasks. To enable attachment sync for tasks, tasks sync should be enabled.
TaskSyncEnable	► True: Task synchronization enabled. ► False: Task synchronization disabled.
TimeZone	Select the required time zone from the list.
To	► csyncDays = 1 ► csyncWeeks = 2 ► csyncMonths = 3

Table 14.2 Profile Parameters Governing Synchronization Behavior in Groupware (Cont.)

The profiles maintained on the server can be seen and edited in Transaction GWIPROFILE.

14.5 Installing cGWI on a Client Machine

Once the SAP CRM server is configured and the profile is maintained, you can install the cGWI client component on a system. The installation is simple and can be done by logging into SAP CRM WebClient UI and going to the PERSONALIZATION section on the home screen, as shown in Figure 14.6. Keep in mind that the current installation requires administrative rights on the client machine to run successfully. This is because of the way the plug-in is integrated with Microsoft Outlook.

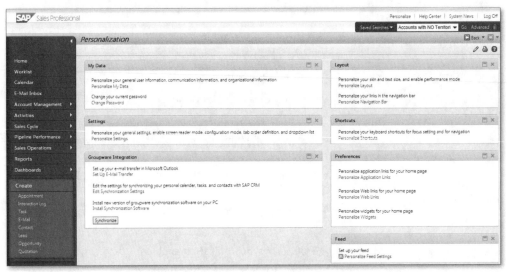

Figure 14.6 Install Client-Based Groupware from SAP CRM WebClient UI

Once the installation is complete, you can launch your mail client (either Microsoft Outlook or IBM Lotus Notes) and check whether the solution is working properly (Figure 14.7 and Figure 14.8).

Before you can begin to use cGWI, you need to download the profile that matches your user identity on the SAP CRM system. You can do this from the same screen in SAP CRM WebClient UI where you just installed the component. One this is done, you will be ready to start working with Client-based Groupware Integration.

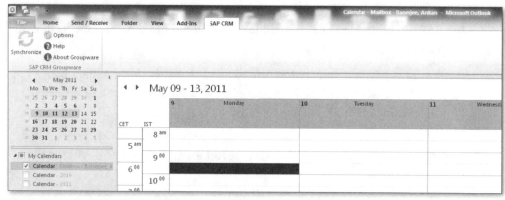

Figure 14.7 Client-based Groupware Add-in in Microsoft Outlook after Installation

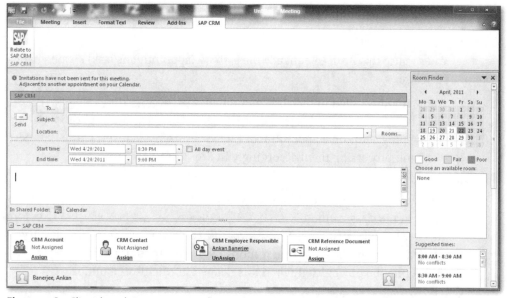

Figure 14.8 Client-based Groupware Interface in the Microsoft Outlook Appointment Screen Showing SAP CRM References

14.6 Extending the Functionality Offered by cGWI

Now that Client-based Groupware Integration is up and running, we can extend cGWI's functionality. Even though cGWI is already a flexible and quick way of offering users collaborative features, there are ways to expand its standard functioning. SAP recently added business add-in (BAdI) support to the component, allowing us to accomplish certain tasks.

Within the BAdI implementation, you will have access to the object being synchronized. The object will be represented as an XML document and we can parse it using existing methods and create our logic.

14.6.1 Extending Activity Transfer between SAP CRM and Microsoft Outlook

The BAdI CRM_GWI_ACTIVITY_REQUEST allows for extensions in the transfer between SAP CRM and Microsoft Outlook for Activities.

The methods used in the BAdI are:

▶ MODIFY_ACTIVITY_REQ
You can use this BAdI to enhance the activity (appointment/task) create/change structure.

The method is called in the class method CL_CRM_XML_GW_SYNC->SET_WRITE_REQ_DATA, before an activity is created or changed. One possible application would be mapping additional appointment categories from Microsoft Outlook to SAP CRM and processing them accordingly in SAP CRM.

▶ DELETE_ACTIVITY_REQ
You can use this BAdI to block activity deletion in SAP CRM. The method is called in the class method CL_CRM_XML_GW_SYNC->GET_WRITE_REQ_DATA, before an activity is deleted from SAP CRM. You could do this, for example, if you wanted to delete the employee responsible for an appointment or task instead of deleting the object itself when it is deleted in Microsoft Outlook.

▶ MODIFY_ACTIVITY_REPLY_REQ
You can use this BAdI to modify the reply XML activity data sent from SAP CRM to Microsoft Outlook. The method is called in the class method CL_CRM_XML_GW_SYNC->SET_REPLY_DATA_ITEM. One possible use would be sending SAP CRM category information to Microsoft Outlook.

You can create an implementation for this BAdI and implement the methods of the interface IF_BADI_CRM_GWI_ACTIVITY_REQ. Be aware that no implementation for the BAdIs is delivered and no fallback class is executed by default.

To modify the activity data before replication, you can read the required child tags of the node and process it accordingly in BAdI implementations. The parameter IV_NODE/CV_NODE contains the current reference of the request XML. The following code snippets show how you can use the data being exchanged and process it.

To read child node from IV_NODE:

```
lv_node_list = iv_node->get_children( ).
WHILE lv_index < lv_node_list->get_length( ).
lv_child = lv_node_list->get_item( lv_index ).
lv_name = lv_child->get_name( ).
lv_value = lv_child->get_value( ).
CASE lv_name.
WHEN 'CATEGORY'.
<...>
ENDCASE.
lv_index = lv_index + 1.
ENDWHILE.
```

Listing 14.1 Reading Activity Data Child Note in BAdI

To set reply data to the child node of CV_NODE:

```
lv_node_list = cv_node->get_children( ).
WHILE lv_index < lv_node_list->get_length( ).
lv_child = lv_node_list->get_item( lv_index ).
lv_name = lv_child->get_name( ).
TRANSLATE lv_name TO UPPER CASE.
CASE lv_name.
WHEN 'STARTDATE'.
lv_value_new = lv_startdate.
lv_rval = lv_child->set_value( lv_value_new ).
WHEN 'CATEGORY'.
<....>
ENDCASE.
lv_index = lv_index + 1.
ENDWHILE.
```

Listing 14.2 Writing Activity Data Child Node in BAdI

14.6.2 Extending Contact Transfer between SAP CRM and Microsoft Outlook

The BAdI `CRM_GWI_CONTACT_REQUEST` allows for extensions in the transfer between CRM and Microsoft Outlook for contacts.

The methods used in the BAdI are:

▶ `CREATE_CONTACT_FIELD_CHECK`
You can use this method to change or validate the contact data and generate an error message in case of a faulty entry.

This BAdI is called in class method `CL_CRM_XML_GW_SYNC->IF_CONTACTS~CREATE_CONTACT` before the contact creation. One possible use is checking the consistency of data, the existence of required entry fields, or the compliance with the check tables.

▶ `DELETE_CONTACT_REQ`
You can use this method to block contact deletion in SAP CRM when a contact is deleted in Microsoft Outlook.

This BAdI is called in class method `CL_CRM_XML_GW_SYNC->IF_CONTACTS~DELETE_CONTACT`. In a standard scenario, when a contact is deleted in Microsoft Outlook, the contact would be marked on synchronization for archiving in SAP CRM. There are several reasons why you might want the contact to be deleted just from Microsoft Outlook and remain as-is in SAP CRM, and you can use this method to do that.

You can create an implementation for this BAdI and implement the methods of the interface IF_BADI_CRM_GWI_CONTACT_REQ. You should note here that no implementation for the BAdIs is delivered and no fallback class is executed by default.

If the result of a check in your BAdI implementation is negative, you can display the error message and block subsequent processes in the synchronization flow.

In case of a negative result, update the changing parameter `CT_RETURN` with an error message (message type `E`).

14.7 Summary

You now are familiar with most of the functionality offered by the Client-based Groupware Integration and understand how to start using it. This functionality allows customers to maintain and synchronize accounts, contacts, tasks and appointment between the Groupware and SAP CRM systems.

We covered the overall architecture of the Groupware integration and showed how to configure it. We showed you not only how to set properties and profiles, but also how to install cGWI on the client machine.

Last but not least, you should also be able to extend some of the functionality by using dedicated BAdIs provided by SAP. Since cGWI is a client component, it undergoes changes more frequently than some other components. The following SAP Notes provide additional valuable information:

▶ Note 1555348 gives details on the functional documentation along with tips on customizing cGWI to your needs.

▶ Note 1549890 has links to the latest versions of the client component of cGWI across all SAP CRM releases from CRM 2007 onwards.

▶ Note 1499833 provides details on BAdIs provided by SAP for cGWI and any new extensibility concepts.

In the next chapter, we conclude our discussion of SAP Web Client with an overview of some lesser-known features and concepts from the Web Client UI framework.

You never use the full potential of a framework in a single project; there are always features left to be discovered later. In this chapter, we address some of these features.

15 Additional Topics

In the following sections, we will present lesser-known features and concepts from the Web Client UI framework. Even though "Additional Topics" sounds like a safe and conservative chapter heading, there is nothing ordinary about the contents of this chapter, Most of the features have been either recently introduced or recently enhanced by SAP. Moreover, we have sections on tips and tricks that we could not fit in our previous examples.

Some of the topics—for example session handling and security—would come in handy in almost any projects you are working on. Others—such as action on fields and task-based UI—will be used in specific situations. No matter how they are used, we will try to provide you with sufficient code listings and displays to help you understand how to use the features. We believe that by now you know enough to skip some of the basic steps.

With the above disclaimer, we can plunge into these last but by no means least pieces of the Web Client UI Framework.

15.1 Task-based UI

Imagine that your users need to enter a large quantity of data that has to be handled as part of a business transaction. The users need to populate many different fields, and select options and checkboxes. Moreover, they need to do so in a particular sequence as there are dependencies between the input fields. If you present the users with one giant page with many blocks and fields to fill, they might be quite confused. Therefore, the best practice is to break such a complex screen into smaller and digestible pages. The user fills one page with related data and then moves to the next page until he reaches the last step to commit the transaction. This interaction pattern is called a *guided activity* or *task-based UI*.

The task-based user interface consists of a series of screens that guides the user through an activity to achieve a specific goal in order to simplify a complex task by breaking it into steps. The Web Client UI provides the visualization of these steps in the so-called *guided activity roadmap*. The roadmap comes with buttons that allow users to navigate between the steps, for example NEXT and PREVIOUS. As of SAP CRM 7.0 EhP1, it is possible to integrate existing guided activities and visualize them as sub-steps (see Figure 15.1).

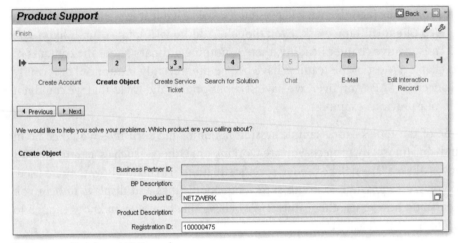

Figure 15.1 Task-based UI Example

We will expand our hotel guest booking scenario in the direction of guided activities. We will create a new application, where users will be able to create new booking records in three steps.

In the first step, the user will provide basic booking data: guest ID, hotel name, and check in date. In Step 2, we will use this data to create a new booking BOL entity and let the end user enter the rest of the booking information (room, stay length, membership, etc). The last step will provide an overview of the entered data and will allow the user to confirm and commit the new booking.

15.1.1 Creating a Guided Activity Page

The framework achieves the task-based UI functionality by providing dedicated runtime infrastructure, APIs, and even a special type of UI elements. A dedicated wizard is integrated with the Component Workbench and facilitates the creation of a view called *guided activity page*. The guided activity page serves as a container that encompasses the task-based UI steps. It is configurable and allows users to assign views (steps), control their sequence, and set title and explanatory text for the steps. The guided activity page derives from the super class CL_BSP_WD_GEN_ROADMAP_VS. In essence it is a specialized view set. For our example, we need to create a new UI component called ZBOOK_TB and add a new guided activity page to it (see Figure 15.2).

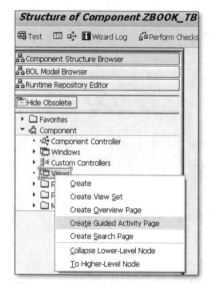

Figure 15.2 Creating Guided Activity Page

If you activate the CONFIGURATION tab of this view set, you will not find any views that you can use. There are three types of elements that you can add into a guided activity page:

▶ Views (steps) from the runtime repository that are assigned to the guided activity view set (local views and component usages)

▶ Reusable views (steps) that are made globally available to all components via customizing (in the so called *view steps repository*)

▶ Reusable guided activity pages that are available to all components in accordance with the customizing in the so-called *guided activity page repository*.

In our example, we will create two local views and one reusable view and assign them to our guided activity page. We will leave the reusable guided activity pages for you to experiment with. As you might have guessed, they are visualized as sub-steps in the task-based UI.

15.1.2   Reusable Guided Activity Page

Let us create another component ZBOOK_TB2. It will have only one view, called CREATE. We will add to it a value node modeled according to the create attribute structure of our Bookings GenIL business object (see Figure 15.3).

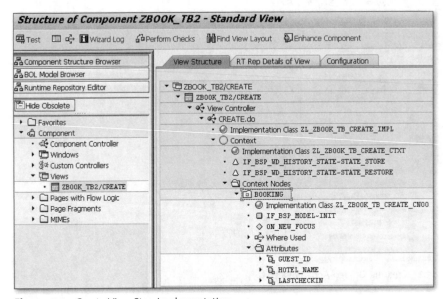

Figure 15.3   Create View Step Implementation

The step view controller class implements two interfaces: IF_BSP_DLC_PROCESS_STEP and IF_BSP_DLC_TBUI. The first interface is used from the task-based UI runtime to check if a given step is in a valid state. IF_BSP_DLC_PROCESS_STEP~IS_COMPLETE is called to determine if the current step is completed. IF_BSP_DLC_PROCESS_STEP~IS_POSSIBLE_TO_LEAVE will be used to determine if the user can navigate to the next page. In our example, we will rely on the implementation of IS_POSSIBLE_TO_LEAVE and call it from our IS_COMPLETE method. Listing 15.1 shows the result.

```
DATA: lr_prop          TYPE REF TO if_bol_bo_property_access,
      lv_guest         TYPE string,
      lv_hotel         TYPE string,
      lv_date          TYPE string.

rv_result = abap_false.
lr_prop = typed_context->BOOKING->collection_wrapper->get_first( ).

IF lr_prop IS BOUND.
  lv_guest = lr_prop->get_property_as_string( 'GUEST_ID' ).
  lv_hotel = lr_prop->get_property_as_string( 'HOTEL_NAME' ).
  lv_date = lr_prop->get_property_as_string( 'LASTCHECKIN' ).
  "check for the mandatory fields
  IF lv_guest is not initial
        AND lv_hotel is not initial
        AND lv_date is not initial.
    rv_result = abap_true.
  ENDIF.
ENDIF.

IF rv_result = abap_false.
  data: LV_MSG_SRV type ref to CL_BSP_WD_MESSAGE_SERVICE.
  LV_MSG_SRV = ME->VIEW_MANAGER->GET_MESSAGE_SERVICE( ).
  LV_MSG_SRV->ADD_MESSAGE( IV_MSG_ID = 'ZBOOK_MSG'
                           IV_MSG_NUMBER = '004'
                           IV_MSG_TYPE = 'E' ).
ENDIF.
```

Listing 15.1 IS_POSSIBLE_TO_LEAVE Implementation in the CREATE View

In our implementation, we require that the GUEST, HOTEL, and CHECKIN fields are mandatory. If one of these field values is missing, we will issue an error message. As mentioned, our IS_COMPLETE calls IS_POSSIBLE_TO_LEAVE implementation. Hence we ensure that the above check is executed there as well.

The IF_BSP_DLC_TBUI interface is more interesting. It enables us to integrate application data into the *shared data context*. This concept allows us to store and retrieve data between steps that are not related via data binding. This is fundamental for enabling the task-based UI to work with reusable views. As you can see from our implementation of WRITE_DATA_CONTEXT in Listing 15.2, the principles of data sharing are quite simple.

```
data: ls_key type ZBOL_BOOKINGS_KEY,
      lr_entity type ref to IF_BOL_BO_PROPERTY_ACCESS.
lr_entity = TYPED_CONTEXT->BOOKING->GET_COLLECTION_WRAPPER( )->GET_
FIRST( ).
check LR_ENTITY is bound.
"get the key attributes
lr_entity->GET_PROPERTIES( importing ES_ATTRIBUTES = ls_key ).
"store the keys in the global context
ir_data_context->set_data_context( iv_viewid = ''
                                   iv_name = 'BOOKING_KEY'
                                   iv_value = ls_key ).
```

Listing 15.2 WRITE_DATA_CONTEXT Implementation for CREATE View

One sets a parameter into the context by assigning it a name and passing the name of the view it should be associated with. How you use these two parameters is up to you. For example, we are not associating the BOOKING_KEY parameter with a specific view as we want to share it among many views. The value is of type ANY, and in our example we pass the obtained create structure attributes. The important thing here is that the parameter names be registered in CUSTOMER RELATIONSHIP MANAGEMENT • UI FRAMEWORK • UI FRAMEWORK DEFINITION • GUIDED ACTIVITY PAGE • DEFINE PARAMETERS FOR SHARED DATA CONTAINER (see Figure 15.4).

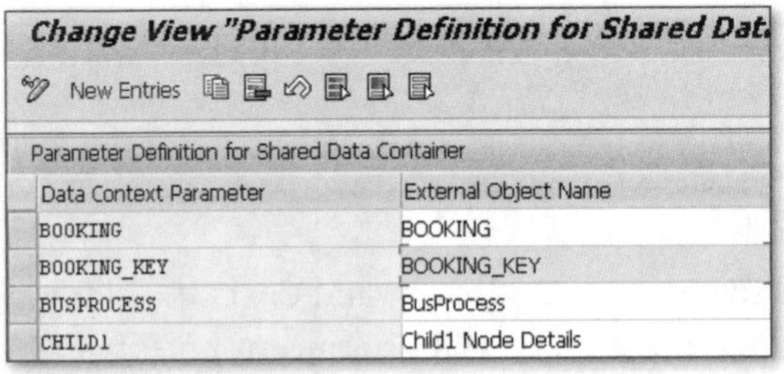

Change View "Parameter Definition for Shared Dat.	
New Entries 🗐 🗎 🗇 📑 📑 📑	
Parameter Definition for Shared Data Container	
Data Context Parameter	External Object Name
BOOKING	BOOKING
BOOKING_KEY	BOOKING_KEY
BUSPROCESS	BusProcess
CHILD1	Child1 Node Details

Figure 15.4 Registering Shared Data Context Parameter

Listing 15.3 shows our READ_DATA_CONTEXT method. We try to fetch a structure from the data context that is stored in parameter BOOKING_KEY. If we find one, we set it to the BOOKING context node.

```
DATA: lr_prop    TYPE REF TO if_bol_bo_property_access,
      lv_guest   TYPE string,
```

```
        ls_key      TYPE ZBOL_BOOKINGS_KEY,
        lr_key      TYPE REF TO ZBOL_BOOKINGS_KEY,
        lr_booking  TYPE REF TO CL_BSP_WD_VALUE_NODE,
        lr_coll     TYPE REF TO if_bol_bo_col.

  TRY.
      ir_data_context->get_data_context(
EXPORTING IV_VIEWID = ''
                   iv_name = 'BOOKING_KEY'
                   iv_free = abap_true
          IMPORTING ev_value = ls_key ).
    CATCH cx_root.
  ENDTRY.

  IF ls_key IS not initial.
    lr_key->* = ls_key.
    create object lr_booking type CL_BSP_WD_VALUE_NODE
          EXPORTING iv_data_ref = lr_key.
    lr_booking->SET_PROPERTIES( ls_key ).
    "clean collection and restore booking
    typed_context->BOOKING->GET_COLLECTION_WRAPPER( )->CLEAR_
COLLECTION( ).
    typed_context->BOOKING->GET_COLLECTION_WRAPPER( )->ADD( lr_booking
).
  ENDIF.
```

Listing 15.3 READ_DATA_CONTEXT Implementation in CREATE View

In order to make one view reusable with respect to guided activities, you need to register it in customizing via the menu path CUSTOMER RELATIONSHIP MANAGEMENT • UI FRAMEWORK • UI FRAMEWORK DEFINITION • GUIDED ACTIVITY PAGE • DEFINE REUSABLE STEP VIEWS. Figure 15.5 shows the entry related to ZBOOK_TB2/CREATE.

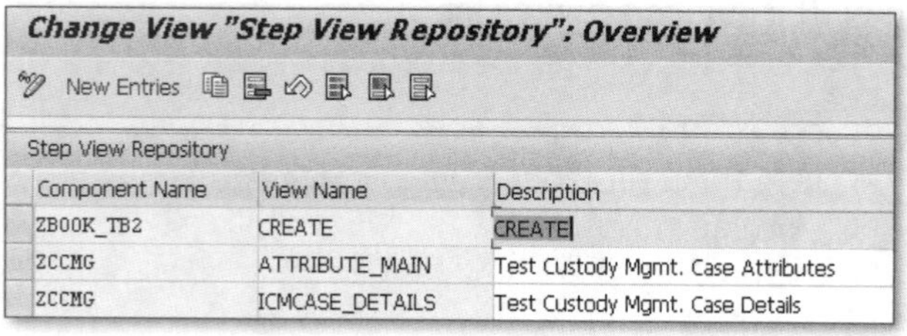

Figure 15.5 Registering Reusable View

Next we will go back into the component where we wanted to create our guided activity page, namely ZBOOK_TB. Let us create two more views: BOOKING and OVERVIEW. The first one will work with the Bookings GeniL business object (Figure 15.6). It will implement both IF_BSP_DLC_TBUI and IF_BSP_DLC_PROCESS_STEP interfaces.

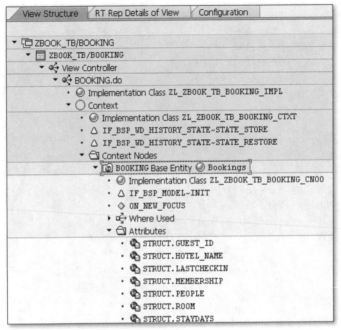

Figure 15.6 BOOKING Step View

The implementation of IF_BSP_DLC_PROCESS_STEP is analogous to that of ZBOOK_TB2\ CREATE. As you can see in Listing 15.4, we ensure that the guest ID, hotel, and check-in date contain values. If not, we ensure that the system sends an error message. The framework provides access to the message service and makes sure that your messages are displayed by the guided activity step.

```
DATA: lv_name        TYPE        string,
      lr_coll        TYPE REF TO if_bol_bo_col,
      lr_prop        TYPE REF TO if_bol_bo_property_access,
      lv_guest       TYPE string,
      lv_hotel       TYPE string,
      lv_date        TYPE string.

rv_result = abap_false.
```

```
lr_coll ?= typed_context->BOOKING->collection_wrapper->get_copy( ).
IF lr_coll IS BOUND.
  lr_prop = lr_coll->get_current( ).
  IF lr_prop IS BOUND.
    lv_guest = lr_prop->get_property_as_string( 'GUEST_ID' ).
    lv_hotel = lr_prop->get_property_as_string( 'HOTEL_NAME').
    lv_date = lr_prop->get_property_as_string( 'LASTCHECKIN').
    "check for the mandatory fields
    IF lv_guest is not initial
        AND lv_hotel is not initial
        AND lv_date is not initial.
      rv_result = abap_true.
    ENDIF.
  ENDIF.
ENDIF.

IF rv_result = abap_false.
  data: LV_MSG_SRV type ref to CL_BSP_WD_MESSAGE_SERVICE.
  LV_MSG_SRV = ME->VIEW_MANAGER->GET_MESSAGE_SERVICE( ).
  LV_MSG_SRV->ADD_MESSAGE( IV_MSG_ID = 'ZBOOK_MSG'
                           IV_MSG_NUMBER = '004'
              IV_MSG_TYPE = 'I' IV_IMPORTANT_INFO = ABAP_TRUE ).
ENDIF.
```
Listing 15.4 IS_POSSIBLE_TO_LEAVE Implementation in Booking View

The write data context method uses the BOOKING parameter that we registered in customizing (Figure 15.4). It simply takes the BOL entity from the context nodes and sets it in the shared data context (container).

```
DATA: lv_name          TYPE      string value 'BOOKING',
      lr_coll          TYPE REF TO if_bol_bo_col.
lr_coll ?= typed_context->BOOKING->collection_wrapper->get_copy( ).
IF lr_coll IS BOUND.
  ir_data_context->set_data_context( iv_viewid = ''
                 iv_name = lv_name iv_value = lr_coll ).
ENDIF.
```
Listing 15.5 WRITE_DATA_CONTEXT Implementation in BOOKING View

In the implementation of the READ_DATA_CONTEXT method, we try to obtain the create attribute structure from the BOOKING_KEY parameter. If successful, we will create a new booking entity and add it into the context node of the view. Remember that the view `ZBOOK_TB2/CREATE` collects basic booking data and pushes it into the shared context for further use.

If we do not find a create structure, we will try to get the `Bookings` entity from the `BOOKING` parameter and set it to the context node (Listing 15.6).

```
DATA: lr_prop     TYPE REF TO if_bol_bo_property_access,
      ls_param type CRMT_NAME_VALUE_PAIR,
      lt_param    TYPE CRMT_NAME_VALUE_PAIR_TAB,
      lr_booking  TYPE REF TO CL_CRM_BOL_ENTITY,
      ls_key      TYPE ZBOL_BOOKINGS_KEY,
      lr_coll     TYPE REF TO if_bol_bo_col.
TRY.
  "get key
  ir_data_context->get_data_context(
EXPORTING IV_VIEWID = '' iv_name = 'BOOKING_KEY'
iv_free = abap_true
      IMPORTING ev_value = ls_key  ).
  IF ls_key-GUEST_ID is not initial.
    "prepare the creation parameters
    ls_param-NAME = 'GUEST_ID'.
    ls_param-VALUE = ls_key-GUEST_ID.
    append ls_param to lt_param.
    ls_param-NAME = 'HOTEL_NAME'.
    ls_param-VALUE = ls_key-HOTEL_NAME.
    append ls_param to lt_param.
    ls_param-NAME = 'LASTCHECKIN'.
    ls_param-VALUE = ls_key-LASTCHECKIN.
    append ls_param to lt_param.
    "obtain Bookings factory
    lr_booking = cl_crm_bol_core=>GET_INSTANCE( )->GET_ENTITY_FACTORY(
'Bookings' )->CREATE( lt_param ).
    create object lr_coll type cl_crm_bol_bo_col.
    lr_coll->ADD( lr_booking ).
    typed_context->BOOKING->set_collection( lr_coll ).
  ELSE.
    "get collection
    ir_data_context->get_data_context(
EXPORTING IV_VIEWID = '' iv_name = 'BOOKING'
               iv_free = abap_true
       IMPORTING ev_value = lr_coll  ).
    IF lr_coll IS BOUND.
      "check if bound
```

```
      lr_prop = lr_coll->get_current( ).
      IF lr_prop IS BOUND.
        "booking restored
        typed_context->BOOKING->set_collection( lr_coll ).
      ENDIF.
    ENDIF.
  ENDIF.
CATCH cx_root.
ENDTRY.
```

Listing 15.6 READ_DATA_CONTEXT Implementation in BOOKING View

If you recall, one can set fields as mandatory via the UI configuration tool. In "normal" views, this is more like a recommendation and will allow users to proceed with their activity even if a mandatory field has no value. The framework simply will issue a warning. However, due to the nature of guided activity, configuring a field as mandatory will enforce this setting and will not allow the user to complete the step. In our example, we will mark the HOTEL ROOM field as mandatory (see Figure 15.7).

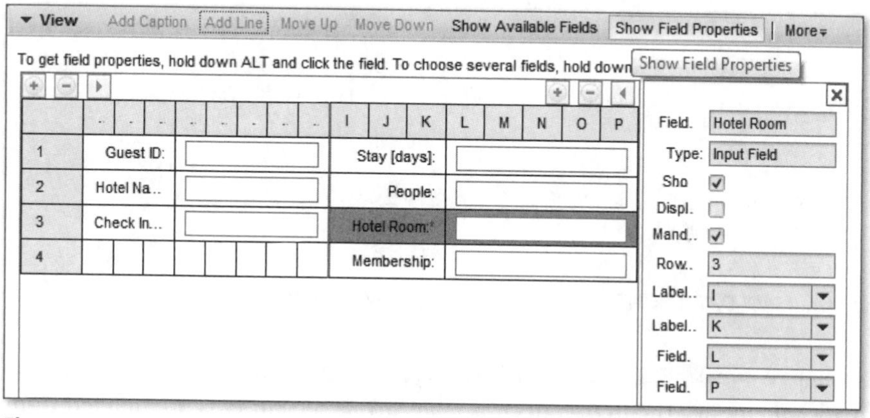

Figure 15.7 UI Configuration of BOOKING Step View

The OVERVIEW step is also based on the Bookings business object. It implements the IF_BSP_DLC_TBUI and IF_BSP_DLC_PROCESS_STEP interfaces. We will not go into details, given that the implementation of the view is analogous to that of the previously discussed views. The only small difference is how we read data from the shared data context (see Listing 15.7). You might have noticed that CL_WCF_DATA_CONTEXT_SRV-> GET_DATA_CONTEXT takes an ABAP_BOOL parameter IV_FREE. When set to

ABAP_TRUE, it will clear the value associated with IV_NAME and IV_VIEWID from the shared context. In the OVERVIEW we will not remove the Bookings entity from the context. We will keep it there by passing ABAP_FALSE to IV_FREE. This will allow us to retrieve the Bookings entity if the user decides to navigate back to the BOOKING step (you can see its GET_DATA_CONTEXT implementation in Listing 15.6).

```
DATA: lr_prop          TYPE REF TO if_bol_bo_property_access,
      lv_name          TYPE string value 'BOOKING',
      lr_coll          TYPE REF TO if_bol_bo_col.

TRY.
    ir_data_context->get_data_context(
EXPORTING IV_VIEWID = '' iv_name = lv_name
                        iv_free = abap_false
          IMPORTING ev_value = lr_coll ).
  CATCH cx_root.
ENDTRY.

IF lr_coll IS BOUND.
  "check if collection empty
  lr_prop = lr_coll->get_current( ).
  IF lr_prop IS BOUND.
    "booking restored
    typed_context->BOOKING->set_collection( lr_coll->get_copy( ) ).
  ENDIF.
ELSE.
 create object lr_coll type cl_crm_bol_bo_col.
 typed_context->BOOKING->set_collection( lr_coll ).
ENDIF.
```
Listing 15.7 READ_DATA_CONTEXT Implementation in OVERVIEW View

To summarize, the OVERVIEW fetches a bookings entity from the context and displays it in read-only mode. The BOL collection that carries the entity is not deleted from the context. In addition, we do not set the original collection to the OVERVIEW's context node. Instead, we create a copy of it by calling the GET_COPY method.

Note that the methods from IF_BSP_DLC_PROCESS_STEP always return ABAP_TRUE. This will ensure that the FINISH button in the OVERVIEW step view is always enabled. It is bound to the ONFINISH event handler in the step view. You could implement your BOL save logic there. But as this is a rather trivial exercise, we will leave it to you to explore.

Now let's go to our guided activity page and open the CONFIGURATION tab. If you have assigned the BOOKING and OVERVIEW views to the view set (our guided activity page), you will see them in the AVAILABLE STEPS VIEW block. You can move them into the STEPS SEQUENCE blocks. However, BOOKING needs a step that will provide the values of the create-attribute structure for the Bookings business object. Such a step view does not exist in our component. However, we can add the reusable step ZBOOK_TB2/CREATE by clicking on the ADD STEP VIEW button. The button next to it, ADD TASK, allows you to add reusable guided activities as sub-steps.

Our final page layout is presented in Figure 15.8. You can rearrange the steps by using the UP and DOWN buttons. Moreover, you can assign explanatory text to steps as part of the guided-activity page configuration.

Figure 15.8 Guided Activity Page Configuration

Once done, click on the TEST button and walk through the application. Be sure to set some breakpoints in your step views and watch how data is passed between steps via the shared data context. If you do not provide a mandatory field, you will get an error message (see Figure 15.9).

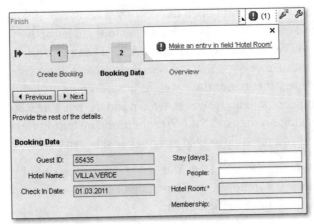

Figure 15.9 Step in the New Guided Activity

Although our application is quite simple, it illustrates the potential of the task-based UI concept and the tools that support it. You can break down complex processes into tangible steps, reuse these steps across different guided activities, and easily change their configurations when needed.

15.2 Field Actions

SAP CRM 7.0 EhP1 delivers new functionality called *action menu*. It allows the system to associate a contextual menu (referred to as an action menu) to a given UI field element (for example, a text area or a disabled input field), and to trigger a custom action when an individual entry in that menu is selected by the user. The menu will be displayed when the user clicks the left mouse button over an icon that signals the existence of the contextual menu. Left-clicking on one of the listed items results in calling the assigned `onclientselect` action and `onselect` server or client events, if assigned. Some of the items could be only text without assigned actions; for example, a presence indicator. Figure 15.10 shows some action menu examples. If you have an Interaction Center (in EhP1) you will find standard implementations of this feature.

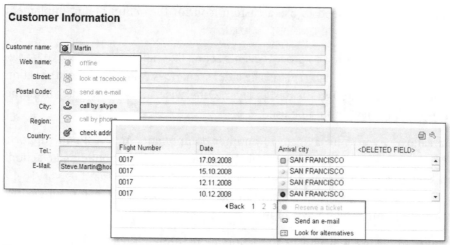

Figure 15.10 Action Menu Examples

There are three ways to implement action menu:

▸ Assign an action menu tag `thtmlb:actionsMenu` to a specific field.

▸ Assign an action menu from configurable page to a field. A special getter method, `GET_AC_<FieldName>`, has to be implemented in the corresponding context node. You can see an example in the Business Role CRM application.

▸ Manage action menus from the design layer (DL). We will discuss this based on an example.

Our example involves the membership type field that we added to the SAP CRM account application. Imagine that we have an external wiki where we store additional information and documents regarding our business process. It would be logical to have a dedicated page with detailed information for each membership type. The business users (agents) want to access these pages straight from the SAP CRM account application. One of the possible solutions is to create an action menu from which the agents open an external wiki page. The exact page URL will be determined dynamically by the system based on the selected membership type.

An action menu is implemented via an action provider class. The easiest way to do this is to create a new class that inherits from `CL_BSP_WD_ACTION_PROVIDER`. The latter implements several interfaces used by the action menu functionality. At the very minimum the `IF_BSP_WD_ACTION_DESCR_EXT~BUILD_ACTIONS` method will be implemented. It returns a table of all the action items that make up the

action menu. If you need to use a custom icon for the action menu, implement
`IF_BSP_WD_ACTION_DESCR_EXT~BUILD_MENU`.

If the action provider has to process events acting like callbacks you have to implement `CALLBACK_EXT~HANDLE_EVENT`. The latter scenario is valid only when the action menu is assigned through the design layer. Otherwise, an event handler from the corresponding view should be used.

In a callback, you can navigate to another component. Action menu supports dynamic navigation, although it is not always possible. Before building an action, you should check whether it is supported via `cl_crm_ui_navigation_service->is_dynamic_nav_supported`. We saw an example of how to do that when we discussed cross-component navigation.

In our example, we will activate the action menu through the DL. This approach is probably the most powerful one. It makes it possible to assign, activate, or deactivate an action provider to a design object attribute. As a consequence all views where that attribute is used will get the same action menu.

In order to implement the exemplary requirement, we will first create an action provider (derived from `CL_BSP_WD_ACTION_PROVIDER`). We will create a class called `ZCL_AC_GOTO_WIKI` and implement `IF_BSP_WD_ACTION_DESCR_EXT~BUILD_ACTIONS` (see Listing 15.8).

```
DATA: ll_action_item TYPE wcfs_thtmlb_action_menu_item,
      lv_url type string.
concatenate `window.open('http://mywiki.com/`
iv_attribute_value
`','welcome','width=1200,height=800,menubar=yes,status=yes,location=yes
,toolbar=yes,scrollbars=yes');`
      into lv_url.

ll_action_item-id = '1'.
ll_action_item-type = if_bsp_wd_action_descriptor=>gc_type_generic_
action.
ll_action_item-text = 'Goto Wiki'.
ll_action_item-icon_src= cl_thtmlb_util=>get_icon_url( 'w_docu_s.gif'
).
ll_action_item-onclientselect = lv_url.

INSERT ll_action_item INTO TABLE et_actions.
```

Listing 15.8 BUILD_ACTIONS Method Implementation

The code is pretty explanatory. We assign a client-side JS event to `ll_action_item-onclientselect`. All it does is open a new window with the specified URL. The URL is created via string concatenation during which the UI element value is appended to the wiki's base URL (*http://mywiki.com/*). We will assign the action provider to the custom field ZZFLD000003C. This way, the `iv_attribute_value` will deliver the current membership type selection. The solution has some shortcomings but serves our main purpose, which is to demonstrate the concepts.

Once done, we shall save and activate our class. Next, we will follow the customizing menu path CUSTOMER RELATIONSHIP MANAGEMENT • UI FRAMEWORK • UI FRAMEWORK DEFINITION • DESIGN LAYER • DEFINE ACTION PROVIDERS and register our action provider class (see Figure 15.11). Because we will use our action provider with the `BuilHeader` BOL object, we shall specify the REFERENCE OBJECT NAME field accordingly. Later, this information will be used in the design object when determining the connection to the BOL object.

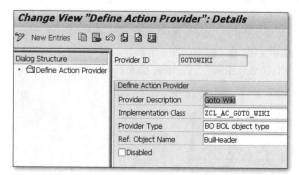

Figure 15.11 Register GOTOWIKI Action Provider

Next, we access the BUSINESSPARTNER design object definition via the menu path CUSTOMER RELATIONSHIP MANAGEMENT • UI FRAMEWORK • UI FRAMEWORK DEFINITION • DESIGN LAYER • DEFINE DESIGN OBJECTS. The GOTOWIKI provider needs to be assigned the membership type field. As you can see on Figure 15.12, the reference object name of the action provider matches the BOL object of the design object.

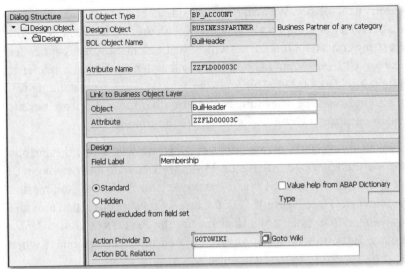

Figure 15.12 Assign Action Provider to Design Object Attribute

Figure 15.13 shows the effect of the above steps on the SAP CRM account application. The standard graphical identifier for the action menu is a grey circle. Clicking on it will bring an action menu that contains one entry, namely the dynamically calculated link to the relevant wiki page.

Figure 15.13 Action Menu for Membership Type Field

If we need to assign an existing action provider to another field we can do so via customizing, without writing code. Moreover, we do not need to implement complex application specific BAdIs nor enhance standard SAP components.

15.3   Flash Islands

Flash Islands (FI) technology lets you incorporate Adobe Flex application into the Web Client UI framework. The framework and Flex components can interact and exchange information. In this section, we will provide you with a quick overview of this feature. This time, we will not provide a concrete example. FI relies on Adobe Flex and is compatible with SAP NetWeaver's Flash Islands. Visit Adobe's Web site for information on the former. SDN has plenty of blogs and tutorials on Adobe Flex with SAP and Flash Islands.

Flash Islands let you create and deploy "best-of-both-world" hybrid Flash-HTML applications where Flash and HTML join forces to deliver interactive content to your users. Figure 15.14 summarizes at a high level what you need to do in order to create a custom Flash Island application. First you need to get a development license for Adobe Flex Builder and install it. You need to understand and apply MXML and ActionScript.

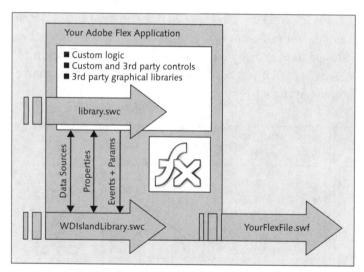

Figure 15.14   Flash Island Overview

In order for an application to be a Web Client UI Flash Island, it has to include the Flash Island library WDIslandLibrary.swc. SAP provides skinning for basic UI controls (for example buttons, checkboxes, input field, label, etc.) via the UI controls library library.swc. You can include it in case you want to use the standard skinning. Next, you need to develop your Adobe Flex application. The integration with Web Client UI framework comes in the form of data and event binding. This way you can pass data between the framework's UI elements and invoke the framework's events from your Flex application. Once you are done, you need to build your Flex application and produce a .SWF file.

Once you have a SWF file, enter the Component Workbench and open the desired component, which could be an enhanced SAP component or a custom one. Add the SWF file to the MIME repository. Next, open the HTM file of a view and define your Flash Island using the Flash Island tag library.

The Flash Island (thtmlbx:flashIsland) tag is a root tag. It creates a special XML document, known as *XBCML*. The latter will be pushed to the Flash Island via a JavaScript function. XBCML is used to define UIs via XML. You can check SDN and your SAP documentation for more details. However, for basic scenarios you do not have to deal with it. The XBCML is created by the root tag and all sub-tags simply insert nodes in the XML document. Applications can have multiple Flash Islands on the same page but they must have distinct IDs.

The data source tag (thtmlbx:flashIslandDataSource) is for binding data to a table or a structure context node. You can point to a context node via a binding string (for example //ContextNode/Table) or by passing the data directly (for example data = "<%= lt_table_entries%>"). If you need only a subset from the data source, you can fill the properties tag attribute.

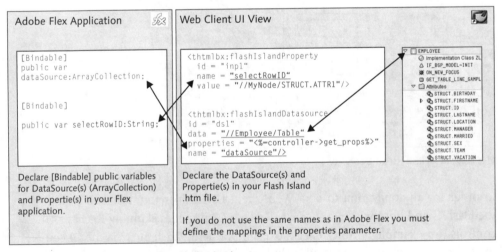

Figure 15.15 Data Binding in Flash Islands

The property (thtmlbx:flashIslandProperty) tag can be used to bind to a specific attribute from a context node. In the case of a model-based context nodes use value = "//MyContextNode/STRUCT.ATTRIBUTE". If you have a value node use // MyContextNode/ATTRIBUTE. You can also use this tag to pass an ABAP variable: value = "<%= myVariable %>.

The event (thtmlbx:flashIslandEvent) tag is used to map events between the Flash Island application and the view controller. Thus you can specify the event handler that shall be called on a specific Flash Island event. Inside the event handler, you can also retrieve event parameters, if provided. To do so, you should cast the htmlb_event_ex into CL_THTMLBX_FI_EVENT and call its GET_PARAM_VALUE method:

```
DATA: lr_fi_event  TYPE REF TO cl_thtmlbx_fi_event,
         lv_id    TYPE string.
*  Cast to FI event type
lr_fi_event ?= htmlb_event_ex.
*  Get an event parameter provided by the FI
lv_id = lr_fi_event->get_param_value( 'ID' ).
```

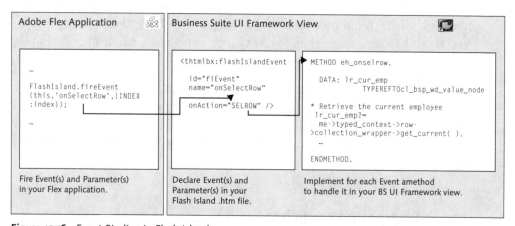

Figure 15.16 Event Binding in Flash Islands

Instead of using the event tag, you can pass a table of events to the EVENTS parameter of the flashIsland root tag. The result will be exactly the same.

The Web Client UI framework provides a user parameter WCF_THTMLBX_FI_DEBUG that one can use in order to debug a FI. Setting this parameter to X will cause the following.

The debug string will be appended to the SWF file name of each FI. For example if your application is called *myApp.swf*, the framework will load myApp-debug.swf. The latter must be in the same MIME folder as the original file. You should have S_DEVELOP rights in order to take advantage of this feature.

With the "–debug" option, the FI trace will be enabled. When you right-click on a Flash Island, you will see in the context menu a new option called COPY SOURCE TO CLIPBOARD. Choosing it will place the produced XBCML file into the clipboard. You can paste it into an editor and examine the results.

Alternatively, one can log into the SAP CRM Web UI with business role UIF. The navigation menu will contain a link called FLEX SANDBOX. One of the TEST APPLICATIONS there is called XBCML VALIDATION. Start it and provide the URL of your SWF file and the XBCML you want to test against. Click the PUSH TO FLASH ISLAND button and observe the results. You can tweak the XBCML as much as you want in the process of your investigation.

The Flash Island tag will prepare two AJAX areas: one for the script and another for the SWF file. This way, your code can perform roundtrips without reloading the Flash movie. You should be careful not to place the flash island in a tajax:area tag. If this happens, then when the AJAX area changes the whole Flash Island tag will be rendered again as part of the round trip.

In summary, Flash Islands are a powerful way to add rich content to your Web applications. They are standard NetWeaver technology and you can reuse them not only across Web Client UI applications but also in Web Dynpro applications (ABAP and Java). However, they require Adobe Flex knowledge and their maintenance might be challenging.

15.4 Transaction Launcher

We saw how you can use the Rapid Application tool to bring content from existing data sources into the Web Client UI. Web mash-ups might help you integrate existing Web resources into the Web UI. However, those of you working in an existing SAP landscape might want to integrate functionalities based on BSP applications, ABAP transactions, or simply display the result of a BOR method using SAP GUI for HTML. For all these scenarios, the Web Client UI provides the *Transaction Launcher*.

The Transaction Launcher helps you integrate external content. However, one should not use it to turn the Web Client UI into some sort of a portal. You should not treat the Transaction Launcher as your main integration tool, and you should use it with care.

We will illustrate the concept with the help of a simple example. Suppose someone in your team has developed a dashboard that brings in content from various social networks and interpolates them against campaign data. The dashboard's specific job is less important than the fact that it feeds directly neither from your local database, nor from your BI systems. As a result it does not make sense to integrate the dashboard in a standard way; for example, by deploying it in a BW system and using SAP CRM report assignments to incorporate it into the Web UI. All you need is contained in a SWF file, and one can visualize it via a simple HTML page.

The requirement is to incorporate SAP BusinessObjects Dashboard Design (formerly known as Xcelsius) into the Web UI. We decided to show you how to do so via the Transaction Launcher. First, we will create a BSP application. The dashboard belongs to the MIME repository. A HTML file (page with flow logic) will render the dashboard (it is an Adobe Flex control). Figure 15.17 shows our BSP application.

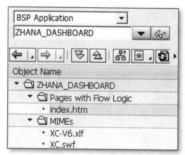

Figure 15.17 BSP Application With Dashboard

We will not show the listing of index.htm, as it is trivial and not related to the Transaction Launcher discussion. The important point is that if you display it, the dashboard will be rendered.

You can define URLs for the Transaction Launcher via customizing by following menu path CUSTOMER RELATIONSHIP MANAGEMENT • UI FRAMEWORK • TECHNICAL ROLE DEFINITION • TRANSACTION LAUNCHER. Figure 15.18 shows how we define a URL to our BSP application. We will use an unsecured HTTP GET request to access it. You can define URLs to non BSP applications, thus incorporating content from virtually everywhere.

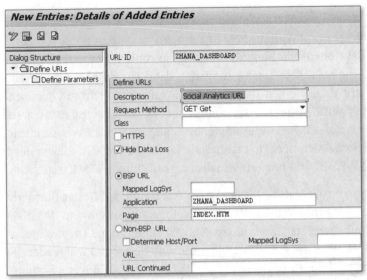

Figure 15.18 Defining URL to BSP Application

We will not use any parameters, but you should keep this option in mind in case your resource requires data input.

What we have done so far is just to create a URL ID that will be used by the Transaction Launcher wizard. You will use this wizard whether you are integrating a URL or *ITS based launch transactions*. The latter is a term used when referring to calling a BOR via SAP GUI for HTML. ITS based launch transactions uses the so-called *mapped logical system* (this specifies the remote system), so you'll have to make sure that the following customizing is maintained:

▶ Define RFC destination (Transaction SM59)

▶ Define logical system (Transaction BD54)

▶ Assignment of RFC destination to logical system for synchronous method calls (Transaction BD97)

▶ Define mapped logical system and ITS URL (define a higher level of abstraction with Transaction CRMS_IC_CROSS_SYS)

The previous steps are not strictly Web Client UI specific (except for the last one) and we will not describe them further.

Finally you can launch the transaction wizard (via menu path CUSTOMER RELATIONSHIP MANAGEMENT • UI FRAMEWORK • TECHNICAL ROLE DEFINITION • TRANSACTION LAUNCHER) and use the mapped logical system or URL within your launch transaction. Figure 15.19 shows Step 1 from the wizard where we specify the URL ID that we want to use.

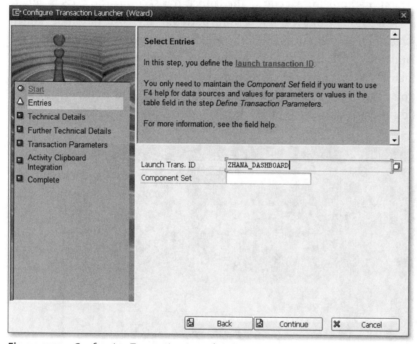

Figure 15.19 Configuring Transaction Launcher Step 1

Because we do not use any URL parameters, we do not need any entry in the COMPONENT SET FIELD. If you need to pass some data from your GenIL business objects to the transaction, you can do so by selecting the required component set and mapping to the transaction parameters in Step 4. The framework assumes that the required BOL entities are passed as part of the navigation collection (cross-component navigation to Transaction Launcher is supported). Alternatively, you can provide one in the handler class (Step 2).

In Step 2 (see Figure 15.20), you can specify a description and some additional technical details; for example, if the transaction is to be launched in a new browser window. If you want to pass data back from the launched transaction, you need the session ID in order to determine the callback mechanism. To pass the session information, you need to select SESSION SOURCE TYPE as `SAM Simple ABAP messaging`. The HANDLER CLASS field contains the name of the class that the wizard will generate upon completion. This class derives from `CL_CRM_UI_LTX_ABSTRACT`, which implements the interface `IF_CRM_IC_ACTION_HANDLER`. This interface provides the most important methods for executing the launch transaction. The class is generated in the local package and will not be transported. If the corresponding launch transaction customizing is transported, the handler class will be generated on the fly when launching the transaction. If you need to influence the standard behavior of the launch transaction, you can redefine the methods of the handler class. In this case you have to assign the class to a normal package and transport it to the appropriate systems. If you rerun the wizard, your coding will be lost.

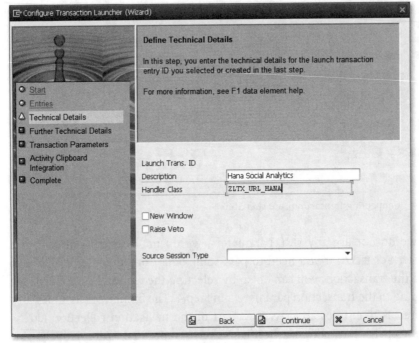

Figure 15.20 Configuring Transaction Launcher Step 2

Figure 15.21 shows Step 3. The fields OBJECT TYPE and OBJECT ACTION are not used. You can leave them blank. The transaction type that corresponds to a URL transaction is B.

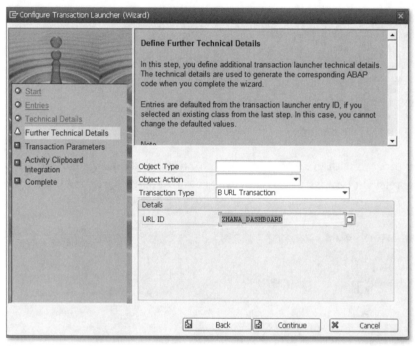

Figure 15.21 Configuring Transaction Launcher Step 3

Because we do not have transaction parameters, we can skip the next two steps. In ACTIVITY CLIPBOARD INTEGRATION, you can specify the return parameter. You can specify only one parameter, and its value will be stored in the clipboard. This is mainly of interest in the Interaction Center environment.

Upon completion, the wizard will generate the handler class and store the relevant customizing in CUSTOMER RELATIONSHIP MANAGEMENT • UI FRAMEWORK - TECHNICAL ROLE DEFINITION • TRANSACTION LAUNCHER • COPY/DELETE LAUNCH TRANSACTIONS. Now you can access the navigation bar profile customizing and create a logical link that points to the target ID of the launch transaction ID. As Figure 15.22 shows, you need to choose TYPE C and TARGET ID EXECLTX. The PARAMETER is the launch transaction ID and the parameter class is always CL_CRM_UI_LTX_NAVBAR_PARAM.

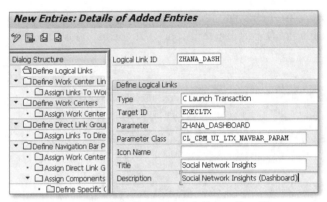

Figure 15.22 Logical Link for the Launch Transaction ID

Next, you proceed with the navigation customizations and finally enable the new link in the relevant business roles. The results of our example are shown in Figure 15.23.

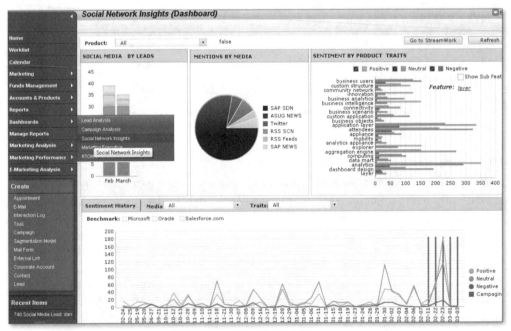

Figure 15.23 Integration of BSP Application into Web UI

As mentioned already, you should use Transaction Launcher with care. The most frequent cause of errors is related to application security: You might run into cross-domain scripting issues, your SSO might not be resolved, and so on. In addition, because of the complexity of the customizing and the fact that two systems are involved, debugging and maintenance might be quite challenging.

15.5 Performance Optimization

Performance has been, is, and will always be one of the most important success factors of any application and software infrastructure. The Web Client UI framework is no exception. Whenever you are dealing with performance in Web Client applications, you always have to look from two different points of view: frontend and backend performance.

When you build your own UI using the Web Client tag libraries, to improve performance and reduce the CPU time used by the browser when rendering your pages, it is of paramount importance that your HTML and CSS are as simple as possible. The following will typically affect rendering performance:

▶ **JavaScript code executed on page load**
  This code always adds its runtime to the frontend rendering time because it is executed after the normal rendering has finished. Thus, onload scripts should be used only in rare cases and should be designed in such a way that they leave their footprints after roundtrips only on those pages where their execution is needed.

▶ **DOM operations in JavaScript**
  Read and write access to DOM elements can have a severe impact on frontend runtime. This is true especially in browsers of older releases, where read accesses to elements can take considerable time with no apparent reason. Furthermore, when you insert new visible elements into the DOM, the browser needs to repaint the modified sections and sometimes the neighboring sections.

▶ **New, duplicate, conflicting, or obsolete CSS rules**
  The more CSS code you add to a page, the longer it will take the browser to evaluate all the CSS rules for each HTML element. And if you happen to have declared more than one rule for an element, the browser needs to resolve which

one to apply. Therefore, you need to regularly clean your CSS files and remove duplicate, conflicting, and obsolete rules.

▸ **Inline script blocks in BSP views**
Because the Web Client UI usually works with automatic delta handling, if a screen area is changed the included scripts blocks also will be changed. Automatic delta handling logic takes such inline script blocks and puts them into the HTML header. This hurts performance. Therefore, if you need to introduce script blocks, you have to make sure that they are introduced on a view which stays stable for a long time; that is, where the content of the view stays unchanged from one roundtrip to another.

▸ **Horizontal scrollbar in a table**
If you need a horizontally scrollable table, you have to use a `div` around the table with overflow in `x` direction instead of setting the `chtmlb:configCellerator` to scrollable, because this last approach hurts performance.

If you are using a Web Client application in the L-Shape and you have performance issues, and if you have reliably excluded the frontend as the source of the performance degradation, you will want to analyze your application performance in the backend. You can use the performance analysis tool—Transaction ST05—that you are already familiar with. Alternatively, the Web Client UI framework comes with a performance tracker that you can start directly from the browser. By pressing [Ctrl] + [Shift] + [F7], you get a window in the upper right corner of the work area frame that shows backend and frontend rendering times for every backend event that happens after the window is opened (Figure 15.24).

You can close the window with the same key combination. The measurements given by the performance tracker will serve as a starting point for your investigation. Using the button START BACKEND RUNTIME ANALYSIS, you can start the runtime analysis that can then be viewed and analyzed in Transaction SAT. You can as well take a memory snapshot by pressing the button CREATE MEMORY SNAPSHOT and then analyze it using Transaction S_MEMORY_INSPECTOR.

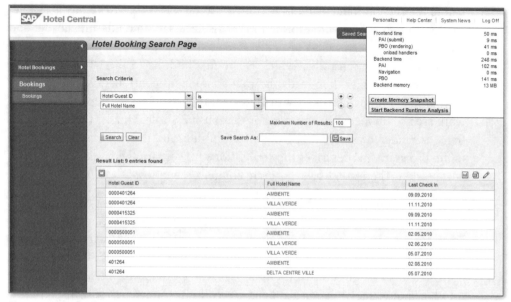

Figure 15.24 Performance Tracker in Web Client UI

15.6 Session Management

Session management is a complex topic. Although you are very unlikely to have to deal with this topic in building Web Client applications, it is a good idea to understand how sessions are opened and closed.

Although it is transparent for them, whenever users start a Web Client application, in reality they start two Web applications. First, the session manager is loaded, and then it requests a new Web Client UI framework session embedded in the session frame. The following describes the start sequence of a Web Client application.

When the user launches an application using the URL that points to the Web Client application frame, the system determines the business roles of the user and returns them along with the session manager. If there are many business roles, the session manager displays the business role selection screen. Upon selection of a business role — or if the system has found only one business role — the session manager starts a new Web Client UI framework session by loading the session frame. However, before the session frame is returned to the browser, it will retrieve business role-specific data such as layout information that is necessary to render the header and the footer. And once the session frame is loaded in the browser, it sends a request to the application controller, which is the first address to the UI runtime. The application controller then loads the root component controller, which provides a dynamic runtime repository with view definitions and usages depending on the work area components customized for that business role. Finally, the application frame is rendered as defined by the layout profile, and the response is sent back to the browser. This describes the straightforward scenario when the user starts a new session. There are, however, more complex scenarios.

When the user reloads the Web Client application—for example by pressing the F5 button—the application will stay in the same session and on the same page except when the session has expired, in which case a new session will start as if the user had launched the application from the beginning. If the user closes the browser or navigates to a foreign, non-Web Client page, the UI framework session is closed. Another interesting situation happens when the session times out. In that case, the Web Client host page will notify the user about the timeout and it will offer a link to start a new session. The user also has the option to end a long-running action, in which case a warning about the risk of losing data is displayed, and the user can decide to proceed or to cancel the action.

In order to ensure that a browser request hits the correct session with the current context and the state of the application, a session identifier (SID) is communicated to the browser. The SID can be stored in a cookie or it can be stored in the URL. However, both methods have some disadvantages and a third method is preferable: the external session ID or eSID. The eSID is an abstract session ID. It is not created by the NetWeaver Web Application Server but by applications themselves, including non-SAP applications. In the Web Client UI framework, the application frame only supports external session IDs. The Web Client UI framework host page is responsible for the generation of the eSIDs and acts the session manager. One eSID is generated per browser window and is valid as long as that window or tab is alive. On the other hand, the eSID does not protect against session disclosure. You need to enable either HTTP Security Session Management using Transaction SICF_SESSIONS or to set system parameter `icf/user_recheck` to the appropriate level.

You can use the technical profile to configure the session behavior in the Web Client UI. Figure 15.25 shows the details of the technical definition that influences the session behavior.

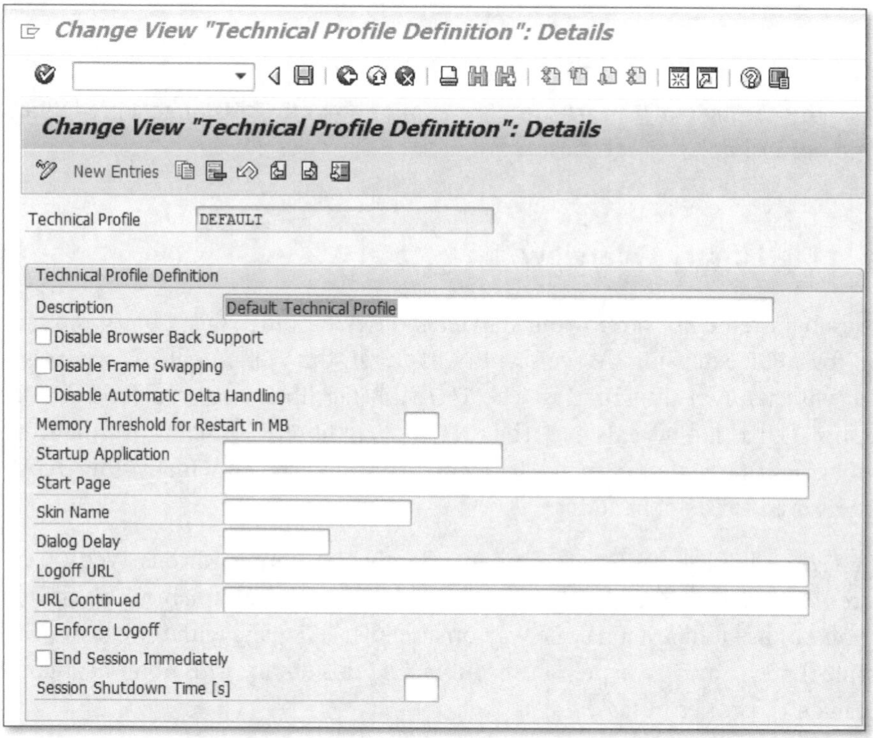

Figure 15.25 Technical Profile Definition

In IMG activity Customer Relationship management • UI Framework • Technical Role Definition • Define Technical Profile, you can:

▶ Enforce Logoff

If this flag is activated, the Web Client UI Framework removes the user's logon credentials when the user uses the logoff link in the L-Shape. It does the same when the user leaves the application in any other way; for instance, if he or she navigates to an external Web site or reloads the page. In that case, the logon credentials are destroyed and the user needs to log on again upon return. If this flag is not checked, the Web Client UI framework only removes the user's logon credentials when he or she uses the logoff link; any other way of leaving the application keeps the credentials and the user does not have to log on again.

▶ ENFORCE IMMEDIATE SESSION END
Use this flag to force the browser to always create a new session when the browser reloads.

▶ SET A SESSION SHUTDOWN DELAY
With this setting, you can schedule the expiration of the session to a predefined time; for example, 10 seconds.

15.7 Tag Library Overview

As you might remember from your BSP technology training, a tag library is a synonym for a BSP extension. As we saw in Chapter 4, the Web Client UI framework comes with its own tag libraries. The THTMLB tag library is used for basic UI elements such as input, texts, etc. The CHTMLB tag library is used for configuring UIs, making it possible to arrange UI elements on the screen. Finally, the TAJAX library is used for delta handling.

The THTMLB library can be used independently from other various Web Client features that we have seen, such as context nodes or UI components. This means that you can use it in a standalone way on a regular BSP page with flow logic. The example that we saw in Chapter 4 was built using this library. This library contains three main categories of tags:

▶ Tags that initialize the runtime and establish the logic for data management and are responsible for the event mechanism. Examples of such tags are `thtmlb:content` and `thtmlb:form`.

▶ Tags that are responsible for layout arrangement. These tags are not necessarily visible but are essential to create a layout that corresponds to your needs. Example: `thtmlb:grid`.

▶ Tags used for creating visible UI elements. Examples: `thtmlb:inputField`, `thtmlb:cellerator`.

The THTMLB tag library comes with native support for accessibility and with support for right-to-left languages.

Unlike the THTMLB library, the CHTMLB library is fully coupled with and dependent on other Web Client components. The CHTMLB tag library requires a usage of context nodes that we have seen in Chapter 4. For this reason, you cannot use CHTMLB tags within the context of simple BSP pages or even native BSP MVC applications. The most important CHTMLB tags are directly related to UI configurations and require for their input an XML document that describes the UI configuration. On the other hand, CHTMLB tags do not render themselves HTML elements; they are rather composite tags that delegate this task to underlying THTMLB tags.

The TAJAX library is very different from the two other libraries. Unlike the THTMLB and CHTMLB libraries, the TAJAX library does not create any visible UI content and it does not take care of any UI layout. TAJAX is used to introduce the concept of delta handling, which is used for automatic delta handling (ADH). Here it is used to define groups of UI elements called areas. The areas are structured so that they comprise UI units, which are likely to change as a group while staying stable when another area changes, unless they are interdependent. An example would be an area comprising the form fields of a sales order header. Another area on the same UI could be a table of sales order items. Changing a field of a sales order header does not necessarily change the content of the sales order item table. This way, after a roundtrip to the server, it is also not necessary to replace or to refresh the whole UI. Instead, only the areas whose content has changed are replaced while the remaining areas of the UI stay stable. This has the advantage of increasing frontend performance because the browser does not have to render the entire page. It also ensures a flicker-free interaction with the application.

For the visible tags, the Web Client UI framework makes it possible to apply a theme, which is a set of colors and visual design that is applied to the UI. Five different themes are offered out of the box. On top of the standard themes, also called skins, you can create your own theme. You can create your own skin from scratch, but this would be a very cumbersome task. For this reason, the Web Client framework comes with the Skin Workbench that you can use to copy a standard skin and use it as the basis for creating your own skin. The standard skins are stored in the MIME repository of BSP application THTMLB_STYLES. Depending on the skin, the files are automatically uploaded by the `thtmlb:content` tag. Every skin consists of a number of cascading style sheet files. The organization of the CSS files is done is such a way as to:

- ▶ Distinguish structural CSS from styles that change from one skin to another—such as background colors—and which you are likely to change to create your own skin.

- ▶ Provide a multitude of styles that are valid for as many purposes as possible for each use and isolate styles that have to differ for special use.

- ▶ Prevent the need for CSS hacks to tackle browser differences.

Styles that are not organized in a CSS file that directly addresses a certain browser version are set up to be compliant to CSS 2.1 standard. Whenever the CSS 2.1 standard is not properly handled in a certain browser, the browser- specific style sheet will have to overwrite the standard compliant version.

THTMLB library comes up with a big library of JavaScript functions. This library is stored in BSP application THTMLB_SCRIPTS and is automatically loaded by the `thtmlb:content` tag. Unlike the CSS files, the JavaScript library is not modularized to upload only functions specific to a browser; it uploads all functions for all browsers. Furthermore, there is no possibility to replace, modification free, the standard JavaScript code. You can, however, add your own JavaScript files on top of the JavaScript files delivered in the standard. See IMG activity CUSTOMER RELATIONSHIP MANAGEMENT • UI FRAMEWORK • TECHNICAL ROLE DEFINITION • DEFINE PATH FOR JS FILES for more details.

If you want to use the Web Client tag libraries, you have two sources of information: the self-explanatory description of individual tag attributes, and the individual tag documentation.

15.8   Summary

In this chapter, we have seen some of the additional features of the Web Client UI. We have built a guided activity page—also known as a task-based UI page—and have seen how you can enrich your fields with new actions using the field actions and action menu. We have also seen how you can use the Flash Island infrastructure to enrich your application with a Rich Internet Application (RIA) built using Adobe Flex, which offers more frontend intelligence than the Web Client UI framework. In case you want to bring your beloved backend traditional transactions to the browser, we showed how you can use the Transaction Launcher to do so. Finally, we discussed performance optimization and how the tag library can be used to build standalone applications styled to meet your needs.

The Authors

Tzanko Stefanov is a director of solution management on the SAP Customer Solution Management team, focusing on the Web Client UI framework, particularly its extensibility and customer enhancements aspects. He works closely with customers, partners, and SAP industries to find optimal ways to incorporate their additions to SAP CRM. Prior to doing this, Tzanko was a member of the Web Client UI Product Management team. He participated in the development of the framework's extensibility, application generation, and mash-ups tools and concepts (among other tasks). In the past, Tzanko was a development manager in SAP CRM and SAP NetWeaver. Before joining SAP, he led teams and designed large enterprise information systems for Morgan Stanley.

Armand Sezikeye is project manager at SAP Custom Development. He joined SAP in 2000 and has held various technical and managerial positions. For the last five years, he has worked as a development manager for the Web UI Tag Library Implementation team, where he has acquired extensive know-how in various aspects of Web Client UI. He was also responsible for the SAP CRM Security Product Standard, and has had the opportunity to appreciate the Web Client from a consumer point of view, as a CRM application developer. Since he became a manager for one of the Web UI Development teams, he has provided technical and functional guidance and leadership on various topics within the Web UI framework. Before joining SAP, Armand worked in various companies and countries as an Enterprise Java Developer.

Sanjeet Mall is the vice president and chief solution architect in the SAP Customer Solution Management team, focusing on common components and the base architecture of the solution. As a key player in the CRM team since the days of SAP CRM 3.0, and with most of his working career in SAP and in CRM, he has been lucky enough to watch SAP CRM grow from its humble beginnings to a world class product. During this journey, he has had the opportunity to play the roles of a consultant, product manager, director, and finally the chief architect of SAP CRM. Sanjeet is presently transitioning into his new role as the vice president and chief architect of the Mobile Applications Unit inside SAP.

Index

C

S

Find everything you need to know in this comprehensive guide to creating forms in SAP

Learn how to solve real-life problems that occur when working with interactive forms

Expand your knowledge with new information on ABAP Offline Infrastructure, XDC Editor

Jürgen Hauser, Andreas Deutesfeld, Thomas Szücs, Stephan Rehmann

SAP Interactive Forms by Adobe

If you've ever had any questions about working with SAP's interactive forms, this comprehensive book will be a valuable addition to your library. Whether you are a beginning or advanced technical consultant developer, or form designer, you will learn everything you need to know about working with SAP Interactive Forms by Adobe. The second edition is updated for SAP NetWeaver 7.20, and includes new coverage of ABAP Offline Infrastructure, XDC Editor, JobProfiles Editor, parallelization of print jobs, and more.

approx. 790 pp., 2. edition, 89,95 Euro / US$ 89.95
ISBN 978-1-59229-398-8, Aug 2011

>> www.sap-press.com

Presents end-to-end process integration from a developer's perspective

Helps you master the development of mappings, adapters, and proxies

Includes a comprehensive example scenario

Valentin Nicolescu, Matthias Heiler, Florian Visintin, Burkhardt Funk, Holger Wittges, Benedikt Kleine Stegemann, Peter Niemeyer, Thomas

Practical Guide to SAP NetWeaver PI – Development

This new edition of Practical Guide to SAP NetWeaver PI – Development is revised and updated to include new functions and practical examples that apply to the newest software release, SAP NetWeaver PI 7.1. As a practical exercise book written for developers, it is devoted to the configuration and development of mappings, adapters, and proxies. Beginning with information about technical prerequisites and basic information on setting up your system, it rounds out explanations with step-by-step exercises and case studies that will prove useful to both the beginner and the advanced user.

498 pp., 2. edition 2010, 79,95 Euro / US$ 79.95
ISBN 978-1-59229-334-6

>> www.sap-press.com

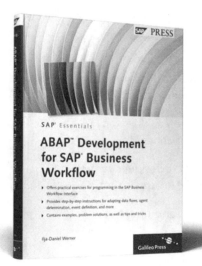

Explore practical exercises for programming in SAP Business Workflow

Utilize step-by-step instructions for adapting data flows, agent determination, event definitions, and more

Learn from examples, problem solutions, and tips and tricks

Ilja-Daniel Werner

ABAP Development for SAP Business Workflow

If you are an ABAP developer interested in the complex programming of SAP Business Workflow, this is the resource for you! This book addresses all aspects of the tools that are directly related to the developer's tasks, explaining when it is necessary to influence the behavior of SAP Business Workflow using custom code, detailing how to write this code, and offering complete listings for download. After reading this book, you will have everything you need to know in order to use ABAP code to program workflows.

approx. 256 pp., 69,95 Euro / US$ 84.95
ISBN 978-1-59229-394-0, July 2011

>> www.sap-press.com

Presents the most important
ABAP statements comprehensively

Covers key object-oriented
programming concepts

Step-by-step techniques to develop
a working ABAP application

2nd, revised, and updated edition
for ABAP 7.0

Günther Färber, Julia Kirchner

ABAP Basics

In this newly revised and updated book, you will become acquainted
with the most important and commonly used ABAP commands and
terminology. Updated for ABAP version 7.0, you will find all of the
typical tasks and issues that a programmer faces within the fast-paced
SAP environment, which will enable you to write your own ABAP
application.

508 pp., 2. edition 2011, 59,95 Euro / US$ 59.95
ISBN 978-1-59229-369-8

>> www.sap-press.com

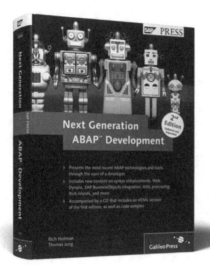

Presents the most recent ABAP technologies and tools through the eyes of a developer

Includes new topics like syntax enhancements, ABAP Test Cockpit, AJAX, SAP BusinessObjects integration, XML processing, Rich Islands, NWBC 3.0, and many more

Rich Heilman, Thomas Jung

Next Generation ABAP Development

After reading this book, you will be able to assess and employ the new tools and features of ABAP within SAP NetWeaver 7.0 to 7.0 EHP2. The updated and revised second edition assumes a scenario where a fictive university has just converted from SAP R/3 4.6C to SAP NetWeaver 7.0 (SAP Business Suite 7.0), this time with the default installation option of EHP2. Readers will experience the entire development process of applications – design, development and testing of all areas – through the eyes of a developer, and will walk away with a firm understanding of many of the newer technologies or design techniques that were not previously available in ABAP.

735 pp., 2. edition 2011, with CD, 69,95 Euro / US$ 69.95
ISBN 978-1-59229-352-0

>> www.sap-press.com

Workshops for custom enhancement of the SAP standard

Examples for purchasing, inventory management, logistics invoice verification, and much more

More than 130 User Exits and BAdIs at a glance

Jürgen Schwaninger

ABAP Development for Materials Management in SAP: User Exits and BAdIs

Find the solution to your user exit problems with "ABAP Programming for SAP Materials Management: User Exits and BAdIs." This book offers helpful advice and insider knowledge to the user exits and Business Add-Ins that are used the most in Materials Management projects. As a developer's guide, you will find basic programming principles, programming examples for the most important user exits and BAdIs, a nd a systematic, complete description of all exits.

270 pp., 2011, 69,95 Euro / US$ 84.95
ISBN 978-1-59229-373-5

>> www.sap-press.com

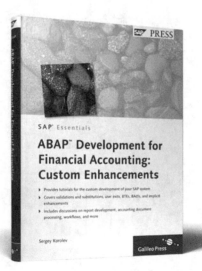

Provides tutorials for the immediate improvement of your SAP system

Covers validations and substitutions, user exits, BTEs, BAdIs, and implicit enhancements

Includes the enhancement of reports, accounting document processing, workflows, and more

Sergey Korolev

ABAP Development for Financial Accounting: Custom Enhancements

With this book, you can learn how to create custom enhancements to standard ABAP code in Financial Accounting for SAP ERP Financials (release 6.0) in order to address all corporate and/or country-specific business rules. It explains how to customize data flow between sub-systems, as well as between external systems (such as those of banks, vendors, customers, etc.). Taking a systematic approach to the topic, you will be introduced to general information about the subject of enhancements, and then benefit from specific coding tutorials consisting of step-by-step instructions and screenshots.

252 pp., 2011, 69,95 Euro / US$ 84.95
ISBN 978-1-59229-370-4

>> www.sap-press.com

Interested in reading more?

Please visit our Web site for all
new book releases from SAP PRESS.

www.sap-press.com